Formal Concept
Artificial Intelligence

CHAPMAN & HALL COMPUTING SERIES

Computer Operating Series
For micros, minis and mainframes
2nd edition
David Barron

Microcomputer Graphics
Michael Batty

The Pick Operating System
Malcolm Bull

A Course of Programming in FORTRAN
3rd edition
V. J. Calderbank

Expert Systems
Principles and case studies
2nd edition
Edited by Richard Forsyth

Machine Learning
Principles and techniques
Edited by Richard Forsyth

Expert Systems
Knowledge, uncertainty and decision
Ian Graham and Peter Llewelyn Jones

Computer Graphics and Applications
Dennis Harris

Artificial Intelligence and Human Learning
Intelligent computer-aided instruction
Edited by John Self

Formal Concepts in Artificial Intelligence
Fundamentals
Rajjan Shinghal

Artificial Intelligence
Principles and applications
Edited by Masoud Yazdani

ACCESS
The Pick enquiry language
Malcolm Bull

Formal Concepts in Artificial Intelligence
Fundamentals

Rajjan Shinghal

CHAPMAN & HALL COMPUTING
London · New York · Tokyo · Melbourne · Madras

Published by Chapman & Hall, 2–6 Boundary Row, London SE1 8HN

Chapman & Hall, 2–6 Boundary Row, London SE1 8HN, UK

Van Nostrand Reinhold Inc., 115 5th Avenue, New York NY10003, USA

Chapman & Hall Japan, Thomson Publishing Japan, Hirakawacho Nemoto Building, 7F, 1-7-11 Hirakawa-cho, Chiyoda-ku, Tokyo 102, Japan

Chapman & Hall Australia, Thomas Nelson Australia, 102 Dodds Street, South Melbourne, Victoria 3205, Australia

Chapman & Hall India, R. Seshadri, 32 Second Main Road, CIT East, Madras 600 035, India

First edition 1992

© 1992 Rajjan Shinghal

Typeset in 10/12 Palatino by Excel Typesetters Company, Hong Kong
Printed in Singapore by Kin Keong Printing Co. Pte. Ltd.

ISBN 0 412 40790 6   0 442 31444 2 (USA)

A catalogue record for this book is available from the British Library

Library of Congress Cataloging-in-Publication data available

Shinghal, Rajjan, 1945 -
    Formal concepts in artificial intelligence : fundamentals / Rajjan Shinghal. - 1st ed.
        p.   cm. - (Chapman & Hall computing)
    Includes bibliographical references and index.
    ISBN 0-442-31444-2
    1. Artificial intelligence. I. Title. II. Series.
Q335.S483 1991
006.3-dc20   91-36004
                                                                          CIP

Contents

Preface

Intended as a first exposure to Artificial Intelligence (AI), this book is aimed at upper-level undergraduate and first-year graduate students. It is assumed that the students have a good grasp of mathematics and computer science fundamentals such as those taught in a typical undergraduate degree programme for computer science.

In the Spring 1985 issue of the *AI Magazine*, published by the American Association for Artificial Intelligence, David Waltz listed 13 topics in AI. The topics contained within them about 500 subtopics. To cover everything and to cover it well would have made this book far too big. Accordingly, after an extensive review of the AI literature and university calendars, I selected the topics and subtopics presented in this book. I grant that not everyone will concur with my selection, but then, I do not know of any selection with which everyone will concur. (In the coming years, I hope to write on the remaining topics separately.)

AI is alive with controversy. As the following three examples will show, there is no unanimity as to what constitutes AI.

1. While reviewing Elaine Rich's text (published by McGraw-Hill in 1983), Roy Rada wrote: 'Elaine Rich in *Artificial Intelligence* claims that AI is most fundamentally concerned with problem solving and knowledge representation. This contrasts with the other popular texts . . .' (*Artificial Intelligence*, 1986, vol. **28**, no. 1, pp. 119–21).
2. While reviewing Michael Genesereth and Nils Nilsson's *Logical Foundations of Artificial Intelligence* (published by Morgan Kaufmann in 1987), Drew McDermott wrote: 'The unsophisticated reader should be warned that the foundations being explored are not exactly the foundations of AI.' Nilsson responded by pointing to the reviewer's 'by-now-tiresome doubts about the value of logic in AI.' (*AI Magazine*, Fall 1989, pp. 103–6)
3. Describing a discussion on AI education, Alan Bundy wrote: 'The debate was between the "scruffies", led by Roger Schank and Ed Feigenbaum, and the "neats", led by Nils Nilsson. The neats argued that no education in AI was complete without a strong theoretical component, containing, for instances, courses on predicate

logic . . . The scruffies maintained that such a theoretical component was not only unnecessary but harmful.' (*AI Magazine*, Winter 1981–2, pp. 13–4; quotation reprinted in Wolfgang Kreutzer and Bruce Mckenzie's *Programming for Artificial Intelligence*, p. 197, published by Addison-Wesley in 1990)

If I were to classify this book, I would classify it as a neat book, not a scruffy one. The book is written to explain AI through its concepts, and not to discuss whether the concepts should be implemented in this or that programming language. One may implement the concepts in the programming language of one's choice. Nonetheless, when I feel it is needed, I do mention a programming language, but I do not emphasize it. The poet Alfred Lord Tennyson said it about brooks and men. I rephrase him: Programming languages may come, and programming languages may go, but concepts go on forever. The world of AI is, however, big enough to accommodate differing viewpoints.

To explain a topic, I choose whichever writing style makes the topic easy to understand, provided I feel I am not sacrificing precision. Thus sometimes my writing is formal, other times informal. My primary concern has been the clarity and precision of the presentation.

The book contains thirteen chapters and an appendix. Material presented later builds on the material presented earlier. In class, the material can easily be covered in the sequence presented in the book. At the end of each chapter, there are exercises and an annotated list of suggested reading. A reader wanting to learn more about the topic under consideration may begin by choosing sources from the list.

Chapter 1 briefly discusses the notion of AI, and what we may justifiably expect of it. Messiah or monster, AI is what we make it.

Till now, predicate logic has played a substantial role in the evolution of AI. Prolog, which for instance has become prevalent in the different areas of AI, after all sprouted from predicate logic. Nonetheless, predicate logic has its shortcomings; for example, we can comfortably express 'All birds fly', but not 'Most birds fly.' I expect that in time predicate logic will develop to become more powerful. The sixth-century development of using zero in the place-value notation (discussed in the Appendix) lead to the flowering of arithmetic, and humankind learnt to easily manipulate numerical knowledge. I trust that, similarly, a powerful predicate logic will lead to the flowering of AI, and humankind will learn to easily manipulate non-numerical knowledge too.

Accordingly, the first area I discuss is the one in which predicate logic is most appropriate, namely automated reasoning (Chapters 2–5).

In class, Chapters 2 and 3 should be covered in full, for they form the basis of automated reasoning. Chapters 4 and 5, which essentially present proof strategies, may be covered in full. Alternatively, a teacher may make selections from these two chapters, keeping in mind class background and interests. From Chapter 4, I recommend that at the very least the fewest literals preference strategy, the deleting of chaste clauses strategy, and the set of support strategy (sections 4.1, 4.2.2, 4.3.3 and 4.4.1) should be covered. I have observed that students often find these strategies easy to understand and to implement. From Chapter 5, backchaining (sections 5.1 to 5.3) should be covered. This is because of the wide application of backchaining in AI. Some of these applications are discussed later in the book.

Chapters 6–8 present natural language processing, the natural language for our consideration being English. The purpose is to describe techniques for communicating with a computer in English. I have noted that even those who speak English fluently by instinct are often not fully aware of English grammar. If, however, one is to implement an English processor, one should be acquainted with English grammar and all its intricacies. Chapter 6 accordingly presents a grammar of English, which can be applied to designing an English processor. The lists of words from the different grammatical classes presented in Chapter 6 should be useful in building a lexicon for the processor. A teacher can use Chapter 6 as a reference for class deliberations. Chapter 7, which deals with parsing English sentences and eliciting meaning from them, should be covered in class fully. Chapter 8 may be covered fully, or a teacher may select from the transformational procedures presented. I recommend that at least contractions, transforming positive to negative sentences, and transforming declarative sentences to questions (sections 8.1–8.4) should be covered. These procedures are likely to be the most often needed in practice.

Expert systems have become popular in business and industry. Chapter 9 presents the fundamental ideas of expert systems. These systems are frequently required to reason with uncertainties. Two schemes for such reasoning are given in Chapter 10. If the class has a good comprehension of probabilities, as I suppose it should, then the teacher should cover the Bayesian scheme of section 10.2; otherwise, the teacher may cover only the *ad hoc* scheme of section 10.3.

Chapters 11–13 present search. Sections 11.1–11.5 should be covered in all classes. They deal with the basic search strategies: breadth-first, depth-first and best-first. The other sections of Chapter 11 may be covered according to the teacher's preferences. Chapter 12, which discusses problem solving by decomposition, may be covered in full, or a teacher may select. I suggest that at the very least AND/OR graphs and means–end analysis (sections 12.1, 12.2 and 12.4) should be covered. They form the foundation of solving problems by decomposition. In Chapter 13, at least sections 13.1–13.3 should be covered. They deal with the notions of game trees and of pruning them by alphabeta search. The remaining sections on scout search, best-first search, performance appraisal, enhancements and alternative search procedures may be covered at the teacher's discretion.

As will become apparent from reading the chapters, for AI to progress further, we need efficient techniques to manipulate knowledge, which is essentially in the form of numerical and non-numerical symbols. Manipulating numerical symbols was a challenge at one time. How big a challenge it was can be gauged from the Appendix. The Appendix also narrates the genius of Charles Babbage, who, by the late 1830s, had proposed a machine that contained the same major components as the twentieth-century computer. His associate, Ada Lovelace, even tackled the question of whether their machine could think ('originate anything'). Questions like that engendered AI in the mid-1950s. The Appendix ends with a review of AI's past, highlights of its present, and hope for its future.

In my writing, I have throughout used the masculine pronouns *he*, *his* and *him* to refer to persons in general, regardless of whether the persons are males or females. For example: 'Before making his move, a player looks ahead . . .'

It was Allen Dykler who repeatedly suggested to me that I write this book. Halina Monkiewicz, Irene Mazis and Mary Smodis typed different portions of the manuscript. Larry Thiel and Stan Swiercz straightened out the word processor SYMSET whenever it misbehaved. Chantal Desjardins and Henry Polley helped draw the figures. Gregg Rabe, Lynne Carson, Michael Assels and Robin Potter read different segments of the manuscript and provided me with their comments. To all these people, I offer my sincere gratitude.

Rajjan Shinghal

1

A view of artificial intelligence

1.1 INTRODUCTION

The term artificial intelligence (AI) is reputed to have been coined in 1956 by American scientist John McCarthy. Since then, AI has come to encompass many different areas of investigation; as examples, six such areas are the following.

1. Automated reasoning: can a computer prove theorems in some domain, say, geometry?
2. Natural language processing: can a computer communicate with humans in an everyday language, say, English?
3. Expert systems: can a computer exhibit expertise in some given domain, say, medicine? If the computer is fed a patient's symptoms, can the computer diagnose the disease and prescribe appropriate therapy?
4. Game playing: can a computer play a game, say, chess?
5. Vision: can a computer, by looking at the photographic image of a scene, interpret what the scene depicts, say, a kitchen with a running tap? (A robot controlled by the computer may then be guided into the kitchen to turn off the tap.)
6. Learning: can a computer operating in areas such as the above learn to improve its performance over time, say, become a better chess player?

From your general understanding of computers, you will know that a computer can do only what its program allows it to do. Hence, in studying AI, we often study techniques to program computers so that they can operate in areas such as those given above.

The overall objective of AI is to build intelligent machines; in other words, machines that display intelligence. (In AI literature, the words **machines** and **computers** are often used synonymously.) AI is expected to complement human intelligence, not replace it, just as the invention of the automobile did not obviate walking. The automobile is meant to help humans; so is AI.

1.2   INTELLIGENCE AND ITS CRITERIA

Since the objective of AI is to build machines that display intelligence, you may wonder whether we can give a precise definition of intelligence. Intelligence is considered to have many facets; loosely speaking, these facets include the ability to reason, to learn from experience and to adapt to new situations. Giving a precise definition of intelligence falls into the realms of philosophy and psychology. In such literature, you will find various definitions of intelligence, not all of them alike. You may have come across the poem by John Godfrey Saxe (1816–87) which opens as follows:

> It was six men of Indostan
>   To learning much inclined,
> Who went to see the Elephant
>   (Though all of them were blind),
> That each by observation
>   Might satisfy his mind.

The poem continues to narrate how the man who touched the elephant's broad side declared that the elephant was like a wall, but the man who touched the elephant's tusk declared that the elephant was like a spear. Similarly touching the trunk, the knee, the ear and the tail, the other four men declared one by one that the elephant was like a snake, a tree, a fan and a rope. The poem closes by saying:

> And so these men of Indostan
>   Disputed loud and long,
> Each in his own opinion
>   Exceedingly stiff and strong,
> Though each was partly in the right,
>   And all were in the wrong!

For us to give a precise definition of intelligence may be akin to those men squabbling over the elephant. A five-year-old who can manipulate fractions (the bugbear of many a child) is likely to be called intelligent, but educated adults are not likely to be called intelligent just because they can manipulate fractions, for the adult is expected to be able to do so. From the child to the adult, the notion of intelligence changes. Altering the well-known dictum of Margaret Wolfe Hungerford (1855–97) we could perhaps say: intelligence is in the eye of the beholder.

To judge whether a given machine is intelligent, British mathematician Alan Mathison Turing (1912–54) proposed a test, now known as the Turing test. In essence, the Turing test can be described thus:

A person, called the interrogator, converses through a teletype with two interlocutors hidden from his view. One interlocutor is a machine, the other a human. The machine attempts to respond to the interrogator's questions as if it were the human interlocutor. The human, of course, responds as a human interlocutor would. After conversing with the two interlocutors for some time, if the interrogator is unable to distinguish the machine from the human, then the machine can be said to be intelligent.

The Turing test is often criticized in the literature because its outcome depends on the gullibility of the interrogator. We can try to overcome this criticism by having many interrogators, each one working independently of the other. Then the outcome of the test depends on whether most of the interrogators can distinguish the machine from the human interlocutor.

The Turing test is also criticized because its outcome depends on observing the behaviour of the machine but not on knowing its internal working. This criticism is confronted by contending that even humans do not know everything about the internal working of their brains, and yet humans are judged capable of intelligent behaviour. Moreover, it is immaterial whether the internal workings of the machine and the human brain are the same. What matters is that both are observed to behave intelligently. A bird flaps its wings, an aeroplane does not, and yet both are observed to fly. The internal working of the sun is known to be different from the internal working of an electric bulb; yet both are observed to emit light. Accordingly, an intelligent machine need not be created in the image of humans.

Analysing the AI literature, you will notice that two fundamental approaches have unfolded.

1. **Neural nets** The machine appears as a network of neurons modelled on the human brain.
2. **Symbol manipulators** Not only does the machine manipulate numeric symbols 0 to 9 required for arithmetic, but it also manipulates non-numeric symbols; for example, the symbols of mathematical logic required in formal reasoning. In this approach, the machine is not modelled on the human brain.

A given book may cover both of these approaches, or it may cover only one of them, depending on the areas of AI discussed, the size of the book and the standpoint of the author. Nonetheless, it is advisable to keep an open mind on the two approaches, for the possibility exists that ultimately their synergism will lead to the building of intelligent machines. There is also the prospect that in building such machines, we may gain sagacious insights into the working and the performance of the human brain: what is not understood about the human brain today may someday become understood.

In building intelligent machines, we should, however, always remember this: there is no known justification for expecting that a machine is intelligent only if it displays intelligence superior to that of a typical human. A machine displaying intelligence in solving problems of, say, medicine should not be expected to write sonnets as well, just as a doctor is expected to be proficient in medicine, not in writing sonnets.

1.3 CLOSING REMARKS

Realizing the objective of AI may take some time. Today we may suffer a set-back or we may achieve only modest success. But today's set-back and modest success are the foundation of tomorrow's bigger success. That has been the way of progress through the ages.

It is incumbent on a surgeon to wield his knife for removing a tumour, not for killing. Likewise, it is incumbent on us that intelligent machines are for benevolent uses, not malevolent: a machine specializing in medicine is meant to promote public health, not germ warfare.

As you read Chapter 2 onwards, you may decide for yourself whether AI can be beneficial. Regardless of what you decide, we hope that you will find the reading useful.

1.4 EXERCISES

1. In your view, what criteria should a machine satisfy before it can be called intelligent? Give justifications for the criteria you establish.
2. What are the potential beneficial and harmful effects of AI? Amplify your essay with examples.
3. What ethical constraints would you place on AI research? Discuss with reasoning.

1.5 SUGGESTIONS FOR FURTHER READING

Waltz (1985) proffered a list of topics and subtopics in AI. Minsky (1968) edited some studies in AI. Shrobe (1988) collected papers surveying several areas of AI. Shapiro (1987) gathered a number of articles on various topics in AI. Haralick, Mackworth and Tanimoto (1989) surveyed machine vision. Kodratoff and Michalski (1990) edited papers on machine learning. Saxe (1884) penned the poem, segments of which were quoted in Section 1.2. Turing (1950) proposed a test for judging whether a machine is intelligent. Disagreeing with Turing,

Gunderson (1971) parodied the Turing test. Lighthill (1973) discouraged AI research. Dreyfus (1979) and Dreyfus and Dreyfus (1986) divined the failure of AI. Graubard (1988) presented papers giving different viewpoints on AI. Anderson (1964), Bellman (1978), and Boden (1977) explored the philosophical issues of AI. Feigenbaum and McCorduck (1983) called for more AI research. Minsky (1986) thought of the human mind as a number of processes, or agents, working together as a society. Weizenbaum (1976) warned of the dangers of AI. Wasserman (1989) explained neural nets. Charniak and McDermott (1984), Charniak, Risebeck, McDermott and Meehan (1987), Firebaugh (1989), Genesereth and Nilsson (1987), Hunt (1975), Kreutzer and McKenzie (1990), Luger and Stubblefield (1989), Nilsson (1980), Rich and Knight (1991), Rowe (1988), Schalkoff (1990), Tanimoto (1987), and Winston (1984) all wrote AI textbooks. Dougherty and Giardina (1988) described methods for linking AI with autonomous systems.

1. Anderson, A. R. (1964) *Minds and Machines*, Prentice-Hall, Englewood Cliffs, New Jersey.
2. Bellman, R. (1978) *An Introduction to Artificial Intelligence; Can Computers Think?*, Boyd and Fraser Publishing Company, San Francisco, California.
3. Boden, M. A. (1977) *Artificial Intelligence and Modern Man*, Basic Books, New York.
4. Charniak, E., and McDermott, D. (1984) *Introduction to Artificial Intelligence*, Addison-Wesley, Reading, Massachusetts.
5. Charniak, E., Risebeck, C. K., McDermott, D. V. and Meehan, J. R. (1987) *Artificial Intelligence Programming* (2nd edition), Lawrence Erlbaum Associates, Hillsdale, New Jersey.
6. Dougherty, E. R. and Giardina, C. R. (1988) *Mathematical Methods for Artificial Intelligence and Autonomous Systems*, Prentice Hall, Englewood Cliffs, New Jersey.
7. Dreyfus, H. (1979) *What Computers Can't Do* (2nd edition), Harper and Row, New York.
8. Dreyfus, H. and Dreyfus, S. (1986) *Mind over Machines, The Power of Human Intuition and Expertise in the Era of the Computer*, Free Press, New York.
9. Feigenbaum, E. A. and McCorduck, P. (1983) *The Fifth Generation: Artificial Intelligence and Japan's Computer Challenge to the World*, Addison-Wesley, Reading, Massachusetts.
10. Firebaugh, M. W. (1989) *Artificial Intelligence: A Knowledge Based Approach*, PWS-KENT Publishing Company, Boston, Massachusetts.

11. Genesereth, M. R. and Nilsson, N. J. (1987) *Logical Foundations of Artificial Intelligence*, Morgan Kaufmann Publishers Inc., Los Altos, California.
12. Graubard, S. R. (ed.) (1988) *The Artificial Intelligence Debate: False Starts, Real Foundations*, MIT Press, Cambridge, Massachusetts.
13. Gunderson, K. (1971) *Mentality and Machines*, Doubleday, Garden City, New York.
14. Haralick, R. M., Mackworth, A. K. and Tanimoto, S. L. (1989) Computer Vision Update, in *The Handbook of Artificial Intelligence*, Volume 4 (eds. A. Barr, P. R. Cohen and E. A. Feigenbaum), Addison-Wesley, Reading, Massachusetts, pp. 519–87.
15. Hunt, E. B. (1975) *Artificial Intelligence*, Academic Press, New York.
16. Kodratoff, Y. and Michalski, R. (eds.) (1990) *Machine Learning: An Artificial Intelligence Approach*, Morgan Kaufmann, San Mateo, California.
17. Kreutzer, W. and McKenzie, B. (1990) *Programming for Artificial Intelligence: Methods, Tools and Applications*, Addison-Wesley, Reading, Massachusetts.
18. Lighthill, J. (1973) *Report to the Science Research Council on Funding for Artificial Intelligence Research*, Her Majesty's Stationery Office, London.
19. Luger, G. F. and Stubblefield, W. A. (1989) *Artificial Intelligence and the Design of Expert Systems*, Benjamin/Cummings Publishing Company Inc., Menlo Park, California.
20. Minsky, M. L. (ed.) (1968) *Semantic Information Processing*, MIT Press, Cambridge, Massachusetts.
21. Minsky, M. L. (1986) *The Society of Mind*, Simon and Schuster, New York.
22. Nilsson, N. J. (1980) *Principles of Artificial Intelligence*, Morgan Kaufmann, Los Altos, California.
23. Rich, E. and Knight, K. (1991) *Artificial Intelligence* (2nd edition), McGraw-Hill, New York.
24. Rowe, N. C. (1988) *Artificial Intelligence Through Prolog*, Prentice-Hall, Englewood Cliffs, New Jersey.
25. Saxe, J. G. (1884) The Blind Men and the Elephant, in *The Poetical Works of John Godfrey Saxe*, Houghton, Mifflin and Company, Boston, Massachusetts, pp. 111–2.
26. Schalkoff, R. J. (1990) *Artificial Intelligence: An Engineering Approach*, McGraw-Hill, New York.
27. Shapiro, S. C. (ed.) (1987) *Encyclopedia of Artificial Intelligence*, Volumes 1 and 2, John Wiley & Sons, New York.
28. Shrobe, H. E. (ed). (1988) *Exploring Artificial Intelligence: Survey Talks from the National Conference on Artificial Intelligence*, Morgan Kaufmann Publishers, San Mateo, California.

29. Tanimoto, S. L. (1987) *The Elements of Artificial Intelligence*, Computer Science Press, Rockville, Maryland.
30. Turing, A. M. (1950) Computing machinery and intelligence, *Mind*, **59**, 433–60.
31. Waltz, D. L. (1985) Scientific data link's artificial intelligence classification scheme, *AI Magazine*, **6**[1], Spring issue, 58–63.
32. Wasserman, P. D. (1989) *Neural Computing*, Van Nostrand Reinhold, New York.
33. Weizenbaum, J. (1976) *Computer Power and Human Reason: From Judgment to Calculation*, Freeman, San Francisco, California.
34. Winston, P. H. (1984) *Artificial Intelligence* (2nd edition), Addison-Wesley, Reading, Massachusetts.

2
Automated reasoning with propositional logic

2.1 INTRODUCTION

Suppose we are given the following four statements:

1. John awakens;
2. John brings a mop;
3. Mother is delighted, if John awakens and cleans his room;
4. If John brings a mop, then he cleans his room.

The statements being true, we can reason intuitively to conclude that Mother is delighted. Thus we have deduced a fact that was not explicitly given in the four statements. But if we were given many statements, say a hundred, then intuitive reasoning would be difficult. Hence we wish to automate reasoning by formalizing it and implementing it on a computer. It is then usually called automated theorem proving. To understand computer-implementable procedures for theorem proving, one should first understand propositional and predicate logics, for these logics form the basis of the theorem proving procedures. It is assumed that you are familiar with these logics.

Nevertheless, in this chapter, you will initially read a review of propositional logic. Then you will read of procedures to prove theorems. The chapter ends with the description of a theorem proving procedure called resolution refutation. This procedure will then be extended to predicate logic in Chapter 3.

2.2 A REVIEW OF PROPOSITIONAL LOGIC

2.2.1 Propositions

Propositions make declarations; for example, 'The earth is round' and 'The moon is made of cheese.' A proposition is either *true* or *false*, but not both. This is called the **truth value** of the proposition. The truth value is assigned to a proposition; it is not inherent to the proposition. Propositions can be denoted by symbols such as A, B, C, D, E; these symbols are called **atoms**. To illustrate, the above propositions may be denoted by atoms as follows.

A = The earth is round.
B = The moon is made of cheese.

2.2.2 Formulae

A **formula** can be built with atoms, parentheses, and these five logical operators: the unary operator $\sim$ (called **not**); and binary operators $\wedge$

Formula	Written in English as ...
$(\sim F)$	"not F" or "negation of F"
$(F \wedge G)$	"F and G" or "conjunction of F and G" where F and G are "conjuncts"
$(F \vee G)$	"F or G" or "disjunction of F and G" where F and G are "disjuncts"
$(F \rightarrow G)$ or $(G \leftarrow F)$	"If F then G" or "F only if G" or "F implies G" or "F is sufficient for G" or "G is necessary for F" where F is the "antecedent" and G is the "consequent"
$(F \leftrightarrow G)$	"F if, and only if, G" or "F iff G" or "F is necessary and sufficient for G" or "G is necessary and sufficient for F"

Figure 2.1 The various ways in which the different kinds of formulae are stated in English.

F	G	(~F)	(F ∧ G)	(F ∨ G)	(F → G)	(F ↔ G)
true	true	false	true	true	true	true
true	false	false	false	true	false	false
false	true	true	false	true	true	false
false	false	true	false	false	true	true

Figure 2.2   Truth tables for the formulae built with the five logical operators.

(and), ∨ (or), → (if . . . then), and ↔ (if, and only if). These operators are also known, respectively, as **negation, conjunction, disjunction, implication**, and **double implication**. For example, B, $(\sim B)$, $((B \vee C) \wedge \sim D)$, $(((A \to D) \wedge C) \vee E)$ are all formulae. A formula in propositional logic has the following recursive definition: an atom is a formula; if F is a formula, then $(\sim F)$ is a formula; if F and G are formulae, then $(F \wedge G)$, $(F \vee G)$, $(F \to G)$ and $(F \leftrightarrow G)$ are formulae. There are no other formulae, other than those just defined. Figure 2.1 shows the various ways in which the different kinds of formulae are stated in English.

Formulae, too, have truth values. The truth value of a formula can be obtained from its atoms and logical operators. To illustrate, the formula $(\sim F)$ is true when F is false, and vice versa. This attribute of the negation operator is shown in the truth table of Figure 2.2. Figure 2.2 also contains the truth tables for $(F \wedge G)$, $(F \vee G)$, $(F \to G)$ and $(F \leftrightarrow G)$. Thus, for example, $(F \wedge G)$ is true only when both F and G are true; otherwise, $(F \wedge G)$ is false.

The precedence of the logical operators in a formula is as follows: $\sim$, $\wedge$, $\vee$, $\to$, $\leftrightarrow$. Accordingly, the formula $(((\sim A) \wedge B) \to (C \vee D))$ can be rewritten without parentheses as

$$\sim A \wedge B \to C \vee D.$$

Nonetheless, for ease in reading, it is customary to write some of the parentheses.

B	C	D	(B∨C)	(~C)	((B∨C)∧~C)	(((B∨C)∧~C)∨D)
true	true	true	true	false	false	true
true	true	false	true	false	false	false
true	false	true	true	true	true	true
true	false	false	true	true	true	true
false	true	true	true	false	false	true
false	true	false	true	false	false	false
false	false	true	false	true	false	true
false	false	false	false	true	false	false

Figure 2.3 Truth table for the formula $(((B \lor C) \land \sim C) \lor D)$. Each row corresponds to an interpretation. Some interpretations of the formula make it true; others make it false. To illustrate, the formula is false in the second row, but true in the third row.

2.2.3   Interpretations of formulae

An interpretation of a formula F is an assignment of a truth value to every atom occuring in F. Assigning, say, true to B, true to C, and false to D is an interpretation of $(((B \lor C) \land \sim C) \lor D)$. Since the formula has three distinct atoms, $(B, C$ and $D)$ and since every atom can be assigned one of two values (either true or false), there can be 2^3 distinct interpretations of the formula. A formula containing n distinct atoms has 2^n distinct interpretations. Under each interpretation, a formula can be evaluated to be true or false, as shown in the truth table of Figure 2.3. The number of rows required to construct a truth table for a formula is equal to the number of distinct interpretations of the formula. An interpretation that makes a formula true is said to **satisfy** the formula. Thus, for example, assigning true to B, false to C, and true to D satisfies the formula $(((B \lor C) \land \sim C) \lor D)$, as can be seen from the third row of the truth table in Figure 2.3.

2.2.4   Tautology and inconsistency

A formula is a **tautology** if, and only if, it is true under all its interpretations. A formula is an **inconsistency** if, and only if, it is false under all its interpretations. Moreover, note that a formula is a tautology if, and only if, its negation is an inconsistency. For example, $(B \lor \sim B)$ is a tautology; its negation, $(\sim B \land B)$, is an inconsistency. A formula is **consistent** if, and only if, it is not inconsistent. In other words, a consistent formula is true under at least one interpretation. The formula $(((B \lor C) \land \sim C) \lor D)$ illustrated in Figure 2.3 is an example of a consistent formula. If a formula is a tautology, it is consistent, but the converse may not hold. In logic literature, a tautology is also known as a **valid formula**, an inconsistency as an **unsatisfiable formula**, and a consistency as a **satisfiable formula**.

2.2.5 Equivalences

A formula F is considered to be **equivalent** to formula G if, and only if, the truth value of F is equal to the truth value of G under every interpretation of F and G. This equivalence is written as $F \equiv G$. As an example, the truth table in Figure 2.4 shows that $\sim(A \lor B) \equiv (\sim A \land \sim B)$. A list of frequently used equivalences is given in Figure 2.5. In section 2.4.2, you will read how these equivalences are employed to restructure formulae to prove theorems.

2.3 FUNDAMENTAL PROOF PROCEDURES

2.3.1 The notion of a proof

Formula G is said to be a **logical consequence** of formulae F1, F2, . . . , Fn if, and only if, every interpretation that satisfies the formula (F1 $\land$ F2 $\land$ . . . $\land$ Fn) also satisfies G. That is to say, whenever F1, F2, . . . , Fn are all true, then so is G. Alternatively, we can say that F1, F2, . . . , Fn imply G (also known as the **goal formula**). F1, F2, . . . , Fn are called the **premisses**. (The spelling 'premiss' is preferred over 'premise' in logic literature.) To demonstrate that G is such a logical consequence is to prove that $((F1 \land F2 \land \ldots F n) \rightarrow G)$ is a **theorem**; the demonstration is the proof. For simplicity in writing, we may, however, say that G has been proved to be a theorem, or even shorter, G has been proved. We shall study only those cases in which (F1 $\land$ F2 $\land$ . . . $\land$ Fn) is consistent, otherwise, it is akin to proving anything one wants, starting from an ever-false premiss: if the moon is made of cheese, then the earth is flat. You will read more about the consistency of premisses later in section 4.4.1.

2.3.2 Direct and refutation proofs

From the discussion above we can see that a formula G is a logical consequence of premisses F1, F2, . . . , Fn if, and only if, $((F1 \land F2 \land$

A	B	(~A)	(~B)	(A∨B)	~(A∨B)	(~A∧~B)
true	true	false	false	true	false	false
true	false	false	true	true	false	false
false	true	true	false	true	false	false
false	false	true	true	false	true	true

Figure 2.4   Truth table to show ~(A ∨ B) ≡ (~A ∧ ~B).

... ∧ Fn) → G) is a tautology. But, since the negation of a tautology is an inconsistency, we can also see that G is a logical consequence of F1, F2, ..., Fn if, and only if, ~ ((F1 ∧ F2 ∧ ... ∧ Fn) → G) is an inconsistency. Then we notice that

$$\sim((F1 \wedge F2 \wedge \ldots \wedge Fn) \to G)$$
$$\equiv \sim(\sim(F1 \wedge F2 \wedge \ldots \wedge Fn) \vee G)$$
$$\equiv (F1 \wedge F2 \wedge \ldots \wedge Fn \wedge \sim G).$$

Hence we can develop two fundamental methods to prove theorems: first, a direct method to demonstrate that ((F1 ∧ F2 ∧ ... ∧ Fn) → G) is a tautology; and second, a refutation method to demonstrate that (F1 ∧ F2 ∧ ... Fn ∧ ~G) is an inconsistency.

As an example, let us prove by both methods that G is a logical consequence of the premises F and (F → G). The truth table in Figure 2.6 shows by the direct method that ((F ∧ (F → G)) → G) is a tautology, and by the refutation method that (F ∧ (F → G) ∧ ~G) is an inconsistency. The formulae require four rows in the truth table because they contain two distinct atoms, F and G. As discussed in section 2.2.3, a formula with n distinct atoms requires 2^n rows. Thus there exists a finite procedure in propositional logic to decide whether a given goal is a theorem, or whether it is not. Therefore, propositional logic is said to be *decidable*. But with increasing n, the number of rows

[1]	~(~F)	≡	F	[involution]
[2]	(F → G)	≡	(~F ∨ G)	
[3]	(F → G)	≡	(~G → ~F)	[contrapositivity]
[4]	(F → (G → H))	≡	(G → (F → H))	
[5]	(F → (G → H))	≡	((F ∧ G) → H)	
[6]	(F ↔ G)	≡	((F ∧ G) ∨ (~F ∧ ~G))	
[7]	(F ↔ G)	≡	((F → G) ∧ (G → F))	
[8]	(F ↔ G)	≡	((~F ∨ G) ∧ (~G ∨ F))	
[9]	(G ∧ G)	≡	G	[idempotence]
[10]	(G ∧ TRUE)	≡	G	
[11]	(G ∧ FALSE)	≡	FALSE	
[12]	(G ∧ ~G)	≡	FALSE	[exclusion]
[13]	(G ∨ G)	≡	G	[factoring]
[14]	(G ∨ TRUE)	≡	TRUE	
[15]	(G ∨ FALSE)	≡	G	
[16]	(G ∨ ~G)	≡	TRUE	[complementation]
[17]	((F ∧ G) ∧ H)	≡	(F ∧ (G ∧ H))	
[18]	((F ∨ G) ∨ H)	≡	(F ∨ (G ∨ H))	[associativity]
[19]	(F ∧ G)	≡	(G ∧ F)	
[20]	(F ∨ G)	≡	(G ∨ F)	[commutativity]
[21]	(F ∨ (G ∧ H))	≡	((F ∨ G) ∧ (F ∨ H))	
[22]	(F ∧ (G ∨ H))	≡	((F ∧ G) ∨ (F ∧ H))	[distributivity]
[23]	~(F ∨ G)	≡	(~F ∧ ~G)	
[24]	~(F ∧ G)	≡	(~F ∨ ~G)	[de Morgan's Laws]
[25]	(F ∨ (F ∧ G))	≡	F	
[26]	(F ∧ (F ∨ G))	≡	F	
[27]	(F ∨ (~F ∧ G))	≡	(F ∨ G)	
[28]	(F ∧ (~F ∨ G))	≡	(F ∧ G)	[absorption]

Figure 2.5   A list of frequently used equivalences. Some of the equivalences are often mentioned in logic literature by their specific names; such names have been written between brackets, next to the equivalences. F, G, and H denote any formulae either in propositional or in predicate logic. TRUE symbolizes any formula that is a tautology; FALSE, an inconsistency.

in the truth table increases exponentially, and so does the computing effort. So for large n, constructing truth tables to prove theorems for either of the two methods is practicable, but not practical.

2.3.3   Rules of inference

Other approaches to theorem proving employ rules (called rules of inference) to deduce logical consequences from premisses. In Figure 2.6 you can see a proof for G being the logical consequence of the premisses F and (F → G); that, in reality, is a well-known rule of inference called **modus ponens**, often written as 'If F and (F → G) then G.' A rule of inference applied to a set of premisses produces a

F	G	~G	(F→G)	(F∧(F→G))	Proof by direct method ((F∧(F→G))→G)	Proof by refutation method (F∧(F→G)∧~G)
true	true	false	true	true	true	false
true	false	true	false	false	true	false
false	true	false	true	false	true	false
false	false	true	true	false	true	false

Figure 2.6 Truth table to prove that G is a logical consequence of the premisses F and (F → G). The table shows the proof by both the direct and the refutation methods.

formula. If we prove in general that a rule of inference applied to a set of premisses produces a formula that is a logical consequence of the premisses, then we say we have verified that the rule is **sound**. Thus modus ponens applied to F and $(F → G)$ produces G, and Figure 2.6 verifies the soundness of modus ponens. Alternatively, we can say that G is **deduced** from F and $(F → G)$ by modus ponens. Some of the commonly used rules of inference are listed in Figure 2.7. Their soundness can be verified in the manner shown in Figure 2.6. These rules of inference are used in a theorem proving procedure called **natural deduction**, described below.

2.3.4 Natural deduction

In this procedure, we apply one of the rules of inference to the given set of premisses to deduce a logically consequent formula such that the deduced formula contains atoms from only those in the premisses and

[1]   If F and G then (F ∧ G).   [introducing conjunction]

[2]   If (F ∧ G) then F.
[3]   If (F ∧ G) then G.   ]   [eliminating conjunction]

[4]   If F then (F ∨ G).
[5]   If G then (F ∨ G).   ]   [introducing disjunction]

[6]   If F and (F → G) then G.   [modus ponens]

[7]   If ~G and (F → G) then ~F.   [modus tollens]

[8]   If (F → G) and (G → H) then (F → H).   [chaining]

[9]   If F and (F ≡ G) then G.

[10] If G and (F ≡ G) then F.

Figure 2.7 Some rules of inference. The names of the rules are written between brackets. F, G, H denote any formulae either in propositional or in predicate logic. Thus, for example, according to [9] and [10] above, if we are given a formula to be true, we can deduce that the equivalent of the formula is true, too.

the goal. The formula is added to the set of premisses. Repeating this, we continue applying rules of inference and continue deducing new formulae. We stop either when we deduce a formula that is identical to the goal (the goal has been proved to be a theorem), or when we can deduce no new formulae (the goal has been proved not to be a theorem). One of the two stopping conditions must ultimately occur since, with a finite number of atoms in the premisses and the goal, we can build only a finite number of distinct formulae. As mentioned in section 2.3.2, propositional logic is decidable. Note that if the goal has been proved not to be a theorem, then it does not necessarily mean that the negation of the goal has been proved to be a theorem; for example, neither proposition D nor $\sim D$ is a logical consequence of the formula $(A \wedge C)$. In Figure 2.8, you can see an example of a proof by natural deduction. Note, natural deduction is a direct method for proving theorems.

There is, however, a deterrent to the computer implementation of natural deduction. For the example shown in Figure 2.8, suppose that at some intermediate stage of the proof, a program had deduced the formula $(A \wedge B)$ by applying to the first and second premisses the introducing-conjunction rule of inference shown in Figure 2.7. This would have wasted computing effort: formula $(A \wedge B)$ is useless as it is not used in finally proving the goal, but to know at an intermediate

Given the premisses:

[i]   John awakens.
[ii] John brings a mop.
[iii] Mother is delighted, if John awakens and cleans his room.
[iv] If John brings a mop, then he cleans his room.

Prove by natural deduction the goal: Mother is delighted.

We denote the different propositions contained in the premisses by these atoms.
A = John awakens.
B = John brings a mop.
C = John cleans his room.
D = Mother is delighted.

The goal to be proved is D.

We can then write the premisses as formulae.
[1]   A
[2]   B
[3]   A ∧ C → D
[4]   B → C

From the above premisses, we can deduce the following logical consequences.   The rules of inference are from Figure 2.7.

[5]   C   [by modus ponens on 2 and 4]
[6]   A ∧ C   [by introducing conjunction on 1 and 5]
[7]   D   [by modus ponens on 3 and 6]

The goal has been deduced as a logical consequence of the premisses.
Hence it has been proved to be a theorem.
In other words, Mother is delighted.

Figure 2.8   An example of natural deduction. This was the problem we saw at the beginning of Chapter 2.

stage that a deduced formula is useless requires foresight, something which is complicated to incorporate into a program. At every stage, the program needs to select judiciously which rule of inference to apply on which of the premisses. One way to reduce the complicacy of the program is to work with fewer rules (we have no control over the number of premisses present in a given problem). A rule of inference called **resolution** is effective enough to make the other rules secondary. The resolution rule (also called the **resolution principle** in logic literature) proves theorems by refutation. This rule and its theorem proving procedure are described next.

2.4   PROVING THEOREMS BY RESOLUTION

2.4.1   Literals and clauses

The resolution rule of inference can be applied only to a formula that is a conjunction of clauses. A **clause** is a disjunction of n literals, for any finite integer $n \geq 0$. A **literal** is an atom or the negation of an atom. Thus A, B, C, D, E, $\sim A$, $\sim B$, $\sim C$, $\sim D$ and $\sim E$ are all examples of literals. An atom and its negation are referred to as **complementary literals**; for instance B and $\sim B$. From literals, we can construct clauses similar to those shown below.

$A \lor C \lor \sim E$
$\sim A \lor D$
B
NIL.

A clause containing only one literal, such as B above, is called a **unit** clause. NIL symbolizes an **empty** clause: a clause with zero literals.

2.4.2   Converting a formula into clause form

Before we learn what the resolution rule is, we may be tempted to ask this question: Is not the resolution rule of limited utility because it can be applied only to a conjunction of clauses? No, for we can convert any formula into an equivalent conjunction of clauses by the four-stage procedure illustrated in Figure 2.9. An example of such a conversion is shown in Figure 2.10. The stages are executed sequentially from the first to the fourth; nevertheless, there may be situations when some of the stages are skipped. If the formula to be converted does not contain, say, any double implication operator, then the first stage would be skipped.

Therefore, before the resolution rule can be applied to any formulae, all of them have to be converted into equivalent conjunctions of clauses. A conjunction of clauses being true signifies that each of the clauses is true. Hence a conjunction of clauses can be written as a set of clauses, once it is understood that there is an implicit conjunction between the clauses. A formula written as a set of clauses is said to be in **clause form**. The clauses in the set are said to be **derived** from the formula.

2.4.3   The resolution rule and its soundness

The resolution rule can be applied to a pair of clauses I1 and I2 when a literal in I1 and a literal in I2 are complementary literals. To illustrate, consider I1 and I2 as the following two clauses

Stage	Objective of executing the stage	The equivalence used in order to execute the stage
1.	Eliminate $\leftrightarrow$	[1] $(F \leftrightarrow G) \equiv ((\sim F \vee G) \wedge (\sim G \vee F))$
2.	Eliminate $\rightarrow$	[2] $(F \rightarrow G) \equiv (\sim F \vee G)$
3.	Reduce scope of negation operator to apply to one atom at the most	[De Morgan's Laws] [3a] $\sim(F \vee G) \equiv (\sim F \wedge \sim G)$ [3b] $\sim(F \wedge G) \equiv (\sim F \vee \sim G)$
4.	Transform into a conjunction of clauses	[Distributivity] [4a] $(F \vee (G \wedge H)) \equiv ((F \vee G) \wedge (F \vee H))$ [4b] $((G \wedge H) \vee F) \equiv ((G \vee F) \wedge (H \vee F))$

Figure 2.9 The four successive stages of the procedure to convert any propositional logic formula into an equivalent conjunction of clauses. At each stage, repeated use any of the corresponding equivalences [that is, replace the left-hand side of the equivalence by its right-hand side] until the objective of the stage has been realized. Then enter the next stage in the sequence. If double negations appear at any time [usually in the first three stages], eliminate them by using involution ($\sim(\sim F) \equiv F$). Figure 2.10 illustrates an example that invokes the above procedure.

(*I1*) $B \vee F$

(*I2*) $\sim B \vee H$

where B is an atom; F and H are each a disjunction of zero or more literals; and the number of literals in F is independent of the number of literals in H. By the resolution rule of inference, we can deduce the following clause I3.

(*I3*) $F \vee H$

Clause I3 is called the **resolvent** deduced by **resolving** the **parent** clauses I1 and I2, by **resolving upon** the complementary literals B and

Convert the formula $((C \lor D) \rightarrow (\sim A \leftrightarrow B))$ into a conjunction of clauses by invoking the procedure of Figure 2.9.

Proceeding stage by stage, we replace the above formula by an equivalent formula, until we get a conjunction of clauses.

$$((C \lor D) \rightarrow (\sim A \leftrightarrow B))$$

$\equiv$ $((C \lor D) \rightarrow ((\sim(\sim A) \lor B) \land (\sim B \lor \sim A)))$
[obtained by using equivalence 1 of Figure 2.9]

$\equiv$ $((C \lor D) \rightarrow ((A \lor B) \land (\sim B \lor \sim A)))$
[by eliminating double negation]

$\equiv$ $(\sim(C \lor D) \lor ((A \lor B) \land (\sim B \lor \sim A)))$
[by equivalence 2]

$\equiv$ $((\sim C \land \sim D) \lor ((A \lor B) \land (\sim B \lor \sim A)))$
[by equivalence 3a]

$\equiv$ $(((\sim C \land \sim D) \lor (A \lor B)) \land ((\sim C \land \sim D) \lor (\sim B \lor \sim A)))$
[by equivalence 4a]

$\equiv$ $(((\sim C \lor A \lor B) \land (\sim D \lor A \lor B)) \land ((\sim C \land \sim D) \lor (\sim B \lor \sim A)))$
[by equivalence 4b]

$\equiv$ $((\sim C \lor A \lor B) \land (\sim D \lor A \lor B) \land (\sim C \lor \sim B \lor \sim A) \land (\sim D \lor \sim B \lor \sim A))$
[by equivalence 4b]

Figure 2.10 An example showing the conversion of a propositional logic formula into an equivalent conjunction of ·clauses. The equivalences are numbered as in Figure 2.9. Note, in this example, equivalence 3b was not used at all, whereas equivalence 4b was used twice.

$\sim B$. (The literals resolved upon must be complementary literals.) Put another way, I1 and I2 are the premises from which I3 is deduced. The literals in the resolvent are the union of the literals in the parents minus the literals resolved upon. If both parents are unit clauses, then the resolvent is the empty clause NIL.

It is easy to verify that I3 is a logical consequence of I1 and I2. Employing the equivalences from Figure 2.5, we can rewrite I1 and I2 as formulae F1 and F2, respectively.

(F1) $\sim F \rightarrow B$
(F2) $B \rightarrow H$

Then, by applying the chaining rule of inference, introduced in Figure 2.7, to F1 and F2, we can deduce $(\sim F \rightarrow H)$, which is equivalent to $(F \lor$

Case	Premises	The Logical Consequence Deduced
1	C C → D	D by modus ponens
	C ~C ∨ D	D by resolution
2	~D C → D	~C by modus tollens
	~D ~C ∨ D	~C by resolution

Figure 2.11 An illustration that the resolution rule is a generalization of the modus ponens and modus tollens rules of inference. Within each case above, the two sets of premises are equivalent. When applying resolution, if one of the parent clauses is a unit clause, then the logical consequence deduced is identical to the logical consequence deduced by applying either modus ponens or modus tollens.

H), and which in turn is identical to clause I3 above. Thus the resolution rule is sound: the resolvent clause is a logical consequence of its parents.

The soundness of the resolution rule could also have been verified by constructing a truth table, as in Figure 2.6, to show that $(((B \lor F) \land (\sim B \lor H)) \to (F \lor H))$ is a tautology.

We can conclude that the resolution rule is sound by another way. There can be two situations: *B* is either true or false. For clauses I1 and I2 to be true under both these situations, we can observe the following: if *B* is true, then *H* must be true; if *B* is false, then *F* must be true. So under both situations, $(F \lor H)$ is true. Thus resolvent clause I3 is true: it is a logical consequence of its parents, I1 and I2.

Figure 2.11 shows that the resolution rule is a generalization of the modus ponens and modus tollens rules of inference, which you saw earlier in Figure 2.7.

2.4.4 Resolution deduction

Suppose we are given a set U of clauses. Then by a procedure called **resolution deduction** we can deduce from U a sequence of resolvent clauses as follows: deduce resolvents by mutually resolving the resolvable clauses of U; further resolve these resolvents with one another or with the clauses of U to deduce more resolvents; keep deducing more and more resolvents in this manner; and stop on meeting a stipulated criterion (for example, until we deduce a specified clause, or until we cannot deduce any new clause, or until the procedure execution exhausts computer resources by overshooting some bound of computer time or memory). Alternatively, we can say that in resolution deduction we deduce a sequence of clauses I1, I2, I3, . . . such that any clause Ij is either in U or is a resolvent of the clauses preceding it in the sequence. An example of resolution deduction is shown in Figure 2.12.

2.4.5 Refutation completeness of resolution

Suppose that the set U of clauses is inconsistent (which means we are supposing that the conjunction of the clauses is inconsistent). It is an

Given a set U comprising the following five clauses:

[I1] ~A ∨ ~C
[I2] ~A ∨   C ∨ D
[I3]   A ∨   D ∨ E
[I4] ~D
[I5] ~E

Below, we see some of the resolvents that can be deduced from the set U.

[I6] ~A ∨ C   [deduced by resolving I2 and I4]
[I7]   A ∨ E   [resolving I3 and I4]
[I8]   D ∨ E ∨ C   [resolving I3 and I6]
[I9]   C ∨ E   [resolving I6 and I7]
      .
      .
      .   [and so on; more resolvents can be deduced]

Figure 2.12 An example of resolution deduction: a sequence of resolvents is deduced from a given set U of clauses.

established mathematical result that as we proceed with resolution deduction on U, we are certain to deduce an inconsistent clause. Say at some time the union of the set U and the set of resolvents contains unit clauses B and $\sim B$. Resolving these unit clauses will produce the empty clause NIL (with no literals) which is not true under any interpretation. Since NIL has been deduced from U by resolution (a sound rule of inference) any interpretation that satisfies U must satisfy NIL. But no interpretation satisfies NIL, and hence no interpretation satisfies U either. Therefore U is inconsistent. Deducing NIL from the set U of clauses thus confirms that U is inconsistent. Remember, in section 2.3.2, it was shown that G is a logical consequence of premisses F1, F2, . . . , Fn if, and only if, (F1 $\wedge$ F2 $\wedge$ . . . $\wedge$ Fn $\wedge$ $\sim G$) is inconsistent. Moreover, in section 2.4.2, you saw a procedure that you can employ to convert any formula into clause form. Thus from our discussion above, we can conclude the following: G is a logical consequence of F1, F2, . . . , Fn if, and only if, by resolution deduction, we can deduce the empty clause NIL from the set of clauses (called the **input** set) derived from F1, F2, . . . , Fn, $\sim G$.

Resolution is thus said to be **complete**: if G is indeed a theorem, then resolution is guaranteed to prove it to be so. Note, however, that resolution is complete only for the refutation method, not for the direct method. Suppose we are given the premisses B and ($\sim B \vee C$), and we are to prove that their logical consequence is the goal ($B \vee C$). Using only the resolution rule (and no other rule) on pairs of clauses, we can prove the goal by the refutation method, but we cannot deduce the goal directly from the premisses. Therefore in logic literature, resolution is more precisely called **refutation complete** but not **deduction complete**. Accordingly in our discussion, when we say that resolution is complete, we really mean that it is refutation complete.

2.4.6   The need for factoring clauses

Here we need words of caution. Resolution is complete provided all clauses in the deduction are factored, whenever they can be. By factoring, introduced in Figure 2.5, multiple occurrences of a literal in a clause are replaced by a single occurrence of the literal. Consider the example of the set of clauses ($B \vee B$) and ($\sim B \vee \sim B$). Clearly the set is inconsistent, but we are unable to prove this by resolving the two clauses; the resolvent of the clauses is ($B \vee \sim B$), a tautology. Nonetheless, if we first factor the two clauses, we get B and $\sim B$, which resolve into the empty clause NIL, thus proving the inconsistency. Accordingly, in saying that resolution is complete, we shall assume that all clauses are factored: first, all clauses in the input set are factored; later, when any resolvent is deduced, it too is factored. The factored clause replaces the original clause.

From section 2.4.3 you know that resolution is a sound rule. Moreover, from the discussion immediately above, you know resolution is complete. The soundness and refutation completeness of resolution assures us of the following: by refutation, resolution will always prove a formula that is a logical consequence of the given premisses, but it will never prove a formula that is not a logical consequence.

2.4.7   The resolution refutation procedure

The procedure by which resolution proves theorems is called **resolution refutation**. You will see below how the resolution refutation procedure is used to prove theorems: in other words, to prove that a goal formula G is a logical consequence of the premisses F1, F2, . . . , Fn.

1. Convert F1, F2, . . . , Fn and $\sim G$ into an equivalent set of clauses. These clauses constitute the input set U.
2. Select from the set two clauses that are resolvable; resolve them; and add the resolvent to the set. Iterate over this, resolving clauses and adding resolvents to the set. Stop when either the resolvent is the empty clause NIL (G has been proved to be a theorem as the input set U has been shown to be inconsistent) or no new resolvents can be deduced (G has been proved not to be a theorem). Since the set U has only a finite number of atoms, one of the two stopping conditions must eventuate (remember, propositional logic is decidable).

Do not forget to factor the clauses in both the steps above. Accordingly, on individual clauses, we apply only the factoring rule of inference; on pairs of clauses, we apply only the resolution rule. Hence, as observed in section 2.3.4, the rules of inference needed for resolution refutation are fewer than those needed for natural deduction.

2.5   CLOSING REMARKS

In Figure 2.13, you can see an example of a proof by resolution refutation. By employing resolution as the sole rule of inference on pairs of clauses we do not need to employ the other rules of inference given in Figure 2.7. Nevertheless, the number of resolvents deduced to finish the proof can depend on which clauses we select to resolve from

Given the premisses:

[i]   A
[ii]   B
[iii]   A ∧ C → D
[iv]   B → C

Prove by resolution refutation that D is a logical consequence of the above premisses. Thus D is the goal.

The premisses and the negation of the goal when converted to clauses constitute the following input set.

[I1]   A   ⎫
[I2]   B   ⎪
[I3]   ~A ∨ ~C ∨ D ⎬   [premisses]
[I4]   ~B ∨ C   ⎪
[I5]   ~D   ⎭
                                            [negation of goal]

From the above clauses, we can deduce the following resolvents.

[I6]   ~A ∨ ~C   [by resolving I3 and I5]
[I7]   ~C   [by resolving I1 and I6]
[I8]   ~B   [by resolving I4 and I7]
[I9]   NIL   [by resolving I2 and I8]

The goal is proved to be a theorem, as the empty clause NIL is deduced.

Figure 2.13 An example of proving a theorem by resolution refutation in propositional logic. Compare this with Figure 2.8, in which there is a proof by natural deduction of the same theorem.

the available resolvable clauses at any time during the proof procedure. We should obviously try to shorten the proof: as a general tenet, the fewer the resolvents, the smaller is the computer time and memory required, and thus the more efficient is the proof. Therefore we need refinements to resolution refutation. Some such refinements are discussed in Chapter 4, after resolution refutation has been extended to predicate logic in Chapter 3.

2.6 EXERCISES

A, B, C, D and E are propositional symbols below.

1. By constructing truth tables, show that
   (a) the pairs of formulae in Figure 2.5 are equivalences, and
   (b) the rules of inference in Figure 2.7 are sound.
2. Convert the following formulae into clause form

(a) $(((A \rightarrow B \wedge C) \rightarrow D))$
(b) $((A \wedge \sim B) \leftrightarrow (C \wedge D))$
(c) $(\sim(\sim A \rightarrow \sim B) \vee (C \wedge D))$

3. Prove by resolution refutation that the given goal is a logical consequence of the corresponding set of premisses.

Premisses	Goal

(a) $\sim A$
$\quad \sim C$
$\quad A \vee B \vee C$
$\left. \right\} \quad \sim A \wedge B$

(b) $\sim A$
$\quad A \vee \sim C$
$\quad A \vee \sim B \vee C$
$\left. \right\} \quad \sim A \wedge \sim B \wedge \sim C$

(c) $\sim B$
$\quad E \vee \quad C$
$\quad \sim E \vee \quad D$
$\quad A \vee \sim D$
$\quad \sim A \vee \quad B$
$\left. \right\} \quad C$

4. You are given the following premisses.
   (a) That Tom does not go to church and Harry does not go to church is false.
   (b) If Alice does not go to church, then Harry does not go to church.
   (c) If Tom goes to church, then Harry goes to church.
   Prove by resolution refutation: Alice goes to church.

5. Write a program to implement resolution refutation in propositional logic. Test the program to
   (a) solve the problem of Figure 2.13;
   (b) solve exercises 3 and 4 above; and
   (c) prove the inconsistency of the following set of clauses:
   $\sim A \vee \sim B$
   $\sim A \vee \quad B$
   $\quad A \vee \sim B$
   $\quad A \vee \quad B$

Study the resolvents deduced by your program. Could the inconsistency have been proved by a shorter proof (that is, by deducing fewer resolvents)? If so, produce manually the shortest possible proof.

2.7 SUGGESTIONS FOR FURTHER READING

Edger (1989), Enderton (1972), Kleene (1967), and Mendelson (1964) described introductory mathematical logic. Newell, Shaw and Simon

(1963) gave examples of proofs in propositional logic. Newell and Simon (1963)presented a problem-solving technique that later became known as means–end analysis. Integrated into a natural deduction procedure, the technique selected the inference rule that it considered to be the most appropriate at any stage of the proof development. Bledsoe (1977) discussed natural deduction. Robinson (1965) introduced the resolution rule of inference.

1. Bledsoe, W. W. (1977) Non-resolution theorem proving, *Artificial Intelligence*, **9**[1], pp. 1–35. Reprinted (1981) in *Readings in Artificial Intelligence* (eds. B. L. Webber and N. J. Nilsson), Tioga Publishing Company, Palo Alto, California, pp. 91–108.
2. Edgar, W. J. (1989) *The Elements of Logic*, Science Research Associate~, Chicago.
3. Enderton, H. B. (1972) *A Mathematical Introduction to Logic*, Academic Press, New York.
4. Kleene, S. C. (1967) *Mathematical Logic*, Wiley, New York.
5. Mendelson, E. (1964) *Introduction to Mathematical Logic*, Van Nostrand, New York.
6. Newell, A., Shaw, J. C. and Simon, H. A. (1963) Empirical explorations with the logic theory machine: a case study in heuristics, in *Computers and Thought* (eds. E. A. Feigenbaum and J. Feldman), McGraw-Hill, New York, pp. 109–33.
7. Newell, A. and Simon, H. A. (1963) GPS, a program that simulates human thought, in *Computers and Thought* (eds. E. A. Feigenbaum and J. Feldman), McGraw-Hill, New York, pp. 279–93.
8. Robinson, J. A. (1965) A machine-oriented logic based on the resolution principle, *Journal of the ACM*, **12**[1], 23–41.

3
Automated reasoning with predicate logic

3.1 INTRODUCTION

You should master the material discussed in Chapter 2 before reading further. In that chapter, you learned how reasoning with propositional logic could be automated, but the power of human reasoning is more than that of propositional logic. Suppose we are given the following two premisses.

1. Every husband argues with his wife.
2. Alan is a husband.

We can reason intuitively to draw the conclusion that Alan argues with his wife. But we cannot draw the same conclusion by using propositional logic, even if we were to represent the two premisses by propositional symbols, say, A and B. As we will see later in section 3.2.4, we can, however, draw the required conclusion by using predicate logic. This logic extends the power of automated reasoning to beyond that of propositional logic. It is assumed that you are familiar with predicate logic.

In this chapter, you will nonetheless initially see a review of predicate logic, intended mainly to establish our notation. You will see some similarities between the nomenclatures for predicate and propositional logic so, to prevent any confusion, all nomenclature will be explained. The resolution refutation procedure that you saw in Chapter 2 will be extended to predicate logic but beware: resolution is more complicated for predicate logic than for propositional logic. Refinements for improving the efficiency of resolution refutation will be discussed in Chapter 4.

3.2 A REVIEW OF PREDICATE LOGIC

3.2.1 Basic nomenclature

Before we use predicate logic for reasoning, we should first decide on some set of elements about which we shall be reasoning. These elements constitute our domain of discourse. An example of a domain is the set of positive integers. Elements in a domain are identified by their specific names. Such names are called **constants**. In the domain of positive integers, the constants are 1, 2, 3, 4, ... **Variables** like u, v, w, x, y, z can take on the values of the constants. Thus u could be 1 or 2 or 3 or 4 . . . . **Functions** map one or more elements of the domain to an element in the same domain. Suppose **add** is a function for adding two integers, and **mult** is a function for multiplying two integers. Then add(x, y) and mult(u, v) each have two **arguments**: add(2, 3) maps 2 and 3 to 5; mult(2, 3) maps 2 and 3 to 6. We can also say that add(2, 3) returns 5, and mult(2, 3) returns 6. Alternatively, we can write add(2, 3) = 5, and mult(2, 3) = 6. **Predicates** map one or more elements of the domain to one of the truth values, either true or false. Suppose we consider ODD, EVEN and GT to be predicates: ODD(3) has one argument, and it is true, as it declares 3 to be an odd number; ODD(2) is false; EVEN(2) is true, as it declares 2 to be an even integer; GT(add(2, 3), 3) is true, as it declares 5 to be greater than 3. We say that ODD(2) returns false, EVEN(2) returns true, and GT(add(2, 3), 3) returns true. Thus predicates tell us about the properties of individual elements of the domain or about the relationships between these elements. Constants, variables, functions and predicates constitute four mutually disjoint sets; thus, for example, a constant cannot be a variable, a function or a predicate.

A **term** is defined recursively as follows: a constant is a term; a variable is a term; $f(t_1, t_2, \ldots, t_n)$ is a term if, and only if, f denotes a function of n arguments, and $t_1, t_2, \ldots, t_n$ are terms. Thus 2, 3, and add(2, 3) are examples of terms. $P(t_1, t_2, \ldots, t_n)$ is said to be an **atom** if, and only if, P denotes a predicate of n arguments, and $t_1, t_2, \ldots, t_n$ are terms. Hence GT(add(2, 3), 3) is an atom.

3.2.2 Formulae

The five logical operators that are used in propositional logic are used in predicate logic, too. The attributes of these operators are identical in both logics, as seen in the truth tables of Figure 2.2. We can thus build formulae like (ODD(3) $\wedge$ GT(5, 2)). Moreover, to build formulae, predicate logic uses two special symbols, $\forall$ and $\exists$; they are called, respectively, the **universal** and **existential quantifiers**. For example, the formula $\forall x(\text{GT}(\text{add}(x, 1), x))$ declares that for all values of x (often alternatively worded as: for every x, or for each x) in the domain, $x + 1$ is greater than x. The occurrence of the variable x is said to be **bound** (or **quantified**) by $\forall x$. The formula GT(add(x, 1), x) is called the **scope** of $\forall x$ because that is the formula to which $\forall x$ applies. The formula

$\exists y(GT(y, 4))$ declares that there exists an element y (often alternatively worded as: for some y, or at least one y) in the domain such that y is greater than 4. The occurrence of y is bound by $\exists y$; the scope of $\exists y$ is $GT(y, 4)$.

Another formula $\forall w(ODD(w) \rightarrow EVEN(add(w, 1)))$ declares that for all w, if w is odd, then $w + 1$ is even. The occurrence of w is bound by $\forall w$; the scope of $\forall w$ is $(ODD(w) \rightarrow EVEN(add(w, 1)))$.

Let us consider one more example. The formula $\forall x(\exists y(GT(y, x)))$ declares that for all x in the domain, there exists a y (also in the domain) such that y is greater than x. The occurrence of y is bound by $\exists y$, and x by $\forall x$. The scope of $\forall x$ is $\exists y(GT(y, x))$, whereas the scope of $\exists y$ is $GT(y, x)$. So the scope of $\exists y$ is within the scope of $\forall x$. The notion of the scope of one quantifier being within the scope of another quantifier will be referred to again in Section 3.3.1, where you will see a discussion on a particular type of functions called Skolem functions.

A variable is said to be **bound** in a formula if, and only if, at least one occurrence of it is bound. A variable is said to be **free** in a formula if, and only if, at least one occurrence of it is not bound. In $\forall u(GT(u, v))$, u is bound, but v is free. Note that a variable can be both free and bound in a formula. In $(\forall u(GT(u, v)) \wedge \exists v(ODD(v)))$, v is both free and bound. The free v is independent of the bound v.

A formula in predicate logic has the following formal recursive definition: an atom is a formula; if F is a formula then $(\sim F)$ is a formula; if F and G are formulae, then $(F \wedge G)$, $(F \vee G)$, $(F \rightarrow G)$ and $(F \leftrightarrow G)$ are formulae; and if F is a formula such that x is a free variable in it, then $\forall xF$ and $\exists xF$ are formulae. There are no formulae other than those just defined. Note, x may be free in F, but in $\forall xF$ and $\exists xF$, it is bound.

The precedence of logical operators in predicate logic is the same as in propositional logic: $\sim$, $\wedge$, $\vee$, $\rightarrow$, $\leftrightarrow$, introduced in section 2.2.2. The quantifiers, however, have precedence over the logical operators. Accordingly, the formula $(\forall u(GT(u, v)) \wedge \exists v(ODD(v)))$ can be rewritten as follows:

$$\forall uGT(u, v) \wedge \exists vODD(v).$$

You must always write the parentheses enclosing the arguments of a predicate or a function. You may also write some of the other parentheses to facilitate reading.

To be precise, the predicate logic we have reviewed here is **first-order predicate logic**, as only variables can be quantified. Predicate and function symbols cannot be quantified: if P and f are predicate and function symbols, respectively, then $\forall P(P(x))$ and $\forall f(P(f(x)))$ are not permitted to be formulae. All our discussions will be limited to first-

Evaluate the truth value of the formula

$$\forall x \exists y (P(x) \wedge Q(x,f(y)))$$

under the following two interpretations.

[i] Given:
Domain = {a,b},
f(a) = b and f(b) = a, and the following truth values for atoms.

P(a)	P(b)	Q(a,a)	Q(a,b)	Q(b,a)	Q(b,b)
false	true	true	true	false	true

[ii] Given:
Domain = {1,2},
f(1) = 2 and f(2) = 1, and the following truth values for atoms.

P(1)	P(2)	Q(1,1)	Q(1,2)	Q(2,1)	Q(2,2)
true	true	true	true	false	true

Evaluating for interpretation [i]
  For x = a, P(x) is false.
  So the formula is not true for all values of x in the domain.
  Hence, $\forall x \exists y (P(x) \wedge Q(x,f(y)))$ is false.
Evaluating for interpretation [ii]
  For x = 1, P(x) is true;
        Q(x,f(y)) is true for both y = 1 and y = 2.
  For x = 2 P(x) is true;
        Q(x,f(y)) is true for y = 1.
  So for all values of x in the domain, there is a value of y in the
  domain that makes the formula true.   Hence, $\forall x \exists y (P(x) \wedge Q(x,f(y)))$
  is true.

Figure 3.1 An example showing the evaluation of a predicate logic formula
under two different interpretations.

order logic. Note that the definitions of a formula and an atom in
predicate logic are different from those in propositional logic.

3.2.3 Interpretations of formulae

An **interpretation** of a predicate logic formula consists of the following:

1. specifying a domain of $m \geq 1$ elements, each element being
   identified by a constant;

2. defining the mapping of every n-argument function $f(c_1, c_2, \ldots, c_n)$, where the c's symbolize constants from the domain; and
3. assigning truth values for every n-argument predicate $P(c_1, c_2, \ldots, c_n)$.

Once a formula has been given an interpretation, the truth value of that formula can be evaluated. Figure 3.1 shows an example of how the truth value of a formula is evaluated under two interpretations. One interpretation makes the formula true, the other false. As we can see from this example, we cannot evaluate a formula that contains free variables. Accordingly, from now on we shall assume that none of our formulae for evaluation contains any free variables.

Formulae that are **equivalent** to one another have the same truth values under all interpretations. Commonly used equivalences are listed in Figures 2.5 and 3.2. Note, whereas the equivalences of Figure 2.5 hold for both propositional and predicate logics, those for Figure

$$
\begin{array}{clcl}
[1] & \forall x F(x) & \equiv & \forall y F(y) \\
[2] & \exists x F(x) & \equiv & \exists y F(y) \\
[3] & \sim\forall x F(x) & \equiv & \exists x(\sim F(x)) \\
[4] & \sim\exists x F(x) & \equiv & \forall x(\sim F(x)) \\
[5] & (\forall x F(x) \ \lor \ \forall x G(x)) & \equiv & (\forall x F(x) \ \lor \ \forall y G(y)) \\
[6] & (\forall x F(x) \ \lor \ \exists x G(x)) & \equiv & (\forall x F(x) \ \lor \ \exists y G(y)) \\
[7] & (\exists x F(x) \ \lor \ \forall x G(x)) & \equiv & (\exists x F(x) \ \lor \ \forall y G(y)) \\
[8] & (\exists x F(x) \ \lor \ \exists x G(x)) & \equiv & (\exists x F(x) \ \lor \ \exists y G(y)) \\
[9] & (\forall x F(x) \ \land \ \forall x G(x)) & \equiv & (\forall x F(x) \ \land \ \forall y G(y)) \\
[10] & (\forall x F(x) \ \land \ \exists x G(x)) & \equiv & (\forall x F(x) \ \land \ \exists y G(y)) \\
[11] & (\exists x F(x) \ \land \ \forall x G(x) & \equiv & (\exists x F(x) \ \land \ \forall y G(y)) \\
[12] & (\exists x F(x) \ \land \ \exists x G(x)) & \equiv & (\exists x F(x) \ \land \ \exists y G(y)) \\
[13] & (\forall x F(x) \ \lor \ \forall y G(y)) & \equiv & \forall x \forall y(F(x) \ \lor \ G(y)) \\
[14] & (\forall x F(x) \ \land \ \forall y G(y)) & \equiv & \forall x \forall y(F(x) \ \land \ G(y)) \\
[15] & (\forall x F(x) \ \lor \ H\{x\}) & \equiv & \forall x(F(x) \ \lor \ H\{x\}) \\
[16] & (\forall x F(x) \ \land \ H\{x\}) & \equiv & \forall x(F(x) \ \land \ H\{x\}) \\
[17] & (\exists x F(x) \ \lor \ H\{x\}) & \equiv & \exists x(F(x) \ \lor \ H\{x\}) \\
[18] & (\exists x F(x) \ \land \ H\{x\}) & \equiv & \exists x(F(x) \ \land \ H\{x\}) \\
[19] & \forall x(F(x) \ \land \ G(x)) & \equiv & (\forall x F(x) \ \land \ \forall x G(x)) \\
[20] & \forall x(F(x) \ \land \ G(x)) & \equiv & (\forall x F(x) \ \land \ \forall y G(y)) \\
[21] & \forall x(F(x) \ \land \ G(x)) & \equiv & \forall x \forall y(F(x) \ \land \ G(y)) \\
[22] & \exists x(F(x) \ \lor \ G(x)) & \equiv & (\exists x F(x) \ \lor \ \exists x G(x)) \\
[23] & \exists x(F(x) \ \lor \ G(x)) & \equiv & (\exists x F(x) \ \lor \ \exists y G(y)) \\
[24] & \exists x(F(x) \ \lor \ G(x)) & \equiv & \exists x \exists y(F(x) \ \lor \ G(y))
\end{array}
$$

Figure 3.2 A list of frequently used equivalences in predicate logic. $F(x)$ and $G(x)$ denote formulae containing a free variable x; $H\{x\}$ denotes a formula that does not contain the variable x. The above list can be extended by the list of equivalences given in Figure 2.5. Note that whereas the equivalences of Figure 2.5 hold for both propositional and predicate logic, those above hold only for predicate logic.

Suppose we are given the following two premisses.

[i]   Every husband argues with his wife.
[ii]   Alan is a husband.

Prove the goal: Alan argues with his wife.

We shall use the following predicates and functions.
HUSBAND(x) : a predicate to declare x is a husband.
ARGUES(x,y) : a predicate to declare x argues with y.
wife(x)   : a function to map x to the wife-of-x; in other
                 words, if z = wife(x), then z is the wife of x.
The goal to be proved is ARGUES(Alan,wife(Alan)).

We can then write the premisses as follows.
[1]   ∀x(HUSBAND(x) → ARGUES(x,wife(x)))
[2]   HUSBAND(Alan)

Note, Alan is a constant in our domain of persons.   So by applying the
rule of universal specialization to [1], we obtain the following deduction.

[3]   HUSBAND(Alan) → ARGUES(Alan,wife(Alan))

Then by applying the modus ponens rule of inference to [2] and [3], we
obtain the following deduction.

[4]   ARGUES(Alan,wife(Alan))
Thus the goal is proved to be a theorem.

Figure 3.3   An example showing the application of the universal specialization
rule of inference. See Figure 2.7 for the modus ponens rule, which too has
been applied above. The above procedure is that of natural deduction, which
was described in section 2.3.4.

3.2 hold only for predicate logic. In section 3.3.1, you will see how
some of these equivalences are used to restructure formulae to prove
theorems.

3.2.4   Rules of inference

Just as in propositional logic, rules of inference can also be used in
predicate logic to deduce logical consequences from premisses. Some
of these rules are listed in Figure 2.7. Besides these, predicate logic has
another intuitively obvious rule: if a formula is true for all elements in a
domain, then it is true for specific elements in the domain. This is
called the rule of **universal specialization** (or **universal instantiation**).
From $\forall x F(x)$, we can deduce $F(b)$, where b is a constant. Put another
way, any element from the domain can be substituted for a universally

quantified variable. In Figure 3.3, you can see an example in which the rule of universal specialization is applied. You will read more about the substitution of variables in section 3.3.2.

3.2.5   Semidecidability of predicate logic

Remember from Chapter 2, a tautology is a formula that is always true (in other words, true under all interpretations); an inconsistency is always false. The negation of a tautology is an inconsistency; for example, $(\forall x P(x) \rightarrow \exists y P(y))$ is a tautology; its negation, $(\forall x P(x) \wedge \sim \exists y P(y))$ is an inconsistency. Similarly, the negation of an inconsistency is a tautology. A formula is consistent if, and only if, it is true under at least one interpretation. Every tautology is a consistent formula, but not vice versa.

To prove that a formula G is a logical consequence of the premises F1, F2, . . . , F_n, we can, as discussed in section 2.3.2, develop two fundamental methods: a direct method to demonstrate that $((F1 \wedge F2 \wedge \ldots \wedge Fn) \rightarrow G)$ is a tautology; and a refutation method to demonstrate that $(F1 \wedge F2 \wedge \ldots \wedge Fn \wedge \sim G)$ is an inconsistency. In predicate logic, in general, there can be an infinite number of domains. Moreover, a single domain can contain an infinite number of elements; for example, the domain of positive integers. There can hence be an infinite number of interpretations of a formula. Therefore, we cannot show that a formula is a tautology or an inconsistency by evaluating it under all interpretations. This is unlike propositional logic, where a formula can be evaluated under all its interpretations.

It is an established mathematical result that in predicate logic there exists no general proof procedure that will prove a goal G if G is a theorem, and that will disprove G if G is not a theorem. Nonetheless, procedures do exist that will prove G if G is a theorem but these procedures may never terminate if G is not a theorem. So predicate logic is said to be **semidecidable**. The resolution refutation procedure can be used in predicate logic but its proving power is limited by the semidecidability of the logic.

3.3   PREREQUISITES FOR RESOLUTION

3.3.1   Converting a formula into clause form

Applying the resolution rule in predicate logic is more complicated than in propositional logic. Nevertheless, it is still required that formulae be converted into a clause form (a set of clauses), that is to say, clauses have to be derived from the formulae. A **clause** is a

Convert the formula $\forall y \forall z (\exists u(P(y,u) \lor P(z,u)) \to \exists u Q(y,z,u))$ into clause form by invoking the ten-stage procedure of Section 3.3.1.

$\forall y \forall z (\exists u(P(y,u) \lor P(z,u)) \to \exists u Q(y,z,u))$
[double implication absent; stage 1 skipped]

$\equiv \quad \forall y \forall z (\sim\exists u(P(y,u) \lor P(z,u)) \lor \exists u Q(y,z,u))$
[implication eliminated; end of stage 2]

$\equiv \quad \forall y \forall z (\forall u(\sim(P(y,u) \lor P(z,u))) \lor \exists u Q(y,z,u))$
$\equiv \quad \forall y \forall z (\forall u(\sim P(y,u) \land \sim P(z,u)) \lor \exists u Q(y,z,u))$
[scope of negations reduced to atoms; end of stage 3]

$\equiv \quad \forall y \forall z (\forall u(\sim P(y,u) \land \sim P(z,u)) \lor \exists x Q(y,z,x))$
[renamed bound variables to make them unique; end of stage 4]

$\equiv \quad \forall y \forall z (\forall u(\sim P(y,u) \land \sim P(z,u)) \lor Q(y,z,f(y,z)))$
[existential quantifiers eliminated; f(y,z) is Skolem term; end of stage 5]

$\equiv \quad \forall y \forall z \forall u((\sim P(y,u) \land \sim P(z,u)) \lor Q(y,z,f(y,z)))$
[quantifiers moved to the left; end of stage 6]

After eliminating the prefix, the following matrix remains.
$(\sim P(y,u) \land \sim P(z,u)) \lor Q(y,z,f(y,z))$
[end of stage 7]
$\equiv \quad (\sim P(y,u) \lor Q(y,z,f(y,z))) \land (\sim P(z,u) \lor Q(y,z,f(y,z)))$
[conjunction of clauses developed; end of stage 8]

After deleting the explicit conjunction, we obtain the following two clauses.
$\sim P(y,u) \lor Q(y,z,f(y,z))$
$\sim P(z,u) \lor Q(y,z,f(y,z))$ [end of stage 9]
After standardizing the clauses so that the clauses do not contain the same variable name, the clauses are written as follows.
$\sim P(y,u) \lor Q(y,z,f(y,z))$
$\sim P(x,v) \lor Q(w,x,f(w,x))$ [end of stage 10]

Figure 3.4 An example showing the conversion of a predicate logic formula into clause form. P and Q are predicates; f is a function; u, v, w, x, y, z are variables.

disjunction of zero or more literals. A **literal** is an atom or the negation of an atom. All variables in a clause are understood to be implicitly universally quantified and, between the clauses themselves, there is an implicit conjunction. To apply resolution to the clauses it is essential that the clauses be **standardized**, that is, no two clauses should contain the same variable. Later, in section 3.4.1, you will see how resolution is applied to a pair of clauses. Formulae in predicate logic can be converted into clause form by the ten-stage conversion procedure described below. As you read the procedure, you should also keep referring to the conversion example given in Figure 3.4. That way, you may find the procedure easier to comprehend. Note, most of the stages in the conversion procedure rely on the use of equivalences, which were listed earlier in Figures 2.5 and 3.2. To review the notation mentioned earlier and in these figures: F, G and H denote any formulae; $F(x)$ and $G(x)$ denote formulae containing a free variable x; and $H\{x\}$ denotes a formula that does not contain the variable x.

Stage 1
Eliminate the double implication operator $\leftrightarrow$. Use the following equivalence to replace the left-hand side by the right-hand side:

$$(F \leftrightarrow G) \equiv (\sim F \lor G) \land (\sim G \lor F).$$

Stage 2
Eliminate the implication operator $\rightarrow$. Use the equivalence

$$(F \rightarrow G) \equiv (\sim F \lor G).$$

Stage 3
Reduce the scope of the negation operators to apply to one atom at the most. Use the following four equivalences

$$\sim(F \lor G) \equiv (\sim F \land \sim G)$$
$$\sim(F \land G) \equiv (\sim F \lor \sim G)$$
$$\sim \forall x F(x) \equiv \exists x(\sim F(x))$$
$$\sim \exists x F(x) \equiv \forall x(\sim F(x)).$$

At any time in the above three stages, apply involution $\sim(\sim F) \equiv F$ to eliminate double negation.

Stage 4
Rename variables so that every quantifier binds a unique variable. The truth value of the formula does not change by doing this because these variables can be viewed as dummy variables. In effect, you will be using the following eight equivalences.

$$(\forall x F(x) \lor \forall x G(x)) \equiv (\forall x F(x) \lor \forall y G(y))$$
$$(\forall x F(x) \lor \exists x G(x)) \equiv (\forall x F(x) \lor \exists y G(y))$$
$$(\exists x F(x) \lor \forall x G(x)) \equiv (\exists x F(x) \lor \forall y G(y))$$
$$(\exists x F(x) \lor \exists x G(x)) \equiv (\exists x F(x) \lor \exists y G(y))$$
$$(\forall x F(x) \land \forall x G(x)) \equiv (\forall x F(x) \land \forall y G(y))$$
$$(\forall x F(x) \land \exists x G(x)) \equiv (\forall x F(x) \land \exists y G(y))$$
$$(\exists x F(x) \land \forall x G(x)) \equiv (\exists x F(x) \land \forall y G(y))$$
$$(\exists x F(x) \land \exists x G(x)) \equiv (\exists x F(x) \land \exists y G(y))$$

Stage 5

Replace all existentially quantified variables by Skolem terms (explained below) and eliminate all existential quantifiers. Suppose we have the following formula

$$\exists u \forall v \forall w \exists x \forall y \exists z F(u, v, w, x, y, z).$$

This is rewritten as the formula below:

$$\forall v \forall w \forall y F(b, v, w, f(v, w), y, g(v, w, y)).$$

In the new formula, the constant b has replaced variable u, $f(v, w)$ has replaced x, and $g(v, w, y)$ has replaced z. Moreover, the three existential quantifiers $\exists u$, $\exists x$ and $\exists z$ have been eliminated. Consider $f(v, w)$, which has replaced x. Since $\exists x$ is within the scope of $\forall v$ and $\forall w$ the value of x that 'exists' depends on v and w. We define this dependence by the function f, which maps values of v and w into the value of x that exists. One can similarly explain why b has replaced u and why $g(v, w, y)$ has replaced z. The replacements b, $f(v, w)$ and $g(v, w, y)$ are called Skolem terms and b, f and g are called Skolem functions; b is viewed as a function of zero arguments. Alternatively, b is referred to as a Skolem constant. None of the symbols b, f and g should have already occurred in the original formula $F(u, v, w, x, y, z)$. The arguments of a Skolem function are those universally quantified variables whose scope includes the scope of the existentially quantified variable being replaced. This is because the value of the existentially quantified variable that makes the formula true can be viewed as a function of such universally quantified variables. For example, the formula $\forall x \exists y GT(y, x)$ would become $\forall x GT(h(x), x)$, where $h(x)$ is a Skolem term. Incidentally, a dual of the Skolemizing discussed here will be presented later in section 5.3.1, wherein we shall be eliminating universal quantifiers instead of existential quantifiers.

Stage 6

Move all quantifiers (only the universal ones remain) so that on the left of the formula there is a string of quantifiers called the **prefix**, and on the right, there is a quantifier-free formula called the **matrix**. The relative order of the quantifiers remains unchanged. The formula is now said to have been converted into **prenex normal form**. In effect, you will be using the following four equivalences

$$(\forall x F(x) \lor \forall y G(y)) \equiv \forall x \forall y (F(x) \lor G(y))$$
$$(\forall x F(x) \land \forall y G(y)) \equiv \forall x \forall y (F(x) \land G(y))$$
$$(\forall x F(x) \lor H\{x\}) \equiv \forall x (F(x) \lor H\{x\})$$
$$(\forall x F(x) \land H\{x\}) \equiv \forall x (F(x) \land H\{x\})$$

Stage 7

Eliminate the prefix; now only the matrix remains. This does not affect the formula as long as it is understood that all variables in the matrix are implicitly universally quantified. According to the assumption we made in section 3.2.3, none of our formulae for evaluation contain free variables. Hence there are never any free variables in the matrix.

Stage 8

Convert the matrix into a conjunction of clauses by repeatedly employing the following distributivity equivalences

$$(F \lor (G \land H)) \equiv ((F \lor G) \land (F \lor H))$$

$$((G \land H) \lor F) \equiv ((G \lor F) \land (H \lor F))$$

Stage 9

Write the conjunction of clauses as a set of clauses by deleting the explicit occurrence of the conjunctions. It should be understood that there is an implicit conjunction between the clauses.

Stage 10

Standardize the clauses by renaming variables so that no two clauses contain the same variables. Since all the variables in the clauses are implicitly universally quantified from stage 7, and since there is an implicit conjunction between the clauses from stage 9, this renaming of variables is justified because it is based on the use of the following equivalence

$$\forall x(F(x) \land G(x)) \equiv \forall x \forall y(F(x) \land G(y)).$$

3.3.2 Substitutions

Before we learn about resolution in predicate logic we should learn about substitution. We saw substitution in the example of Figure 3.3, where a universally quantified variable was replaced by a constant. In general, variables can be replaced by terms. Substitution is required so that we can apply the resolution rule to clauses.

Let **expression** be a generic appellation for a term, an atom, a function, a predicate, or a formula. A set of ordered pairs constitutes a **substitution**

$$\alpha = \{t_1/y_1, t_2/y_2, \ldots, t_n/y_n\}$$

where the t's are terms, the y's are distinct variables, and t_i is not equal to y_i, for any $i = 1, 2, \ldots, n$. When a substitution α is applied to any expression K, then every occurrence of y_i in K is simultaneously replaced by t_i; the resulting expression is symbolized by $K\alpha$, which is said to be an **instance** of K. Suppose the substitution

$$\alpha = \{a/x, g(u)/z\}$$

is applied to $P(w, f(x), z)$; the resulting expression is $P(w, f(a), g(u))$. The **empty substitution** is denoted by the symbol ε; when ε is applied to any expression K, then $K\varepsilon = K$.

3.3.3 Composition of substitutions

If α and β are two substitutions, then the **composition** of α with β is defined to be another substitution $\alpha \circ \beta$ such that

$$K(\alpha \circ \beta) = (K\alpha)\beta$$

for any expression K. In other words, applying the substitution $\alpha \circ \beta$ to K gives the same result as first applying α to K to get $K\alpha$, and then applying β to $K\alpha$.

$\alpha \circ \beta$ can be derived from α and β by the procedure described below. As you read the procedure, keep referring to the example of Figure 3.5. That should facilitate your understanding of the procedure. Suppose α and β are the following substitutions

$$\alpha = \{t_1/y_1, t_2/y_2, \ldots, t_n/y_n\}$$
$$\beta = \{s_1/x_1, s_2/x_2, \ldots, s_m/x_m\}$$

The procedure to generate $\alpha \circ \beta$ consists of two steps.

Step 1
From α and β, construct sets $\lambda 1$, $\lambda 2$ and $\lambda 3$.

$$\lambda 1 = \{t_1\beta/y_1, t_2\beta/y_2, \ldots, t_n\beta/y_n, s_1/x_1, s_2/x_2, \ldots, s_m/x_m\}$$
$$\lambda 2 = \{t_i\beta/y_i \mid t_i\beta/y_i \ \varepsilon \ \lambda 1 \text{ and } t_i\beta = y_i, \text{ for } 1 \leq i \leq n\}$$
$$\lambda 3 = \{s_i/x_i \mid s_i/x_i \ \varepsilon \ \lambda 1 \text{ and } x_i \ \varepsilon \ \{y_1, y_2, \ldots, y_n\}\}$$

Step 2
Derive the composition $\alpha \circ \beta$ from the following equation

$$\alpha \circ \beta = \lambda 1 - \lambda 2 - \lambda 3.$$

Figure 3.6 lists the properties of the composition of substitutions. Being conversant with these properties may help you when you read how substitutions are used in unification. This is described next.

3.3.4 Unifiers

Expressions K_1 and K_2 are said to be **unifiable** if, and only if, there exists a substitution γ such that $K_1\gamma = K_2\gamma$. Substitution γ is called the

Given substitutions α and β.

$$\alpha = \{z/u,\ h(u)/w\}$$
$$\beta = \{a/u,\ z/w,\ u/z\}$$

Derive the composition $\alpha \circ \beta$ by the procedure of Section 3.3.3. Then show that for a specimen expression
$$K = P(u,w,f(z)),$$

$$K(\alpha \circ \beta) = (K\alpha)\beta.$$

We begin executing the procedure to generate $\alpha \circ \beta$.

[Step 1]
$$\lambda 1 = \{z\beta/u,\ h(u)\beta/w,\ a/u,\ z/w,\ u/z\}$$
$$ = \{u/u,\ h(a)/w,\ a/u,\ z/w,\ u/z\}$$
$$\lambda 2 = \{u/u\}$$
$$\lambda 3 = \{a/u,\ z/w\}$$

[Step 2]
$$\alpha \circ \beta = \lambda 1 - \lambda 2 - \lambda 3$$
$$ = \{h(a)/w,\ u/z\}$$

Next, to show $K(\alpha \circ \beta) = (K\alpha)\beta$ for $K = P(u,w,f(z))$.
$$K(\alpha \circ \beta) = P(u,h(a),f(u))$$

$$K\alpha = P(z,h(u),f(z))$$
$$(K\alpha)\beta = P(u,h(a),f(u))$$

Therefore, $K(\alpha \circ \beta) = (K\alpha)\beta$.

Figure 3.5   An example to show the derivation of the composition $\alpha \circ \beta$ from given substitutions α and β. Furthermore, it shows that $K(\alpha \circ \beta) = (K\alpha)\beta$ for some specimen expression K.

---

1. $(\alpha \circ \beta) \circ \gamma = \alpha \circ (\beta \circ \gamma)$ [associativity holds]

2. $\epsilon \circ \alpha = \alpha$ [ϵ is left identity]

3. $\alpha \circ \epsilon = \alpha$ [ϵ is right identity, too]

4. It is usually not true that $\alpha \circ \beta = \beta \circ \alpha$. Thus composition of the substitutions is not commutative.

Figure 3.6   Properties of the composition of substitutions. α, β, and γ denote any substitutions; ε is the empty substitution.

unifier and $K_i\gamma$ (that is, $K_1\gamma$ or $K_2\gamma$) is called the **common instance** of the two expressions. Alternatively, the two expressions are said to have been **unified** by γ.

Any given expressions may have more than one unifier. Consider the atoms $P(x)$ and $P(y)$, where x and y are both variables. With a unifier $\gamma_1 = \{b/x, b/y\}$ the common instance is $P(b)$; with $\gamma_2 = \{z/x, z/y\}$ the common instance is $P(z)$. Taking b to be a constant and z to be a variable, we can say that of the two common instances, $P(z)$ is more general than $P(b)$: note that $P(b)$ is an instance of $P(z)$, but not vice versa. Put another way, if in a clause (where all variables are understood to be universally quantified) $P(z)$ is true, then by universal specialization $P(b)$ is true; but if $P(b)$ is true, $P(z)$ need not be true. We say that for $P(x)$ and $P(y)$, unifier γ_2 is **more general** then unifier γ_1. You may have observed that $P(x)$ and $P(y)$ have other unifiers, too, for example, $\{x/y\}$ and $\{y/x\}$. Since two expressions can have many unifiers, there arises the idea of a **most general unifier**, abbreviated as **mgu**.

3.3.5   Most general unifiers

A unifier δ of expressions K_1 and K_2 is called an **mgu** if, and only if, for every unifier γ of K_1 and K_2, common instance $K_i\delta$ is more general than common instance $K_i\gamma$. In other words, $K_i\gamma$ is an instance of $K_i\delta$. The expresion $K_i\delta$ is called the **most general common instance** of K_1 and K_2, that is to say, there exists a substitution θ such that

$$K_i\gamma = (K_i\delta)\theta$$
$$= K_i(\delta \circ \theta)$$

by the definition of composition of substitutions described in section 3.3.3. From this, we can conclude that $\gamma = \delta \circ \theta$. An mgu makes the least possible changes to unify the expressions. Suppose, during the process of finding a common instance of the expressions, there is a choice: a variable can be replaced either by another variable or by a constant. An mgu would then choose to replace the variable by the other variable, rather than by the constant. As we shall see later in this section, two expressions may have more than one mgu. In that case, the different most general common instances are all equally general.

An mgu of two expressions K_1 and K_2 can be found by invoking the recursive procedure MGUNIFIER given in Figure 3.7. You will notice that the procedure uses the notions of the **head** and the **tail** of an expression. To understand what the head and tail signify, consider the expression as a list, where each element of the list is itself an expression, sometimes called a **subexpression**. Thus an expression

[1]   procedure MGUNIFIER(K_1,K_2);

[2]   If either K_1 or K_2 symbolizes a constant, a variable, a function, or a predicate, then do:

    [2.1]   If K_1 and K_2 are identical, then return the empty substitution ϵ.

    [2.2]   If K_1 symbolizes a variable, then do:

        [2.2.1]   If K_1 occurs in K_2 then return failure, else return $\{K_2/K_1\}$.

    [2.3]   If K_2 symbolizes a variable, then do:

        [2.3.1]   If K_2 occurs in K_1 then return failure, else return $\{K_1/K_2\}$.

    [2.4]   If neither K_1 nor K_2 symbolizes a variable, then return failure.

[3] α := MGUNIFIER(head of K_1, head of K_2).

[4]   If α is equal to failure, then return failure.

[5]   K3 := result of applying α to the tail of K_1.

[6]   K4 := result of applying α to the tail of K_2.

[7] β := MGUNIFIER(K_3,K_4).

[8]   If β is equal to failure, then return failure.

[9]   Return the composition $\alpha \circ \beta$.

[10]   end.

Figure 3.7 A recursive procedure to return a most general unifier of two expressions K_1 and K_2. The notions of the head and the tail of an expression are explained in section 3.3.5. Steps 2.2.1 and 2.3.1 conduct the so-called occurrence check. You will read more about this in section 5.4.2.

such as $P(x, y, f(b))$ can be considered as the list $(P \quad x \quad y \quad (f \quad b))$. The four successive elements of the list are P, x, y and $(f \quad b)$; the fourth element $(f \quad b)$ is itself a list of two elements, f and b. The head of a list is the first element of a list; the tail is the rest of the elements. For $(P \quad x \quad y \quad (f \quad b))$, the head is P and the tail is the list $(x \quad y \quad (f \quad b))$. Figure 3.8 shows an example of finding the mgu of two expressions.

You will also notice that procedure MGUNIFIER sometimes returns failure. This happens when the two expressions to be unified cannot be unified. A few examples of expressions that cannot be unified are given in Figure 3.9. As is apparent from these examples, two expressions cannot be unified when unifying them requires (a) that a variable be replaced by a term containing the same variable, or (b) that a predicate or a function symbol be replaced. The former causes

Find an mgu of expressions $K_1 = P(g(u),z,f(z))$ and
$$K_2 = P(x,y,f(b)).$$

Developing the mgu.
$\{g(u)/x\}$ unifies the first mismatched subexpressions of K_1 and K_2.

$K_1\{g(u)/x\} = P(g(u),z,f(z))$
$K_2\{g(u)/x\} = P(g(u),y,f(b))$

$\{y/z\}$ unifies the next mismatched subexpressions.
The composition $\{g(u)/x\}\circ\{y/z\} = \{g(u)/x, \ y/z\}$.

$K_1\{g(u)/x, \ y/z\} = P(g(u), \ y, \ f(y))$
$K_2\{g(u)/x, \ y/z\} = P(g(u), \ y, \ f(b))$

$\{b/y\}$ unifies the next mismatched subexpressions.
The composition $\{g(u)/x, \ y/z\}\circ\{b/y\} = \{g(u)/x, \ b/z, \ b/y\}$
is the mgu, which we call δ.

Applying δ to K_1 and K_2, we generate a most general common instance.
$K_i\delta = P(g(u),b,f(b))$, for $i = 1$ and 2.

Figure 3.8 An example showing how to find a most general unifier of two expressions. P is a predicate; f and g are functions; u, x, y, z are variables; b is a constant.

indefinite recursion; the latter violates the definition of a substitution in first-order predicate logic.

Figure 3.10 shows another example: for two expressions, K_1 and K_2, we find an mgu δ and we also find one other specimen unifier γ. It is then shown that $K_i\delta$ is more general than $K_i\gamma$.

Earlier in this section it was mentioned that two expressions may not have a unique mgu. Figure 3.11 illustrates an example where a pair of expressions have two different mgu's. Thus there are two different most general common instances. This outcome looks like a contradiction, but it is not. Both the most general common instances are equally general; each is an instance of the other. They are said to be **alphabetic variants** of each other: they are similar except that they contain differently named variables. It is an established mathematical result that different mgu's for a set of expressions produce most general common instances which are only alphabetic variants of one another. In section 3.4.1 we shall see the need to find an mgu of literals, so we can apply the resolution rule to clauses. Because of the

Examples of expressions K_1 and K_2 that cannot be unified; procedure MGUNIFIER will return failure.		Cause of the failure in unification.	The step number of procedure MGUNIFIER in Figure 3.7 at which the procedure returns failure.
K_1	K_2		
$P(x)$	$P(f(x))$	To try to unify these, we need substitution $\{f(x)/x\}$. But that can cause indefinite recursion, as the expressions become $P(f(x))$ and $P(f(f(x)))$.	2.2.1
$P(f(x))$	$P(x)$	ditto	2.3.1
$P(x)$	$Q(x)$	One predicate symbol P cannot be replaced by another predicate symbol Q.	2.4
$P(f(x))$	$P(g(x))$	One function symbol f cannot be replaced by another function symbol g.	2.4

Figure 3.9 Examples of expressions that cannot be unified. P is a predicate; f and g are functions; x is a variable.

above result, it is immaterial which mgu we find, as long as we find any one mgu.

3.3.6 Unification of literals

Two literals L and M are said to be **unifiable literals** if, and only if, (a) either both L and M denote negated atoms, or they both denote unnegated atoms, and (b) these atoms can be unified. To illustrate, $P(x)$ and $P(y)$ are unifiable literals; similarly $\sim P(x)$ and $\sim P(y)$ are unifiable literals.

Two literals are said to be **complementary unifiable** literals if, and only if, (a) one of the literals denotes a negated atom, and the other an

In Figure 3.8, we found that for expressions

$$K_1 = P(g(u),z,f(z)) \text{ and}$$
$$K_2 = P(x,y,f(b)),$$

an mgu $\delta = \{g(u)/x,\ b/z,\ b/y\}$,
and a most general common instance

$$K_i\delta = P(g(u),b,f(b)).$$

For the specimen unifier

$$\gamma = \{g(c)/x,\ c/u,\ b/z,\ b/y\},$$

show that $K_i\delta$ is more general than $K_i\gamma$.

We observe that $K_i\gamma = P(g(c),b,f(b))$.

Next we observe that there exists substitution $\theta = \{c/u\}$ such that $K_i\gamma = (K_i\delta)\theta$. $K_i\gamma$ is thus an instance of $K_i\delta$. Hence $K_i\delta$ is more general than $K_i\gamma$.

Figure 3.10   An example to show that the common instance produced by an mgu is more general than the common instance produced by another specimen unifier. P is a predicate; f and g are functions; u, x, y, z are variables; b and c are constants.

unnegated atom, and (b) these atoms can be unified. For example, $P(x)$ and $\sim P(y)$ are complementary unifiable literals; similarly $\sim P(x)$ and $P(y)$ are complementary unifiable literals.

3.4   RESOLUTION

3.4.1   Resolving two clauses

Resolution in predicate logic is similar to resolution in propositional logic but more laborious. Before we attempt to resolve two clauses in predicate logic we must ensure that the clauses are standardized. If they are not, they can be standardized by renaming variables so that no variable name occurs in both clauses. Consider the following standardized clauses I1 and I2:

(I1) $L_1 \lor L_2 \lor L_3 \ldots \lor L_i$
(I2) $M_1 \lor M_2 \lor M_3 \ldots \lor M_j$

Given expressions $P(g(u),w,f(z))$ and $P(x,y,f(b))$, we can find two different mgu's of these expressions, by invoking procedure MGUNIFIER(K_1,K_2) of Figure 3.7.

If we take $K_1 = P(g(u),w,f(z))$

and $K_2 = P(x,y,f(b))$,

then MGUNIFIER returns mgu
$$\delta 1 = \{g(u)/x,\ y/w,\ b/z\}.$$

But if we take $K_1 = P(x,y,f(b))$

and $K_2 = P(g(u),w,f(z))$,

then MGUNIFIER returns mgu
$$\delta 2 = \{g(u)/x, w/y, b/z\}.$$

We notice that the two mgu's $\delta 1$ and $\delta 2$ are not identical. Let us now examine the two most general common instances $K_i \delta 1$ and $K_i \delta 2$.

$$K_i \delta 1 = P(g(u),y,f(b))$$
$$K_i \delta 2 = P(g(u),w,f(b))$$

$K_i \delta 1$ and $K_i \delta 2$ are instances of each other; they are equally general. We can also say that $K_i \delta 1$ and $K_i \delta 2$ are alphabetic variants of each other.

Figure 3.11   An example to show that even if the mgu's of two expressions are different, their most general common instances are equally general. P is a predicate; f and g are functions; u, w, x, y, z are variables; b is a constant.

The L's and the M's are literals, some of them denoting negated atoms and some denoting unnegated atoms. Suppose a literal of clause I1 and a literal of clause I2 are complementary unifiable literals. Since, from Figure 2.5, we know that disjunction is commutative, the sequence of literals within a clause is immaterial. So, without loss of generality, we assume that L_1 and M_1 are the complementary unifiable literals. We also assume that this unification can be done by an mgu δ. We can then resolve parent clauses I1 and I2 by resolving upon literals L_1 and M_1 to deduce the resolvent clause I3.

(I3) $L_2\delta \lor L_3\delta \lor \ldots \lor L_i\delta \lor M_2\delta \lor M_3\delta \lor \ldots \lor M_j\delta$.

Thus the literals in the resolvent are obtained by applying δ to the union of the literals in the parent clauses minus the literals resolved upon. On resolving two unit clauses (that is, clauses with one literal each) we deduce the empty clause NIL. An example of resolving two clauses is shown in Figure 3.12.

By the rule of universal specialization, $I1\delta$ (the clause obtained by

Find the resolvent of the following clauses.

P(g(y),x,f(z)) ∨ Q(z,b) ∨ R(x)
S(x,y) ∨ ~P(x,y,f(a))

The two clauses are not standardized: variable names x and y occur in both clauses.   To standardize the clauses, rename the variables in the first clause above; rename x as w, and y as u.   The standardized clauses are written as I1 and I2.

[I1] P(g(u),w,f(z)) ∨ Q(z,b) ∨ R(w)
[I2] S(x,y) ∨ ~P(x,y,f(a))

By using mgu δ = {g(u)/x, y/w, a/z}, we can observe that P(g(u), w, f(z)) of I1 and ~P(x, y, f(a)) of I2 are complementary unifiable literals. Thus we resolve upon these two literals to deduce the following resolvent I3.

[I3] Q(a,b) ∨ R(y) ∨ S(g(u),y)

Figure 3.12 An example showing how to resolve two clauses in predicate logic. P, Q, R, S are predicates; f and g are functions; u, w, x, y, z are variables; a and b are constants. See Figure 3.7 for the procedure to find an mgu of two expressions.

applying δ to the literals of I1) is a logical consequence of I1. Similarly, I2δ is a logical consequence of I2. Moreover, by following ratiocinations similar to what we did for propositional logic in section 2.4.3, we can see that I3 is a logical consequence of I1δ and I2δ. Therefore I3 is a logical consequence of I1 and I2, and we can conclude that even for predicate logic, the resolution rule is sound.

We unified literals L_1 and M_1 by an mgu, rather than by just any unifier, because by doing that, the resolvent clause I3 was deduced in its most general form. This increases the likelihood of I3 resolving with other clauses, as is required for the resolution refutation procedure, about which we shall soon see more.

3.4.2   Resolution is refutation complete

Just as for propositional logic, the resolution rule is refutation complete for predicate logic, too. A formula G is a logical consequence of premises F1, F2, . . . , Fn if, and only if, we can show the input set (clauses derived from F1, F2, . . . , Fn, ~G) to be inconsistent by deducing from the set the empty resolvent clause NIL. The soundness and refutation completeness of resolution assures us that by resolution we can always prove G to be a theorem if it is indeed so, but we can never prove G to be a theorem if it is not so. But when G is indeed not

48   *Automated reasoning with predicate logic*

Given the premisses:
[i]   John awakens.
[ii] John brings a mop.
[iii] Mother is delighted, if John awakens and cleans his room.
[iv] If John brings a mop, then he cleans his room.

Prove by resolution refutation the goal: Mother is delighted.

The premisses and the negation of the goal when converted to clause form constitute the following input set.
[I1] AWAKENS(John)
[I2] BRINGS(John,Mop)
[I3] ~AWAKENS(John) ∨ ~CLEANS(John,Room) ∨ DELIGHTED(Mother)
[I4] ~BRINGS(John,Mop) ∨ CLEANS(John,Room)
[I5] ~DELIGHTED(Mother)

From the above clauses we can deduce the following resolvents.

[I6] ~AWAKENS(John) ∨ ~CLEANS(John,Room)   [by resolving I3 and I5]
[I7] ~CLEANS(John,Room)   [by resolving I1 and I6]
[I8] ~BRINGS(John,Mop)   [by resolving I4 and I7]
[I9] NIL   [by resolving I2 and I8]

The goal is proved to a theorem, as the empty clause NIL is deduced.

Figure 3.13 An example of a resolution refutation proof in the subclass of predicate logic that does not allow the occurrence of variables. AWAKENS, BRINGS, CLEANS and DELIGHTED symbolize predicates; John, Mop, Mother and Room symbolize constants. Earlier, the same theorem was proved in propositional logic by two approaches: natural deduction in Figure 2.8, and resolution refutation in Figure 2.13.

a theorem, the resolution refutation procedure may never terminate because predicate logic is semidecidable, as discussed in section 3.2.5. A subclass of predicate logic that does not allow the occurrence of variables is, however, decidable. Such a subclass allows the occurrence of only constants, functions and predicates. An example of a resolution refutation proof in this subclass is given in Figure 3.13. Such a subclass of predicate logic has the same power of reasoning as propositional logic. In logic literature, literals with no variables in them are referred to as **ground literals**; in turn, a disjunction of ground literals is a **ground clause**.

3.4.3   Factor clauses to retain completeness

Just as in propositional logic, clauses in predicate logic should be factored for resolution to retain its refutation completeness, but in predicate logic, factoring takes on a wider connotation. A clause can be factored if, and only if, it contains unifiable literals. Consider the following clause.

(J) $L_1 \vee L_2 \vee L_3 \vee \ldots \vee L_i$.

Let us assume without loss of generality that L_1 and L_2 are unifiable literals. Moreover, we assume that this unification can be carried out by an mgu δ. The above clause can then be factored, giving the following clause.

(J') $L_2\delta \vee L_3\delta \vee \ldots \vee L_i\delta$.

Clause J' is then known as a **factor** of clause J. In general, a factor of a factor of clause J will also be known as a factor of J. Put another way, if a set of literals in a clause J have an mgu δ, then Jδ is a factor of J, where multiple occurrences of a literal in Jδ have been replaced by a single occurrence of the literal. For an example of factoring, consider the clause

$$P(x, y, f(b)) \vee S(x, y) \vee P(g(u), w, f(z)).$$

P and S are predicate symbols; f and g are function symbols; u, w, x, y, z are variables; and b is a constant. The first and the third literals can be

Consider the clauses:
[I1] $P(u) \vee P(w)$
[I2] $\sim P(x) \vee \sim P(y)$

By using mgu $= \{u/x\}$ to resolve upon $P(u)$ of I1 with $\sim P(x)$ of I2, we deduce the following resolvent.

[I3] $P(w) \vee \sim P(y)$

Resolving upon any other literals of I1 and I2, we deduce resolvents that are alphabetic variants of I3.

But if we factor I1 by using mgu $= \{w/u\}$, we obtain the clause
$$P(w).$$
Similarly, if we factor I2 by using mgu $= \{y/x\}$, we obtain the clause
$$\sim P(y).$$
Resolving the unit clause $P(w)$ and $\sim P(y)$ by using mgu $= \{w/y\}$, we deduce the empty clause NIL.

Thus the set of clauses I1 and I2 is inconsistent. We would not have been able to show this inconsistency had we not factored I1 and I2.

Figure 3.14 An example to show that if clauses are not factored before resolving, then the resolution rule may lose its refutation completeness. P is a predicate; u, w, x, y are variables.

unified by an mgu δ = {g(u)/x, y/w, b/z}. Then the factor of the above clause is as follows:

$P(g(u), y, f(b)) \lor S(g(u), y)$.

A factor that contains only one literal is called a **unit** factor. In Figure 3.14 you can see an example of how resolution loses its completeness when clauses are not factored before they are resolved.

From now on, resolution in predicate logic will be assumed to have a more general meaning. A resolvent I3 is considered to be deduced from clauses I1 and I2 if, and only if, we obtain I3 by any of the following ways:

1. resolving I1 and I2; or
2. resolving I1 and a factor of I2; or
3. resolving I2 and a factor of I1; or
4. resolving a factor of I1 and a factor of I2.

Moreover, I1 and I2 will be considered to be resolvable if, and only if, resolvent I3 can be deduced as above. We shall assume that in resolving clauses not only will we resolve the clauses as they are but also their factors, if any, unless otherwise stated.

3.4.4   The resolution refutation procedure

The resolution refutation procedure for predicate logic is based on the discussion above. Before reading any further, you should look at the preparatory example of resolution refutation given in Figure 3.15. To prove that a goal formula G is a logical consequence of the premises F1, F2, . . . , Fn, execute the procedure described below.

1. Convert F1, F2, . . . , Fn and ~G into clause form. The set of clauses derived constitutes the input set U.
2. Select from the set two clauses that are resolvable; standardize them if necessary; deduce the resolvent; and add the resolvent to the set. Iterate over this, resolving clauses and adding resolvents to the set. Stop when any one of the following criteria is met.
   2.1 The resolvent is the empty clause NIL (the goal has been proved to be a theorem; input set U is inconsistent).
   2.2 No clauses can be resolved, or no new resolvent can be deduced (the goal has been proved not to be a theorem; this criterion will be met if we tried to prove that, say, $\forall y(\sim P(y))$ is a logical consequence of $\forall x P(x)$).
   2.3 Some prescribed amounts of computing resources are exhausted (no decision reached about G; remember, predicate logic is semidecidable).

Given as premises:
[i] ∀x(HUSBAND(x) → ARGUES(x,wife(x)))
[ii] HUSBAND(Alan)

Prove by resolution refutation the goal:
ARGUES(Alan,wife(Alan))

The premises and the negation of the goal when converted to clauses constitute the following input set.
[I1] ~HUSBAND(x) ∨ ARGUES(x,wife(x))
[I2] HUSBAND(Alan)
[I3] ~ARGUES(Alan,wife(Alan))

From the above clauses, we can deduce the following resolvents.
[I4] ~HUSBAND(Alan)   [by using mgu = {Alan/x} to resolve I1 and I3]
[I5] NIL   [by using empty substitution to resolve I2 and I4]

The goal is proved to be a theorem, as the empty clause NIL is deduced.

Figure 3.15 A preparatory example of proving a theorem by resolution refutation in predicate logic. Compare this with Figure 3.3, in which there is a proof by natural deduction of the same theorem.

See another example of resolution refutation in Figure 3.16. Next we shall look at a technique which uses the resolution refutation procedure to answer questions from a set of premises.

3.4.5 Answering questions by using resolution

If a formula of the type $\exists vG(v)$ is a logical consequence of some premises then we can prove it to be so by the resolution refutation procedure. We shall see below that we can extend resolution refutation to answer this question: For what value of v is $G(v)$ a logical consequence of the premises? As you read the question-answering procedure below, keep referring to the example of Figure 3.17.

Step 1
From the input set of clauses derived from the premises F1, F2, . . . , Fn, and the negation of the goal $\sim\exists vG(v)$, deduce by resolution, clauses I1, I2, I3, . . . until for some $m \geq 1$, clause Im is the empty clause NIL. The goal has then been proved to be a theorem.

Step 2
Modify the input set of clauses from step 1 so as to convert into a tautology each clause derived from $\sim\exists vG(v)$. A clause with, say, literal $H(v)$ can be converted into a tautology by writing the clause as ($H(v)$ ∨ $\sim H(v)$). In general, append to the clause the complement of every

The following premises are given as English sentences, together with their synonymous formulae in predicate logic.

[i]   Amity is the ma of Betsy.   MA(Amity,Betsy).
[ii]   For all u and w: if u is the daughter of w, then w is the ma of u.
       ∀u∀w(DAUGHTER(u,w) → MA(w,u)).
[iii] Cindy is the daughter of Betsy.   DAUGHTER(Cindy,Betsy).
[iv]   For all x, y, and z: if x is the ma of y, and y is the ma of z, then x is the grandma of z.   ∀x∀y∀z((MA(x,y) ∧ MA(y,z)) → GRANDMA(x,z)).

Prove by resolution refutation the goal: Cindy has a grandma; that is, ∃v(GRANDMA(v,Cindy)); in other words, there exists a v such that v is the grandma of Cindy. The premises and the negation of the goal when converted to clauses constitute the following input set.

[I1]   MA(Amity,Betsy)
[I2]   ~DAUGHTER(u,w) ∨ MA(w,u)
[I3]   DAUGHTER(Cindy,Betsy)
[I4]   ~MA(x,y) ∨ ~MA(y,z) ∨ GRANDMA(x,z)
[I5]   ~GRANDMA(v,Cindy)

From the above clauses, we can deduce the following resolvents.

[I6]   ~MA(x,y) ∨ ~MA(y,Cindy)
                   [by mgu = {x/v, Cindy/z} to resolve I4 and I5]
[I7]   ~DAUGHTER(Cindy,y) ∨ ~MA(x,y)
                   [by mgu = {y/w, Cindy/u} to resolve I2 and I6]
[I8]   ~MA(x,Betsy)   [by mgu = {Betsy/y} to resolve I3 and I7]
[I9]   NIL   [by mgu = {Amity/x} to resolve I1 and I8]

The goal is proved to be a theorem, as the empty clause NIL is deduced. Therefore, Cindy has a grandma.

Figure 3.16 An example of proving a theorem by resolution refutation in predicate logic. With a slight modification, the above proof can be used to answer the question: Who is Cindy's grandma? To do this, we need to maintain a record of the term that replaced the variable v of clause I5 above. See Figure 3.17 for one method as to how such a record can be maintained.

literal already present in the clause. Perform the same resolutions as in step 1 to deduce clauses J1, J2, J3, ... Clause J*m* will contain the answer to the question. Note, J*m* of step 2 tallies with I*m* of step 1; I*m* was the empty clause NIL.

Clause J*m* in step 2 has been deduced by resolution from the premises and the tautologies. Since the resolution rule is sound, J*m* is a logical consequence of the premises and the tautologies. That is, (F1 ∧ F2 ∧ ... ∧ F*n* ∧ TRUE → J*m*), where TRUE symbolizes the tautologies. From the tenth equivalence of Figure 2.5, we can then say that (F1 ∧ F2 ∧ ... ∧ F*n* → J*m*). Thus J*m* is a logical consequence of the premises

For the example in Figure 3.16, the premisses are represented as the following clauses.

[J1] MA(Amity,Betsy)
[J2] ~DAUGHTER(u,w) ∨ MA(w,u)
[J3] DAUGHTER(Cindy,Betsy)
[J4] ~MA(x,y) ∨ ~MA(y, z) ∨ GRANDMA(x, z)

By resolution refutation, answer the question: Who is Cindy's grandma? To find the answer, we not only prove the goal ∃v(GRANDMA(v,Cindy)) as in Figure 3.15, but we also evaluate the value of v. Each clause derived from the negation of the goal is converted into a tautology. We thus get the following clause.

[J5] ~GRANDMA(v,Cindy) ∨ GRANDMA(v,Cindy)

We now proceed by resolving exactly the same clauses and by resolving upon exactly the same literals as we did in Figure 3.15.

[J6] ~MA(x,y) ∨ ~MA(y, Cindy) ∨ GRANDMA(x, Cindy)
                    [by mgu = {x/v, Cindy/z} to resolve J4 and J5]
[J7] ~DAUGHTER(Cindy,y) ∨ ~MA(x,y) ∨ GRANDMA(x, Cindy)
                    [by mgu = {y/w, Cindy/u} to resolve J2 and J6]
[J8] ~MA(x,Betsy) ∨ GRANDMA(x, Cindy)
                    [by mgu = {Betsy/y} to resolve J3 and J7]
[J9] GRANDMA(Amity, Cindy)
                    [by mgu = {Amity/x} to resolve J1 and J8]

At this point in Figure 3.16, we had deduced the NIL clause. But now, to the question posed above, we have the answer: Amity is the grandma of Cindy.

Figure 3.17 An example showing how resolution refutation can be used to answer questions from a set of premisses. The literal GRANDMA(v, Cindy) of clause J5 is employed to keep a record of the term that replaced the variable v during resolution refutation: x replaced v, and Amity replaced x; in effect, Amity replaced v.

alone, and hence the answer present in Jm is a logical consequence of the premisses, too. (You will read more about question answering, later in section 5.3.5.)

3.5 MANIPULATING THE EQUALITY LITERAL

3.5.1 Semantics of equality

Until now, there has been no mention of a special literal called the equality literal. EQUAL symbolizes a predicate that declares the equality of its two arguments. Thus in the domain of integers the

The following premisses are given as English sentences together with their synonymous formulae in predicate logic.

[i]   For all x, the mother of the mother of x is the grandmother of x.
      ∀xEQUAL(mother(mother(x)),grandmother(x))
[ii] The mother of the mother of Cindy likes garlic.
      LIKES(mother(mother(Cindy)),Garlic)

Reasoning intuitively, we can conclude that the grandmother of Cindy likes garlic. We can arrive at the same conclusion by demodulation. Converted to clause form, the above premisses become the following:

[I1] EQUAL(mother(mother(x)),grandmother(x))
[I2] LIKES(mother(mother(Cindy)),Garlic)

We notice that the first argument of LIKES is an instance of the first argument of EQUAL by using mgu δ = {Cindy/x}. If we were to apply δ to clause I1, we would generate this clause:

[J1] EQUAL(mother(mother(Cindy)),grandmother(Cindy))

We can replace the first argument of LIKES in clause I2 by the second argument of EQUAL in clause J1 to deduce the following demodulant.

[I3] LIKES(grandmother(Cindy), Garlic)

Thus, the grandmother of Cindy likes garlic.

Figure 3.18   A preparatory example of demodulation. Note, clause I3 is syntactically simpler than clause I2, although the two clauses are semantically identical. Clause J1 need not be generated in practice; it is shown above only for clarity.

equality literal EQUAL(7, 7) is true, but EQUAL(8, 7) is false. If equality literals are present in the input set of clauses then we can employ two special techniques, called **demodulation** and **paramodulation**, to make use of the semantics of these literals. Each technique is described separately below. The techniques can be incorporated into the resolution refutation procedure and you will see details and examples of how this is done.

3.5.2 Demodulation

You should first glance over the preparatory example of demodulation given in Figure 3.18. Then as you read the formal description of demodulation below, keep referring to the example. This will help you in your understanding.

Consider two standardized clauses of the following form:

(I1) EQUAL(*r*, *s*)

(I2) $P(\ldots t \ldots) \lor H$

I1 is a unit clause; it contains only an unnegated equality literal; *r* and *s* are terms that denote the arguments of the equality literal. In clause I2, $P(\ldots t \ldots)$ is a literal, *P* is a predicate symbol that can have any number of arguments, and *t* is a term occurring in one of the arguments of *P*. *H* symbolizes the rest of the clause I2; in other words, it is a disjunction of zero or more literals.

Suppose *t* is an instance of either *r* or *s*. Without loss of generality let us assume *t* is an instance of *r*. Then there exists an mgu δ such that *r*δ is syntactically identical to *t*. If we were to apply δ to clause I1, we would generate the clause

EQUAL(*r*δ, *s*δ)

which is syntactically identical to the clause.

(J1) EQUAL(*t*, *s*δ).

Thus *t* is semantically identical to *s*δ, so in clause I2, we can replace the term *t* by *s*δ to deduce the following clause:

(I3) $P(\ldots s\delta \ldots) \lor H$.

I1 is called the **demodulator** or the 'from' clause, I2 is the **demodulated** or the 'into' clause, and I3 is the **demodulant** deduced. We say that we have demodulated from I1 into I2 by demodulating upon the literals EQUAL(*r*, *s*) and $P(\ldots t \ldots)$. I1 and I2 are also referred to as the **parents** of I3. The demodulant I3 is semantically identical to its 'into' parent I2, but it is not so syntactically.

The generation of clause J1 is only conceptual; J1 need not actually be generated. The main symbol manipulation to be done is this: if *r*δ is identical to *t*, the demodulant is

$P(\ldots s\delta \ldots) \lor H$;

conversely, if *s*δ is identical to *t*, the demodulant is

$P(\ldots r\delta \ldots) \lor H$.

You should now look at the example of demodulation in Figure 3.19. As we can see from the examples in Figures 3.18 and 3.19, demodulation administers a generality from the equality literal into a less general term of the demodulated clause to obtain a syntactically simplified term in the demodulant.

Suppose we have the following two standardized clauses:
[I1]   EQUAL(mult(x,1),x)
[I2]   P(c,f(mult(b,1))) ∨ Q(y) ∨ S(u,z)

The term mult(b, 1) in the arguments of P is an instance of the first argument of EQUAL by using mgu δ = {b/x}. If we were to apply δ to clause I1, we would generate this clause:

[J1]   EQUAL(mult(b,1),b)

We can replace the second argument of P in clause I2 by the second argument of EQUAL in clause J1 to deduce the following demodulant.

[I3]   P(c,f(b)) ∨ Q(y) ∨ S(u,z)

Figure 3.19   An example of demodulation. Clause I3 is syntactically simpler than clause I2, although the two clauses are semantically identical. Clause J1 need not be generated in practice; it is shown above only for clarity. P, Q, S are predicates; mult and f are functions; u, x, y, z are variables; b, c, 1 are constants.

You are given the following premisses in clause form.
[I1]   ~EQUAL(f(a),f(b))
[I2]   EQUAL(g(a,z),f(a)) ∨ ~R(b,a)
[I3]   EQUAL(g(w,b),f(b)) ∨ ~R(b,w) ∨ Q(u,b)
[I4]   ~R(x,y) ∨ R(y,x)
[I5]   ~Q(a,b)

Using resolution and demodulation, prove by refutation that goal ~R(a,b) is a logical consequence of the above premisses. The negation of the goal is written as follows.
[I6]   R(a,b)

From the input set of clauses I1 to I6, we can deduce the following clauses.
[I7]   R(b,a)   [by using mgu = {a/x,b/y} to resolve I4 and I6]
[I8]   EQUAL(g(a,z),f(a))   [by using empty substitution to resolve I2 and I7]
[I9]   EQUAL(g(a,b),f(b)) ∨ Q(u,b)
                             [by using mgu = {a/w} to resolve I3 and I7]
[I10] EQUAL(f(a),f(b)) ∨ Q(u,b)
                             [by using mgu = {b/z} to demodulate from I8 into I9]
[I11] Q(u,b)   [by using empty substitution to resolve I1 and I10]
[I12] NIL   [by using mgu = {a/u} to resolve I5 and I11]

The goal is proved to be a theorem, as the empty clause NIL is deduced.

Figure 3.20   An example of proving a theorem by refutation, using resolution and demodulation. EQUAL symbolizes equality; R and Q are predicates; f and g are functions; u, w, x, y, z are variables; a and b are constants.

3.5.3   Demodulation with resolution

Demodulation can be incorporated into the resolution refutation procedure; this means that not only do we resolve clauses, but we also demodulate from one clause into another clause. The resolvents and the demodulants are added to the set of clauses. There is an example of this in Figure 3.20.

Should you incorporate demodulation with resolution, you need to take care of the following.

1. Any time a unit clause containing an unnegated equality literal is deduced, match it against the already existing clauses to demodulate them, if possible. This is called **backward demodulation**.
2. On deducing any other clause, test to see whether it can be demodulated by any of the already existing unit clauses that contain unnegated equality literals. This is called **forward demodulation**.

Having learned demodulation, you will now read about paramodulation. There is some repetition in the description because paramodulation has some similarities with demodulation, but this repetition is unavoidable if you are to learn of both the similarities and the differences between the two types of modulation.

3.5.4   Paramodulation

You should first glance over the preparatory example of paramodulation given in Figure 3.21. It may look like demodulation but it is not. The following description of paramodulation should dispel your doubts. Later you will see a comparison of demodulation with paramodulation.

Consider two standardized clauses of the following form:

(I1) EQUAL$(r, s) \vee F$
(I2) $P(\ldots t \ldots) \vee H$

The predicate symbol P and terms r, s and t are defined as for demodulation in section 3.5.2. F and H are each a disjunction of zero or more literals; the number of literals in F is independent of the number of literals in H.

Suppose t is unifiable with either r or s. Without loss of generality, let us assume that t is unifiable with r. Then there exists an mgu δ such that $r\delta$ is syntactically identical to $t\delta$. If we were to apply δ to clause I1 we would generate the clause

EQUAL$(r\delta, s\delta) \vee F\delta$

The following premisses are given as English sentences together with their synonymous formulae in predicate logic.

[i]   The mother of Cindy is Betsy.
      EQUAL(mother(Cindy),Betsy)
[ii] For all x, the mother of x is senior to x.
      ∀xSENIOR(mother(x),x)

Reasoning intuitively, we can conclude that Betsy is senior to Cindy. We can arrive at the same conclusion by paramodulation. Converted to clause form, the above premisses become the following:

[I1]   EQUAL(mother(Cindy),Betsy)
[I2]   SENIOR(mother(x),x)

The first argument of EQUAL and the first argument of SENIOR can be unified by mgu δ = {Cindy/x}. If we were to apply δ to clauses I1 and I2, we would generate these clauses:

[J1]   EQUAL(mother(Cindy),Betsy)
[J2]   SENIOR(mother(Cindy),Cindy)

We can replace the first argument of SENIOR in clause J2 by the second argument of EQUAL in clause J1 to deduce the following paramodulant.

[I3]   SENIOR(Betsy,Cindy)

Thus, Betsy is senior to Cindy.

Figure 3.21   A preparatory example of paramodulation. Clauses J1 and J2 need not be generated in practice; they are shown above only for clarity.

which is syntactically identical to the clause

(J1) EQUAL($t\delta$, $s\delta$) ∨ $F\delta$.

Similarly, if we were to apply δ to clause I2, we would generate the clause

(J2) $P(\ldots t\delta \ldots) ∨ H\delta$.

Then from J1 and J2 we can deduce the following clause.

(I3) $P(\ldots s\delta \ldots) ∨ H\delta ∨ F\delta$.

I1 is called the **paramodulator** or 'from' clause; I2 is the **paramodulated** or 'into' clause; and I3 is the **paramodulant** deduced. We say that we have paramodulated from I1 into I2 by paramodulating upon the literals EQUAL(r,s) and $P(\ldots t \ldots)$. I1 and I2 are also referred to as the **parents** of I3.

If we are told that clauses I1 and I2 are true, then their instances J1 and J2 must also be true. There can be two situations: EQUAL($t\delta$, $s\delta$) is

Suppose we have the following two standardized clauses:

[I1]   EQUAL(f(a), g(a,z)) ∨ S(w,z)
[I2]   P(f(g(u,b)), h(c)) ∨ Q(u,y)

The term g(u, b) in the arguments of P can be unified with the second argument of EQUAL by using mgu $\delta = \{a/u, b/z\}$. If we were to apply δ to clauses I1 and I2, we would generate these clauses:

[J1]   EQUAL(f(a), g(a,b)) ∨ S(w,b)
[J2]   P(f(g(a,b)), h(c)) ∨ Q(a,y)

We can replace the first argument of P in clause J2 by the first argument of EQUAL in clause J1, and then append the rest of the literals of J1 to deduce the following paramodulant.

[I3]   P(f(f(a)), h(c)) ∨ Q(a,y) ∨ S(w,b)

Figure 3.22   An example of paramodulation. Clauses J1 and J2 need not be generated in practice; they are shown above only for clarity. P, Q, S are predicates; f, g, h are functions; u, w, y, z are variables; a, b, c are constants.

either true or false. If it is true, then since clause J2 is also true, $(P(\ldots t\delta \ldots)) \lor H\delta)$ must be true. Now since $t\delta$ and $s\delta$ are semantically identical, $(P(\ldots s\delta \ldots)) \lor H\delta)$ must be true. But if EQUAL($t\delta$, $s\delta$) is false, then for clause J1 to be true, $F\delta$ must be true. So in both situations,

$$P(\ldots s\delta \ldots) \lor H\delta \lor F\delta$$

is true. Note, this is identical to the paramodulant I3 above. Hence I3 is a logical consequence of its parents I1 and I2, and we can say that paramodulation is a sound rule of inference.

The generation of clauses J1 and J2 is only conceptual; they have been shown above only to provide a justification for deducing the paramodulant clause I3. In practice, J1 and J2 need not be generated. The main symbol manipulation to be done is this: if $r\delta$ is identical to $t\delta$, the paramodulant is

$$P(\ldots s\delta \ldots) \lor H\delta \lor F\delta;$$

conversely, if $s\delta$ is identical to $t\delta$, the paramodulant is

$$P(\ldots r\delta \ldots) \lor H\delta \lor F\delta.$$

You should now look at the example of paramodulation in Figure 3.22.

3.5.5   Paramodulation with resolution

Paramodulation can be incorporated into the resolution refutation procedure; this means that not only do we resolve clauses, but we also

You are given the following premises in clause form.
[I1] ~EQUAL(f(a), f(b))
[I2] EQUAL(g(a,z), f(a)) ∨ ~R(b,a) ∨ Q(a,z)
[I3] EQUAL(g(u,b), f(b)) ∨ Q(u,b) ∨ ~R(b,w)
[I4] ~R(x,y) ∨ R(y,x)
[I5] ~Q(a,b)

Using resolution and paramodulation, prove by refutation that goal ~R(a,b) is a logical consequence of the above premises. The negation of the goal is written as follows.
[I6] R(a,b)

From the input set of clauses I1 to I6, we can deduce the following clauses.
[I7] R(b,a)   [by using mgu = {a/x, b/y} to resolve I4 and I6]
[I8] EQUAL(g(a,z), f(a)) ∨ Q(a,z)
                      [by using empty substitution to resolve I2 and I7]
[I9] EQUAL(g(u,b), f(b)) ∨ Q(u,b)
                      [by using mgu = {a/w} to resolve I3 and I7]
[I10] EQUAL(f(a), f(b)) ∨ Q(a,b)
                      [by using mgu = {a/u, b/z} to paramodulate from I8
                       into I9, and factoring the paramodulant]
[I11] Q(a,b)   [by using empty substitution to resolve I1 and I10]
[I12] NIL   [by using empty substitution to resolve I5 and I11]

The goal is proved to be a theorem, as the empty clause NIL is deduced.

Figure 3.23 An example of proving a theorem by refutation, using resolution and paramodulation. EQUAL symbolizes equality; R and Q are predicates; f and g are functions; u, w, x, y, z are variables; a and b are constants.

paramodulate from one clause into another clause. The resolvents and the paramodulants are added to the set of clauses. There is an example of this in Figure 3.23.

Both paramodulation and resolution are sound rules of inference. When incorporated together they retain their refutation completeness. Thus they will always prove a goal that is indeed a theorem but they will never prove a goal that is not a theorem.

Should you incorporate paramodulation with resolution, you need to take care of the following.

1. Any time a clause containing an unnegated equality literal is deduced, match it against the already existing clauses to paramodulate them, if possible. This is called **backward paramodulation**.

2. On deducing any other clause, test to see whether it can be paramodulated by any of the already existing clauses that contain unnegated equality literals. This is called **forward paramodulation**.

	Demodulation	Paramodulation
1	The "from" clause containing the unnegated equality literal must be a unit clause.	The "from" clause containing the unnegated equality literal need not be a unit clause.
2	Replacement of variables is allowed only in the "from" clause.	Replacement of variables is allowed in both the "from" and the "into" clauses.
3	One demodulation usually triggers further attempts at demodulation, as terms are progressively simplified.	Not so.

Figure 3.24 Highlights comparing demodulation with paramodulation. If a 'from' clause I1 can demodulate an 'into' clause I2, then I1 can also paramodulate I2. But if I1 can paramodulate I2, then it is not necessarily true that I1 can also demodulate I2.

You have now learned both demodulation and paramodulation. The highlights comparing the two are given in Figure 3.24.

It is now time you learned of refinements to resolution refutation that make the proof procedure more efficient. Such refinements are discussed in Chapter 4.

3.6 EXERCISES

In some exercises below, the semantics of the formulae and clauses are stated in English. These semantics help to determine which of the names symbolize predicates, functions, variables and constants; for example, see Exercise 11. In the remaining exercises, the formulae and clauses have only an abstract denotation: P, Q, R, S are predicate symbols; f, g, h are function symbols; u, v, w, x, y, z are variables; and a, b, c are constants.

1. Convert into clause form the following formulae:
   (a) $\forall z(\exists x(P(z, x) \land Q(x)) \rightarrow \exists x(R(x, z) \land S(z,x)))$
   (b) $\exists y(Q(y) \land P(y) \land \forall z(R(y, z) \rightarrow Q(z)))$
   (c) $\forall u \exists w \forall z((S(w, u) \rightarrow R(u, w, z)) \land (R(z, w, u) \leftrightarrow P(u, w))) \rightarrow \exists u \forall w \exists z(S(w, u) \rightarrow R(u, z, w))$
2. You are given the following substitutions α and β.

$$\alpha = \{g(y)/x,\ x/y,\ b/z\}$$
$$\beta = \{y/x,\ h(z)/y,\ c/z\}$$

Find the compositions $\alpha \circ \beta$ and $\beta \circ \alpha$. Is $\alpha \circ \beta = \beta \circ \alpha$? Let K be an expression such that $K = P(g(x),\ h(y),\ f(h(x),\ z))$. Show that $(K\alpha)\beta = K\ (\alpha \circ \beta)$ and that $(K\beta)\alpha = K(\beta \circ \alpha)$.

3. If the following pairs of atoms are unifiable, find an mgu for them and their most general common instance. Otherwise, state why they are not unifiable.
   (a) $Q(c)$ and $Q(b)$
   (b) $P(b,\ h(z,\ y))$ and $P(x,\ h(x,\ c))$
   (c) $R(x,\ f(x))$ and $R(y,\ y)$
   (d) $Q(y,\ g(y))$ and $Q(g(x),\ x)$
   (e) $S(u,\ f(u),\ z)$ and $S(w,\ x,\ g(x))$
   (f) $P(x,\ f(x))$ and $P(b,\ g(b))$
   (g) $P(x)$ and $Q(v)$
   (h) $R(z,\ y,\ x)$ and $R(w,\ h(u,\ u),\ w)$
   (i) $P(g(x),\ y,\ f(g(z),\ z))$ and $P(u,\ u,\ f(w,\ b))$

4. If the following clauses can be factored, then find their factors. Otherwise, state why they cannot be factored.
   (a) $P(u,\ v) \lor P(x,\ f(x))$
   (b) $Q(b) \lor Q(c) \lor {\sim}Q(y) \lor Q(z)$
   (c) $S(x) \lor S(f(x)) \lor R(x,\ y) \lor R(b,\ c)$
   (d) $P(x,\ y) \lor P(y,\ z) \lor P(x,\ b)$
   (e) $R(z,\ y,\ x) \lor {\sim}R(w,\ h(u,\ u),\ w)$

5. If the following pairs of clauses are resolvable, find a resolvent. Otherwise, state why they are not resolvable.
   (a) ${\sim}P(x,\ y) \lor Q(y,\ b)$
       ${\sim}P(b,\ a) \lor Q(a,\ b)$
   (b) $R(z,\ y,\ x) \lor S(y)$
       $Q(w,\ a)\quad \lor {\sim}R(w,\ h(u,\ u),\ w)$

6. Prove by resolution refutation that the following set of clauses is inconsistent.

$$R(x)$$
$${\sim}Q(c) \lor {\sim}R(c)$$
$$P(c) \lor Q(y)$$
$${\sim}P(z) \lor Q(z)$$

7. Prove by resolution refutation that
   (a) $\exists x(R(x) \land S(x))$ is a logical consequence of the premisses:

$$\exists y(P(y) \land R(y))$$
$$\forall z(P(z) \to (Q(z) \land S(z)))$$

(b) $\forall y(Q(y) \rightarrow \sim R(y))$ is a logical consequence of the premises:

$$\forall u(S(u) \rightarrow \forall z(R(z) \rightarrow \sim P(u, z)))$$
$$\exists y(S(y) \land \forall w(Q(w) \rightarrow P(y, w)))$$

8. Find a demodulant of the following sets of clauses:
   (a) EQUAL(b, c)
       $Q(b) \lor R(c)$
   (b) EQUAL(mum(sister(x)), mum(x))
       MAN(brother(mum(sister(Cindy))))

9. Find all possible paramodulants of the following pairs of clauses:
   (a) $R(c) \lor$ EQUAL(b, c)
       $Q(b) \lor R(c)$

   (b) $R(c) \lor$ EQUAL(b, c)
       $Q(y) \lor R(x)$

   (c) $Q(f(c)) \lor$ EQUAL($g(f(c))$, b)
       $R(f(g(y))) \lor P(y, b)$

   (d) EQUAL($h(u, w)$, $g(u, f(w))$) $\lor R(u, w)$
       $P(f(g(f(x)), f(b))))$

10. Incorporate paramodulation into resolution refutation to prove that $\sim$EQUAL(b, c) is a logical consequence of the following set of premises given in clause form.

    $$Q(b) \lor \sim S(b)$$
    $$\sim Q(x) \lor R(b, x)$$
    $$S(c) \lor \sim P(c)$$
    $$P(b) \lor P(c)$$
    $$\sim P(z) \lor \sim S(u) \lor \sim R(z, u)$$

11. You are given the following three premises:
    (a) for all x, if x is a king, then the wife of x is a queen

    $$\forall x(\text{KING}(x) \rightarrow \text{QUEEN}(\text{wife}(x)))$$

    (b) Bozo is a king

    $$\text{KING(Bozo)}$$

    (c) Dumbell is the wife of Bozo

    $$\text{EQUAL(wife(Bozo), Dumbell)}.$$

    By incorporating either paramodulation or demodulation into resolution refutation, answer the question: Who is a queen?

12. Write a program to implement resolution refutation in predicate logic. Test the program by solving exercises 6, 7, 10 and 11 above.

3.7 SUGGESTIONS FOR FURTHER READING

Edgar (1989), Enderton (1972), Kleene (1967), Mendelson (1964), and Pospesel (1976) wrote introductory books on logic. Hayes (1977) advocated the utility of logic. Church (1936) and Turing (1936) independently proved the semidecidability of predicate logic. Davis and Putnam (1960) developed the procedure to convert a formula into clause form. Robinson (1965) introduced the resolution rule of inference. Green (1969) proposed the method of question answering; Luckham and Nilsson (1971) extended it. Wos, Robinson, Carson and Shalla (1967) and Winker and Wos (1982) described demodulation. Robinson and Wos (1969) presented paramodulation; Wos and Robinson (1973) proved its refutation completeness. Lusk, McCune and Overbeek (1982) discussed the organization of computer programs for automated reasoning. Suppes and Takahashi (1989) described a theorem prover for the foundations of differential and integral calculus. Bibel (1982), Chang and Lee (1973), Gallier (1986), Loveland (1978) and Wos, Overbeek, Lusk and Boyle (1984) wrote about theorem proving in general. Andrews (1970), Huet (1973) and Pietrzykowski (1973) extended resolution to higher-order logic. Turner (1984) surveyed other kinds of logics besides propositional and predicate logics.

1. Andrews, P. B. (1970) Resolution in type theory, *Journal of Symbolic Logic*, **36**[3], 414–32.
2. Bibel, W. (1982) *Automated Theorem Proving*, Friedr Viewneg, Braunschweig, Wiesbaden.
3. Chang, C. and Lee, R. C. (1973). *Symbolic Logic and Mechanical Theorem Proving*, Academic Press, New York.
4. Church, A. (1936) An unsolvable problem of number theory, *American Journal of Mathematics*, **58**, 345–63.
5. Davis, M. and Putnam, H. (1960) A computing procedure for quantification theory, *Journal of the ACM*, 7[3], 201–15.
6. Edgar, W. J. (1989) *The Elements of Logic*, Science Research Associates, Inc., Chicago.
7. Enderton, H. B. (1972) *A Mathematical Introduction to Logic*, Academic Press, New York.
8. Gallier, J. H. (1986) *Logic for Computer Science: Foundations of Automatic Theorem Proving*, Harper and Row, New York.
9. Green, C. C. (1969) Theorem proving by resolution as a basis for question answering in *Machine Intelligence*, 4 (eds. B. Meltzer and D. Michie), American Elsevier, New York, pp. 183–205.
10. Hayes, P. J. (1977) In defense of logic, in *Proceedings of the International Joint Conference on Artificial Intelligence*, 5, pp. 559–65.

11. Huet, G. (1973) A mechanization of type theory, in *Proceedings of the International Joint Conference on Artificial Intelligence*, 3, pp. 139–46.
12. Kleene, S. C. (1967) *Mathematical Logic*, Wiley, New York.
13. Loveland, D. W. (1978) *Automated Theorem Proving: A Logical Basis*, North Holland, New York.
14. Luckham, D. C. and Nilsson, N. J. (1971) Extracting information from resolution proof trees, *Artificial Intelligence*, 2[1], 27–54.
15. Lusk, E., McCune, W. and Overbeek, R. (1982) Logic machine architecture, in *Proceedings of the Sixth Conference on Automated Deduction* (ed. D. W. Loveland), Springer-Verlag, New York, pp. 70–108.
16. Mendelson, E. (1964) *Introduction to Mathematical Logic*, Van Nostrand, New York.
17. Pietrzykowski, T. (1973) A complete mechanization of second-order theory, *Journal of the ACM*, **20**, 333–64.
18. Pospesel, H. (1976) *Introduction to Logic: Predicate Logic*, Prentice-Hall, Englewood Cliffs, New Jersey.
19. Robinson, G. A. and Wos, L. (1969) Paramodulation and theorem proving in first order theories with equality, in *Machine Intelligence*, 4 (eds. B. Meltzer and D. Michie), American Elsevier, New York, pp. 135–50.
20. Robinson, J. A. (1965) A machine-oriented logic based on the resolution principle, *Journal of the ACM*, **12**[1], 23–41.
21. Suppes, P. and Takahashi, S. (1989) An interactive calculus theorem-prover for continuity properties, *Journal of Symbolic Computation*, **7**[6], 573–90.
22. Turing, A. M. (1936) On computable numbers with an application to the entscheindungsproblem, in *Proceedings of the London Mathematical Society*, **42**, pp. 230–65.
23. Turner, R. (1984) *Logics for Artificial Intelligence*, Ellis Horwood, West Sussex.
24. Winker, S. and Wos, L. (1982) Procedure implementation through demodulation and related tricks, in *Proceedings of the Sixth Conference on Automated Deduction* (ed. D. W. Loveland), Springer-Verlag, New York, pp. 109–31.
25. Wos, L., Overbeek, R., Lusk, E. and Boyle, J. (1984) *Automated Reasoning: Introduction and Applications*, Prentice Hall, Englewood Cliffs, New Jersey.
26. Wos, L. and Robinson, G. A. (1973) Maximal Models and Refutation Completeness: Semidecision Procedures in Automatic Theorem Proving, in *Word Problems: Decision Problems and the*

Burnside Problem in Group Theory (eds. W. Boone, F. Cannonito and R. Lyndon), North Holland, New York, pp. 609–39.

27. Wos, L., Robinson, G. A., Carson, D. F. and Shalla, L. (1967) The concept of demodulation in theorem proving, *Journal of the ACM*, **14**, 698–704.

4

Refinements to resolution refutation

4.1 INTRODUCTION

As you read in Chapters 2 and 3, the problem of proving a theorem has been transformed into a problem of proving the inconsistency of a set of clauses by resolution refutation. The set, called the input set, contains clauses derived from the premises and from the negation of the goal to be proved. The set is proved to be inconsistent if, and only if, we are able to deduce the empty clause NIL as a resolvent. Before we are able to deduce NIL, however, we may have to deduce many other resolvents. Quite a few of these resolvents might be useless as they do not lead to the deduction of NIL. Such useless resolvents make the proof procedure inefficient: there is a needless increase in the computing time required to deduce these resolvents and in the computer memory required to store them.

As refinements to resolution refutation, we can adopt certain strategies to make the proof procedure more efficient. Such strategies can be categorized into three classes:

1. ordering strategies which delineate the sequence in which the clauses are to be resolved;
2. pruning strategies which delete from the set those clauses and literals that have been appraised to be dispensable for the proof; and
3. restriction strategies which regulate the application of the resolution rule to only those clauses that are considered to be vital to the proof.

Adopting a strategy may require extra computing time and memory resources. Nevertheless, should the computing resources saved in generating a more efficient proof be more than the extra resources required in adopting a strategy, then we may adopt it.

A strategy is said to be **complete** if, and only if, by our adopting it, resolution (with factoring) is able to retain its refutation completeness. Do not confuse the completeness of a strategy with the completeness of the resolution rule. By adopting an incomplete strategy for resolution refutation we may not succeed in deducing the empty clause

NIL, even though the given input set is inconsistent. Ideally, the strategy should be complete but occasionally we can risk adopting an incomplete strategy, provided we realize that whenever the strategy does succeed, it does so with a sizable increase in the efficiency of the proof.

In this chapter, you will read descriptions of various kinds of ordering, pruning and restriction strategies. Examples to illustrate the strategies have been drawn from both propositional and predicate logics. Unless otherwise stated, the strategies can be adopted for either of the logics. You may think of propositional symbols A, B, C, D and E

Names in alphabetical order	Notation
Clauses	I, J
Constants	a, b, c, 1, 2, 3, ...
Empty Clause	NIL
Expression	K
Formulae	F, G, H
Functions	f, g, h
Input Set	U
Integer Counters	i, j, k, m, n
Literals	L, M
Predicates	P, Q, R, S
Propositional Symbols	A, B, C, D, E
Quantifiers	$\forall$, $\exists$
Substitutions	α, β, γ, δ, ϵ, θ, λ, where ϵ is the empty substitution
Terms	r, s, t
Variables	u, v, w, x y, z

Figure 4.1 The notation used for our abstract examples in propositional and predicate logics. Symbols may be appended by integers and diacritical marks; for examples, clauses may be numbered: I1, I2, I3, . . . , J1, J2, J3, . . . , I_1, I_2, I_3, . . . , I_1', I_2', I_3', . . .

Class of Strategy	Name of Strategy
ORDERING	1. Depth Saturating 2. Fewest Literals Preference 3. Weighting
PRUNING	1. Deleting Chaste Clauses 2. Deleting Tautologies 3. Deleting Subsumed Clauses 4. Evaluating Ground Literals
RESTRICTION	1. Set of Support 2. Negative Resolution 3. Negative Hyperresolution 4. Positive Resolution 5. Positive Hyperresolution 6. Ancestry Filtered 7. Input Resolution 8. Unit Resolution 9. Insight

Figure 4.2 A foreglimpse of the strategies described in this chapter to refine resolution refutation.

as predicate symbols of zero arguments. Moreover, since propositional logic has no variables, any substitution applied to its literals can be taken to be the empty substitution. For your convenience, the notation developed in Chapters 2 and 3 for propositional and predicate logics is summarized in Figure 4.1. Then in Figure 4.2, there is a foreglimpse of the strategies described in this chapter.

4.2 ORDERING STRATEGIES

At any time during resolution refutation we may have a list of pairs of clauses that are resolvable. The question arises: Which pair of clauses should we select to resolve? Ordering strategies help us make that selection. This, in effect, results in a delineation of the sequence in which clauses are resolved. Below in sections 4.2.1 to 4.2.3 you will read descriptions of three ordering strategies.

4.2.1 Depth saturating strategy

All clauses in the input set are defined to be at **depth** 0. A resolvent is said to be at depth $n + 1$ if, and only if, it has one parent from depth n and the other parent from anywhere between depths 0 to n. To illustrate, a resolvent at depth 1 has both its parents from the input set (depth 0); a resolvent at depth 3 has one parent from depth 2, and the other parent from depths 0, 1, or 2.

In this strategy, we first deduce all possible resolvents at depth 1, then at depth 2, and so on. Thus, in general, we saturate depth n with all its resolvents before proceeding to deduce resolvents at depth $n + 1$. In the literature, this strategy is also known as the breadth-first strategy or the level saturating strategy, the depth being referred to as the **level**. See an example extending over Figures 4.3 and 4.4.

Clauses in a set are said to be **catalogued** in the sequence in which they are written when displaying the members of the set. As we can see from this example, the sequence in which clauses are resolved to deduce resolvents at any depth is as follows. To start, the clauses at depth 0 are catalogued in any given sequence; thereafter, the resolvents shall be catalogued in the sequence in which they are deduced. Suppose that we have clauses available from depths 0, 1, 2, ..., n. To deduce resolvents at depth $n + 1$, resolve all resolvable clauses I and J such that

1. I is catalogued before J,
2. I belongs to any of the depths 0 to n, and
3. J belongs to depth n.

By depth saturating [breadth first] resolution refutation, prove the inconsistency of the following set of four clauses.

[J1]	~A	∨	~B	
[J2]	~A	∨	B	Input set; that is, depth 0 clauses
[J3]	A	∨	~B	
[J4]	A	∨	B	

We deduce the following depth 1 resolvent clauses, with both parents for each resolvent being from depth 0 clauses.

[J5]	~A			[by resolving J1 and J2]
[J6]	~B			[by resolving J1 and J3]
[J7]	~B	∨	B	[by resolving upon A and ~A of J1 and J4]
[J8]	~A	∨	A	[by resolving upon B and ~B of J1 and J4; note, we deduced two resolvents J7 and J8 from the same parents J1 and J4]
[J9]	~B	∨	B	[by resolving J2 and J3]
[J10]	~A	∨	A	[by resolving J2 and J3]
[J11]	B			[by resolving J2 and J4]
[J12]	A			[by resolving J3 and J4]

Figure 4.3 An example to show resolution refutation by adopting the depth saturating strategy. Above, you will see only the input set [depth 0] and the depth 1 resolvents. The example is continued on to Figure 4.4, where the depth 2 resolvents are shown.

The strategy is complete. But as you can observe from the example in Figures 4.3 and 4.4, numerous useless resolvents are deduced. So, whereas this strategy provides a systematic manner of deducing resolvents, it usually does not provide an efficient proof procedure.

4.2.2 Fewest literals preference strategy

The number of literals in a clause is called the **length** of the clause; the fewer the literals in it, the shorter is the clause. Resolving a clause of length i with a clause of length j produces a resolvent of length $i + j - 2$, as shown in section 3.4.1. Thus the length of a resolvent varies directly with the sum of the lengths of its parents.

We now deduce the following depth 2 resolvents from clauses J1 to J12 of Figure 4.3. At least one parent of each depth 2 resolvent is from the depth 1 clauses, J5 to J12.

[J13]	~A ∨ ~B	[by resolving J1 and J7]
[J14]	~A ∨ ~B	[by resolving J1 and J8]
[J15]	~A ∨ ~B	[by resolving J1 and J9]
[J16]	~A ∨ ~B	[by resolving J1 and J10]
[J17]	~A	[by resolving J1 and J11]
[J18]	~B	[by resolving J1 and J12]
[J19]	~A	[by resolving J2 and J6]
[J20]	~A ∨ B	[by resolving J2 and J7]
[J21]	~A ∨ B	[by resolving J2 and J8]
[J22]	~A ∨ B	[by resolving J2 and J9]
[J23]	~A ∨ B	[by resolving J2 and J10]
[J24]	B	[by resolving J2 and J12]
[J25]	~B	[by resolving J3 and J5]
[J26]	A ∨ ~B	[by resolving J3 and J7]
[J27]	A ∨ ~B	[by resolving J3 and J8]
[J28]	A ∨ ~B	[by resolving J3 and J9]
[J29]	A ∨ ~B	[by resolving J3 and J10]
[J30]	A	[by resolving J3 and J11]
[J31]	B	[by resolving J4 and J5]
[J32]	A	[by resolving J4 and J6]
[J33]	A ∨ B	[by resolving J4 and J7]
[J34]	A ∨ B	[by resolving J4 and J8]
[J35]	A ∨ B	[by resolving J4 and J9]
[J36]	A ∨ B	[by resolving J4 and J10]
[J37]	~A	[by resolving J5 and J8]
[J38]	~A	[by resolving J5 and J10]
[J39]	NIL	[by resolving J5 and J12]

Figure 4.4 The depth saturating resolution refutation example continued from Figure 4.3. Notice that of all the resolvents deduced from J5 to J39, only J5, J12, and J39 are essential to the proof; the rest are useless.

In this strategy, we prefer to deduce shorter resolvents over longer resolvents: our preference is based on the conjecture that it will be quicker to deduce the empty clause NIL (of length 0) from shorter clauses than from longer clauses. So, from the available list of pairs of resolvable clauses, we resolve that pair of clauses the sum of whose lengths is the least.

A special case of this strategy is the **unit preference strategy**, wherein unit clauses (of length 1) are resolved before non-unit clauses (of length greater than 1).

4.2.3 Weighting strategy

Based on your intuitive understanding of the theorem proving problem, associate literals and clauses of the input set with numerical weights: those that you consider more important for the proof are associated with, say, higher weights; hence they are resolved first. This strategy is only as reliable as your intuition, so adopt it with care.

4.3 PRUNING STRATEGIES

Sometimes in a set of clauses, there is a clause I that is dispensable. This signifies that the set is inconsistent if, and only if, it is inconsistent after I has been deleted. Similarly, there can be a literal L in some clause J in the set, such that L is dispensable. In such cases, the set is **pruned** by deleting clause I and literal L.

We need less computer memory to store the pruned set. Moreover, we may need fewer resolutions to prove the inconsistency of the pruned set, thus resulting in a shortened proof. In sections 4.3.1 to 4.3.4 below, you will read of four pruning strategies.

4.3.1 Deleting chaste clauses

A clause I is called an **ancestor** of a clause J if, and only if, either I is a parent of J, or I is a parent of an ancestor of J. Moreover, J is said to be a **descendant** of I if, and only if, I is an ancestor of J.

L is called a **chaste literal** if, and only if, it occurs in a set of clauses but its complementary unifiable literal ~L does not occur in the set. Such an L can never be resolved upon because ~L is absent. Furthermore, the empty clause NIL can never be a descendant of a clause containing L, for every descendant of such a clause will contain L. That is to say, it serves no purpose to resolve the clause, and it can be deleted from the set. A clause containing a chaste literal is called a **chaste clause**. (From the above definition of chaste literals, we exclude

Suppose we are asked to prove by resolution refutation the inconsistency of the following set of clauses.

[J1]   A
[J2]   ~ C
[J3]   C ∨ ~ D   ⎫
[J4]   ~ A ∨ ~ B   ⎬   Input Set
[J5]   ~ A ∨   B ∨ C   ⎭

Note that in clause J3 above, ~D is a chaste literal. We can never resolve upon ~D because no other clause contains its complementary literal D. Clause J3 is thus a chaste clause. We could resolve J3 with J2 by resolving upon C and ~C. But that would be futile, for the empty clause NIL can never be a descendant of clause J3: any descendant of J3 will contain the literal ~D. Thus J3 can play no role in the resolution refutation proof; it can be deleted from the input set. After deleting J3 and renumbering the clauses, we get the following pruned input set.

[I1]   A
[I2]   ~C
[I3]   ~A ∨   ~B
[I4]   ~A ∨   B ∨ C

Incidentally, later in Figure 4.11, you will see a resolution refutation proof for the inconsistency of the pruned input set.

Figure 4.5   An example to show the deletion of a chaste clause from an input set.

those *L*'s which are appended to clauses that have been derived from the negation of the goal, to convert such clauses to tautologies, when we are using resolution refutation to answer questions. Section 3.4.5 dealt with such question answering.)

In this strategy, we delete all chaste clauses from the input set. An example is given in Figure 4.5. In the literature, this strategy is also known as the **purity principle**.

4.3.2   Deleting tautologies

In this strategy we delete clauses that are tautologies. The set of clauses is inconsistent before the deletion if, and only if, it is inconsistent after the deletion. A clause containing complementary literals is a tautology; for example, $P(x) \lor Q(x, z) \lor \sim P(x)$. Look at Figures 4.3 and 4.4 delete all tautologies, and observe how the proof shrinks.

In this discussion on deleting tautologies, we should exclude the cases where we use resolution refutation to answer questions which was explained earlier in section 3.4.5. In those cases, clauses derived from the negation of the goal are intentionally converted into tautologies. Do not delete such tautologies, of course.

4.3.3   Deleting subsumed clauses

A clause J is said to be **subsumed** by a clause I if, and only if, there exists a substitution δ such that all the literals in the clause Iδ occur in the clause J. In other words, either Iδ is identical to J, or Iδ is a subclause of J. Subsumption can be viewed as a rule of inference: if J is subsumed by I, then J is a logical consequence of I. Fugure 4.6 shows examples of pairs of clauses wherein one of the clauses subsumes the other.

If, within a set of clauses, a clause J is subsumed by another clause I, then J can be deleted from the set. The set is inconsistent before the deletion if, and only if, it is inconsistent after the deletion. One effect of deleting subsumed clauses is the deletion of a clause that is an instance of another. For example, from clauses $P(x)$ and $P(b)$, we delete $P(b)$, but retain $P(x)$; that is, we retain the most general instance;

Clause I	Clause J, which is subsumed by clause I	The substitution δ such that all the literals in Iδ occur in J
A A ∨ B ~A ∨ B A ∨ B	A A ∨ B ~A ∨ B A ∨ B ∨ C	Since propositional logic clauses contain no variables, δ can be taken to be the empty substitution for all such clauses.
$P(x)$	$P(x)$	The empty substitution ϵ
$\sim P(x)$	$\sim P(a)$	$\{a/x\}$
$P(x) \vee Q(y)$	$P(a) \vee Q(z)$	$\{a/x,\ z/y\}$
$P(x) \vee \sim Q(y)$	$P(a) \vee \sim Q(b)$	$\{a/x,\ b/y\}$
$P(x) \vee Q(y)$	$P(f(z)) \vee Q(b) \vee R(w)$	$\{f(z)/x,\ b/y\}$
$S(u,\ b) \vee S(c,\ w)$	$S(c,\ b)$	$\{c/u,\ b/w\}$

Figure 4.6 Examples of clauses I and J, such that J is subsumed by I. Remember, Iδ is the clause obtained by applying substitution δ to the literals of clause I.

Rewrite the depth saturating resolution refutation proof of Figures 4.3 and 4.4 after incorporating the following stipulation: if a newly deduced resolvent is a tautology, or if it is subsumed by an already existing clause, then delete this new resolvent.

[I1]   ~A ∨ ~B   ⎫
[I2]   ~A ∨   B   ⎬ Input Set
[I3]   A ∨ ~B   ⎪
[I4]   A ∨   B   ⎭

We deduce the following first-level resolvent clauses from J1 to J4.

[I5]	~A	[by resolving I1 and I2]
[I6]	~B	[by resolving I1 and I3]
[I7]	B	[by resolving I2 and I4]
[I8]	A	[by resolving I3 and I4]

We now deduce the following second-level resolvent.

[I9]   NIL   [by resolving I5 and I8]

Figure 4.7 An example of a resolution refutation proof after we have deleted resolvents that are tautological or subsumed. Notice that in spite of these deletions, there are still two useless resolvents: I6 and I7. These two clauses are not used in deducing I9.

remember, in our notation, b is a constant and x is a variable. As a result of this, we delete multiple copies of any clause.

In this strategy we initially delete all subsumed clauses from the input set. Then, whenever we deduce a resolvent, we delete it if it is subsumed by an already existing clause. One common practice is to delete the subsumed resolvents at each depth only after all the resolvents at that depth have been deduced. The example in Figure 4.7 shows a resolution refutation proof in which we delete tautologies (discussed earlier in section 4.3.2) and subsumed clauses. Observe from the example that in spite of such deletions a few useless resolvents may still survive in the proof.

4.3.4 Evaluating ground literals

In this strategy, truth value evaluating procedures are built into the theorem prover. These built-in procedures are invoked whenever we encounter a ground literal (that is, a predicate logic literal with no variables) in a clause. If the ground literal is evaluated to be false then the literal is deleted from the clause, but if the ground literal is evaluated to be true then the clause is a tautology and hence the clause

Suppose an input set contains the following two clauses, where GT is the name for the predicate GREATER-THAN.

[I1]   R(9) ∨ S(z) ∨ P(w)
[I2]   GT(6, y) ∨ ~R(y)

We resolve the two clauses, by resolving upon R(9) and ~R(y), with mgu = {9/y}, to deduce the following resolvent.

$$GT(6, 9) \lor S(z) \lor P(w)$$

A built-in procedure is invoked to evaluate the ground literal GT(6, 9). Since 6 is not greater than 9, the literal is evaluated to be false. The ground literal is deleted, and the resolvent of I1 and I2 becomes the following.

[I3]   S(z) ∨ P(w)

Figure 4.8   An example of deleting a ground literal that has been evaluated to be false. We can look upon this from another viewpoint: as if the input set contains an implicit unit clause ~GT(6, 9). We call this an implicit clause to distinguish it from an explicit clause, one that is actually contained in the input set. The implicit clause could be resolved with the [explicit] clause (GT(6, 9) ∨ S(z) ∨ P(w)) to deduce the resolvent I3 shown above.

Suppose an input set contains the following two clauses, where GT is the name for the predicate GREATER-THAN.

[I1]   P(4) ∨ Q(z)
[I2]   GT(6, x) ∨ ~P(x)

We resolve the two clauses, by resolving upon P(4) and ~P(x), with mgu = {4/x}, to deduce the following resolvent.

[I3]   GT(6, 4) ∨ Q(z)

A built-in procedure is invoked to evaluate the ground literal GT(6, 4). Since 6 is greater than 4, the literal is evaluated to be true. That makes clause I3 to be a tautology. So I3 is deleted.

Figure 4.9   An example of deleting a clause that is a tautology, because a ground literal in the clause has been evaluated to be true. Just as we did for Figure 4.8, we can look upon the above, too, from a different viewpoint: as if the input set contains an implicit unit clause GT(6, 4). This implicit clause would subsume the [explicit] clause (GT(6, 4) ∨ Q(z)). Then according to the discussion in section 4.3.3, we would delete the subsumed clause I3.

itself is deleted. The set of clauses is inconsistent if, and only if, it is inconsistent after either of the two kinds of deletions discussed above. See the examples in Figures 4.8 and 4.9. As is evident from the foregoing description, this strategy of evaluating ground literals is adoptable only for predicate logic, not propositional logic.

Read the legend below Figures 4.8 and 4.9 carefully to understand how we could have effected the same deletion of literals and clauses, provided we had assumed the existence of **implicit clauses** not actually present in the input set, but only assumed to be so present.

If, on deleting a literal that has been evaluated to be false, only the empty clause NIL remains, then it is akin to our deducing NIL and we can say that we have proved the inconsistency of the input set. This happens when, for example, a unit clause contains the literal GT(6, 9). The literal is evaluated to be false, it is deleted, and the empty clause NIL remains. It is like resolving an implicit unit clause ~GT(6, 9) with the explicit (actually present) unit clause GT(6, 9) to deduce NIL.

By evaluating ground literals we can reduce the computer memory required because fewer explicit clauses need to be stored. In all our discussions from now on, all clauses are explicit unless otherwise indicated.

4.4 RESTRICTION STRATEGIES

By adopting pruning strategies we may reduce the amount of computer memory required because dispensable literals and clauses are deleted, but we may still waste some computer time. For example, to delete resolvents that are tautologies or subsumed, we first have to deduce them, then inspect them for being tautologies or subsumed, and finally, perhaps delete them. Computer time is, of course, expended in all this effort.

One way to reduce this time is to lessen the number of resolvents deduced. Restriction strategies strive to do this by imposing some constraints on the types of clauses that may be resolved. These restriction strategies may be adopted together with ordering and pruning strategies. The three classes of strategies synergize with one another to improve the efficiency of resolution refutation. Before you read below about the different restriction strategies you should be conversant with the following definitions.

A literal denoting an unnegated atom is called a **positive literal**; a literal denoting a negated atom is a **negative literal**. To illustrate, $P(x, y)$ and B are positive literals, and $\sim P(x, y)$ and $\sim B$ are negative literals. Thus every literal is either a positive literal or a negative literal, but not both.

A **positive clause** is a clause that contains only positive literals; a **negative clause** contains only negative literals; a **mixed clause** contains at least one positive literal and at least one negative literal. For example, $(A \lor B)$ is a positive clause, $(\sim A \lor \sim B)$ is a negative clause and $(A \lor \sim B)$ is a mixed clause. Every non-empty clause must be one of the following types: a positive, a negative or a mixed clause.

Below in sections 4.4.1 to 4.4.9 you will read of nine restriction strategies.

4.4.1   Set of support strategy

A set U_s is called a **set of support** if, and only if, U_s is a subset of an input set U of clauses, and set U_c is consistent, where $U_c = U - U_s$. Later you will read about how to select U_s from a specific U. In this strategy we never resolve two clauses that are both from U_c. The outcome of this is that at least one ancestor of every resolvent belongs to U_s. Put another way, every resolvent is a descendant of at least one of the clauses in U_s. Every resolvent is said to be supported by U_s.

The strategy is complete. The intuitive justification is this: since U_s is a likely cause of the inconsistency of U, the empty clause NIL must be supported by U_s and hence every resolvent that is an ancestor of NIL must also be supported by U_s. If, however, you adopt the strategy for deleting subsumed clauses, as described in section 4.3.3, along with adopting the set of support strategy, then heed the following. Suppose you have deduced a resolvent J which is subsumed by a clause I, such that I belongs to U_c. Now J will be supported by U_s and so, if you delete J, you must add clause I to U_s otherwise some of the essential resolutions may not occur and the set of support strategy may lose its completeness.

There are three customary approaches to selecting the set of support U_s from a specific input set U.

1. U_s = set of clauses derived from the negation of the goal. Thus U_c becomes the set of clauses derived from the premises. As mentioned in section 2.3.1, we are studying only those cases where the premises are consistent. Therefore U_c is consistent. Look at the example in Figure 4.10. (A proof cluttered with useless resolvents is usually baffling and so only those resolvents essential to the proof have been shown in this example. Such shall be the case for the remaining examples in this chapter.)

2. U_s = set of negative clauses in U. Thus U_c becomes the set of positive and mixed clauses, that is, each clause in U_c has at least one

Given the following premisses:

[I1]   A
[I2]   ~C
[I3]   ~A   ∨   ~B

Prove by resolution refutation that the goal (A ∧ ~B ∧ ~C) is a logical consequence of the above premisses. Let the negation of the goal constitute the set of support. The negation of the goal in clause form is the following:

[I4]   ~A   ∨   B   ∨   C

Since I4 constitutes the set of support, all our resolvents should be descendants of I4. We then deduce the following resolvents.

[I5]   ~A   ∨   B   [by resolving I2 and I4; so I5 is a descendant of I4]
[I6]   ~A   [by resolving I3 and I5; so I6 is a descendant of I5, and thus in turn I6 is a descendant of I4]
[I7]   NIL   [by resolving I1 and I6; so I7 is a descendant of I6, and thus in turn I7 is a descendant of I4]

The goal is proved to be a theorem, as the empty clause NIL is deduced.

Figure 4.10   An example of resolution refutation by adopting the set of support strategy. The set of clauses derived from the negation of the goal constitutes the set of support. For clarity, only those resolvents essential to the proof have been shown.

positive literal. As one interpretation (see sections 2.2.3 and 3.2.3 for the definition of the interpretation of a formula) these positive literals can be assigned the value true. So U_c is consistent because there exists an interpretation that makes the clauses of U_c true. Look at the example in Figure 4.11. Note that if U_s is an empty set, then $U_c = U$ and so U is consistent. In other words if the input set contains no negative clauses then the set is consistent. The converse, however, may not always hold.

3. U_s = set of positive clauses in U. Thus U_c becomes the set of negative and mixed clauses, that is, each clause in U_c has at least one negative literal. As one interpretation, these negative literals can be assigned the value true. So U_c is consistent because there exists an interpretation that makes the clauses of U_c true. Look at the example in Figure 4.12. Note that if U_s is an empty set then $U_c = U$ and so U is consistent. In other words if the input set contains no positive clauses then the set is consistent. The converse, however, may not always hold.

Using the negative clauses as the set of support, prove by resolution refutation the inconsistency of the following set of clauses.

[I1]   A
[I2]   ~C   } Input Set
[I3]   ~A ∨ ~B
[I4]   ~A ∨   B ∨ C

Since I2 and I3 are the negative clauses present above, they constitute the set of support. Thus all our resolvents should be descendants of I2 or I3, or both. We then deduce the following resolvents.

[I5]   ~A ∨ C   [by resolving I3 and I4; so I5 is
                                        a descendant of I3]
[I6]   C   [by resolving I1 and I5; so I6 is a descendant of
                                 I5, and thus in turn I6 is a descendant of I3]
[I7]   NIL   [by resolving I2 and I6; so I7 is a descendant
                                    of I2: moreover, I7 is a descendant of I6,
                                 and thus in turn I7 is also a descendant of I3]

The input set is proved to be inconsistent, as the empty clause NIL is deduced.

Figure 4.11   An example of resolution refutation by adopting the set of support strategy. The negative clauses of the input set constitute the set of support.

Of the three approaches to selecting U_s described above, the first is the most common. You may augment any of the above U_s by clauses specific to the given theorem proving problem such as to make them intuitively essential for the proof.

4.4.2   Negative resolution strategy

A resolvent is said to be deduced by **negative resolution** if, and only if, one of its parents is a negative clause. Both its parents cannot be negative clauses because two negative clauses (containing only negative literals) can never be resolved with each other.

In this strategy, we apply only negative resolutions. The strategy is complete and an example is given in Figure 4.13.

Note, the set of support strategy, described in section 4.4.1, with negative clauses as the set of support is not identical to the negative resolution strategy. The former strategy demands that at least one ancestor of every resolvent be a negative clause from the input set; the latter strategy demands that one parent of every resolvent be a negative clause. The example in Figure 4.11 uses negative clauses as the set of support; nonetheless, the proof shown does not meet the

Using the positive clauses as the set of support, prove by resolution refutation the inconsistency of the following set of clauses.

[I1]   A
[I2]   ~C   } Input Set
[I3]   ~A ∨ ~B
[I4]   ~A ∨   B ∨ C

Since I1 is the only positive clause present above, it constitutes the set of support. Thus all our resolvents should be descendants of I1. We then deduce the following resolvents.

[I5]   B ∨ C   [by resolving I1 and I4; so I5 is a
                                            descendant of I1]
[I6]   ~B   [by resolving I1 and I3; so I6 is a
                                            descendant of I1]
[I7]   C   [by resolving I5 and I6; so I7 is a descendant
                          of I5 and I6, and thus in turn I7 is a descendant of I1]
[I8]   NIL   [by resolving I2 and I7; so I8 is a descendant of
                                            I7, and thus in turn I8 is a
                                            descendant of I1]

The input set is proved to be inconsistent, as the empty clause NIL is deduced.

Figure 4.12   An example of resolution refutation by adopting the set of support strategy. The positive clauses of the input set constitute the set of support.

By applying only negative resolutions, prove by refutation the inconsistency of the following set of clauses.

[I1]   ~A ∨ ~B   }
[I2]   ~A ∨   B | Input Set
[I3]   A ∨ ~B |
[I4]   A ∨   B   }

We have to ensure that for each resolvent, one of the two parents is a negative clause. We then deduce the following resolvents.

[I5]   ~A   [by resolving I1 and I2; parent I1 is a
                                            negative clause]
[I6]   ~B   [by resolving I3 and I5; parent I5 is a
                                            negative clause]
[I7]   B   [by resolving I4 and I5; parent I5 is a
                                            negative clause]
[I8]   NIL   [by resolving I6 and I7; parent I6 is a
                                            negative clause]

The input set is proved to be inconsistent, as the empty clause NIL is deduced.

Figure 4.13   An example of resolution refutation by adopting the strategy of negative resolution.

demand of the negative resolution strategy. Any proof generated by the negative resolution strategy will also meet the demand of a set of support strategy proof, where the set of support comprises the negative clauses of the input set. The converse, however, may not always hold.

4.4.3   Negative hyperresolution strategy

Applying **negative hyperresolution** is tantamount to applying several negative resolutions simultaneously. Such a hyperresolution is applied to a positive or mixed clause, called the **nucleus**, and a number of negative clauses, called **satellites**. A preparatory example is given in Figure 4.14 and you are invited to refer to it often while you read the description below.

Consider as nucleus the clause J and as satellites the n clauses I1, I2, ..., In. The satellites need not be distinct clauses. The number of positive literals in the nucleus J should be equal to n, the number of satellites.

Suppose a literal from each satellite is a complementary unifiable pair with a literal from the nucleus. Thus there are n pairs of complementary unifiable literals, each positive literal from the nucleus

Suppose that a set contains the following four clauses.

[I1]	∼A						
[I2]	∼B	∨	∼C				
[I3]	∼D	∨	∼E				
[I4]	A	∨	C	∨ D ∨	∼E		

Then by applying negative resolutions, we can deduce the following resolvents.

[I5]	C	∨	D	∨ ∼E		[by resolving I1 and I4]
[I6]	∼B	∨	D	∨ ∼E		[by resolving I2 and I5]
[I7]	∼B	∨	∼E			[by resolving I3 and I6]

To deduce I7, we had to apply negative resolutions thrice. Alternatively, we could have deduced a hyperresolvent clause identical to I7, by applying negative hyperresolution once. The nucleus would have been the mixed clause I4, the satellites being the negative clauses I1, I2, and I3. We would not have deduced clauses I5 and I6; thus we would have used less computer memory.

Figure 4.14   A preparatory example of negative hyperresolution. The satellites must be negative clauses; the nucleus can be a positive or a mixed clause. The hyperresolvent is to be either a negative clause or the empty clause NIL.

By applying negative hyperresolution at least once, prove by refutation the inconsistency of the following set of clauses.

$$
\left.\begin{array}{lll}
\text{[I1]} & \text{Q(b)} & \\
\text{[I2]} & \sim\!\text{P(z, a)} \quad \vee \quad \text{R(c)} \\
\text{[I3]} & \text{P(c, u)} \quad \vee \quad \text{R(w)} \\
\text{[I4]} & \sim\!\text{Q(x)} \quad \vee \quad \sim\!\text{R(y)}
\end{array}\right\} \quad \text{Input Set}
$$

We deduce the following resolvents and hyperresolvents.

[I5]	~R(y)	[by mgu = {b/x} to resolve I1 and I4]
[I6]	~P(z, a)	[by mgu = {c/y} to resolve I2 and I5]
[I7]	NIL	[by mgu = {a/u, w/y, c/z} to hyperresolve nucleus I3 with satellites I5 and I6]

The input set is proved to be inconsistent, as the empty clause NIL is deduced.

Figure 4.15 An example of using negative hyperresolution to prove the inconsistency of a set of clauses.

appearing in one pair. Let us assume that this unification can be achieved by using some mgu δ. Then we can deduce a hyperresolvent clause whose literals make up the following set.

$$
\{\text{I1}\delta\} \ \cup \ \{\text{I2}\delta\} \ \cup \ \ldots \ \cup \ \{\text{I}n\delta\} \ \cup \ \{\text{J}\delta\} \ - \ \{\text{the } n \text{ pairs of}
$$
complementary unifiable literals}.

In our notation, $\{\text{I1}\delta\}$ denotes the set of literals in the clause $\text{I1}\delta$. Notice, all the n positive literals of the nucleus have been removed from the hyperresolvent so the hyperresolvent is a negative clause; it can also be the empty clause NIL. The same hyperresolvent can be deduced by applying n negative resolutions. By negative hyperresolution we deduce fewer clauses and thus use less computer memory. Negative hyperresolution is refutation complete. Figure 4.15 shows an example in which negative hyperresolution is used to prove the inconsistency of a set of clauses.

4.4.4 Positive resolution strategy

A resolvent is said to be deduced by **positive resolution** if, and only if, one of its parents is a positive clause. Both of its parents cannot be positive clauses because two positive clauses (containing only positive literals) can never be resolved with each other. Resolving a positive clause with a negative clause can be viewed either as a positive resolution or as a negative resolution.

By applying only positive resolutions, prove by refutation the inconsistency of the following set of clauses.

[I1]   ~A ∨   ~B ⎫
[I2]   ~A ∨   B ⎪   Input Set
[I3]   A ∨   ~B ⎬
[I4]   A ∨   B ⎭

We have to ensure that for each resolvent, one of the two parents is a positive clause. We then deduce the following resolvents.

[I5]   A   [by resolving I3 and I4; parent I4 is a positive clause]

[I6]   ~B   [by resolving I1 and I5; parent I5 is a positive clause]

[I7]   B   [by resolving I2 and I5; parent I5 is a positive clause]

[I8]   NIL   [by resolving I6 and I7; parent I7 is a positive clause]

The input set is proved to be inconsistent, as the empty clause NIL is deduced.

Figure 4.16   An example of resolution refutation by adopting the strategy of positive resolution. Compare this with Figure 4.13, where the same input set was proved to be inconsistent by adopting the strategy of negative resolution.

In this strategy, we apply only positive resolution; the strategy is complete. Look at the example in Figure 4.16.

Note, the set of support strategy (described in section 4.4.1) with positive clauses as the set of support is not identical to the positive resolution strategy. The former strategy demands that at least one ancestor of every resolvent be a positive clause from the input set; the latter strategy demands that one parent of every resolvent be a positive clause. Any proof generated by the positive resolution strategy will also meet the demand of a set of support strategy proof, where the set of support comprises the positive clauses of the input set. The converse, however, may not always hold. In the literature, positive resolution is also known as **P1** resolution.

4.4.5   Positive hyperresolution strategy

Having understood negative hyperresolution from section 4.4.3, you should be able to understand positive hyperresolution readily. Interchange the words positive and negative in section 4.4.3 and you will have the description of positive hyperresolution but if you find

Suppose that a set of clauses contains the following three clauses.

[I1] ~Q(x) V ~R(b) V S(x)
[I2] Q(a) V S(b)
[I3] R(y)

Then by applying positive resolutions, we can deduce the following resolvents.

[I4] ~R(b) V S(a) V S(b)   [by mgu = {a/x} to resolve I1 and I2]
[I5] S(a) V S(b)   [by mgu = {b/y} to resolve I3 and I4]

To deduce I5, we had to apply positive resolutions twice. Alternatively, we could have deduced a hyperresolvent clause identical to I5, by applying positive hyperresolution once. The nucleus would have been the mixed clause I1, the satellites being the two positive clauses I2 and I3, and mgu = {a/x, b/y}. We would not have deduced clause I4, thus using less computer memory.

Figure 4.17 A preparatory example of positive hyperresolution. The satellites must be positive clauses; the nucleus can be a negative or a mixed clause. The hyperresolvent is to be either a positive clause or the empty clause NIL.

that disconcerting, you may read about positive hyperresolution below.

Applying positive hyperresolution is tantamount to applying several positive resolutions simultaneously. Such a hyperresolution is applied to a negative or mixed clause J, called the **nucleus**, and n positive clauses I1, I2, . . ., In, called **satellites**. The satellites need not be distinct clauses. The number of negative literals in the nucleus J should be equal to n, the number of satellites. A preparatory example is given in Figure 4.17.

Suppose that a literal from each satellite is a complementary unifiable pair with a literal from the nucleus. Thus there are n pairs of complementary unifiable literals, each negative literal from the nucleus appearing in one pair. Let us assume that this unification can be achieved by using some mgu δ. Then we can deduce a hyperresolvent clause whose literals make up the following set.

{I1δ} U {I2δ} U . . . U {Inδ} U {Jδ} − {the n pairs of complementary unifiable literals}.

Notice, all the n negative literals of the nucleus have been removed from the hyperresolvent so the hyperresolvent is a positive clause; it can also be the empty clause NIL. The same hyperresolvent can be deduced by applying n positive resolutions. By positive

By applying positive hyperresolution at least once, prove by refutation the inconsistency of the following set of clauses.

[I1]	~ Q(x) V ~ R(b) V S(x)	
[I2]	Q(a) V S(b)	
[I3]	~ P(x, a) V R(x)	Input Set
[I4]	P(y, a) V R(y)	
[I5]	~ S(w)	

We deduce the following resolvents and hyperresolvents.

[I6]	R(y)	[by mgu = {y/x} to resolve I3 and I4]
[I7]	S(a) V S(b)	[by mgu = {a/x, b/y} to hyperresolve nucleus I1 with satellites I2 and I6]
[I8]	S(a)	[by mgu = {b/w} to resolve I5 and I7]
[I9]	NIL	[by mgu = {a/w} to resolve I5 and I8]

The input set is proved to be inconsistent, as the empty clause NIL is deduced.

Figure 4.18 An example of using positive hyperresolution to prove the inconsistency of a set of clauses.

By ancestry filtered resolution refutation, prove the inconsistency of the following set of clauses.

[I1]	~A V ~B	
[I2]	~A V B	Input Set
[I3]	A V ~B	
[I4]	A V B	

We have to ensure that for each resolvent, either at least one parent is in the input set, or one parent is an ancestor of the other parent. We then deduce the following resolvents.

[I5]	~A	[by resolving I1 and I2; both parents I1 and I2 are in the input set]
[I6]	~B	[by resolving I3 and I5; parent I3 is in the input set]
[I7]	A	[by resolving I4 and I6; parent I4 is in the input set
[I8]	NIL	[by resolving I5 and I7; parent I5 is an ancestor of parent I7]

The inconsistency of the input set is proved, as the empty clause NIL is deduced.

Figure 4.19 An example of resolution refutation by adopting the ancestry filtered strategy.

hyperresolution we deduce fewer clauses and thus use less computer memory. Positive hyperresolution is refutation complete. Figure 4.18 shows an example in which positive hyperresolution is used to prove the inconsistency of a set of clauses.

4.4.6 Ancestry filtered strategy

In this strategy, for every resolvent, either at least one parent is in the input set or one parent is an ancestor of the other parent. The strategy is complete. An example is shown in Figure 4.19.

The strategy remains complete even if we incorporate paramodulation, described earlier in section 3.5.5, into resolution refutation. In that case, however, the strategy takes on an extended definition: for every resolvent or paramodulant, either at least one parent is in the input set or one parent is an ancestor of the other parent.

4.4.7 Input resolution strategy

In this strategy, for every resolvent, at least one parent is in the input set. Comparing this with section 4.4.6, we observe the following: every input resolution is an ancestry filtered resolution, but not vice versa, so the input resolution strategy is more constrained. Because of the extra constraint, the input resolution strategy is incomplete.

In the example of Figure 4.20 the strategy succeeds in proving a given input set to be inconsistent but in the example in Figure 4.21 it fails to prove the inconsistency of an input set that is known to be inconsistent.

From Figure 4.21 we can draw this conclusion: for the input resolution strategy to succeed it is necessary that the input set contain either at least one unit clause or at least one clause that can be factored into a unit clause. The presence of such a clause in the input set, however, does not guarantee that the strategy will succeed.

Although the input resolution strategy is incomplete in general, it is complete for a subclass of clauses called **Horn clauses**. You will read more about Horn clauses and input resolution in Chapter 5.

Paramodulation can be incorporated into resolution refutation by extending this strategy: for every resolvent or paramodulant, at least one parent is in the input set. The strategy remains incomplete.

4.4.8 Unit resolution strategy

In this strategy, for every resolvent, at least one parent is either a unit clause or the unit factor of a clause. The strategy is incomplete.

By adopting the input resolution strategy, prove by refutation the inconsistency of the following set of clauses.

[I1]	A					⎫
[I2]	~C					⎬ Input Set
[I3]	~A	∨	~B			⎪
[I4]	~A	∨	B	∨	C	⎭

We have to ensure that for each resolvent, at least one of the two parents is in the input set. We then deduce the following resolvents.

[I5]	~A ∨ C	[by resolving I3 and I4; both parents I3 and I4 are in the input set]
[I6]	~A	[by resolving I2 and I5; parent I2 is in the input set]
[I7]	NIL	[by resolving I1 and I6; parent I1 is in the input set]

The input set is proved to be inconsistent, as the empty clause NIL is deduced.

Figure 4.20 An example in which the input resolution strategy succeeds in proving the inconsistency of a given input set.

By adopting the input resolution strategy, can you prove the inconsistency of the following set of clauses?

[I1]	~A	∨	~B		⎫ We know that this input set is
[I2]	~A	∨	B		⎬ inconsistent. It was proved to be so
[I3]	A	∨	~B		⎪ in Figure 4.16
[I4]	A	∨	B		⎭

We must ensure that for each resolvent, at least one parent is in the input set. Remember that when the resolvent is the empty clause NIL, both the parents are unit clauses. So to deduce resolvent NIL, we should have in the input set either at least one unit clause or at least one clause that can be factored into a unit clause. But since there are no such clauses in the above input set, we can never deduce NIL. Thus we are unable to prove the inconsistency of the set by adopting the input resolution strategy.

Figure 4.21 An example to show the incompleteness of the input resolution strategy. Although the given input set is known to be inconsistent, we cannot prove it to be so by this strategy.

By adopting the unit resolution strategy, prove by refutation the inconsistency of the following set of clauses.

[I1]	A				
[I2]	~C				Input Set
[I3]	~A	∨	~B		
[I4]	~A	∨	B	∨ C	

We have to ensure that for each resolvent, at least one of the two parents is either a unit clause or the unit factor of a clause. We then deduce the following resolvents.

[I5]   ~A ∨ B   [by resolving I2 and I4; parent I2
                                        is a unit clause]
[I6]   B   [by resolving I1 and I5; parent I1 is a unit clause]
[I7]   ~A   [by resolving I3 and I6; parent I6 is a unit clause]
[I8]   NIL   [by resolving I1 and I7; both parents I1 and
                                        I7 are unit clauses]

The input set is proved to be inconsistent, as the empty clause NIL is deduced.

Figure 4.22 An example in which the unit resolution strategy succeeds in proving the inconsistency of a given input set.

In the example of Figure 4.22 the strategy succeeds in proving a given input set to be inconsistent but in the example of Figure 4.23 it fails to prove the inconsistency of an input set that is known to be inconsistent.

From Figure 4.23 we can draw this conclusion: for the unit resolution strategy to succeed it is necessary that the input set contain

By adopting the unit resolution strategy, can you prove the inconsistency of the following set of clauses?

[I1]	~A	∨	~B		We know that this set is
[I2]	~A	∨	B		inconsistent. It was proved to
[I3]	A	∨	~B		be so in Figure 4.16.
[U4]	A	∨	B		

We must ensure that, for every resolvent, at least one parent is either a unit clause or the unit factor of a clause. Since the above input set contains no such clauses, we cannot deduce any resolvents whatsoever. Thus we are unable to prove the inconsistency of the set by adopting the unit resolution strategy.

Figure 4.23 An example to show the incompleteness of the unit resolution strategy. Although the given input set is known to be inconsistent, we cannot prove it to be so by this strategy.

either at least one unit clause or at least one clause that can be factored into a unit clause. The presence of such a clause in the input set, however, does not guarantee that the strategy will succeed.

It is an established mathematical result that a set of clauses can be proved to be inconsistent by the unit resolution strategy if, and only if, they can be proved to be inconsistent by the input resolution strategy.

Paramodulation can be incorporated into resolution refutation by extending this strategy: for every resolvent or paramodulant, at least one parent is a unit clause. The strategy remains incomplete.

4.4.9 Insight strategy

Based on your insight into the theorem proving problem, mark those clauses of the input set that you presume will play no role in the generation of the proof. These marked clauses are then never resolved. This strategy is incomplete; it is only as reliable as your insight so take care before you adopt it. You may have noticed that the insight strategy has similarities with the weighting strategy of section 4.2.3.

4.5 CLOSING REMARKS

By now you may be wondering which is the best strategy. The answer is not known but the set of support strategy is popular. Experiment with the different strategies on the class of problems to which you want to apply resolution refutation and adopt whichever looks promising.

In section 4.4.1 it was explained that if an input set contains either no negative clauses or no positive clauses then the set can be shown to be consistent. Hence, for a set of clauses to be inconsistent, it is necessary (but not sufficient) that the set contain at least one negative clause and at least one positive clause. Either or both of these types of clauses may be implicit if, and only if, we are building into the theorem prover procedures to evaluate the truth values of ground literals (see the discussion on implicit clauses in section 4.3.4).

Therefore suppose that you have been given an input set. Further, suppose that you are not building ground literal evaluating procedures into the theorem prover. Then first scan the clauses. If you discover at least one positive clause and at least one negative clause, begin resolution refutation; otherwise, declare the set to be consistent. If, however, you are building in ground literal evaluating procedures then there is no need to scan the set, for the positive and negative clauses may be implicit; promptly begin resolution refutation.

As discussed above, there is a lower limit (that of one each) on the number of positive and negative clauses to be necessarily present in an inconsistent input set. There is no such limit for mixed clauses: an inconsistent set may contain no mixed clauses, or any number of them.

As mentioned in sections 4.4.2 and 4.4.4, a negative clause can never resolve with another negative clause, and a positive clause can never resolve with another positive clause. Hence, the only combinations of types of clauses that resolve with one another are as follows:

1. a mixed clause with a positive clause;
2. a mixed clause with a mixed clause;
3. a mixed clause with a negative clause; and
4. a positive clause with a negative clause.

Should you want to resolve a pair of clauses, first test whether the pair belongs to one of the four combinations above. If it does, then probe into the clauses to locate complementary unifiable literals. If such literals are found, you may resolve the clauses.

Chapters 2, 3 and 4 have described how logic is used for automated reasoning. The next chapter will discuss how logic can be used to write computer programs.

4.6 EXERCISES

1. Prove the inconsistency of the following input set:

$$\sim D$$
$$\sim A \lor C$$
$$B \lor D$$
$$A \lor C$$
$$\sim B \lor \sim C \lor D$$

Generate the proofs by adopting each of the following strategies: (a) positive resolution, (b) negative resolution, (c) applying either positive or negative hyperresolution at least once, (d) ancestry filtered, (e) input resolution, and (f) unit resolution.

2. Adopting the set of support strategy, prove the inconsistency of the following input set.

$$C$$
$$B \lor \sim C$$
$$\sim A \lor \sim B$$
$$A$$

Let the set of support comprise the positive clauses of the input set. Generate two proofs, where
(a) all resolvents are deduced by applying positive resolution; and

    (b) at least one resolvent is deduced by applying a resolution that is not a positive resolution.

3. Figure 4.10 shows an example of the set of support strategy but the proof shown also happens to meet the demand of the input resolution strategy. For each of the Figures 4.10, 4.11, 4.12, 4.13, 4.16, 4.19, 4.20 and 4.22 list all the restriction strategies whose demands happen to be met by the proof shown.

4. Prove the inconsistency of the input set

$$\sim B \lor \sim C$$
$$\sim A \lor \sim C$$
$$\sim B \lor \sim D$$
$$A \lor B$$
$$B \lor C$$
$$C \lor D$$

Generate the proofs by each of the following:
(a) ancestry filtered strategy;
(b) set of support strategy with the positive clauses of the input set constituting the set of support; and
(c) set of support strategy with the negative clauses of the input set constituting the set of support.

5. Identifying the nucleus and the satellites, deduce a hyperresolvent from the following set of clauses:

$$\sim A$$
$$\sim B \lor \sim C$$
$$A \lor \quad B \lor \sim D \lor E$$
$$\sim E \lor \sim D$$

Did you apply positive or negative hyperresolution? Deduce a resolvent identical to the hyperresolvent by applying a sequence of either only positive or only negative resolutions.

6. Adopting some suitable restriction strategy, prove the inconsistency of the following input set:

$$EQUAL(b, c)$$
$$\sim R(c) \lor \sim S(b)$$
$$\sim R(b) \lor \quad S(c)$$
$$R(b) \lor \sim S(c)$$
$$R(c) \lor \quad S(b)$$

7. Write a program to implement resolution refutation so as to solve exercises 1, 2 and 4 above.

4.7 SUGGESTIONS FOR FURTHER READING

Wos, Robinson and Carson (1965) proposed the set of support strategy and demonstrated its completeness. Wos and Robinson (1970) extended the strategy to the case where paramodulation is incorporated into resolution refutation. Robinson (1965) and Slagle (1967) presented hyperresolution and Overbeek (1975) described its implementation. Wos, Carson and Robinson (1964) introduced unit resolution. Chang (1970) showed that a set of clauses can be proved to be inconsistent by the unit resolution strategy if, and only if, it can be proved to be inconsistent by the input resolution strategy. In their books, Chang and Lee (1973), Loveland (1978), and Wos, Overbeek, Lusk and Boyle (1984) surveyed and discussed the different strategies for refining resolution refutation. Wos (1987) presented research problems in automated reasoning. Nie and Plaisted (1989) advanced a procedure for theorem proving.

1. Chang, C.L. (1970) The unit proof and the input proof in theroem proving, *Journal of the ACM*, **17**, 698–707.
2. Chang, C. and Lee, R. C. (1973) *Symbolic Logic and Mechanical Theorem Proving*, Academic Press, New York.
3. Loveland, D. W. (1978) *Automated Theorem Proving: A Logical Basis*, North Holland, New York.
4. Nie, X. and Plaisted, D. A. (1989) Refinements to depth-first iterative-deepening search in automatic theorem proving, *Artificial Intelligence*, **41**[2], 223–35.
5. Overbeek, R. (1975) An implementation of hyper-resolution, *Computers and Mathematics with Applications*, **1**, 201–14.
6. Robinson, J. A. (1965) Automatic deduction with hyper-resolution, *International Journal of Computer Mathematics*, **1**, 227–34.
7. Slagle, J. R. (1967) Theorem proving with renamable and semantic resolution, *Journal of the ACM*, **14**, 687–97.
8. Wos, L. (1987) *Automated Reasoning: Thirty-three Basic Research Problems*, Prentice Hall, Engelwood Cliffs, New Jersey.
9. Wos, L., Carson, D. F. and Robinson, G. A. (1964) The unit preference strategy in theorem proving, in *Proceedings of the AFIPS Fall Joint Computer Conference*, **26**, Thompson Book Company, New York, pp. 615–21.
10. Wos, L., Overbeek, R., Lusk, E. and Boyle, J. (1984) *Automated Reasoning: Introduction and Applications*, Prentice Hall, Engelwood Cliffs, New Jersey.
11. Wos, L. and Robinson, G. A. (1970) Paramodulation and set of support, in *Symposium on Automatic Deduction*, Springer-Verlag, Berlin, pp. 276–310.

12. Wos, L., Robinson, G. A. and Carson, D. F. (1965) Efficiency and completeness of the set of support strategy in theorem proving, *Journal of the ACM*, **12**, 536–41.

5
Using logic to write programs

5.1 INTRODUCTION

The refinements to resolution refutation you read about in Chapter 4 comprised three ordering strategies, four pruning strategies, and nine restriction strategies. These strategies decrease the number of resolvents deduced to varying extents but ordinarily no individual strategy succeeds in eradicating all useless resolvents.

A new strategy is described later in this chapter. This strategy, known in the literature as SLD, amalgamates within it quite a few of the refinements presented in Chapter 4. SLD is exacting, for it dictates

1. the kind of clauses that are to be resolved,
2. the manner in which the clauses are to be constituted,
3. the specific literals of the clauses that are to be resolved upon,
4. the order in which the clauses are to be resolved, and
5. the type of resolution to be carried out.

The strategy has a mechanism that enables it to judge when useless resolvents have been deduced. It then deletes the useless resolvents, goes back (called **backtracking**) and begins to deduce a new sequence of resolvents. Informally speaking, this is somewhat like taking up a different line of reasoning, after a previous line of reasoning appears to be unfruitful.

SLD has a twin called LBS; the proofs of SLD and LBS are analogous. SLD and LBS can be adopted for logic programming, that is, writing programs by using logic and this has led to the evolution of a programming language called Prolog.

The SLD strategy is described in section 5.2, LBS in section 5.3, and the fundamentals of Prolog in section 5.4.

5.2 THE SLD STRATEGY

You will read below in sections 5.2.1 to 5.2.4 the description of the strategy called SLD (Linear resolution with Selector function on

Definite clauses). The justification for this name will become apparent to you by the end of the description. As mentioned in section 5.1, some of the refinements to resolution refutation presented in Chapter 4 are amalgamated in the SLD strategy. To adopt SLD, we need a special kind of input set which is described next.

5.2.1   Streamlined input set

A **Horn clause** is a clause that contains one positive literal at the most. Under this definition the empty clause NIL is a Horn clause, every negative clause is a Horn clause, a positive clause is a Horn clause if, and only if, it contains a single positive literal (it is a positive unit clause), and a mixed clause is a Horn clause if, and only if, it contains one positive literal and at least one negative literal. The following are examples of Horn clauses.

$$\sim P(z, y) \lor \sim Q(z) \lor \sim R(u, v, w) \qquad \text{(negative clause)}$$
$$P(x, y) \qquad \text{(positive clause)}$$
$$Q(y) \lor \sim S(u, w) \lor \sim P(b, c) \qquad \text{(mixed clause)}$$

As mentioned in sections 2.4.6 and 3.4.3, resolution with factoring is refutation complete for a set of clauses in general but, for a set of Horn clauses, resolution is refutation complete even without factoring. In other words, to prove the inconsistency of a set of Horn clauses, we need to apply resolution but we need not apply factoring.

In the literature, a mixed Horn clause is often written with the positive literal leftmost, the negative literals thus being on the right. We have observed this convention in the example above and we shall continue to do so. You will read in section 5.2.2 how this convention affects resolution in the SLD strategy.

Suppose that an input set has been streamlined to contain only the following types of Horn clauses:

1. at least one positive clause,
2. zero or more mixed clauses, and
3. one negative clause.

The sole negative clause in the input set is derived from the negation of the goal to be proved; the remaining clauses are derived from the premises. We said above that there must be at least one positive clause in the input set. This clause may be implicit if, and only if, we build procedures into the theorem prover to evaluate ground literals, as described in sections 4.3.4 and 4.5.

For the rest of this chapter we shall assume that all our clauses are Horn clauses and that all our input sets are streamlined as specified above. The inconsistency of such sets can be proved by adopting the SLD strategy for resolution refutation.

The strategy has two components. The first component, described in section 5.2.2, restricts us to a constricted form of input resolution. The second component, described in section 5.2.3, guides us in selecting a pair of clauses for resolution when more than one pair is resolvable. The overall description of this strategy is more protracted and more complicated than the description of any strategy you read in Chapter 4 so you may want to read attentively.

5.2.2 Linear input resolution upon leftmost literals

As part of the first component of the SLD strategy, two clauses are considered to be resolvable if, and only if, their leftmost literals are complementary unifiable literals, that is to say, we resolve upon only the leftmost literals of the clauses. This reduces the time and effort required to search for complementary unifiable literals; we need to examine only the leftmost literals of the clauses.

We will never resolve a mixed clause with another mixed clause because, by our convention of section 5.2.1, the leftmost literals of the two mixed clauses will both be positive literals, and hence they are not complementary unifiable literals. Neither will we ever resolve a mixed clause with a positive clause (being a positive literal, the leftmost literal of the mixed clause is not a complementary unifiable literal with the single positive literal of the positive clause). Thus we shall resolve only either (a) a mixed clause with a negative clause, or (b) a positive clause with a negative clause. Since one of the clauses to be resolved will always be a negative clause, all our resolution will be negative resolutions, as defined in section 4.4.2.

A typical resolution between two clauses I and J will then be as follows.

(I) $F_1 \lor \sim F_2 \lor \sim F_3 \lor \ldots \lor \sim F_i$

(J) $\sim G_1 \lor \sim G_2 \lor \sim G_3 \lor \ldots \lor \sim G_j$

The F's and G's are atoms, J is a negative clause and I is a mixed clause. But should the literals $\sim F_2, \sim F_3, \ldots, \sim F_i$ be absent then I becomes a positive clause, containing only the atom F_1. Suppose that F_1 and G_1 can be unified by an mgu δ. Then the resolvent J', deduced by resolving I with J, is written as

(J') $\sim F_2\delta \lor \sim F_3\delta \lor \ldots \lor \sim F_i\delta \lor \sim G_2\delta \lor \sim G_3\delta \lor \ldots \lor \sim G_j\delta$.

Take note of the sequence in which the literals are written in the negative clause J'. The subclause

$$\sim F_2 \delta \vee \sim F_3 \delta \vee \ldots \vee \sim F_i \delta$$

is written at the left, that is, it is written in the place of the literal resolved upon. From the point of view of logic, it does not matter in what sequence we write the literals of the resolvents; all sequences are equivalent. Nevertheless, in the SLD strategy, the literals of a resolvent are written in the sequence shown above. A resolvent is, of course, the empty clause NIL when both its parents are unit clauses.

It was mentioned earlier in this section that all the resolutions will be negative resolutions. Clearly, the resolution shown above is a negative resolution, but we can also look upon it as a negative hyperresolution, as defined in section 4.4.3. The nucleus, which must be a positive or a mixed clause, is the clause I. Because I has one positive literal it needs one negative clause as the satellite. The satellite is the clause J. Clause J' should then be called the hyperresolvent. Such a hyperresolvent is required to be either a negative clause or the empty clause NIL and Clause J' fulfils that requirement. Thus the above negative resolution also exemplifies negative hyperresolution.

Continuing with our description of the first component of SLD, we shall now blend the above negative resolution with input resolution, as defined in section 4.4.7.

As mentioned in section 5.2.1, the streamlined input set contains a single negative clause, which is derived from the negation of the goal. We shall refer to this clause as J_0 and we can think of it as constituting a set of support, as defined in section 4.4.1. The resolvents we deduce sequentially will then be referred to as J_1, J_2, J_3, $\ldots$ which are all descendants of J_0. We adopt a constricted form of input resolution known as **linear input resolution**. In input resolution, the only stipulation is that, for any resolvent, at least one parent must be in the input set. In linear input resolution, for any resolvent J_{m+1} ($m = 0, 1, 2, \ldots$), not only must one parent be in the input set, the other parent must be J_m. Put another way, we start by resolving J_0 with another clause from the input set; thereafter, we always resolve the latest resolvent, with a clause from the input set, to deduce the next resolvent.

Remember, however, that whereas linear input resolution allows us in general to resolve upon any literal in a clause, the SLD strategy allows us to resolve upon only the leftmost literal in the clause. Thus the SLD strategy restrains us even more than linear input resolution. An example of this is given in Figure 5.1. It is mentioned in the example that you may assume we were lucky in arbitrarily selecting a particular clause for resolution. In fact, our selection was guided by the

Given the premisses:
[i]   Amity is the ma of Betsy, Anna of Bill, and Betsy of Cindy.
[ii]   Bill is the pa of Cindy.
[iii]   For all x, y, z: if x is the ma of y, and y is either the pa or
         the ma of z, then x is the grandma of z.

The following Horn clauses are derived from the above premisses.
[I1]   MA(Amity, Betsy)
[I2]   MA(Anna, Bill)
[I3]   MA(Betsy, Cindy)
[I4]   PA(Bill, Cindy)
[I5]   GRANDMA(x1, z1) ∨ ~MA(x1, y1) ∨ ~PA(y1, z1)
[I6]   GRANDMA(x2, z2) ∨ ~MA(x2, y2) ∨ ~MA(y2, z2)

Adopt linear input resolution on the leftmost literals of the clauses to prove the goal GRANDMA(Anna, Cindy). The negation of the goal is clause J0 below.
[J0]   ~GRANDMA(Anna, Cindy)

Resolve J0 with I5 by mgu = {Anna/x1, Cindy/z1} to deduce J1 below.
[J1]   ~MA(Anna, y1) ∨ ~PA(y1, Cindy)

Resolve J1 with I2 by mgu = {Bill/y1} to deduce J2 below.
[J2]   ~PA(Bill, Cindy)

Resolve J2 with I4 to deduce the empty clause NIL. Thus the goal is proved to be a theorem: Anna is a grandma of Cindy.

Above, J0 was resolvable with both I5 and I6. After you have read about the second component of the SLD strategy in Section 5.2.3, you will know why J0 was resolved with I5 and not with I6. At present, you may assume we were lucky in arbitrarily selecting I5.

Figure 5.1   An example of a refutation proof by linear input resolution upon the leftmost literals of clauses [the first component of the SLD strategy]. J_0, J_1, J_2, ... used in the textual description of Chapter 5 to denote clauses in general, have been indicated specifically as J0, J1, J2, ... in the examples in the chapter.

second component of the SLD strategy. This component is described in the next section.

5.2.3   Selecting definite clauses and backtracking

A clause that has exactly one positive literal is known as a **definite clause**. Every mixed or positive clause is hence a definite clause. It was mentioned in section 5.2.1 that the mixed and positive clauses in the input set are derived from the premisses. Therefore, the only definite clauses in the input set are those that are derived from the premisses. Definite clauses are also known as **regular clauses** in the literature.

From section 5.2.2 we can say that whenever we apply resolution in the SLD strategy we resolve a negative clause J_m ($m \geq 0$) with one of the definite clauses. Those definite clauses that are resolvable with J_m are called the **consorts** of J_m.

When J_m has only one consort then we do not have to make a selection: we resolve that consort with J_m. But when J_m has more than one consort then we do have to make a selection: Which one of these consorts shall we select to resolve with J_m? A good selection will lead us to finishing the proof; a bad selection will not. In case we make a bad selection, we need a mechanism that, at some stage of the proof, indicates to us that we had made a bad selection. We receive this indication when we deduce a resolvent such that (a) it is not resolvable with any of the definite clauses, or (b) the resolvent is a tautology because its leftmost literal is a ground literal that has been evaluated to be true by procedures we may have built into the theorem prover (these procedures were discussed in section 4.3.4).

On becoming aware that we had made a bad selection, we backtrack and select a different consort to resolve with J_m. In case we make a bad selection again, we backtrack again. Making a selection and then backtracking is said to **constitute one** J_m**-rooted iteration**. These iterations continue until either we have made a selection that leads us to finishing the proof, or we have exhausted all the selections without finishing the proof. The number of J_m-rooted iterations will at the most be equal to the number of consorts of J_m.

Since we have discussed the fundamental notion of selecting and backtracking we can now study how consorts are selected for resolution in the SLD strategy.

Let the $n \geq 1$ consorts of J_m be symbolized by $I'_1, I'_2, \ldots, I'_n$ such that I'_1 is catalogued before I'_2 in the input set, I'_2 before $I'_3 \ldots$. (As defined in section 4.2.1, clauses in a set are said to be catalogued in the order in which they are written when displaying the members of the set.) Then in the first J_m-rooted iteration we resolve J_m with I'_1, in the second iteration we resolve J_m with I'_2, and so on. The consorts are thus selected in successive iterations in the order in which they are catalogued in the input set.

Before you read any further, pause for a while and look again at the example in Figure 5.1. In this example it was mentioned that you may assume we were lucky in arbitrarily selecting a particular clause for resolution. Our selection was in fact guided by the preceding paragraph.

By now you may have thought of different approaches to control the J_m-rooted iterations. Nonetheless, you will read below one such approach.

[1] Resolve J_m with its consort I'_k to deduce J_{m+1}.

[2] Decrease the value of the c-index of J_m by 1, because there is now one less consort yet to be resolved with J_m.

[3] Continuing with linear input resolution upon the leftmost literals of clauses, commence iterations successively rooted in J_{m+1}, J_{m+2}, ..., until we deduce a resolvent J_{m+i} [$i \geq 1$] such that

[3a] J_{m+i} is the empty clause NIL; we stop because the goal is proved;

or

[3b] either J_{m+i} is not resolvable with any definite clause, or the leftmost literal of J_{m+i} is a ground literal that has been evaluated to be true by procedures built into the theorem prover; we then scan clauses J_{m+i-1}, J_{m+i-2}, ..., until we find a bluebeard, and to that we backtrack [we thus backtrack to the nearest bluebeard ancestor of J_{m+i}]; but suppose we scan all the way to J_0 and do not find a bluebeard; then we know we have exhausted all the selections, and so we stop [the proof can never be finished].

Figure 5.2 Steps to be executed in the k-th [$1 \leq k \leq n$] J_m-rooted iteration for the SLD strategy. At the beginning of the first iteration, the value of the c-index is n, which is equal to the number of consorts of J_m. The first step above can alternatively be written as follows: Resolve J_m with its consort I'_{n-j+1}, where j is the value of the c-index at the beginning of the current iteration.

We associate with J_m an integer valued **c-index**, which is short for **consort index**. Its value at any time reflects the number of consorts that are yet to be resolved with J_m. Since J_m initially has n consorts, we assign an initial value of n to its c-index. Thereafter, in each J_m-rooted iteration, the value of this c-index is decreased by 1 because there is one less consort yet to be resolved with J_m. While its c-index has a value greater than zero, J_m is called a **bluebeard**. Note, bluebeard is a status of the clause: it signifies that there is at least one consort yet to be resolved with J_m. During the last J_m-rooted iteration the value of the c-index becomes zero, and J_m no longer remains a bluebeard.

Figure 5.2 summarizes the steps to be executed in a J_m-rooted iteration for SLD. As the figure shows, when we backtrack from some resolvent, we backtrack to its nearest bluebeard ancestor. Suppose we

Given the following definite clauses derived from some premisses:

[I1]   MA(Amity, Betsy)
[I2]   MA(Anna, Bill)
[I3]   MA(Betsy, Cindy)
[I4]   PA(Bill, Cindy)
[I5]   GRANDMA(x1, z1) $\lor$ $\sim$MA(x1, y1) $\lor$ $\sim$PA(y1, z1)
[I6]   GRANDMA(x2, z2) $\lor$ $\sim$MA(x2, y2) $\lor$ $\sim$MA(y2, z2)

Adopt the SLD strategy to prove by refutation the goal GRANDMA(Amity, Cindy). The negation of the goal is clause J0 below.

[J0] $\sim$GRANDMA(Amity, Cindy)

The c-index of J0 above is 2, with consorts I5 and I6. Resolve J0 with I5 by mgu = {Amity/x1, Cindy/z1} to deduce J1 below. The c-index of J0 becomes 1.

/line1/   [J1] $\sim$MA(Amity, y1) $\lor$ $\sim$PA(y1, Cindy)

Resolve the above J1 with I1 by mgu = {Betsy/y1} to deduce J2 below.

/line2/   [J2] $\sim$PA(Betsy, Cindy)

The J2 above is not resolvable with any definite clause. So backtrack to J0, the nearest bluebeard ancestor. Resolve J0 with I6 by mgu = {Amity/x2, Cindy/z2} to deduce J1 below. The c-index of J0 becomes zero.

/line3/   [J1] $\sim$MA(Amity, y2) $\lor$ $\sim$MA(y2, Cindy)

Resolve J1 of line 3 with I1 by mgu = {Betsy/y2} to deduce J2 below.

/line4/   [J2] $\sim$MA(Betsy, Cindy)

Resolve J2 of line 4 with I3 to deduce the empty clause NIL. Thus the goal is proved to be a theorem: Amity is a grandma of Cindy.

Figure 5.3   An example of resolution refutation by adopting the SLD strategy. The c-index of any J clause after its resolution is zero, unless otherwise specified.

are backtracking from J_5 and its bluebeard ancestors are J_0, J_1 and J_3. Then we backtrack to J_3 because that is the nearest bluebeard ancestor of J_5, and we commence the next J_3-rooted iteration. We must be careful, for iterations may be nested inside one another; J_3-rooted iterations may be nested inside J_1-rooted iterations, which in turn may be nested inside J_0-rooted iterations. During each J_0-rooted iteration, we must execute all J_1-rooted iterations; similarly, during each J_1-rooted iteration, we must execute all J_3-rooted iterations.

In other words we backtrack to that clause (a) where we made chronologically the most recent selection, and (b) where another selection is still available. In the literature, this kind of backtracking is thus often called chronological backtracking. Figures 5.3 and 5.4 show examples of resolution refutation by adopting the SLD strategy.

5.2.4   Remarks on SLD

When we deduce resolvents J_1, J_2, J_3, ..., we need not retain all of them in computer memory for all the time. We need to retain them

Given the following definite clauses derived from some premisses:

[I1] MA(Amity, Betsy)
[I2] MA(Anna, Bill)
[I3] MA(Betsy, Cindy)
[I4] PA(Bill, Cindy)
[I5] GRANDMA(x1, z1) ∨ ~MA(x1, y1) ∨ ~PA(y1, z1)
[I6] GRANDMA(x2, z2) ∨ ~MA(x2, y2) ∨ ~MA(y2, z2)

Adopt the SLD strategy to prove by refutation the goal ∃v(GRANDMA(v, Cindy)). The negation of the goal is clause J0 below.

[J0] ~GRANDMA(v, Cindy)

The c-index of J0 above is 2, with consorts I5 and I6. Resolve J0 with I5 by mgu = {v/x1, Cindy/z1} to deduce J1 below. The c-index of J0 becomes 1.

/line 1/ [J1] ~MA(v, y1) ∨ ~PA(y1, Cindy)

The c-index of J1 above is 3, with consorts I1, I2, and I3. Resolve J1 with I1 by mgu = {Amity/v, Betsy/y1} to deduce J2 below. The c-index of J1 becomes 2.

/line 2/ [J2] ~PA(Betsy, Cindy)

The J2 above is not resolvable with any definite clause. So backtrack to J1 of line 1, the nearest bluebeard ancestor. Resolve that J1 with I2 by mgu = {Anna/v, Bill/y1} to deduce J2 below. The c-index of J1 becomes 1.

/line 3/ [J2] ~PA(Bill, Cindy)

Resolve J2 of line 3 with I4 to deduce the empty clause NIL. Thus the goal is proved to be a theorem.

Figure 5.4   An example of resolution refutation by adopting the SLD strategy. The c-index of any J clause after its resolution is zero, unless otherwise specified. Above, we backtracked from J2 of line 2 to J1 of line 1, and not to J0, because J1 was the nearer bluebeard ancestor of J2.

only for the time they are bluebeards: should we ever backtrack, we backtrack to a bluebeard. Suppose that, after resolving a J_m with some definite clause, we notice that the c-index of J_m has become zero. We can then delete J_m for, having employed J_m to deduce J_{m+1}, we shall not require J_m any more. This will free computer memory for other future use but, of course, we must retain all resolvents, if we want to keep a chronicle of the full proof.

It should be clear by now that the two components of the SLD strategy you have read above are (a) linear input resolution upon the leftmost literals of the clauses, and (b) selection of definite clauses for resolution in the order in which the clauses are catalogued in the input set, together with chronological backtracking. Thus, as mentioned at the beginning of section 5.2, the expansion of the name SLD is Linear resolution with Selection function on Definite clauses. In the literature this strategy is also known as LUSH (Linear resolution with Unrestricted Selection for Horn clauses) but we shall continue to use the name SLD. In the following section we discuss LBS, another technique for automated reasoning.

5.3   THE LBS TECHNIQUE

Programs for automated reasoning are often designed for conversational (interactive) use. From a terminal, we load into the computer the premisses of a problem. We then enter the goal and activate the reasoning program. As the proof evolves, we scrutinize its trace and possibly discover that we have formulated the problem incorrectly. Thereupon, for example, we may modify some premisses or add new ones, and activate the program again. We thus employ the reasoning program to augment our own power of reasoning. For our convenience, it is desirable that the premisses and the proof be displayed at the terminal in a manner that we can easily understand.

By using resolution refutation, a program can reason with clauses. Most people, however, may find it difficult to reason with clauses. Consider the following clause

CLEANS(John, Room) ∨ ~BRINGS(John, Mop).

In English, the clause can be read as this: John cleans the room, or he does not bring the mop. Now consider the following implication.

CLEANS(John, Room) ← BRINGS(John, Mop).

This implication, in turn, can be read as this: John clean the room, if he brings the mop. Logically, the above clause and the above implication are equivalent but most people would understand the purport of the implication more easily than that of the clause. If you are like most people, then the LBS (Linear Backchaining with Selector function on assertions) technique of reasoning would be of interest to you. It is described below in sections 5.3.1–5.3.4. The justification for its name will become apparent to you by the end of the description. The word *backchaining* is a short form for **backward chaining**.

LBS is closely related to the SLD strategy so make sure you have mastered SLD before you begin to read about LBS. You will then readily appreciate LBS and its relationship with SLD and, in turn, an appreciation of LBS will help you in logic programming. You will read next how the premisses and the goal of a problem are to be formulated for LBS.

5.3.1   Formulation of premisses and the goal

It was mentioned in section 5.2.1 that, for the SLD strategy, the input set is streamlined to contain positive and mixed Horn clauses, derived from the premisses, and one negative clause, derived from the negation of the goal. For LBS these clauses are formulated as described below.

The positive clauses in the streamlined input set are unit clauses. No change is made in writing them for LBS. They are, however, now called **verities**. The following are examples of verities.

> AWAKENS(John)
> GT(add(x,1), x)

All variables occurring in verities are understood to be implicitly universally quantified. We can informally say that a verity is a fact that has been given to us. Accordingly, in the literature, a verity is also called a **fact**.

The mixed clauses in the streamlined input set contain one positive literal and any number of negative literals. For LBS they are written as equivalent implications. Hence the clause

$$F_1 \lor \sim F_2 \lor \sim F_3 \lor \ldots \lor \sim F_i$$

is written as the following equivalent implication.

$$F_1 \leftarrow F_2 \land F_3 \land \ldots \land F_i.$$

The consequent in the implication is a single atom; the antecedent is a conjunction of any number of atoms (observing the practice for LBS in the literature, we shall write the consequent on the left and the antecedent on the right). The following are examples of such implications.

> DELIGHTED(Mother) ← AWAKENS(John) ∧
>   CLEANS (John, Room)
> ARGUES(x, wife(x)) ← HUSBAND(x)

All variables occurring in these implications are understood to be implicitly universally quantified.

An **assertion** is a verity or an implication of the kind described above. We shall write an assertion as

$$F_1 \leftarrow F_2 \land F_3 \land \ldots \land F_i.$$

When the assertion is a verity, then F_2, F_3, . . ., F_i are understood to be absent. Since assertions correspond to the positive and mixed Horn clauses of a streamlined input set, we can say that assertions are derived from the premisses of the problem.

In the goal to be proved, all universally quantified variables are replaced by Skolem terms, and all universal quantifiers are eliminated. To illustrate, the goal formula

$$\exists u \forall v \forall w \exists x \forall y \exists z F(u, v, w, x, y, z)$$

is rewritten as the following goal formula

$$\exists u \exists x \exists z F(u, f(u), g(u), x, h(u, x), z).$$

In the new goal formula, $f(u)$ has replaced v, $g(u)$ has replaced w, and $h(u, x)$ has replaced y. Moreover, the three universal quantifiers have been eliminated. The replacements $f(u)$, $g(u)$ and $h(u, x)$ are Skolem terms, and f, g, and h are Skolem functions. None of the symbols f, g and h should have already occurred in the original goal formula $F(u, v, w, x, y, z)$. The arguments of a Skolem function are those existentially quantified variables whose scope includes the scope of the universally quantified variable being replaced. (You may have noticed that this Skolemizing is a dual of the Skolemizing discussed earlier in section 3.3.1.)

We next eliminate the existential quantifiers and write the formula as $F(u, f(u), g(u), x, h(u, x), z)$. This does not affect the formula as long as it is understood that variables in the formula are implicitly existentially quantified.

Examples of goals, which are written as conjunctions of atoms, are given below.

> AWAKENS(John) $\wedge$ CLEANS(John, Room)
> GRANDMA(v, Cindy)

Note that, whereas for SLD we negate the goal, for LBS we do not. While Skolemizing the negation of the goal for SLD, we eliminate existential quantifiers; while Skolemizing the goal for LBS, we eliminate universal quantifiers.

Until now, symbols I and J have been used to denote clauses. Because of the kinship of the clauses for SLD with the assertions and the goal for LBS, just described, symbols I and J will be used to denote the assertions and goal, too.

Just as there are two components in SLD, so there are two components in LBS. The first component of LBS is described in section 5.3.2, and the second in section 5.3.3. Before you read about the first component (backchaining), look at the two preparatory examples given

Given the following assertions derived from some premisses:
[I1]   AWAKENS(John)
[I2]   BRINGS(John, Mop)
[I3]   DELIGHTED(Mother) ← AWAKENS(John) ∧ CLEANS(John, Room)
[I4]   CLEANS(John, Room) ← BRINGS(John, Mop)

Adopt backchaining to prove the goal J0.
[J0]   DELIGHTED(Mother)

J0 is identical to the consequent in I3. So to prove J0, it is sufficient to prove the antecedent of I3, written as J1 below. J1 becomes our new goal. We say that J0 is backchained through I3 to produce J1.
[J1]   AWAKENS(John) ∧ CLEANS(John, Room)

To prove J1, we must prove both its atoms. Either of these two atoms can be proved first. But it will be our practice that when we have to prove many atoms, we will try to prove the leftmost atom first. The leftmost atom of J1 is trivially proved because it is identical to the verity I1. Thus what remains to be proved is J2 below.
[J2]   CLEANS(John, Room)

J2 is backchained through I4 to produce J3 below.
[J3]   BRINGS(John, Mop)

J3 is trivially proved because it is identical to the verity I2. Hence it can be said that goal J0 is proved to be a theorem.

Figure 5.5 A preparatory example to show backchaining through assertions in which there are only ground literals. Compare the above proof with Figure 3.13, wherein the same theorem was proved by resolution refutation.

in Figures 5.5 and 5.6. Then as you read the description in the following section, keep referring to the examples. This will help you understand backchaining better.

5.3.2 Linear backchaining of the leftmost atom

You will read below a description of the backchaining of the leftmost literal of a goal. It constitutes a part of the first component of LBS. Suppose we have the following goal J.

(J) $G_1 \wedge G_2 \wedge G_3 \wedge \ldots \wedge G_j$

where the G's are atoms. To prove goal J, we have to prove each of the G's. We could prove any of them first, but in LBS we try to prove the leftmost atom G_1 first. To do this, we peruse the set of assertions for an assertion

Given the following assertions derived from some premisses:
[I1]   ARGUES(x, wife(x)) ← HUSBAND(x)
[I2]   HUSBAND(Alan)

Adopt backchaining to prove the goal J0.
[J0]   ARGUES(Alan, wife(Alan))

The atom in J0 is unified with the consequent of I1 by mgu = {Alan/x}. So to prove J0, it is sufficient to prove the antecedent of I1, after applying the mgu to I1. We write it as J1 below. J1 becomes our new goal. We say that J0 is backchained through I1 by mgu = {Alan/x} to produce J1.
[J1]   HUSBAND(Alan)

J1 is trivially proved because it is identical to the verity I2.   Hence it can be said that J0 is proved to be a theorem.

Figure 5.6 A preparatory example to show backchaining through assertions that may contain variables. All variables in the assertions are understood to be implicitly universally quantified. Compare the above proof with Figure 3.15, wherein the same theorem was proved by resolution refutation.

(I) $F_1 \leftarrow F_2 \wedge F_3 \wedge \ldots \wedge F_i$

such that G_1 and F_1 are unifiable by some mgu δ. In other words, the leftmost atom in goal J is unifiable with the consequent in some assertion I. Then to prove goal J, it is sufficient to prove the following goal J'.

(J') $F_2\delta \wedge F_3\delta \wedge \ldots \wedge F_i\delta \wedge G_2\delta \wedge G_3\delta \wedge \ldots \wedge Gj\delta.$

The problem of proving goal J has thus been transformed into the problem of proving goal J'. We say that J is backchained through I by mgu δ to produce J'. To be precise, it is the leftmost atom of J that is backchained through I but, since in LBS that is the only atom we will ever backchain, we may not explicitly mention it every time. Take note of the sequence in which the atoms are written in J'. From the point of view of logic, it does not matter in what sequence we write the literals of J'. Nevertheless, it is the practice in LBS to write the atoms of J' in the sequence shown above.

Goal J is called a parent of J', and J' is called a **bourne** of J. Given a set of assertions, it is likely that J can be backchained through more than one assertion. Thus goal J can have more than one bourne. Remember that, just as a resolvent is also a clause, a bourne is also a goal. An empty bourne (goal) is a bourne (goal) of zero atoms.

A goal J is called an **ancestor** of a goal J″ if, and only if, either J is a parent of J″ or J is a parent of an ancestor of J″. Moreover, J″ is said to be a **descendant** of J if, and only if, J is an ancestor of J″. An atom G_1 is said to be **trivially proved** if, and only if, either

1. backchaining G_1 through some assertion produces an empty bourne (this happens when the assertion is a verity F_1, and G_1 is unifiable with F_1); or
2. G_1 is a ground literal that is evaluated to be true by procedures we may have built into the theorem prover, as discussed in section 4.3.4.

A goal J is said to be **trivially proved** if, and only if, either (a) J is an empty goal, or (b) J contains only one atom G_1 such that G_1 is trivially proved.

As described in section 5.3.1, our theorem proving problem consists of a set of assertions derived from the premises, and a goal to be proved. Let this goal be referred to as J_0. To prove J_0 by backchaining, we would need to produce a sequence of bournes $J_1, J_2, J_3, \ldots$ such that they are all descendants of J_0. Goal J_0 is then proved if, and only if, in the sequence of goals $J_0, J_1, J_2, \ldots$, we obtain a goal that is trivially proved. In LBS, however, we adopt a constricted form of backchaining, called linear backchaining, according to which any J_{m+1} ($m = 0, 1, 2, \ldots$) must be a bourne of J_m. That is to say, in linear backchaining we start by producing a bourne of J_0. Thereafter, the latest bourne becomes the parent of the next bourne. We say we have finished the proof when we produce a bourne that is trivially proved. Look at the example in Figure 5.7.

Take note of the following relationship between backchaining and resolution: we can produce bourne J′ by backchaining the leftmost literal of goal J through assertion I if, and only if, we can deduce resolvent ~J′ by resolving upon the leftmost literals of clause ~J and the clause equivalent of assertion I. Check the veracity of the preceding sentence by comparing the proofs given in Figures 5.1 and 5.7. Make sure you understand this relationship before you begin reading the description of the second component of LBS, given in the next section.

5.3.3 Selecting assertions and backtracking

The second component of LBS resembles the second component of SLD, which was described in section 5.2.3. Having understood it for SLD, you may have already guessed it for LBS, in which case, you may skip this section and go on to read section 5.3.4, but should you have any doubts, then continue to read this section. The fundamental

Given the following assertions derived from some premisses:
[I1]   MA(Amity, Betsy)
[I2]   MA(Anna, Bill)
[I3]   MA(Betsy, Cindy)
[I4]   PA(Bill, Cindy)
[I5]   GRANDMA(x1, z1) ← MA(x1, y1) ∧ PA(y1, z1)
[I6]   GRANDMA(x2, z2) ← MA(x2, y2) ∧ MA(y2, z2)

Adopt linear backchaining of the leftmost atoms of goals to prove the goal J0.
[J0]   GRANDMA(Anna, Cindy)

Backchain J0 through I5 by mgu = {Anna/x1, Cindy/z1} to produce J1 below.
[J1]   MA(Anna, y1) ∧ PA(y1, Cindy)

Backchain J1 through I2 by mgu = {Bill/y1} to produce J2 below.
[J2]   PA(Bill, Cindy)

J2 is identical to I4. Put another way, backchaining J2 through I4 produces the empty bourne. J2 is thus trivially proved. Therefore goal J0 is proved to be a theorem: Anna is a grandma of Cindy.

Above, J0 was backchainable through both I5 and I6. After you have read about the second component of LBS in Section 5.3.3, you will know why J0 was backchained through I5 and not through I6.

Figure 5.7   An example of a proof by adopting linear backchaining of the leftmost atom of a goal [the first component of LBS]. Compare the above proof with Figure 5.1, wherein the same theorem was proved by linear input resolution upon the leftmost literals of clauses.

notions of selecting and backtracking will not be explained again; they were previously explained in section 5.2.3. Here you will read only how LBS specifically employs selecting and backtracking. This section is similar to section 5.2.3, but it is not identical.

A goal is said to be **inert** if, and only if, either (a) it is not backchainable through any assertion, or (b) its leftmost literal is a ground literal that has been evaluated to be false by procedures we may have built into the theorem prover (these procedures were discussed in section 4.3.4).

From the description in section 5.3.2, we can say that whenever we apply backchaining, we backchain a goal J_m ($m \geq 0$) through one of the assertions. Those assertions through which J_m is backchainable are called the **consorts** of J_m.

Let the $n \geq 1$ consorts of J_m be symbolized by I_1', I_2', . . . , I_n' such that I_1' is catalogued before I_2' in the set of assertions, I_2' before

I_3', ... (Assertions in a set are said to be **catalogued** in the order in which they are written, when displaying the members of the set.) We next commence J_m-rooted iterations. In the first such iteration, we select I_1' and backchain J_m through it. Continuing with linear backchaining, we produce bournes J_{m+1}, J_{m+2}, ... until we produce either a bourne that is trivially proved, in which case we stop since the proof is finished, or we produce a bourne that is inert. In the latter case, we backtrack and commence the second J_m-rooted iteration: we select I_2' and backchain J_m through it. If we again produce an inert bourne, we backtrack again. In the kth ($1 \leq k \leq n$) J_m-rooted iteration, we backchain J_m through I_k'. Thus the consorts are selected in successive iterations in the order in which they are catalogued in the set of assertions.

Look again at the example in Figure 5.7 where there was a statement about a particular goal being backchainable through two assertions. One of the assertions was selected, and the goal was backchained through it. Our selection was in fact guided by the preceding paragraph.

The approach to controlling the J_m-rooted iteration in LBS can be similar to the approach described for SLD in section 5.2.3. We associate with J_m an integer valued c-index, whose value at any time reflects the number of consorts through which J_m is yet to be backchained. With J_m having initially n consorts, the initial value of the c-index is n. Thereafter, the value of the c-index is decreased by 1 in each J_m-rooted iteration. For the duration that its c-index has a value greater than zero, J_m is referred to as a **bluebeard**. The steps to be executed in a J_m-rooted iteration for LBS are summarized in Figure 5.8. Note that the backtracking in LBS is also chronological backtracking, as it is in SLD Figure 5.9 gives an example of a proof generated by adopting LBS.

5.3.4   Remarks on LBS

When we produce bournes J_1, J_2, J_3, ..., we need not retain all of them in computer memory all the time. We need to retain them only for the time they are bluebeards: whenever we backtrack, we backtrack to a blubeard. If after backchaining a J_m through an assertion, the c-index of J_m becomes zero, we can then delete J_m for having employed J_m to produce J_{m+1}', we shall not be requiring J_m any more. This will free computer memory for other future use, but we must obviously retain all bournes if we want to keep a chronicle of the full proof.

To recapitulate, the two components of LBS are (a) linear backchaining of the leftmost atoms of goals, and (b) selection of assertions to be backchained through in the order in which they are

[1]   Backchain J_m through its consort I'_k to produce J_{m+1}.

[2]   Decrease the value of c-index of J_m by 1, because there is now one less consort through which J_m is yet to be backchained.

[3]   Continuing with linear backchaining of the leftmost atoms of goals, commence iterations successively rooted in J_{m+1}, J_{m+2}, ..., until we produce a bourne J_{m+1} [i $\geq$ 1] such that

[3a] J_{m+i} is trivially proved; we stop because the goal J_0 is proved;

or

[3b] J_{m+i} is an inert bourne; this happens when either J_{m+i} is not backchainable through any assertion, or the leftmost literal of J_{m+i} is a ground literal that has been evaluated to be false by procedures built into the theorem prover; we then backtrack to the nearest bluebeard ancestor of J_{m+i}; but suppose we do not find a bluebeard even up to J_0; then we know we have exhausted all the selections, and so we stop [the proof can never be finished].

Figure 5.8   Steps to be executed in the k-th [1 $\leq$ k $\leq$ n] J_m-rooted iteration for LBS. At the beginning of the first iteration, the value of the c-index is n, which is equal to the number of consorts of J_m. The first step above can alternatively be written as follows: Backchain J_m through its consort I'_{n-j+1}, where j is the value of the c-index at the beginning of the current iteration.

catalogued, together with chronological backtracking. Thus, as mentioned at the beginning of section 5.3, the expansion of the name LBS is Linear Backchaining with Selector function on assertions.

To prove the goal $(G_1 \wedge G_2 \wedge \ldots \wedge G_j)$ in LBS, we in effect first prove G_1, second G_2, third G_3, and so on. In other words, we finish the task on hand no matter how deep we have to go into its working before we begin to toil on the next task in the sequence. In the literature, this kind of approach to solving problems is known as a **depth-first** approach.

Suppose, for a given theorem proving problem, the definite clauses for SLD are catalogued in the same sequence as the equivalent assertions for LBS. Then, in the proof for SLD, we deduce a resolvent J_m of the form

$$\sim G_1 \vee \sim G_2 \vee \sim G_3 \vee \ldots$$

Given the following assertions derived from some premisses:

[I1] MA(Amity, Betsy)
[I2] MA(Anna, Bill)
[I3] MA(Betsy, Cindy)
[I4] PA(Bill, Cindy)
[I5] GRANDMA(x1, z1) ← MA(x1, y1) ∧ PA(y1, z1)
[I6] GRANDMA(x2, z2) ← MA(x2, y2) ∧ MA(y2, z2)

Adopt LBS to prove the goal J0.
[J0] GRANDMA(Amity, Cindy)

The c-index of J0 above is 2, with consorts I5 and I6. Backchain J0 through I5 by mgu = {Amity/x1, Cindy/z1} to produce J1 below. The c-index of J0 becomes 1.

/line 1/   [J1] MA(Amity, y1) ∧ PA(y1, Cindy)

Backchain the J1 above through I1 by mgu = {Betsy/y1} to produce J2 below.

/line 2/   [J2] PA(Betsy, Cindy)

The J2 above is inert because it is not backchainable through any assertion. So backtrack to J0, the nearest bluebeard ancestor. Backchain J0 through I6 by mgu = {Amity/x2, Cindy/z2} to produce J1 below. The c-index of J0 becomes zero.

/line 3/   [J1] MA(Amity, y2) ∧ MA(y2, Cindy)

Backchain J1 of line 3 through I1 by mgu = {Betsy/y2} to produce J2 below.

/line 4/   [J2] MA(Betsy, Cindy)

J2 of line 4 is trivially proved because backchaining it through I3 produces the empty bourne. Therefore goal J0 is proved to be a theorem: Amity is a grandma of Cindy.

Figure 5.9 An example of a proof by adopting LBS. The c-index of any goal after its backchaining is zero, unless otherwise specified. Compare the above proof with Figure 5.3, wherein the same theorem was proved by adopting the SLD strategy.

if, and only if, in the proof for LBS, we produce a corresponding bourne of the form

$$G_1 \wedge G_2 \wedge G_3 \wedge \dots$$

You may check the correctness of the preceding sentence by comparing the proofs of Figure 5.1 with Figure 5.7, and Figure 5.3 with Figure 5.9.

The above correspondence between the proofs of LBS and SLD should not be surprising. The former uses the chaining rule of inference, the latter, resolution. In sections 2.4.3 and 3.4.1, we had employed chaining to demonstrate the soundness of resolution. Chaining and resolution are kindred: a theorem proved by LBS can also be proved by SLD, and vice versa. However, there is one difference between the two: LBS proves theorems by the direct method, SLD by refutation. These two fundamental methods of proving theorems were discussed in section 2.3.2.

In sections 5.3.6 to 5.3.8, you will read about the order in which you should catalogue the assertions, about the care you should take in writing assertions, and about how you can write programs with them. But before that, you will read in the next section how you can adopt LBS to answer questions about a goal.

5.3.5   Answering questions by adopting LBS

In section 3.4.5, we discussed how resolution refutation can be extended so that, in proving a goal of the form $\exists vG(v)$, we are also able to answer this question: For what value of v is $G(v)$ a logical consequence of the given premisses? When the proof is finished, the

> Given the following assertions derived from some premisses:
> [I1]   MA(Amity, Betsy)
> [I2]   MA(Anna, Bill)
> [I3]   MA(Betsy, Cindy)
> [I4]   PA(Bill, Cindy)
> [I5]   GRANDMA(x1, z1) ← MA(x1, y1) ∧ PA(y1, z1)
> [I6]   GRANDMA(x2, z2) ← MA(x2, y2) ∧ MA(y2, z2)
>
> Adopt LBS to find the values of v for which the goal ∃v(GRANDMA(v, Cindy)) is a logical consequence of the above premisses. The goal to be proved is written as J0.
> [J0]   GRANDMA(v, Cindy)
>
> The c-index of J0 above is 2 with consorts I5 and I6. Backchain J0 through I5 by mgu = {v/x1, Cindy/z1} to produce J1 below. The c-index of J0 becomes 1.
> /line 1/   [J1]   MA(v, y1) ∧ PA(y1, Cindy)
>
> The c-index of the J1 above is 3, with consorts I1, I2, and I3. Backchain J1 through I1 by mgu = {Amity/v, Betsy/y1} to produce J2 below. The c-index of J1 becomes 2.
> /line 2/   [J2]   PA(Betsy, Cindy)
>
> The J2 above is inert because it is not backchainable through any assertion. So backtrack to J1 of line 1, the nearest bluebeard ancestor. Backchain that J1 through I2 by mgu = {Anna/v, Bill/y1} to produce J2 below. The c-index of J1 becomes 1.
> /line 3/   [J2]   PA(Bill, Cindy)
>
> J2 of line 3 is trivially proved because backchaining it through I4 produces the empty bourne. Therefore goal J0 is proved to be a theorem. Variable v was instantiated to Anna; hence, Anna is a grandma of Cindy.

Figure 5.10   An example showing how to find an answer to a question, by adopting LBS. The c-index of any goal after its backchaining is zero, unless otherwise specified. Compare the above proof with Figure 5.4, wherein the same theorem was proved by adopting the SLD strategy.

value to which v gets instantiated is the value of v for which $G(v)$ is a logical consequence of the premises. The value of this instantiation is known by maintaining a record of the term that replaces v in any unification. Since the SLD strategy proves theorems by resolution refutation, we can answer the above question by adopting SLD, but, as discussed in section 5.3.4, there is a correspondence between the proofs of SLD and LBS. Thus we can answer the same question by adopting LBS, too. The example in Figure 5.10 illustrate this.

Furthermore, we can attune LBS to find multiple answers to the question. In other words, we can find multiple values of v, provided such values exist. To find these multiple values, we generate different proofs; all proofs have the same set of assertions and the same goal, but no two proofs have identical sequences of the bournes produced. The variable v may thus get instantiated to different values in the different proofs. We now discuss how we can generate these different proofs.

Suppose we have generated a proof in which at some stage we have produced a bourne J_m that is trivially proved. The proof is then finished. To generate another proof, we force backtracking. We scan $J_m, J_{m-1}, J_{m-2}, \ldots$ until we find a bluebeard, and we backtrack to that

To find a second value of v for the example in Figure 5.10, force backtracking to J1 of line 1, the nearest bluebeard. Backchain J1 through I3 by mgu = {Betsy/v, Cindy/y1} to produce J2 below. The c-index of J1 becomes zero.

/line 4/   [J2] PA(Cindy, Cindy)

The J2 above is inert because it is not backchainable through any assertion. So backtrack to J0, the nearest bluebeard ancestor. Backchain J0 through I6 by mgu = {v/x2, Cindy/z2} to produce J1 below. The c-index of J0 becomes zero.

/line 5/   [J1] MA(v, y2) ∧ MA(y2, Cindy)

The c-index of the J1 above is 3, with consorts I1, I2, and I3. Backchain J1 through I1 by mgu = {Amity/v, Betsy/y2} to produce J2 below. The c-index of J1 becomes 2.

/line 6/   [J2] MA(Betsy, Cindy)

J2 of line 6 is trivially proved because backchaining it through I3 produces the empty bourne. Therefore goal J0 is again proved to be a theorem, this time by a proof different from that of Figure 5.10. Now v is instantiated to Amity; hence, Amity is a grandma of Cindy.

Figure 5.11 An example showing how we can force backtracking in LBS to find multiple answers to a question. The c-index of any goal after its backchaining is zero, unless otherwise specified.

bluebeard. We then proceed to produce new bournes to try to finish the proof again. This is illustrated in Figure 5.11.

We can continue to force backtracking after each proof, until there are no bluebeard ancestors remaining. Then we can backtrack no further; there are no more proofs, and we have found by then all the values of v for which $G(v)$ is a logical consequence of the given premisses. An example is shown in Figure 5.12.

5.3.6   Ordering of assertions

In this section, you will read about the order in which assertions should be catalogued to improve the efficiency of LBS, but first we need to discuss how a collection of assertions can constitute a procedure. The predicate in the leftmost atom of an assertion is said to be the **label** of the assertion. To illustrate, the following two assertions have the label MA.

MA(Amity, Betsy)
MA(w, u) ← DAUGHTER(u, w)

The first assertion says Amity is the ma of Betsy; the second, w is the ma of u if u is the daughter of w. The collection of assertions with the same label is said to constitute a procedure for that label.

To find a third value of v for the example extending over Figures 5.10 and 5.11, force backtracking to J1 of line 5, the nearest bluebeard. Backchain J1 through I2 by mgu = {Anna/v, Bill/y2} to produce J2 below. The c-index of J1 becomes 1.

/line 7/   [J2] MA(Bill, Cindy)

The J2 above is inert because it is not backchainable through any assertion. So backtrack to J1 of line 5, the nearest bluebeard ancestor. Backchain J1 through I3 by mgu = {Betsy/v, Cindy/y2} to produce J2 below. The c-index of J1 becomes zero.

/line 8/   [J2] MA(Cindy, Cindy)

The J2 above is inert because it is not backchainable through any assertion. We try to backtrack. But J2 has no bluebeard ancestors. So we cannot backtrack. There are no further values of v. From Figures 5.10 and 5.11, we can thus see that v has only two values: Anna and Amity. In other words, Anna and Amity are the two grandmas of Cindy.

Figure 5.12   An example showing how we can repeatedly force backtracking in LBS to find all the answers to a question, till we can backtrack no more.

Suppose, in a set of assertions, the above two are the only assertions labelled MA. Then these two assertions constitute a procedure named MA.

An implication in which the same predicate appears in the consequent and in the antecedent is called a **recursive implication**. Since the predicate JEWISH appears both in the consequent and the antecedent, the following is an example of a recursive implication:

JEWISH(x) ← JEWISH(y) ∧ MA(y, x).

The implication says: if y is Jewish, and y is the ma of x, then x is Jewish. To prove that a person is Jewish, it is thus sufficient to prove that the person's ma is Jewish. A procedure containing a recursive implication is called a **recursive procedure**.

The consorts of a goal are drawn from the procedure whose name is identical to the predicate in the leftmost atom of the goal. Hence only the assertions in the procedure MA can be the consorts of a goal whose leftmost atom contains the predicate name MA. Therefore, to reduce the time required by the reasoning program to search for a goal's consorts, catalogue all the assertions of a procedure together, one immediately after another. This will also turn out to be convenient to us: to correct a suspected error in a procedure, we do not have to look for the assertions of the procedure over the entire set of assertions.

The next question that arises is this: In what order should we catalogue the assertions within a given procedure? As described in section 5.3.3, a goal backchains through assertions catalogued earlier before it backchains through assertions catalogued later. It is as if the assertions catalogued earlier had been weighted, as described in section 4.2.3, to be backchained through before those assertions catalogued later. Therefore, if we have an intuitive understanding of the problem, we should catalogue earlier those assertions that we consider to be important for the proof, but if we lack this intuitive understanding, then as a heuristic (rule of thumb) we should catalogue the assertions in such an order that they contain an increasing number of atoms: the fewer the atoms in the assertion, the earlier it is catalogued. This ordering of assertions is based on the fewest literals preference strategy, discussed earlier in section 4.2.2. A goal is thus backchained through an assertion containing few atoms before it is backchained through an assertion containing many atoms.

An obvious outcome of the above heuristic is that verities are catalogued earlier than implications, and a goal backchains through a verity before it backchains through an implication. In recursive procedures, there is an additional motivation for cataloguing verities

Given the premisses:
[i]   Amity is the ma of Betsy.
[ii]   For all x and y: if y is Jewish, and y is the ma of x, then x
           is Jewish.
[iii]   Amity is Jewish

The following assertions are derived from the above premisses.
[I1]   MA(Amity, Betsy)
[I2]   JEWISH(x) ← JEWISH(y) ∧ MA(y, x)
[I3]   JEWISH(Amity)

Adopt LBS to find the values of z for which the goal $\exists z(JEWISH(z))$ is a
logical consequence of the above premisses.   The goal to be proved is
written as J0.
[J0]   JEWISH(z)

The c-index of J0 is 2, with consorts I2 and I3.   Backchain J0 through
I2 by mgu = {z/x} to produce J1.   The c-index of J0 becomes 1.
[J1]   JEWISH(y) ∧ MA(y, z)

We note that to prove JEWISH(z) of J0, we have to prove JEWISH(y)
[the leftmost atom of J1] first.   The goal remains essentially the same,
and it will again remain essentially the same, if we backchain J1 through
I2.   The proof generation enters indefinite recursion.   We are unable to
prove goal J0 even though intuitively we know that it should be provable
for two values of z: Amity and Betsy.

Figure 5.14, shows a way of removing the impediment to this proof.

Figure 5.13   An example in which the proof generation by LBS enters indefinite recursion. We cannot finish the proof, even though we intuitively
know that the proof exists. Above, JEWISH is a recursive procedure.

earlier than implications. If this is not done, the proof generation may
enter indefinite recursion so that the proof may not be finished, even
though it exists. Such an example is shown in Figure 5.13. A proof for
the same problem is then generated in Figure 5.14, after having
catalogued the verity earlier than the implication in a recursive
procedure. Furthermore, it is recommended that within a procedure
the recursive implications be always catalogued last.

The different procedures, however, can be in any sequence. It is
thus immaterial in Figure 5.14 whether we catalogue procedure
MA earlier or later than procedure JEWISH.

Based on the above discussion in this section, one can make the
following overall suggestions:

1. catalogue the assertions of a procedure immediately after one
   another;

To remove the impediment to the proof generation for the example in Figure 5.13, interchange the assertions of the recursive procedure JEWISH, so that the verity is catalogued before the implication. By doing so, we obtain the following assertions.

[I1]   MA(Amity, Betsy)
[I2]   JEWISH(Amity)
[I3]   JEWISH(x) ← JEWISH(y) ∧ MA(y, x)

Now we can try to find the values of z to prove the goal J0.

[J0]   JEWISH(z)

The c-index of J0 is 2, with consorts I2 and I3. Backchain J0 through I2 by mgu = {Amity/z} to produce the empty bourne. Therefore J0 is trivially proved, with z being instantiated to Amity; hence, Amity is Jewish. The c-index of J0 becomes 1.

To find whether another value of z exists, force backtracking from the empty bourne to J0, the nearest bluebeard ancestor. Backchain J0 through I3 by mgu = {z/x} to produce J1. The c-index of J0 becomes zero.

[J1]   JEWISH(y) ∧ MA(y, z)

The c-index of J1 is 2, with consorts I2 and I3. Backchain J1 through I2 by mgu = {Amity/y} to produce J2. The c-index of J1 becomes 1.

[J2]   MA(Amity, z)

J2 is trivially proved because backchaining it through I1 by mgu = {Betsy/z} produces the empty bourne. Therefore goal J0 is proved, with z being instantiated to Betsy; hence, Betsy is Jewish. Thus from the full proof above, we can say that Amity and Betsy are Jewish.

Figure 5.14 An example to show why we should catalogue a verity before an implication in a procedure.

2. unless your intuition commands otherwise, catalogue verities before implications in a procedure;
3. catalogue the recursive implications last within a procedure; and
4. catalogue the different procedures themselves in any sequence.

5.3.7 Avoidance of circularities in assertions

As described in section 5.3.2, to prove goal J_0 by adopting LBS, we produce a sequence of bournes $J_1, J_2, J_3, \ldots$. Suppose in this sequence we produce a bourne J_n ($n \geq 1$) such that J_n is identical to some J_m ($0 \leq m < n$). Then J_{n+1} will be identical to J_{m+1}, J_{n+2} to J_{m+2}, and so on. We shall be unable to finish the proof, since the proof generation loops indefinitely. This may come about when we have circularity in the assertions. To illustrate, the following three assertions together have circularity:

Given the premisses:

[i]   Amity is the ma of Betsy, and Betsy of Cindy.

[ii]   For all u and w: the grandchild of w is u if, and only if, w is the grandma of u.

[iii]   For all x, y, and z: if x is the ma of y, and y is the ma of z, then x is the grandma of z.

The following assertions are derived from the above premisses:

[I1]   MA(Amity, Betsy)

[I2]   MA(Betsy, Cindy)

[I3]   GRANDCHILD(u1, w1) ← GRANDMA(w1, u1)

[I4]   GRANDMA(w2, u2) ← GRANDCHILD(u2, w2)

[I5]   GRANDMA(x, z) ← MA(x, y) ∧ MA(y, z)

Adopt LBS to prove the goal J0.

[J0]   GRANDCHILD(Cindy, Amity)

Backchain J0 through I3 by mgu = {Cindy/u1, Amity/w1} to produce J1.

[J1]   GRANDMA(Amity, Cindy)

The c-index of J1 is 2, with consorts I4 and I5. Backchain J1 through I4 by mgu = {Amity/w2, Cindy/u2} to produce J2. The c-index of J1 becomes 1.

[J2]   GRANDCHILD(Cindy, Amity)

Note that J2 is identical to J0. If we backchain J2 through I3, the new bourne J3 will be identical to J1. Thus we shall loop indefinitely between bournes GRANDCHILD(Cindy, Amity) and GRANDMA(Amity, Cindy). The circularity between assertions I3 and I4 causes the looping. We are unable to finish the proof, even though we intuitively know that the proof exists. Nevertheless, we can finish the proof if either we interchange the positions in which I4 and I5 are catalogued, or we delete I4.

Figure 5.15 An example in which proof generation loops indefinitely because of circularity between two assertions.

(I1) F1 ← F2

(I2) F2 ← F3

(I3) F3 ← F1

From I1, to prove F1, we need to prove F2; from I2, to prove F2, we need to prove F3; from I3, to prove F3, we need to prove F1. In Figure 5.15, there is an example of a proof generation looping indefinitely because of circularity between two assertions. It should be evident from the above discussion that we must formulate our assertions so as to avoid circularities.

A limiting case of circularity occurs when, in a recursive implication, the consequent and the antecedent are identical. Consider, for example, a set of assertions that contains the following recursive implication I.

(I) F1 ← F1.

Now if we backchain a goal, say J_m, through I then the bourne J_{m+1} is identical to J_m. Backchaining J_{m+1} through I will produce J_{m+2} to be identical to J_{m+1}. Proceeding in this way, the proof generation will loop indefinitely. Although the above implication may look harmless since it is a tautology, we should not include any such implications in our set of assertions.

The following assertions in logic constitute a procedure FAC(x, y) such that it returns with y equal to the factorial of x.
[I1]   FAC(x, 1) ← LE(x, 1)
[I2]   FAC(x, y) ← GT(x, 1) ∧ ASSIGN(x1, sub(x, 1)) ∧
             FAC(x1, y1) ∧ ASSIGN(y, mult(x, y1))

To instantiate a variable w to the value of the factorial of 2, we invoke the above procedure by J0.
[J0]   FAC(2, w)

The c-index of J0 is 2, with consorts I1 and I2. Backchain J0 through I1 by mgu = {2/x, 1/w} to produce J1 below. The c-index of J0 becomes 1.

/line 1/   [J1]   LE(2, 1)

J1 above is inert because a built-in procedure evaluates LE(2, 1) to be false. So backtrack to J0, the nearest bluebeard ancestor. Backchain J0 through I2 by mgu = {2/x, w/y} to produce J1 below. The c-index of J0 becomes zero.

/line 2/   [J1]   GT(2, 1) ∧ ASSIGN(x1, sub(2, 1)) ∧ FAC(x1, y1) ∧ ASSIGN(w, mult(2, y1))

In J1 above, GT(2, 1) is trivially proved because it is evaluated to be true by a built-in procedure. Another built-in procedure evaluates ASSIGN(x1, sub(2, 1)) and assigns the value 1 to x1. So the J1 above is reduced to the following J1.

/line 3/   [J1]   FAC(1, y1) ∧ ASSIGN(w, mult(2, y1))

The c-index of the J1 above is 2, with consorts I1 and I2. Backchain J1 through I1 by mgu = {1/x, 1/y1} to produce J2 below. The c-index of J1 becomes 1.

/line 4/   [J2]   LE(1, 1) ∧ ASSIGN(w, mult(2, 1))

In J2 above, LE(1, 1) is trivially proved because it is evaluated to be true by a built-in procedure. Another built-in procedure evaluates ASSIGN(w, mult(2, 1)) and assigns the values 2 to w. Thus the factorial of 2 is equal to 2.

Figure 5.16   A procedure to calculate factorials. Figure 5.17 contains an explanation of built-in procedures LE, GT, ASSIGN, sub, and mult used above. We assume that these procedures are available to us.

5.3.8   Writing programs with assertions

Until now we have discussed how we can adopt LBS to automate reasoning with assertions. We shall now see how we can write programs with assertions, just as we can with, say, FORTRAN or Pascal.

As mentioned in section 5.3.1, an assertion is of the following form:

$$F_1 \leftarrow F_2 \wedge F_3 \wedge \ldots \wedge F_i.$$

For the purpose of reasoning, we decipher the assertion thus: to prove atom F_1, we need to prove atoms F_2 and F_3 and . . . and F_i, but for the purpose of programming, we decipher the assertion thus: to execute routine F_1, we need to execute routines F_2 and F_3 and . . . and F_i in a left-to-right sequence.

If we were to write a program in, say, Pascal, we would first design an algorithm, and then code the algorithm in Pascal. To write a program as a set of assertions, we would still first design the algorithm, but now we would code it as verities and implications. An example should clarify our discussion. Suppose we want to write a procedure FAC(x, y) so that when we invoke the procedure, we supply it with an integer value for x, and the procedure returns with y equal to the factorial of x; that is, y = factorial(x). Based on the definition of factorial in mathematics, we can observe the following.

$$y = \begin{cases} 1 & \text{if } x \leq 1 \\ x \times \text{factorial}(x - 1) & \text{if } x > 1. \end{cases}$$

Figure 5.16 shows the procedure written as a set of assertions. The figure also shows an annotated trace of the procedure when it is invoked to calculate the factorial of 2. As is apparent from the figure, to write FAC(x, y), we also needed a few built-in procedures. Some of the built-in procedures usually required to write programs to do arithmetic are given in Figure 5.17.

You should now have an initial understanding of how logic in the form of assertions can be used to write programs. Using logic to write programs has spawned the programming language Prolog (*Pro*gramming in *log*ic). An abecedarian to Prolog is provided in the next section.

5.4   PROLOG

5.4.1   The nature of the language

Prolog is a conversational programming language of which many implementations are available nowadays. Suppose one such imple-

Built-in Procedures	Value Returned	
minus(v)	$-v$	
add(u, v)	$u + v$	
sub(u, v)	$u - v$	
mult(u, v)	$u \times v$	
div(u, v)	$u \div v$	
EQ(u, v)		$u = v$
NE(u, v)		$u \neq v$
LE(u, v)	True if, and only if,	$y \leq v$
LT(u, v)		$u < v$
GE(u, v)		$u \geq v$
GT(u, v)		$u > v$
ASSIGN(u, v)	True. As a side effect, the value of v is assigned to u.	

Figure 5.17 Some typical built-in procedures usually required to write programs for doing arithmetic. When writing logic programs, we shall assume that these procedures are available to us.

mentation is available to us. From a computer terminal, we can then load the assertions into the computer, activate the Prolog interpreter, or compiler, and enter the goal to be proved. In Prolog terminology, the goal is often referred to as the **question**. Prolog displays its response to our question on the terminal.

The syntax of Prolog varies among the different implementations. Many implementations have taken up a syntax developed at the University of Edinburgh which is referred to as the Edinburgh syntax of Prolog, or for short, Edinburgh Prolog. To get acquainted with Edinburgh Prolog, look at the examples in Figures 5.18 and 5.19. The examples show typical Prolog responses to our questions. Most Prolog implementations have the facility by which we can trace the execution of a program, and such traces can help us debug Prolog programs.

By perusing the examples in Figures 5.18 and 5.19, we notice that Prolog appears to adopt LBS, but LBS and SLD are so closely related that either of them can double for the other. Thus it is often mentioned in the literature that Prolog adopts the SLD strategy. In effect, SLD looks like LBS: internally, Prolog may adopt SLD, but externally to us it appears as LBS. You may also find mentioned in the literature that Prolog uses the negative hyperresolution rule of inference. This is because resolution under SLD can at the same time be looked upon as negative hyperresolution, as discussed in section 5.2.2.

In Figure 5.16, you saw a procedure to calculate factorials. That procedure was written in the language of mathematical logic. Below you see the same procedure coded in Edinburgh Prolog.

```
/*  The following procedure fac(X, Y) returns with Y equal to the
    factorial of X.  */

/*  1    */ fac(X, 1) :- X =< 1.
/*  2    */ fac(X, Y) :- X > 1, X1 is X - 1,
                         fac(X1, Y1), Y is X * Y1.
```

Prolog being a conversational language, we program from a computer terminal. After loading the above assertions into the computer, suppose we want the procedure to calculate the factorial of 2 and store the result in a variable W. Then we enter the question
?- fac(2, W).

Prolog responds by displaying on the terminal
W = 2

Figure 5.18 An example in Edinburgh Prolog of a procedure to calculate factorials. In Figure 5.16, you saw the above procedure written as a set of assertions in logic. Comparing the above with Figure 5.16 may help you get an idea of the syntax of Edinburgh Prolog. The symbols '/*' and '*/' enclose any comments written among the assertions. A non-numeric constant or a predicate name is in lower-case letters. The first letter of a variable name is in upper-case. In an implication, the sign ':-' appears between the consequent on the left and the antecedent on the right. The conjuncts in the antecedent are separated by commas. An assertion may continue on more than one line. Every assertion ends with a period (full stop). The question begins with a question mark and ends with a period. The built-in procedures compare numbers [for example, $X < 1$ and $X > 1$] or do arithmetic operations [for example, $X - 1$ and $X * Y1$].

Given that the following assertions in Edinburgh Prolog have been loaded into the computer:

```
/*1*/    ma(amity, betsy).
/*2*/    ma(anna, bill).
/*3*/    ma(betsy, cindy).
/*4*/    pa(bill, cindy).
/*5*/    grandma(X1, Z1) :- ma(X1, Y1), pa(Y1, Z1).
/*6*/    grandma(X2, Z2) :- ma(X2, Y2), ma(Y2, Z2).
```

Suppose we enter the question [that is, goal]
?-   grandma(amity, cindy).
Prolog responds by displaying
yes

But to our question
?-   pa(betsy, anna).
Prolog responds by displaying
no
By which, Prolog means "not as far as I know."

Now, to our question
?-   grandma(V, cindy).
Prolog responds by displaying
V = anna;
By which, Prolog means that the goal is provable for V = anna. We enter the semicolon above immediately after Prolog's printing of the word "anna" to tell Prolog we want more values of V. Prolog is forced to backtrack [see Section 5.3.5], and it responds by displaying
V = amity;
We enter the semicolon again, forcing Prolog to backtrack once more. But this time, no more value of V is found. So Prolog responds by displaying
no

Figure 5.19 An example of reasoning in a conversational session with an implementation of Edinburgh Prolog. See the legend below Figure 5.18 for an explanation of the syntax of the language.

5.4.2   Characteristics of implementations

Most Prolog implementations have built-in procedures for list and symbol manipulation, input and output, controlled backtracking, and arithmetic operations. To program well in Prolog, we should familiarize ourselves with the built-in procedures, the design, and the syntax of the implementation available to us, otherwise, it is always tempting to ascribe the mistakes in our own programs to some alleged shortcomings in the implementation.

To illustrate, let us consider Edinburgh Prolog, whose examples we saw in Figures 5.18 and 5.19. We can think of variables bearing some likeness to English common nouns and constants bearing some likeness to English proper nouns. The common noun 'female' is loosely akin to a variable: it can stand for (be instantiated to), say, Amity, Betsy or Cindy. The proper noun Amity is loosely akin to a constant: being the name of a specific female, it cannot be instantiated. In Edinburgh Prolog, variable names begin with an upper-case letter (they can also begin with an underline sign), and constants with lower-case. Thus, in Edinburgh Prolog we would write as follows: Female, amity, betsy, cindy. This reverses the capitalization convention of English. Moreover, Edinburgh Prolog reverses even the capitalization convention of predicate logic when writing predicate names: where predicate logic writes $R(a, b)$, Edinburgh Prolog writes $r(a, b)$. if we are to program in any implementation of Prolog, we have no choice but to adjust ourselves to it.

It is better to get an understanding of the fundamental notion of logic programming rather than become burdened with the syntactic mannerisms of any particular implementation of Prolog, so in any discussion on the topic, it is preferable to use the language of mathematical logic. You may translate it into the syntax of the Prolog implementation available to you. Let the reference manual of your implementation be your consultant.

Take note, however of the manner in which many Prolog implementations carry out unification. Suppose the two literals to be unified are $P(x)$ and $P(f(x))$. As shown in Figure 3.9, we cannot unify these literals because x occurs in $f(x)$. To quicken the execution of Prolog programs, many implementations do not have the occurrence check, that is, the check to prevent unifying a variable with a term containing the same variable. Hence, in attempting to unify such literals, these implementations may unify them wrongly, or they may enter indefinite recursion. A wrong unification can cause resolution to lose its soundness (sections 2.4.3 and 3.4.1 discussed the soundness of resolution). Thus responses printed by Prolog may on occasion have errors. The designers of such implementations presumably fancy that only rarely will a program be harmed by the absence of the occurrence check.

In the last four chapters, you have read how you can use logic for reasoning and for writing programs on a computer. In the next chapter, you will begin to read how you can use an everyday language like English for communicating with a computer.

5.5   EXERCISES

1. Given the premisses:
   (I1) B
   (I2) $E \leftarrow D$
   (I3) $A \leftarrow B$
   (I4) $C \leftarrow E$
   (I5) $D \leftarrow A$
   prove that C is a logical consequence of the above premisses by (a) linear input resolution upon the leftmost literals of clauses, and (b) linear backward chaining of the leftmost atom of a goal.
2. Given the premisses:
   (I1) MA(Amity, Betsy)
   (I2) MA(w, u) $\leftarrow$ DAUGHTER(u, w)
   (I3) DAUGHTER(Cindy, Betsy)
   (I4) GRANDMA(x, z) $\leftarrow$ MA(x, y) $\wedge$ MA(y, z)

   by adopting LBS, manually find a value of v for which the goal $\exists v$(GRANDMA(Amity, v)) is a logical consequence of the above premisses. Repeat the proof by rewriting I4 above as shown below.

   GRANDMA(x, z) $\leftarrow$ MA(y, z) $\wedge$ MA(x, y)

3. Given the premisses:
   (I1) MA(Amity, Betsy)
   (I2) JEWISH(Amity)
   (I3) JEWISH(x) $\leftarrow$ MA(y, x) $\wedge$ JEWISH(y)
   by adopting LBS, manually find the values of z for which the goal $\exists z$(JEWISH(z)) is a logical consequence of the above premisses. Compare your proof with the proof given in Figure 5.14.
4. Manually develop the trace for the procedure FAC(x, y) of Figure 5.16, when the procedure is invoked by the goal FAC(3, w).
5. Given the following procedure:
   (I1) INT(0)
   (I2) INT(x) $\leftarrow$ INT(z) $\wedge$ ASSIGN(x, add(z, 1))
   where the built-in procedures ASSIGN and add are defined in Figure 5.17, answer manually the following.
   1. Is the goal INT[3] a logical consequence of I1 and I2?
   2. What is the value to which y is instantiated when the procedure is invoked by the goal INT(y)? What is the instantiation of y if we force backtracking? What are the successive instantiations of y if the we continue to force backtracking?

6. Write a procedure $F(x, y, z)$ with assertions in logic such that when we invoke the procedure we supply it with a value for x and a value for y, and the procedure returns z calculated as shown below:

$$z = \begin{cases} -x + y & \text{if } x \le 4 & \text{and } y \ge 5 \\ xy & \text{if } 4 < x \le 7 & \text{and } 3 < y < 5 \\ x - y & \text{if } x > 7 & \text{and } y \le 3. \end{cases}$$

You may use any of the typical built-in procedures given in Figure 5.17. Test your procedure by manually invoking it with different values of x and y.

7. Write a procedure SUMINT(u, w) with assertions in logic such that when we invoke the procedure we supply it with a value for u, and the procedure returns w as calculated below.

$$w = \begin{cases} 0 & \text{if } u < 1 \\ \displaystyle\sum_{i=1}^{u} i & \text{if } u \ge 1. \end{cases}$$

For writing the procedure, you may find it convenient to reformulate the above equation as follows:

$$w = \begin{cases} 0 & \text{if } u < 1 \\ 1 & \text{if } u = 1 \\ u + \displaystyle\sum_{i=1}^{u-1} i & \text{if } u > 1. \end{cases}$$

You may use any of the typical built-in procedures given in Figure 5.17. Test your procedure by manually invoking it with different values of u.

8. You must have solved the above seven exercises manually. Now take the solutions of exercises 2–7 above and code them into whichever implementation of Prolog is available to you. Run your code on the computer available to you.

5.6   SUGGESTIONS FOR FURTHER READING

Horn (1951) proposed the form of clauses that later became known as Horn clauses. Hogger (1984), Kowalski (1979), and Lloyd (1984) explained the theoretical background of logic programming. Clark and

Tärnlund (1982) edited a collection of papers on theory, implementation and application of logic programming. Clocksin and Mellish (1984), Rogers (1986), Bratko (1986), and Saint-Dizier and Sabatier (1990) described Edinburgh Prolog. Coelho and Cotta (1988) presented Edinburgh Prolog code for many examples. De Saram (1985), Clark and McCabe (1984), Giannesini, Kanoui, Pasero and van Caneghem (1986), and Sterling and Shapiro (1986) described versions of Prolog with syntax diffrent from Edinburgh Prolog. Warren (1979) discussed a Prolog compiler/interpreter on the DEC 10 computer. Kluźniak and Szpakowicz (1985) reviewed the principles of Prolog implementation.

1. Bratko, I. (1986) *Prolog Programming for Artificial Intelligence*, Addison-Wesley, Reading, Massachusetts.
2. Clark, K. L. and McCabe, F. G. (1984) *Micro-Prolog Programming in Logic*, Prentice Hall, Englewood Cliffs, New Jersey.
3. Clark, K. L. and Tärnlund, S.-A. (eds.) (1982) *Logic Programming*, Academic Press, New York.
4. Clocksin, W. F. and Mellish, C. S. (1984) *Programming in Prolog* (2nd edition), Springer-Verlag, New York.
5. Coelho, H. and Cotta, J. C. (1988) *Prolog by Example: How to Learn, Teach and Use It*, Springer-Verlag, New York.
6. De Saram, H. (1985) *Programming in Micro-Prolog*, Ellis Horwood, Chichester, West Sussex.
7. Giannesini, F., Kanoui, H., Pasero, R. and van Caneghem, M. (1986) *Prolog*, Addison-Wesley, Reading, Massachusetts.
8. Hogger, C. J. (1984) *Introduction to Logic Programming*, Academic Press, New York.
9. Horn, A. (1951) On sentences which are true of direct unions of algebras, *Journal of Symbolic Logic*, **16**, 14–21.
10. Kluźniak, F. and Szpakowicz, S. (1985) *Prolog for Programmers*, Academic Press, New York.
11. Kowalski, R. (1979) *Logic for Problem Solving*, Elsevier Science, New York.
12. Lloyd, J. W. (1984) *Foundations of Logic Programming*, Springer-Verlag, New York.
13. Rogers, J. B. (1986) *A Prolog Primer*, Addision-Wesley, Reading, Massachusetts.
14. Saint-Dizier, P. and Sabatier, P. (1990) *An Introduction to Programming in Prolog*, Springer-Verlag, New York.
15. Sterling, L. and Shapiro, E. (1986) *The Art of Prolog: Advanced Programming Techiques*, MIT Press, Cambridge, Massachusetts.

16. Warren, D. (1979) Prolog on the DEC System 10, in *Expert Systems in the Micro Electronic Age* (ed. D. Michie), Edinburgh University Press, Edinburgh, pp. 112–21.

6
Natural language processing: a prescriptive grammar

6.1 INTRODUCTION

In Chapters 2–5, you learned that if you entered into a computer mathematical logic formulae denoting some premisses and a goal, then you could automate reasoning to prove whether the goal was a logical consequence of the premisses. Entering the premisses and the goal exemplifies communicating with the computer in the language of mathematical logic.

You may, however, find it easier to communicate with a computer in a language you employ in your everyday life, say, English. Rather than enter the logic formula MA (Amity, Betsy), you may prefer to enter 'Amity is the ma of Betsy.' In general, you would enter the premisses and the goal as English sentences. The computer translates your sentences into mathematical logic formulae and then proceeds with the reasoning, ultimately telling you whether the goal is a logical consequence of the premisses.

English is an example of a natural language. Other examples are Arabic, French, Hindi and Spanish. Used for ordinary speaking and writing through the ages, these languages have evolved over time. Contrast these with artificial languages, which are invented by some individual or committeee for a particular purpose. Programming languages like Lisp, Pascal or Prolog are examples of artificial languages.

Having learnt at least one natural language from your childhood days, it is likely that you may find it handy to understand and to express your thoughts. A given thought can often be expressed by different sentences, with varying emphases and nuances. See Figure 6.1 for an illustration in English. In processing these sentences, the computer will have to check whether they are grammatical and elicit

1. Archie has broken the window with a massive stone.
2. Archie has used a massive stone to break the window.
3. The window has been broken by Archie with a massive stone.
4. A massive stone has been used by Archie to break the window.
5. It is Archie who has broken the window with a massive stone.
6. It is the window that Archie has broken with a massive stone.
7. It is the window that has been broken with a massive stone by Archie.
8. It is a massive stone that Archie has used to break the window.
9. It is with a massive stone that Archie has broken the window.
10. It is with a massive stone that the window has been broken by Archie.
11. What Archie has done is to break the window with a massive stone.
12. What has been done by Archie is to break the window with a massive stone.
13. What Archie has used is a massive stone to break the window.
14. What has been used by Archie is a massive stone to break the window.
15. With a massive stone, Archie has broken the window.
16. The window is what Archie has broken with a massive stone.
17. A massive stone is what Archie has used to break the window.
18. That Archie has used a massive stone to break the window is true.
19. It is true that Archie has used a massive stone to break the window.

Figure 6.1 An example to show how a given thought can be expressed by different sentences with varying emphases and nuances.

the meaning from them. Different sentences can have the same meaning. In the literature, it is sometimes said that different surface structures can map into the same deep structure. The deep structure is *what to say*; the surface structure is *how to say* it.

A set of programs that can process English sentences is called an English language processor (ELP). In this and the next two chapters, you will read about ELPs. Having learnt of ELPs, you may adapt the fundamentals to design a processor in a natural language of your predilection.

Entering premises and a goal is not the only application of ELPs, for they can also be used for, say, understanding stories or querying databases. While designing an ELP, one should be aware of the specific purpose for which the ELP will be used.

6.1.1 Template fitting

In one of the methods of designing an ELP, the ELP is made to process only those sentences that fit a template. In other words, the numerous variations in the sentences, illustrated in Figure 6.1, may not be processed.

Course Number	Course Name	Course Instructor
COMP351	Data Structures	Merriwether
COMP383	Programming Languages	Beefly
COMP475	Artificial Intelligence	Merriwether
COMP497	Operating Systems	Devotion
COMP523	Software Engineering	Sharma

Figure 6.2   A specimen database to be queried in English

Suppose the ELP was for querying the database of Figure 6.2. Let us define the following sets:

$\alpha = \{$Who, Which instructor$\}$
$\beta = \{$COMP351, COMP383, COMP475, COMP497, COMP523, Data Structures, Programming Languages, Artificial Intelligence, Operating Systems, Software Engineering$\}$

We can then decree that a question to be processed by the ELP must fit the following template:

α' teaches β'?

In the template, α' can be replaced by any member of the set α, and β' by any member of the set β. Typical questions that can be processed are then the following.

1. Who teaches COMP351?
2. Which instructor teaches Programming Languages?
3. Who teaches Software Engineering?

The ELP checks to see whether a given question fits the template. If so, the ELP translates the question into a formal query language, through which some database management system can access the database.

We may permit more than one template. We may, for instance, permit also this template:

γ' courses does δ' teach?

We define:

$\gamma = \{$What, Which$\}$
$\delta = \{$Merriwether, Beefly, Devotion, Sharma$\}$

Then a typical question can be: Which courses does Sharma teach?

You may find the template fitting approach, also known in the literature as the semantic grammar approach, too constraining. You may prefer to use the full power of English. The discussion below should then be of interest to you.

6.1.2 The lexicon

We saw in Chapter 3 that for reasoning with predicate logic, we confine ourselves to some domain of discourse. Similarly, to design an ELP, we confine ourselves to some domain, say, a university calendar. We are then confined to using the vocabulary prevalent in that domain. The vocabulary resides in a data structure called a lexicon. Just as our everyday vocabulary and its use are regulated by the dictionary, so the ELP's vocabulary and its use are regulated by the lexicon. Associated with every word in the lexicon is all the information required for the word. At different places in this chapter you will read about the nature of this information. Then in the next chapter you will see a specimen lexicon.

6.1.3 Knowing grammar

It is assumed that you are familiar with English grammar: looking at a sentence, you can instinctively tell whether the sentence is grammatical. Nevertheless, in sections 6.2 to 6.11 below, a review of English grammar is given. The review should remind you of the intricacies of English, for you may have to incorporate these intricacies into an ELP, and its lexicon, which you may want to design. Chapter 7 will then present you with a technique for incorporating these intricacies. In that chapter, you will also learn that the meaning you elicit from a sentence can depend on your grammatical analysis of the sentence. Consider the following sentence.

(T1) The visitor saw the old painting in the den.

Sentence T1 is ambiguous, for it can be paraphrased as either of the following.

1. The visitor saw the old painting that is in the den.
2. In the den, the visitor saw the old painting.

As you will see later, you can elicit the two meanings by two different grammatical analyses of sentence T1. It is thus essential that you master English grammar, however humdrum it may seem to be. If you have already mastered English grammar, you may skim over sections 6.2 to 6.11. These sections will acquaint you with the terminology used in our discussion of ELPs; not all grammar books use the same terminology.

There are two renditions of English grammar: prescriptive and descriptive. Prescriptive grammar, as the name suggests, prescribes how English should be spoken or written:

> It is I.

Similarly, descriptive grammar, as the name suggests, describes how English is often actually spoken or written:

> It is me.

Prescriptive grammar is used in formal or official communication, say, in writing a scientific treatise, descriptive grammar in informal or colloquial communication, say, writing to a friend. The review given below is of prescriptive grammar. Now and then colloquial usage is also mentioned. In designing an ELP, it is your choice whether to follow prescriptive or descriptive grammar.

Note, however, that there can always be exceptions to the prescripts of grammar given below. Suppose it is said that the word *to* is needed to specify destination:

> Archie went *to* school.
> Gilda went *to* Nairobi.

Do not follow the prescript blindly, for here is an exception:

> Anita went home.

The next section begins the review of English grammar.

6.2   A PRELUSORY TO GRAMMAR

6.2.1   Sentences

A sentence is a grammatically autonomous word group that makes sense by expressing a thought. For example,

> Archie ate the cake.

A sentence is said to have positive or negative polarity:

> Archie has gone to school. (positive polarity)
> Anita has not gone to school. (negative polarity)

Sometimes there are words that do not occur explicitly in a sentence, but they are presumed to occur implicitly. We say these words have been elided (deleted) from the sentence; in other words, the occurrence of these words is optional. Such optional words are shown parenthesized below:

> Archie is taller than Anita (is tall).
> He went to the doctor's (office).
> (I) beg your pardon.
> (I am) sorry for that.

Sentences from which words have been elided are called elliptical (or elliptic) sentences, and the practice of writing elliptical sentences is called ellipsis. Aphorisms have often developed over time from elliptical sentences:

> (If) garbage (goes) in, (then) garbage (comes) out.
> (As) easy (they) come, (so) easy (they) go.
> The more (they are), the merrier (they are).

6.2.2   Subjects and predicates

The subject of a sentence is those words that tell us what the sentence is about:

(T1) *Anita* climbed up the mountain. (*Anita* is the subject.)
(T2) *The tourists* were cheated by the guide.
(T3) *He* looked ill.

The predicate of a sentence is those words that do not constitute the subject. The predicate tells us what action the subject did (as in sentence T1 above), what action was done to the subject (T2), or what state of existence the subject is in (T3). Do not confuse the predicate of a sentence with the predicate of mathematical logic that you saw earlier in Chapters 3–5.

As shown in the above examples, the subject usually occurs before (to the left of) the predicate. For rhetoric, however, the words in a sentence may be transposed:

> Up the mountain Anita climbed.
> Cheated by the guide were the tourists.
> Ill looked he.

Now consider the sentence:

> There are several books on the table.

The subject of the sentence is not *There*, but *several books*. The sentence is called an existential sentence (in grammar books, the word *there* in an existential sentence is known as an expletive). The wording of an existential sentence emphasizes the subject. The above existential sentence can be reworded:

Several books are on the table.

Other typical existential sentences are:

There is a boy in the room.
There was a drunk at the party.

When the subject of a sentence comprises more than one part (connected by the words *and*, *but* or *or*), then the subject is said to be a compound subject:

Archie and Anita helped the old man.
Anita or Archie will fetch the uniforms.

When the predicate narrates either more than one action or more than one state of existence (connected by *and*, *but* or *or*), then the predicate is said to be a compound predicate:

She *hopped, skipped and jumped.*
They *came but left immediately.*
He *cooks the supper or washes the dishes.*
He *is ill but remains cheerful.*

A sentence can have both a compound subject and a compound predicate:

Anita and her sister came but left immediately.

Note the following sentence:

Archie ate rice and lentils.

The predicate is not compound because it narrates only one action, that of eating.

The sentences you have seen as examples above are called declarative sentences: they make a statement. There are three other types of sentences: imperative, which issue a command or a request; interrogative, which ask a question; and exclamatory, which express emotion. In an imperative sentence, the subject is often elided:

Learn grammar.
Please lend me the book.

It can be presumed that the subject is the one who is addressed, usually *you*. As can be seen from the above, a sentence that is declarative or imperative ends with a period (the symbol '.', also known as a full stop).

An interrogative sentence ends with a question mark '?'. To obtain the subject of an interrogative sentence, look upon the question as though it were a declarative sentence. The subject of the question is the same as the subject of the corresponding declarative sentence.

Is Anita eating the cake?

The above question, when looked upon as a declarative sentence, would be the following:

Anita is eating the cake.

Hence the subject is *Anita*. Other examples:

Are there *several books* on the table?
Which is *the best restaurant*?
(Does) *anybody* want some fruit?
Who teaches COMP351?
Which instructor teaches Programming Languages?

Ending with an exclamation mark '!', an exclamatory sentence takes on the structure of a declarative, imperative or interrogative sentence. The subject can be obtained from the structure of the sentence:

Ah, there *you* are!
(*You*) get out of here!
Isn't *she* gracious!

6.2.3   Finite clauses

A group of words containing a subject and a predicate constitutes a finite clause. A sentence has at least one finite clause:

Archie knows the way.
    (the sentence has one finite clause: *Archie . . . way*)
Archie knows where Anita has gone.
    (the finite clause *where . . . gone* is embedded in the finite clause *Archie . . . gone*)
When he came, I was out.
    (this has two finite clauses: *when . . . came* and *I . . . out*)

Words may be elided from a finite clause:

Anita is leaving tomorrow, but Archie (is leaving) the day after (tomorrow).

As the above examples show, a finite clause can exist by itself and so become a sentence. A sentence may contain more than one finite clause.

6.2.4 Non-finite clauses

A non-finite clause is a group of words that express some sense of action or a state of existence. Nevertheless, a non-finite clause never exists by itself, but is connected to some finite clause:

I appreciated *his visiting me.*
To pass chemistry is his sole desire.
The argument being over, we went out for dinner.
Torn from his friends, he was lonely.

The above explanation will give you only a preliminary comprehension of non-finite clauses. You will read a more detailed explanation in section 6.5.6, by which time, you will have learned enough grammar to achieve a better comprehension of non-finite clauses.

6.2.5 Grammatical classes

A word in a sentence belongs to one of these nine grammatical classes: interjections, nouns, pronouns, verbs, prepositions, adjectives, adverbs, conjunctions, and determiners. These nine classes are also known as the nine parts of speech. A foretaste of these nine classes, discussed later in this chapter, is given in Figure 6.3.

6.2.6 Interjections

Interjections are words that express emotion:

Alas, he failed!
Good grief, what a mess!
Look, I am warning you!
Ouch, it hurts!

A list of frequently used interjections is given in Figure 6.4. In this chapter, you will find lists of many types of words. These lists are intended to help you pick the vocabulary for your ELP.

Number	Grammatical Class	What its words do	Examples	Details in Section
1	Interjections	express emotion	<u>Wow</u>, what chocolates!	6.2.6
2	Nouns	denote persons, places, or things	<u>Anita</u> drove the <u>car</u> to <u>Paris</u>.	6.3
3	Pronouns	replace nouns	<u>She</u> met <u>him</u> in the library.	6.4
4	Verbs	portray actions or states of existence	He <u>littered</u> the park. She <u>seemed</u> pale.	6.5
5	Prepositions	reveal relationships	The cottage is <u>beside</u> the river.	6.6
6	Adjectives	modify nouns or pronouns	A <u>fat</u> man threatened me. She was <u>angry</u>.	6.7
7	Adverbs	modify verbs, sentences, adjectives, or other adverbs	<u>Besides</u>, that <u>very</u> fat man drives <u>extremely</u> <u>recklessly</u>.	6.8
8	Conjunctions	connect words or groups of words	Archie <u>and</u> I play football. <u>When</u> you are ready, call me.	6.9
9	Determiners	call attention to nouns	<u>A</u> mob damaged <u>his</u> bicycle.	6.10

Figure 6.3   A foreglimpse of the grammatical classes discussed in this chapter.

aha, ah, alas, boy, eeks, good grief, hey, jumping jellyfish, look, oh, ooh, oops, ouch, ow, phew, phooey, say, shucks, ugh, wow, yahoo, yipee, yipes

Figure 6.4   A list of interjections.

6.3 NOUNS

Nouns are words that are traditionally defined to denote persons, places or things. The things may be those we can perceive through our senses, that is, those we can smell, hear, taste, touch and see, or they may be those we can conceive of in our minds as ideas. Animals are also considered to be things in the definition of a noun. The following are examples of nouns: *army, blackboard, beauty, city, colt, dramatist, flavour, fragrance, freedom, honesty, justice, man, Montreal, mountain, Shakespeare, shrub, steel, truth, thought, voice* and *woman*. Nouns can be used in sentences as follows:

Shakespeare was a *dramatist*.
That *woman* is known for her *honesty*.

6.3.1   The number of a noun

A noun is associated with a number, which can be singular or plural. A singular noun denotes one person, place or thing; a plural noun denotes more than one person, place or thing. To illustrate: *child, city, hen, man, mouse, ox, plough, tooth, voice* and *wolf* are singular nouns; *children, cities, hens, men, mice, oxen, ploughs, teeth, voices* and *wolves* are the corresponding plural nouns. Converting a noun from singular to plural usually requires that the spelling of the noun be changed; most plural nouns end with the letter *s*, but there are exceptions: *mathematics, classics* and *physics* are among nouns used as singular.

Weights, measurements, periods of time, and amounts of money may look like plural, but they are often treated as singular. Each of them is thought to be a single quantity:

Twenty kilograms is a heavy load to carry.
Three metres is the length of this pole.
Seven years is a long time.
Two billion dollars is a steep price for that property.

Contrast these with nouns like *annals, archives, cattle, culottes, earnings, environs, pants, pliers, remains, scissors, thanks, tidings, trousers* and *tweezers*. These nouns are always considered to be plural; none of them has a corresponding singular.

There also exist nouns whose singular and plural are identical; for example, *deer, salmon* and *sheep*. The number of a polysemous noun can depend on how it is used in a sentence. Consider the noun *means*: it is singular when it indicates *method*, but plural when it indicates *wealth*.

The means he adopted is questionable. (singular)
His means are substantial. (plural)

If you are ever unsure whether a noun is singular or plural, consult a dictionary. Note, when a family, clan or tribe name is converted to plural so that it ends with an *s*, then the noun denotes all the members of the family, clan or tribe. We can thus have the *Roosevelts*, the *Mayas* and the *Tasadays*.

It is customary to use the plural when writing or talking about zero *persons*, zero *places* or zero *things*. You can see this being done in the preceding sentence and also in the following sentence: The poor farmer had two oxen, one hen, and zero *pigs*. Nevertheless, with the word *no*, either the singular or the plural noun can be used.

The poor farmer had no *pig/pigs*. (either *pig* or *pigs* can be used)

You may look upon the singular and the plural as two forms of a noun.

6.3.2   The genitive of a noun

A noun can have two more forms; these forms, known as genitives, or possessives, indicate ownership, origin or association. One form is the singular genitive, the other the plural genitive. The following are the prescripts for writing genitives.

The singular genitive is written by affixing *'s* to the end of the singular, as in *wolf's* lair (meaning the lair of a wolf), *Roosevelt's* hospitality, a *man's* trousers, and a *sheep's* nose.

The plural genitive is written as follows: if the plural ends with an *s* then affix an apostrophe to its end; otherwise, affix *'s*. Examples are: *wolves'* lair, *Roosevelts'* hospitality, *men's* trousers, and *sheep's* noses.

There are a few exceptions to the above. Often developed for ease in speaking, these exceptions have become acceptable in writing, too. In these exceptions, we do not affix any symbols whatsoever. Thus we may write the *school* team, a *hen* house, the *student* files, the *family* name, and the *Toronto* subway.

The genitive of a person whose name ends with an *s* is written as follows: if the name contains no other *s*, then you may affix to its end either the apostrophe or *'s*. *Dickens'* novels and *Dickens's* novels are both correct. If, however, the name contains any other *s*, then affix only the apostrophe: *Jesus'* suffering is preferred over *Jesus's* suffering.

Certain expressions may employ the so-called double genitive: an *opera* of my *teacher's*, and a *symphony* of *Beethoven's*. The noun after the word 'of' should denote some definite person. The noun before the 'of' usually denotes some person, place or thing taken from an indefinite number of persons, places or things: a *friend* of my brother's. However, if the noun before the 'of' denotes some definite person, place or thing, then the double genitive is usually not employed: the friend of my brother. Nevertheless, there are exceptions in popular usage:

Heaven help that brother of Anita's!
Who can read this report of Archie's!

6.3.3 The case of a noun

A noun can thus have four forms, as in: *colt, colts, colt's* and *colts'*. The four forms are, respectively, singular, plural, singular genitive, and plural genitive. All the four forms need not be distinct; the singular and plural of *sheep* are identical. Moreover, all nouns need not have all the four forms; the noun *trousers* has no singular, and consequently no singular genitive either.

When a genitive form of a noun occurs in a sentence, the noun is said to be in the genitive, or possessive, case. A noun can be in two other cases: nominative (or subjective) and accusative (or objective) cases. A noun is in the nominative case when

1. it is the subject, or
2. it is a part of the predicate such that it identifies the subject, in which instance, it is also known as the predicate nominative.

If, in a sentence, a noun is neither in the nominative case nor in the genitive case, then it is in the accusative case. In such an instance, the noun is usually the object of an action or of a relationship. The action is portrayed by a verb, and the relationship is revealed by a preposition (defined in Figure 6.3). A few examples of sentences with nouns in

Nouns in the Nominative Case:

    The girls bought one each.
    It is the painter. [predicate nominative]
    The bully was confronted by her.

Nouns in the Accusative Case:

    She confronted the bully.
    He cooked the girls a dinner.
    He cooked a dinner for the girls.
    She saw a boy walking across the street.
    They had Archie come over.
    She told the painter to go away.
    We elected her captain.

Nouns in the Genitive Case:

    A book of Archie's was lost. [employs double genitive]
    The bicycle is Anita's.
    The sheep's nose was cold.
    The farmer's fields looked dry.
    The farmers' fields looked dry.

Figure 6.5 Examples of sentences with nouns in the nominative, accusative, and genitive cases.

nominative, accusative, and genitive cases are given in Figure 6.5.

You may have noticed from Figure 6.5 that it is the singular and plural forms of nouns which occur in the nominative and accusative cases. For a given number (singular or plural) of a noun, the spelling of its nominative and accusative cases is the same, but the spelling may change for the genitive case. Thus the spelling of a noun may change with its case and number. This is expressed in grammar books by saying that a noun undergoes declension, or that a noun is declined, to signify its case and number. Figure 6.6 gives the declension of a few nouns. The study of nominative and accusative cases for nouns may be of theoretical interest only, because the spellings are the same in both cases. The case of a noun, however, affects the choice of the pronoun (defined in Figure 6.3) that can be used in place of the noun.

Applying the prescripts for spelling changes, discussed in sections 6.3.1 and 6.3.2, among the different forms, an ELP can for many nouns develop the other forms, provided one form, usually the singular, is stored in the lexicon. More than one form may need to be stored for those nouns to which the prescripts are not applicable; for example, *child*, *man* and *wolf*.

Nominative and Accusative Cases		Genitive Case	
SINGULAR	PLURAL	SINGULAR	PLURAL
blackboard	blackboards	blackboard's	blackboards'
child	children	child's	children's
city	cities	city's	cities'
man	men	man's	men's
mother-in-law	mothers-in-law	mother-in-law's	mothers-in-law's
sheep	sheep	sheep's	sheep's
-	trousers	-	trousers'
wolf	wolves	wolf's	wolves'

Figure 6.6 Table to show the declension of a few nouns to signify their case and number. It is not necessary that every noun have all the four possible forms. For instance, as shown above, there are only two forms for *trousers*: the plural and the plural genitive.

6.3.4 The genus of a noun

Nouns are of various genera. When a noun is stored in the ELP lexicon, then as discussed later in this section, we may need to store its genus also. The genera for nouns are enumerated below.

1. Proper nouns name specific persons, places or things, such as *Shakespeare, Montreal, Fido* and *Mount Everest*. These nouns are written beginning with an upper-case letter.
2. Common nouns name non-specific persons, places or things, such as *dramatist, city, colt, mountain, woman, pebble, flock, milk, ambition* and *thought*. A common noun cannot be a proper noun, and vice versa.
3. Count nouns are those that can be counted, as in one *woman*, two *women*, three *women*, and so on. Other such nouns are *assignment, colt*, and *pebble*. When used in sentences, such nouns are frequently preceded by words like *a, an, each, every*, or *many*:

   Many women were disappointed by the speech.

4. Mass nouns, also called non-count nouns, are those that are not counted; these nouns do not usually have a plural form. Examples are *dirt, foam, homework, honesty, steel* and *water*. Note that *assignment* and *homework* have similar meanings, but whereas *assignment* is a count noun, *homework* is a mass noun:

   Anita has two *assignments* due today. (grammatical)
   Anta has two *homeworks* due today. (ungrammatica)

   In certain stock expressions, however, mass nouns are used in the plural form:

   Anita bathed in the *waters of Lourdes*.

   Some nouns can be used both as count nouns and as mass nouns:

   Anita pulled out two *hairs*. (count noun)
   Anita cut her *hair*. (mass noun)

   When used in sentences, mass nouns are frequently preceded by words like *much, more, little*, or *less*:

   Anita asked for *more water*.

5. Collective nouns name a group, with the members of the group sharing some characteristics: an *army* (of soldiers), a *crowd* (of merrymakers), a *flock* (of geese), a *herd* (of cows), and a *team* (of players). A collective noun is usually considered to be singular:

The *army* was called out to quell the riot.

6. Compound nouns are those that were originally written as two or more words. Depending on how the practice has evolved for a specific noun, it may now be written as a sequence of separate words, as a sequence of hyphenated words, or as one word derived from merging the original sequence of words. Some examples are: *funny bone*, *mother-in-law* and *blackboard*. As a dictionary would show, the plurals of these nouns are *funny bones*, *mothers-in-law* and *blackboards*.

7. Concrete nouns name tangibles like *book, blackboard, colt, crowd, water* and *Mount Everest*.

8. Abstract nouns name intangibles like *ambition, fragrance, honesty, integrity, truth* and *thought*. An abstract noun cannot be a concrete noun, and conversely.

You will find the above eight genera of nouns in most grammar books, but for ELPs these eight genera may not be adequate.

Suppose that the domain of discourse for our ELP does not include fantasy, and that we do not use metaphoric or poetic language. Let our domain be the everyday world, the world of men and women and boys and girls and plants and shrubs and chalk and blackboard. . . . Then the sentence *A shrub began to sing* does not make sense, but *A girl began to sing* makes sense because a girl is a human, and we know that humans are capable of singing.

Similarly we can say that the sentence *The blackboard is thirsty* does not make sense, but both the sentences *The shrub is thirsty* and *The boy is thirsty* make sense.

To enable an ELP to decide whether a given sentence makes sense, we may need to store in the lexicon, in addition to the eight genera discussed above, more genera of nouns, what actions the nouns from each genus can do, what actions can be done to them, and what states of existence they can be in. We call these the permissible roles for the various nouns in our domain of discourse. (You will read more about such roles in section 7.3, when we discuss the eliciting of meaning from a sentence.) Hence we may supplement the above eight genera of nouns by the following specimen genera:

9. living nouns (plant, shrub, man, woman, boy, girl, colt, filly, . . .),
10. animate nouns (man, woman, boy, girl, colt, filly, . . .),
11. human nouns (man, woman, boy, girl, . . .),
12. masculine nouns (man, boy, colt, ...),
13. feminine nouns (woman, girl, filly, . . .), and
14. neuter nouns (plant, shrub, . . .).

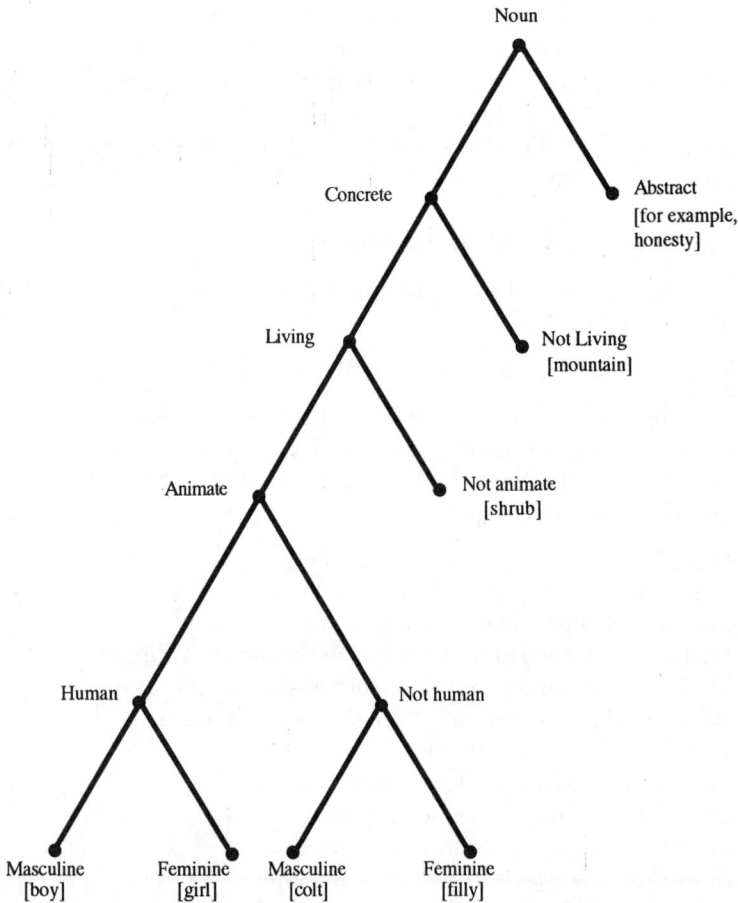

Figure 6.7 A suggested relationship among some of the genera of nouns. Every animate noun is a living noun, but not conversely: a *shrub* is a living noun and a concrete noun, but it is not an animate noun. If in our domain of discourse, we permit that all animate nouns can, say, jump, then the sentence *The colt jumped* will make sense.

A noun may be of more than one genus; to illustrate, a *colt* is a common, count, concrete, living, animate, masculine noun. *Man* and *woman* are hyponyms (instances) of *person*. Therefore, person is both a masculine and feminine noun. Similarly, *child*, *parent* and *relative* are also both masculine and feminine nouns.

The relationships among some of the genera of nouns can be shown by the tree-structured graph of Figure 6.7. According to the figure, every animate noun is a living noun, but not conversely, so if every living noun is permitted to be thirsty, then every animate noun too can be thirsty, but if every animate noun is permitted to jump, then it is not necessary that every living noun too can jump.

Should you find the above genera of nouns inadequate for your ELP, you may set up more genera.

6.3.5   Finite and non-finite noun clauses

When a finite clause behaves like a noun in a sentence, it is called a finite noun clause:

> *Where I want to go* is far from here.

The finite clause *Where . . . go* is a finite noun clause because it behaves like a noun; we can replace the clause by an appropriate noun, say, *Cairo*; the clause is broached by the word *where*. Other examples of finite noun clauses are:

> I could not decide on *which bicycle I should buy.*
> I know *who is coming to dinner.*
> I know *whom you have invited to dinner.*
> Mr Devotion bought *whoever was in the concert* a dinner.
> Mr Devotion bought a dinner for *whoever was in the concert.*
> We elected Anita *what/whatever she wanted to be.*
> *That you hit her* is disgusting.
> I know *how/when/why she is coming.*
> Give some money to *whosoever this is.*
> *Whether he will come* is of no importance.
> She asked me *whether I will go to the game.*
> > (in colloquial usage, the *whether* in such a sentence is often supplanted by *if*)
> The reason was *that he overslept.*
> I realized *(that) I had eaten enough.*
> > (when *that* broaches a finite noun clause as the object of an action, the *that* can be elided).
> Just *because you are big* does not mean *(that) you can bully me.*

A list of words that can broach finite noun clauses is given in Figure 6.8.

Just as we have finite noun clauses, we can also have non-finite noun clauses. In such instances, non-finite clauses behave like nouns:

> *To swim* is fun.
> His *winning the election* is a tragedy.
> She likes *skiing in the Alps.*

Words that usually broach a finite noun clause	Alternative words that can broach a finite noun clause to give a nuance to the clause		
because	-	-	-
how	-	-	-
that	-	-	-
what	whatever	whatso	whatsoever
when	whenever	whenso	whensoever
where	wherever	whereso	wheresoever
whether	-	-	-
which	whichever	whichso	whichsoever
who	whoever	whoso	whosoever
whom	whomever	whomso	whomsoever
whose	whosever	whoseso	whosesoever
why	-	-	-

Figure 6.8 A list of words that can broach a finite noun clause. Although you may find the words *whatso, whenso, whereso, whichso, whoso, whomso,* and *whoseso* in many an English dictionary, you may notice these words being used in writing and speaking only rarely, if at all.

You will read details about non-finite clauses in section 6.5.6.

6.3.6 Noun phrases

A noun phrase is a group of words that is not a clause but that, as a unit, behaves like a noun:

The rowdy boys were punished.

The word *boys* is the vital constituent of the noun phrase. The other words in the phrase tell us only about some characteristics of the *boys*. The essence of the sentence can be expressed thus: *boys were punished.* The word *boys* is called the headword of the noun phrase.

The number, gender and case of a noun phrase are, respectively, identical to the number, gender and case of its headword. A noun phrase behaves grammatically like its headword. Accordingly, a noun phrase is said to be endocentric. An endocentric structure behaves like one or more of its immediate constituents. For clarity, only one noun phrase is highlighted in each specimen sentence below:

> Mr Devotion bought *the students in the concert* a dinner.
> We elected Anita *captain of the team.*
> *A thin man with two children* crossed the street.
> *The fat man who called me yesterday* called again today.

In the last sentence, the finite clause *who . . . yesterday* is embedded in the noun phrase *The . . . yesterday.* As you can see from the specimen sentences above, words that tell us about the characteristics of the headword can appear both before and after the headword. You will read more about noun phrases in sections 6.4.6 and 6.8.3.

6.4   PRONOUNS

Pronouns are words that are usually used in place of nouns or noun phrases. The noun or noun phrase that is replaced by a pronoun is known as the referent of the pronoun:

> Anita walked to the door where *she* saw her younger brother leaning on crutches; *he* was wearing a cast on his left foot.

The referent of the pronoun *she* is *Anita*; the referent of the pronoun *he* is *Anita's younger brother.* In some grammar books, a pronoun's referent is known as a pronoun's antecedent. (Do not confuse the antecedent of a pronoun with the antecedent of an implication in mathematical logic that you saw earlier in Figure 2.1.) To elicit the meaning from a sentence that contains pronouns, one of the essentials is to decide upon the referents of the pronouns, but sometimes this is difficult:

> Anita and her sister, Gilda, were walking home when *she* said, 'Let's hurry, or Mother will be angry.'

It is not apparent whether the referent of *she* is *Anita* or *Gilda.* To be specific, we should write either *Anita* or *Gilda* instead of *she.*

The referent of a pronoun need not always be a particular noun or noun phrase:

> He cheated, but *it* did not help him to succeed.

The referent of *it* is *his cheating*, and not any particular noun or noun phrase. The referent of a pronoun can often be found by seeing how the pronoun is declined. Just as nouns undergo declension, so do pronouns. The declension of a pronoun signifies the number, gender, person and case of the pronoun. This is discussed next.

6.4.1   The number of a pronoun

The number (singular or plural) of a pronoun should be the same as the number of its referent:

> When Archie said *he* was going to the game, Anita and Gilda said *they* were going to the library.

The referent of the singular *he* is the singular *Archie*; the referent of the plural *they* is the plural *Anita and Gilda.*

6.4.2   The gender of a pronoun

The gender (masculine, feminine or neuter) of a pronoun should be the same as the gender of its referent:

> Father said *he* would tell Anita that *she* should water the plant because *it* had wilted.

The referent of the masculine *he* is the masculine *Father*; that of the feminine *she*, the feminine *Anita*; and that of the neuter *it*, the neuter *plant*.

6.4.3   The person of a pronoun

The person of a pronoun can be first, second or third. A writer or speaker uses first person when referring to himself (for example, *I, me, mine,* . . .), second person when referring to the one addressed or spoken to (*you, your, yours*), and third person when referring to humans, places and things written or spoken about (*he, she, they, it,* . . .):

> While discussing Mr Merriwether, Archie asked Anita, 'Don't *you* agree with *me* that *he* is a good teacher?'

The referent of the first person *me* is *Archie*; of the second person *you*, *Anita*; and of the third person *he*, *Mr Merriwether*.

6.4.4   The case of a pronoun

The case (nominative, accusative or genitive) of a pronoun should be the same as the case of its referent:

Since Archie's name was written on the book, I thought the book was *his*.

The referent of the genitive *his* is the genitive *Archie's*.

6.4.5   The genus of a pronoun

We can summarize the discussion of sections 6.4.1–6.4.4 by the prescript that a pronoun should concord with its referent on number, gender, person and case. In other words, the number, gender, person and case of a pronoun should be the same as those of its referent. Given a sentence containing pronouns, an ELP can apply the prescript to decide upon the referents of the pronouns. The ELP can supplement the prescript by:

1. the heuristic that the referent of a pronoun is almost always in the same sentence as the pronoun, or in the immediately preceding sentence; and
2. the information stored in the lexicon about the genus of the pronoun; like nouns, pronouns are of various genera; the referents of some pronouns, for example, are mostly humans.

Number	Case	First Person	Second Person	Third Person		
		All Genders	All Genders	Mascu-line	Femi-nine	Neuter
Singular	Nominative	I	you	he	she	it
	Accusative	me	you	him	her	it
	Genitive	mine my	yours your	his	hers her	its
Plural	Nominative	we	you	they		
	Accusative	us	you	them		
	Genitive	ours our	yours your	theirs their		

Figure 6.9 Declension of personal pronouns signifying their number, gender, person and case. The pronouns *his, its, my, our, your, her* and *their* are also considered to be determiners [see Section 6.10 and Figure 6.49].

Pronouns in the Nominative Case:

> They bought a book.
> It is he. [predicate nominative]
> He was confronted by Anita.

Pronouns in the Accusative Case:

> Anita confronted him.
> Archie cooked them dinner.
> Archie cooked dinner for them.
> Anita saw him walking across the street.
> The members had him come over.
> Anita told him to go home.
> We elected her captain.

Pronouns in the Genitive Case:

> A book of his was lost. [employs double genitive]
> The bicycle is hers.
> Its nose was cold.
> His fields looked dry.
> Their fields looked dry.

Figure 6.10 Examples of sentences with personal pronouns in the nominative, accusative, and genitive cases. Compare the above with Figure 6.5.

Six genera for pronouns are enumerated below.

Personal pronouns refer mostly to humans; for example, *I, me, mine, you* and *his*. The personal pronouns together with their number, gender, person and case are listed in Figure 6.9. A few examples of sentences with personal pronouns in nominative, accusative and genitive cases are given in Figure 6.10.

As Figure 6.10 shows, the double genitive, discussed in section 6.3.2, can also be employed for personal pronouns. The pronoun *it* is considered to be of neuter gender, but it can be used for masculine and feminine, too:

> Who is *it*?
> *It* is Archie/Anita.

Several speakers and writers use *it* to refer to animals and babies whose gender is not known:

> My new neighbour's dog kept me awake. *It* braked all night.
> A baby in the next cabin kept me awake. *It* cried all night.

Similarly, many speakers and writers use the masculine pronoun for a referent whose gender is not known:

> When a doctor comes, tell *him* to see the injured girl.

It is not known whether the doctor will be a man or woman. By using the pronoun *him*, one avoids the longer sentence:

> When a doctor comes, tell *him* or *her* to see the injured girl.

One could as well have used only *her*:

> When a doctor comes, tell *her* to see the injured girl.

The pronouns *we, our, ours* and *us* are first person plural. The examples below will, however, show that these pronouns are sometimes used differently:

> Mother to child: 'Have *we* done *our* homework?' Mother means (second person): 'Have *you* done *your* . . .'

all	another	any	any other
anybody	anybody else	anyone	anyone else
anything	anything else	both	each
each one	each other	either	enough
everybody	everybody else	everyone	everyone else
everything	everything else	few	fewer
fewest	it	less	many
more	most	much	neither
no one	no one else	nobody	nobody else
none	nothing	nothing else	one
one another	ones	other	others
several	some	somebody	somebody else
someone	someone else	something	something else
such	they	we	you

Figure 6.11 A list of indefinite pronouns.

Author in a book: '*We* shall assume for *our* presentation that the set of premises is consistent.' The author means (first person singular): '*I* shall assume for *my* presentation . . .'

Monarch in a speech: 'You countrymen of *ours* make *us* proud.' The monarch means (first person singular): 'You countrymen of *mine* make *me* . . .'

Indefinite pronouns refer to humans, places and things in a general sense, not in a specific sense. A list of indefinite pronouns is given in Figure 6.11. Indefinite pronouns like *both, few, many, ones, others* and *several* are plural, as in:

Both were at the party.
Anita was studying while *others* were sleeping.

Pronouns like *all, any, more, most, none* and *some* may be singular or plural depending on the sense of their usage:

Of the cake, only *some* was eaten. (singular)
Of the trees, only *some* were damaged. (plural)

Pronouns like *anybody, anyone, each, either, everyone, neither, nobody, one, other* and *something* are singular:

Each receives an apple.
Nobody was present.

A few grammar books list *each other* and *one another* not as indefinite pronouns but as a separate genus called **reciprocal pronouns**. These pronouns are used in sentences such as the following:

The two of us helped *each other*.
All of us helped *one another*.

It may be surprising to see the pronouns *it, they, we* and *you* listed as indefinite pronouns in Figure 6.11, since earlier in Figure 6.9 they were listed as personal pronouns. This is so because there can be sentences in which *it, they, we* and *you* are used as indefinite pronouns:

Archie will never make *it* in life.
They say, 'Crime never pays.'
We/You never know about the future.

The last sentence is akin to writing: *One never knows about the future.* Indefinite pronouns, except *they* and *we*, are spelled the same in both the nominative and the accusative cases:

Many helped Archie. (nominative)
Archie helped *many*. (accusative)

Number	First Person	Second Person	Third Person		
	All Genders	All Genders	Masculine	Feminine	Neuter
Singular	myself	yourself	himself oneself	herself oneself	itself
Plural	ourselves	yourselves	themselves		

Figure 6.12 Reflexive pronouns in the nominative and accusative cases. They are never in the genitive case.

Indefinite pronouns with the following endings can be written in the genitive by affixing *'s* to the end of the pronoun:

1. *body* as in *anybody* and *everybody*;
2. *else* as in *everybody else*, and *everything else*;
3. *one* as in *anyone*, *everyone*, *one* except *none*;
4. *ther* as in *another*, *any other*, *either* and *other*; and
5. *thing* as in *anything*, *everything* except *nothing*.

Hence, for example, we can write *everybody's* responsibility, *everyone else's* responsibility, *one's* responsibility, *other's* responsibility. The genitive of *ones* and *others* is written as *ones'* and *others'*. A few indefinite pronouns like *all*, *any*, *many* and *more* are never in the genitive case.

Reflexive pronouns are pronouns like *myself*, *yourself* and *himself*. See Figure 6.12 for the reflexive pronouns together with their number, person, gender and case. Reflexive nouns, which are spelled the same in both nominative and accusative cases, are never in the genitive case.

Although a reflexive pronoun can be in the nominative case, it connot be the subject of a sentence. It is ungrammatical to write:

Myself cooked the dinner.

However, a reflexive pronoun in the nominative case can be appended to the subject for emphasis. The pronoun must concord on number, person and gender with the subject:

I *myself* cooked the dinner.
She *herself* donated time and money.
We *ourselves* were at the concert.

In the nominative case, a reflexive pronoun can also be the predicate nominative, to express a natural state of affairs:

> Archie was soon *himself* after the accident.
> (You should) try to be *yourself*.
> Let's not pretend; let's be *ourselves*.

When the object of an action is also be doer of the action, then the object of the action is denoted by a reflexive pronoun in the accusative case:

> Anita saw *herself* in the mirror.
> Archie drove *himself* to the hospital.
> It rolled down *itself*.
> We shall treat *ourselves* to dinner.
> One can easily cut *oneself* while shaving.

The doer of the action may sometimes be implicit in the sentence:

> To cut *onself/yourself/ourselves* while shaving is easy.

Demonstrative pronouns point to their referents directly. There are four such pronouns: *this*, *that*, *these* and *those*. The pronouns *this* and *that* are singular; *these* is the plural of *this*; and *those* is the plural of *that*. The pronouns can be used for any gender. They can be used in nominative and accusative cases, but not in the genitive case. A few specimen sentences containing demonstrative pronouns in the nominative case are given below.

> *This* is the girl I told you about.
> It is *this*.
> *That* was broken.
> *These* have rotted.
> *Those* are ripe.

The specimen sentences below contain demonstrative pronouns in the accusative case.

> Archie likes *this*.
> Anita broke *that*.
> She will throw *these* away.
> I bought *those*.

Note that, in expressions like 'this pretty girl,' 'that window,' 'these tomatoes,' and 'those yellow mangoes,' *this*, *that*, *these* and *those* are not demonstrative pronouns. They are instead determiners, which you will read about later, in section 6.10.

Interrogative pronouns are employed to broach a question. These

Interrog-ative pronouns	Kinds of referents	Genders of the pronouns	Cases in which the pronouns may be used	Alternative pronouns that may be used to give a nuance
which	humans, animals, places, and things	masculine, feminine, and neuter	nominative and accusative	whichever whichso whichsoever
who	humans	masculine and feminine	nominative	whoever whoso whosoever
whom	humans	masculine and feminine	accusative [of who]	whomever whomso whomsoever
whose	humans, animals, places, and things	masculine, feminine, and neuter	genitive [of who and which]	whosever whoseso whosesoever
what	animals, places,and things	masculine, feminine, and neuter	nominative and accusative	whatever whatso whatsoever

Figure 6.13 The interrogative pronouns; they may be singular or plural depending on the sense in which they are used. Although some grammar books consider animals to be things too, the two have been mentioned separately above only for added clarity. The above pronouns, except *what*, can also be used as relative pronouns, but note that when *which* is used as a relative pronoun, its referents can be animals, places and things, but not humans.

essentially are *which, who, whom, whose* and *what*. Figure 6.13 lists the different interrogative pronouns, the kinds of referents they may have, the number and gender of the pronouns, the cases in which the pronouns may be used, and the alternative pronouns that may be employed to give a nuance to the question. Here are examples of questions broached by interrogative pronouns.

Which are your favorite singers?
Which is their pet?
Which will you wear?

Who are your favorite singers?
Who called Anita?
Whom did Anita call?
Whomever did Anita call? (compare with the question above)
Whose is this jacket?
What are the results?
I want to know *what* does Archie do.
  (Indirect question; the other examples were direct questions.
  You will read more about questions later in section 8.4.)

In colloquial practice, *whom* is often supplanted by *who*:

Who did Anita call?

Relative pronouns are essentially *which, who, whom, whose* and *that*.
The kind of referents, the number, the gender, the possible cases, and
the alternatives of *which, who, whom* and *whose* are as given in Figure
6.13. Relative pronouns can be used to broach a kind of finite clause
called a relative clause. Relative clauses behave like nouns, adjectives
or adverbs. These grammatical classes are given in Figure 6.3.
  You have already seen in section 6.3.5 how *which, who, whom* and
whose are among words that can be used to broach finite clauses that
behave like nouns. Such kinds of relative clauses are in fact finite noun
clauses:

I know *which is your favorite novel.*
I do not care *who it is.*
Whom you see is none of my business.
Do you know *whose is this house*?

Note, when *that* is used to broach a finite noun clause, *that* does not
behave like a relative pronoun but like a conjunction (see Figure 6.3):

His plea was *that the court show him mercy.*

The relative pronoun *which* can also be used to broach a relative clause
that behaves like an adverb. Such kinds of relative clauses are among
clauses that are called finite adverb clauses, which are further
discussed later in section 6.8.6:

He lent her money, *which I find suspicious.*

The referent of *which* is the finite clause *He . . . money.* When a relative
clause is a finite adverb clause, the referent of *which* is the sentence or
another finite clause:

Mother asked me to fetch milk, *which I did.*

The most frequent usage of relative pronouns is to broach relative clauses that behave like adjectives. Such kinds of relative clauses are among clauses that are called finite adjective clauses, which are further discussed later in section 6.7.5:

> We met a man, *who helped us.*

The referent of *who* is *man*; the relative clause gives us some information about the referent. Other examples are:

> This is the room *whose door is broken.*
> Give some money to *whose/whosoever this is.*
> He is one of the boys *who are always fighting.*
> (the referent of *who* is *boys*)
> He is the only one of the boys *who is always fighting.*
> (the referent of *who* is *one*)
> Archie, *whom the bully hit,* had a black eye.

As the above examples show, within a relative clause, *who* is in the nominative case, and *whom* is in the accusative case. In colloquial practice, however, *whom* is often supplanted by *who*:

> Archie, *who the bully hit,* had a black eye.

The referent of the relative pronoun *that* can be a human, animal, place or thing. A relative clause broached by *that* restricts the referent, whereas a clause broached by *which* does not do so. Consider:

> The bicycle *that is broken* is in the shed.
> The bicycle, *which is broken,* is in the shed.

In the first example, there are many bicycles, one of them is broken, and the broken bicycle is in the shed. The pronoun *that* has restricted the referent to one bicycle from among many. In the second example, there is one bicycle, it is broken, and it is in the shed. The pronoun *which* does not restrict the referent; it merely adds some information about the bicycle being broken. Relative clauses that do not restrict the referent are usually placed between commas. An ELP can apply the above prescript, whenever applicable, to decide whether the referent in a sentence has been restricted.

The relative clauses broached by *who* or *whom* may restrict the referent, or they may not. When such relative clauses restrict the referent, then *who* and *whom* can be replaced by *that*:

> I invited the student *who/that helped me.*
> The students (*whom/that*) *I met* were polite.
> (if the relative pronoun is the object of the action in a relative

clause that restricts the referent, the relative pronoun may be elided)

However, when such relative clauses do not restrict the referent, then *who* and *whom* cannot be replaced by *that*:

Archie, *who rescued the child*, was given an award.
Anita, *whom I have met*, is polite.

In colloquial practice, *that* is often supplanted by *which* for non-human referents, and by *who* for human referents.

6.4.6 Pronouns as noun phrase headwords

Earlier, in section 6.3.6, you read about noun phrases. A pronoun, too, can be the headword of a noun phrase:

Our school expels *anyone who cheats*. (headword is *anyone*)
Mr Devotion bought *those in the concert* a dinner. (*those*)
Someone with two children crossed the street. (*Someone*)
Somebody who called me yesterday called again today. (*Somebody*)
Everyone in our class fell asleep during the lecture. (*Everyone*)
No one I know would do such a thing. (*No one*)
Gilda took the big room, Anita *the small one*. (*one*)

You will read more about pronoun headwords in section 6.11.1. It is often convenient in the discussion to:

1. consider an individual noun or an individual pronoun as the headword of a noun phrase that contains only the headword; and
2. employ the generic appellation nounal to a noun phrase or a noun clause (finite or non-finite). In a few grammar books, a nounal is also known as a nominal or a substantive.

6.4.7 Nounals as appositives

In a sentence, if a noun phrase N_1 is elucidated by a nounal (or a sequence of nounals) N_2, then we say that N_2 is an appositive of N_1. Alternatively, we say that N_2 is in apposition to N_1, or that N_2 apposits N_1. Barring a few exceptions, N_2 occurs immediately after N_1 in a sentence:

Mr Sharma, *a friend of my father's*, treated me to lunch.

The noun phrase *a friend . . . father's* is the appositive; it apposits *Mr Sharma*. Sometimes, the appositive can be viewed to be part of an elliptical relative clause:

Mr Sharma, *(who is) a friend of my father's,* treated me to lunch.

But suppose we were to write:

A friend of my father's, *Mr Sharma,* treated me to lunch.

Then the appositive is *Mr Sharma;* it apposits the noun phrase *A friend . . . father's.* Now we cannot view the appositive as part of an elliptical relative clause. Neither can we do so for the following example:

He, *Mr Sharma,* treated me to lunch.

An appositive may be non-restrictive or restrictive. A non-restrictive appositive merely adds some information to the noun phrase it apposits. The appositive can be deleted from the sentence since it is not essential to the meaning of the sentence. When such an appositive occurs in the middle of a sentence, the appositive is usually placed between commas:

Mr Beefly, *the departmental chairman,* spoke to us.

To prevent ambiguity, the commas are sometimes replaced by dashes:

Two professors – Mr Devotion and Mr Merriwether – spoke to us.

If we were to use commas instead of dashes above, the sentence would become ambiguous. It could then be paraphrased as either of the following:

Two professors, whose names are Mr Devotion and Mr Merriwether, spoke to us.
Two professors and Mr Devotion and Mr Merriwether spoke to us.

When a non-restrictive appositive occurs at the end of a sentence, the appositive is preceded by a colon if the appositive contains an enumeration, but, if the appositive does not contain an enumeration, then either a colon or a comma is used.

He won the first prize, *a holiday in Europe.* (the comma can be replaced by a colon)
His room contained the barest of furniture: *a chair, a cot and a stool.* (the appositive should be preceded by a colon, as shown)

A restrictive appositive cannot be deleted from a sentence since it is essential to the meaning of the sentence.

I went to see Mr Sharma *my father's friend,* not Mr Sharma *the software engineering professor.*

The number, gender and case of a noun phrase in the appositive should be, respectively, the same as the number, gender and case of the noun phrase apposited:

They – *Archie and he* – did all the work.
Two boys – *Archie and he* – did all the work.
All the work was done by two boys: *Archie and him*.
The bicycles stolen were theirs: *Archie's and his*.

Sometimes appositives are broached by words like *as, chiefly, especially, for example, for instance, mainly, namely, notably, or, particularly, such as,* and *that is*:

Only two of our professors, *namely Mr Devotion and Mr Merriwether*, speak clearly in class.
Anita, *as our new captain*, gave us a pep talk.
Mass, *or non-count*, nouns do not usually have a plural form.

Noun clauses, too, can be appositives. Here are examples of non-finite noun clauses as appositives:

His love – *acting in college plays* – kept him busy.
Her desire – *to improve her grades* – was not fulfilled.

(You will read more about non-finite clauses in section 6.5.6.) Similarly, here are examples of finite noun clauses as appositives:

Our last hope, *that the police would rescue us*, was soon to be realized.
The news *that he was expelled* was correct.

The above appositives may appear to be relative clauses behaving like adjectives. In such relative clauses, the *that* can be colloquially supplanted by *which* or *who*, and the clauses still make some sense. The *that* in the above examples cannot be so supplanted. Hence the finite clauses shown above are appositives.

Appositives may also be used when we address someone specific in a crowd:

You, *the one in the blue shirt*, step forward.
You, *the one who is wearing a blue shirt*, step forward.

In both instances, the appositives elucidate *you*. In all the examples we have seen until now, the appositive occurs immediately after the noun phrase apposited, but when it is not so, we say that the appositive is displaced:

Mr Sharma, he treated me to lunch. (apposits *he*)
Whoever comes first, give him this. (apposits *him*)

Whichever you like, pick it up. (apposits *it*)
Whatever happened yesterday, it taught me a lesson. (apposits *it*)

6.5   VERBS

A verb is a word that portrays an action or a state of existence:

He *ran*. (action)
They *are* students. (state of existence)

The action may be a physical action, such as, *buy, cook, jump,* or a mental action, such as, *learn, think, understand*. Several words that behave like nouns can also behave like verbs:

The *plant* grew rapidly. (noun)
We *plant* corn every year. (verb)
This *shop* is new. (noun)
I *shop* at the flea market. (verb)

6.5.1   Properties of a verb

A verb can have six properties: person, number, voice, tense, aspect and mood. These properties are explained below. In a sentence, the spelling of a verb may depend on the values of its properties. This change in spelling is known as conjugation. We say that the verb undergoes conjugation, or that the verb is conjugated, based on its properties.

Person and number of a verb
Just as a noun or a pronoun has a person (first, second or third) and a number (singular or plural), so does a verb. In a sentence, the person and number of the verb must be identical to the person and number of its subject. We say that the subject and verb must concord on person and number.

He *shows* the book. (third person singular)
They *show* the book. (third person plural)
I *am* a singer. (first person singular)
We *are* singers. (first person plural)

By looking at the verb, we can sometimes decide whether the subject is singular or plural:

The sheep is grazing. (singular subject)
The sheep are grazing. (plural subject)

1.	Singular parts connected by <u>and</u>: [a] If the parts denote the same person, place, or thing, then the subject is singular: <u>Our leader and coach</u> is Anita. [b] Otherwise, the subject is plural: <u>Anita and Gilda</u> were singing. In practice, however, some people treat interrelated items as singular: <u>Bread and butter</u> is all I want. <u>Tea and coffee</u> has been served.
2.	Singular parts connected by <u>or</u>: The subject is singular: <u>Anita or Gilda</u> visits Grandma every day.
3.	One singular part and one plural part connected by <u>or</u>: The number of the subject is the same as the number of the part nearer to the verb: <u>A few grapes or an apple</u> is sufficient. <u>An apple or a few grapes</u> are sufficient.

Figure 6.14 Examples to illustrate the number of a compound subject wherein at least one part is singular. If a compound subject does not have at least one singular part [that is, all parts are plural], then the subject is plural, too.

Figure 6.14 gives examples to illustrate the number of a compound subject. In a compound predicate, all the verbs in the predicate must agree with the subject:

He *eats and/or sleeps.* (third person singular)
They *eat and/or sleep.* (third person plural)

Voice of a verb
The voice of a verb denotes the relationship of the verb with its subject. The voice is said to be active or passive. In active voice, the subject does the action portrayed by the verb:

  . Archie *showed* the book.

In passive voice, the action is done to the subject:

  The book *was shown* by Archie.

We say that the voice of a finite clause is the same as the voice of its verb.

Tense and aspect of a verb
The tense of the verb indicates the time of the action or the state of

existence portrayed by the verb. There are three tenses: past, present and future. Verbs are conjugated for the past and present tenses:

I *show*. (present tense)
I *showed*. (past tense)

The present tense is also used for statements that are always (in the past, present and future) true:

A kilogram *contains* a thousand grams.

The future tense can be depicted by employing a word like *will* or *shall* with the verb:

I *will/shall show*.

Within each tense, there are four aspects: simple, perfective, progressive and perfective progressive. For, say, an action in the future tense, the four aspects bring out the following:

1. simple: action happens in the future (I *will show*);
2. perfective: action completed in the future (I *will have shown*);
3. progressive: action continues in the future (I *will be showing*); and
4. perfective progressive: action combines the perfective and the progressive aspects (I *will have been showing*).

We similarly have the four aspects in each of the present and past tenses. In some grammar books, the progressive aspect is called the **continuous** aspect.

According to the above discussion, the present tense is used for actions performed at the present time. In practice, however, it is not always so. The present tense is occasionally used to denote actions in the future:

I *leave* for Singapore tomorrow.
I *am leaving* for Singapore tomorrow.
In two weeks, I *leave* for Melbourne.

In such usage, usually some other words, like *tomorrow* and *two weeks* above, in the sentence suggest that the action is to be done in the future. The context of the sentence can also tell us that the action is to be done in the future:

I shall return on Sunday. Then I *leave* for Singapore.

Similarly, the present tense can also be used to denote actions of the past:

I *am coming* down the escalator when this man *steps* out from behind a pillar and *points* a gun at me.

Such usage is intended to convey a sense of suspense. It is on occasion practiced in story telling. Also note that the past tense is sometimes used for the actions of the present:

It is time you *went* to school.

Mood of a verb

The mood, also known as mode, of a verb tells us about the attitude and understanding of the speaker or writer, regarding the action or state of existence portrayed by the verb. A verb can have three moods: indicative, imperative, and subjunctive. The indicative mood makes a statement or asks a question:

She *will be* a singer.
Will she *be* a singer?

The imperative mood issues a command, an exhortation, or a request:

Show your book.
Have mercy on me.
Please *lend* me your book.

The subjunctive mood always uses the plural verb, even when the subject of the verb is singular, but there is a codicil to this prescript: if the verb to be used is *are* under the prescript, which can happen when the tense is present, then *are* is replaced by *be*. The subjunctive mood is prescribed for the following three situations:

1. when we employ certain stock expressions, such as *be that as it may, come one come all, come what may, far be it, heaven help us, long live freedom, so be it, suffice it to say;*
2. when we express a condition contrary to fact; in other words, a condition that we know in reality is not true:

   If I *were* you, I would have greeted her.
   (in reality, I am not you)
   He behaved as though he *were* the host.
   (in reality, he was not the host)

3. when we express a desire, a recommendation or a requirement rendered by employing words like *ask, demand, essential, important, insist, move, necessary, obligatory, recommend, request, suggest:*

   I insist that he *show* his book.
   I move that the committee *appoint* a task force.
   It is necessary that she *be* at home.
   (the verb would have been *are* under the subjunctive prescript, but observing the codicil mentioned earlier, we replaced *are* by *be*)

The subjunctive is disappearing gradually in practice, except in stock expressions. Many speakers and writers avoid the subjunctive by alternative wording. Thus the last example above can be rewritten:

It is necessary that she *should be* at home.
It is necessary for her *to be* at home.

In colloquial usage, you may now and then hear the subjunctive being disregarded:

It is necessary that she *is* at home.
If I *was* you, I would have greeted her.

Of the three moods of a verb, the indicative mood is the most frequent in everyday English. In all our discussion from now on, we shall assume that the mood of a given verb is indicative, unless otherwise specified.

We have seen above that the conjugation of a verb is based on its person, number, voice, tense, aspect and mood. We now need to see the possible forms of a verb over which the verb can be conjugated. These forms are presented next.

6.5.2 Forms of a verb

All verbs (except one verb, to be discussed later) have at the most five forms. A verb can be conjugated only over its forms; that is to say, the spelling of a verb must be identical to one of its forms. Consider the verb *show*. Its five forms are: *show, shows, showed, showing* and *shown*

1. The form *show* is called the basal form of the verb. This form is symbolized as SHOW-b for *show* in particular, or as VERB-b for any verb in general. It is the form usually listed in dictionaries. The tense of VERB-b is present. VERB-b concords with subjects of all persons and numbers, except third person singular:

   I/We/You/They *show*.

2. The form *shows* is called the third person singular form. It is symbolized as SHOW-s for *show* in particular, or as VERB-s for any verb in general. The tense of VERB-s is present. VERB-s concords with third person singular subjects:

   He/She/It *shows*.

This form can be written by affixing s to the end of the basal form of the verb, sometimes requiring a minor change in spelling at the place s is affixed. To illustrate, *goes* is the VERB-s form obtained from *go*, the VERB-b form. Similarly, for a VERB-b ending in *ch*, *sh*, *ss*, *x* or *zz* we affix *es* to the end of the VERB-b as in *catch*, *catches*, *wish*, *wishes*, *hiss*, *hisses*, *mix*, *mixes*, *buzz*, *buzzes*; for a VERB-b ending in a consonant followed by a *y*, we substitute *i* for *y* and affix *es* as in *study*, *studies*. Since VERB-b and VERB-s are both in the present tense, they are on occasion symbolized together as VERB-pr; in other words, VERB-pr may symbolize either VERB-b or VERB-s.

3. The form *showed* is called the past tense form. It is symbolized as SHOW-ed for *show* in particular, or as VERB-ed for any verb in general. VERB-ed concords in the past tense with subjects of all persons and numbers:

> I/We/You/He/They *showed*.

For most, but not all, verbs, this form ends with the letters *ed*, as in *jumped*, *pealed* and *walked*.

4. The form *showing* is called the present participle. It is symbolized as SHOW-ing for *show* in particular, or as VERB-ing for any verb in general. VERB-ing is employed to portray a continuing action or state of existence:

Person and number of the subject with which the form of the verb concords	Verb BE	
	Present	Past
First person singular: I	am	was
First person plural: We	are	were
Second person singular and plural: You	are	were
Third person singular: He/She/It	is	was
Third person plural: They	are	were
Participles	being	been

Figure 6.15 Conjugation of the verb BE. This is the only verb in English that has eight forms: *am*, *are*, *be*, *been*, *being*, *is*, *was*, *were*. The present tense forms *am*, *are*, and *is* can be symbolized as BE-pr, the past tense forms *was* and *were* as BE-ed, the present participle *being* as BE-ing, the past participle *been* as BE-en, and the basal form *be* as BE-b.

We *were showing*.

This form can be written by affixing *ing* to the end of the basal form of the verb, sometimes requiring a minor change in spelling at the place *ing* is affixed. To illustrate, *cutting* is the VERB-ing form obtained from *cut*, the VERB-b form.

5. The form *shown* is called the past participle. It is symbolized as SHOW-en for *show* in particular, or as VERB-en for any verb in general. VERB-en is employed to portray a completed action or state of existence:

We *have shown*.

Nearly all past participles end with the letters *en* (as in broken), *ed* (walked), *n* (worn), *d* (sold) or *t* (spent).

abide, arise, awake, be, bear, beat, become, befall, beget, begin, behold, bend, bereave, beseech, beset, bestride, bet, betake, bethink, bid, bind, bite, bleed, blend, bless, blow, break, breed, bring, broadcast, build, burn, burst, buy, cast, catch, chide, choose, cleave, cling, clothe, come, cost, creep, crow, cut, deal, dig, dive, do, draw, dream, dress, drink, drive, dwell, eat, fall, feed, feel, fight, find, flee, fling, fly, forbear, forbid, forget, forgive, forsake, forswear, freeze, gainsay, get, gild, gird, give, go, grave, grind, grow, hamstring, hang, have, hear, heave, hew, hide, hit, hold, hurt, inlay, keep, kneel, knit, know, lade, lay, lead, lean, leap, learn, leave, lend, let, light, lose, make, mean, meet, melt, miscast, misdeal, misgive, mislay, mislead, misspell, misspend, mistake, misunderstand, mow, outbid, outdo, outgrow, outride, outrun, outshine, overbear, overcast, overcome, overdo, overhang, overhear, overlay, overleap, override, overrun, oversee, oversleep, overshoot, overtake, overthrow, overwrite, partake, pay, pen, plead, prove, put, quit, rap, read, reave, rebind, rebuild, recast, redo, relay, remake, rend, repay, rerun, reset, retell, rewind, rewrite, rid, ride, ring, rise, rive, run, saw, say, see, seek, sell, send, set, sew, shake, shave, shear, shed, shine, shoe, shoot, show, shred, shrink, shrive, shut, sing, sink, sit, slay, sleep, slide, sling, slink, slit, smell, smite, sow, speak, speed, spell, spend, spill, spin, spit, split, spoil, spread, spring, stand, stave, stay, steal, stick, sting, stink, strew, stride, strike, string, strive, strow, swear, sweat, sweep, swell, swim, swing, take, teach, tear, tell, think, thrive, throw, thrust, tread, unbend, unbind, underbid, undergo, understand, undertake, underwrite, undo, unwind, uphold, upset, wake, wax, waylay, wear, weave, wed, weep, wet, whet, win, wind, wit, withdraw, withhold, withstand, work, wring, write

Figure 6.16 A list of irregular verbs. The modal auxiliaries [discussed in section 6.5.5] have not been included above. In some grammar books, the modal auxiliaries are considered to be irregular verbs.

At the beginning of this section, it was mentioned that there is one verb which is an exception. This is the verb BE, for it is the only verb that has eight forms. The conjugation of the verb BE is given in Figure 6.15.

As mentioned above, past participles have different endings. Those verbs for which

1. the past participle ends with *ed*, and
2. the past participle is identical to the past tense form

are called regular verbs; for example, *jump*, *peal* and *walk*. Verbs that are not regular are called irregular verbs. In English, around three hundred verbs are irregular; the rest are regular. A list of irregular verbs is given in Figure 6.16. The conjugations of a few specimen irregular verbs are illustrated in Figure 6.17.

According to the legend of Figure 6.17, several verbs can be

Number of parts to the VERB	Present tense VERB-pr		Past tense	Present Participle	Past Participle
	VERB-b	VERB-s	VERB-ed	VERB-ing	VERB-en
1	cost	costs	cost	costing	cost
	cut	cuts	cut	cutting	cut
	hurt	hurts	hurt	hurting	hurt
	put	puts	put	putting	put
	spread	spreads	spread	spreading	spread
2	beat	beats	beat	beating	beaten
	come	comes	came	coming	come
	get	gets	got	getting	got
	have	has	had	having	had
	run	runs	ran	running	run
	swing	swings	swung	swinging	swung
3	do	does	did	doing	done
	eat	eats	ate	eating	eaten
	fall	falls	fell	falling	fallen
	go	goes	went	going	gone
	show	shows	showed	showing	shown

Figure 6.17 Table to show the conjugations of a few irregular verbs. If the number of different forms of a verb from among VERB-b, VERB-ed, and VERB-en is n [where $1 \leq n \leq 3$], then we say there are n parts to the verb. There are several verbs which in practice are conjugated as irregular or regular, depending on the choice of the speaker or writer; for example, *show*. When *show* is conjugated as a regular verb, the past participle is *showed*, not *shown*.

conjugated as regular or irregular, for example, verbs like *burn, learn, prove, sew, show, spill* and *spoil*. More and more verbs once conjugated as irregular are nowadays being conjugated as regular. Occasionally, the conjugation of a verb depends on the meaning ascribed to it: *hang* is regular for *to execute*, irregular for *to suspend; lie* is regular for *to falsify*, irregular for *to repose; pen* is regular for *to write*, but it can be regular or irregular for *to enclose*. Always consult a dictionary to find the allowable conjugations of a verb.

For a regular verb, you may not need to store all its forms in the ELP lexicon. You may store mostly the basal form and then develop the other forms from the basal form, but it will not suffice to store only one form for an irregular verb.

6.5.3   Verb–particle composites

A particle is a word that appears with a verb to compose an idiom called a verb–particle composite, also called a merged verb or a phrasal verb in some grammar books. Being an idiom, the composite has a meaning different from the meaning of its constituents. Moreover, the meaning of the composite may change with the particle used. Consider the following specimen sentences in which the verb *turn* has been used once without a particle and then with different particles:

> She *turned* left. (no particle, so no change in meaning)
> The economy should *turn around* soon. (improve)
> He *turned down* my suggestion. (rejected)
> I *turned in* my term paper. (submitted)
> It was late at night when I *turned in*. (went to bed)
> We were *turned off* by his vulgarity. (disgusted)
> Anita *turned over* half the library. (searched)
> They *turned up* late for the party. (arrived)

A list of frequently used particles is given in Figure 6.18, and some typical verb–particle composites are given in Figure 6.19.

Some verb–particle composites may optionally be separated by other words:

> He *turned* my suggestion *down*.
> She *took* her accusation *back*.
> Archie *knocked* the burglar *out*.
> The man *on* whom I *called* was not at home.

In the above examples, the particle may be moved so that it occurs immediately after the verb, but there exist verb–particle composites that connot be separated by other words:

about	across	after	against
around	at	away	back
by	down	for	in
into	of	off	on
onto	out	over	through
to	up	upon	with

Figure 6.18 A list of particles.

blow up, break off, bring about, bring out, bring up, burn up, call off, call on, call up, catch on, depend on, drink up, fill out, find out, get over, get up, give in, give up, knock out, look after, look out, look up, look upon, make up, pick out, put on, put up, run across, run into, run out, run over, run through, shoot at, sit down, set off, stand by, take back, take in, take off, take on, take out, take over, take to, tear up, turn around, turn down, turn in, turn off, turn out, turn over, turn up, wash up, waste away, weather through

Figure 6.19 A list of verb–particle composites, wherein every composite contains one particle. The above pairs of words need not always be used as composites. Consider, for example, *sit down*: Tired, I *sat down* [not used as a composite]; The army *sat down* for a long siege [used as a composite].

> She *shot at* the burglar.
> I *stand by* my decision.
> You can *depend on* Archie.
> Anita *looked after* Mother.

Now consider the verb–particle composite *look up*:

> I *looked* Mr Sharma *up*.
> I *looked up* Mr Sharma.

Both the above sentences are grammatical. Suppose we replace the noun *Mr Sharma* by the pronoun *him*. We obtain:

(T1) I *looked* him *up*.
(T2) I *looked up* him.

back out of	break in on	break out in
catch up on	catch up with	check up on
cut down on	do away with	drop in on
face up to	get away with	get down to
look down on	look out for	make away with
make up with	put up with	set up in
stand up for	stand up to	walk out on

Figure 6.20 A list of verb–particle composites, wherein every composite contains two particles.

Whereas sentence T1 is grammatical, sentence T2 is not. *Look up* exemplifies a verb–particle composite in which the verb and the particle need not be separated by a noun, but they must be separated by a pronoun that replaces the noun. Another such composite is *call up*. To verify for yourself, substitute *call up* for *look up* in the above sentences T1 and T2.

In the discussion until now, a verb has formed a composite with one particle. A verb can also form a composite with two particles:

The thieves *got away with* some jewellery.
She *broke in on* our conversation.

Some typical verb–particle composites with two particles are listed in Figure 6.20.

The lexicon should contain all the verb–particle composites that are required for the ELP.

6.5.4 The genus of a verb

For sentences in active voice, there are five genera of verbs. These genera are enumerated below:

A **linking verb** portrays a prevalent state of existence or a resultant state of existence, where the state of existence is characterized by words called the subject complement. Examples about prevalent states of existence are:

She *appeared* ill.
(subject complement is the adjective *ill*)

He *is* a writer.
(subject complement is the noun phrase *a writer*)

Examples on resultant state of existence are:

She *became* ill.
He *became* a writer.

The subject complement either modifies or identifies the subject. When the subject complement modifies the subject, as *ill* does in the above examples, the subject complement is also known as a predicate adjective. You will read more about predicate adjectives in section 6.7.2. When the subject complement identifies the subject, as *a writer* does in the above examples, the subject complement is also known as a predicate nominative. The predicate nominative is a nounal. You have seen examples of predicate nominatives in Figures 6.5 and 6.10. Remember that predicate nominatives are in the nominative case. Here are more examples of subject complements:

She *remained* in a sullen mood. (subject complement is the predicate adjective *in . . . mood*)
He *is* what every mother likes. (subject complement is the predicate nominative *what . . . likes*)

When the subject complement has more than one part (connected by the words *and*, *but* or *or*) then the subject complement is called a compound subject complement:

The apples *seemed* fresh and ripe.
He *appeared* ill but cheerful.
She *is* stupid or insane.

A few frequently used linking verbs are listed in Figure 6.21. In some grammar books, linking verbs are also called copula or intensive verbs.

An **intransitive verb** portrays an action that is not carried over to any object:

Archie *stumbled*.
Anita *gave up*. (a verb–particle composite)
She *hopped*, *skipped* and *jumped*.

A few verbs that can be used intransitively are listed in Figure 6.22.

A **unitransitive verb** portrays an action that is carried over to some object called the direct object. A direct object is a nounal.

appcar	be	become
cost	continue	fall
feel	get	grow
look	lie	prove
remain	resemble	seem
smell	sound	stay
taste	turn	weigh

Figure 6.21 A list of linking verbs.

arrive	bake	blow up	boil	break
change	come	depart	eat	emerge
fall	give up	go	happen	hop
jump	leave	look	occur	prove
rest	run	shine	sing	skip
sleep	smoke	speak	stumble	think
tremble	trip	vanish	walk	work

Figure 6.22 A list of intransitive verbs. Above, *blow up* and *give up* exemplify intransitive verb particle composites.

> They *hit* him. (direct object is the pronoun *him*)
> I *ran across* Archie. (direct object is the noun *Archie*)
> I *know* who is coming to dinner.
>   (direct object is the finite noun clause *who . . . dinner*)
> I *enjoyed* meeting him.
>   (direct object is the non-finite noun clause *meeting . . . him*)
> We *thanked* the old man.
>   (direct object is the noun phrase *the . . . man*)

When the direct object has more than one part (connected by the words *and*, *but* or *or*), then the direct object is called a compound direct object:

accept, acknowledge, admire, admit, advise, allow, ask, avoid, bake, believe, blow up, boil, borrow, break, buy, cause, cook, change, claim, clean, command, complete, consider, criticize, cut, demand, deny, deserve, detest, discover, discuss, dislike, doubt, drive, eat, enjoy, expect, fancy, feel, fill, find, finish, force, forget, frighten, guess, help, hit, indicate, know, learn, leave, make, miss, move, name, need, notice, order, permit, pick, play, postpone, propose, prove, push, recognize, recommend, remark, require, rescue, resent, resist, ride, ring, risk, run across, see, sell, shake, show, smell, stop, study, suggest, surprise, surround, take, taste, teach, tell, thank, trust, understand, urge, visit, wash, weigh, write

Figure 6.23 A list of unitransitive verbs. Above *blow up* and *run across* exemplify unitransitive verb particle composites.

Verb used intransitively	Verb used unitransitively
The bridge blew up.	They blew up the bridge.
The window broke.	Archie broke the window.
The weather changed.	I changed my shirt.
He ate all day.	He ate an apple.

Figure 6.24 Examples of verbs used intransitively and unitransitively.

She *sells* tea and biscuits.

A few verbs that can be used unitransitively are listed in Figure 6.23. Figure 6.24 gives examples of verbs that have been used intransitively and unitransitively. In some grammar books, unitransitive verbs are also called monotransitive verbs.

A **complex transitive** (abbreviated as cotransitive) verb portrays an action that is carried over to a direct object, where the direct object is modified or identified by an object complement:

> Mr Devotion *considers* Archie intelligent.
> > (the object complement *intelligent* is an adjective that modifies the direct object *Archie*)
> We *elected* Anita whatever she wanted to be.
> > (the object complement *whatever . . . be* behaves like a noun to identify the direct object *Anita*)
> We *appointed* Anita captain.
> > (the object complement *captain* is a noun that identifies the direct object *Anita*)

appoint	believe	call	choose
christen	consider	crown	elect
find	imagine	keep	leave
make	name	paint	proclaim
pronounce	prove	select	serve
suppose	think	vote	wash

Figure 6.25   A list of cotransitive verbs.

An object complement behaves like an adjective or a noun. When an object complement has more than one part (connected by the words *and, but* or *or*) then the object complement is called a compound object complement:

We *named* Anita our leader and coach.

A few verbs that can be used cotransitively are listed in Figure 6.25.

A **bitransitive verb** portrays an action that is carried over to a direct object, where an indirect object occurs before the direct object. The indirect object tells us for whom or for what, or to whom or to what the action is done. Either a *for* or a *to* can be inserted before the indirect

ask	bake	bring	build
buy	cook	draw	feed
find	get	give	grant
hand	leave	lend	make
offer	order	owe	peel
prove	read	save	sell
send	show	spare	take
teach	tell	throw	write

Figure 6.26   A list of bitransitive verbs.

object without changing the meaning of the sentence. Both the indirect and the direct objects are nounals:

> Anita *took* Gilda a book. (the indirect object is *Gilda*; the direct object is *a book*)
> Mr Devotion *bought* the boys in the concert a dinner.
> (the indirect object is the noun phrase *the boys . . . concert*; the direct object is *a dinner*)

When the indirect object has more than one part (connected by the words *and, but* or *or*), then the indirect object is called a compound indirect object:

> Mother *baked* Anita and Gilda a cake.

A few verbs that can be used bitransitively are listed in Figure 6.26.

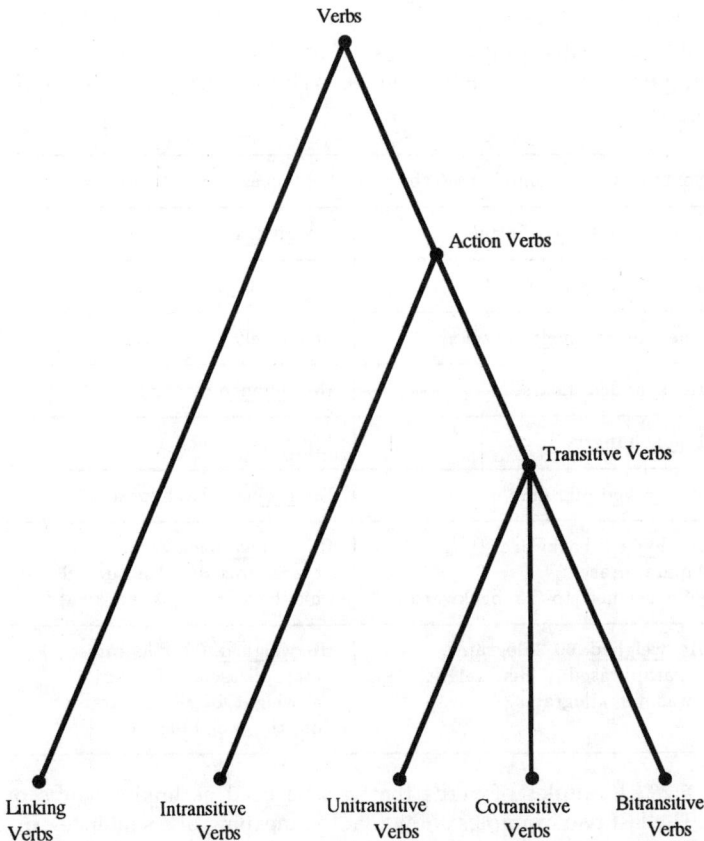

Figure 6.27 A tree to show the relationship among the five genera of verbs.

In some grammar books, bitransitive verbs are also called ditransitive verbs.

The relationships among the five genera of verbs discussed above is shown by a tree-structured graph in Figure 6.27. A verb that is intransitive, unitransitive, cotransitive or bitransitive is generically known as an action verb.

A verb can belong to more than one genus. Consider the action verb *leave*:

> He *left*. (intransitive)
> He *left* her. (unitransitive)
> He *left* her broke. (cotransitive)
> He *left* her the house. (bitransitive)

Similarly there are verbs that can be used as linking verbs or action verbs, examples of which are shown in Figure 6.28.

As two of the examples in Figure 6.28 show, a sentence can be ambiguous; its meaning can depend on whether we view its verb as a linking verb or as an action verb. When storing verbs in the ELP

Sentences with Linking Verbs	Sentences with Action Verbs
The soup <u>tasted</u> bitter.	I <u>tasted</u> the soup.
The table <u>felt</u> smooth.	I <u>felt</u> the table.
The clover <u>smelt</u> pleasant.	She <u>smelt</u> the clover.
He <u>sounded</u> hoarse.	He <u>sounded</u> the gong.
I <u>got</u> hungry.	I <u>got</u> my lunch.
He <u>proved</u> unreliable.	He <u>proved</u> the hypothesis.
He <u>looked</u> backward. [paraphrased: He seemed to be backward.]	He <u>looked</u> backward. [paraphrased: He turned his head to look backward.]
He <u>weighed</u> 60 kilograms. [paraphrased: His weight was 60 kilograms.]	He <u>weighed</u> 60 kilograms. [paraphrased: He put a weight of 60 kilograms on the weighing scale.]

Figure 6.28 Examples of verbs that can be used as linking verbs or action verbs. The last two examples show that the meaning of a sentence can depend on whether we view the verb as a linking verb or as an action verb; in other words, such a sentence can be ambiguous.

lexicon, we should store with every verb, the names of the genera to which the verb can belong.

6.5.5   Finite verb phrases

The VERB-pr and VERB-ed forms of a verb are known as the finite forms of the verb, or for brevity, finite verbs. Auxiliaries are verbs that help another verb manifest its six properties: person, number, voice, tense, aspect and mood:

I will have been showing.

In the above example, *will*, *have* and *been* are auxiliaries helping the present participle form of the verb *show*. The word sequence *will have been showing* exemplifies a finite verb phrase. The above finite verb phrase manifests the following values for its properties: first person, singular number, active voice, future tense, perfective progressive aspect, and indicative mood.

There are two kinds of auxiliaries: modal and primary. The modal auxiliaries, often called modals for brevity, are *can, could, may, might, must, shall, should, will* and *would*. The primary auxiliaries are BE, HAVE

Using a word as an auxiliary	Using the same word as another part of speech
I <u>can</u> show you the strawberries.	Ma and Pa <u>can</u> strawberries every year. [verb] That <u>can</u> is dented. [noun]
I <u>did</u> finish my homework.	I <u>did</u> my homework. [verb]
She <u>has</u> bought a new coat.	She <u>has</u> a new coat. [verb]
He <u>is</u> becoming the manager.	He <u>is</u> the manager. [verb]
I <u>might</u> show you the strawberries.	The people's <u>might</u> defeated the dictator's tyranny. [noun]
I <u>will</u> show you the strawberries.	He should <u>will</u> the house to his wife. [verb] She read her husband's <u>will</u>. [noun]

Figure 6.29 Examples of words being used as auxiliaries and as other parts of speech.

and DO, together with their various forms as given in Figure 6.15 and 6.17. The usage of a word as a verb or as any other part of speech is different from its usage as an auxiliary. Some examples are in shown in Figure 6.29.

In the indicative mood for declarative sentences, there can be two kinds of finite verb phrases. These are discussed below.

The first kind of finite verb phrases can be developed from the following formula:

(MODAL|b) (HAVE|en) (BE$_1$|ing) (BE$_2$|en) VERB (PARTICLES)

The symbols *b*, *ing* and *en* are called stubs; they will be discussed a little later in this section. According to the formula, a finite verb phrase can contain up to four auxiliaries in the following sequence:

1. at the most one MODAL;
2. at the most one primary auxiliary HAVE; and
3. at the most two primary auxiliaries BE; which have been symbolized as BE$_1$ and BE$_2$.

The parenthesization of the auxiliaries signifies that the auxiliaries are optional. The vital constituent of a finite verb phrase is the verb; it occurs after the auxiliaries, if any. The verb is the headword of the finite verb phrase. The verb may be associated with particles; the occurrence of the particles is optional. Should the particles occur, they may be separated from the verb by other words, as discussed in section 6.5.3. Nevertheless, the particles are considered to be a part of the verb phrase.

Before you read how to use the above finite verb phrase formula, see Figure 6.30 for the possible first person singular, finite verb phrases. Keep consulting the figure as you read the explanation below.

The form of the first word in a finite verb phrase must be such that

1. it concords with the subject on person and number; and
2. its tense is the same as the tense desired for the verb phrase.

The person, number and tense of the first word in a finite verb phrase become the person, number and tense of the verb phrase. Accordingly, we say that the finite verb phrase must concord with its subject on person and number:

> He *is/was showing*.
> They *are/were showing*.

Thus the first word in a finite verb phrase will be a finite form of an auxiliary or of the verb. Modals are considered to be of finite form. Note that the modals are not affected by person and number:

The auxiliaries used	Subject of the verb phrase:	Finite Verb Phrase				
		The four possible auxiliaries				VERB (Particles)
	first	1	2	3	4	
	person singular	(MODAL|b)	(Have|en)	(BE₁|ing)	(Be₂|en)	
none	I					show/showed
1	I	will				show
2	I		have/had			shown
3	I			am/was		showing
4	I				am/was	shown
1, 2	I	will	have			shown
1, 3	I	will		be		showing
1, 4	I	will			be	shown
2, 3	I		have/had	been		showing
2, 4	I		·have/had		been	shown
3, 4	I			am/was	being	shown
1, 2, 3	I	will	have	been		showing
1, 2, 4	I	will	have		been	shown
1, 3, 4	I	will		be	being	shown
2, 3, 4	I		have/had	been	being	shown
1, 2, 3, 4	I	will	have	been	being	shown

Figure 6.30   The possible first person singular, finite verb phrases. The mood is indicative; the sentences are declarative. Any line with a slash displays two sentences: for instance, the third line of the table displays the two sentences *I have shown* and *I had shown*. The above twenty-four sentences have been arranged according to their tense, aspect, and voice in Figure 6.31.

They/He/You/We/I *can show.*

The modal can, however, be affected by tense:

He *can show.* (present)
He *could show.* (past)
He *shall/will show.* (future)

The choice of the modal can also give a nuance to the finite verb phrase:

He *may/might/must/should/would show.*

As mentioned earlier in this section, *b, ing* and *en* are stubs. Each auxiliary has a stub; the stubs of MODAL, HAVE, BE$_1$ AND BE$_2$ are *b, en, ing* and *en*, respectively. When an auxiliary occurs in a finite verb phrase, its stub dictates the form of the word immediately after the auxiliary. Accordingly, if a modal occurs, the word immediately after it has the *-b* (basal) form:

He *will show.* (*show* is in its basal form)

If HAVE occurs, the word immediately after it has the *-en* (past participle) form:

He *will have shown.*
He *has shown.*

If BE$_1$ occurs, the word immediately after it has the *-ing* (present participle) form:

He *is showing.*
He *has been showing.*

If BE$_2$ occurs, the word immediately after it has the *-en* (past participle) form:

He *was shown.*
He *will have been shown.*
He *will have been being shown.*

When you see only one form of BE as an auxiliary in a finite verb phrase, you may wonder whether it represents BE$_1$ or BE$_2$. Look at the word immediately after the form of BE. If the word is a present participle, then the form of BE represents BE$_1$, but if the word is a past participle, then the form of BE represents BE$_2$. The particles, if any, in a finite verb phrase are not conjugated:

I *show up.*
I *had shown up.*
I *have been showing up.*

Therefore, for simplicity, no particles have been written for the finite verb phrases in our examples of Figure 6.30. The finite verb phrases of Figure 6.30 have been arranged according to their tense, aspect and voice in Figure 6.31.

The finite verb phrases in Figure 6.31 are for first person singular subjects. These have been generalized for subjects of any person and

Aspect	Voice	Present Tense	Past Tense	Future [with modal will]
Simple	Active	I show	I showed	I will show
	Passive	I am shown	I was shown	I will be shown
Perfective	Active	I have shown	I had shown	I will have shown
	Passive	I have been shown	I had been shown	I will have been shown
Progressive	Active	I am showing	I was showing	I will be showing
	Passive	I am being shown	I was being shown	I will be being shown
Perfective Progressive	Active	I have been showing	I had been showing	I will have been showing
	Passive	I have been being shown	I had been being shown	I will have been being shown

Figure 6.31 First person singular, finite verb phrases of Figure 6.30 arranged according to their tense, aspect, and voice. The mood is indicative; the sentences are declarative. For all tenses, the perfective progressive aspect in the passive voice is rarely used in practice.

any number in Figure 6.32–6.34. Remember that all verb phrases in Figure 6.32–6.34 have been derived from the formula of a finite verb phrase, given above.

Examining Figure 6.32–6.34, we have summarized in Figure 6.35 the effects of the primary auxiliaries on the aspect and the voice of a finite verb phrase.

As we can see from Figure 6.35, the occurrence of BE_2 is necessary and sufficient for the finite verb phrase to be in the passive. However, certain verbs, mostly linking and intransitive, cannot be used in the passive. The following, for instance, cannot be paraphrased in the passive.

He *is* ill.
She *skipped*.
Archie *is being* polite.

Aspect	Voice	Generalized Finite Verb Phrases in Present Tense, Indicative Mood, Declarative Sentences
Simple	Active	VERB-pr
	Passive	BE-pr VERB-en
Perfective	Active	HAVE-pr VERB-en
	Passive	HAVE-pr been VERB-en
Progressive	Active	BE-pr VERB-ing
	Passive	BE-pr being VERB-en
Perfective Progressive	Active	HAVE-pr been VERB-ing
	Passive	HAVE-pr been being VERB-en

Figure 6.32 Generalized finite verb phrases in the present tense. The first word of the verb phrase must concord with the subject on person and number. To illustrate, for third person singular subject with perfective progressive aspect in active voice, we can obtain the expression *He has been showing.*

Aspect	Voice	Generalized Finite Verb Phrases in Past Tense, Indicative Mood, Declarative Sentences
Simple	Active	VERB-ed
	Passive	BE-ed VERB-en
Perfective	Active	had VERB-en
	Passive	had been VERB-en
Progressive	Active	BE-ed VERB-ing
	Passive	BE-ed being VERB-en
Perfective Progressive	Active	had been VERB-ing
	Passive	had been being VERB-en

Figure 6.33 Generalized finite verb phrases in the past tense. The first word of the verb phrase must concord with the subject on person and number. To illustrate, for third person plural subject with progressive aspect in passive voice, we can obtain the expression *They were being shown.*

Aspect	Voice	Generalized Finite Verb Phrases with a Modal, Indicative Mood, Declarative Sentences
Simple	Active	MODAL VERB-b
	Passive	MODAL be VERB-en
Perfective	Active	MODAL have VERB-en
	Passive	MODAL have been VERB-en
Progressive	Active	MODAL be VERB-ing
	Passive	MODAL be being VERB-en
Perfective Progressive	Active	MODAL have been VERB-ing
	Passive	MODAL have been being VERB-en

Figure 6.34 Generalized finite verb phrases with a modal. The modal, which is the first word of the verb phrase, concords with subjects of all persons and number. For denoting future tense, the modals usually employed are *shall* or *will*. To illustrate, for perfective aspect in passive voice, we can obtain the expression *They/He/You/We/I will have been shown.*

Hence, if the verb is such that it cannot be used in the passive, then BE$_2$ cannot occur in the finite verb phrase.

It was mentioned above that the vital constituent of a finite verb phrase is the verb. Nevertheless, the verb is sometimes elided:

He has not finished the assignment, but I *have* (finished the assignment).

The verb *finished* has been elided from the finite verb phrase *have finished*. We can then assume that the verb *finished* occurs implicitly in the given verb phrase.

In colloquial practice, the auxiliary BE$_2$ in a finite verb phrase is often supplanted by *get*: *I got robbed* instead of *I was robbed*. Then the formula for a finite verb phrase becomes:

(MODAL|b) (HAVE|en) (BE|ing) (GET|en) VERB (PARTICLES)

Several grammar books call GET a pseudo-auxiliary. Similarly there are other pseudo-auxiliaries. For instance, *I had better play* can be considered an alternative to *I should play*. Thus *had better* can be called a pseudo-auxiliary. Similarly, we can have *I had better be playing* and *The*

For any finite verb phrase to be in	Primary auxiliaries that must occur in the verb phrase	Primary auxiliaries that must not occur in the verb phrase
Simple aspect	-	HAVE and BE_1
Perfective aspect	HAVE	BE_1
Progressive aspect	BE_1	HAVE
Perfective Progressive aspect	HAVE and BE_1	-
Passive voice	BE_2	-

Figure 6.35 Table to summarize how the aspect and voice of a finite verb phrase are governed by the primary auxiliaries. We can read above, for instance, that a finite verb phrase is in perfective aspect if, and only if, HAVE occurs and BE_1 does not occur [the occurrence of BE_2 is immaterial]. We can view the effect of the auxiliaries in a finite verb phrase to be in the following sequence: (modal) (perfective) (progressive) (passive).

game had better be played. Examples of a few other pseudo-auxiliaries used in finite verb phrases are given in Figure 6.36.

The only primary auxiliaries used in the finite verb phrases discussed above have been HAVE and BE. Another kind of finite verb phrase can be developed by using the primary auxiliary DO:

She *does show.*
They *did show.*

The verb phrases are said to have DO-support, and such verb phrases lend emphasis to a statement. These verb phrases can be in either present tense or past tense, but not in future tense. There is no aspect. DO-support finite verb phrases can be developed from the following formula:

DO VERB-b (PARTICLES)

The VERB cannot be BE. The form of DO used manifests tense, and it concords with the subject on person and number. A few examples of DO-support finite verb phrases are given in Table 6.37.

Pseudo auxiliary	A specimen sentence using the pseudo auxiliary in a finite verb phrase
be able to	I <u>was able to play</u>.
be about to	They <u>are about to play</u>.
be going to	She <u>is going to play</u>.
be supposed to	You <u>are supposed to play</u>.
dare to	He <u>dares to play</u>.
get to	We <u>get to play</u>.
had better	We <u>had better play</u>.
had best	We <u>had best play</u>.
have got to	They <u>have got to play</u>.
have to	We <u>had to play</u>.
keep	They <u>kept playing</u>.
need to	She <u>needs to play</u>.
ought to	He <u>ought to play</u>.
used to	I <u>used to play</u>.
will get to	She <u>will get to play</u>.

Figure 6.36 Examples of finite verb phrases containing pseudo auxiliaries. In speech, the *had* of *had better* is sometimes elided, as in 'We better be going now.'

In section 6.5.4, you read about the five genera of verbs. We can have similar genera for finite verb phrases:

He *has been* ill. (linking)
She *has been sleeping*. (intransitive)
I *can see* the concert tomorrow. (unitransitive)
We *were electing* Anita captain. (cotransitive)
Anita *will be taking* Gilda a book. (bitransitive)

In section 6.2.3, you read about finite clauses. You can now enrich your understanding of finite clauses: a clause containing a finite verb phrase is a finite clause. Finite clauses in a sentence can have their own

Subject	DO-support finite verb phrase: DO VERB-b (PARTICLES)	
	Present Tense	Past Tense
First person singular	I do show.	I did show.
First person plural	We do show.	We did show.
Second person singular and plural	You do show.	You did show.
Third person singular	He/She/It does show.	He/She/It did show.
Third person plural	They do show.	They did show.

Figure 6.37   Examples of DO-support finite verb phrases. Such verb phrases do not exist when the verb is BE.

subjects, subject complements, direct objects, object complements, and indirect objects. In the next section, we shall study non-finite verb phrases.

6.5.6   Non-finite verb phrases

An infinitive is written by placing a *to* before the basal form of a verb, for example, *to be, to cheat, to have,* and *to show.* The infinitives, present participles and past participles of a verb are known as the non-finite forms of the verb, or for brevity, non-finite verbs. Some grammar books refer to non-finite verbs as verbals. Thus *to cheat, to show, cheating, showing, cheated* and *shown* exemplify non-finite verbs. A non-finite verb phrase is constructed from a non-finite verb; see Figure 6.38 for examples of non-finite verb phrases. Keep consulting the figure as you read the explanation below.

Non-finite verb phrases are contained in non-finite clauses (defined in Section 6.2.4):

> Having been cheated by the vendor, Gilda was consoled by Anita.

The non-finite verb phrase *Having been cheated* is contained in the non-finite clause *Having . . . vendor.* As you read in section 6.2.4, a

Formula of a nonfinite verb phrase	Voice of the non-finite verb phrase	A specimen sentence that contains a nonfinite verb phrase corresponding to the formula
VERB-ing	active	He was caught <u>cheating</u>.
having been VERB-ing	active	<u>Having been cheating</u>, he is now sorry.
VERB-en	passive	<u>Cheated</u>, she became angry.
being VERB-en	passive	She became angry on <u>being cheated</u>.
having VERB-en	active	<u>Having cheated</u>, he is now sorry.
having been VERB-en	passive	<u>Having been cheated</u>, she was angry.
to VERB-b	active	<u>To cheat</u> was his mistake.
to be VERB-en	passive	<u>To be cheated</u> angered her.
to have VERB-en	active	He is known <u>to have cheated</u>.
to have been VERB-ing	active	He is known <u>to have been cheating</u>.
to have been VERB-en	passive	She is known <u>to have been cheated</u>.

Figure 6.38 Examples of non-finite verb phrases.

non-finite clause expresses some sense of either action or state of existence. A non-finite clause does not exist by itself as a sentence; instead it is connected to some finite clause. In the example above, the non-finite clause is connected to the finite clause *Gilda was consoled by Anita*. A non-finite clause is said to be dependent on the finite clause to which it is connected.

If the non-finite clause does not explicitly contain a subject, as in the example above, then it is assumed that the subject of the non-finite clause is the same as the subject of the finite clause on which the non-finite clause depends; thus the subject of the non-finite clause above is *Gilda*. Moreover, the non-finite clause is in passive voice

Genus of the nonfinite verb phrase	Specimen nonfinite clauses containing the nonfinite verb phrase
Linking	<u>Monday being Easter</u>, there will be no class. <u>The argument (being) over</u>, we went out. I want <u>you to be happy.</u>
Intransitive	<u>Hands trembling</u>, he signed the contract. <u>The lunch eaten</u>, we boarded the bus. He asked <u>me to go.</u>
Unitransitive	<u>Eating ice-cream</u> is fun. <u>To eat ice-cream</u> is fun. I am happy <u>to have visited my aunt.</u>
Cotransitive	<u>Electing him captain</u> was a mistake. <u>Having elected him captain</u>, we obeyed him. <u>To elect him captain</u> was a mistake.
Bitransitive	<u>Lending him the book</u> was a mistake. <u>Having lent him the book</u>, I could not get it back. I wanted <u>him to offer me some tea.</u>

Figure 6.39 Examples of linking, intransitive, unitransitive, cotransitive, and bitransitive non-finite verb phrases.

because the action (of cheating) was done to the subject; the finite clause incidentally is also in the passive voice. Other illustrations are:

> Having been cheated by the vendor, Gilda flew into a rage.
> (non-finite clause is passive; finite clause, active)
> Having cheated the vendor, he was punished by Mother.
> (non-finite clause is active; finite clause, passive)
> Having cheated the vendor, he boasted to his friends.
> (both non-finite and finite clauses are active)

Now look again at the examples in Figure 6.38 to review the voices of the given non-finite verb phrases; in all those examples, the non-finite clause contains only the non-finite verb phrase, and no other words. Compare:

> *Shaking*, I began my speech.
> (the subject of the non-finite clause is assumed to be *I*)
> *Knees shaking*, I began my speech.
> (the subject of the non-finite clause is *Knees*)

A non-finite verb phrase need not concord with its subject on person and number. Non-finite verb phrases can contain particles:

Having lost *out* on the deal, he is bitter.

Non-finite verb phrases can be linking, intransitive, unitransitive, cotransitive or bitransitive, and examples are given Figure 6.39.

It should be evident from Figure 6.39 that just like finite clauses, non-finite clauses too can have their subjects, subject complements, direct objects, object complements, and indirect objects.

Moreover, as with non-finite noun clauses discussed earlier in sections 6.3.5 and 6.4.7, non-finite clauses can behave like nouns in a sentence:

Swimming is fun.
To swim is fun.
He likes *going home*.
He likes *to go home*.
I gave *singing* my best try.
His passion – *to race cars* – cost him his life.

Non-finite clauses can behave like adjectives (defined in Figure 6.3) too:

A man *holding a dog* crossed the street.
The tenant *thrown out on the street* had not paid his rent.
The place *to visit for a holiday* is Ulan Bator.

Such non-finite clauses are called non-finite adjective clauses. You will read more about non-finite adjective clauses in section 6.7.4. By then you will have a better understanding of adjectives. Similarly non-finite clauses can behave like adverbs (defined in Figure 6.3) too:

We ate *standing under the tree*.
When shown by Mother, Anita learnt to knit.
I hurried *to be on time*.

Such non-finite clauses are called non-finite adverb clauses. You will read more about non-finite adverb clauses in section 6.8.5. By then, you will know more about adverbs. To sum up, any non-finite clause in a sentence will behave like a noun, an adjective or an adverb.

In some grammar books, non-finite clauses are known by the form of the verb in them: they are called present participial phrases, past participial phrases, and infinitive phrases. Moreover, a present participle behaving like a noun is known as a gerund, as in: *Studying* is his hobby.

aboard, about, above, according to, across, after, against, ahead of, along, along with, alongside of, amid, among, apart from, around, aside from, as, as for, at, away from, because of, before, behind, belonging to, below, beneath, beside, besides, between, beyond, but, by, by means of, by way of, concerning, contrary to, despite, down, during, except, except for, for, for the sake of, from, in, in addition to, in advance of, in case of, in comparison with, in consideration of, in front of, in lieu of, in light of, in line with, in place of, in reference to, in relation to, in spite of, in the event of, inside, inside of, instead of, into, like, near, of, off, on, on account of, on behalf of, on top of, over, out of, outside, owing to, past, rather, save, since, through, throughout, till, to, together with, toward, under, underneath, until, unto, up, up at, up on, up to, upon, with, with regard to, with respect to, within, without

Figure 6.40 A list of prepositions. In colloquial practice, the preposition *owing to* is often supplanted by *due to*, as in 'Due to her tardiness, we all were late,' instead of 'Owing to . . . late.'

6.6 PREPOSITIONS

A preposition is a word or a group of words that reveals the relationship between a nounal, called the object of the preposition, and some other word in the sentence. The preposition and its object constitute a prepositional phrase, and the preposition is said to be the headword of the prepositional phrase:

The cost *of this book* is high.

In this example the noun phrase *this book* is the object of the preposition *of*; the preposition reveals the relationship between *cost* and *this book*; the prepositional phrase is *of this book*.

A list of prepositions is given in Figure 6.40. As the figure shows, a preposition can comprise more than one word. Consider the preposition *in front of*:

He sat in front of me.

Prepositions comprising more than one word are called compound prepositions or complex prepositions, in grammar books.

Unlike a noun or a verb, which can change its spelling to signify, say, number, a preposition never changes its spelling. Remember that as the object of a preposition, a noun or a pronoun is in the accusative case (see sections 6.3.3 and 6.4.4 together with Figures 6.5 and 6.10):

No one went *but me*.

Do not confuse the usage of *to* in an infintive with *to* in a prepositional phrase:

> To listen to him is a pleasure.

Here *to listen* is an infinitive, but *to him* is a prepositional phrase. Likewise, do not confuse a particle (defined in section 6.5.3) with a preposition:

> I ran *across* Archie. (particle)
> I ran *across* the street. (preposition)

Below are more examples of prepositional phrases:

> He sat *on the green fence*. (noun phrase *the green fence* is the object of the preposition *on*)
> I shall not go *until after supper*. (*supper* is the object of *after*; the prepositional phrase *after supper* behaves like a noun in being the object of the preposition *until*; hence a prepositional phrase is embedded in another prepositional phrase)
> She wrote a program *for playing chess*. (non-finite clause *playing chess* is the object of preposition *for*)
> Being torn up *over his divorce*, he attempted suicide. (the prepositional phrase *over his divorce* is embedded in the non-finite clause *Being . . . divorce*)
> He has learnt a lesson *from what happened yesterday*. (the finite clause *what . . . yesterday* is the object of the preposition *from*; hence a finite clause is embedded in a prepositional phrase)

In the examples until now, the object of the preposition has occurred after the preposition. In colloquial usage, it is not always so; the object is then said to be displaced:

> I need a pen to write *with*.
> What did he do that *for*?
> Beethoven is enjoyable to listen *to*.

The above sentences can be rewritten so that the prepositions are no longer displaced:

> I need a pen *with which to write*.
> *For what* did he do that?
> To listen *to Beethoven* is enjoyable.

Nevertheless, you will often come across sentences like:

> I am well cared *for*.
> I was yelled *at*.

The object of a preposition can be elided:

It is Archie (whom) I want to talk *to*.

If we do not write *whom* above, then the object of *to* has been elided. You can, of course, rewrite the sentence:

It is Archie *to whom* I want to talk.

A prepositional phrase in a sentence always behaves like a noun, an adjective or an adverb (see Figure 6.3):

Beside the river is where I jog. (noun as subject)
We elected him *as captain*. (noun as object complement)
He came out from *under the bed*. (noun as object of the preposition *from*)
After lunch is when I sleep. (noun as subject)
Inside the room is warmer than outside. (noun as subject)
The house *beside the river* burnt down. (adjective)
The milk spilt *on the floor*. (adverb)

The first six examples above are said to have nounized prepositional phrases, which are considered to be a kind of nounal. In section 6.7.3, you will read more about prepositional phrases behaving like adjectives, and in section 6.8.4 about prepositional phrases behaving like adverbs. By then you will have a better understanding of adjectives and adverbs.

6.7   ADJECTIVES

Adjectives are words that modify nouns or pronouns. In *a red flower*, the adjective *red* modifies the noun *flower*. As you know by now, a word can behave like more than one part of speech. Several words can behave like nouns or adjectives:

The *young* woman married the *old* man.
(*young* and *old* are adjectives)
The *young* die in wars that the *old* declare.
(*young* and *old* are nouns; they are, respectively, the headwords of the noun phrases *the young* and *the old*)
The *unemployed* men lined up for soup. (adjective)
The mayor promised help to the young *unemployed*. (noun)

When storing adjectives in an ELP lexicon, we may also need to store what nouns each adjective can modify, for instance, *red* can modify *flower*, but it cannot modify *honesty*.

Adjectives can modify compound nouns. In *a fractured funny bone*, the adjective *fractured* modifies the compound noun *funny bone*. Similarly, there can be, so to speak, a *charming mother-in-law*. A compound adjective is two or more hyphenated words behaving together like a single adjective, for example, an *up-to-date* dictionary, a *soft-fur* cat, *freeze-dried* coffee, and a *sixty-year-old* mother-in-law. A noun or a pronoun can be modified by more than one adjective at the same time:

a *soft furry* cat
a *hot, humid* summer
a *hot* and *humid* summer

Note that whereas *a soft-fur cat* and *a soft furry cat* may have similar meanings, the former expression contains one adjective (albeit compound), whereas the latter contains two adjectives. Any number of adjectives may modify a noun or a pronoun, but in practice it is rare for more than three adjectives to modify a noun or pronoun. In the ELP lexicon, we would also need to specify which adjectives are incompatible with one another; for instance, both *young* and *old* can modify *man*, but the two of them cannot modify the same *man* at the same time. It would not make literal sense to write the expression *a young old man*. So *young* and *old* are incompatible with each other.

Non-finite verbs (infinitives and participles) can behave like adjectives. Here are examples of infinitives behaving like adjectives:

The fruit *to buy* are mangoes. (the infinitive modifies *fruit*)
She wants a chance *to sing*.
I had raisins *to eat*.

Now we give examples of participles behaving like adjectives:

1. for present participles: *cheering* crowd, *crying* baby, *exciting* project, *losing* proposition, *stinging* rebuke, and *winning* team;
2. for past participles: *baked* potato, *broken* vase, *burnt* toast, *fallen* tree, *stolen* jewels, and *worn-out* trousers.

6.7.1   The grade of an adjective

When adjectives modify nouns or pronouns, we can affiliate words with the adjectives that tell us to what extent the adjectives are doing the modifying. Such words are called intensifiers in grammar books. In *somewhat tall woman* and *very tall woman*, the words *somewhat* and *very* are intensifiers.

An adjective together with its intensifiers is called an adjective phrase. Accordingly, *somewhat tall* and *very tall* are adjective phrases.

The headword of an adjective phrase is the adjective in the phrase.

Not all adjectives are intensifiable. We can say *dead man*, but it makes no sense to say *very dead man*. Hence *dead* cannot be intensified. Some of the other adjectives that cannot be intensified are *endless, everlasting, eternal, infinite, matchless, mortal, perfect, unique* and *universal*. Nonetheless, some of these adjectives are intensified in practice:

> After the accident, he is *more dead than alive*. (idiomatic)
> Anita handed in a *very unique* assignment. (colloquial)

You will read more about intensifiers in section 6.8.

Adjectives that can be intensified can have three forms. These forms are said to be the three grades: absolute, also called positive in some grammar books; comparative; and superlative. Thus, for instance, we can say:

> Archie is *tall*. (absolute grade)
> Archie is *taller* than Anita. (comparative grade for comparing the two)
> Archie is the *tallest* among them. (superlative grade for comparing three or more)

For grading, adjectives can be divided into the following three groups:

Group 1
This group usually contains the polysyllabic adjectives. The comparative grade is written with the intensifier *more*, and the superlative grade with the intensifier *most*. Accordingly, we write *careful, more careful* and *most careful*. To weaken the intensification, we write *less careful* and *least careful*.

Group 2
This group usually contains the monosyllabic adjectives. The comparative grade ends with *er*, and the superlative grade ends with *st*. Accordingly, we write *tall, taller* and *tallest* as the grades for *tall*.

Group 3
There is no uniformity in the grades of the adjectives from this group. For example, we write *good, better* and *best* as the grades for *good*.

An adjective can be considered to belong to more than one of the above groups. Adjectives like *fancy, happy* and *lively* can be considered to be in group 1 or group 2. Thus we can write *fancy*, either *more fancy* or *fancier*, and either *most fancy* or *fanciest*. See Figure 6.41 for the grades of a few adjectives from each group.

Group	ABSOLUTE	COMPARATIVE	SUPERLATIVE
1	careful	more careful	most careful
	obedient	more obedient	most obedient
2	far	farther	farthest
	far	further	furthest
	late	later	latest
	late	latter	last
	tall	taller	tallest
3	bad	worse	worst
	good	better	best

Figure 6.41 Grades of a few adjectives from each of the three groups. Adjectives like *far* and *late* each have two sets of grades depending on the meaning for which they are used.

An adjective is said to undergo declensions to signify its grade. Consult a dictionary whenever you want to find out the declensions of an adjective. You may need to store the declensions in the ELP lexicon.

6.7.2   The position of an adjective

In a sentence, an adjective can occur in the four positions enumerated below.

Predicate adjective position
As you read in section 6.5.4, a predicate adjective occurs in the predicate to modify the subject of the sentence:

Archie/He is *tall*.

Prenominal position
In this position, the adjective occurs immediately before the noun or pronoun it modifies, as in *tall boy, angry girl, fresh apples* and *broken vase*. Pronouns, however, cannot be modified in the manner shown in the examples. It is ungrammatical to write *tall he, angry she, fresh they* or *broken it*. One way to modify pronouns is to use predicate adjectives:

He is tall.
She is angry.
They are fresh.
It is broken.

Several adjectives can be prenominal to both nouns and pronouns, provided there is a comma between the adjective and the noun or pronoun.

Afraid, Archie/he whistled in the dark.
Fuming, Anita/she slammed the door.
Injured, Gilda/she screamed.
To visit, the place is Ulan Bator.

Without the comma as shown in the above examples, some adjectives cannot be prenominal at all. It is ungrammatical to say *the afraid boy*, although it is grammatical to say *the frightened boy*. Nevertheless, *afraid* can be a predicate adjective:

The boy is afraid.

An adjective like *sharp* can be a prenominal adjective or a predicate adjective without any change in meaning: *The sharp knife*, as compared to *The knife is sharp*. But there are adjectives whose meanings as prenominal adjectives are different from their meanings as predicate adjectives. *His late uncle* does not mean the same as *His uncle is late*. Similarly, *The civil servant* may not mean that *The servant is civil*.

Then there are words that can be prenominal adjectives but not predicate adjectives. Such words are usually nouns that behave like adjectives to modify other nouns. The expression *the iron knife* means *the knife made out of iron*; the expression cannot be paraphrased as *the knife is iron*. There is no uniformity in the meanings of expressions in which nouns behave like adjectives to modify other nouns. Figure 6.42 lists a few such expressions. None of them can be paraphrased with a predicate adjective.

Postnominal position
In this position, the adjective occurs immediately after the noun or pronoun it modifies:

Her success made him *envious*. (note, *envious* is object complement)
She, *pale* and *frightened*, faced her abductor.
Anyone *interested* should come to the lecture.
Something *odd* is going on here.
The place *to visit* is Ulan Bator.
The girl *injured* began to scream.
The baby *gurgling* is my niece.

Expression	A Paraphrase of the Expression
wood shelf	shelf made out of wood
book shelf	shelf for books
grammar book	book discussing grammar
newspaper headlines	headlines in the newspaper
television reporter	reporter on television
car maintenance	maintenance done on the car
clearance sale	sale to clear stock
warehouse sale	sale at the warehouse
shirt sale	sale of shirts
bride sale	sale for brides
December sale	sale during December
Montreal man	man from Montreal

Figure 6.42   The paraphrases of some expressions in which nouns behave like adjectives to modify other nouns. There is no uniformity in the paraphrases of the expressions. None of them can be paraphrased with a predicate adjective.

A postnominal adjective can sometimes be considered to be part of an elliptical relative clause, as for the last two examples above:

The girl *(who was) injured* began to scream.
The baby *(who is) gurgling* is my niece.

Some adjectives can be postnominal, but not prenominal. We can say that *The office below was burgled*; but we cannot say *The below office was burgled*.

Displaced position
In this position, the adjective occurs a few words after the noun or pronoun it modifies:

She remained sitting, *angry*.

The adjective *angry* modifies the pronoun *she*. The usage of displaced adjectives is infrequent.

When storing an adjective in the ELP lexicon, we need to also store the postitions in which the adjective can occur.

6.7.3   Adjectivized prepositional phrases

An adjectivized prepositional phrase is a prepositional phrase behaving like an adjective (see section 6.6). Such prepositional phrases occur usually in the postnominal or predicate adjective positions, and occasionally in the displaced position.

> Someone *in the crowd* threw an egg. (postnominal)
> The cause *of this brawl* is unknown. (postnominal)
> The boy *on the fence* jumped. (postnominal)
> She was *in an angry mood*. (predicate adjective)
> The flowers are *in full bloom*.(predicate adjective)
> The flowers are in the garden, *in full bloom*. (displaced)

6.7.4   Non-finite adjective clauses

As you read earlier in section 6.5.6, non-finite adjective clauses are non-finite clauses that behave like adjectives. The examples below show that such clauses can occur in all the four positions (predicate adjectives, prenominal, postnominal and displaced):

> She was *exhausted by the heat*.
> *Holding a dog*, a man crossed the street.
> *Torn from his friends*, he was lonely.
> *To visit for a holiday*, the place is Ulan Bator.
> All boys *leaving now* will not be allowed back.
> I bought the shirt *displayed in the shop window*.
> Mr Devotion is the man *to see about the new course*.
> He turned away, *smiling at his wickedness*.
> The woman fainted, *exhausted by the heat*.

6.7.5   Finite adjective clauses

One kind of finite clause that can behave like an adjective is the relative clause, mentioned in section 6.4.5. Nonetheless, other finite clauses can also behave like adjectives. All finite clauses that behave like adjectives are called finite adjective clauses. Such clauses usually occur in the postnominal position:

> We found a hotel *that had a vacancy*.
> This is the book *(that) I am reading*.

I was sad the day *(when) Father scolded me.*
I am going to the office *where I work.*
I know the place *(where) Archie had an accident.*
This car, *which I bought last year,* is no good.
I bought several books, *the price of which was steep.*
Gilda, *who is always humorous,* is enjoyable company.
The girl *who,* I heard, *painted this picture* is eight years old.
  (*I heard* is a parenthetical comment; it is not considered to be a
  part of the finite adjective clause)
A man *(whom) I met yesterday* called today.
He has two sons, *one of whom is a singer.*
The woman *whose car was stolen* called the police.
The reason *(why) he came late* is not known.

It is often convenient to refer to an adjective, an adjective phrase, an adjectivized prepositional phrase, or a finite or non-finite adjective clause as an adjectival.

6.8   ADVERBS

Adverbs are words that modify verbs (both finite and non-finite), sentences, adjectives or other adverbs. The six genera of adverbs are enumerated below.

1. A manner adverb modifies a verb to tell us how (the manner in which) an action is done. This includes within it the means or the instruments adopted to do the action. A manner adverb can be replaced by the word *thus,* and the sentence will still make sense:

   She replied *frankly.* (tells us how she replied)
   They examined the hair *microscopically.*
   He waited *eagerly.*
   I saw him studying *furiously.*(modifies the non-finite verb *studying*)

2. A place adverb modifies a verb to tell us where (the place in which) an action is done. A place adverb can be replaced by the word *there,* and the sentence will still make sense:

   She lives *nearby.*
   He walked *down.*

3. A time adverb modifies a verb to tell us when (the time at which, or during which, or how frequently) an action is done. A time adverb can be replaced by the word *then,* and the sentence will still make sense:

She arrived *early*. (when she arrived)
He is *temporarily* unemployed. (the duration of unemployment)
We meet *weekly*. (the frequency of meeting)

4. A degree adverb modifies a verb to tell us how much of (the degree to which) an action is done:

She *nearly* had an accident.
He agrees with her *completely*.

5. A sentence adverb modifies a sentence to tell us about one's comments on what one is saying. In the sentence *Luckily, no one was hurt*, the word *Luckily* is a sentence adverb: the speaker is informing us that no one was hurt; moreover, the speaker is commenting that, in his opinion, it was lucky for such to happen. Other examples:

Frankly, he is a snob.
She sings *besides*.

Note that earlier *frankly* was used as a manner adverb. Thus an adverb can belong to more than one genus.

6. An intensifier adverb modifies an adjective or another adverb:

She is *rather* tall. (adverb *rather* modifies adjective *tall*)
He lives *very* frugally. (adverb *very* modifies another adverb *frugally*)
He lives *completely* frugally.

You will notice that in this last example, *completely* is exemplified as an intersifier adverb; earlier in this section, it was exemplified as a degree adverb. The two genera share many adverbs, but the genera are not identical. To illustrate: *quite, rather* and *very* are intensifier adverbs, but not degree adverbs; it is ungrammatical to say *He very agrees with me*.

For brevity, intensifier adverbs are also known as intensifiers. You read about intensifiers in section 6.7.1, during the discussion on intensifying adjectives.

Specimen adverbs from the six genera discussed above are given in Figure 6.43. Do not confuse adverbs with adjectives. Two sentences may have a similar structure, but one may use an adjective, the other an adverb:

The lecture is *boring*. (the word *boring* is an adjective)
The lecture is *daily*. (time adverb)

Genus of the adverbs	Specimen adverbs from the genus				
Manner	aloud headlong	carefully politely	deliberately skillfully	eagerly thus	frankly well
Place	away nearby	behind overhead	far somewhere	forward there	inside up
Time	ago late	always seldom	before temporarily	continually usually	early weekly
Degree	barely lavishly	completely moderately	definitely nearly	entirely scarcely	hardly thoroughly
Sentence	admittedly luckily	besides naturally	certainly offhand	frankly perhaps	indeed theoretically
Intensifier	almost pretty	completely quite	enough rather	moderately somewhat	no very

Figure 6.43 Specimen adverbs from the six genera of adverbs. The most frequent ending for adverbs is *ly*. The genera are not disjoint: for example, *frankly* is both a manner and a sentence adverb.

Father is *ill*. (adjective)
Father is *inside* (adverb)

Moreover, what looks like an adverb can sometimes behave like a noun. In the last example above, *inside* behaved like an adverb; below it behaves like a noun:

Inside is better. (*inside* is the subject of the sentence)

6.8.1 The grade of an adverb

An adverb together with its intensifiers is called an adverb phrase:

He drove *somewhat recklessly*.
He ate *very rapidly*.

The headword of an adverb phrase is the intensified adverb. Not all adverbs are intensifiable. We can say:

He spoke *perfectly*.

but it makes no sense to say:

He spoke *very perfectly*.

Some of the other adverbs that cannot be intensified are *endlessly*, *everlastingly*, *eternally*, *infinitely*, *matchlessly*, *mortally*, *uniquely* and *universally*. Nonetheless, colloquially some of these adverbs are intensified:

The argument continued *rather endlessly*.
She behaved *very uniquely*.

Just as for intensifiable adjectives, there can be three grades for intensifiable adverbs:

Anita replied *politely*. (absolute grade)
Anita replied *more politely* than Gilda. (comparative grade)
Anita replied *most politely* from among them. (superlative grade)

For grading, adverbs can be divided into three groups. As will become apparent from the explanation below, these groups are based on the nature of the correspondence that many adverbs have with adjectives.

Group 1
This group contains mostly those adverbs that are written by affixing *ly* to the end of their corresponding adjectives; to illustrate, the adverb *politely* corresponds to the adjective *polite*. The comparative and superlative grades are written with the intensifiers *more* and *most*, respectively. Accordingly, we write *politely*, *more politely* and *most politely*. To weaken the intensification, we write *less politely* and *least politely*. In embodying this prescript into your ELP, be careful, however: not every word ending with an *ly* is an adverb; for instance, *fatherly*, *friendly*, *homely*, *lonely*, *lovely*, *manly*, *motherly*, *neighbourly*, *orderly*, *portly*, and *scholarly* can be used as adjectives, but not as adverbs.

Group 2
This group contains mostly those adverbs that are identical to their corresponding adjectives; for example, *early*, *far* and *late*:

He was an *early* arrival. (adjective)
He arrived *early*. (time adverb)

The grades for the adverbs are identical to the grades of the corresponding adjectives. Hence we write *late*, *later* and *latest* as the grades for *late*.

Group 3
This group contains mostly those adverbs whose spelling bears no resemblance to their corresponding adjectives; for instance, the adverb *well* corresponds to the adjective *good*:

Group	Adjective	Grades of the Adverb corresponding to the Adjective		
		ABSOLUTE	COMPARATIVE	SUPERLATIVE
1	careful	carefully	more carefully	most carefully
	polite	politely	more politely	most politely
2	early	early	earlier	earliest
	far	far	farther	farthest
	far	far	further	furthest
	late	late	later	latest
3	bad	badly	worse	worst
	good	well	better	best

Figure 6.44   Grades of a few adverbs from each of the three groups. An adverb like *far* has two sets of grades depending on the meaning for which it is used. The adverb *badly* may appear to belong to Group 1 [since the adverb is formed by affixing *ly* to the end of the corresponding adjective], but in fact it belongs to Group 3.

He wrote a *good* essay. (adjective)
He wrote his essay *well*. (manner adverb)

There is no uniformity in the grades of the adverbs of this group; *well*, *better* and *best* are the grades of *well*. Note that *well* is used as an adjective when talking about health: *I feel well*. Figure 6.44 shows the grades of a few adverbs from each group.

There are adverbs from group 1 that are colloquially used as if they were from group 2:

He fought *dirty*.
Play *fair*.

An adverb is said to undergo declension to signify its grade. Consult a dictionary whenever you want to find out the declensions of an adverb. You may need to store the declensions in the ELP lexicon.

By now you have read that verbs undergo conjugation, and that nouns, pronouns, adjectives and adverbs undergo declension. Some grammar books refer to both conjugation and declension as inflection, that is to say, nouns, pronouns, verbs, adjectives and adverbs all undergo inflection.

6.8.2   The position of an adverb

In a sentence, an intensifier or a degree adverb usually occurs immediately before the word it modifies. Changing its position can alter the meaning of the sentence:

> I *only* gave him a book today. (only gave, did nothing else)
>
> I gave him a book *only* today. (gave only today, not any other day)

Some of the other such adverbs, which can alter the meaning of a sentence by changing their positions, are *almost, even, just, merely* and *nearly*. As mentioned above, such adverbs occur before the words they modify. An exception is the intensifier *enough*. It can occur immediately after the word it modifies:

> He ran fast *enough*.
> She is tall *enough* to be a pilot.

There are instances where the meaning of a sentence is not sensitive to the change in position of an adverb:

> *Certainly* we will elect him.
> We *certainly* will elect him.
> We will *certainly* elect him.
> We will elect him *certainly*.

The four sentences above illustrate the four positions in which an adverb can essentially occur in a clause (non-finite or finite). The positions can be described as follows:

Position 1
In this position, the adverb occurs before the subject of the clause, thus usually at the beginning of the clause:

> *Rapidly* walking into the room, she picked up a book.
>   (the subject of the non-finite clause is implicitly *she*)
> *Rapidly* she walked into the room.
> *Finally* he arrived.
> *Inside*, the man continued to yell.

Position 2
In this position, the adverb occurs after the subject, but before the verb phrase (finite or non-finite):

> Knees *badly* shaking, I began my speech.
> He *finally* arrived.
> I *really* must be careful.

Position 3
In this position, the adverb occurs within the verb phrase. Although the adverb occurs within the verb phrase, it is not considered to be part of the verb phrase:

Having *vilely* cheated the vendor, he boasted to his friends.
I must *really* be careful.
I will *not* go to Vancouver.
I might *never* have learnt about it.
We could *easily* have finished the job.

The adverb occurs mostly after the first auxiliary in the verb phrase, as it does in the examples above. Nevertheless, the verb can occur after the other auxiliaries, too:

We could have *easily* finished the job.
   (adverb occurs after the second auxiliary)
We could have been *easily* finishing the job.
   (adverb occurs after the third auxiliary)
The job could have been being *easily* finished.
   (adverb occurs after the fourth auxiliary; rare usage)

Some of the adverbs that can occur within a verb phrase are *always*, *barely*, *certainly*, *easily*, *fortunately*, *frequently*, *hardly*, *little*, *never*, *not*, *often*, *probably*, *rarely*, *really*, *scarcely*, *seldom* and *usually*.

Position 4
In this position, the adverb occurs after the verb phrase. If, however, the clause contains an object (direct or indirect) of the verb phrase, then the adverb occurs after the object, and not between the verb phrase and the object:

Having been cheated *vilely* by the vendor, she was angry.
He was *never* at school.
She was walking *rapidly* into the room.
He drove *carefully*.

None of the above examples contained an object of the verb phrase. The examples below contain such objects:

Driving the car *carefully*, he took the injured to the hospital.
He drove the car *carefully*.
I gave him the book *happily*.
We consider him elected *fairly*.
   (adverb occurs after the adjectival object complement *elected*)
Gilda kept the children *very* quiet.

(adverb occurs after the direct object *children*, but before the adjectival object complement *quiet*)
We elected him captain *fortunately*.
(adverb occurs after the nounal object complement *captain*)

As the last example illustrates, an adverb does not occur between a direct object and a nounal object complement.

When storing an adverb in the ELP lexicon, we need to also store the positions in which the adverb can occur.

6.8.3   Adverbized noun phrases

A noun phrase (see section 6.3.6) that behaves like an adverb is called an adverbized noun phrase. In a clause (finite or non-finite), such noun phrases occur usually before the subject or after the verb phrase.

> *Last Sunday*, he came. (behaves like a time adverb)
> He went *home*. (place)
> She practiced *a whole lot*. (degree)
> He came *one hour* later. (intensifier)
> She resides *a long way* away. (intensifier)
> Residing *a long way* away from here, she cannot come every day.
>   (intensifier)

6.8.4   Adverbized prepositional phrases

An adverbized prepositional phrase is a prepositional phrase behaving like an adverb (see section 6.6). In a clause, such a prepositional phrase occurs usually before the subject or after the verb phrase.

> He came *on Friday*. (behaves like a time adverb)
> *On Friday*, he came. (time)
> She acted *with pride*. (manner)
> *In all frankness*, (I think) he is a snob. (sentence)
> I walked *through the park*. (place)
> Walking *through the park*, I saw an old man. (place)
> He came *in order to see me*. (purpose)

In the last example above, the prepositional phrase modifies the verb *came* to tell us the purpose of his coming. Here we have brought in for adverbs a new genus called purpose. In section 6.8, we had not enumerated the purpose genus; there we were discussing single-word adverbs, and single-word adverbs can never belong to the purpose genus, but prepositional phrases can belong to the purpose genus, as the last example above shows.

Adjectivized prepositional phrases, described in section 6.7.3, and adverbized prepositional phrases can themselves be modified by other adverbs:

He is *totally* in error.
(adverb *totally* modifies adjectivized prepositional phrase *in error*)
I left *just* before his arrival.
(adverb *just* modifies adverbized prepositional phrase *before . . . arrival*)

From an adverbized prepositional phrase, if we delete all words except the preposition itself, then the preposition alone may sometimes behave like an adverb:

She walked *by me*.
She walked *by*.
I had never seen him *before today*.
I had never seen him *before*.
He lives *below this floor*.
He lives *below*.
Looking *up the tree*, I saw a cat.
Looking *up*, I saw a cat.

6.8.5 Non-finite adverb clauses

As you read earlier in section 6.5.6, non-finite adverb clauses are non-finite clauses that behave like adverbs:

He stood *staring at the window*. (manner)
Putting it frankly, (I think) he is a snob. (sentence)
We stood *frozen*. (manner)
When shown by Mother, Anita learnt to knit. (time)
Spoken frankly, (I think) he is a snob. (sentence)
He came *to see me*. (purpose)

Note that in the last example if we insert *in order* between *came* and *to*, then the non-finite clause *to see me* becomes an adverbized prepositional phrase *in order to see me*.

6.8.6 Finite adverb clauses

One kind of finite clause that can behave like an adverb is the relative clause (see section 6.4.5). Nonetheless, other finite clauses can also behave like adverbs. All finite clauses that behave like adverbs are called finite adverb clauses. Finite adverb clauses can belong to ten genera. Of these you are already familiar with five (manner, place, time, sentence and purpose), since they were discussed in sections 6.8 and 6.8.4. Specimen sentences containing finite adverb clauses from those five genera are given below:

1. The cake tasted *as it should.* (manner)
   He acted *as though he owned the place.* (manner)
2. I will go *wherever you go.* (place)
   I hid the cake *where nobody would find it.* (place)
3. *Whenever I argue with Mother,* she pulls rank on me. (time)
   We ate dinner *after Father returned.* (time)
4. *If I can put it frankly,* (I think) he is a snob. (sentence)
   He came late, *which surprised me.* (sentence)
5. I hurried *so that I would be on time.* (purpose)
   He came *in order that he would see me.* (purpose)

The other five genera to which finite adverb clauses can belong are as follows:

6. Contrast: the finite adverb clause modifies a verb by presenting itself as a contrast to an action narrated in another finite clause:

   Although she needed help, no one helped her.
   However he tried, he failed.

7. Condition. the finite adverb clause modifies a verb by presenting itself as a condition for an action narrated in another finite clause:

   I will not come *unless you invite me.*
   If you invite me, I will come.
   If you do not invite me, I will not come.

   The last two examples above can be colloquially written as follows:

   Invite me, and I will come.
   Invite me, or I will not come.

8. Cause: the finite adverb clause modifies a verb by presenting itself as a cause of the action narrated in another finite clause:

   Since I am late, I should hurry.
   Mother hurried *because she had an appointment.*

9. Result: the finite adverb clause modifies a verb by presenting itself as a result of the action narrated in another finite clause:

   Mother told me to go to the store, *so I did.*
   I was *so* terrified *that I could not speak.*

Number	Genus of finite adverb clauses	Words typically used to broach a finite adverb clause of the genus
1	Manner	as, as if, as though, like [colloquial]
2	Place	where, wherever, wheresoever, whereso
3	Time	as, after, as soon as, before, once, since, until, while, when, whenever, whenso, whensoever
4	Sentence	if I may be frank, if I can speak frankly, if I can put it frankly
5	Purpose	in order that, so, so that
6	Contrast	although, however (much), no matter how, though, whereas, while
7	Condition	if, in case, provided (that), unless
8	Cause	as, because, inasmuch as, in that, now that, since, seeing that
9	Result	so, so that, so ... that
10	Comparison	as ... as, less ... than, less than, more ... than, more than, than

Figure 6.45 Words that are typically used to broach finite adverb clauses from each of the ten genera. Note that the use of the word *like* to broach a finite clause is colloquial. In the sentence *The cake tasted like it should*, the word *like* should be replaced by *as*. Also note that a word can broach finite adverb clauses of more than one genus; for example, *as* can broach finite adverb clauses of manner, time, and cause.

10. Comparison: the finite adverb clause modifies an adjective or an adverb, but not a verb, to make a comparison:

> I am *as* tall *as you (are)*.
> She helped *more than he (did)*.
> It is easier *than it seems*.
> He arrived earlier *than she (did)*.

As the last two examples above show, the word *than* occurs after the comparative grades of adjectives or adverbs.

You may have observed from the examples above that some typical words are used to broach finite adverb clauses. A few such words for each of the ten genera are given in Figure 6.45.

A finite adverb clause can ordinarily be moved about in a sentence, but it usually occurs close to the finite clause whose verb the adverb clause modifies. A finite adverb clause can itself be modified by other adverbs:

> Immediately after we arrived, he left. (adverb *immediately* modifies the finite adverb clause *after we arrived*)
> Sobbing while she talked, Gilda told her story. (adverb *sobbing* modifies the finite adverb clause *while she talked*.)

6.8.7 Adverbials

It is often convenient to refer to an adverb, an adverb phrase, an adverbized noun phrase, an adverbized prepositional phrase, or an adverb clause (finite or non-finite) as an adverbial. In some grammar books, sentence adverbials are also known as disjuncts; the other adverbials are then known as adjuncts.

A finite clause in a sentence may contain any number of adverbials, but you will rarely find more than four; otherwise, the finite clause becomes difficult to understand:

> Yesterday Anita remained all day in her room to study for an examination.

In the example above, these are the four adverbials:

> *Yesterday,*
> *all day,*
> *in her room,* and
> *to study for an examination.*

Try inserting more adverbials in the example to see how difficult it becomes to understand.

If the words *how, when, where* or *why* are used to broach a question, then these words are called interrogative adverbs. The answer to the question lies in the adverbial of the respones. For examples:

> *How* did Archie cook lunch?
> Archie cooked lunch *carefully.*
> . . . *with care.*
> . . . *as though he were an expert.*
> *When* did Archie cook lunch?
> . . . *yesterday.*

. . . last Sunday.
. . . when Father asked him to do so.
Where did Archie cook lunch?
. . . nearby.
. . . in the camp ground.
. . . where we had pitched the tent.
Why did Archie cook lunch?
. . . to please Father.
. . . so that Father would be pleased.

The interrogative adverbs can also broach indirect questions:

I wonder *how* Archie cooked.

Moreover, to give a nuance to the question, we can replace *when* by *whenever, whenso* or *whensoever*; similarly, we can replace *where* by *wherever, whereso* or *wheresoever*. You will read more about questions in section 8.4.

6.9 CONJUNCTIONS

A conjunction is employed to connect words, phrases or clauses:

We ate dinner *after* Father returned.
However she tried, she did not succeed.
He is a miser *and* a grouch.
He is *as* tall *as* she.

Just like a preposition, a conjunction is never inflected. (Do not confuse a conjunction in English with the conjunction in mathematical logic, which you saw in Figure 2.1) A conjunction can belong to any of the three genera enumerated below:
   A **subordinating conjunction** connects two finite clauses by making one clause subordinate to the other:

When I went to his house, I saw him studying.

The subordinating conjunction *when* makes *I . . . house* subordinate to *I . . . studying*. Other examples are:

I know *where* he hid the presents.
I will not come *unless* you invite me.

A list of subordinating conjunctions is given in Figure 6.46.

   A finite clause C_1 subordinate to another finite clause C_2 is said to be dependent on C_2. Alternatively, it is said that the rank of C_1 is less than

according as, admitting that, after, although, as, as if, as far as, as long as, as soon as, as though, assuming that, because, before, but that, considering that, except that, fewer than, for all that, given that, granted that, granting that, how, however, if, immediately that, in case, in that, in order that, inasmuch as, insofar as, less than, more than, no matter how, now that, once, presuming that, provided that, providing that, rather than, save that, seeing that, since, so as, so far as, so long as, sooner than, so that, such that, supposing that, than, that, though, till, unless, until, when, whenever, whenso, whensoever, where, whereas, whereby, wherever, whereso, wheresoever, whereupon, whether, while, whilst

Figure 6.46 A list of subordinating conjunctions. Such conjunctions are usually used to broach finite adverb clauses. Being a preposition, the word *like* is not listed above. Nonetheless, *like* is colloquially used as a subordinating conjunction. See legend of Figure 6.45. In some grammar books, one-word subordinating conjunctions are called simple subordinating conjunctions; the rest are compound subordinating conjunctions. Compound subordinating conjunctions ending with *that* may sometimes be used without the *that* as in: *Supposing (that)* it is true, what can we do!

the rank of C_2. A finite clause not dependent on any other clause is called an independent clause. In several grammar books, an independent clause is also called a main clause or a principal clause. It should have been apparent from the discussion since section 6.2 that any sentence contains at least one independent clause.

Co-ordinating conjunctions are *and*, *but* and *or*. They are employed to connect words of the same formation and grammatical class, for example, adjectives to adjectives, noun phrases to noun phrases, non-finite adverb clauses to non-finite adverb clauses, finite adjective clauses to finite adjective clauses, and independent clauses to independent clauses. Moreover, when connecting finite clauses, co-ordinating conjunctions connect clauses of the same rank. Examples:

Archie and *I* play football. (connects noun phrases)
I will *eat* or *sleep*. (verbs)
He is *kind* and *generous*. (adjectives)
He drove *quickly* but *steadily*. (adverbs)
She walked *through the fields* and *through the forests*.
(adverbized prepositional phrases)
On seeing him and *talking to him*, remind him of the money.
(non-finite adverb clauses)
When you see him and *talk to him*, remind him of the money.
(finite adverb clauses of the same rank, both clauses
being dependent on *remind . . . money*)

The man *who came yesterday* and *called today* is a snob.
    (finite adjective clauses of the same rank)
I know *who is coming to dinner* and *who is not (coming)*.
    (finite noun clauses of same rank)
I went to see him, but *I could not find him.*
    (independent clauses)

Three or more items are connected by a single *and* or *or,* which occurs between the last two items:

    I awakened, shaved, bathed *and* ate.
    You can sit here, move to the next room, *or* go home.

Correlative conjunctions are pairs of conjunctions that behave together like co-ordinating conjunctions:

    As it is with Pa, *so* it is with Ma.
    He *neither* works *nor* studies.

Correlative conjunctions help give emphasis to what can often be said by employing co-ordinating conjunctions. Compare the above two examples with the sentences below:

    It is the same with Pa *and* Ma.
    He does not work *or* study.

Here are some more examples with correlative conjunctions:

    The more (they are), *the* merrier (they are).
    Both Archie *and* I play football.
    Either you will go, *or* I will (go).

A list of correlative conjunctions is given in Figure 6.47.

although ... nevertheless	although ... yet	as ... yet
as ... so	both ... and	either ... or
fewer ... than	if ... then	less ... than
more ... than	neither ... nor	no sooner ... than
not only ... but (also)	so ... as	so ... that
such ... as	such ... that	the ... the
though ... nevertheless	though ... yet	whether ... or

Figure 6.47 A list of correlative conjunctions.

accordingly	afterward	also
as a result	besides	consequently
earlier	for example	for instance
furthermore	hence	however
in addition	in the meantime	indeed
instead	later	meanwhile
moreover	nevertheless	nonetheless
on the contrary	otherwise	so
still	then	therefore
thus	to illustrate	yet

Figure 6.48   A list of conjunctive adverbs.

Some words can be used as conjunctions or prepositions. Do not confuse them:

My table is fine, *but* my chair is broken. (conjunction)
I have everything *but* a chair. (preposition)

As he was not home, I could not meet him. (conjunction)
He was elected *as* our chairman. (preposition)

She has stopped visiting me *since* she failed. (conjunction)
She has stopped visiting me *since* her failure. (preposition)

Apart from conjunctions, a few adverbs can also be employed to connect finite clauses. These adverbs are called conjunctive adverbs. A list of conjunctive adverbs is given in Figure 6.48.

Consider the sentence:

Mother sent me to the store, and I went.

The above sentence can be rewritten with the conjunctive adverb *therefore*, as shown below:

Mother sent me to the store; *therefore* I went.
    . . .   ; I *therefore* went.
    . . .   ; I went *therefore*.
Mother sent me to the store, and *therefore* I went.

. . .   , and I *therefore* went.

. . .   , and I went *therefore*.

Conjunctive adverbs help provide a smooth transition from one finite clause to the next. Such adverbs can usually be moved around the clause in which they occur. In the examples above, *therefore* has been so moved. Moreover, as the examples show, the finite clause containing a conjunctive adverb is preceded by either a semicolon or a co-ordinating conjunction. In practice, however, the co-ordinating conjunction before the conjunctive adverbs *so* and *yet* is often elided.

> Mother sent me to the store, (and) so I went.
> He was angry, (and) yet he appeared calm.

Because this practice is widely prevalent, some grammar books prefer to call *so* and *yet* not conjunctive adverbs, but co-ordinating conjunctions. Conjunctive adverbs are called conjuncts when they provide a transition from one sentence to the next:

> Mother sent me to the store. *Therefore* I went.
>
> . . .   . I *therefore* went.
>
> . . .   . I went *therefore*.

6.10 DETERMINERS

Determiners are words that call attention to nouns by occurring before the nouns. The determiners used frequently are *a, an* and *the*. The determiner *the* makes the noun it determines (calls attention to) as definite:

> *The* tree fell down.

The above example is about some definite tree. The context in which the sentence would appear would tell us which tree fell down. The determiners *a* and *an*, however, make the noun they determine as indefinite:

> *A* tree fell down.
> *An* ant climbed over my hand.

The is also known as a definite article; *a* and *an* are also known as indefinite articles. *A* is used mostly before words beginning with consonant sounds, *an* before vowel sounds.

The number (singular or plural) of a determiner must be the same as the number of the noun it determines: *a* and *an* are singular; *the* can be both singular or plural: *a* tree, *an* ant, *the* tree, *the* trees, *the* ant. We say that a determiner and the noun it determines must concord on number.

a, a few, all, an, another, another's, any, any other, any other's, anybody else's, anybody's, anyone else's, anyone's, anything else's, anything's, both, each, each one's, each other's, either, either's, enough, every, everybody's, everybody else's, everyone's, everyone else's, everything's, everything else's, few, fewer, fewest, half, her, his, its, least, less, many, more, most, much, my, neither, neither's, no, no one's, no one else's, nobody else's, nobody's, nothing else's, one, one's, other's, our, several, some, somebody, somebody's, someone else's, someone's, something else's, something's, that, the, their, these, this, those, what, whatever, whatso, whatsoever, which, whichever, whichso, whichsoever, who, whoever, whoso, whosoever, whose, whosever, whoseso, whosesoever, your

Figure 6.49   A list of mid-determiners. In addition to the above, the genitives of nouns are also considered to be mid-determiners; for example, *Archie's*, *wolf's*, and *men's* as in *Archie's coat, wolf's lair,* and *men's trousers.*

Determiners belong to the three genera enumerated below.

Mid-determiners include within them the three articles *a, an* and *the*; every mid-determiner, however, is not an article. Consider:

I have lost *the* new keys.
I have lost *my* new keys.

The words *the* and *my* are mid-determiners; *new* is an adjective; *the new keys* and *my new keys* are noun phrases. A list of mid-determiners is given in Figure 6.49. Looking at Figure 6.49, we can say that mid-determiners contain the following categories of words:

1. the articles *a, an, the,* as in *a boy, an egg,* and *the student*;
2. the demonstratives *this, that, these* and *those,* as in *this girl* and *those boys*;
3. genitives of nouns and pronouns, as in *Archie's coat* and *my shoes*;
4. several of the words that denote quantity like *all, half, many* and *some,* as in *some students*; and
5. a few of the words like *what, which* and *whose,* as in *which book.*

It may be surprising to see *one* listed as a mid-determiner in Figure 6.49, but consider:

Come and see me *one* day.

Here *one* is akin to *some,* as in:

Come and see me *some* day.

Do not confuse mid-determiners with pronouns:

all	almost	both
double	especially	even
half	just	merely
nearly	one-third	only
particularly	quite	rather
such	three times	triple
twice	two-sevenths	what

Figure 6.50　A list of predeterminers.

Many helped Archie. (*Many* is a pronoun)
Many people helped Archie. (*Many* is a mid-determiner)

Mid-determiners like *what, which* and *whose* are often used to broach questions:

What mistake have you now made?
Which/Whose book did you borrow?

Nevertheless, these mid-determiners can also be used in sentences that are not questions:

I know *which/whose* book to borrow.

There can be more than one mid-determiner in a noun phrase:

The girl's new coat is torn.

Both *The* and *girl's* are mid-determiners. The mid-determiners should occur before any adjectives (*new*) modifying the headword (*coat*) of the noun phrase (*The girl's new coat*). Now compare the above example with the following:

The new girl's coat is torn.

Here the adjective *new* is not modifying the headword (*coat*) of the noun phrase. Instead, *new* is modifying a noun (*girl's*), which is behaving like a mid-determiner.

Predeterminers usually occur before mid-determiners in a noun phrase:

I have lost all my new keys.

The predeterminer is *all*, the mid-determiner is *my*, and the noun phrase is *all my new keys*. A list of predeterminers is given in Figure 6.50.

Earlier it was said that predeterminers usually occur before mid-determiners, but there are two exceptions: the predeterminers *all* and *both*. They can occur even after the noun phrase:

> *Both/All* the boys went home.
> (occur before the mid-determiner *the*)
> The boys *both/all* went home.
> (occur after the noun phrase *The boys*)

Besides *all* and *both*, predeterminers contain several other words that denote quantity, for instance, *half, double, twice, three times*, and so on, and also fractions such as *one-third* and *two-sevenths*.

Predeterminers like *quite, rather, such* and *what* are used in sentences such as:

> It is *quite/rather/such* a cold day.
> *What* a cold day it is!

Compare, however, the above examples with the following, where the noun phrase headwords are plural:

> These are *quite/rather/such* cold days.
> *What* cold days these are!

Now *quite, rather, such* and *what* are not predeterminers, but they are intensifiers to the adjective *cold*.

Predeterminers like *almost, especially, even, just, merely, nearly, only* and *particularly* can be used to modify other predeterminers:

> I have lost *nearly* all my new keys.

Here predeterminer *nearly* modifies the predeterminer *all*. A noun phrase can contain more than one predeterminer. In the above example, the noun phrase *nearly all my new keys* contains two predeterminers: *nearly* and *all*.

Postdeterminers occur after mid-determiners but before any adjectives that modify the headword of the noun phrase:

> I have lost my other new keys.

The mid-determiner is *my*, the postdeterminer is *other*, and the noun phrase is *my other new keys*. A list of postdeterminers is given in Figure 6.51.

Postdeterminers contain cardinals (like *zero, one, two, three, . . .*),

another	every	few
fewer	first	fourth
further	good deal of	great deal of
great number of	large amount of	large number of
last	less	little
lot of	many	next
one	other	same
second	several	single
small amount of	such	third
three	two	zero

Figure 6.51 A list of postdeterminers.

general ordinals (like *another, further, last, other* ...), and numeric ordinals (like *first, second, third*, ...):

The last two days have been awful.

The above example shows that a noun phrase can contain more than one postdeterminer: the noun phrase *The last two days* contains postdeterminers *last* and *two*.

Postdeterminers also contain several words or groups of words to denote quantity, such as *few, many, little, lot of* and *great deal of*:

Archie helped his *many* friends.
She owes a *lot of* money.

It should be evident from the above discussion that a word can belong to more than one genus of determiners. Consider:

This is only *half* the solution. (predeterminer)
I do not want *half* solutions. (mid-determiner)

On the one hand, a noun phrase may have no determiners:

Tigers are ferocious.
I went *home*.

On the other hand, a noun phrase may have determiners from all the three genera:

a few	a little	all
any	both	double
each	either	enough
every	few	fewer
fewest	half	least
less	little	many
more	most	much
neither	no	one
one-third	several	some
three times	twice	two-sevenths

Figure 6.52 A list of determiners that are used as quantifiers. Phrasal quantifiers [that is, those containing the preposition *of* as in *lot of*] have not been listed above. See them in Figure 6.51. Note that several words in the list above are also in the list of Figure 6.53.

I lost *all my other* new keys.

In some grammar books, determiners are considered to be kinds of adjectives. For developing an ELP, however, it may be better to keep the determiners separate from the adjectives. It may then be easier to incorporate checks to ensure that determiners precede any adjectives modifying the headword of a noun phrase.

6.11   A CODA TO GRAMMAR

6.11.1   Quantifiers

Quantifiers are words that denote quantity. Do not confuse the quantifiers of English with the quantifiers of predicate logic, about which you read in section 3.2.2.

You must have noticed from section 6.10 that all the three genera of determiners contain quantifiers. Note that the quantifiers are not a distinct grammatical class; they are either determiners or pronouns. We shall discuss them separately.

We shall first discuss the quantifiers that are determiners. A list of such quantifiers is given in Figure 6.52.

To illustrate, consider from Figure 6.52, the quantifiers *all* and *no*:

All my friends were at the party. (predeterminer)
He has *no* friends. (mid-determiner)

These quantifiers can be modified:

Nearly all my friends were at the party.
He has *almost no* friends.

In the ELP lexicon, we would need to specify which quantifiers are incompatible with one another. Compatible quantifiers taken together make sense: *half several boys* does not make sense, whereas *twice every month* makes sense. The ELP would not permit incompatible quantifiers to be in the same noun phrase.

A few of the quantifiers that are postdeterminers also contain the preposition *of* (examples of which are given in Figure 6.51), as in the following expressions: a *lot of* friends, a *large amount of* money, and a *great deal of* nonsense.

Quantifiers containing *of* are called phrasal quantifiers. Phrasal quantifiers have not been listed in Figure 6.52; you can get an idea about them by seeing Figure 6.51, instead. It may perhaps be obvious, but all the same we emphasize that in noun phrases, such as the above examples, the headword is the noun occurring after the phrasal quantifier.

A lot of *friends were* at the party.
(plural verb *were* concords with plural headword *friends*)
A lot of *effort has* been put into it.
(singular verb *has* concords with singular headword *effort*)

You may, of course, think of *a lot* as a noun phrase embedded in another noun phrase, say, *a lot of friends*. These phrasal quantifiers can be modified:

Quite a lot of friends were at the party.

Moreover, phrasal quantifiers can be used to treat mass nouns (defined in section 6.3.4) as if they were count nouns. For examples, *a good piece of* news, *one bucket of* water, and *two cups of* milk.

We next discuss quantifiers that are pronouns. A list of such quantifiers is given in Figure 6.53. To illustrate, consider from Figure 6.53, the quantifiers *all* and *everyone*:

All were at the party.
Everyone is invited.

all, any, anybody, anyone, anything, both, each, either, enough, everybody, everyone, everything, few, fewer, fewest, half, least, less, little, many, more, most, much, neither, no one, one, several, some

Figure 6.53   A list of pronouns that are used as quantifiers. Note that several words in the list above are also in the list of Figure 6.52.

These quantifiers can be modified:

Nearly all were at the party.
Almost everyone is invited.

Quantifiers that are pronouns can take on the preposition *of* to be used as phrasal quantifiers. Note, however, that when a pronoun is part of a phrasal quantifier, the pronoun is the headword of the noun phrase:

All of my friends *were* at the party.
    (plural verb *were* concords with *All*)
Everyone of the boys *is* invited.
    (singular verb *is* concords with *Everyone*)

These phrasal quantifiers can be modified:

Almost all of my friends were at the party.
Nearly everyone of the boys is invited.

Finite adjective clauses (see section 6.7.5) can be broached by such phrasal quantifiers:

We put out the food, *little of which was eaten.*
He has two daughters, *one of whom is a musician.*

6.11.2   Closed and open classes

By now, you have read about the different grammatical classes (or parts of speech). Interjections, pronouns, prepositions, conjunctions and determiners are called closed classes. A new word is rarely added to these classes. If a new word is ever added, it is mostly to interjections.

Nouns, verbs, adjectives and adverbs are called open classes. New words are continually being added to these classes. The new words are either coined (for example, minicomputer), or they are taken from other languages (for example, *kowtow* from Chinese, *dandelion* from French, and *guru* from Sanskrit). If we consider auxiliaries to be a subclass of verbs (as several grammar books do), then auxiliaries are said to be a closed subclass.

6.11.3 Structures of finite clauses

The structure of a finite clause depends on the genus of the finite verb, or finite verb phrase, contained in the clause. In this section, we shall learn about a few details of finite clauses. We were unable to discuss these details in section 6.5.4 because by then we had not learnt enough grammar to comprehend them. We give below the five basic structures of finite clauses in active voice.

1. When a finite clause contains a linking verb, then the verb is followed by a subject complement (predicate nominative or predicate adjective) or an adverbial (of time or place). Sometimes we have the option of inserting the expression *to be* between the verb and the subject complement. The predicate nominative as a subject complement is a noun phrase or finite noun clause:

   > He seemed (to be) *a successful accountant*.
   > (noun phrase as subject complement)
   > This is *what we should do*.
   > (finite noun clause as subject complement)
   > He seemed (to be) *impatient*.
   > (adjective as subject complement)

   In the following examples, an adverbial occurs after the verb:

   > He is *outside*. (place adverbial)
   > The books are *on the couch*. (place adverbial)
   > She was *where I saw her last*. (place adverbial)
   > The concert will be *in July*. (time adverbial)

2. When a finite clause contains an intransitive verb, then the verb is followed by nothing, a prepositional phrase, or a non-finite clause constructed from an infinitive or a present participle.

   > He jumped. (the verb is followed by nothing)
   > They yelled *at her*. (the verb is followed by a prepositional phrase)
   > He lives *to eat*. (non-finite clause from infinitive)
   > She came *screaming*. (non-finite clause from present participle)

3. When a finite clause contains a unitransitive verb, then the direct object of the verb is a nounal, that is, a noun phrase, a finite noun clause, or a non-finite noun clause. When the non-finite noun clause is constructed from an infinitive, then sometimes the word *to* is elided:

   > She typed *the letter*. (noun phrase)
   > I forgot *what you wanted*. (finite noun clause)

I understand *(that) you are offended.* (finite noun clause)
We have stopped *seeing him.* (non-finite noun clause)
I promise *to go home.* (non-finite noun clause)
I helped *(to) clean the floor.* (non-finite noun clause)

The direct object can be followed by a non-finite clause. When the non-finite clause is constructed from an infinitive, then sometimes the word *to* is elided.

I saw him *running the marathon.*
I had my room *redone.*
    (non-finite clause constructed from a past participle)
He allowed me *to borrow his pen.*
I helped her *(to) clean the floor.*

4. When a finite clause contains a cotransitive verb, then the direct object is a nounal, and the object complement (which modifies or identifies the direct object) is an adjectival or a nounal. Sometimes we insert the expression *to be* or *as* between the direct object and the object complement:

We elected him (to be/as) *our leader.* (noun phrase)
The court found him (to be) *innocent.* (adjective)
They chose to distribute soup as *their contribution.*
    (noun phrase)
Regular scrubbing kept whatever he owned *sparkling clean.*
    (adjective phrase)
We painted the wall *green.* (adjective)

5. When a finite clause contains a bitransitive verb, then the indirect and the direct objects are both nounals:

She gave him the book.
She told me that she was hungry.
I asked her whether she was hungry.

For each of the above five finite clause structures, we can optionally insert adverbials at different positions within a clause (see also sections 6.8.2 to 6.8.4):

This is what we should (definitely) do.
He seemed (exceedingly) impatient.
He is (certainly) outside.
He jumped (on the trampoline).
She (quickly) typed the letter.
We elected him our leader (immediately).
She gave him the book (without any argument).

6.11.4 The genus of a sentence

The genus of a sentence depends on the number of independent clauses (see section 6.9) it contains, and whether any finite clauses are dependent on these independent clauses. The presence or absence of phrases and non-finite clauses does not affect the genus of a sentence. The four genera of sentences are enumerated below.

1. A simple sentence contains a single independent clause, that is to say, a simple sentence contains no other finite clauses. A simple sentence may have a compound subject or a compound predicate or both:

   > Archie ran ahead and caught up with Mr Merriwether.
   > Anita and Gilda went to the park.
   > I lost my suitcase on the bus.
   > Who is coming to dinner?

2. A compound sentence contrains two or more independent clauses connected by co-ordinating conjunctions (*and*, *but*, *or*) or by semicolons. In other words, a compound sentence does not contain any finite clauses that are dependent. If more than two independent clauses are to be connected by *and* or *or*, then the conjunction is required only between the last two clauses. Examples:

   > I arrived, but he left.
   > I go, or he goes.
   > The rain began, and I got wet.
   > The vase was broken, the chair was overturned, and the floor
   >   was littered with broken glass.
   > The lightening struck; the house burned down.
   > Politicians may come, and politicians may go, but bureaucrats
   >   go on forever.

3. A complex sentence contains one independent clause and at least one finite clause that is dependent on it:

   > Boys who helped with the concert were treated to dinner.
   > I will not come unless you invite me.
   > What I do is none of your business!
   > When he heard the news, I know what he did.

4. A compound complex sentence contains two or more independent clauses such that there is at least one independent clause having at least one finite clause dependent on it:

I know what you want, but I cannot help you.
Although we left early, we were delayed in the traffic;
  Mr Sharma was waiting for us.
When Pa came home, Ma began to sing, and we all joined
in.

A sentence may contain any number of finite clauses. Nonetheless, you will often find that a sentence containing more than three finite clauses is difficult to understand.

In this chapter, you have read about English grammar. In the next chapter, you will read how English grammar can be adapted for embodying into an ELP.

6.12   EXERCISES

1. Write a program to implement an ELP to query the database of Figure 6.2. Suppose the query is:

   Who teaches Programming Languages?

   The system uses template matching to respond:

   Beefly.
   Think of the different ways the queries may be posed and incorporate these into the ELP. Here are some typical queries that may be posed:

   What courses does Sharma teach?
   What is the course number of Data Structures?
   What is the course name of COMP351?
   How many courses does Beefly teach?

2. Given the following sentences:

   He called his wife dear because of her expensive habits.
   Friends we choose; relatives we do not.
   Rights without responsibilities for all leads to no rights at all.
   It was a government of merchants, by the politicians, and for
     their mutual profit.
   Capitalism flourishes best under socialism.
   Right of centre is good economics; left of centre is good
     politics.
   He was rich enough to live very happily in poverty.
   A journalist's pen is mightier than a bureaucrat's.
   It was so scary as to make a bald man grow hair.

I ask not when the world began; I ask not when it will end; all
I ask is to live in it; until it and I are both around.
It is human wrongs that trample human rights.

Identify:

1. the grammatical class (part of speech) of every word in each of
   the above sentences;
2. all noun, verb, prepositional, adjective and adverb phrases; and
3. all finite and non-finite noun, adjective and adverb clauses.

3. Identify the grammatical class of every word in the following
   sentence:

   The tilpy habads had rupuxly dronken the blaktox to a rekup.

   The sentence contains many words that do not make sense. Did
   you need to know their meaning to identify their grammatical
   class? What helped you most to identify their grammatical classes?
   Was it words from the closed classes or from the open classes? Do
   the nonsensical words belong to the closed classes or the open
   classes? Does the above sentence have the same structure as the
   following sentence? The eager scouts had quickly taken the injured
   to a hospital.

6.13 SUGGESTIONS FOR FURTHER READING

Hendrix, Sacerdoti, Segalowicz and Slocum (1978) described an
application of template fitting for an English interface. Blumenthal
(1981) presented a programmed course in English grammar. Winograd
(1983) discussed the syntactic structure of English. Quirk, Greenbaum,
Leech and Svartvik (1985) treated English grammar comprehensively.
Quirk and Greenbaum (1973) wrote a concise version of English
grammar. Leech and Svartvik (1975) explained nuances of English.
Courtney (1983) and Long (1979) gave meanings of English verb–
particle composites and idioms, respectively.

1. Blumenthal, J. C. (1981) *English 3200* (3rd edition), Harcourt, Brace
   Jovanovich Inc., New York.
2. Courtney, R. (1983) *Longman Dictionary of Phrasal Verbs*, Longman
   Group Limited, London.
3. Hendrix, G. G., Sacerdoti, E. D., Segalowicz, D. and Slocum, J.
   (1978). Developing a natural language interface to complex data,
   ACM Transactions on Database Systems, **3**[2], 105–47.
4. Leech, G. and Svartvik, J. (1975) *A Communicative Grammar of
   English*, Longman Group Limited, London.

5. Long, T. H. (editorial director) (1979). Longman Dictionary of English Idioms, Longman Group Limited, London.
6. Quirk, R. and Greenbaum, S. (1973) *A Concise Grammar of Contemporary English*, Seminar Press, New York.
7. Quirk, R., Greenbaum, S., Leech, G. and Svartvik, J. (1985) *A Comprehensive Grammar of the English Language*, Longman Group Limited, London.
8. Winograd, T. (1983) *Language as a Cognitive Process: Syntax*, Addison-Wesley, Reading, Massachusetts.

7
Natural language processing: syntax and semantics

7.1 INTRODUCTION

Before you learn how English grammar can be adapted for embodying into an ELP, you should become conversant with the material discussed in Chapter 6. As mentioned in that chapter, the ELP vocabulary is stored in a lexicon. Every word in the lexicon is associated with the grammatical classes in which the word is permitted to be used. Suppose, for instance, the ELP permits the word *man* to be used both as a noun and as a verb, as in:

> I saw that *man* yesterday. (noun)
> These two fellows *man* our production lines. (verb)

Then *man* will need to be stored both as a noun and as a verb. The grammatical class of a word is an element of a set of features associated with the word in the lexicon. The features delineate the word. To illustrate, the features for *man* as a noun could delineate that the word is a common noun, singular, masculine and human. Figure 7.1 shows the typical contents of a lexicon.

7.1.1 Parsing

To parse a word group (phrase, clause or sentence), we analyse the word group syntactically to discover (a) the grammatical class of each word in the word group, and (b) how the word relates to the other words in the word group. By parsing, we can formally decide whether the word group is grammatical. Consider the word group *the old painting*. We know that *the* is a determiner, *old* is an adjective, and *painting* is a noun. Together, the three words constitute a noun phrase. This parsing of the noun phrase can be illustrated by a graph called a

Word	Features of the Word	
	Grammatical Class	Supplementary Information
a	determiner	singular, indefinite, middeterminer, ...
...	...	...
Archie	noun	third person, singular, animate, count, human, living, masculine, proper, ...
...	...	...
broken	verb	BREAK-en, intransitive and unitransitive
...	...	...
has	...	HAVE-s, perfective aspect auxiliary, ...
...	...	...
massive	adjective	prenominal, absolute grade, ...
...	...	...
stone	noun	third person, singular, not animate, count, not human, not living neuter, common, ...
...	...	...
the	determiner	singular and plural, definite, middeterminer, ...
...	...	...
window	noun	third person, singular, not animate, not human, not living, neuter, common, ...
...	...	...
with	preposition	...
...	...	...

Figure 7.1 Typical contents of a lexicon. Depending on the needs of the ELP, you may store more or fewer features for a word. For example, the noun *Archie* has been delineated as both animate and living. You may delete living provided you record as in Figure 6.7, for example, that every animate noun is a living noun.

parse tree, also known in the literature as a phrase marker, as illustrated in Figure 7.2.

Just as we built a parse tree for a noun phrase, we can build a parse tree for a sentence. Figure 7.3 gives a parse tree for the sentence:

The visitor saw the old painting in the den.

which you had earlier seen in section 6.1.3. But this sentence also has another parse tree, given in Figure 7.4. Comparing the legends below Figures 7.3 and 7.4, we can see that the sentence above is ambiguous. A sentence having more than one parse tree can be ambiguous. It was

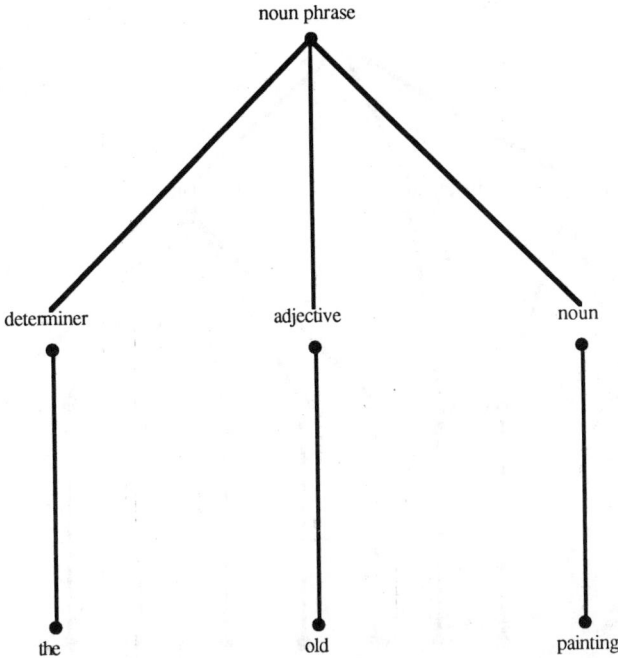

Figure 7.2   The parse tree for the noun phrase *the old painting*.

mentioned in section 6.1 that different surface structures can map into the same deep structure. For ambiguous sentences, different deep structures are mapped into the same surface structure. An ELP will, in essence, need to parse a given sentence and to elicit the meaning of the sentence.

A word in a sentence can sometimes be allotted to a grammatical class only after examining the other words in the sentence. Take, for instance, the sentence:

The jeep trails across the meadow.

In parsing this sentence, we say that *jeep* is a noun and *trails* is a verb. Now suppose we append a few words to the sentence:

The jeep trails across the meadow have been obliterated.

Allotting grammatical classes to the words from left to right, we may initially declare *jeep* to be a noun, and *trails* a verb, but on reaching the end of the sentence, we shall have to backtrack, and then declare *jeep* to be an adjective, and *trails* a noun. In designing a parser, that is, the parsing procedure, for an ELP, we may need to incorporate such backtracking capability into the parser.

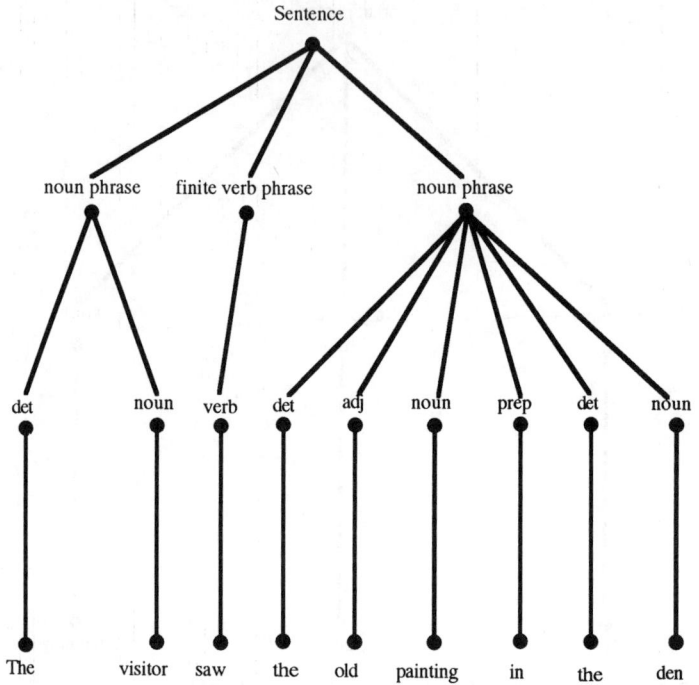

Figure 7.3   A parse tree for the sentence *The visitor saw the old painting in the den*. The prepositional phrase *in the den* is embedded in the noun phrase *the old . . . den*. Hence the prepositional phrase is an adjectival modifying *painting*. Paraphrased, the sentence could be *The visitor saw the old painting that is in the den*.

Apart from allotting the words of a sentence to grammatical classes, a parser must also check whether the words abide by their context. We know from Chapter 6 that the form of a word can depend on other words in the sentence. For example, a determiner and the noun determined must concord on number (as in *a boy* but not in *a boys*); the choice of a determiner will also depend on whether the noun determined is a count noun or a mass noun (*many boys* but *much water*); and furthermore, a finite verb phrase and its subject must concord on person and number. Because the words in a sentence must abide by their context, English is said to be a context-sensitive language.

7.1.2   Synthetic grammars

We shall call synthetic grammar the grammar that we embody into an ELP. To simplify the design of an ELP, the synthetic grammar may

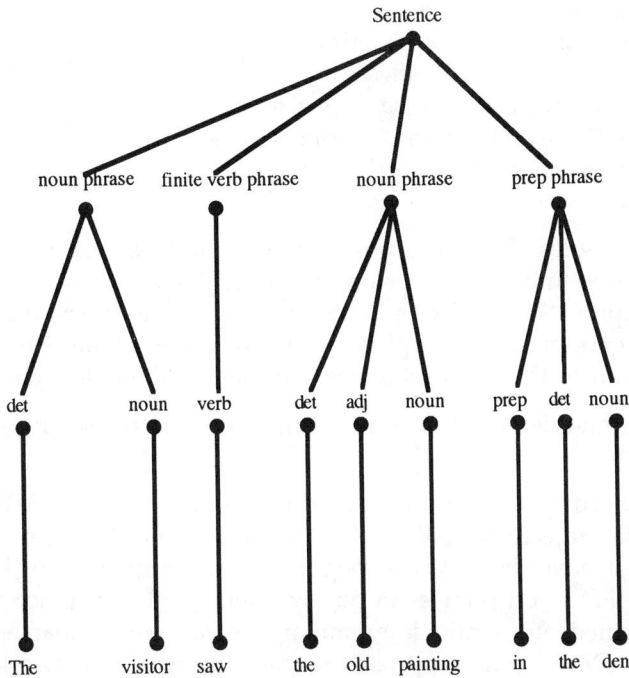

Figure 7.4   A parse tree different from that of Figure 7.3 for the sentence *The visitor saw the old painting in the den*. The prepositional phrase *in the den* is an adverbial of place. Paraphrased the sentence could be *In the den, the visitor saw the old painting*.

contain only some of the prescripts of English grammar. Hence the variations allowed in the structures of phrases, clauses and sentences under a synthetic grammar may be fewer than those under full English grammar. For instance, to prevent the ambiguity caused by sentences that can be parsed in more than one way, a synthetic grammar may not permit such sentence structures. Any grammar that can parse a sentence in more than one way is said to be an ambiguous grammar.

Let us consider a noun phrase. Under English grammar, a noun phrase is typically based on the following formula:

(determiners) (prenominal adjectivals) headword (postnominal adjectivals),

where the headword is a noun or a pronoun. Besides the noun phrases that you saw in Chapter 6, here are a few more examples of noun phrases, to refresh your memory.

> *Archie* owns *a very sharp iron knife.*
> *The fat boy standing on the dais* is *a braggart.*
> *Anita* had *some fresh mangoes to eat.*
> *The boy expelled from school* began to cry.
> *Our school* expels *anyone who cheats.*
> *A girl from our class* won *the contest.*
> *He* was wearing *a worn-out shirt.*

As the examples show, the postnominal adjectivals are usually non-finite clauses, finite clauses or prepositional phrases.

To simplify the syntax of noun phrases, let us posit that in our synthetic grammar, a noun phrase is restricted to contain either only a proper noun or the word sequence specified by the following formula:

> (one mid-determiner) (any number of adjectives) one common noun.

In other words, when the headword is a common noun, we can have prenominal adjectives, but no postnominal adjectivals. Accordingly, *Archie, boys, iron, the fat boy, a sharp iron knife, sharp knife, knife* and *the boy* exemplify noun phrases in our synthetic grammar. Once we have fully designed our synthetic grammar, we can build a parser for the grammar. One popular approach to parsing employs networks called augmented transition networks.

7.2   AUGMENTED TRANSITION NETWORKS

To reach a preliminary understanding of an augmented transition network (abbreviated as ATN), see in Figure 7.5 an ATN for the noun phrase specified in section 7.1.2 by our synthetic grammar.

In general, an ATN contains a finite set of nodes, which are called states $S_1, S_2, \ldots, S_n$. S_1 is called the initial state. There exists an m ($1 \leq m \leq n$), for which $S_m, \ldots, S_{m+1}, \ldots, S_n$ are called final states. A state S_i may be joined to state S_j by an arc A_{ij} directed from S_i to S_j, where A_{ij} carries a label L_{ij}, which may be parenthesized. L_{ij} typically specifies a class or subclass of words, such as noun, proper noun, adjective, verb, noun phrase, prepositional phrase, relative clause, and {boy, girl, Archie, . . . }. The label may be empty, thus specifying the empty class. Note that it is not necessary for a state S_i to be joined by an arc to every state in the ATN. Integrated into an ATN is a set of registers for storing the words being parsed, together with their features as obtained from the lexicon. This in effect gives an ATN its name: a transition network augmented by registers. The purpose of the registers will be discussed in sections 7.2.2 and 7.2.3.

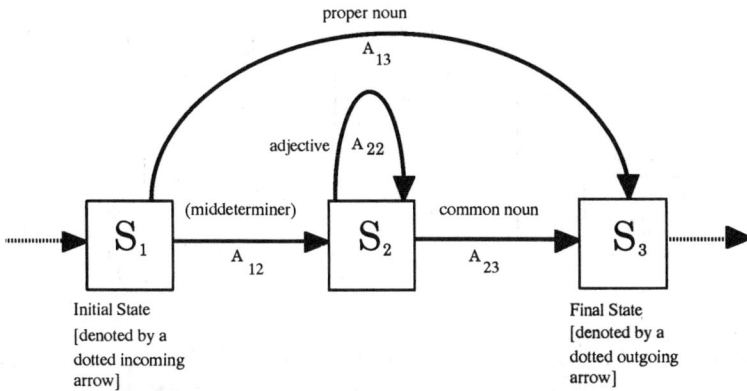

Figure 7.5 An ATN to depict a noun phrase that can contain either a proper noun or the word sequence specified by the following formula:

(one mid-determiner) (any number of adjectives) one common noun

S_1, S_2, and S_3 are states, of which S_1 is called the initial state, and S_3 a final state. The parenthisization of the mid-determiner as the label of arc A_{12} denotes that a mid-determiner is optional. We can view arc A_{12} as denoting two arcs: an arc A_{12}^1 labelled mid-determiner, and an arc A_{12}^2 labelled empty.

Given an input string of words, a parser employs an ATN to report whether the given input string is grammatical according to the ATN. Let the input string W contain the words W_1, W_2, W_3 ..., where W_1 is the leftmost word, and W_{k+1} is to the right to W_k, for $k \geq 1$. To start, the parser is in the initial state S_1.

In essence, the parser examines the words of W from the left and transits over arcs from one state to another. While transiting, the parser may breathe to change the contents of W, by inhaling some words from W or exhaling some words into W. To inhale words from W, the parser deletes them from the left of W and transfers them to the ATN registers. To exhale words into W, the parser deletes words from the ATN registers and transfers them to the left in W.

7.2.1 Transiting through an ATN

The parser can change from one state to another state of the ATN by two kinds of transitions: foretracking and backtracking. Figure 7.6 illustrates the distinction between foretracking and backtracking.

Generalizing the comments in the legend of Figure 7.5, we say that words corresponding to the parenthesized label of an arc are optional.

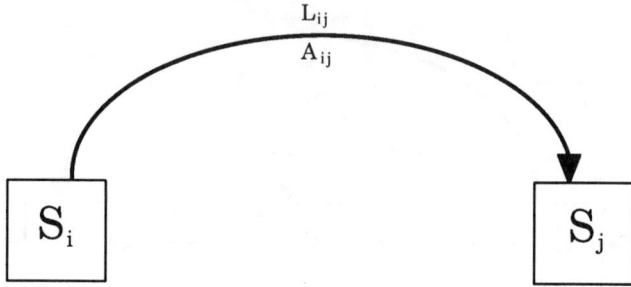

Foretracking: In foretracking, the parser transits over A_{ij} in the direction of the arrow to change state from S_i to S_j. Arc A_{ij} is foretrackable if, and only if, in the input string W, a leftmost substring W' belongs to L_{ij}. If the parser foretracks over A_{ij}, it inhales W'. Note, if the parser foretracks over an arc labeled empty, then the parser holds its breath; that is, it does not inhale W'. In effect, the parser can fortrack over such an arc regardless of the contents of W.

Backtracking: In backtracking, parser transits over A_{ij} in the opposite direction of the arrow to change from state S_j to S_i. The parser can backtrack over A_{ij} only if earlier sometime it had foretracked over A_{ij}. When backtracking over A_{ij}, the parser exhales any words it may have inhaled while earlier foretracking over A_{ij}.

Figure 7.6 Distinguishing foretracking from backtracking. L_{ij} is the label of arc A_{ij}.

From a state S_i to a state S_j, if there accordingly exists an arc A_{ij} labelled with a parenthesized L_{ij}, then A_{ij} denotes two arcs: an arc A_{ij}^1 labelled the unparenthesized L_{ij}, and an arc A_{ij}^2 labelled empty. A parser may then foretrack over one of these arcs, say, A_{ij}^1. In the event that the parser backtracks over A_{ij}^1 to state S_i, it may then foretrack over A_{ij}^2. Often, diagrams of ATNs become visually confusing because of the clutter produced by the numerous arcs. By observing the above convention, we try to reduce the clutter. Moreover, by representing optional words with parenthesized labels, we conform to the convention adopted in Chapter 6 and continued in this chapter, according to which we parenthesize words that may be elided, that is, optional words. Figure 7.7 provides the trace of a parser foretracking through the ATN of Figure 7.5.

The procedure for a parser transiting through an ATN in general can be developed from Figure 7.8. After studying Figure 7.8, see Figure 7.9 for an example of a parser foretracking and backtracking through an ATN.

Step	Contents of W	State of parser	Action taken by the parser		
			Direction and arc transited	How parser breathes	New state of parser
1	sharp knife	S_1	ft A_{12}^2	holds breath	S_2
2	sharp knife	S_2	ft A_{22}	in <u>sharp</u>	S_2
3	knife	S_2	ft A_{23}	in <u>knife</u>	S_3

After step 3, W becomes empty, and the parser is in a final state.
Hence the input string is accepted. Moreover, the words in the input
string abide by their context. So the string is reported to be
grammatical.

Figure 7.7 Trace of the parser as it foretracks through the noun phrase ATN of
Figure 7.5 to process the input string *sharp knife*. Abbreviations used: foretrack
[ft] and inhale [in]. Note that in Step 1 above, the parser holds its breath since
it foretracks over an arc labelled empty. Remember that arc A_{12} of Figure 7.5
denotes two arcs: an arc A_{12}^1 labelled mid-determiner, and an arc A_{12}^2 labelled
empty.

Conditions satisfied when the parser is in a state S_i			Action to be taken by the parser
[1]	[2]	[3]	
Input string W is not empty	Foretrackable arcs are available from S_i.		Employ heuristics to select an arc A_{ij}. Foretrack over A_{ij}. Change to new state S_j.
	No new foretrackable arcs are available from S_i.	$S_i = S_1$	Report input string to be ungrammatical.
		$S_i \neq S_1$	Backtrack chronologically to the nearest state S_k [where $S_k \geq 1$], such that another arc can be selected from S_k for foretracking. If no such state is found, then backtrack to S_1.
Input string W is empty	S_i is not a final state.		
	S_i is a final state.		Accept input string. If the words in the ATN abide by their context, report string to be grammatical; otherwise, ungrammatical.

Figure 7.8 Outline of the action to be taken by the parser when it is in a state
S_i, while transiting through an ATN.

Step	Contents of W	State of parser	Action taken by parser		
			Direction and arc transited	How the parser breathes	New state of parser
1	a sharp iron knife	S_1	ft A^1_{12}	in $\underline{a}$	S_2
2	sharp iron knife	S_2	ft A_{22}	in $\underline{sharp}$	S_2
3	iron knife	S_2	ft A_{23}	in $\underline{iron}$	S_3
4	knife	S_3	bt A_{23}	ex $\underline{iron}$	S_2
5	iron knife	S_2	ft A_{22}	in $\underline{iron}$	S_2
6	knife	S_2	ft A_{23}	in $\underline{knife}$	S_3

W becomes empty; the parser is in a final state; the input string is accepted. The parser next checks whether words in the input string abide by their context: the middeterminer $\underline{a}$ concords with the noun phrase headword $\underline{knife}$. So the input string is reported to be grammatical.

Figure 7.9 Trace of a parser as it transits across the noun phrase ATN of Figure 7.5 to process the input string *a sharp iron knife*. Abbreviations used: backtrack [bt], exhale [ex], foretrack [ft], inhale [in]. Note that in Step 3, the parser could have foretracked over A_{22} or A_{23}. It employed the heuristic that *iron* is used more often as a noun than as an adjective, this information being obtained from the lexicon, so the parser selected A_{23}, then in Step 4 backtracked over A_{23}, and then in Step 5 selected A_{22}.

You may have noticed, from Figures 7.8 and 7.9, that the backtracking done by a parser in an ATN is chronological backtracking, akin to the chronological backtracking discussed in sections 5.2.3 and 5.3.3.

According to our above description, the input string contains words, and the labels of arcs specify word classes. In general, the input string will contain not only words, but also punctuation marks. Therefore,

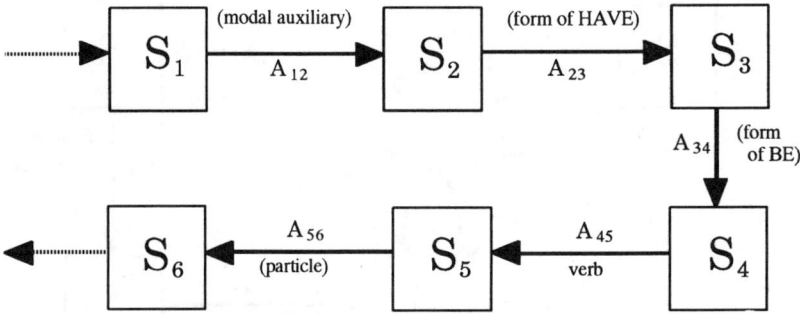

Figure 7.10 An ATN for an indicative mood, active voice finite verb phrase that may contain one particle at the most. After an input string of words is accepted, the parser checks whether the words abide by their context, according to the formula [see section 6.5.5]:

$$(\text{MODAL}|b) \ (\text{HAVE}|en) \ (\text{BE}|ing) \ \text{VERB} \ (\text{PARTICLE})$$

If so, the string is reported to be grammatical. Thus *has broken, will have been breaking, will break up,* and *shall break* exemplify input strings that will be reported to be grammatical as finite verb phrases.

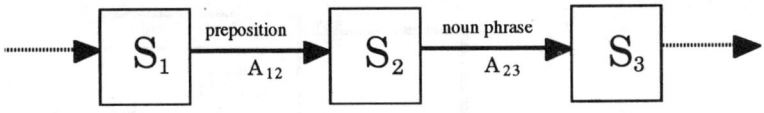

Figure 7.11 An ATN for a prepositional phrase. To foretrack over arc A_{23}, the parser will invoke the noun phrase ATN of Figure 7.5. The parser will then transit through the noun phrase ATN. If a noun phrase is found, the parser will return to the ATN above, and it will foretrack over A_{23}. Hence *with a massive stone* exemplifies an input string that will be reported to be grammatical as a prepositional phrase.

the label of an arc can also specify any punctuation marks that are needed. We, however, shall not be considering punctuation marks to keep our discussion simple.

7.2.2 Invoking one ATN from another ATN

To extend our synthetic grammar, we give ATNs for a finite verb phrase, a prepostional phrase, and a sentence in Figures 7.10–7.12. As Figures 7.11 and 7.12 show, a parser transiting through an ATN may invoke another ATN. It is like one procedure invoking another.

Note that there is a difference between a string of words being

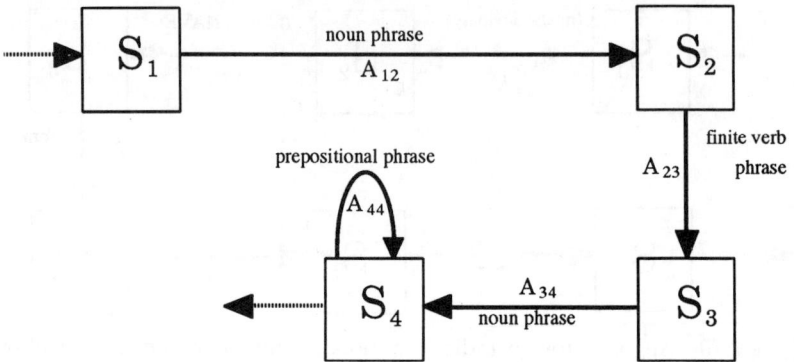

Figure 7.12 An ATN for a sentence containing a unitransitive finite verb phrase. To transit through the above ATN, the parser will invoke the noun phrase ATN of Figure 7.5, the finite verb phrase ATN of Figure 7.10, and the prepositional phrase ATN of Figure 7.11. After an input string of words is accepted, the parser checks whether the words abide by their context; for instance, whether the finite verb phrase and its subject concord on person and number. Hence the input string *Archie has broken the window with a massive stone* will be reported to be grammatical as a sentence. For simplicity, we have not shown the end-of-sentence punctuation mark (usually a full stop/period) in the ATN above.

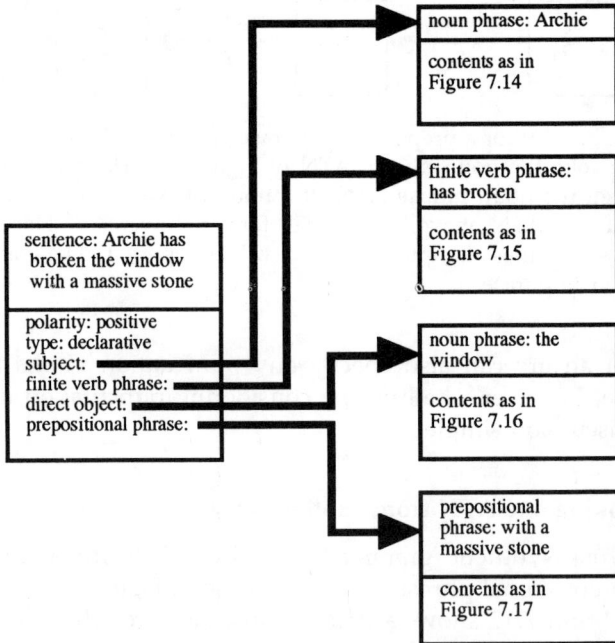

Figure 7.13 The contents of the ATN registers after parsing the sentence *Archie has broken the window with a massive stone* according to the ATN of Figure 7.12.

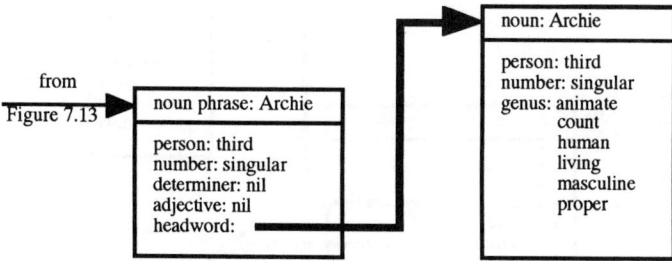

Figure 7.14 The contents of the ATN registers for the noun phrase *Archie* of Figure 7.13.

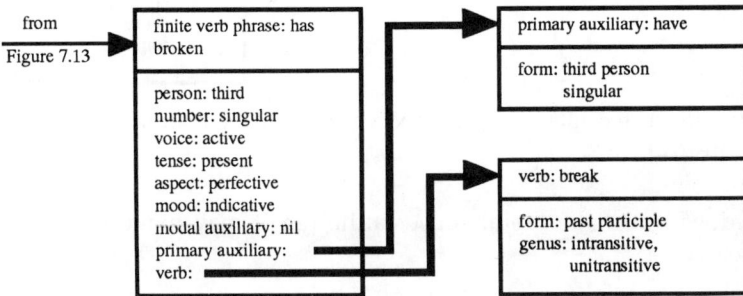

Figure 7.15 The contents of the ATN registers for the finite verb phrase *has broken* of Figure 7.13.

accepted on an ATN, and the string being found grammatical. The string *Archie have broken the window* will be accepted on the ATN of Figure 7.12. Nevertheless, the string is not grammatical because the finite verb phrase *have broken* does not concord on number with the subject *Archie*. That is to say, the words in the string do not abide by their context. Transiting through the ATN ensures that the words are in the appropriate sequence in the string; checking for the words to abide by their context ensures that the words are in the appropriate form.

As is apparent from our discussion above, an accepted string is stored in the ATN registers. Together with each word we store its features as obtained from the lexicon. These features can be used to check whether the words abide by their context. Moreover, as you will read in section 7.3, these features can also be used to elicit the meaning of a sentence. You can do some preliminary checking on meaning right here: to illustrate, incompatible adjectives (see section 6.7) should not modify the same noun in a noun phrase; a noun phrase like *a young old*

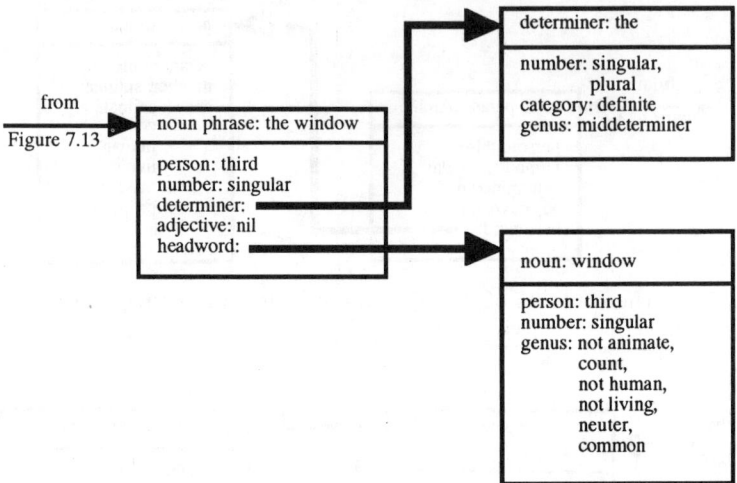

Figure 7.16 The contents of the ATN registers for the noun phrase *the window* of Figure 7.13.

man does not make literal sense, although it may make metaphorical sense.

7.2.3 Contents of ATN registers

For an example of the contents of the ATN registers after parsing a sentence, see Figure 7.13. The figure, in turn, cites Figures 7.14–7.17. You may consider each register in Figures 7.13–7.17 to be a node in a parse tree.

The contents of the ATN registers can be manipulated to transform sentences, which you will read about in Chapter 8, but first we discuss the roles of noun phrases, which can be employed to elicit the meaning from a sentence.

7.3 ELICITING THE MEANING FROM A SENTENCE

Before we discuss eliciting the meaning from a sentence, we need to discuss the trait and annunciation of a sentence. To simplify the discussion, let us for the time being consider only those sentences that contain one finite clause. The discussion can then be extended to sentences containing more than one finite clause. The trait of a sentence comprises the following:

1. type of sentence: declarative, interrogative, imperative or exclamatory;

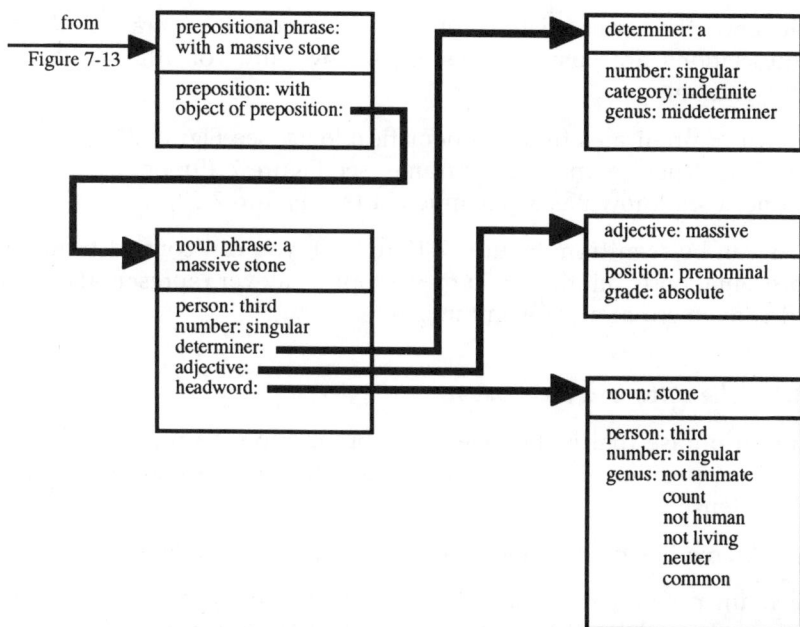

Figure 7.17 The contents of the ATN registers for the prepositional phrase *with a massive stone* of Figure 7.13.

2. polarity: positive or negative;
3. modal auxiliary, if any, used in the finite verb phrase: *can, could, may, might, must, shall, should, will, would* or *nil* (in the event that no modal auxiliary is used);
4. tense: past, present or future;
5. aspect: simple, perfective, progressive or perfective progressive;
6. mood: indicative, imperative or subjunctive; and
7. voice: active or passive.

The annunciation of a sentence comprises the roles of the different noun phrases with respect to the verb in the sentence. Every noun phrase in a sentence is said to have a role:

Archie has broken the window with a massive stone.

We say that the noun phrase *Archie* has the role of the agent (the doer of the action), *the window* has the role of the target (being the direct object of the finite verb phrase, it is the entity affected by the action), and *a massive stone* has the role of the instrument (the entity that is used to do the action).

One way to represent the meaning of a sentence is by displaying the trait and the annunciation of the sentence. The trait and the annunciation are usually displayed by any of the following representations:

1. a set of predicates from mathematical logic (see Figure 7.18);
2. a data structure known as a frame (see Figure 7.19); or
3. a network known as a semantic net (see Figure 7.20).

As can be seen from Figures 7.18 to 7.20, you can convert from one representation to another. You may adopt whatever representation you find convenient at any given time.

7.3.1 The roles and their flags

A noun phrase that is the object of a preposition is said to be flagged by the preposition. Not all noun phrases in a sentence are flagged. In the sentence

Archie has broken the window with a massive stone.

the noun phrases *Archie* and *the window* are unflagged, but *a massive stone* is flagged by the preposition *with*. Whether a noun phrase is flagged, and if so, by which preposition, can often help us discover the role of the noun phrase.

We saw above an example containing three roles: agent, target and instrument. In designing an ELP, we may set up the list of possible roles for the noun phrases in the ELP. On scrutinizing the roles, we may decide upon the prepositions (such as those listed in Figure 6.40) that may flag the noun phrases for these roles. For brevity, we say that we decide upon the prepositions that flag the various roles. We list below some typical roles together with examples to illustrate the prepositions that usually flag such roles.

The **agent** is the animate entity that does the action portrayed by the verb. In the active voice, the agent is unflagged; in the passive voice, the agent is flagged by the preposition *by*:

Archie read the story.
The story was read *by Archie.*

The **coagent** is the animate entity that, in doing the action portrayed by the verb, is secondary to the agent. The coagent is usually flagged by the preposition *with*:

Archie baked a cake *with Anita.*

The **target** is the entity directly affected by the action portrayed in the verb. The entity can be living or non-living. The target is

```
TYPE-OF-SENTENCE(declarative)
POLARITY(positive)
MODAL-AUXILIARY(nil)
TENSE(present)
ASPECT(perfective)
MOOD(indicative)
VOICE(active)
VERB(break)
AGENT(Archie)
TARGET(the window)
INSTRUMENT(a massive stone)
```

Figure 7.18   A set of logical predicates to represent the meaning of the sentence *Archie has broken the window with a massive stone.*

Name of the slot	Value stored in the slot
TYPE-OF-SENTENCE	declarative
POLARITY	positive
MODAL-AUXILIARY	nil
TENSE	present
ASPECT	perfective
MOOD	indicative
VOICE	active
VERB	break
AGENT	Archie
TARGET	the window
INSTRUMENT	a massive stone

Figure 7.19   The above table exemplifies a frame to represent the meaning of the sentence *Archie has broken the window with a massive stone.* A frame is viewed as a data structure containing slots into which values are stored.

unflagged. It most often corresponds to the direct object of the verb in active voice:

Archie hit *the bully.*
Archie watered *the plant.*
Archie gave Anita *a book.*

In the passive voice, the target can be the subject of the sentence:

The bully was hit by Archie.
The plant was watered by Archie.
A book was given Anita by Archie.

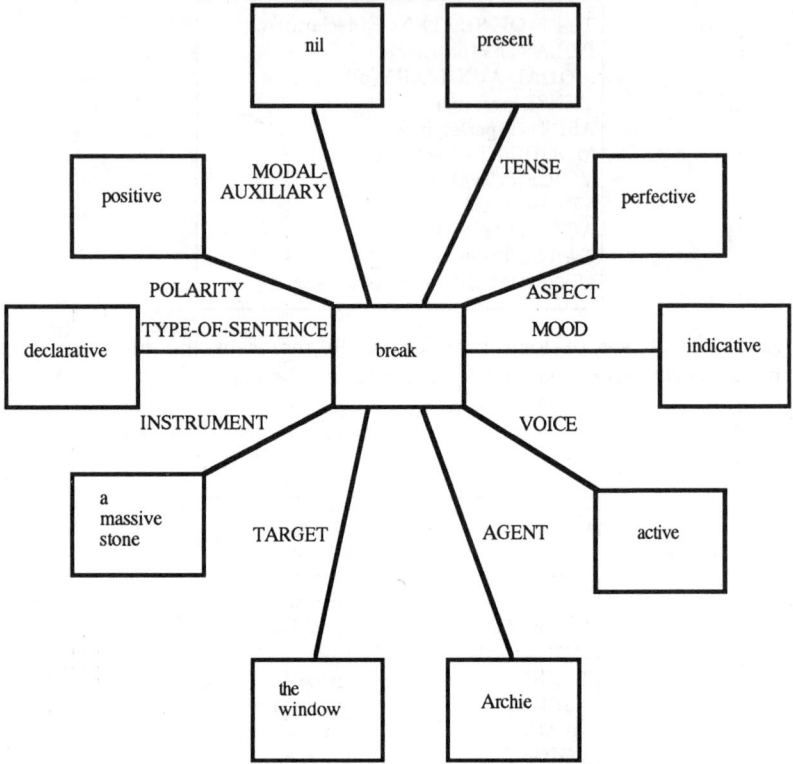

Figure 7.20   A network known as a semantic net to represent the meaning of the sentence *Archie has broken the window with a massive stone.*

For a few verbs, the target can be the subject of an active voice sentence, too:

The window broke.

But we cannot say:

The window cleaned.

The **instrument** is the inanimate entity that is used as a tool to do the action portrayed by the verb. When it is the subject of a sentence, the instrument is unflagged:

A stone broke the window.

When, however, the instrument is not the subject of a sentence, it is usually flagged by the prepositions *by* or *with*:

Anita took the photograph *with a 35 mm camera.*
The photograph was taken *by/with a 35 mm camera.*

The **recipient** is the entity (living or non-living) that benefits from the action portrayed by the verb. The recipient is unflagged when it is the indirect object of the verb in an active voice sentence, or when it is the subject of a passive voice sentence:

I gave *the bicycle* an overhaul. (active voice)
Gilda cooked *Anita* a dinner. (active voice)
Anita was cooked a dinner by Gilda. (passive voice)

Prepositions *for* and *to* can be used to flag the recipient:

He sang *for father.*
I bought a cover *for the chair.*
A cover was bought *for the chair* by me.
Anita threw a ball *to Gilda.*
A ball was thrown *to Gilda* by Anita.

The choice of the preposition depends on the verb: as shown in the above examples, the preposition *for* is used with the verbs *buy* and *sing*, and *to* with the verb *throw*.

The **location** is the place of action portrayed by the verb:

He ran *in the gym.*
She sat *by the wall.*

In the above examples, the location is flagged by the prepositions *in* and *by*. Other prepositions that can flag a location are typically *above, beside, on* and *under*.

The **route** is the path through which the action portrayed by the verb is done. The route is usually flagged by prepositions *over* and *through*:

Anita ran *over the bridge.*
Archie walked *through the puddle.*

The **source** is the place from which something or someone moves. It is flagged mostly by *from*:

He walked *from* school.

The **destination** is the place to which something or someone moves. It is flagged mostly by *to*:

He walked *to* school.

Occasionally, the destination may be unflagged:

He walked *home*.

The **conveyance** is the entity by which something or someone travels. It is usually flagged by the preposition *by*:

I went home *by bus*.

The **ingredient** is the entity that is contained in something else. Prepositions that can flag an ingredient are typically *from, in, of, out of* and *with*:

She built a hut *from straw*.
Anita carved a statue *in stone*.
The jar is full *of water*.
The chair is made *(out) of wood*.
She made a cake *with raisins*.

The **time** is the period when the action portrayed by the verb occurs. The time is usually flagged by the prepositions *after, at, before, for, in, till* and *until*.

She came *after two hours*.
The enemy attacked *at dawn*.
She eats *before noon*.
He sang *for an hour*.
Mozart was born *in the eighteenth century*.
Archie waited *till/until noon*.

The **target identifier** is said to be the role of the noun phrase that constitutes an object complement. The target identifier is unflagged:

They consider him *a cheat*.
We elected Anita *captain*.

The **subject identifier** is said to be the role of the noun phrase that constitutes a subject complement. The subject identifier is unflagged:

He is *a cheat*.
Anita became *the captain*.

The **subject identified** is said to be role of the subject when a noun phrase constitutes the subject complement. The subject identified is unflagged:

He is a cheat.
Anita will be the captain.

The **prop** is said to be the role of the pronoun *it* when it broaches a sentence, usually while mentioning the weather or some state of existence:

Preposition	Specimen sentences containing the preposition	Role of the noun phrase flagged by the preposition
by	The story was read by <u>Archie</u>. I went home by <u>bus</u>. The photograph was taken by <u>a 35 mm camera</u>. She sat by <u>the wall</u>.	agent conveyance instrument location
from	She built a hat from <u>straw</u>. He walked from <u>school</u>.	ingredient source
for	He sang for <u>father</u>. He sang for <u>an hour</u>.	recepient time
in	Anita carved a statue in <u>stone</u>. He ran in <u>the gym</u>.	ingredient location
with	Archie baked a cake with <u>Anita</u>. Archie baked a cake with <u>raisins</u>. The photograph was taken with <u>a 35 mm camera</u>.	coagent ingredient instrument

Figure 7.21 Specimen sentences to show that a preposition can flag more than one role.

> *It* is sunny.
> *It* is noisy here.

As shown in the above examples, the prop is unflagged. Sentences with *it* as a prop cannot be paraphrased to remove the *it*.

We emphasize that the above list of roles is not exhaustive. You may develop your own list of roles depending on the ELP you want to design. You must have noticed from the list of roles above that many a preposition can flag more than one role, as illustrated in Figure 7.21. It may be useful to store in the lexicon the roles a noun is permitted to fill. This can help us discover the role of a noun phrase in a sentence. To illustrate, an animate noun can be an agent, coagent, target or recipient; however, it cannot be an instrument. Consider the animate noun *Anita*:

> *Anita* knit a sweater. (agent)
> Archie baked a cake with *Anita*. (coagent)
> Archie helped *Anita*. (target)
> Archie gave *Anita* a book. (recipient)

The role of a noun phrase may depend on the other words in the sentence:

> *Anita* is reluctant to cheat. (*Anita* is agent)
> *Anita* is easy to cheat. (*Anita* is target)

Although the two sentences have the same structure, the role of *Anita* is different in the two sentences. The role of *Anita* depends on the adjectives *reluctant* and *easy*.

The different roles that the subject of an active voice sentence typically fills are the following:

> Agent: *An old woman* helped me.
> Target: *The window* broke.
> Instrument: *The key* opened the door.

No.	English name of the case	Sanskrit name of the case	Purpose in brief of the case
1.	Nominative	Karta	Subject of a sentence
2.	Accusative	Karma	direct object
3.	Instrument	Karna	tool used for action
4.	Dative	Sampradana	indirect object
5.	Ablative	Apadana	place of departure
6.	Genitive	Sambandha	possession
7.	Locative	Adhikarna	place of action
8.	Vocative	Sambodhan	addressing the listener

Figure 7.22   Whereas English has three cases [nominative, accusative, and genitive], Sanskrit has eight, as shown above. The inflection [ending] of a Sanskrit noun depends on its case in the sentence, except that the vocative inflection is identical to the nominative inflection. The words in a Sanskrit sentence may be in any order, depending on the style of the writer or speaker. Latin has six of the above cases: nominativus, accusativus, dativus, ablativus, genitivus, and vocativus. The instrument and locative cases of Sanskrit are collapsed into the ablativus case of Latin. It is an open question whether Sanskrit or Latin would be more suitable than, say, English or French for a natural language processor.

Time: *Tomorrow* is the concert.

Prop: *It* is cold.

In the passive voice sentence, the subject usually fills the role of the target or the recipient:

Target: *The window* has been broken by Archie.

Recipient: *Anita* was given a book by Archie.

In our examples till now, the different noun phrases in a sentence have been filling different roles, but it need not always be so: that is to say, different noun phrases within the same sentence can fill the same role:

Anita sat by *the wall* near *a window*. (location)
She eats lunch before *noon* on *Sunday*. (time)
I ate with *a knife* and *a fork*. (instrument)

Noun phrases filling the same role can be connected by conjunctions like *and*, as in the last example above. For humour, however, noun phrases filling different roles are sometimes connected by *and*:

Archie and *a stone* broke the window.
   (agent and instrument are connected by *and*)
Anita and *the rice* were cooking.
   (agent and the target are connected by *and*)

The notion of roles in English is akin to the notion of cases in Sanskrit and Latin, as illustrated in Figure 7.22. Hence this notion of roles is also known in the literature as semantic roles, semantic cases or case grammars.

7.3.2 Discovering the roles

In this section, we discuss the outline of a method to find out the roles of the noun phrases in a sentence. Such a method can be incorporated into an ELP.

As mentioned in section 7.3.1, we can say *The window broke*, but we cannot say *The window cleaned*. Hence, the possible structures of a sentence can depend on the verb in the sentence.

Suppose we want to find out the roles of noun phrases containing the polysemous verb *break*. Let us examine the different sentence structures permissible for the different meanings of *break*. To keep the discussion brief, we shall restrict ourselves to active voice sentences.

When *break* means *to damage*, we have three permissible sentence structures, but when *break* means *to disobey*, we have only one permissible sentence structure. These structures are shown in Figure

Meaning of break	Permissible sentence structures	Constraints on Roles
to damage	Agent Verb Target (with instrument) Examples: Archie broke the window. Archie broke the window with a stone.	Agent is an animate noun; target is an inanimate concrete noun; instrument belongs to the set {hammer, stone, rock, ...}.
	Instrument Verb Target Example: A stone broke the window.	
	Target Verb Example: The window broke.	
to disobey	Agent Verb Target Example: Archie broke the rules.	Agent is a human noun; target is an abstract noun from the set {curfew, law, rules, ...}.

Figure 7.23 Permissible sentence structures for the verb *break*. The three structures for *break* meaning *to damage* can alternatively be viewed as follows: if there is an agent, it is the subject of the sentence; otherwise, if there is an instrument, it is the subject; otherwise, the target is the subject. The agent and the target are always unflagged. If the instrument is the subject, it is unflagged; otherwise, it is flagged by *with*.

7.23. The figure also shows the constraints that have been placed on the roles for each meaning of *break*.

Now suppose we are to find out the roles in the sentence *The glass broke*. We see that the sentence matches a sentence structure for break meaning *to damage*; moreover, according to that, *The glass* is the target.

Similarly, in the sentence *Anita broke the curfew*, we can find out that here *break* means *to disobey*, *Anita* is the agent, and *the curfew* is the target.

Let us assume that we have to find out the roles in the following sentence:

The law broke.

The sentence does not match any of the sentence structures of Figure 7.23, while at the same time satisfying the corresponding constraints on the roles. The sentence matches the structure:

Target Verb

But then the target should be an inanimate concrete noun according to the constraints we have placed. The lexicon tells us that *law* is an abstract, not concrete, noun. We can say that we cannot find out the roles in the given sentence.

If we allow particles with verbs, we can similarly set up the permissible sentence structures for the different meanings of the verb–particle composites:

The law *broke down*. (failed)
He *broke down* at the funeral. (wept)
A fire *broke out* in the building. (began)
The men *broke out* of the prison. (escaped)
She *broke into* the conversation. (interrupted)

The method to find out the roles of the noun phrases in a sentence can be summarized as follows.

1. Parse the sentence to locate its verb and all its noun phrases.
2. By examining the permissible sentence structures for the verb, assign a meaning to the verb and assign the roles to the noun phrases. In assigning a role to a noun phrase, make use of the flag (or its absence) of the noun phrase and whether the noun phrase satisfies the constraints placed on the noun phrase for that role.

Until now, the roles in our examples have been explicit. Nevertheless, roles can be implicit. Implicit roles are associated with specific verbs. Consider:

Anita wrote a letter.

Although the instrument role is not explicitly mentioned, we can assume that the instrument is a *pen*, since people mostly use a pen to write. The instrument role of a *pen* is thus implicit in the example above. Alternatively, we can say that a *pen* is the default instrument for the verb *write*. When a *pen* is not the instrument for *write*, the instrument will be explicitly mentioned:

Anita wrote a letter with *her bleeding index finger*.

Such default roles associated with a verb can be stored with the verb in the lexicon.

The sentences we have considered up to now have contained only

NAME OF THE SLOT	Value Stored in the Slot
TYPE-OF-FINITE-CLAUSE	declarative
POLARITY	positive
MODAL-AUXILIARY	nil
TENSE	past
ASPECT	simple
MOOD	indicative
VOICE	active
VERB	fume
AGENT	father
BECAUSE	

NAME OF THE SLOT	Value Stored in the Slot
TYPE-OF-FINITE-CLAUSE	declarative
POLARITY	positive
MODAL-AUXILIARY	nil
TENSE	past
ASPECT	perfective
MOOD	indicative
VOICE	passive
VERB	cheat
TARGET	Anita

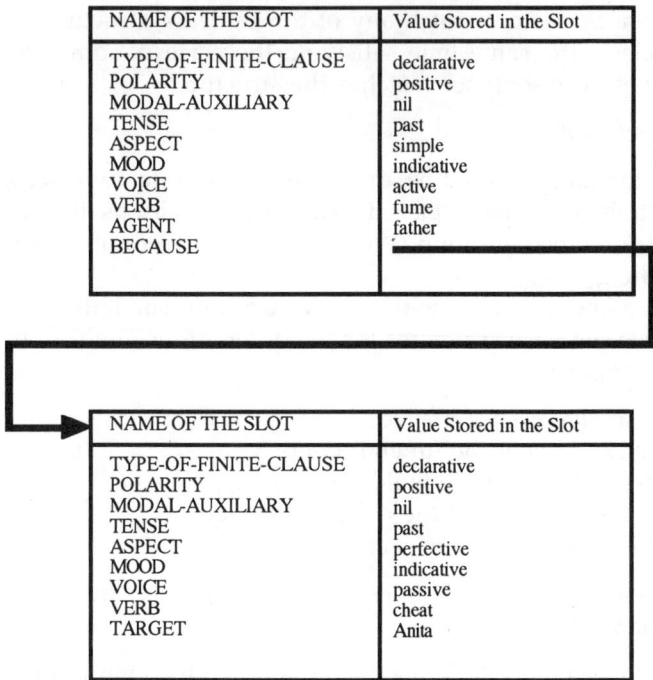

Figure 7.24 Frames to represent the meaning of the sentence *Father fumed because Anita had been cheated.*

one finite clause. When a sentence contains more than one finite clause, the meaning representations of the individual clauses can be joined to show the relationship between the clauses. An example is shown in Figure 7.24.

7.3.3 Expressing verbs as primitive sequences

A refinement to representing the meaning of a sentence is to define a set of primitive actions or states. Then every verb in the ELP vocabulary is expressed as a sequence of a subset of these primitives. Consider:

Archie picked the book.

If, say, *grasp* and *lift* belong to our set of primitives, then in the representation of the meaning of the above example, we replace the verb *picked* by *grasped*, followed by *lifted*. Note, however, that in defining the primitives, we should ensure that the primitives are independent of one another; in other words, no primitive should be expressible by other primitives. The sequence of primitives for every verb in the ELP lexicon is stored in the lexicon.

Expressing verbs as a sequences of primitives is akin to explaining a complicated idea in terms of simpler ideas, for example, explaining *picking* in terms of *grasping* and *lifting*.

7.4   UNDERSTANDING STORIES

Quite often the meaning of a sentence is apparent only from the context of the sentence; that is, from the relationship of the sentence with the other sentences around it. Take, for instance, the sentence:

Archie visited her two days later.

We do not know two days after what event Archie visited her. Neither do we know the referent of the pronoun *her*. But suppose we have the following two sentences:

Anita returned last Thursday. Archie visited her two days later.

Now we know that the referent of *her* is Anita, and that Archie visited Anita two days after her return.

We often understand stories by understanding individual sentences from their context. Multiple sentences related to one another are considered to constitute a story. In section 6.1 it was mentioned that one purpose of an ELP could be to understand stories. One approach to understanding stories is by using the notions of scripts and plans.

7.4.1   Scripts and plans

Scripts provide possible action sequences for stereotyped situations. Consider, for example, the stereotyped situation of students taking a university course. It is usual that to pass a course they need to pass both the term work and the final examination. This can be viewed as a script to pass a course. We can represent this script as a sequence of frames: a frame for the term work and a frame for the final examination. If we want more details, then each frame in the frame sequence can designate, say, a primitive action: completing the first assignment, completing the second assignment, presenting a class seminar, and so on. Now suppose the ELP reads the following story:

In the Operating Systems course, Gilda passed the term work. Yet she failed the course.

If we ask the ELP:

Why did Gilda fail the Operating Systems course?

The ELP should be able to respond:

It seems Gilda failed the final examination.

Given the two-line story, the ELP cannot be certain of the correctness of its response, and so it speculates. This is what humans would possibly do, if they were to read the story. Without the script, the ELP would not have been able to speculate.

An ELP can be given alternative scripts to understand a story. For example, the grade of a course can be based on the following alternatives:

1. the term work alone;
2. the final examination alone; or
3. both the term work and the final examination.

The ELP can select from the alternative scripts to understand variations to stories about courses. Consider:

Anita's term project for the Data Structures course was excellent. She received an A grade.

The ELP should be able to speculate that the grade was based on the term work.

Having discussed scripts, we shall now discuss plans. A plan provides an appropriate sequence of actions to meet the goal of a character in the story. Suppose an ELP reads the following story:

Archie wanted to get good marks in the examination for the Programming Languages course next day. He stayed up all night.

If the ELP was asked what Archie was doing in the night, the ELP should be able to speculate that Archie was studying, but to be able to make this speculation, the ELP should have been provided with the different plans of what students would do to meet their goals of getting good marks in an examination.

Just as scripts can be stored as a sequence of frames, so can plans. Overall, by using scripts and frames, an ELP tries to understand the details of a story that are not explicitly mentioned in the story.

7.5 CLOSING REMARKS

7.5.1 Ambiguity

In understanding sentences, we need to be wary of ambiguous sentences. As you saw in section 7.1.1, a sentence that may be parsed in more than one way can be ambiguous. We discuss below the other frequent causes of ambiguity.

A sentence can be ambiguous when the referent of a pronoun is not apparent. Consider the following two examples:

> The broker rejected Mr Sharma as a client because *he* did low business.
>
> The broker rejected Mr Sharma as a client because *he* did high business.

The sentences in the two examples have the same structure. The sentences are ambiguous, because it is not apparent whether the referent of *he* is *the broker* or *Mr Sharma*. We can, however, resolve the ambiguity by using knowledge (which may be in the form of scripts and plans) about brokers. A broker may not want a new client who brings in only low business to the broker, because the little profit from such a client may not be worth the broker's time. One the other hand, a broker who is already doing high business may not want new clients, because the broker may not have the extra time required to handle new clients. The above knowledge about brokers can tell us that the referent of *he* is *Mr Sharma* in the first example, and that the referent of *he* is *the broker* in the second example.

Now consider the example you saw in section 6.4: Anita and her sister, Gilda, were walking home when *she* said, 'Let's hurry, or Mother will be angry.' It is not apparent whether the referent of *she* is *Anita* or *Gilda*. We are not able to resolve the ambiguity.

An elliptical sentence can be ambiguous:

> Anita helped Archie more than Gilda.

The above sentence is ambiguous, for it could be paraphrased as either of the following:

> Anita helped Archie more than (she helped) Gilda.
>
> Anita helped Archie more than Gilda (helped Archie).

A sentence can be ambiguous when it contains polysemous words, or expressions:

> When the going gets tough, the tough get going.

The expression *get going* is polysemous. Spoken in sarcasm, the above example can be paraphrased as:

> When the going gets tough, the tough leave.

Spoken as part of a pep talk, the example can be paraphrased as:

> When the going gets tough, the tough begin working.

Terminology	Examples from mathematical logic	Examples from English
Clause	~P(x,a) ∨ R(y)	When father returned, ...
Complement	~B is the complement of B	She is a lawyer. [subject complement] We appointed him coach. [object complement]
Conjunction	A ∧ B is the conjunction of A and B	and, when, or, ...
Existential	∃ is the existential quantifier	There is a bee in your bonnet. [existential sentence]
Predicate	P is the predicate in P(x,a)	He bought a radio.
Quantifier	∀ and ∃ are quantifiers	all, many, some,...

Figure 7.25 A review of the terminology that is used in both mathematical logic and English grammar, but with different meanings.

You may have also noticed that some of the terminology used in mathematical logic in Chapters 2–5 is the same as the terminology in English grammar. This terminology, which is reviewed in Figure 7.25 is polysemous. The meaning of a word from this terminology depends on the context of the sentence in which the word is used.

7.5.2 Superficial versus actual meaning

The actual meaning of a sentence is not always what it appears to be. You read in section 6.5.3 that a verb and a particle compose an idiom, the meaning of an idiom being different from the meaning of its constituents. For example:

I must *put up with* his antics. (tolerate)

Idioms are formed from other words, too:

He *had me over a barrel*. (gave me no choice)
She can talk *until the cows come home*. (endlessly)

There also exist idioms whose meaning is the opposite of the meaning of its constituents. It is as if the polarity of the sentence had been switched from positive to negative, or vice versa:

His kindness *cannot be underestimated*.

Superficially, it would seem that the sentence were saying *He is not kind*, but actually the sentence is saying *He is kind*. Here are two other examples of such idioms:

There is *no love lost* between the two of them.
(means: they dislike each other)

You *picked a fine time* to do this to me!
(spoken often in sarcasm, the sentence means: you picked a terrible time . . .)

Sometimes, while describing the attributes of one member in a particular class, we are really describing the attributes of all members in the class:

An elephant has a tail.

This can be paraphrased as:

Every elephant has one tail.

But suppose we were to say:

All elephants have tails.
All elephants have eyes.

The two sentences have the same structure; they are both ambiguous because they do not specify how many tails (or eyes) elephants have. Our knowledge about elephants, however, tells us that the first sentence is about one tail for each elephant, the second sentence about two eyes for each elephant.

Now consider the following two sentences, which have the same structure:

We have ten students from Mathematics and Computer Science.
We have ten students from Belgium and Brazil.

The first sentence could mean that we have ten students who are studying both mathematics and computer science, perhaps in a joint programme. But the second sentence means that we have ten students who are either from Belgium or from Brazil (our prior knowledge about nationalities tells us that a student cannot be both from Belgium and Brazil at the same time).

The meaning of a sentence can depend on the speaker and the situation. If, in the cafeteria, a friend asks you:

Do you have any change on you?

Your friend perhaps means:

Could you lend me some change?

But, say, you are leaving home to go to school in another city. At the train station, your father, who has come to see you off, asks:

Do you have any change on you?

Your father perhaps means:

Shall I give you some change, if you don't have any? You may need the change for petty expenses during the journey.

From the above discussion, we can say that, to understand the meaning of a sentence, we may need the following three kinds of analyses.

1. Syntactic analysis: parse the sense to check whether it is grammatical.
2. Semantic analysis: elicit the superficial meaning from the sentence.
3. Pragmatic analysis: elicit the actual meaning from the sentence using prior knowledge (called pragmatics) about the domain of discourse.

To enable an ELP to elicit the actual meaning from a sentence, we shall need to incorporate the pragmatics into the ELP. Pragmatics can also help us to speculatively answer questions. Suppose we are given the following statement T1:

(T1) Every boy who fetched a mop cleaned his room.

Then we are asked:

Was there a boy who cleaned his room?

Using predicate logic, discussed in Chapter 3, we cannot answer the question, but using pragmatics we can say: There must have been at least one boy who cleaned his room; otherwise, it is pointless for anyone to make statement T1.

Having read about syntax and semantics in this chapter, you will read in the next chapter how a sentence can be transformed into another sentence of related meaning.

7.6 EXERCISES

1. Design an ATN for parsing sentences that contain one finite clause such that the finite verb phrase in the clause is unitransitive. Write a parsing program that transits through the ATN to parse a few sentences of your choice. The vocabulary in your lexicon will depend on the vocabulary in the sentences you will be parsing.

2. Repeat exercise 1 for finite verb phrases that are each of the following:
   (a) linking,
   (b) intransitive,
   (c) cotransitive, and
   (d) bitransitive.

3. Modify the ATN of Figure 7.5 to also include an arc A_{33} from state S_3 to S_3 labelled prepositional phrase. Employing the ATNs of Figures 7.10, 7.11, 7.12, and the modified ATN of Figure 7.5, obtain manually a parse tree for the sentence: *The thief hit the old woman with an umbrella.* After you have obtained one parse tree, force backtracking to obtain another parse tree. Alter the parsing program of exercise 1 so that, after it has parsed a given sentence, it is repeatedly forced to backtrack to obtain all possible parses of the sentence. Use the altered program to test whether any of the synthetic grammars depicted by your ATNs of exercises 1 and 2 are ambiguous.

4. What modification is required in the definition of the trait of a sentence to distinguish a DO-support sentence (such as, *Archie did finish the homework*) from a non-DO-support sentence (such as, *Archie finished the homework*)? Suppose you are given a frame that contains the trait of a sentence, a verb, and up to three roles. The roles are to be from those listed in section 7.3.1. Write a program that can read the frame and generate the sentence corresponding to the frame. Remember that the sentence might need DO-support. If your program were to read the frame of Figure 7.19, it would generate this sentence: Archie has broken the window with a massive stone. Test your program on a few frames of your choice.

5. Which of the following sentences are ambiguous? If a sentence is ambiguous, what causes the ambiguity?

   I saw Anita running down the street.
   Archie was told that he was not needed by Father.
   The Mayas constructed this way.
   I found him a puzzle.
   She was arrested for robbing a bank last Wednesday.

I offered Archie more food than Anita.
It was the shirt displayed in the store window that I bought.
Archie is taller than Anita, and Gilda, too.
Which students have high grades in Computer Science?
What hurt Gilda was being ignored by Mother.
She decided on the truck.
The lamb is ready to eat.
Call me a taxi.
Where is J.F. Kennedy?
You should waste no time in visiting New York.
She pleaded guilty to the crime in the court.
He is blooming late.
I met a man with my brother.
I saw the child in the photograph in the school room.
Who are the students from Mathematics or Computer Science?
A cat can jump higher than a cow.
I do not understand clauses.
Deposit the money in the bag.
He failed me.
The aircraft sprayed the locusts.
He loves his yacht more than his wife.
He is the only one who counts.
I cut the cheese on the table with a knife.
Mr Sharma, he treated me to lunch.

6. Write a program for automated understanding and reasoning. The input to the program is English sentences that denote (a) premisses and (b) either a goal or a question. The program translates the sentences into predicate logic formulae. If a goal has been input, then the program tries to prove that the goal is a logical consequence of the premisses. If a question has been input, then the program tries to answer it.

Specimen input to the program

Premiss: Amity is the ma of Betsy.
Premiss: For all u and w, if u is the ma of w, then w is the daughter of u.
Goal: Betsy is the daughter of Amity.

Output from the program

Goal proved.

The possible outputs are *Goal proved*, *Goal disproved*, and *Unable to prove goal since time/memory exhausted*.

If, in the specimen input to the program above together with the given premises, we had said:

Question: Who is the daughter of Amity?

then the output from the program would have been *Betsy*. For this program, select your domain of discourse, vocabulary and permitted sentence structures. To implement the 'proving' portion of your program, you would need to be familiar with the material discussed in Chapters 3 and 4.

7. Write a program to implement an ELP to query the database of Figure 6.2. Use ATNs to parse your queries. Suppose the query is:

Who teaches Programming Languages?

The system responds:

Beefly.

Think of the different ways the queries may be posed and incorporate these into the ELP. Here are some typical queries that may be posed:

What courses does Sharma teach?
What is the course number of Data Structures?
What is the course name of COMP351?
How many courses does Beefly teach?

This exercise may seem to be the same as the first exercise of section 6.12. Note, however, that there you were to use template matching, but here you are to use ATNs.

8. (a) Read the following story entitled *A Friend of His*:

He was waiting when she came bouncing down the steps of the university library. 'You know, there was this guy who came up to me, and . . . '
They began to walk toward the car park while she continued her chatter. Then suddenly she fell silent.
'Anything the matter?' he asked. In their brief friendship, he had known her to be moody.
'Nothing.' There was ice in her voice.
The only further sound was the rhythmic ringing of her heels on the asphalt. Her face had become flushed and her chin was cocked high. With every breath, her nostrils flared from east to west.
At the entrance to the car park, she erupted. 'What's the use of dressing up when no one notices!'
From the corner of his eye, he stole a glance. She was wearing a

pale ruffled skirt with a matching blouse adorned by a loosely tied bow. Her long black hair glistened in the evening sun. Her eyes, big and round and brown, were full of tears.

(b) Design and implement an ELP to read and understand the above story. You may paraphrase the sentences in the story, or you may let the ELP read a synopsis of the story. What pragmatics is needed to understand the story? Will it help to understand the story better if the two characters in the story were given names? Test your ELP to see whether it can answer the following questions.

(i)   What is her state of mind at the beginning of the story?

(ii)   Why did she fall silent? What emotion was she expressing? At what point in the story does this become apparent?

(iii) What are her feelings toward him? At the beginning of the story? At the end of the story? What are his feelings toward her?

(iv)   Was she crying at the end of the story? If so, why?

(v)   Is the title of the story appropriate? If yes, why? If no, why not? What other title can the story have?

Before attempting the above exercise, you should also read exercises 9 and 10 given below. The exercises are similar: even the titles of the stories in the three exercises are similar. Of exercises 8, 9 and 10, it would be adequate to attempt any one exercise.

9. (a) You may have found the story in exercise 8 too restrictive since it describes only one scene. The story may not have been to your liking. We give below a longer story. Select any scene from the story, and design and implement an ELP to understand that scene. You may paraphrase the sentences in the scene, or you may make a synopsis of the scene. To understand one scene, you may need the knowledge gained from the other scenes. Alternatively, as a class project, different students may select different scenes from the story, thus covering the full story. The story assumes that you know about universities. Nevertheless, we wish to emphasize that the events and characters in the story are all imaginary, and any similarity to real events or characters, living or dead, is a coincidence. The story is entitled *A Friend of the School*:

When Donald Merriwether returned to his office after lunch, he found a note dangling from a piece of tape stuck to the door. 'Professor Merriwether, could you please come over and see Professor Beefly as soon as possible. It's urgent – Alice.'

'Oh, no!' said Donald to himself.

Donald turned around and began to trudge toward Beefly's

office, thirty metres down the corridor. By the time he arrived at the grey, sombre departmental office, he had quickened his pace. He exchanged a cheery 'Hi' with Alice who, flicking her red hair, signalled that Beefly was in. Donald knocked sharply on the heavy oak door marked CHAIRMAN.

A shrill voice cried, 'Come in.'

Donald pushed the door open. Dressed in a custom-tailored blue suit and a red tie, Beefly sat in a swivel chair behind a mahogany desk, sucking vigorously at his pipe, with his short, chubby legs sticking out as the feet were propped on a side table. His belly was bursting out of the waistband of his trousers, and his breath came in shallow wheezes.

Beefly put a book down as he swung in his chair and from behind a screen of smoke said, 'Donald! Glad you came. Sorry, I had to send for you. Sit down, sit down.' Beefly motioned to the chair opposite.

Donald slowly lowered his six-foot frame into the chair. He ran his fingers through his thinning black hair, adjusted his glasses and cleared his throat. The air in the room was stuffy. Beefly is back to his coarse tobacco, Donald thought.

'A girl called Liz Thorpe in your COMP475 class, Don?' Beefly's voice was a low whistle.

'Why, yes,' said Donald. He clearly remembered the peroxide blonde painted up in cherry-red lipstick. 'Something wrong?'

'Nothing much. There was a call from the Dean. How did she do in your course?'

'I'll have to look up my class records. They're in my office. I can fetch them if you . . .'

'No, no, you don't have to. Just tell me what you remember.'

Donald remembered Liz as one who was often absent from class. Whenever she managed to turn in her assignments, they were shoddily done and usually incomplete. She always had an excuse though, spoken softly in a caressing, finishing-school voice. 'I don't think she did well,' said Donald.

'Donald, you failed her. Well, the Dean wants her passed; says it's the wish of the Vice-President, Academic. You do know, I suppose, that the grades haven't been released officially yet.'

'Is my judgement under question?' Donald arched his eyebrows.

'No, Donald, I know you better than that. I can't say why they want her passed, but I can guess. The kid's old man is Edgar J., the textile king who's promised to finance our new computer lab. In the past, he has helped us get many government grants, in spite of all the budget cuts. Knows all the ropes, he does. Plays golf with the Education Minister. He's being given an honorary doctorate at the next convocation. Does that make sense, Donald?'

'Are you telling me that I should pass her?' Donald's voice quivered as he emphasized the word 'telling'.

'No, I'm not telling you anything yet.' Beefly also emphasized the word 'telling'. His breathing became shallower and his voice began to screech. 'I would advise you to think it over. Tonight. Can you come and see me tomorrow morning at ten?' Beefly went back to his book.

Donald rose quietly and walked out of the room. Beefly's voice followed him. 'I'll let you know if they've turned on the heat.'

Thoughts of his encounter with Beefly were still crowding him when Donald went home that evening. His wife, Caroline, was waiting for him. During supper he mentioned the incident, trying to sound casual.

'Can Beefly force you to pass this girl?' Caroline asked.

'Of course, not! The instructor is the final arbiter. That's the rule.' He reached out to pat her on the shoulder, comforting her.

'You mean a student can't dispute his grade?'

'Sure, he can. Pay a fee and appeal. The chairman appoints someone else in the department to review the student's record. If the grade changes, the fee is refunded.'

Caroline rose to bring the blueberry pie she had baked for dessert. She returned with two plates and put one down in front of Donald, who greedily smacked his lips. She was quiet for a while and then blurted, 'You really mean Beefly can't do a thing?'

'Yes, he can. He can get this girl to appeal her grade, and then review the record himself. But I doubt if he can even find her. She might be raising hell somewhere in Europe for all anyone knows.' Donald paused as his gaze rested on Caroline's golden-brown hair and the playful dimple on her chin. 'Sometimes I feel I should give up this rat race and go back to Dad and start milking cows again on his farm.' He sounded distant.

'Is that why you did a PhD? Milk cows? If that was what you wanted, why did you leave the farm at all?'

'This life looked beautiful then. It's not what you publish, but how many times you publish it; that's what I've found. Mom and Dad are getting old, and they need help. As a kid, I could never think that one day they'd get old.'

Donald picked up the glass of apple juice beside him and drank slowly. 'Say, Carr, if someday I did return to the farm, would you come with me? Mind you, we'll have to work a lot harder and earn a lot less.'

Caroline looked thoughtfully at Donald and smiled. 'Mind you, I'm not complaining about our present life, but as Mother always said, "Whither thou goest . . ." '

'I didn't know my mother-in-law talks like that. Remind me to get her something nice next Christmas.' Donald laughed as he pushed back his plate, stood up and tweaked Caroline's nose. 'Need any help cleaning up?'

'Thanks. I'll manage. There isn't much anyway.'

Later they went for a short walk, and when they came back they were arguing about what to give Donald's parents on their fortieth wedding anniversary next weekend. At eleven that evening they were preparing to turn in when the phone rang. Bob Devotion was on the line.

'Donny, you old skunk!' The voice rang out. 'You ain't in bed yet? Well, stay out. Listen, I'm calling from a pay phone. Sam and I are coming over. Put on some coffee, willya.' Sam was Samantha, Bob's wife.

'Everything okay, Bob?' Donald said.

'Now shut up and do as Uncle Bob tells you to. Hey, you got company?'

'No.'

'Good.' The line went dead.

What's Bob up to, Donald thought. He had known Bob since they were doctoral candidates together in Toronto. After graduation, they had both applied to the University of Sheepville, four hundred kilometres away. Both had been accepted.

In graduate school, Bob had a reputation for hard drinking, but once, after smashing his car into a lamp-post, which put him in the hospital for two months, Bob sobered up.

The Devotions arrived soon. Bob was of Donald's height, rugged and tanned, but walked with a limp, the result of his car accident. Samantha was short, with thin lips, a slender waist, and blond hair falling over her shoulders.

Bob greeted Caroline with a bear hug. 'Yes, Caroline, I'll have coffee in the big cup,' and then looking at Donald, he added, 'You want to know why we're here? Well, I ain't gonna tell you. Not until I've had my coffee.'

They all sat around the kitchen table, and Caroline served the coffee.

'Sam and I went down to El Passo's for dinner today,' Bob began. 'Guess who was there? Only three tables away. Beefly and his wife. We stopped by to say "hello." It was the little woman's birthday, and they were celebrating.'

Bob paused as he looked around the kitchen. 'Later, we got the chef to take them a cake with a few candles stuck on it. They invited us to join them at their table. Then for the next one hour we listened to a drunk Beefly blabbering. He must have been drinking the whole evening.'

Donald tensed and exchanged a glance with Caroline.

'So now you know why we're here,' Bob said. 'Beefly's hopping mad at you, Donny boy. Told us about the to-do you had with him this afternoon. He shouldn't have talked, but as I said, he was drunk. He said you were uppity, and if you're not a friend of the school, he's gonna make it hot for you. He wouldn't like it to be known that he can't keep his profs in line. It's December, and he has to send in the recommendations for renewing the next year's teaching contracts. What are you gonna do?'

'What's there to do?' Donald said faintly. Beefly can't get away with that, Donald thought. He could appeal Beefly's decision to the Faculty Council. Beefly wouldn't have a leg to stand on.

'I know what you're thinking. Faculty Council and all that,' Bob said. 'Beefly also bragged that, after you left, he called the Dean, and together they polled the members of the Council. They have a majority. Who wants to be on the wrong side of the Dean, eh!'

'I don't know what to say.' Donald knew it was the talk of the department that Beefly was angling to be the Associate Dean.

'They'll throw mud on you . . . attack your teaching . . . attack your research. Beefly told of some other guy who stood up to him a few years ago. The guy lost his job, couldn't get another, as he couldn't get references . . . finally emigrated to England. Seems Beefly has a pretty good old-boy network operating around these parts.'

They all sat silently, the only noise being the tick-tock of the wall clock.

'I could tell the Council what Beefly said tonight. But who'd believe me if I said Beefly was drunk. Me, untenured, a brand-new assistant professor, and a former drunk; he, the chairman, and a member of the National Committee for Research.' Bob sounded sincere and Donald was touched.

There was silence again, till Samantha said, 'Bob, we better be going now. Caroline, I hope you didn't mind our coming so late. Bob said the final grades are due in the Records Office tomorrow, and there isn't much time.'

They all stood up and walked toward the door. Bob turned. 'Don, we've come a long way together. I promise to be with you, through all the councils, through all the appeals. But give me the word on what you want. Later tonight, if you want to talk, call me up. I'll sleep with my eyes and ears open.' He reached out and squeezed Donald's elbow. For a few moments, the two men stood staring into each other's eyes. The women looked on.

'Youse a ratface, son,' said Bob to Donald, as he and Samantha walked out of the door.

Donald returned to the kitchen table and sat down, cradling his head in his hands. Caroline sat beside him for a while; she then rose and tiptoed to the bedroom.

Donald remained sitting alone with his thoughts. He still owed money on the loan he took from the government when he was a student. He was repaying it in monthly instalments. Without this job, it would be hard to repay, but he'll have to. The fight with Beefly could be a long drawn affair. If he lost, he would carry the stigma for the rest of his life. If he won, would he want to remain in a department where the chairman and the dean were thirsting for his blood? His research grants would dry up. What a Pyrrhic victory that would be! To fight, he would have to lean on Bob. But could Bob himself be hurt? What strain would the fight put on Caroline, on himself, on their marriage? Could he fight and not heed the wounds? Or he could do what Beefly wanted and be over with it. But if he caved in now, would he have to cave in again in the future? He, like Hamlet, had to make up his mind.

Around three in the morning, he raised his head, and with a determined step walked to the Smith-Corona lying on his study table. He rolled in a fresh sheet of paper and stayed there pecking on the typewriter for the next half hour. Finally, he shrugged, rose, stretched, yawned and with a great sense of relief toddled to the bedroom.

Caroline lay curled fully dressed on the bed, asleep. Donald lay down gently beside her and fell asleep, too, fully dressed.

At seven, Caroline was the first to stir, and that woke both of them up. Caroline cooked buckwheat pancakes, Donald's favourite, for breakfast. They ate in silence.

Donald was standing in Beefly's office at ten. Beefly was wearing dark glasses, looked groggy and tired, and kept massaging his forehead with his left palm. Beefly held out the grade sheet to Donald. 'Do initial the correction, Don.'

From his jacket pocket, Donald pulled out the letter he had typed early that morning. He handed it over to Beefly.

'What's that!' said Beefly.

'I'll be giving myself to Dad as his anniversary present.' Donald turned around sharply and strode out of Beefly's office.

(b) The questions that your ELP answers will depend on the scene you select from the above story. You can think up the questions yourself. To give you an idea, however, here are a few typical questions.

(i)   What is Beefly's goal?

(ii)   What is Donald's goal?

(iii) Does the meeting between Beefly and Donald at the beginning of the story follow the script of a usual meeting?

(iv)   Does Bob like Donald? Remember Bob called Donald a skunk once, and later a ratface.

(v)   What did Donald do at the end?

(vi)   Did Donald act honourably at the end? In answering this question, your ELP will have to make a judgement. Can your ELP make a judgement?

(vii) Is the title of the story appropriate? If yes, why? If no, why not?

10. (a) The stories in exercises 8 and 9 were fictitious. You may prefer a true story. Such a story is given below. Select any segment of the story, and design and implement an ELP to understand that segment. You may paraphrase the sentences in the segment, or you may make a synopsis of the segment. To understand one segment, you may need the knowledge gained from the other segments. Alternatively, as a class project, different students may select different segments from the story, thus covering the full story. The story assumes you know about public life. The story is entitled: *A Friend of the Poor*.

Early in 1948, when Mahatma Gandhi was shot and killed in New Delhi, India, statesmen, diplomats and journalists the world over paid tribute, comparing him to Buddha and Jesus. Many saw Gandhi through the eyes of the cartoonist: wrapped in a dhoti, a pocket watch dangling from his waist, bare kneed, hollow-cheeked with a toothless grin and wire-rimmed glasses, walking his goat.

In his *Stride Toward Freedom*, American civil rights leader Martin Luther King wrote: 'Gandhi was probably the first person in history to lift the love ethic . . . to a powerful . . . social force . . .' To do this, Gandhi blended Jesus' Sermon on the Mount with Krishna's Bhagavad Gita discourse. Then he led India's struggle for freedom from British rule.

British politician Winston Churchill roared: 'Gandhism and all that it stands for must ultimately be . . . crushed.' But, in time, Churchill's roar became a meow.

Mohandas Karamchand Gandhi was born on the west coast of

India on 2 October 1869 in the then principality of Porbander, where his father (Kaba) was chief minister to the local ruler. Gandhi was married at the age of thirteen to Kasturba, also thirteen. In his autobiography, he recalled his earlier years as those being swayed by temptations: defying his family's vegetarianism, he ate meat secretly for a while; he visited a brothel, but his courage failed, and he fled amidst a shower of obscenities from the woman; to pay off a debt, he clipped off a piece from his brother's gold amulet, but later wrote a confession to his father.

At eighteen, he sailed for Britain to train as a barrister. He was leaving his wife behind; his mother, Putlibai, extracted from him a vow that he would abstain from wine, women and meat: a vow he reported he fulfilled. Once he did find himself drawing close to an English girl. After a bout with his conscience, he wrote a letter to a mutual friend, explaining that he was already married.

In England, he initially affected the English gentleman: bought a morning suit, a silk top hat and a silver-headed cane; took lessons in dancing, elocution and the violin; wrote home for a double watch chain of gold. This phase soon wore off.

It was in Britain that he first read the Bible; he slept through most of it but woke up during the Sermon on the Mount. He was bewildered by the biblical reference to Jesus' divinity. 'If God can have sons, all of us were his sons.' Divine characters exist in other religions, too, and on all these he commented: '. . . ascribing to the chief actors superhuman or subhuman origins . . . made short work of . . . history . . .'

He returned to India after his studies but soon departed for South Africa on being retained by a merchant there. In South Africa he faced the colour bar: at Pietermaritzburg he was evicted from a first-class railway carriage; on a stagecoach from Charlestown to Johannesburg, he sat shivering outside as he was not allowed in; when he walked by President Kruger's house, he was kicked by a sentry. It was the same President Kruger who once dismissed a delegation's plea for justice by saying: 'You are the descendants of Ishmael, and therefore from your very birth, you are bound to slavery.'

The leader in Gandhi was aroused. Soon he was protesting against discriminatory statutes. For this, he spent many days in jail. One frightful night, two felons propositioned him. He did not respond. Fearing assault, he lay silently in his bunk while in front of him, the two men busied themselves.

In and out of the slammer, Gandhi continued his campaign. Meanwhile, the saint in him was arising, too. On being beaten up by a few Pathans on a Johannesburg street, he (by now, a well-recognized public figure) was carried, unconscious, by passers-by to the office of one Mr J. C. Gibson and then to the house of Joseph Doke, a Baptist minister from New Zealand and Gandhi's friend. Gandhi was in pain when he came around, but his immediate request was that his assailants be released, if they had been arrested. He would not press charges. Yes, he had one more request: Would Reverend Doke's little girl, Olive, please sing 'Lead, Kindly Light.'

Gandhi hadn't always been like that. He would tell how once during a spat with his wife, he lunged at her, grabbed her hand, and began to push her out of the house. As Kasturba began to cry, he loosened his grip.

He, however, could also be a jittery husband. On learning that some guests were to arrive within an hour, he instructed an assistant to prepare a meal. Quietly. Kasturba, taking a nap in an adjoining room, was not to be disturbed because he did not want her to 'go for me.' But a crashing brass platter exposed his conspiracy, and Kasturba, akimbo, burst upon him: Why hadn't she been woken up?

'Ba,' said the man, 'I am afraid of you on such occasions.'

Though Gandhi was continually squabbling with the government, his sense of duty did not betray him. During the 1899 Boer War and the 1906 Zulu 'Rebellion,' he raised an ambulance corps and walked as many as sixty kilometres a day, carrying the wounded on stretchers, often inside the firing line.

Meanwhile, other changes were taking place in his life. He cancelled his life insurance policy; he and his family were now to rely solely on Providence. Feeling that 'Chastity is one of the greatest disciplines without which the mind cannot attain requisite firmness,' he, at the age of thiry-seven, consulted Kasturba and took the vow of celibacy. He was now embracing proverty and godliness and expected his wife and four sons to do the same. When some friends gave Kasturba the gift of a gold necklace, he would not let her keep it.

He denied his sons a formal education because he considered character-building more important. 'Knowledge without character is a power for evil only, as seen in the instances of so many talented "thieves" and "gentlemen rascals" . . .' The sons resented their father's attitude. Kasturba remonstrated: 'You want my sons to be holy men before they are men!' Harilal, the oldest son, left home and became a derelict.

In 1915, Gandhi returned to India and embroiled himself in social and political reform.

He denounced the practice of Untouchability. The Untouchables were the outcastes who bore the burden of society but enjoyed no privileges. They scoured the lavatories and swept the streets, but could not draw water from the village well or worship at the temple. Many of them subsisted on carrion. Gandhi gave the Untouchables a new name: Harijans (People of God). To his vexation, he got a new name, too; he started being addressed as Mahatma (Great Souled). Exasperated, he said: 'The woes of Mahatmas are known to Mahatmas alone.'

He toured the villages by train, by bicycle, by bullock-cart, by foot and made the cause of the poor his own. He began to dress as they did; he had already given up drinking cow's milk in favour of the goat's. To those who could find work for only a few months in a year, he said: 'Spin and weave,' for the villages must bustle with cottage industries, as they had before the British conquest, a century earlier. To create a market for her industrial goods, Britain by predatory taxation had forced Indian handicrafts to wilt.

Gandhi called for a boycott of cloth imported from Lancashire, Britain, and said that those who possessed such cloth should burn it in public bonfires. Thousands complied.

He raved against industrialization that installed huge machines but left millions jobless. 'To a people famishing and idle, the only acceptable form in which God can dare appear is work and promise of food as wages.'

In politics, he started off as a loyal subject of the British empire. But as his disenchantment grew, he called for India's freedom. In 1922, he was arrested and tried for sedition. As evidence, the prosecution produced three articles he had written. Gandhi pleaded guilty, asked for the highest penalty, was sentenced to seventy-two months imprisonment, but released in twenty-two.

His speeches and writing became strident (he called the government 'Satanic'), but his deeds remained non-violent. Describing a confrontation between some Gandhi marchers and police in 1930, American newsman Web Miller of the United Press wrote; 'The police rushed out and methodically and mechanically beat down the second column. There was no fight, no struggle; the marchers simple walked forward until struck down.'

In 1931, Gandhi sailed for Britain to discuss India's future at a conference with British leaders. He stopped briefly at Marseilles in France. Ranking town officials lined up at the gangplank to greet

him. They had come to see a crepehanger; they saw a quipster
Word spread: *'Le Mahatma est un grand comique.'*

The *grand comique* arrived in London and set up house at
Kingsley Hall in the city's East End slums. The neighbourhood
children gathered to stare.

'Hey, Gandhi, where's your trousers?' one lad shouted.

Gandhi laughed. The children clustered around him. One three
year-old boy addressed him as 'Uncle Gandhi.' The others picked
up the refrain.

Gandhi stayed in England for three months. At 5.30 every
morning, he went for a walk. Children stood in their doorways to
holler him a greeting. One day a rumour buzzed around that it was
Uncle Gandhi's birthday. The children dug into their pockets. They
presented him with a letter and a basket.

The letter wished 'you had a birthday cake with icing and a
bird . . .' It went on to invite him to a party with a promise that 'we
will . . . play music about "daisy" and "away in a manger" . . .' The
basket contained two woolly dogs, a tin plate, a blue pencil, some
jelly sweets and three pink birthday candles.

At a folk festival, Gandhi was invited to dance. 'Yes, certainly,'
he chirped, and then swinging his walking stick, he whirled
merrily.

He visited Colonel Maddock, a surgeon, now retired, who had
performed an appendectomy on him seven years earlier in
Bombay. He and Maddock had a pleasant time gabbing and
convincing each other that neither looked a day older. British
writer Bernard Shaw called on Gandhi, felt a spirit of kindredness
and proclaimed himself to be a 'Mahatma Minor.'

Gandhi joined King George and Queen Mary for tea at
Buckingham Palace; he parleyed with Prime Minister Ramsay
Macdonald; lectured at Oxford, Cambridge, Eton and the London
School of Economics; addressed MPs in the committee rooms of
the parliament; and journeyed to Lancashire, explaining to the
unemployed there why he got the Indians to boycott cloth from
their mills. The boycott had aggravated the unemployment.
Gandhi agreed that their conditions were bad, but said the Indian
conditions were worse. 'Your average unemployment dole is
seventy shillings. Our average income is seven shillings and six
pence a month.' One man rose to respond: 'I am one of the
unemployed, but if I was in India, I would say the same thing that
Mr Gandhi is saying.'

Winston Churchill refused to meet the 'seditious fakir.'

The conference with the British leaders was a failure and

Gandhi, disappointed, set out for India. In Rome, he visited the Sistine Chapel and wept on seeing the figure of Christ.

Then a storm broke. The *Giornale d'Italia* published an interview with Gandhi in which he had threatened to start civil disobedience on his return to India. British leaders were enraged. They accused him of treachery. Gandhi denied giving the interview.

Shortly after his arrival in India, he was arrested. From detention, one of the first letters he wrote was to his 'Dear little friends' in London, thanking them for the woolly dogs, the tin plate, the . . . .

Even in jail, he remained a force. In August 1932, the British announced a new constitution for India, granting limited self-rule. Gandhi was appalled because the Untouchables were being given separate electorates. This amounted to creating a permanent wall between the Untouchables and the rest. To oppose the British decision, he announced a 'fast unto death.' Messages from all over poured in, advising him against the fast. He was in delicate health and would surely die. His lieutenant, Jawaharlal Nehru, 'felt annoyed with him for choosing a side issue for his final sacrifice.' Gandhi ignored all requests. Nevertheless, just before commencing the 'fast unto death,' he placed an order for new dentures.

On 20 September he began his fast. His condition deteriorated rapidly as he lay on a cot in the prison yard. No politician, Indian or British, wanted a dead Gandhi on his public conscience. Cablegrams flashed between New Delhi and London as India faced an upheaval. One by one the politicians capitulated. Nehru said he realized that Gandhi 'could pull the strings that move people's hearts.' On 26th September, Gandhi sipped orange juice. Eight months later, he was released.

Told that fasting in politics was coercion, he replied that one who had love in his heart 'even for opponents' was 'privileged to fast.' He had interpreted Jesus' homily, 'If any man take away thy coat, let him have thy cloak also,' as a plea for 'non-violent non-co-operation' with one's oppressor. This was Satyagraha: the 'vindication of truth not by infliction of suffering on the opponent but on one's self.' He cited the examples of the Christians in first-century Rome and the Dukhobors in eighteenth-century Russia.

His detractors said he was mixing religion with politics. He replied that he took Krishna's call to fight a righteous war as a call for action. He declared that Buddha and Christ had both been men of action. 'Buddha fearlessly carried the war into the enemy's camp and brought down on its knees an arrogant priesthood. Christ drove out money-changers from the temple...' In Gandhi's righteous war, the battlefield was politics, 'and I can say... in all humility, that those who say that religion has nothing to do with politics do not know what religion means.'

He continued his agitation for India's freedom, and in August 1942 he was again imprisoned, this time with his wife. In jail, Kasturba contracted bronchitis, and she began to sink. Hour after hour, he sat by her bed. On 22 February 1944, her head resting in her husband's lap, Kasturba died. She was cremated, and her ashes were buried in the prison grounds. Shaken, Gandhi said: 'We lived together for sixty-two years.'

Two-and-a-half months later, he was freed. His last confinement had ended. In South Africa and in India, six-and-a-half years of his life he had spent in jail.

Meanwhile, the Second World War had ravaged Europe. In July 1945, a weakened Britain held an election. Winston Churchill, the war-time prime minister, went out; Clement Attlee came in. Imperialism was fast becoming a dirty word. On 15th August 1947 the British withdrew, leaving behind two independent nations: India and Pakistan. The sun had set on the British empire.

But independence brought strife. Riots broke out between the Hindus and the Muslims. The riots, they brought looting, they brought rape, they brought murder. Gandhi was on the move again, applying his balm to a people gone mad. Some listened, some did not, and some blamed him for everything that had gone wrong. 'Have I led the country astray!' he wondered.

He said his life's work was a failure, and he had lost the will to live.

New Delhi, 30 January 1948: Gandhi was striding to his daily meeting of public prayers. Nathuram Godse, 37, journalist, unmarried, thickset, medium height, closely cropped hair, wearing a khaki bush jacket, pushed past the crowds and stood in front. He held a black Beretta automatic pistol. Thrice he fired. Two bullets passed through Gandhi; the third lodged in his lung.

His arms folded. He gasped. He fell backward. It was 5.17 in the evening.

News of his assassination blazed across the world. The United Nations Organization lowered its flag to half-staff; the Security Council suspended its deliberations; Philip Noel-Baker, the British delegate, said Gandhi was 'the friend of the poorest and lowliest and lost.'

(b) The questions that your ELP answers will depend on the segment you select from the story above. You can think up the questions yourself. To give you an idea, however, here are a few typical questions:

(i)   What was Gandhi's goal?
(ii)   What was the British goal?
(iii)   What were Gandhi's views on formal education?
(iv)   Did the neighbourhood children like Gandhi when he visited London in 1931?
(v)   What could have been Gandhi's motive in ordering new dentures just before commencing his 'fast unto death'?
(vi)   What could have been the motive of the man who shot Gandhi?
(vii)   Is the title of the story appropriate? If yes, why? If no, why not?

Note that the story contains a French sentence (*Le Mahatma est un grand comique*) with a structure like that of an English sentence. Did the ELP have to make special provisions to process the French sentence?

11. The titles of the stories in exercises 8, 9 and 10 all contain the word *friend*. Does the word *friend* have the same meaning in the three titles? Design and implement an ELP that reads the titles and the synopses of the three stories. Each synopsis may be around four sentences long. From a list of possible meanings of the word *friend*, the ELP should be able to select the appropriate meaning for each title.

7.7   SUGGESTIONS FOR FURTHER READING

Sager (1981) presented a grammar for processing English text. Bates (1978) explained augmented transition networks. Marcus (1986) illustrated the use of Prolog for parsing. Marcus (1980) described a scheme for parsing English. Grosz, Appelt, Martin and Pereira (1987) put forward a natural language interface called TEAM. Harris (1985) gave Pascal codes for the procedures in English processing. Similarly, Gazdar and Mellish (1989a) and (1989b) gave codes in Lisp and Prolog. Fillmore (1968) provided an account of the roles of noun phrases. Mellish (1985) investigated the meaning of noun phrases. Black (1988) reported three methods of discriminating the word senses for English. Hirst (1988) explored semantic interpretation to remove ambiguities. Minsky (1975) proposed the use of frames. Allen (1987) surveyed the processing of English. Procter (1978) listed possible sentence structures for frequently used verbs. Simmons (1984) employed logic to represent and understand English. Schank and Risebeck (1981) proposed a set of primitives, called conceptual dependency, for expressing actions.

Cullingford (1986) and Wilensky (1983) explained scripts and plans, respectively. Courtney (1983) and Long (1979) gave meanings of verb–particle composites and other idioms. Jacobs (1987) reviewed a system called KING to generate English.

1. Allen, J. (1987) *Natural Languages Understanding*, Banjamin/ Cummings Publishing Co. Inc., Menlo Park, California.
2. Bates, M. (1978) The theory and practice of augmented transition networks in *Natural Language Communication with Computers* (ed. L. Bolc), Springer-Verlag, New York, pp. 191–259.
3. Black, E. (1988) An experiment in computational discrimination of English word senses, IBM Journal of Research and Development, **32**[2], 185–93.
4. Courtney, R. (1983) *Longman Dictionary of Phrasal Verbs*, Longman Group Limited, London.
5. Cullingford, R. E. (1986) *Natural Language Processing: A Knowledge Engineering Approach*, Rowman & Littlefield Publishers, Totowa, New Jersey.
6. Fillmore, C. (1968) The case for case, in *Universals in Linguistic Theory* (eds. E. Bach and D. Michie), Holt, Rinehart, and Winston, New York, pp. 1–90.
7. Gazdar, G. and Mellish, C. (1989a) *Natural Language Processing in LISP*, Addison-Wesley, Wokingham.
8. Gazdar, G. and Mellish, C. (1989b) *Natural Language Processing in PROLOG*, Addison-Wesley, Wokingham.
9. Grosz, B. J., Appelt, D. E., Martin, P. A. and Pereira, F. C. N. (1987). TEAM: an experiment in the design of transportable natural-language interfaces, *Artificial Intelligence*, **32**[2], 173–243.
10. Harris, M. D. (1985) *Natural Language Processing*, Reston Publishing Company, Reston, Virginia.
11. Hirst, G. (1988) Semantic interpretation and ambiguity, *Artificial Intelligence*, **34**[2], 131–77.
12. Jacobs, P. S. (1987) Knowledge-intensive natural language generation, *Artificial Intelligence*, **33**[3], 325–78.
13. Long, T. H. (editorial director) (1979) *Longman Dictionary of English Idioms*, Longman Group Limited, London.
14. Marcus, C. (1986) *Prolog Programming*, Addison Wesley, Reading, Massachusetts.
15. Marcus, M. P. (1980) *A Theory of Syntatic Recognition for Natural Language Parsing*, MIT Press, Cambridge, Massachusetts.
16. Mellish, C. S. (1985) *Computer Interpretation of Natural Language Descriptions*, Ellis Horwood, Chichester.
17. Minsky, M. (1975) A framework for representing knowledge, in

The Psychology of Computer Vision (ed. P. H. Winston), McGraw-Hill, New York, pp. 211–77.

18. Procter, P. (ed.) (1978) *A Dictionary of Contemporary English*, Longman Group Limited, London.

19. Sager, N. (1981) *Natural Language Information Processing*, Addison-Wesley, Reading, Massachusetts.

20. Schank, R. C. and Risebeck, C. K. (1981) *Inside Computer Understanding: Five Programs Plus Miniatures*, Lawrence Erlbaum Associates, Hillsdale, New Jersey.

21. Simmons, R. F. (1984) *Computations from the English*, Prentice-Hall, Englewood Cliffs, New Jersey.

22. Wilensky R. (1983). *Planning and Understanding: A Computational Approach to Human Understanding*, Addison-Wesley, Reading, Massachusetts.

8
Natural language processing: a transformational grammar

8.1 INTRODUCTION

Two or more sentences that do not look identical can have the same or related meaning:

> I am reading the book.
> I'm reading the book.

The two sentences have the same trait and annunciation, as explained in section 7.3. The *I am* of the first sentence has been contracted to *I'm* of the second sentence. Now consider:

> I am reading the book. (positive polarity)
> I am not reading the book. (negative polarity)

Except for the change in polarity, the two sentences have the same trait and annunciation. We can say that the meaning of the two sentences is related. Similarly, consider:

> I am reading the book. (active voice)
> The book is being read by me. (passive voice)

Now except for the change in voice, the two sentences have the same trait and annunciation.

There exist procedures that can transform a sentence into a sentence of related meaning. Such procedures are called transformational procedures. In the literature, transformational procedures are also known as transformational rules. It is beneficial to embody transformational procedures in an ELP, so that if two sentences are related in meaning, the ELP can discover the nature of this relationship. Moreover, the ELP can express a given thought by generating different sentences with variations in emphasis and nuance.

Sentence before transformation [with an example in brackets]	Sentence after transformation [with an example in brackets]	Details discussed in Section
without contractions [It is he.]	with contractions [It's he.]	8.2
positive polarity [She may go.]	negative polarity [She may not go.]	8.3
declarative [He has eaten.]	question [Has he eaten?]	8.4
without tag question [She has gone.]	with tag question [She has gone, hasn't she?]	8.5
declarative [You will go.]	imperative [Go.]	8.6
active voice [He broke the window.]	passive voice [The window was broken by him.]	8.7

Figure 8.1 A foreglimpse of transformation procedures discussed in this chapter.

You saw an example of such sentences in Figure 6.1. The transformational procedures embodied in an ELP constitute the transformational grammar embodied in the ELP.

Applying a transformational procedure to a sentence usually entails executing one or more of the following operations on the words of the sentence: copying, deleting, inserting, and moving the words. If the words of the sentence reside in registers, such as the ATN registers discussed in section 7.2.3, then these operations are executed by manipulating the contents of the registers.

In sections 8.2–8.7, you will read about a few transformational procedures for simple sentences, defined in section 6.11.4. A foreglimpse of these procedures is given in Figure 8.1. Reading these procedures will give you an idea of how they work. You can then develop your own procedures for any ELP you may design.

8.2 UNCONTRACTED TO CONTRACTED EXPRESSIONS

The word *not* can occur within a finite verb phrase although it is not considered to be part of the verb phrase (see section 6.8.2):

Auxiliary	Expression to be Contracted	Contracted Expression
MODAL	can not <u>or</u> cannot could not might not must not shall not should not will not would not	can't couldn't mightn't mustn't shan't shouldn't won't wouldn't
HAVE	have not has not had not	haven't hasn't hadn't
BE	am not is not are not was not were not	aren't isn't aren't wasn't weren't
DO	do not does not did not	don't doesn't didn't

Figure 8.2 The word *not* can often be contracted when it appears after an auxiliary. The above expressions to be contracted can appear anywhere in a sentence: beginning, middle or end. In colloquial usage, the expressions *aren't*, *hasn't*, *haven't* and *isn't* are sometimes supplanted by *ain't*. Rarely, *may not* is contracted into *mayn't*.

I *could not* have gone.
She is not going.

In such instances, the word *not* and the auxiliary before it are often contracted into one word. The sentences in the above examples can then be rewritten as follows:

I *couldn't* have gone.
She isn't going.

Expressions obtained by contracting auxiliaries and *not* are listed in Figure 8.2.

An auxiliary can often also be contracted with the word immediately before it. Consider:

They have gone.

Expression to be Contracted	Contracted Expression	Expression to be Contracted	Contracted Expression
he has	he's	he is	he's
he will	he'll	he would/had	he'd
here is	here's	I have	I've
I am	I'm	I will	I'll
I would/had	I'd	it is	it's
it will	it'll	she has	she's
she is	she's	she will	she'll
she would/had	she'd	that is	that's
that will	that'll	there is	there's
they are	they're	they have	they've
they will	they'll	they would/had	they'd
we are	we're	we have	we've
we will	we'll	we would/had	we'd
what is	what's	when is	when's
where is	where's	who is	who's
who will	who'll	why is	why's
you are	you're	you have	you've
you will	you'll	you would/had	you'd

Figure 8.3 Specimen expressions in which an auxiliary contracts with the word before it. Different expressions may have the same contraction: *he's* is the contraction for both *he has* and *he is*. Even proper nouns can be contracted, as in: *Anita's* for *Anita has* and *Anita is*. Contracting *Anita's* for *Anita has* or *Anita is* is practised more often in speaking than in writing. Similarly, *he'd* is a contraction for both *he would* and *he had*.

Contracting the auxiliary *have* with the pronoun *They*, we can rewrite the above sentence as follows:

They've gone.

Figure 8.3 shows a list of expressions obtained by contracting auxiliaries with the words immediately before them. Such contracted expressions, however, occur only at the beginning or middle of a finite clause, but not at the end of the finite clause. *There we are* cannot be contracted to *There we're*; but *We are there* can be contracted to *We're there*.

Because an auxiliary can contract with a word before it and also with the word *not* (if *not* occurs) after it, we can have alternative contracted expressions in a sentence. Consider:

They have not gone.

The alternative contracted expressions for the above sentence are the following:

Expression to be Contracted	Alternative Contracted Expressions	
	According to Figure 8.2	According to Figure 8.3
I would not go.	I wouldn't go.	I'd not go.
We are not ready.	We aren't ready.	We're not ready.
That will not do.	That won't do.	That'll not do.
They have not finished.	They haven't finished.	They've not finished.
What is not true?	What isn't true?	What's not true?
He is not coming.	He isn't coming.	He's not coming.
He has not come.	He hasn't come.	He's not come.

Figure 8.4   Examples that have alternative contracted expressions. Whether *he's* is a contraction of *he is* or *he has* can be found out by looking at the context in which *he's* occurs, as in the rightmost column of the last two rows above. For such context, remember that the formula of a finite verb phrase, as given in section 6.5.5, is

$$\text{(MODAL}|\text{b) (HAVE}|\text{en) (BE}_1|\text{ing) (BE}_2|\text{en) VERB (PARTICLES)}.$$

Accordingly, look at the word in the finite verb phrase immediately after *he's*. If the word is a present participle, then *he's* is a contraction of *he is*; but if the word is a past participle, then *he's* is a contraction of *he has*. Keep in mind that the word *not* is not considered to be part of the finite verb phrase.

> They haven't gone.
> They've not gone.

A few other examples with alternative contracted expressions are given in Figure 8.4.

Let's, the contracted expression for *Let us*, exemplifies an expression in which neither of the words contracted is an auxiliary. Note that the expression *let's* can occur only at the beginning of a finite clause. *Mother, let us go* can be rewritten as *Mother, let's go*; but *Mother let us go* cannot be rewritten as *Mother let's go*.

To sum up, in carrying out contractions, two words are contracted into one word. Contracted expressions are widely prevalent. Hence it is useful for an ELP to be able to transform uncontracted expressions into contracted expressions, and vice versa. A procedure to contract expressions will need to look up Figures 8.2 and 8.3.

8.3   DECLARATIVE SENTENCES: POSITIVE TO NEGATIVE

Before you read the procedure to transform a declarative positive sentence (that is, a declarative sentence with positive polarity) into a declarative negative sentence, you should read below the examples and the accompanying comments. That should help you understand the procedure better. The instances mentioned in the examples are based on the finite verb phrases in the declarative positive sentences.

Example 1
Consider the instances when the finite verb phrase contains at least one auxiliary:

> He will go.
> She had been cheated.

Insert the word *not* immediately after the first auxiliary:

> He will not go.
> She had not been cheated.

Carry out contractions, if desired, to obtain:

> He won't go.
> She hadn't been cheated.

Example 2
Consider the instances when the finite verb phrase does not contain any auxiliaries, and when the verb is not BE:

> Archie finished his homework.
> I have a coat.

Transform the verb into a DO-support finite verb phrase (see section 6.5.5), without changing the tense:

> Archie did finish his homework.
> I do have a coat.

Proceed as in example 1 above by inserting *not* immediately after the auxiliary:

> Archie did not finish his homework.
> I do not have a coat.

Carry out contractions, if desired, to obtain:

> Archie didn't finish his homework.
> I don't have a coat.

Example 3

Consider the instances when the finite verb phrase does not contain any auxiliaries, and when the verb is either BE or HAVE:

He is in the room.
I have a coat.

Insert the word *not* immediately after the verb:

He is not in the room.
I have not a coat.

Carry out contractions, if desired, to obtain:

Grammatical class of word to be replaced	Sentence with positive polarity	Corresponding sentence with negative polarity
	He has left <u>already</u>.	He has not left <u>yet</u>.
	She finished the job <u>somehow</u>.	She did not finish the job <u>at all</u>.
	You will see him <u>sometime</u>.	You will not see him <u>ever</u>.
Adverb	They see him <u>sometimes</u>.	They do not see him <u>ever</u>.
	He rested <u>somewhat</u>.	He did not rest <u>at all</u>.
	You could buy it <u>somewhere</u>.	You could not buy it <u>anywhere</u>.
	She is working <u>still</u>.	She is not working <u>any more</u>.
	He is going <u>too</u>.	He is not going <u>either</u>.
Determiner	They bought <u>some</u> grain.	They did not buy <u>any</u> grain.
	She will hit <u>somebody</u>.	She will not hit <u>anybody</u>.
Pronoun	He called <u>someone</u>.	He did not call <u>anyone</u>.
	She said <u>something</u>.	She did not say <u>anything</u>.

Figure 8.5 Examples of adverbs, determiners, and pronouns that are to be replaced when transforming a declarative positive sentence into a declarative negative sentence. See also Figure 8.7.

He isn't in the room.
I haven't a coat.

You must have noticed that when the finite verb phrase does not contain any auxiliaries, and when the verb is HAVE, you can proceed as in example 2 or example 3 above. In practice, it is more frequent to proceed as in example 2 than as in example 3. Hence, we shall observe the more frequent practice and prefer, say, *I don't have a coat* over *I haven't a coat*.

The steps to be executed in transforming a positive sentence into a negative sentence, as informally explained in the three examples above, may occasionally not be enough. Suppose we want to so transform the following sentence:

He ate some porridge.

According to example 2 above, the corresponding negative sentence would be *He did not eat some porridge*. But that is not enough. The

Conditions to be satisfied in the declarative positive sentence		Step to be executed
finite verb phrase contains	**the verb is**	
at least one auxiliary	any verb	Insert <u>not</u> after the first auxiliary in the finite verb phrase.
no auxiliaries	not BE	Transform the verb into a DO-support finite verb phrase, and then insert <u>not</u> after the auxiliary.
	BE	Insert <u>not</u> after the verb.

After executing the above first step, the following steps may need to be executed:

[Step 2]   Replace adverbs, determiners, and pronouns as shown in Figure 8.5.

[Step 3]   Carry out contractions, if desired.

Figure 8.6 Outline of the procedure to transform a declarative positive sentence into a declarative negative sentence.

Grammatical class of word to be replaced	Sentence with positive polarity	Corresponding sentence with positive polarity but with a negative sense
Adverb	He has left <u>already</u>.	He has left <u>not yet</u>.
	She finished the job <u>somehow</u>.	She finished the job <u>not at all</u>.
	You will see him <u>sometime</u>.	You will see him <u>never</u>.
	They see him <u>sometimes</u>.	They see him <u>never</u>.
	He rested <u>somewhat</u>.	He rested <u>not at all</u>.
	You could buy it <u>somewhere</u>.	You could buy it <u>nowhere</u>.
	She is working <u>still</u>.	She is working <u>no more</u>.
	He is going <u>too</u>.	He is going <u>neither</u>.
Determiner	They bought <u>some</u> grain.	They bought <u>no</u> grain.
Pronoun	She will hit <u>somebody</u>.	She will hit <u>nobody</u>.
	He called <u>someone</u>.	He called <u>no one</u>.
	She said <u>something</u>.	She said <u>nothing</u>.

Figure 8.7 Examples of declarative sentences [rightmost column] that have positive polarity but negative sense. Compare with the examples of Figure 8.5. You may find a few sentences in the rightmost column somewhat unusual.

determiner *some*, which is contained in the noun phrase direct object of the verb *eat*, should be replaced by *any*:

He did not eat any porridge.

A word that may need such a replacement is an adverb, a determiner or a pronoun as illustrated in Figure 8.5. The procedure to transform a declarative positive sentence into a declarative negative sentence is now outlined in Figure 8.6.

Incidentally, there is an alternative for the examples of Figure 8.5. In the alternative, a sentence retains its positive polarity, but it takes on a negative sense. Figure 8.7 lists some examples.

8.4 DECLARATIVE SENTENCES TO QUESTIONS

You saw in section 6.4.5 that questions can be direct or indirect:

Where are you going? (direct question)
I want to know where you are going. (indirect question)

Whereas a direct question has the structure of a interrogative sentence, an indirect question has the structure of a declarative sentence. An indirect question begins with an expletory expression like 'I want to know,' 'I wonder,' and 'I would like to know.' Apart from making an inquiry, a question can also be used to express an emphatic statement, an emotion, an offer, a request or a suggestion as illustrated in Figure 8.8.

A question can be positive or negative. If the response expected from a question is a *yes* or a *no*, then it is called a yn-question; otherwise, it is called a wh-question. Hence we can have eight kinds of questions as listed in Figure 8.9.

A direct yn-question is usually broached by one of the auxiliaries: *can, could, may, might, must, shall, should, will, would*, BE, HAVE and DO. It can also be broached by the verbs BE or HAVE:

Purpose of questions	Specimen questions
inquiry	Who is that man?
emphatic statement	Am I to allow myself to be cheated by you? [This exemplifies a rhetorical question that means "I won't allow myself to be cheated by you." A positive rhetorical question emphasizes a negative statement, and vice versa.]
emotion	Isn't she kind! [Such a question ends with an exclamation mark.]
offer	Would you like some tea? I wonder whether you'd like some tea. [indirect question]
request	Can you lend me your pen?
suggestion	Why don't you have some tea?

Figure 8.8 Specimen questions to show that apart from making an inquiry, a question can be used to express an emphatic statement, an emotion, an offer, a request, or a suggestion.

Kind of question			A specimen question
direct or indirect	polarity	yn or wh	
direct	positive	yn	Is he eating?
		wh	When is he eating?
	negative	yn	Isn't he eating?
		wh	When isn't he eating?
indirect	positive	yn	I want to know whether he is eating.
		wh	I wonder when he is eating.
	negative	yn	I wonder whether he isn't eating.
		wh	I would like to know when he isn't eating.

Figure 8.9 The eight kinds of questions. As mentioned in section 8.4, an indirect question begins with an expletory expression like *I want to know, I wonder,* and *I would like to know.*

Will/Did he go to the library? (an auxiliary broaches the question)
Is he in the room? (the verb BE broaches the question)
Have you a coat? (the verb HAVE broaches the question)

A direct wh-question is broached by one of the words known as the wh-words. The wh-words are essentially *how, what, when, where, which, who, whom, whose* and *why.* The alternatives of these words (like *whatever, whensoever, whomever*) can also broach a wh-question. A wh-word can be preceded by a preposition, as illustrated in Figure 8.10. You may have noticed that the wh-words are adverbs, determiners or pronouns.

We discuss below how to transform declarative sentences (they make statements, as discussed in section 6.2.2) into the different kinds of questions.

8.4.1 Direct positive yn-questions

In this section, we shall develop the procedure to transform a declarative positive sentence into a direct positive yn-question, but before that, we need to look at the examples below. Understanding

1.	How are you?
2.	How many apples did you buy?
3.	How much milk did you buy?
4.	How often does he visit you?
5.	What isn't the matter with him?
6.	When will you leave for Tokyo?
7.	Where aren't you going?
8.	Which boy broke the window?
9.	Who broke the window?
10.	With whom are you?
11.	Whose bicycle is broken?
12.	Why are you angry?

Figure 8.10 Examples of direct wh-questions. Apart from the wh-words that are broaching the questions shown above, the following are also considered to be wh-words: *whatever, whatso, whatsoever, whenever, whenso, whensoever, wherever, whereso, wheresoever, whichever, whichso, whichsoever, whoever, whoso, whosoever, whomever, whomso, whomsoever, whosever, whoseso,* and *whosesoever.* The tenth question is an instance where a preposition precedes the wh-word. In colloquial usage, the question can be reworded: Whom are you with?

these examples will help you not only in understanding the transformation procedure of this section but also in understanding the transformation procedures developed later in sections 8.4.2–8.4.4. The instances mentioned in the examples are based on the finite verb phrases in the declarative positive sentences.

Example 1
Consider the instances when the finite verb phrase contains at least one auxiliary:

> He will go.
> She had been cheated.

Move the first auxiliary to the beginning of the sentence:

> Will he go?
> Had she been cheated?

Example 2
Consider the instances when the finite verb phrase does not contain any auxiliaries, and when the verb is not BE:

> Archie finished his homework.
> You have a coat.

Transform the verb into a DO-support finite verb phrase (see section 6.5.5), without changing the tense:

Archie did finish his homework.
You do have a coat.

Proceed as in example 1 above by moving the auxiliary to the beginning of the sentence:

Did Archie finish his homework?
Do you have a coat?

Example 3
Consider the instances when the finite verb phrase does not contain any auxiliaries, and when the verb is either BE or HAVE:

He is in the room.
You have a coat.

Move the verb to the beginning of the sentence:

Grammatical class of word replaced	Declarative positive sentence	Corresponding direct positive yn-question
Adverb	He has left already.	Has he left yet?
	She finished the job somehow.	Did she finish the job at all?
	You will see him sometime.	Will you see him ever?
	They see him sometimes.	Do they see him ever?
	He rested somewhat.	Did he rest at all?
	You could buy it somewhere.	Could you buy it anywhere?
Determiner	They bought some grain.	Did they buy any grain?
Pronoun	She will hit somebody.	Will she hit anybody?
	He called someone.	Did he call anyone?
	She said something.	Did she say anything?

Figure 8.11 Examples of adverbs, determiners, and pronouns that may need to be replaced when transforming a declarative positive sentence into a direct positive yn-question. Compare these with Figure 8.5

Is he in the room?
Have you a coat?

You must have noticed that when the finite verb phrase does not contain any auxiliaries, and when the verb is HAVE, you can proceed as in example 2 or example 3 above. It is more frequent in practice to proceed as in example 2 than as in example 3. Hence we shall observe the more frequent practice and prefer, say, *Do you have a coat* over *Have you a coat*.

The steps for transformation, as informally explained in the three examples above, may not always be enough. Suppose we want to transform into a question the following sentence:

He ate some porridge.

According to example 2 above, the corresponding question would be *Did he eat some porridge?* You may, however, prefer to replace the determiner *some*, which is contained in the noun phrase direct object of the verb *eat*, by *any*:

Conditions to be satisfied in the declarative positive sentence		Step to be executed
finite verb phrase contains	the verb is	
at least one auxiliary	any verb	Move the first auxiliary of the finite verb phrase to the beginning of the sentence.
no auxiliaries	not BE	Transform the verb into a DO-support finite verb phrase, and then move the auxiliary to the beginning of the sentence.
	BE	Move the verb to the beginning of the sentence.

After executing the above first step, the following step may also need to be executed:

[Step 2] Replace adverbs, determiners, and pronouns as shown in Figure 8.11.

Figure 8.12 Outline of the procedure to transform a declarative positive sentence into a direct positive yn-question.

Did he eat any porridge?

A word that may be so replaced is an adverb, a determiner or a pronoun. Some examples are listed in Figure 8.11. The procedure to transform a declarative positive sentence into a direct positive yn-question is now outlined in Figure 8.12.

8.4.2 Direct positive wh-questions

To be able to transform a declarative positive sentence that may already be understood as a question into a direct positive wh-question, the declarative sentence should contain a wh-word:

It is *what*.
He bought *how* much milk.

If, however, the wh-word is already a part of the subject of the sentence, then no transformation is needed. The sentence is itself a wh-question:

Who came to see you?
Whose bicycle is broken?
Which boy broke the window?

Accordingly, we shall assume for the examples below that the wh-word is not such a part of the subject. The instances mentioned in the examples are based on the finite verb phrases in the declarative positive sentences.

Example 1
Consider the instances when the finite verb phrase contains at least one auxiliary:

You will visit whom.
You have been sitting on what.
He is reading which book.

Move the first auxiliary to the beginning of the sentence:

Will you visit whom.
Have you been sitting on what.
Is he reading which book.

Move the wh-word, together with any prepositional phrase or noun phrase in which it may be contained, to the beginning of the sentence:

Whom will you visit?
On what have you been sitting?
Which book is he reading?

Example 2
Consider the instances when the finite verb phrase does not contain any auxiliaries, and when the verb is not BE:

> You visit whom.
> You swim in which pool.
> He bought how much milk.

Transform the verb into a DO-support finite verb phrase (see section 6.5.5), without changing the tense:

> You do visit whom.
> You do swim in which pool.
> He did buy how much milk.

Proceed as in example 1 above by moving the auxiliary to the beginning of the sentence:

> Do you visit whom.
> Do you swim in which pool.
> Did he buy how much milk.

Move the wh-word, together with any prepositional phrase or noun phrase in which it may be contained, to the beginning of the sentence:

> Whom do you visit?
> In which pool do you swim?
> How much milk did he buy?

Example 3
Consider the instances when the finite verb phrase does not contain any auxiliaries, and when the verb is BE:

> The train is when.
> You are with whom.

Move the verb to the beginning of the sentence:

> Is the train when.
> Are you with whom.

Move the wh-word, together with any prepositional phrase or noun phrase in which it may be contained, to the beginning of the sentence:

> When is the train?
> With whom are you?

The procedure to transform a declarative positive sentence into a direct positive wh-question is now outlined in Figure 8.13.

Conditions to be satisfied in the declarative positive sentence		Step to be executed
finite verb phrase contains	the verb is	
at least one auxiliary	any verb	Move the first auxiliary of the finite verb phrase to the beginning of the sentence.
no auxiliaries	not BE	Transform the verb into a DO-support finite verb phrase, and then move the auxiliary to the beginning of the sentence.
	BE	Move the verb to the beginning of the sentence.

After executing the above the first step, execute the following step:

[Step 2] Move the wh-word [together with any prepositional phrase or noun phrase in which it may be contained] to the beginning of the sentence.

Figure 8.13 Outline of the procedure to transform a declarative positive sentence into a direct positive wh-question. It is assumed that the wh-word is not already a part of the subject of the sentence to be transformed, for then no transformation would be needed. Note that the first step above is identical to the first step of Figure 8.12.

8.4.3   Direct negative yn-questions

In this section, we discuss how to transform a declarative negative sentence into a direct negative yn-question. Consider:

> He will not go.
> Anita had not been at school.
> Archie did not finish his homework.
> He is not in the room.

Step 1
Move the word *not* and the word immediately before it (which will be either an auxiliary or the verb BE as in section 8.3) to the beginning of the sentence:

> Will not he go?
> Had not Anita been at school?

Given the following declarative negative sentences:

> He will not go.
> Anita had not been at school.
> Archie did not finish his homework.
> He is not in the room.

Move the word before the <u>not</u> to the beginning of each sentence to obtain direct negative yn-questions:

> Will he not go?
> Had Anita not been at school?
> Did Archie not finish his homework?
> Is he not in the room?

Figure 8.14 Examples on transforming declarative negative sentences into direct negative yn-questions by a procedure that in practice is used less frequently than the procedure described in section 8.4.3.

> Did not Archie finish his homework?
> Is not he in the room?

Step 2
Carry out contractions:

> Won't he go?
> Hadn't Anita been at school?
> Didn't Archie finish his homework?
> Isn't he in the room?

A less frequently practiced alternative to step 1 above, and illustrated in Figure 8.2, is to move only the word before the *not* to the beginning of the sentence. Observing the more frequent practice, we shall usually prefer the procedure above to the procedure of Figure 8.14. In other words, we shall usually prefer, say, *won't he go* to *will he not go*.

8.4.4 Direct negative wh-questions

To be able to transform a declarative negative sentence that may already be understood as a question into a direct negative wh-question, the declarative sentence should contain a wh-word:

> It is not what.
> You will not visit whom.

If, however, the wh-word is already a part of the subject of the sentence, then no transformation is needed. The sentence is itself a wh-question:

Who did not come to see you?
Whose bicycle is not broken?
Which boy did not break the window?

Accordingly, in describing the transformation procedure, we shall assume that the wh-word is not such a part of the subject. Consider:

You will not visit whom.
He is not reading which book.
You do not swim in which pool.
They are not where.

Step 1
Move the word *not* and the word before it (which will be either an auxiliary or the verb BE; see section 8.3) to the beginning of the sentence:

Will not you visit whom.
Is not he reading which book.
Do not you swim in which pool.
Are not they where.

Step 2
Move the wh-word, together with any prepositional phrase or noun phrase in which it may be contained, to the beginning of the sentence:

Whom will not you visit.
Which book is not he reading.
In which pool do not you swim.
Where are not they.

Step 3
Carry out contractions:

Whom won't you visit?
Which book isn't he reading?
In which pool don't you swim?
Where aren't they?

8.4.5   Indirect questions

An indirect question (shown in Figure 8.9) contains a finite noun clause that is broached by *whether* for a yn-question and by a wh-word for a wh-question:

I want to know *whether* he is going. (yn-question)
I would like to know *where* you are not going. (wh-question)

In colloquial usage, the *whether* of the yn-question is often supplanted by *if*, as in *I want to know if he is going*.

Below we describe a procedure to transform declarative sentences (the kind seen in sections 8.4.1–8.4.4) into indirect questions. Consider:

> He is in the room.
> Who came to see you.
> You swim in which pool.
> She has not gone.
> You are not going where.
> He is not in what business.

Step 1
If the sentence has a wh-word, then move the wh-word, together with any prepositional phrase or noun phrase in which it may be contained, to the beginning of the sentence; otherwise, insert the word *whether* at the beginning of the sentence:

> Whether he is in the room.
> Who came to see you.
> In which pool you swim.
> Whether she has not gone.
> Where you are not going.
> What business he is not in.

Step 2
Insert an expletory expression, like *I wonder*, as suggested in the legend of Figure 8.9, at the beginning of the sentence, and, if desired, carry out contractions:

> I wonder whether he is in the room. (positive yn-question)
> I wonder who came to see you. (positive wh-question)
> I wonder in which pool you swim. (positive wh-question)
> I wonder whether she hasn't gone. (negative yn-question)
> I wonder where you aren't going. (negative wh-question)
> I wonder what business he isn't in. (negative wh-question)

You must have noticed that the above procedure can be used for all four kinds of indirect questions. If the declarative sentence is positive, then the question obtained is positive; otherwise, the question obtained is negative. Furthermore, if the declarative sentence contains a wh-word, then we obtain a wh-question; otherwise we obtain a yn-question.

8.5 APPENDING TAG QUESTIONS

A direct yn-question appended to the end of a statement is called a tag question.

>Archie ate, didn't he?

The tag question is *didn't he*. Note that the statement *Archie ate* is positive, but the tag question is negative. It seems the speaker is merely seeking a confirmation of his statement: he is expecting the response *Yes, he did*. Similarly, a positive tag question is sometimes appended to the end of a negative statement.

>Anita didn't eat, did she?

Here the speaker is seemingly expecting the response *No, she didn't*. Below we discuss how to append tag questions to the end of statements. Before appending any words to the end of a statement, the full stop/period at the end of the statement is replaced by a comma. A question mark is then later put in after the appended tag question. First we discuss the appending of negative tag questions, and then the appending of positive tag questions.

8.5.1 Negative tag questions

Before you read about the procedure to transform a postive statement into a positive statement appended by a negative tag question, read the examples below. The instances mentioned in the examples are based on the finite verb phrase in the statement.

Example 1
Consider the instance when the finite verb phrase contains at least one auxiliary:

>Archie will have eaten.

Append a copy of the first auxiliary of the finite verb phrase:

>Archie will have eaten, will . . .

Append *not*:

>Archie will have eaten, will not . . .

Append a pronoun in the nominative case whose referent is the subject of the statement:

>Archie will have eaten, will not he . . .

Append copies of the remaining auxiliaries, that is, all auxiliaries except the first auxiliary, of the finite verb phrase:

Archie will have eaten, will not he have?

Carry out contractions:

Archie will have eaten, won't he have?

Example 2
Consider the instance when the finite verb phrase does not contain any auxiliaries, and when the verb is not BE:

Archie ate.

Transform the verb into a DO-support finite verb phrase (see section 6.5.5), without changing the tense:

Archie did eat.

Proceed as in example 1 above by appending in sequence a copy of the auxiliary, the word *not*, and a pronoun in the nominative case whose referent is the subject of the statement:

Archie did eat, did not he?

Carry out contractions:

Archie did eat, didn't he?

Example 3
Consider the instance when the finite verb phrase does not contain any auxiliaries, and when the verb is BE:

Anita is at school.

Append in sequence a copy of the verb, the word *not*, and a pronoun in the nominative case whose referent is the subject of the statement:

Anita is at school, is not she?

Carry out contractions:

Anita is at school, isn't she?

The procedure to transform a positive statement into a positive statement appended by a negative tag question is now outlined in Figure 8.15.

8.5.2   Positive tag questions

In this section, we discuss how to transform a negative statement into a negative statement appended by a positive tag question. Consider:

Archie would not have eaten.
Anita is not at school.

Conditions to be satisfied in the positive statement		Step to be executed
finite verb phrase contains	the verb is	
at least one auxiliary	any verb	Append a copy of the first auxiliary of the finite verb phrase to the end of the statement.
no auxiliaries	not BE	Transform the verb into a DO-support finite verb phrase, and then append a copy of the auxiliary to the end of the statement.
	BE	Append a copy of the verb to the end of the statement.

After executing the above first step, execute the following steps:

[Step 2] Append to the end of the statement the following words in sequence:

> the word <u>not</u>;
> a pronoun in the nominative case whose referent is the subject of the statement; and
> copies of the remaining auxiliaries, if any, of the finite verb phrase.

[Step 3] Carry out contractions.

Figure 8.15 Outline of the procedure to transform a positive statement into a positive statement appended by a negative tag question.

Step 1

Append a copy of the word immediately before the *not* (this word will be either an auxiliary or the verb BE as discussed in section 8.3) to the end of the statement:

> Archie would not have eaten, would . . .
> Anita is not at school, is . . .

Step 2

Append in sequence a pronoun in the nominative case whose referent is the subject of the statement, and copies of the remaining auxiliaries, if any, of the finite verb phrase:

> Archie would not have eaten, would he have?
> Anita is not at school, is she?

Step 3
Carry out contractions, if desired:

> Archie wouldn't have eaten, would he have?
> Anita isn't at school, is she?

8.6   DECLARATIVE TO IMPERATIVE SENTENCES

As mentioned in section 6.2.2, the subject in an imperative sentence is often elided. It can be presumed that the subject is the one who is addressed, usually *you*. The procedure below will describe how a declarative positive sentence can be transformed into an imperative sentence provided that in the declarative sentence, (a) the subject is *you*, and (b) the finite verb phrase has the structure of:

> MODAL VERB-b   in active voice, or
> MODAL be VERB-en   in passive voice.

Remember from section 6.5.2 that VERB-b is the basal form of the verb, and VERB-en is the past participle. The aspect of the finite verb phrase should thus be simple, as can be noticed from Figure 6.34. Consider:

> You will see.
> You will be seen.

Step 1
Delete the subject and the modal auxiliary to obtain the imperative:

> See.
> Be seen.

You now have the following choices:

> stop here,
> execute step 2a below,
> execute step 2b below, or
> execute steps 2a and 2b.

Step 2a
To obtain an imperative with emphasis, insert the word *Do* at the beginning of the sentence for a positive imperative, or insert *Don't* (or *Do not*) for a negative imperative:

> Do see.
> Do be seen.
> Don't see.
> Don't be seen.

Step 2b
To obtain a courteous imperative, insert words of request, like *please* or *kindly*, either at the beginning or at the end of the sentence. If we execute this step immediately after step 1, then we typically obtain:

Please/kindly see.
See, please/kindly.
Please/kindly be seen.
Be seen, please/kindly.

If, however, we execute step 2b after executing step 2a, then we typically obtain:

Please/kindly do see.
Do see, please/kindly.
Please/Kindly do be seen.
Do be seen, please/kindly.
Please/kindly don't see.
Don't see, please/kindly.
Please/kindly don't be seen.
Don't be seen, please/kindly.

8.7   ACTIVE TO PASSIVE VOICE

In transforming a declarative sentence from active voice to passive voice, the polarity, tense, aspect and mood remain unchanged. In so transforming a sentence, the subject of the sentence nearly always changes: the finite verb phrase must be suitably modified to concord with the new subject on person and number:

He is reading those books.
(active voice; third person singular subject)
Those books are being read by him.
(passive voice; third person plural subject)

As mentioned in section 7.3.1, the agent (the doer of the action) in passive voice is flagged by the preposition *by*. There are, however, situations in which the agent is often elided. Such situations are usually the following:

1. when mentioning the agent could cause embarrassment:

The dinner was burnt (by Anita).

2. when the agent is not known:

Gilda's bicycle was stolen (by someone).

3. when the agent is obvious:

She was elected mayor (by the townspeople).

Below we discuss how to transform a declarative sentence from the active to the passive voice. The transformation procedure depends on the genus of the finite verb, or finite verb phrase, in the sentence. It is suggested that, before reading any further, you should look over section 6.11.3 to refresh your memory. To simplify the discussion below, we assume that the finite verb phrases do not have DO-support.

(1) Active voice sentences with linking verbs cannot be transformed into the passive. Consider:

The soup tasted awful.
He remained unmarried.

An attempt to transform them into the passive would lead to the awkward sentences *Awful was tasted by the soup* and *Unmarried was remained by him*.

(2) Most of the active voice sentences with intransitive verbs cannot be transformed into the passive. Consider:

He jumped.
She came screaming.

These sentences cannot be transformed into the passive. Nonetheless, when the verb is followed by an adverbized prepositional phrase (discussed in section 6.8.4), then sometimes the active sentence can be transformed into the passive. The sentence *He ran at a slow pace* cannot be transformed into the passive, but the following sentence can be transformed:

They will yell at her.

When transformed into the passive, the sentence becomes:

She will be yelled at by them.

Transformations into the passive of such sentences can be expressed by formulae. Let N_i (where $i \geq 1$) symbolize a nounal such that N_i^n designates N_i in the nominative case, and N_i^a designates N_i in the accusative case. To prevent unnecessarily cluttering our formulae below, we have not shown the presence of particles (see section 6.5.3) with the verbs. The particles, however, may be present. They are not affected by the transformation.

An active voice sentence with an intransitive verb and an adverbized prepositional phrase will essentially be structured (as in sections 6.5.5 and 6.11.3) according to the formula:

N_1^n (MODAL|b) (HAVE|en) (BE$_1$|ing) VERB PREPOSITION N_2^a

Then after transformation, the structure of the corresponding passive sentence will be:

N_2^n (MODAL|b) (HAVE|en) (BE$_1$|ing) BE VERB-en
PREPOSITION by N_1^a

(3) Most of the active voice sentences with unitransitive verbs can be transformed into the passive. Sentences that cannot be transformed into the passive are, for example:

Archie has a bicycle.
Father blew his top.
The punishment suits him.
The key fits the lock.

Active voice sentences that can be transformed into the passive can be of two kinds: sentences in which the subject and the direct object denote the same person, place or thing; and sentences in which the subject and the direct object denote different persons, places or things. We shall discuss the two kinds of sentences one by one. Let us first discuss sentences in which the subject and the direct object denote the same person, place or thing. Consider:

Archie hurt himself.
Anita had driven herself.

When transformed into the passive, the sentences become:

Archie was hurt by himself.
Anita had been driven by herself.

Hence, if the structure of the active voice sentence is the following:

N_1^n (MODAL|b) (HAVE|en) (BE|ing) VERB N_2^a

then, after transformation, the structure of the corresponding passive sentence is:

N_1^n (MODAL|b) (HAVE|en) (BE|ing) BE VERB-en by N_2^a

Now let us discuss sentences in which the subject and the direct object denote different persons, places or things:

He is reading those books.
That man cheated Archie.

The corresponding passive sentences are:

Those books are being read by him.
Archie was cheated by that man.

Therefore, if the structure of the active voice sentence is the following:

N_1^n (MODAL|b) (HAVE|en) (BE|ing) VERB N_2^a

then, after transformation, the structure of the corresponding passive sentence is:

N_2^n (MODAL|b) (HAVE|en) (BE|ing) BE VERB-en by N_1^a

As the above formula shows, we insert the preposition *by* immediately before N_1^a in the passive. There are instances, however, when we either do not insert any preposition before N_1^a, or we insert the prepositions *from, for* or *in*. This usually happens when the subject in the active voice sentence is not the agent:

To eat spaghetti requires grace.
Your symptoms tell your disease.
Eating spaghetti requires grace.
The library requires silence.

The corresponding passive sentences are:

Grace is required to eat spaghetti.
    (no preposition inserted before N_1^a, *to eat spaghetti*)
Your disease is told *from* your symptoms. (inserted *from*)
Grace is required *for* eating spaghetti. (inserted *for*)
Silence is required *in* the library. (inserted *in*)

The agent had been elided from the above active and passive voice sentences. If, however, we do not elide the agent, the active voice sentences can become:

One requires grace to eat spaghetti.
The doctor tells your disease from your symptoms.
One requires grace for eating spaghetti.
The librarian requires silence in the library.

Then the corresponding passive sentences are:

Grace is required *by one* to eat spaghetti.
Your disease is told *by the doctor* from your symptoms.
Grace is required *by one* for eating spaghetti.
Silence is required *by the librarian* in the library.

(4) Active voice sentences with cotransitive verbs can usually be transformed into the passive. Consider:

We have elected him (to be/as) mayor.
She painted the wall green.

The corresponding passive sentences are:

He has been elected (to be/as) mayor by us.
The wall has been painted green by her.

Accordingly, if the structure of the active voice sentence is the following:

N_1^n (MODAL|b)(HAVE|en)(BE|ing) VERB N_2^a (to be/as) ADJECTIVAL/N_3^a

then, after transformation, the structure of the corresponding passive sentence is:

N_2^n (MODAL|b)(HAVE|en)(BE|ing) BE VERB-en (to be/as) ADJECTIVAL/N_3^a by N_1^a

(5) Active voice sentences with bitransitive verbs can usually be transformed into the passive. Consider:

Archie has given Anita a book.

The above sentence can be transformed into either of the two following passive sentences:

Anita has been given a book by Archie.
(*a book* is called the retained object)
A book has been given Anita by Archie.
(now *Anita* is called the retained object)

We can, therefore, say that if the structure of the active voice sentence is the following:

N_1^n (MODAL|b) (HAVE|en) (BE|ing) VERB N_2^a N_3^a

then, after transformation, the structure of the corresponding passive sentence can be either of the following:

N_2^n (MODAL|b) (HAVE|en) (BE|ing) BE VERB-en N_3^a by N_1^a
(N_3^a is the retained object)
N_3^n (MODAL|b) (HAVE|en) (BE|ing) BE VERB-en N_2^a by N_1^a
(N_2^a is the retained object)

8.8 EXERCISES

1. Develop and program a procedure to transform declarative positive sentences containing pseudo-auxiliaries into declarative negative sentences. For example:

   He dares to drink.

   The above positive sentence can be transformed into either of the following negative sentences:

   He dare not drink.
   He does not dare to drink.

   Figure 6.36 contains a list of pseudo-auxiliaries.

2. Develop and program a procedure to transform declarative active positive sentences into declarative passive negative sentences. To illustrate, the sentence *Archie hit the ball* will be transformed into *The ball was not hit by Archie*. Will you transform first to the passive and then to the negative, or first to the negative and then to the passive?

3. Develop and program a procedure to transform declarative active sentences containing DO-support finite verb phrases into declarative passive sentences. Examples are:

   They do yell at her. (intransitive)
   He does hit her. (unitransitive)
   We did elect him mayor. (cotransitive)
   I did give him a book. (bitransitive)

   The corresponding passive sentences are:

   She is indeed yelled at by them.
   She is indeed hit by him.
   He was indeed elected mayor by us.
   He was indeed given a book by me.
   A book was indeed given him by me.

   Note that the word *indeed* is inserted in all the passive sentences. Moreover, a sentence containing a bitransitive verb can be transformed into two alternative passive sentences.

4. Develop and program a procedure to transform active voice non-finite verb phrases in a sentence to passive voice non-finite verb phrases. For example:

   You are to read this book.
   He departed without anyone seeing him.

After transformation, the sentences become:

> This book is to be read by you.
> He departed without being seen by anyone.

Figure 6.38 lists some non-finite verb phrases.

5. Declarative sentences with noun clauses (finite or non-finite) can often be transformed into sentences called it-expletive sentences. Consider:

> To eat so much is a folly.
> Listening to Grandma's stories is fun.
> That you behaved so badly shocked Mother.
> Whether he will get the job is not known.

After transformation, the sentences become:

> It is a folly to eat so much.
> It is fun listening to Grandma's stories.
> It shocked Mother that you behaved so badly.
> It is not known whether he will get the job.

Note, however, that *Whoever came to dinner was polite* cannot be transformed into an it-expletive sentence. Develop and program a procedure to carry out the transformation discussed above.

6. Declarative sentences can usually be transformed into sentences called it-cleft sentences. For example:

> Anita needs new shoes.

The above sentence can be transformed into either of the following it-cleft sentences:

> It is Anita who needs new shoes.
> It is new shoes that Anita needs.

In both the transformed sentences, *it* is a pronoun: in the first sentence the referent of *it* is *Anita*; in the second sentence, the referent of *it* is *new shoes*. It-cleft sentences provide emphasis to the referent of *it*. Develop and program a procedure to transform declarative sentences into it-cleft sentences, whenever possible. Do not confuse it-expletive sentences, introduced in exercise 5 above, with it-cleft sentences.

7. Declarative sentences can usually be transformed into sentences called what-cleft sentences. For example:

> Anita needs new shoes.

The above sentence can be transformed into either of the following what-cleft sentences:

What Anita needs is new shoes.
New shoes are what Anita needs.

What-cleft sentences provide emphasis to the finite noun clause broached by the word *what*. Develop and program a procedure to transform declarative sentences into what-cleft sentences, whenever possible.

8. Declarative sentences whose subjects are indefinite and whose finite verb phrases contain BE can usually be transformed into existential sentences (see section 6.2.2). Examples are:

A boy has been ill. (linking)
Someone was yelling at her. (intransitive)
Somebody will be buying a bicycle. (unitransitive)
No one is electing him mayor. (cotransitive)
Many people have been causing her pain. (bitransitive)

The above sentences can be transformed into the following existential sentences:

There has been a boy ill.
There was someone yelling at her.
There will be somebody buying a bicycle.
There is no one electing him mayor.
There have been many people causing her pain.

Develop and program a procedure to transform declarative sentences into existential sentences, whenever possible.

9. Redo exercise 6 of Chapter 7, permitting a greater variety in the English sentences input to the program. Different sentences with the same meaning are translated into the same predicate logic formula. For instance, the formula MA (Amity, Betsy) is obtained from any of the following premises:

Amity is the ma of Betsy.
It is Amity who is the ma of Betsy.
The ma of Betsy is Amity.

Embody suitable transformational procedures in your ELP.

10. Redo any one of exercises 8, 9 or 10 of Chapter 7. Embody in your ELP the transformational procedures you require. Comment on the usefulness of embodying transformational procedures in an ELP.

8.9 SUGGESTIONS FOR FURTHER READING

Akmajian and Heny (1975), Chomsky (1965), Jacobs and Rosenbaum (1968), Jacobsen (1986), Lester (1971), and Radford (1981) all discussed transformational grammar for English.

1. Akmajian, A. and Heny, F. W. (1975) *An Introduction to the Principles of Transformational Syntax*, MIT Press, Cambridge, Massachusetts.
2. Chomsky, N. (1965) *Aspects of the Theory of Syntax*, MIT Press, Cambridge, Massachusetts.
3. Jacobs, R. A. and Rosenbaum, P. S. (1968) *English Transformational Grammar*, Blaidsell Publishing, Waltham, Massachusetts.
4. Jacobsen, B. (1986) *Modern Transformational Grammar*, Elsevier Science, Amsterdam.
5. Lester, M. (1971) *Introductory Transformational Grammar of English*, Holt, Rinehart and Winston, New York.
6. Radford, A, (1981) *Transformational Syntax*, Cambridge University Press, New York.

9

Production rules for expert systems

9.1 INTRODUCTION

Suppose we were asked to calculate the area of a rectangle whose length is 3 centimetres and breadth is 2 centimetres. Since there is a well-known mathematical procedure (available in books on mensuration) according to which the area can be obtained by multiplying the length and the breadth, we cannot say that it required any expertise to solve the problem. We do not change the procedure by developing heuristics with our experience in calculating the areas of rectangles. Neither do we know of any mathematician who disputes the procedure.

Now consider the domain of medicine, in which a typical problem is to prescribe therapy by observing a patient's symptoms. To solve the problem, a doctor may use the knowledge he has learnt in medical school together with heuristics he has developed with experience. Each doctor may develop his own heuristics. Two doctors examining a patient with the same sincerity and thoroughness may prescribe differently. This may often be because of the different heuristics employed by the two doctors. In other words, different doctors may not follow identical procedures. You may have heard of patients who consulted a doctor and then consulted another doctor to get a second opinion. You may have also heard of patients who prefer to consult a doctor with a few years' experience rather than a doctor fresh out of medical school. A common belief is that the experienced doctor has more expertise. As a doctor increases his experience, he develops more heuristics in medicine, thus increasing his expertise.

Similarly, with experience, a geologist increases his expertise in geology, a mechanic in car repair, and a general in warfare. Employers pay employees with experience more than those without under the impression that, having increased their expertise, the experienced will perform better than the inexperienced.

But human experts, no matter of what domain, do suffer from a handicap: fatigue or emotion can cloud their working. A doctor, tired or irritated, may not be able to prescribe optimal therapy to a patient. Moreover, human expertise is mortal: when human experts die, so does their expertise. It is thus desirable to formalize the human expertise in a domain and implement it on a computer. Such an implementation is known as an expert system for the domain. The expert system's working is not hampered by human fatigue, emotion or mortality. Furthermore, an expert system can be used in environments hazardous for humans: a place contaminated by, say, nuclear radiation.

To build expert systems for a particular domain, we need not restrict ourselves to only one human expert of the domain. By conferring with different human experts of the domain (known in the literature as the **domain experts**), we can pool their expertise to examine whether they contradict or reinforce one another. The expert system then becomes a repository of the relevant knowledge of the domain experts. By continually refining and editing this knowledge, we may succeed in building an expert system that can perform as well as a typical domain expert, if not better. Copies of such an expert system can then be distributed for widespread usage.

In this chapter, you will read how production rules (**prodrules**, for short) can be employed to build expert systems. Prodrules are statements of the form **if . . . then . . .**, similar to the implications in mathematical logic (depicted in Figure 2.1). Examples of prodrules are:

If you're leaving, **then** close the front door.
If you overeat, **then** you will be uncomfortable.

Prodrules help formalize the relevant knowledge of the domain experts. In the literature, the set of prodrules in an expert system is known as a **rule base** or **knowledge base**, the embedding of the knowledge in the expert system is known as **knowledge engineering**, and the persons who do the embedding are known as **knowledge engineers**, since they engineer the knowledge of the domain experts into a formal representation.

Prodrules can help solve mainly two kinds of problems: synthesis and analysis. In section 9.2, you will read about synthesis, and in section 9.3 about analysis.

9.2   PRODRULES FOR SYNTHESIS

A problem of synthesis calls for putting together an arrangement. Writing an English sentence exemplifies synthesis. The components (the individual words and punctuation marks) must be put together under the constraints of English grammar to constitute a sentence that makes sense. To express a given thought, different writers may word the sentence differently. An example is shown in Figure 6.1.

Designing a computer network also exemplifies synthesis. The designer must know about the components that can go into the network and also about the constraints under which the components can be linked to one another. To meet a given objective of the network, different designers may link the components differently.

9.2.1   A problem of synthesis

To illustrate the writing of prodrules for synthesis, let us consider the problem of packing a suitcase with articles that someone (that is, the *user* of the system) is taking with him on a trip. You may think of prodrules as directives that a robot obeys to do the actual packing. The collection of articles that a user gives the robot to pack will be known as the **mound**. To make our discussion easy to read, we shall avoid many of the details of packing, thus simplifying the problem. Let us assume that, after having conferred with the domain experts, we come to know the following.

1. There are a few articles that are essential for taking on a trip, for example, toiletry, so if the user has not included an essential article in the mound, then the robot should add the article to the mound.
2. When one wears a suit, then usually one wears a tie also. A tie can be said to be the **mate** of a suit. Similarly, other articles too can have mates. A person taking an article on a trip should take the article's mate, if any, as well, so if the user has included an article in the mound, but not its mate, then the robot should add the mate to the mound.
3. The robot should know the size (length, breadth and height) of the suitcase and of each article, so that before putting the article in the suitcase, the robot can ensure that there is enough space in the suitcase to fit the article.

The above information about articles can be stored in a data structure called a **roster**. The roster contains the list of all the articles from which the user can choose to include in the mound. The robot too can pick up articles from the roster to add them to the mound. The properties of the articles (whether they are essential for a trip; whether they have a mate, and if so which is the mate; and the sizes of the articles) are also stored in the roster. See Figure 9.1.

In general, a roster contains the list of components that may be

Article	Is the article essential for taking on a trip?	Mate, if any, of the article	Size of the article
alarm clock	•	•	•
belt	•	•	•
coat	•	•	•
clothes brush	•	•	•
dressing gown	•	•	•
handkerchief	•	•	•
pyjamas	•	•	•
reading material	•	•	•
shirt	yes	•	•
shoe brush	•	•	•
shoe polish	•	•	•
shoes	•	•	•
shorts	•	•	•
slippers	•	•	•
socks	•	•	•
suit	•	tie	•
sweater	•	•	•
tie	•	•	•
toiletry	yes	•	•
towel	•	•	•
trousers	•	•	•
underclothes	•	•	•
writing material	•	•	•

Figure 9.1   A roster to store the list of articles [that may be taken on a trip] together with their properties. To prevent cluttering the figure, not all of the entries have been filled in above.

required to solve the problem, together with the properties of these components. You may consider a roster as analogous to a lexicon, as shown in Figure 7.1, in natural language processing.

Let us now decide that we shall write the production rules such that the robot can attempt to pack the articles in the mound by executing the following two steps.

Step 1: Checking-articles
First, check that all articles essential for a trip are in the mound; otherwise, add them to the mound. Second, check that for all articles

in the mound, their mates, if any, are also in the mound; otherwise, add the mates to the mound.

Step 2: Putting-articles
Provided there is space in the suitcase, put the articles from the mound together with their mates, if any, into the suitcase. Should the suitcase run out of space, packing cannot be finished.

Based on the above, we can write the following six prodrules, J1 to J6.

(J1) **If**   the step is checking-articles,
    and there is an essential article not in the mound,
    then add the article to the mound.
(J2) **If**   the step is checking-articles,
    and there is an article in the mound,
    and the article has a mate,
    and the mate is not in the mound,
    then add the mate to the mound.
(J3) **If**   the step is checking-articles,
    then abandon the step of checking-articles,
    and begin the step of putting-articles.
(J4) **If**   the step is putting-articles,
    and there is an article in the mound,
    and there is enough space in the suitcase to fit the article,
    then put the article into the suitcase.
(J5) **If**   the step is putting-articles,
    and there is an article in the mound,
    and there is not enough space in the suitcase to fit the article,
    then announce, 'Unable to finish packing because the suitcase is full,'
    and stop.
(J6) **If**   the step is putting-articles,
    then announce 'Packing finished,'
    and stop.

We shall refer to the above set of six prodrules as PACKER. Before we see an example in the next section, let us get an overview of how PACKER is used. At any time during the packing process, a data structure called **blotter** contains the name of the step being executed, the list of the articles in the mound, and the list of the articles in the suitcase. In other words, the blotter delineates the situation prevailing at that time. In the literature, a blotter is known variously as a context list, dynamic database, data memory, global database, short-term memory or working memory.

Now let us look at the prodrules of PACKER. Being a statement of the **if . . . then . . .** form, each prodrule has an antecedent (the words between the **if** and the **then**) and a consequent (the words after the **then**). The antecedent specifies a situation, and the consequent an action. Such prodrules are thus sometimes more precisely known as situation–action prodrules.

9.2.2   Forechaining for synthesis

If, at any time, the situation delineated by the blotter matches the situation specified by the antecedent of a prodrule (that is, the two situations are the same), then we say that the prodrule has become

Line number	Information stored in the blotter		Prodrules heated	Prodrule fired
	Contents of the mound	Contents of the suitcase		
1	shirts(2), suit(1)		J1, J2, J3	J1
2	shirts(2), suit(1) toiletry(1)		J2, J3	J2
3	shirts(2), suit(1) toiletry(1), tie(1)		J3	J3
4	shirts(2), suit(1) toiletry(1), tie(1)		J4, J6	J4
5	shirt(1), suit(1) toiletry(1), tie(1)	shirt(1)	J4, J6	J4
6	suit(1), toiletry(1) tie(1)	shirts(2)	J4, J6	J4
7	toiletry(1), tie(1)	shirts(2), suit(1)	J4, J6	J4
8	tie(1)	shirts(2), suit(1) toiletry(1)	J4, J6	J4
9		shirts(2), suit(1) toiletry(1), tie(1)	J6	J6

Figure 9.2   An example of firing the prodrules of PACKER. The contents of the mound given by the user for packing are shown in the first line. This provoked prodrules J1, J2, and J3 to become heated. J1, catalogued as the earliest of the heated rules, fired. This caused the contents of the mound to become as shown in the second line. The solution then progresses in the same way. In addition to that shown above, the blotter also contained the name of the step being executed: in the first three lines, it was the checking-articles step; in the remaining lines, it was the putting-articles step.

heated. If the action specified by the consequent of the heated prodrule is carried out, then we say that the prodrule has been **fired**. It can happen that sometimes more than one prodrule becomes heated. Then one of the heated prodrules is selected for firing, and the selected prodrule is fired. Later, in section 9.4, you will read of different techniques for selecting a prodrule to fire. For the example below, we shall, however, adopt the following technique: fire the prodrule that is catalogued as the earliest among the heated prodrules. Prodrules are said to be catalogued in the order in which they are written when displaying them. Accordingly, prodrule J1 is catalogued before J2 in PACKER, J2 before J3, and so on.

After a prodrule has been selected and fired, all the heated rules are said to become **chilled**, that is, they are no longer heated. The firing of the prodrule can result in a change of situation, which is reflected by the change in the contents of the blotter. The new situation provokes another prodrule to fire, and so on, as the solution of the problem progresses.

As an example, suppose the mound contains two shirts and one suit in the beginning. The solution with PACKER is shown in Figure 9.2.

The strategy to control the processing of prodrules, discussed above, is known as **forechaining** (short for forward chaining). We say that in forechaining we match the antecedent of a prodrule to act out the consequent. The practice of repeatedly heating prodrules and firing one of them is known in the literature as a recognize–act cycle/loop or as a select–execute cycle/loop, and the heated prodrules are also known as the triggered prodrules.

9.2.3 Remarks on synthesis

In general, to solve a problem of synthesis, we usually break the problem down into a sequence of steps to be executed. Prodrules are then written for executing each step such that while executing a step only prodrules for that step are heated and fired. Alternatively worded, each step provides a context for the heating and the firing of the prodrules. In the next section, we discuss the writing of prodrules for problems of analysis.

9.3 PRODRULES FOR ANALYSIS

A problem of analysis calls for inferring **hypotheses** from some given data, which are said to serve as **evidence** for the hypotheses. Parsing an English sentence (discussed in section 7.1.1) exemplifies analysis.

The evidence is the words of the sentence, and the hypotheses inferred are the grammatical classes of the words.

Examining soil samples to decide whether oil is present also exemplifies analysis. The evidence is the soil samples, and the hypothesis inferred is that 'oil is present,' or its negation.

Prescribing therapy by observing a patient's symptoms is analysis too. The evidence is the patient's symptoms, and the hypothesis inferred is the prescribed therapy.

9.3.1 A problem of analysis

To illustrate the writing of prodrules for analysis, let us consider the following problem: by observing a person on a university campus, infer whether the person is a undergraduate student, a graduate student, a secretary, a professor or a dean. If you are unable to infer any of the above, then by default infer that the person is a visitor to the campus. After having conferred with the pertinent domain experts, we can tongue in cheek write the following ten prodrules, I1 to I10.

(I1) **If** he is a student,
    and he is emaciated,
    and he wears a helmet,
    then he is an undergraduate student.

(I2) **If** he is a student,
    and he is emaciated,
    then he is a graduate student.

(I3) **If** he is an academic,
    and he eats junk food,
    then he is a student.

(I4) **If** he is an administrator,
    and he talks to himself,
    then he is a secretary.

(I5) **If** he is an academic,
    and he talks to himself,
    and he takes long lunches,
    then he is a professor.

(I6) **If** he is an administrator,
    and he writes memos,
    and he takes long lunches,
    then he is a dean.

(I7) **If** he wears a suit,
    and he shuffles papers,
    then he is an administrator.

(I8) **If**   he looks confused,
     then he is an academic.
(I9) **If**   he looks sleepy,
     then he is an academic.
(I10) **If**   TRUE
     then he is a visitor.

We shall refer to the above set of ten prodrules as UNPERS (UNiversity PERSons). As a user of UNPERS, if you see a person who looks confused, then you can infer from prodrule I8 that the person is an academic. We say that prodrule I8 was fired.

The antecedent of each prodrule in UNPERS specifies some evidence, and the consequent specifies the hypothesis that can be inferred from the evidence. Such prodrules are thus sometimes more precisely known as evidence–hypothesis prodrules. Contrast these with the situation–action prodrules you saw in section 9.2.1.

Let us discuss a few details about evidence–hypothesis prodrules. There are two kinds of hypotheses: final and intermediate. A final hypothesis is in the consequent of at least one prodrule, but never in the antecedent of any prodrule. In UNPERS, *he is a dean* exemplifies a final hypothesis: it is in the consequent of prodrule I6, but not in the antecedent of any prodrule.

An intermediate hypothesis is in the consequent of at least one prodrule and also in the antecedent of at least one prodrule. A hypothesis cannot be both intermediate and final. Intermediate hypotheses serve as steps toward inferring other hypotheses as illustrated in Figure 9.3. Humans are reputed to employ similar

Suppose we have the following two evidence-hypothesis prodrules:

$$\text{If } e_1 \wedge e_2 \wedge e_3 \wedge e_4 \text{ then } h_1.$$
$$\text{If } e_1 \wedge e_2 \wedge e_5 \wedge e_6 \text{ then } h_1.$$

The e's are evidence, and the h's are hypotheses. It is often opined that humans make inferences in steps. If we were to imitate such human behaviour, we can replace the above two prodrules by the following three prodrules:

$$\text{If } e_1 \wedge e_2 \qquad \text{then } h_0.$$
$$\text{If } h_0 \wedge e_3 \wedge e_4 \quad \text{then } h_1.$$
$$\text{If } h_0 \wedge e_5 \wedge e_6 \quad \text{then } h_2.$$

We say that h_0 is an intermediate hypothesis, which serves as a step toward inferring hypotheses h_1 and h_2. Worded alternatively, h_0 serves as evidence for h_1 and h_2.

Figure 9.3   An example to show how an intermediate hypothesis can serve as a step toward inferring other hypotheses.

steps for their inferencing. In UNPERS, the intermediate hypothesis *he is an administrator* (inferred in prodrule I7) serves as a step toward inferring the final hypotheses *he is a secretary* (prodrule I4) or *he is a dean* (prodrule I6).

There are two kinds of evidence: intermediate and initial. Intermediate evidence is an alternative name for an intermediate hypothesis: when in the consequent of a prodrule, it is an intermediate hypothesis; when in the antecedent of a prodrule, it is intermediate evidence. Such nomenclature is intended only for adding clarity to a discussion.

Initial evidence is in the antecedent of at least one prodrule, but never in the consequent of any prodrule. Evidence cannot be both initial and intermediate. The user of an expert system supplies some initial evidence. For example, the initial evidence a doctor, using an expert system for prescribing therapy, would supply may include

Kind of Evidence or Hypothesis	Evidence or Hypothesis	Prodrule of UNPERS in which it is in the	
		Antecedent	Consequent
final hypothesis	he is an undergraduate student		I1
	• a graduate student		I2
	• a secretary		I4
	• a professor		I5
	• a dean		I6
	• a visitor		I10
intermediate hypothesis / evidence	he is a student	I1, I2	I3
	• an academic	I3, I5	I8, I9
	• an administrator	I4, I6	I7
initial evidence	he is emaciated	I1, I2	
	• wears a helmet	I1	
	• eats junk food	I3	
	• talks to himself	I4, I5	
	• takes long lunches	I5, I6	
	• writes memos	I6	
	• wears a suit	I7	
	• shuffles papers	I7	
	• looks confused	I8	
	• looks sleepy	I9	

Figure 9.4 The list of final hypotheses, intermediate hypotheses/evidence, and initial evidence for UNPERS.

1. the doctor's observations of the patient, such as dilated pupils, rapid pulse, shortness of breath; and
2. the results of laboratory tests, such as the level of sugar in the patient's blood.

From the initial evidence, hypotheses can be inferred by firing the appropriate prodrules. In UNPERS, *he looks sleepy* exemplifies initial evidence; it is in the antecedent of prodrule I9, but not in the consequent of any prodrule. Figure 9.4 shows the list of final hypotheses, intermediate hypotheses/evidence, and initial evidence in UNPERS.

A control strategy for prodrules is, as the name suggests, a strategy to control the processing of prodrules. In the literature, a control strategy is also known as a control mechanism, an inference engine or a knowledge-base interpreter. In section 9.2.2, you read of a control strategy called forechaining as applied to the processing of prodrules for a problem on synthesis. In the next section, you will read of applying forechaining for analysis.

9.3.2 Forechaining for analysis

Suppose a user supplies some initial evidence about a person. We are to infer hypotheses about the person by using UNPERS of section 9.3.1. The initial evidence is stored in the blotter, a data structure similar to that shown in Figure 9.2. At any time, all prodrules whose antecedents can be matched by the contents of the blotter become heated. Of the heated prodrules, one prodrule is selected and fired. You will read in section 9.4 different techniques for selecting a prodrule to fire. For the example below, we shall adopt the same technique that we adopted in section 9.2.2: fire the prodrule that is catalogued as the earliest among the heated prodrules.

After the firing, all prodrules are chilled (none remain heated). The hypothesis inferred by firing the prodrule is stored in the blotter. The updated contents of the blotter can provoke another prodrule to fire. The solution of the problem thus progresses until all possible hypotheses have been inferred. Note that, at any particular time, the blotter contains all that is known till then: the initial evidence and the inferred hypotheses. An example is shown in Figure 9.5.

As the legend of Figure 9.5 mentions, the final hypotheses of UNPERS are not mutually exclusive, because there can be evidence from which more than one final hypothesis may be inferred. Now consider the example where the initial evidence for a person is *he wears a rubber nose* and *he chews gum*. With this evidence, none of the

Line Number	Information stored in the blotter			Prodrules heated	Prodrule fired
	Initial evidence	Inferred Hypotheses			
		Intermediate	Final		
1	he is emaciated, wears a helmet, eats junk food, looks confused			I8	I8
2		he is an academic		I3, I8	I3
3		he is a student		I1, I2, I3, I8	I1
4			he is an undergraduate student		

Figure 9.5 An example of firing the prodrules of UNPERS [introduced in section 9.3.1] by forechaining. The initial evidence supplied by the user is shown in the first line. This provoked prodrule I8 to fire. The hypothesis inferred *he is an academic* was added to the blotter [see the second line above]. Next, prodrule I3 fired, and so on. At any time, if more than one prodrule was heated, then the one catalogued the earliest was fired. In line 3, had we fired I2 instead of I1, we would have inferred the hypothesis *he is a graduate student.* So with the given initial evidence, we can infer two final hypotheses. The final hypotheses in UNPERS are not mutually exclusive. If the final hypotheses were mutually exclusive, only one final hypothesis could be inferred at the most, given any initial evidence.

prodrules I1 to I9 will fire. Prodrule I10, however, can always fire because its antecedent is TRUE, which specifies an evidence that is assumed to be always present: in the language of mathematical logic (see Figure 2.5), TRUE is a tautology, so I10 will fire, and the default final hypothesis will be inferred that *he is a visitor* (although, in reality, he may well be the president of the university). Prodrule I10 exemplifies a default prodrule. Thus no matter what the initial evidence is, at least one of the final hypotheses will be inferred. We say that the final hypotheses of UNPERS are **exhaustive**.

Accordingly, in UNPERS, the final hypotheses are exhaustive,but not mutually exclusive. It can be so in many an expert system: for example, a medical diagnostic expert system can have final hypotheses that are exhaustive (one hypothesis for each disease, and a default hypothesis for no disease); but the final hypotheses may not be mutually exclusive (a patient can have more than one disease). If the final hypotheses are exhaustive and mutually exclusive, then for any initial evidence exactly one final hypothesis is inferred.

You may have noticed that in forechaining we do not try to infer any particular hypothesis, that is, we do not focus on a hypothesis. Given the initial evidence, we try to infer whatever we can.

Forechaining, described above and in section 9.2.2, is known in the literature by various names: antecedent processing, bottom-up processing, data-driven processing, event-driven processing, and pattern-directed processing. Sometimes the word *processing* in these names is replaced by the word *reasoning*.

9.4   SELECTING A PRODRULE TO FIRE

When more than one prodrule becomes heated, we can fire all of the heated prodrules. Alternatively, we can select one of the heated prodrules to fire. Below we discuss seven techniques that can help select a prodrule to fire from a set of heated prodrules.

Catalogued ordering of prodrules
Of the heated rules, fire the rule that is catalogued as the earliest. This was the technique we adopted for the examples in Figure 9.2 and 9.5. Earlier, in sections 5.2.3 and 5.3.3, you had seen an approach similar to this technique.

Priority ordering of prodrules
Based on the advice of the domain experts, order the prodrules according to some priority scheme. Of the heated prodrules, fire the prodrule that has the highest priority. Note that a default prodrule always has the lowest priority.

Specificity ordering of prodrules
A prodrule J is said to be more specific than a prodrule J' if, and only if, the instances matched by the antecedent of J are a proper subset of the instances matched by the antecedent of J'. Consider the example of J and J' below:

(J) If $e_1 \wedge e_2$ then h_1.
(J') If e_1 then h_2.

Here, J is more specific than J'. Thus in UNPERS of section 9.3.1, prodrule I1 is more specific than prodrule I2. Now consider:

(I) If $P(b)$ then h_3.
(I') If $\forall x\ P(x)$ then h_4.

Here, I is more specific than I', where P is a predicate, b is a constant, and x is a variable (predicate logic nomenclature was defined in section 3.2.1). Note that if a prodrule is heated then its more general prodrule will also be heated, but it need not be so conversely. In this technique, if a prodrule and its more specific prodrule are heated, then fire the more specific prodrule. Intuitively, this is like giving more importance to specific evidence than to general evidence.

Priority ordering of evidence
Based on the advice of the domain experts, order all the possible evidence according to some priority scheme. Of the heated prodrules, fire the prodrule that is being heated by the highest priority evidence. For example, in medical diagnosis, observing the symptoms of a failing heart and of a broken leg, a doctor may ponder first over the failing heart, that is to say, the evidence for the heart received higher priority than the evidence for a broken leg.

Recency ordering of evidence
Of the heated prodrules, fire the prodrule whose antecedent contains the most recently inferred intermediate hypothesis/evidence. This is intuitively akin to following through a line of reasoning once we have taken it up.

Ordering by meta-prodrules
The prodrules we have seen until now are about a particular domain. We can use meta-prodrules to select the firing of the prodrules of the domain. Thus, for example, together with UNPERS of section 9.3.1, we can incorporate the following meta-prodrule:

> **If**   a prodrule with undergraduate student in the consequent is heated,
> **and**   a prodrule with graduate student in the consequent is heated,
> **then** fire the prodrule with undergraduate student in the consequent.

Chill refractory prodrules
If the hypothesis of a prodrule is already contained in the blotter, then such a heated prodrule, called a refractory prodrule, is forced to get chilled. In other words, a refractory prodrule is never fired. If we were to fire a refractory prodrule, we shall not infer any new hypothesis. Moreover, firing a refractory prodrule can lead to endless looping, as the same prodrule gets fired repeatedly. By chilling the refractory prodrules, the number of heated prodrules is reduced.

The different techniques described above can often be amalgamated. Suppose we amalgamate the catalogued ordering of prodrules with the chilling of refractory prodrules. Then the example of Figure 9.5 would be as shown in Figure 9.6.

Line Number	Information stored in the blotter			Prodrules heated	Prodrule fired
	Initial evidence	Inferred Hypotheses			
		Intermediate	Final		
1	he is emaciated, wears a helmet, eats junk food, looks confused			I8	I8
2		he is an academic		I3	I3
3		he is a student		I1, I2	I1
4			he is an undergraduate student		

Figure 9.6 The forechaining example of Figure 9.5 after the catalogued ordering of the prodrules was amalgamated with the chilling of refractory prodrules. Fewer prodrules are heated above than in Figure 9.5.

In the literature, the set of heated prodrules is known as the conflict set. Then selecting a prodrule to fire is known as conflict resolution. We have not used this terminology, to avoid any misconception with the different kinds of resolution that were discussed in Chapter 4.

9.5 BACKCHAINING THROUGH PRODRULES

As an alternative to forechaining through prodrules, another control strategy is backchaining. You had read about backchaining earlier in section 5.3.2, so we need not describe backchaining in detail again. The following discussion will be only to highlight backchaining as it pertains to the processing of prodrules.

In backchaining, we first make a conjecture about a hypothesis being true. We then check to see whether there is evidence present such that the hypothesis can be inferred from the evidence. If so, then we have **confirmed** the hypothesis.

Suppose the hypothesis to be confirmed is h. We locate a prodrule of the form:

If $e_1 \wedge e_2 \wedge e_3 \ldots$ then h.

To confirm h, we backchain h through the prodrule, that is, we need to confirm e_i for $i \geq 1$. An e_i can be confirmed in either of two ways, depending on whether e_i is an initial or an intermediate evidence. An initial evidence is confirmed if it is in the blotter. An intermediate

Line number	To confirm hypotheses	by prodrules	we need to confirm the evidence	Evidence confirmed since it is in the blotter
1	he is an undergraduate student	I1	he is a student, and he is emaciated, and he wears a helmet	he is emaciated he wears a helmet
2	he is a student	I3	he is an academic, and he eats junk food	he eats junk food
3	he is an academic	I8 or I9	he looks confused, or he looks sleepy	he looks confused

Figure 9.7   An example of backchaining through the prodrules of UNPERS [see section 9.3.1]. The blotter contains the initial evidence *he is emaciated, he wears a helmet, he eats junk food,* and *he looks confused.* We conjecture the hypothesis *he is an undergraduate student,* as in the first line above. To confirm the hypothesis, by prodrule I1, we need to confirm the evidence *he is a student, he is emaciated,* and *he wears a helmet.* The last two are confirmed since they are in the blotter. The first one is an intermediate hypothesis, for which we proceed in the second line above. Backchaining progresses in this way. The above problem is the same as that solved by forechaining in Figures 9.5 and 9.6.

evidence is confirmed by considering it to be an intermediate hypothesis, backchaining it through a prodrule, and proceeding as described above. An example is shown in Figure 9.7. We are writing the mass noun *evidence* as a count noun for simplicity. Such practice is on occasion considered acceptable (see section 6.3.4). Moreover, for euphony, we shall be spelling both the singular and the plural forms of *evidence* identically. Thus, for example, instead of writing *one piece of evidence* and *two pieces of evidence* as prescribed by English grammar, we shall be writing *one evidence* and *two evidence.* Otherwise, some of our sentences below would have sounded jarring.

If there is more than one prodrule through which hypothesis *h* can be backchained, then we shall have to select one prodrule for backchaining. This selection can be done by techniques similar to those described in section 9.4. If *h* cannot be confirmed by backchaining through any of the prodrules, then we say we have failed to confirm the hypothesis *h.*

Should we fail to confirm the hypothesis conjectured, we can conjecture another hypothesis and try to confirm the newly conjectured hypothesis. If the need arises, we can conjecture and try to confirm the different hypotheses one by one. We can take up either of the following approaches to decide on the order in which the hypotheses are to be conjectured.

1. Order the final hypotheses according to their decreasing frequency of occurrence. For UNPERS of section 9.3.1, we may, say, conjecture in the following order:

> he is an undergraduate student,
>> a graduate student,
>> a secretary,
>> a professor,
>> a dean,
>> a visitor.

The above ordering is based on the viewpoint that, on a university campus, a person is most likely to be an undergraduate student, a little less likely to be a graduate student, and so on. The ordering of the hypotheses can be built into the expert system.

2. In this approach for ordering the hypotheses, the expert system can display the different hypotheses, and ask the user in what order the hypotheses are to be conjectured. Thus the expert system takes advantage of the user's insight into the problem. The user too may find this advantageous; for example, on observing a patient's symptoms, a doctor may conjecture what the patient's disease is, and then try to confirm his conjecture by using a medical diagnostic expert system. The expert system can thus complement the doctor's own understanding of medical diagnosis.

We can, of course, amalgamate the above two approaches. The ordering of hypotheses on their decreasing frequency of occurrence (the first approach above) can be built into the expert system. This ordering can, however, be changed at the user's behest.

At any given time, backchaining focuses on a hypothesis: the hypothesis that has been conjectured. This is unlike forechaining (described in section 9.3.2), which does not focus on any hypothesis.

Backchaining can be utilized in problems of trouble-shooting. In such problems, we know the effect, but not its cause. Suppose a car will not start. We examine the different prodrules whose consequent contains the hypothesis *car will not start*:

> **If** the battery is weak,
> **then** *the car will not start.*

> **If** the starter is broken,
> **then** *the car will not start.*

The antecedent of the prodrules tell us about causes for the car not starting: a weak battery or a broken starter.

Backchaining is known in the literature by various names: consequent processing, expectation-driven processing, goal-driven processing, and top-down processing. Sometimes the word *processing* in these names is replaced by the word *reasoning*.

You may have noticed the parallels between our discussion in this section and the discussion in section 5.3.1: the kinship of initial evidence here with verities there, prodrules here with implications there, and a final hypothesis here with a goal there. You may loosely think of initial evidence and prodrules as premises, of which a final hypothesis is a logical consequence.

For a problem on analysis, you have seen backchaining immediately above and forechaining in section 9.3.2, but for the problem on synthesis, you saw only forechaining in section 9.2.2. Backchaining can be carried out for problems on synthesis, too. It is, however, a lot more complicated. You will see an example of such backchaining much later, in section 12.5.1. It was felt that the example will be understood better by putting it in that section. By then, you will have read about searching, which is discussed from Chapter 11 onward.

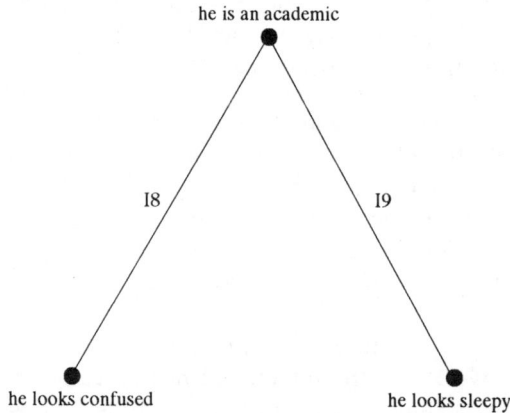

Figure 9.8 The tree-structured inference net for the hypothesis *he is an academic* of UNPERS [see section 9.3.1]. The root of the tree is labelled with the hypothesis, the leaves with the initial evidence, and the arcs with the number of the corresponding prodrules. Thus the above net depicts the two prodrules:

> [I8] *If* he looks confused,
>   *then* he is an academic.
> [I9] *If* he looks sleepy,
>   *then* he is an academic.

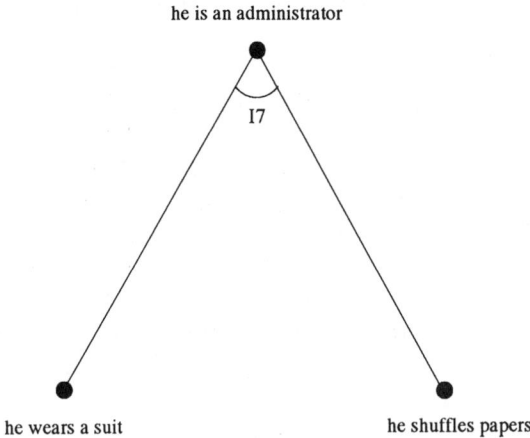

he is an administrator

I7

he wears a suit   he shuffles papers

Figure 9.9 The inference net for the hypothesis *he is an administrator* of UNPERS. The above net depicts the prodrule:

> [I7] *If* he wears a suit,
>   *and* he shuffles papers,
>   *then* he is an administrator.

The circular mark joining the two arcs denotes the conjunction [*and*] of the two evidence. To reduce cluttering in the net, we labelled the circular mark by the number of the prodrule, rather than label both the arcs by the same number of the prodrule.

9.6 INFERENCE NETS

Inference nets provide a pictorial depiction of the inferences we make with prodrules. Figures 9.8 and 9.9 show two examples. The figures also explain the notation used in inference nets.

We can say that, in general, an inference net for a given hypothesis shows the sequence of inferences needed to infer the hypothesis. Figure 9.10 shows the inference net for the final hypothesis *he is an undergraduate student* of UNPERS. As the legend of the figure mentions, forechaining can be viewed as traversing upward toward the final hypothesis in the net, and backchaining can be viewed as traversing downward toward the initial evidence in the net.

You may find it easier to implement forechaining and backchaining as traversing of the inference nets rather than as processing of the prodrules. In that case, you would need to incorporate a procedure in

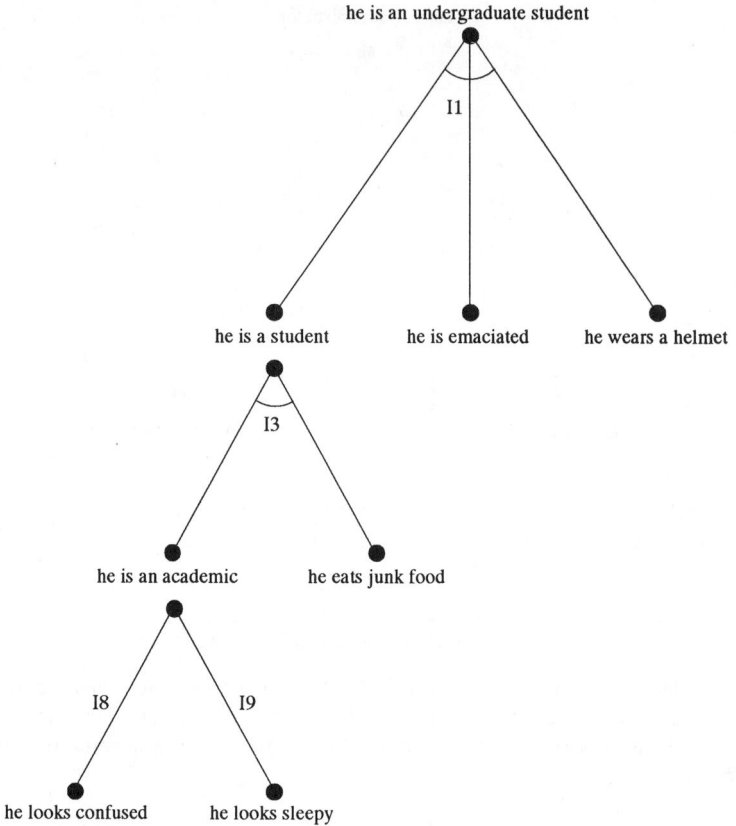

Figure 9.10 The inference net for the final hypothesis *he is an undergraduate student* of UNPERS. During forechaining, traverse upward from the initial evidence to the final hypothesis. During backchaining, traverse downward from the final hypothesis to the initial evidence.

the expert system such that it can generate inference nets, given the prodrules.

For your convenience, the inference nets for the other final hypotheses of UNPERS are given in Figures 9.11–9.15. It is recommended that you examine the prodrules of UNPERS (defined in section 9.3.1) and verify the correctness of the inference net for each final hypothesis. That should give you a better comprehension of inference nets.

Inference nets can also be handy to an expert system for responding to a user's questions, as discussed in the next section.

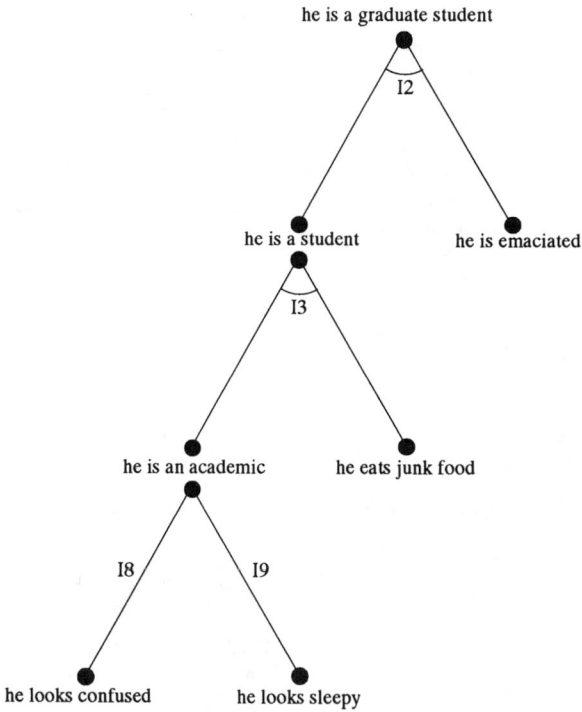

Figure 9.11 The inference net for the final hypothesis *he is a graduate student* of UNPERS.

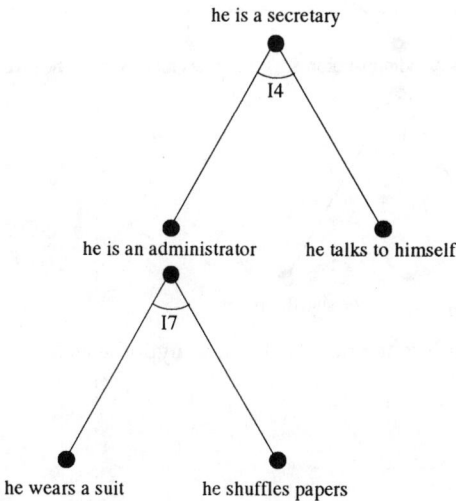

Figure 9.12 The inference net for the final hypothesis *he is a secretary* of UNPERS.

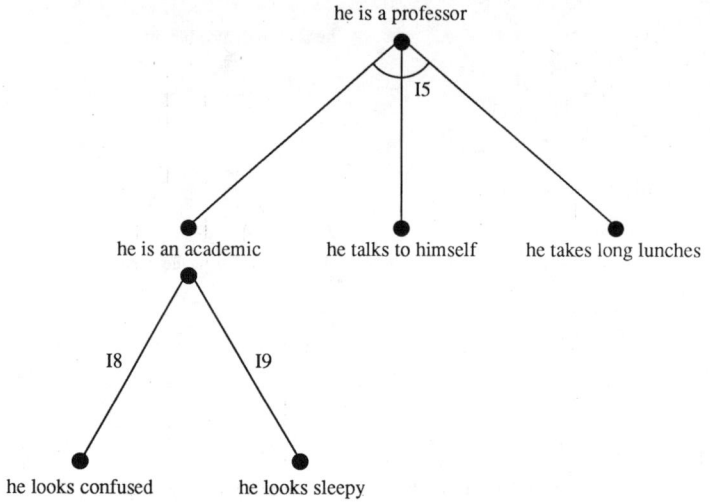

Figure 9.13   The inference net for the final hypothesis *he is a professor* of UNPERS.

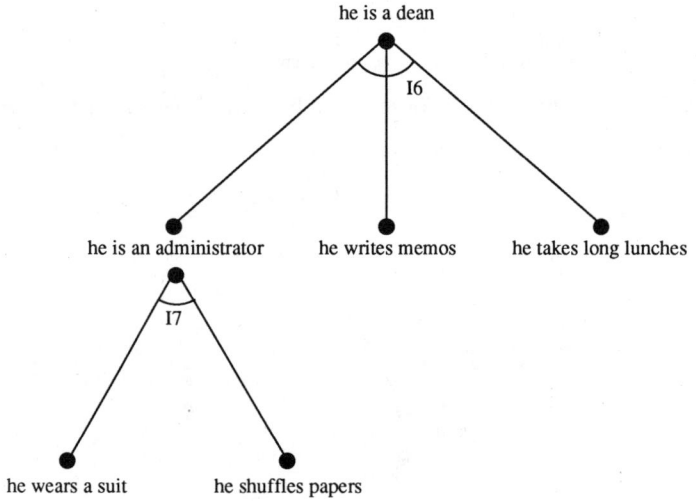

Figure 9.14   The inference net for the final hypothesis *he is a dean* of UNPERS.

he is a visitor

I10

TRUE

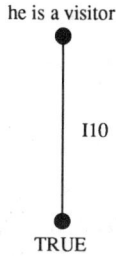

Figure 9.15   The inference net for the default final hypothesis *he is a visitor* of UNPERS.

9.7   DESIDERATA FOR EXPERT SYSTEMS

It is desirable to have a natural language processor embedded in an expert system so that a user can communicate with the system easily. You read about natural language processing in Chapters 6–8. For our discussion, we shall assume that the natural language processor is an English interface between the user and the expert system: thus the user can communicate with the system in English.

Expert systems should be easily usable for consultation. Typically, a user will activate the expert system and interactively enter some initial evidence to see what hypotheses are inferred by the system; for example, a doctor enters a patient's symptoms into a medical diagnostic system and receives recommendations on therapy.

In sections 9.3.2 and 9.5, it was said that the initial evidence supplied by the user is stored in the blotter. All of the initial evidence might not, however, be stored in the blotter. It can happen that a user overlooks the supplying of some evidence. The expert system should be able to ask for any evidence it needs. Suppose the system is backchaining to confirm the hypothesis *he is an undergraduate student* (see Figure 9.7 and Figure 9.10). Further, suppose that the user has overlooked entering the initial evidence *he eats junk food*. On not finding the needed evidence in the blotter, the system may ask:

Does he eat junk food?

Say the user replies:

Yes.

Then the system stores the newly found evidence in the blotter and proceeds with its backchaining. But it can come about that the user, baffled by the system's question, replies by asking another question:

Why do you want to know that?

From its position on the inference net (Figure 9.10), the system looks upwards and responds:

> Because I am trying to fire prodrule I3 to infer that he is a student.

Note that, to respond to a user's question broached by a *why*, the system needed to look upwards toward the final hypothesis in the inference net. The system should maintain a record of its inferencing. Suppose some time later, the user asks:

> How did you confirm that he was a student?

From the position of the hypothesis on the inference net, the system looks downwards and responds:

> By firing prodrule I3 on the evidence that he is an academic and that he eats junk food.

Now note that, to respond to a user's question broached by a *how*, the system needed to look downwards toward the initial evidence in the inference net. Let us also suppose that the user asks one of the following questions:

> What have you confirmed?
> Which hypothesis did you confirm?

The system responds:

> That he is an undergraduate student.

Apart from the wh-questions (which are broached by *why*, *what*, *how*, ..., as discussed in section 8.4), the system should also respond to a user's yn-questions (questions whose response is a *yes* or a *no*). A user could, for example, ask one of these questions:

> Did you fire prodrule I3?
> Have you fired prodrule I3?

The system should respond appropriately.

From our description above, we can say that an expert system should be able to explain its working and to justify any advice that the system gives. Therefore an expert system can be employed to train students.

An expert system should also detect any contradictions in the evidence supplied by the user. Suppose a doctor tells a medical diagnostic expert system that the patient is a male, but later refers to the patient as a female. The system should signal this to the user:

Earlier you said the patient is a male. Now you say the patient is a female. Which information is correct?

Let us now assume the system is backchaining, and it finds out that the patient is male. It can be annoying to a doctor, if the system next asks:

Is the patient pregnant?

The system should have fired a prodrule:

If the patient is male,
then the patient cannot be pregnant.

In other words, the system did some forechaining. So, on occasion, some forechaining needs to be mixed with backchaining to make the system convenient to use.

The capability of an expert system to explain its working can help us make changes in the system. Studying a system's explanation, a domain expert may indicate some flaws in the working of the system. To remove the flaws, we may have to edit the prodrules, that is, modify or delete existing prodrules, and add new ones. The system should have procedures to watch us in the required editing. As an example of such a procedure, suppose we add the following prodrule:

If e_1 then h.

The procedure compares this prodrule with other prodrules that contain h in the consequent, and points out to us, say, the following:

80% of the prodrules that contain h in the consequent also contain e_2 in the antecedent. Do you want to modify the prodrule just added to contain e_2 in the antecedent?

If we reply *yes*, then the new prodrule added to the system becomes:

If $e_1 \wedge e_2$ then h.

Otherwise, the prodrule remains as it was.

To recapitulate our above discussion, we say that it is desirable for an expert system to

1. have a natural language interface,
2. be easily usable for consultation,
3. be able to explain its working, and
4. have procedures to aid us in editing the system.

It is also desirable for an expert system that the prodrules in it be independent of the control strategy required to process the prodrules.

Editing the prodrules should not affect the control strategy. The control strategy and the natural language interface, together with the capability of consultation, explanation and editing, are known in the literature as an expert system shell. Replacing a set of prodrules by another set of prodrules should ideally not harm the functioning of an expert system shell. That is to say, once an expert system shell has been built, it should ideally be able to function on prodrules of different domains, thus giving us expert systems from different domains, but what ideally should be may not always be so in reality.

9.8 WRITING THE PRODRULES

As a knowledge engineer, after you have acquired the knowledge imparted by the domain experts, you may need to encode the knowledge as prodrules. You may write the prodrules in a language like Prolog (outlined in section 5.4). Alternatively, you may write them in a natural language like English, and then have a natural language processor translate them into a formal representation for the expert system. (Chapters 6–8 discussed natural language processing.) In our discussion, we have been writing the prodrules in English so that they are easier to read. Regardless of the language in which you will write the prodrules, you should be wary of circularities (see section 5.3.7) in your prodrules. To illustrate, the following three prodrules have circularity:

> If x_2 then x_1.
> If x_3 then x_2.
> If x_1 then x_3.

Circularities can cause the processing of prodrules to loop indefinitely.

You should also be aware of the following issues in the writing of prodrules.

(1) You can, if you want, avoid having any disjunctions in the antecedent of a prodrule. Suppose you want to write this prodrule:

> If $e_1 \lor e_2$ then h.

You can rewrite it as two prodrules:

> If e_1 then h.
> If e_2 then h.

Similarly, suppose you want to write the prodrule:

> If $((e_1 \lor e_2) \land e_3)$ then h.

Convert the formula in the antecedent into a disjunction of conjunctions. This is the dual of converting a formula into clause form (a conjunction of disjunctions) that you read about in sections 2.4.2 and 3.3.1. After the conversion, the prodrule would become:

If $((e_1 \wedge e_3) \vee (e_2 \wedge e_3))$ then h.

This, in turn, can be written as two prodrules after eliminating the disjunction:

If $e_1 \wedge e_3$ then h.
If $e_2 \wedge e_3$ then h.

By having only conjunctions in the antecedents of prodrules, you may inject some uniformity in the prodrules, thus making chaining through them easier to implement. Let the prodrule being forechained be the following:

If $e_1 \wedge e_2 \wedge e_3 \ldots$ then h.

Then the moment one of the e's is found to be false, the rest of the antecedent need not be examined any further, for the prodrule cannot be heated, and thus it cannot be fired.

(2) You can, if you want, avoid conjunctions of hypotheses in the consequent of a prodrule. Suppose you want to write the prodrule:

If e then $(h_1 \wedge h_2)$.

You can rewrite it as two prodrules:

If e then h_1.
If e then h_2.

(3) Suppose you want to write:

If e then h_1 else h_2.

You can write it as two prodrules:

If e then h_1.
If $\sim e$ then h_2.

(4) You are not restricted to having only one set of prodrules. You can have different sets of prodrules. They communicate with one another through a central data structure called a **blackboard**. Accordingly, if one set of prodrules infers a hypothesis, it writes the hypothesis into the blackboard. The other sets of prodrules can read the hypothesis from the blackboard to use it for making their own inferences. This form of organization is known as a blackboard architecture.

(5) Finally, remember that an expert system is only as good as the prodrules in it. Carelessly written prodrules will result in an expert system giving substandard performance. As mentioned in section 9.1, an expert system should perform as well as a typical domain expert, if not better.

Expert systems allow us to engage in a form of reasoning called plausible reasoning. This reasoning is different from the mathematical logic reasoning that you saw in Chapters 2–5. In the next chapter, you will read about plausible reasoning.

9.9   EXERCISES

1. Extend the prodrules of PACKER (section 9.2.1) to enable the packing of a suitcase and a handbag. You will have to modify the roster of Figure 9.1. Each article to be packed will need to be designated as a suitcase article or a handbag article, depending on the container (suitcase or handbag) in which it is to be packed. If you were travelling by air, you would carry the handbag with you on board, and you would check in the suitcase. The articles in your handbag should be such that you can live with the least possible inconvenience during the trip, should the airline lose your suitcase.

2. Suppose the priority ordering of prodrules of UNPERS (section 9.3.1) is the following:

I8, I9, I7, I3, I1, I2, I5, I4, I6 and I10.

In other words, I8 has the highest priority of firing, and I10 has the lowest priority of firing. You are given the following initial evidence:

he is emaciated,
he wears a helmet,
he eats junk food, and
he looks confused.

By forechaining, can you infer the final hypothesis that *he is an undergraduate student*? If not, why not? Can you infer the final hypothesis if you were to chill the refractory prodrules?

3. Give algorithmic formulations for each of the forechaining and backchaining control strategies.

4. In Chapter 5, you read how Prolog does backchaining. In this chapter, you read about forechaining. Can you use Prolog to implement forechaining? If so, how?

5. In section 7.2, you read how ATNs (augmented transition networks) can be employed to parse English sentences. Can the ATN of Figure

7.12 be represented as a set of prodrules? If it can be so represented, then write the relevant prodrules; otherwise, explain why it cannot be done.

6. Design and implement an English language processor that can translate prodrules written in English into assertions in predicate logic, discussed in section 5.3. Test your processor on the prodrules of UNPERS.
7. Can you write prodrules to elicit the meaning from a sentence (see section 7.3)? Explain your answer.
8. Make a list of ten problems each of synthesis and analysis. You should be a domain expert in at least one problem of synthesis and one problem of analysis. Write prodrules for the problems of your expertise.
9. Design and implement an expert system shell. Test your shell on one of the problems whose prodrules you wrote for exercise 8 above.

9.10 SUGGESTIONS FOR FURTHER READING

Newell and Simon (1972) argued that prodrules model human cognition. Hart (1986) discussed knowledge acquisition for expert systems. Chadwick and Hannah (1987) explained the implementation of expert systems. Forgy (1982) presented a matching algorithm suitable for prodrules. Leigh and Smith (1987) and Marcus (1986) illustrated the use of Prolog for building expert systems. Brownston, Farrel, Kant and Martin (1985) described a version of a language called OPS to write prodrules. Englemore and Morgan (1988) edited a collection of papers on blackboard systems, and Adeli (1990) on knowledge engineering.

1. Adeli, H. (ed.) (1990) *Knowledge Engineering: Volume 1, Fundamentals; Volume 2, Applications*, McGraw-Hill, New York.
2. Brownston, L., Farrel, R., Kant, E. and Martin, N. (1985) *Programming Expert Systems in OPS5: An Introduction to Rule-Based Programming*, Addison-Wesley, Reading, Massachusetts.
3. Chadwick, M. and Hannah, J. (1987) *Expert Systems for Microcomputers*, Tab Books Inc., Blue Ridge Summit, Pennsylvania.
4. Engelmore, R. and Morgan, T. (eds.) (1988) *Blackboard Systems*, Addison-Wesley, Reading, Massachusetts.
5. Forgy, C. L. (1982) A fast algorithm for the many pattern/many object pattern match problem, *Artificial Intelligence*, **19**, 17–37.
6. Leigh, W. and Smith, A. (1987) *Prolog to Expert Systems*, Mitchell Publishing Inc., Santa Cruz, California.

7. Marcus, C. (1986) *Prolog Programming*, Addison-Wesley, Reading, Massachusetts.
8. Hart, A. (1986) *Knowledge Acquisition for Expert Systems*, McGraw-Hill, New York.
9. Newell, A. and Simon, H. (1972) *Human Problem Solving*, Prentice Hall, Englewood Cliffs, New Jersey.

10
Plausible reasoning in expert systems

10.1 INTRODUCTION

As you read in Chapter 9, prodrules are a means of formalizing the knowledge of domain experts. This knowledge is often based on heuristics, but heuristics, being rules of thumb, can be fallible. This raises the question: how reliable are the prodrules? Consider the following prodrule taken from UNPERS of Section 9.3.1:

> **If** he looks confused,
> **then** he is an academic.

There may be domain experts who dispute the viewpoint put forward by the prodrule. The prodrule may not always hold up: there can be people who look confused, but who are not academics. We can say that the prodrule is only partly reliable. We need a measure, say a numeric value, of the reliability of a prodrule. The value of the reliability measure of a prodrule is supplied by the domain expert, for it is only he who can judge the reliability of a prodrule. Now consider the evidence *he looks confused*, in the above prodrule. In describing a person who looks confused, we may intensify the adjective *confused*, as described in section 6.7.1, to be *somewhat confused* and *very confused*. In general, in observing some evidence, we may be certain about the evidence to varying degrees; for example, moderately certain or strongly certain. Accordingly, just as we need a measure of the reliability of a prodrule, we also need a measure of the certainty of an evidence. The value of the certainty measure of an initial evidence is supplied by the user of the expert system, for it is he who supplies the evidence, and the certainty of the evidence rests on his observation of the evidence.

The hypothesis inferred by firing a prodrule has a certainty that is a function of the certainty of the evidence and the reliability of the prodrule. This kind of inferring is known as **plausible reasoning**. In this chapter you will read about two schemes for plausible reasoning: a Bayesian scheme in section 10.2, and an *ad hoc* scheme in section 10.3.

10.2   A BAYESIAN SCHEME

To understand the Bayesian scheme for plausible reasoning, you should be conversant with probability theory. It is assumed that this is the case. Nonetheless, a review of some of the equations of probability theory is given in section 10.2.1 to refresh your memory. The equations given later in the section are obtained from those given earlier. The later equations are then cited in other parts of the chapter. You may skim this section and refer back to the relevant equation whenever it is cited.

10.2.1   A review of probability theory

Let z symbolize an event. For this chapter, an event will be an evidence e or a hypothesis h. The event z is said to occur if, and only if, its negation, symbolized as $\sim z$, does not occur.

Let $P(z)$, where $0 \leq P(z) \leq 1$, denote the probability of the event z occurring. It is known as the prior probability of z. The prior probability of an event is not conditioned on the occurrence of any other event. If $P(z) = 0$, then z never occurs (z is an impossible event); if $P(z) = 1$, then z always occurs.

Suppose it is noted in an experiment that for $1 \leq i \leq n$, the event z_i occurred d_i times. Then under the conventional evaluation, called the maximum likelihood evaluation:

$$P(z_i) = \frac{d_i}{\sum_{i=1}^{n} d_i}$$

but under an alternative evaluation, called the Bayesian evaluation:

$$P(z_i) = \frac{d_i + 1}{\sum_{i=1}^{n} d_i + n}$$

Under this evaluation, we implicitly assume that each event has already occurred once even before we commenced the experiment. For a large sample size (that is, $d_1 + d_2 + \ldots + d_n = $ a large number), the two evaluations will give approximately equal results. Nevertheless, note that, under the Bayesian evaluation, $0 < P(z_i) < 1$. In other words, $P(z_i)$ will never be equal to either 0 or 1. If $P(z_i)$ is to be used in an equation that becomes discontinuous when $P(z_i)$ is equal to 0 or 1 (say, $P(z_i)$ or $(1 - P(z_i))$ is the sole denominator in the equation), then the Bayesian evaluation of $P(z_i)$ may be more practical than the maximum likelihood evaluation.

Let $P(z_1|z_2)$ denote the probability of event z_1 occurring, conditioned on event z_2 having already occurred. It is known as the posterior probability of z_1 conditioned on z_2.

We list below a few equations of probability theory, accompanied by remarks every now and then.

1. $P(z_1 \wedge z_2) = P(z_2 \wedge z_1)$ by definition.
2. $P(z_1 \wedge z_2) = P(z_1|z_2)P(z_2)$ by definition.
3. For independent events z_1 and z_2, that is, the occurrence of one event does not influence the occurrence of the other:

$$P(z_1|z_2) = P(z_1).$$

4. For independent events z_1 and z_2, from 2. and 3. above:

$$P(z_1 \wedge z_2) = P(z_1)P(z_2).$$

The above equation is a special case of mutually independent events $z_1, z_2, \ldots, z_n$, for which:

$$P(z_1 \wedge z_2 \ldots \wedge z_n) = P(z_1)P(z_2) \ldots P(z_n).$$

5. For mutually exclusive events z_1 and z_2, that is, both events cannot occur at the same time (as you read in the discussion on mutually exclusive hypotheses in section 9.3.2):

$$P(z_1 \wedge z_2) = 0.$$

6. $P(z_1 \vee z_2) = P(z_2 \vee z_1)$ by definition.
7. $P(z_1 \vee z_2) = P(z_1) + P(z_2) - P(z_1 \wedge z_2)$ by definition.
8. For completely correlated events z_1 and z_2, that is, z_1 occurs if, and only if, z_2 occurs:

$$P(z_1 \vee z_2) = P(z_1 \wedge z_2)$$
$$= P(z_1)$$
$$= P(z_2)$$

9. For mutually exclusive events z_1 and z_2, from 5. and 7. above:

$$P(z_1 \vee z_2) = P(z_1) + P(z_2).$$

10. For mutually exclusive events $z_1, z_2, \ldots, z_n$, by generalizing 9. above:

$$P(z_1 \vee z_2 \vee \ldots \vee z_n) = P(z_1) + P(z_2) + \ldots + P(z_n).$$

11. For exhaustive events $z_1, z_2, \ldots, z_n$, that is, at least one of the events will occur (as you read earlier in the discussion on exhaustive hypothese in section 9.3.2):

$$P(z_1 \vee z_2 \vee \ldots \vee z_n) = 1.$$

12. For exhaustive and mutually exclusive events $z_1, z_2, \ldots, z_n$, from 10. and 11. above:

$$P(z_1) + P(z_2) + \ldots + P(z_n) = 1.$$

Take note of this equation for expert systems in which the final hypotheses are exhaustive and mutually exclusive.

13. Since events z and $\sim z$ are exhaustive and mutually exclusive, from 12. above, $P(z) + P(\sim z) = 1$, and hence:

$$P(\sim z) = 1 - P(z).$$

14. For events $z_1, z_2, \ldots, z_n$:

$$P(z_1 \lor z_2 \lor \ldots \lor z_n) = 1 - P(\sim(z_1 \lor z_2 \lor \ldots \lor z_n))$$
$$\text{from 13. above}$$

$$= 1 - P(\sim z_1 \land \sim z_2 \land \ldots \land \sim z_n)$$
$$\text{from de Morgan's law in Figure 2.5.}$$

If $z_1, z_2, \ldots, z_n$ are mutually independent, then the above expression can be written as:

$$1 - P(\sim z_1)P(\sim z_2) \ldots P(\sim z_n) \quad \text{from 4. above}$$
$$= 1 - (1 - P(z_1))(1 - P(z_2)) \ldots (1 - P(z_n)) \quad \text{from 13. above.}$$

For the special case when $n = 2$, the above equation can be written as:

$$P(z_1 \lor z_2) = P(z_1) + P(z_2) - P(z_1)P(z_2),$$

which incidentally can be obtained also from 4. and 7. above.

15. Similar to 13. above, it can be shown that for events z_1 and z_2:

$$P(\sim z_1 | z_2) = 1 - P(z_1 | z_2).$$

16. $O(z)$, known as the prior odds on event z, is defined to be:

$$O(z) = \frac{P(z)}{P(\sim z)}.$$

17. From 13. and 16. above, it can shown that:

$$O(z) = \frac{P(z)}{1 - P(z)}.$$

18. By algebraic manipulation of 17. it can be shown that:

$$P(z) = \frac{O(z)}{1 + O(z)}.$$

19. $O(z_1|z_2)$, known as the posterior odds on event z_1 conditioned on event z_2, is:

$$O(z_1|z_2) = \frac{P(z_1|z_2)}{P(\sim z_1|z_2)}.$$

20. From 15. and 19. it can be shown that:

$$O(z_1|z_2) = \frac{P(z_1|z_2)}{1 - P(z_1|z_2)}.$$

21. By algebraic manipulation of 20., it can be shown that:

$$P(z_1|z_2) = \frac{O(z_1|z_2)}{1 + O(z_1|z_2)}.$$

22. When the events are an evidence e and a hypothesis h, then

$$P(h \wedge \sim e) \quad = P(\sim e \wedge h) \quad \text{from 1.}$$
$$P(h|\sim e)P(\sim e) = P(\sim e|h)P(h) \quad \text{from 2.}$$
$$P(h|\sim e) \quad = \frac{P(\sim e|h)P(h)}{P(\sim e)} \quad \text{by cross multiplying.}$$

The equation obtained by cross multiplying is a traditional formulation of a theorem called Bayes theorem.

23. As in 22., we can obtain from $P(\sim h \wedge \sim e) = P(\sim e \wedge \sim h)$ another traditional formulation of the Bayes theorem:

$$P(\sim h|\sim e) = \frac{P(\sim e|\sim h)P(\sim h)}{P(\sim e)}.$$

24. We obtain:

$$O(h|\sim e) = \frac{P(h|\sim e)}{P(\sim h|\sim e)} \quad \text{from 19.}$$

$$= \frac{P(\sim e|h)P(h)}{P(\sim e|\sim h)P(\sim h)} \quad \text{from 22. and 23.}$$

$$= \frac{P(\sim e|h)}{P(\sim e|\sim h)}O(h) \quad \text{from 16.}$$

This is called an odds likelihood formulation of the Bayes theorem. It will be cited by us later in section 10.2.3. The following expressions can be used synonymously: *e does not occur, e is absent, e does not exist,* and *e is false,* so the above formulation of the Bayes theorem gives us the odds on h conditioned on e being absent.

25. As in 22. and 23., we can obtain, from $P(h \wedge e) = P(e \wedge h)$, another traditional formulation of the Bayes theorem:

$$P(h|e) = \frac{P(e|h)P(h)}{P(e)}.$$

26. As in 22. 23. and 25., we can obtain, from $P(\sim h \wedge e) = P(e \wedge \sim h)$, another traditional formulation of the Bayes theorem:

$$P(\sim h|e) = \frac{P(e|\sim h)P(\sim h)}{P(e)}.$$

27. We obtain:

$$O(h|e) = \frac{P(h|e)}{P(\sim h|e)} \qquad \text{from 19.}$$

$$= \frac{P(e|h)P(h)}{P(e|\sim h)P(\sim h)} \qquad \text{from 25. and 26.}$$

$$= \frac{P(e|h)}{P(e|\sim h)}O(h) \qquad \text{from 16.}$$

This too is an odds likelihood formulation of the Bayes theorem that will be cited by us later in section 10.2.3. The following expressions can be used synonymously: *e occurs, e is present, e exists,* and *e is true,* so the above formulation of the Bayes theorem gives us the odds on *h* conditioned on *e* being present.

28. Generalizing 24. and 27. , we get:

$$O(h|\sim e_1 \wedge \sim e_2 \wedge \ldots \wedge \sim e_k \wedge e_{k+1} \wedge \ldots \wedge e_m)$$
$$= \frac{P(\sim e_1 \wedge \sim e_2 \wedge \ldots \wedge \sim e_k \wedge e_{k+1} \wedge \ldots \wedge e_m|h)}{P(\sim e_1 \wedge \sim e_2 \wedge \ldots \wedge \sim e_k \wedge e_{k+1} \wedge \ldots \wedge e_m|\sim h)}O(h).$$

To reduce the amount of computation required to evaluate the above equation, we assume that $\sim e_1, \sim e_2, \ldots, \sim e_k, e_{k+1}, \ldots, e_m$ are conditionally independent on *h* and on $\sim h$. (We concede that you may find this assumption debatable.) We can then write:

$$O(h|\sim e_1 \wedge \sim e_2 \wedge \ldots \wedge \sim e_k \wedge e_{k+1} \wedge \ldots \wedge e_m)$$
$$= \left(\prod_{i=1}^{k} \frac{P(\sim e_i|h)}{P(\sim e_i|\sim h)}\right)\left(\prod_{i=k+1}^{m} \frac{P(\sim e_i|h)}{P(\sim e_i|\sim h)}\right)O(h).$$

We shall cite the above equation in section 10.2.11.

29. If $h_1, h_2, \ldots, h_n$ are exhaustive and mutually exclusive hypotheses, then by definition:

$$P(e_1 \wedge e_2 \wedge \ldots \wedge e_m) = \sum_{i=1}^{n} P(e_1 \wedge e_2 \wedge \ldots \wedge e_m|h_i)P(h_i).$$

30. Since h and $\sim h$ are exhaustive and mutually exclusive, from 29. above, we get:

$$P(e) = P(e|h)P(h) + P(e|\sim h)P(\sim h).$$

31. Since from 13. $P(\sim h) = 1 - P(h)$, we can rewrite 30. as follows:

$$P(e) = P(h)(P(e|h) - P(e|\sim h)) + P(e|\sim h).$$

The above equation will be cited in Figure 10.13.

10.2.2 Applying fuzzy set theory

As we shall see in section 10.2.5, we may often need, for plausible reasoning, the value of a joint probability like $P(z_1 \wedge z_2 \wedge \ldots \wedge z_n)$. Generalizing equation 2. of section 10.2.1, we can obtain the value of $P(z_1 \wedge z_2 \wedge \ldots \wedge z_n)$ from the following equation:

$$P(z_1 \wedge z_2 \wedge \ldots \wedge z_n) = P(z_1|z_2 \wedge \ldots \wedge z_n)P(z_2|z_3 \wedge \ldots \wedge z_n)$$
$$P(z_3|z_4 \wedge \ldots \wedge z_n) \ldots P(z_{n-1}|z_n)P(z_n).$$

But the values of the posterior probabilities, as shown in the right-hand side of the above equation, may not always be known. This is mainly because of the practical difficulties encountered in estimating them; for example, we would need large sample sizes, which may not be available. The prior probabilities $P(z_1)$, $P(z_2)$, $\ldots$, $P(z_n)$ are, however, usually known because they are easier to estimate. If $z_1, z_2, \ldots, z_n$ are mutually independent, then as given in 4. of section 10.2.1:

$$P(z_1 \wedge z_2 \wedge \ldots \wedge z_n) = P(z_1)P(z_2) \ldots P(z_n).$$

But it mostly happens that $z_1, z_2, \ldots, z_n$ are not mutually independent. We can then obtain the value of $P(z_1 \wedge z_2 \wedge \ldots \wedge z_n)$ by using an equation from a branch of mathematics called fuzzy set theory. According to that equation:

$$P(z_1 \wedge z_2 \wedge \ldots \wedge z_n) = \min(P(z_1), P(z_2), \ldots, P(z_n)).$$

In other words, $P(z_1 \wedge z_2 \wedge \ldots \wedge z_n)$ is equal to the minimum of the values of $P(z_1)$, $P(z_2)$, $\ldots$, $P(z_n)$. Intuitively, it is akin to saying that a chain is as strong as its weakest link. Note that the value of $P(z_1 \wedge z_2 \wedge \ldots \wedge z_n)$ that could have been obtained by probability theory may be different from the value obtained by fuzzy set theory.

We can face similar hurdles in obtaining the value of $P(z_1 \vee z_2 \vee \ldots \vee z_n)$ if we were to apply probability theory, so we apply fuzzy set theory, according to which:

$$P(z_1 \vee z_2 \vee \ldots \vee z_n) = \max(P(z_1), P(z_2), \ldots, P(z_n)).$$

in other words, $P(z_1 \lor z_2 \lor \ldots \lor z_n)$ is equal to the maximum of the values of $P(z_1)$, $P(z_2)$, $\ldots$, $P(z_n)$. Intuitively, it is akin to saying that a rope is as strong as its strongest strand.

10.2.3   Necessity and sufficiency measures

Remember from Figure 2.1 that the logic formula for e implies h, that is, $e \rightarrow h$, can be alternatively read as 'e is sufficient for h' or as 'h is necessary for e.' In this section, we shall view the reliability of a prodrule

If e then h

in terms of the necessity and sufficiency of e for h. The notion of the reliability of a prodrule was discussed in section 10.1. These necessity and sufficiency measures are usually weaker for a prodrule than for a logic implication.

As we shall see below, the necessity and sufficiency measures for a prodrule are functions of the prior and posterior probabilities of e and h. We shall assume that the values of these probabilities, as and when needed, have been supplied to us.

An evidence e can usually be in two states: absent or present. When e is always absent ($P(e) = 0$), or when e is always present ($P(e) = 1$), it is of no practical interest. Either way there is nothing to observe. Similarly, when $P(h) = 0$ or $P(h) = 1$ it is of no practical interest; either way there is nothing to infer. Therefore, we shall assume that $0 < P(e) < 1$ and $0 < P(h) < 1$.

To study the necessity and sufficiency measures of e for h, we need to explore the influence that a state of e has on h. If the state makes h more plausible, then we say that the state of e **encourages** h. If the state makes h less plausible, then we say that the state of e **discourages** h. If the state neither encourages nor discourages h, then the state of e has no influence on h: worded alternatively, e and h are independent of each other.

Let us first explore how the absence of e influences h. According to equation 24. of section 10.2.1, by Bayes theorem:

$$O(h \,|\, {\sim}e) = NO(h)$$

where

$$N = \frac{P({\sim}e \,|\, h)}{P({\sim}e \,|\, {\sim}h)}.$$

The value of N ranges in the closed interval zero to infinity. As Figure 10.1 shows: when $N = 0$, then e is necessary for h; when $N = 1$, then e

Value of N	How the absence of e influences h
N = 0	Discourages h as O(h | ~e) < O(h), and hence P(h | ~e) < P(h). In fact, h is discouraged to the extent that O(h | ~e) = 0, thus making P(h | ~e) = 0. We say that the absence of e has invalidated h: that is, ~e → ~h. By contrapositivity [see Figure 2.5], h → e. Thus e is necessary for h.
0 < N < 1	Discourages h as O(h | ~e) < O(h), and hence P(h | ~e) < P(h).
N = 1	No influence on h as O(h | ~e) = O(h), and hence P(h | ~e) = P(h). Thus e and h are independent of each other.
1 < N < ∞	Encourages h as O(h | ~e) > O(h), and hence P(h | ~e) > P(h).
N = ∞	Encourages h as O(h | ~e) > O(h), and hence P(h | ~e) > P(h). In fact, h is encouraged to the extent that O(h | ~e) = ∞, thus making P(h | ~e) = 1. We say that the absence of e has validated h: that is, ~e → h. By contrapositivity [see Figure 2.5], ~h → e. Thus e is necessary for ~h

Figure 10.1 Table to show how the absence of e influences h in the equation O(h|~e) = N O(h) for different values of N. If N < 1, then h is discouraged; if N = 1, then h is not influenced; if N > 1, then h is encouraged.

and *h* are independent of each other; and when $N = \infty$, then *e* is necessary for ~*h*. Thus *N* is a measure of the necessity of *e* for *h*.

We now explore how the presence of *e* influences *h*. According to equation 27. of section 10.2.1, by Bayes theorem

$$O(h|e) = SO(h)$$

Where

$$S = \frac{P(e|h)}{P(e|\sim h)}.$$

The value of *S* ranges in the closed interval infinity to zero. As Figure 10.2 shows: when $S = \infty$, then *e* is sufficient for *h*; when $S = 1$, then *e* and *h* are independent of each other; and when $S = 0$, then *e* is sufficient for ~*h*. Thus *S* is a measure of the sufficiency of *e* for *h*.

The values of *N*, *S* and *O(h)* needed to evaluate $O(h|\sim e)$ and $O(h|e)$ are supplied by the domain expert. The domain expert supplies these values for each prodrule. Quite often these values are subjective estimates supported by the intuition of the domain expert. Instead of supplying the values of *N* and *S*, the domain expert may supply the values of $P(e|h)$ and $P(e|\sim h)$. The values of *N* and *S* can then be calculated:

Value of S	How the presence of e influences h
$S = \infty$	Encourages h as O(h | e) > O(h), and hence P(h | e) > P(h). In fact, h is encouraged to the extent that O(h | e) = ∞, thus making P(h | e) = 1. We say that the presence of e has validated h: that is, e → h. Thus e is sufficient for h.
$1 < S < \infty$	Encourages h as O(h | e) > O(h), and hence P(h | e) > P(h).
$S = 1$	No influence on h as O(h | e) = O(h), and hence P(h | e) = P(h). Thus e and h are independent of each other.
$0 < S < 1$	Discourages h as O(h | e) < O(h), and hence P(h | e) < P(h).
$S = 0$	Discourages h as O(h | e) < O(h), and hence P(h | e) < P(h). In fact, h is discouraged to the extent that O(h | e) = 0, thus making P(h | e) = 0. We say that the presence of e has invalidated h: that is, e → ~h. By contrapositivity [see Figure 2.5], ~h → e. Thus e is sufficient for ~h.

Figure 10.2   Table to show how the presence of e influences h in the equation O(h|e) = S O(h) for different values of S. If S > 1, then h is encouraged; if S = 1, then h is not influenced; if S < 1, then h is discouraged.

$$N = \frac{P(\sim e|h)}{P(\sim e|\sim h)} = \frac{1 - P(e|h)}{1 - P(e|\sim h)}$$

$$S = \frac{P(e|h)}{P(e|\sim h)}$$

By algebraic manipulation of the above equations, the following can be derived:

$$P(e|h) = \frac{S(1 - N)}{S - N}$$

$$P(e|\sim h) = \frac{1 - N}{S - N}$$

$$N = \frac{1 - SP(e|\sim h)}{1 - P(e|\sim h)}$$

The above equations show that the values of S and N are not independent of each other. Moreover, it is apparent from Figure 10.3 that: $S > 1$ if, and only if, $N < 1$; $S = 1$ if, and only if, $N = 1$; and $S < 1$ if, and only if, $N > 1$.

As mentioned above, the domain expert should also supply the value of $O(h)$ to enable us to evaluate $O(h|e)$ and $O(h|\sim e)$. It is

Supposed values of		Corresponding values of			Influence on h as substantiated by Figures 10.1 and 10.2	
$P(e \mid h)$	$P(e \mid \sim h)$	$S = \dfrac{P(e \mid h)}{P(e \mid \sim h)}$	$N = \dfrac{1 - P(e \mid \sim h)}{1 - P(e \mid h)}$		presence of e	absence of e
1	$0 < P(e \mid \sim h) < 1$	$1 < S < \infty$	0		encourages h	invalidates h
	0	∞	0		validates h	invalidates h
$0 < P(e \mid h) < 1$	1	$0 < S < 1$	∞		discourages h	validates h
	$0 < P(e \mid \sim h) < 1$	If $P(e\mid h) > P(e\mid\sim h)$ then $1 < S < \infty$	$0 < N < 1$		encourages h	discourages h
		If $P(e\mid h) = P(e\mid\sim h)$ then $S = 1$	$N = 1$		does not influence h	does not influence h
		If $P(e\mid h) < P(e\mid\sim h)$ then $0 < S < 1$	$1 < N < \infty$		discourages h	encourages h
	0	∞	$0 < N < 1$		validates h	discourages h
0	1	0	∞		invalidates h	validates h
	$0 < P(e \mid \sim h) < 1$	0	$1 < N < \infty$		invalidates h	encourages h

Figure 10.3 How e influences h for different ranges of values of $P(e \mid h)$ and $P(e \mid \sim h)$. The two cases not shown are of no practical interest: evidence always present $[P(e \mid h) = P(e \mid \sim h) = 1]$, or evidence always absent $[P(e \mid h) = P(e \mid \sim h) = 0]$. As apparent from Figures 10.1 and 10.2, validation is a special case of encouragement, and invalidation is a special case of discouragement.

immaterial whether $O(h)$ or $P(h)$ is supplied, for knowing the value of one we can find out the value of the other:

$$O(h) = \frac{P(h)}{1 - P(h)} \text{ from equation 17. of section 10.2.1,}$$

and

$$P(h) = \frac{O(h)}{1 + O(h)} \text{ from equation 18. of section 10.2.1.}$$

Rather than evaluate $O(h \mid \sim e)$ and $O(h \mid e)$, we may often prefer to evaluate $P(h \mid \sim e)$ and $P(h \mid e)$ by the equations derived in Figure 10.4.

From equation [21] of section 10.2.1:

$$P(h \mid \sim e) = \frac{O(h \mid \sim e)}{1 + O(h \mid \sim e)} \cdot$$

In the above equation, replace $O(h \mid \sim e)$ by $NO(h)$ [as justified by Section 10.2.3] to derive:

$$P(h \mid \sim e) = \frac{N\, O(h)}{1 + N\, O(h)} \cdot$$

Replace $O(h)$ in the above equation by

$$\frac{P(h)}{1 - P(h)} \quad \text{from equation [17] of section 10.2.1,}$$

to derive:

$$P(h \mid \sim e) = \frac{N\, P(h)}{1 + (N - 1)\, P(h)} \cdot$$

Similary, from

$$P(h \mid e) = \frac{O(h \mid e)}{1 + O(h \mid e)}$$

we can derive:

$$P(h \mid e) = \frac{S\, P(h)}{1 + (S - 1)\, P(h)} \cdot$$

Figure 10.4   Derivations of equations to evaluate $P(h \mid \sim e)$ and $P(h \mid e)$ from N, S, and $P(h)$.

As an example, suppose that for a prodrule, $P(h) = 0.2$, $P(e \mid h) = 0.8$, and $P(e \mid \sim h) = 0.05$. Then, from the definitions of N and S as given above:

$$N = \frac{1 - P(e \mid h)}{1 - P(e \mid \sim h)} = 0.2105$$

$$S = \frac{P(e \mid h)}{P(e \mid \sim h)} = 16.$$

Furthermore, from the equations of Figure 10.4:

$$P(h \mid \sim e) = \frac{NP(h)}{1 + (N - 1)P(h)} = 0.05$$

$$P(h|e) = \frac{SP(h)}{1 + (S - 1)P(h)} = 0.8.$$

Thus, in the above example, the absence of e discourages h since $P(h|\sim e) < P(h)$, and the presence of e encourages h since $P(h|e) > P(h)$.

10.2.4   Certainty of an evidence

Having studied the necessity and sufficiency measures in a prodrule, we shall now study the certainty measure of evidence, to which we adverted in section 10.1. During our discussion in the previous section, we thought of evidence as being either absent or present, but oft-times one may not be certain about the presence or absence of an evidence. Consider the evidence about the confusedness of a person that the user of an expert system is observing. The user may, for example, say any of the following.

1. I am 20% certain that he looks confused, that is, on a scale of 0 to 1, the user has a certainty of 0.2 regarding the evidence.
2. I am 40% certain that he does not look confused, that is, the user has a certainty of −0.4 regarding the evidence.
3. I do not know whether he looks confused, that is, the user has a certainty of zero regarding the evidence.

So, certainty of an evidence is a measure of how certain the observer is regarding the evidence. Let $C(e)$ denote the certainty of an evidence e such that:

1. if $-1 \le C(e) < 0$, then the user is certain to varying degrees that e is absent; when $C(e) = -1$, the user is fully certain, otherwise partly;
2. if $C(e) = 0$, then the user does not know whether e is absent or present;
3. if $0 < C(e) \le 1$, then the user is certain to varying degrees that e is present. When $C(e) = 1$, the user is fully certain, otherwise partly.

To employ $C(e)$ (which for initial evidence is a subjective estimate supplied by the user and supported by the user's intuition) in our Bayesian scheme, we need to establish a relationship between $C(e)$ and probabilities. Let $P_c(e)$ denote the probability of e based on the user's certainty of e. A more precise notation would have been $P(e|$user's certainty according to the user's observation of $e)$, but for simplicity of notation we shall adopt $P_c(e)$. Now let us establish the· following relationship:

1. when $C(e) = -1$, then the user is fully certain that e is absent, so we assume that $P_c(e) = 0$;

2. when $C(e) = 0$, then the user does not know whether e is absent or present, so we assume that e is present with its prior probability, that is, $P_c(e) = P(e)$;

3. when $C(e) = 1$, then the user is fully certain that e is present, so we assume that $P_c(e) = 1$.

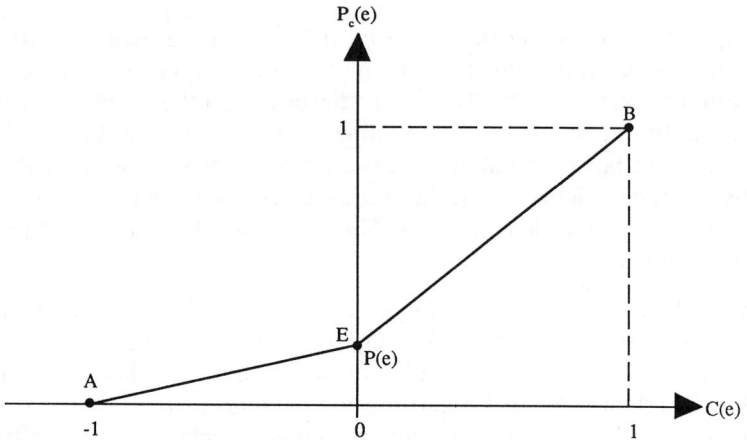

The plot is to pass through the following three points:

point A	$C(e) = -1$	$P_c(e) = 0$
point E	$C(e) = 0$	$P_c(e) = P(e)$
point B	$C(e) = 1$	$P_c(e) = 1$

For piecewise linear interpolation, we join A to E by a straight line, and E to B by another straight line. We derive the equations of these lines:

$$P_c(e) = \begin{cases} (1 + C(e))\, P(e) & \text{if } -1 \leq C(e) \leq 0 \\ P(e) + (1 - P(e))\, C(e) & \text{if } 0 < C(e) \leq 1 \end{cases}$$

We can rewrite the above equation as follows:

$$C(e) = \begin{cases} \dfrac{P_c(e) - P(e)}{P(e)} & \text{if } P_c(e) \leq P(e) \\[3mm] \dfrac{P_c(e) - P(e)}{1 - P(e)} & \text{if } P_c(e) > P(e) \end{cases}$$

Figure 10.5   Plot of $P_c(e)$ versus $C(e)$ for $0 < P(e) < 1$. For $P(e) = 0$, we could consider $C(e) = 0$; and for $P(e) = 1$, we could consider $C(e) = 1$. Note, however, that $P(e) = 0$ and $P(e) = 1$ are of no practical interest, as mentioned in section 10.2.3.

For other values of $C(e)$, we can evaluate $P_c(e)$ by piecewise linear interpolation as shown in Figure 10.5. Remember that the equation of a straight line passing through the coordinates (x_1, y_1) and (x_2, y_2) in the xy plane is obtained from

$$y - y_1 = \frac{(y_2 - y_1)}{(x_2 - x_1)} (x - x_1).$$

To illustrate, let $P(e) = 0.1$. We are to evaluate $P_c(e)$ for $C(e) = -0.2$ and for $C(e) = 0.5$. From the equations of Figure 10.5:

for $C(e) = -0.2$, $\quad P_c(e) = (1 + C(e))P(e) = 0.08.$
for $C(e) = 0.5$, $\quad P_c(e) = P(e) + (1 - P(e))C(e) = 0.55.$

As a check, let us do the converse calculations by evaluation $C(e)$ for $P_c(e) = 0.08$ and for $P_c(e) = 0.55$. Then, again from the equations of Figure 10.5:

for $P_c(e) = 0.08$, $\quad C(e) = \dfrac{P_c(e) - P(e)}{P(e)} = -0.2.$

for $P_c(e) = 0.55$, $\quad C(e) = \dfrac{P_c(e) - P(e)}{1 - P(e)} = 0.5.$

Note, however, that there can be evidence e_1 and e_2 such that $C(e_1) < C(e_2)$, but that $P_c(e_1) > P_c(e_2)$. You may find this going against your intuition. Nonetheless, this can happen when one evidence has high prior probability but low certainty, and the other evidence has low prior probability but high certainty. As an example, suppose that $C(e_1) = 0.2$, $C(e_2) = 0.8$, $P(e_1) = 0.9$ and $P(e_2) = 0.3$. Then, from the equations in Figure 10.4:

$P_c(e_1) = P(e_1) + (1 - P(e_1))C(e_1) = 0.92$
$P_c(e_2) = P(e_2) + (1 - P(e_2))C(e_2) = 0.86.$

Thus, although $C(e_1) < C(e_2)$, we obtain $P_c(e_1) > P_c(e_2)$.

10.2.5 Certainty of a formula of evidence

We next discuss the recommended approaches to find the values of $C(e)$, $P(e)$ and $P_c(e)$ for evidence e that is a formula containing conjunctions. Suppose e is the formula:

$e = e_1 \wedge e_2 \wedge \ldots \wedge e_n.$

We know the values of $C(e_1)$, $C(e_2)$, $\ldots$, $C(e_n)$ and also of $P(e_1)$, $P(e_2)$, $\ldots$, $P(e_n)$. Since the values of $C(e_i)$ and $P(e_i)$, for $1 \leq i \leq n$, are subjective estimates, there are two recommended approaches for finding the values of $C(e)$, $P(e)$ and $P_c(e)$. Both approaches are based on fuzzy set theory, which was discussed in section 10.2.2.

Approach 1

Let $C(e) = \min(C(e_1), C(e_2), \ldots, C(e_n))$. Say we found $C(e)$ to be equal to $C(e_i)$, for some i such that $1 \leq i \leq n$. Then let $P(e) = P(e_i)$. Knowing $C(e)$ and $P(e)$, we can evaluate $P_c(e)$ by the equations given in Figure 10.5.

Approach 2

Evaluate $P_c(e_1)$, $P_c(e_2)$, \ldots, $P_c(e_n)$ by the equations of Figure 10.5. Then let $P_c(e) = \min(P_c(e_1), P_c(e_2), \ldots, P_c(e_n))$. Say we found $P_c(e)$ to be equal to $P_c(e_i)$, for some i such that $1 \leq i \leq n$. Then let $P(e) = P_c(e_i)$ and $C(e) = C(e_i)$. The two approaches may not always give the same results. An example is given in Figure 10.6.

We can similarly have two approaches based on fuzzy set theory, mentioned in section 10.2.2, to find the values of $C(e)$, $P(e)$ and $P_c(e)$ for evidence e that is a formula containing disjunctions. Suppose e is the formula

$$e = e_1 \vee e_2 \vee \ldots \vee e_n.$$

Given e = $e_1 \wedge e_2$, where $C(e_1) = 0.2$, $C(e_2) = 0.8$, $P(e_1) = 0.9$, and $P(e_2) = 0.3$.

To find C(e), P(e), and $P_e(e)$ by the two approaches discussed in Section 10.2.5.

[Aproach 1]

$C(e) = \min(C(e_1), C(e_2)) = 0.2$

Since $C(e) = C(e_1)$,

$P(e) = P(e_1) = 0.9$; and from Figure 10.5,

$P_e(e) = P(e) + (1 - P(e)) C(e) = 0.92$.

[Approach 2]

$P_e(e_1) = P(e_1) + (1 - P(e_1)) C(e_1) = 0.92$

$P_e(e_2) = P(e_2) + (1 - P(e_2)) C(e_2) = 0.86$

$P_e(e) = \min(P_e(e_1), P_e(e_2)) = 0.86$

Since $P_e(e) = P_e(e_2)$,

$P(e) = P(e_2) = 0.3$, and

$C(e) = C(e_2) = 0.8$.

Figure 10.6   An example to show that the values of C(e), P(e), and $P_c(e)$ for the formula $e = e_1 \wedge e_2$ can be different by the two approaches discussed in section 10.2.5. This happened because $C(e_1) < C(e_2)$, but $P_c(e_1) > P_c(e_2)$.

Then, by the first approach:

$$C(e) = \max(C(e_1), C(e_2), \ldots, C(e_n)).$$

In turn, by the second approach:

$$P_c(e) = \max(P_c(e_1), P_c(e_2), \ldots, P_c(e_n)).$$

The above discussion can be extended for evidence that is a formula containing both conjunctions and disjunctions. Consider:

$$e = e_1 \wedge e_2 \vee e_3.$$

By the first approach:

$$C(e) = \max(\min(C(e_1), C(e_2)), C(e_3)).$$

By the second approach:

$$P_c(e) = \max(\min(P_c(e_1), P_c(e_2)), P_c(e_3)).$$

Given a prodrule

If e then h.

where e is any formula, we shall assume that $C(e)$ and $P_c(e)$ have been evaluated by choosing either of the approaches discussed above. So from now on, whenever we refer to an evidence, during the discussion on this Bayesian scheme, we shall be referring to the formula of evidence in the antecedent of a prodrule, unless otherwise stated.

10.2.6   Certainty of a hypothesis

Just as there is a certainty associated with an evidence, there is also certainty associated with the hypothesis that is inferred. The two ideas of certainty are similar. Nevertheless, we shall briefly discuss the certainty of a hypothesis h to avoid any misunderstanding.

Let $C(h|e)$ denote the certainty of h conditioned on the certainty of e, where $-1 \leq C(h|e) \leq 1$. Let $P_c(h|e)$ denote the probability of h conditioned on the certainty of e, where $0 \leq P_c(h|e) \leq 1$.

The following relationship is established between $C(h|e)$ and $P_c(h|e)$. If $C(h|e) = -1$, then $P_c(h|e) = 0$. If $C(h|e) = 0$, then $P_c(h|e) = P(h)$. If $C(h|e) = 1$, then $P_c(h|e) = 1$. For other values of $C(h|e)$, we can evaluate $P_c(h|e)$ by piecewise linear interpolation as illustrated in Figure 10.7.

To illustrate, let $P(h) = 0.2$. We are to evaluate $P_c(h|e)$ for $C(h|e) = -0.15$ and for $C(h|e) = 0.375$. From the equations of Figure 10.7:

for $C(h|e) = -0.15$, $P_c(h|e) = (1 + C(h|e))P(h) = 0.17$,

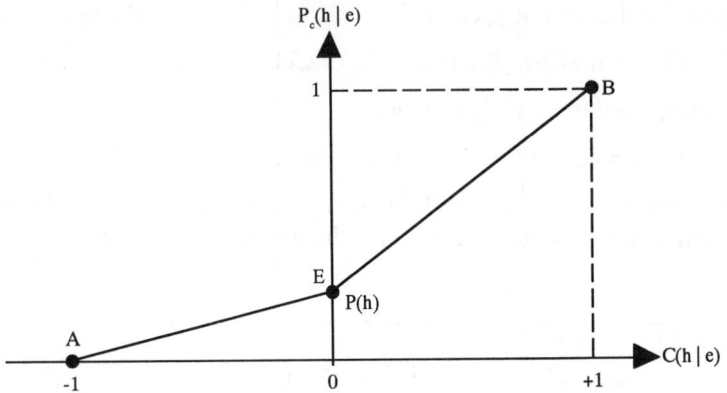

For piecewise linear interpolation [as in Figure 10.5], we derive the equations of straight lines AE and EB.

$$P_c(h \mid e) = \begin{cases} (1 + C(h \mid e))\, P(h) & \text{if } -1 \leqslant C(h \mid e) \leqslant 0 \\ P(h) + (1 - P(h))\, C(h \mid e) & \text{if } 0 < C(h \mid e) \leqslant 1 \end{cases}$$

We can rewrite the above equation, as follows:

$$C(h \mid e) = \begin{cases} \dfrac{P_c(h \mid e) - P(h)}{P(h)} & \text{if } P_c(h \mid e) \leqslant P(h) \\[2em] \dfrac{P_c(h \mid e) - P(h)}{1 - P(h)} & \text{if } P_c(h \mid e) > P(h) \end{cases}$$

Figure 10.7   Plot of $P_c(h|e)$ versus $C(h|e)$ for $0 < P(h) < 1$. For $P(h) = 0$, we could consider $C(h|e) = 0$; and for $P(h) = 1$, we could consider $C(h|e) = 1$. Note, however, that $P(h) = 0$ and $P(h) = 1$ are of no practical interest, as mentioned in section 10.2.3.

for $C(h|e) = 0.375$, $P_c(h|e) = P(h) + (1 - P(h))C(h|e) = 0.5$.

As a check, let us do the converse calculations by evaluation $C(h|e)$ for $P_c(h|e) = 0.17$ and for $P_c(h|e) = 0.5$. Then, again from the equations of Figure 10.7:

for $P_c(h|e) = 0.17$, $C(h|e) = \dfrac{P_c(h|e) - P(h)}{P(h)} = -0.15$,

for $P_c(h|e) = 0.5$, $C(h|e) = \dfrac{P_c(h|e) - P(h)}{1 - P(h)} = 0.375$.

In a typical prodrule *If e then h*, if we know the values of $P_c(e)$ or $C(e)$, we can evaluate $P_c(h|e)$ and $C(h|e)$. Four alternative sets of equations are derived in the next four sections to enable us to do the necessary calculations.

10.2.7 Evaluating $P_c(h|e)$ given $P_c(e)$

In this section, we derive equations by which we can evaluate $P_{\bar{c}}(h|e)$ having been given the value of $P_c(e)$. We establish the following relationship between $P_c(e)$ and $P_c(h|e)$.

1. When $P_c(e) = 0$, then one is fully certain that *e* is absent, so $P_c(h|e) = P(h|\sim e)$.
2. When $P_c(e) = P(e)$, then one does not know whether *e* is absent or present, so $P_c(h|e) = P(h)$.
3. When $P_c(e) = 1$, then one is fully certain that *e* is present, so $P_c(h|e) = P(h|e)$.

For other values of $P_c(e)$ we can evaluate $P_c(h|e)$ by piecewise linear interpolation as shown in Figure 10.8.

To illustrate, let $P(h) = 0.2$, $N = 0.2105$, $S = 16$ and $P(e) = 0.1$. We are to evaluate $P_c(h|e)$ for $P_c(e) = 0.08$ and for $P_c(e) = 0.55$. Then from the equations of Figure 10.4:

$$P(h|\sim e) = \frac{NP(h)}{1 + (N - 1)P(h)} = 0.05$$

$$P(h|e) = \frac{SP(h)}{1 + (S - 1)P(h)} = 0.8.$$

Now from the equations of Figure 10.8:

for $P_c(e) = 0.08$,

$$P_c(h|e) = P(h|\sim e) + \frac{P_c(e)(P(h) - P(h|\sim e))}{P(e)}$$

$$= 0.17,$$

for $P_c(e) = 0.55$,

$$P_c(h|e) = \frac{P(h) - P(h|e)P(e) + P_c(e)(P(h|e) - P(h))}{1 - P(e)}$$

$$= 0.5.$$

In the above example: when $P_c(e) < P(e)$, then $P_c(h|e) < P(h)$, and so *h* is discouraged; and when $P_c(e) > P(e)$, then $P_c(h|e) > P(h)$, and so *h* is encouraged. If needed, we can next obtain $C(h|e) = -0.15$ for $P_c(h|e) =$

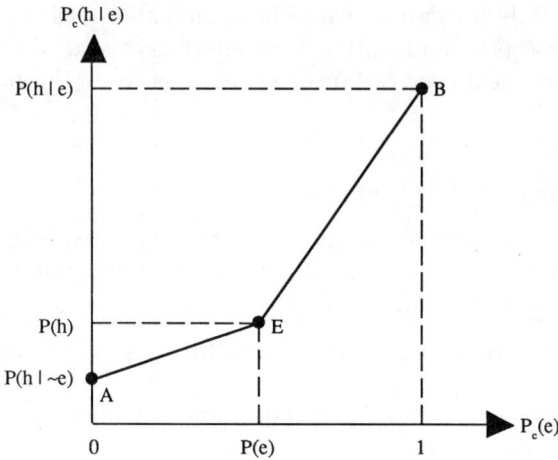

For piecewise linear interpolation, we derive the equations of straight lines AE and EB.

$$
P_c(h \mid e) =
\begin{cases}
P(h \mid \sim e) + \dfrac{P_c(e)\,(P(h) - P(h \mid \sim e))}{P(e)} & \text{if } 0 \le P_c(e) \le P(e) \\[3mm]
\dfrac{P(h) - P(h \mid e)\,P(e) + P_c(e)(P(h \mid e) - P(h))}{1 - P(e)} & \text{if } P(e) < P_c(e) \le 1
\end{cases}
$$

Figure 10.8 Plot of $P_c(h \mid e)$ versus $P_c(e)$.

0.17 and $C(h \mid e) = 0.375$ for $P_c(h \mid e) = 0.5$, as shown in the example of section 10.2.6.

10.2.8 Evaluating $P_c(h \mid e)$ given $C(e)$

As an alternative to section 10.2.7, we shall next derive equations by which we can evaluate $P_c(h \mid e)$ directly from $C(e)$ without knowing the value of $P_c(e)$. We establish the following relationship between $C(e)$ and $P_c(h \mid e)$.

1. When $C(e) = -1$, then one is fully certain that e is absent, so $P_c(h \mid e) = P(h \mid \sim e)$.
2. When $C(e) = 0$, then one does not know whether e is absent or present, so $P_c(h \mid e) = P(h)$.
3. When $C(e) = 1$, then one is fully certain that e is present, so $P_c(h \mid e) = P(h \mid e)$.

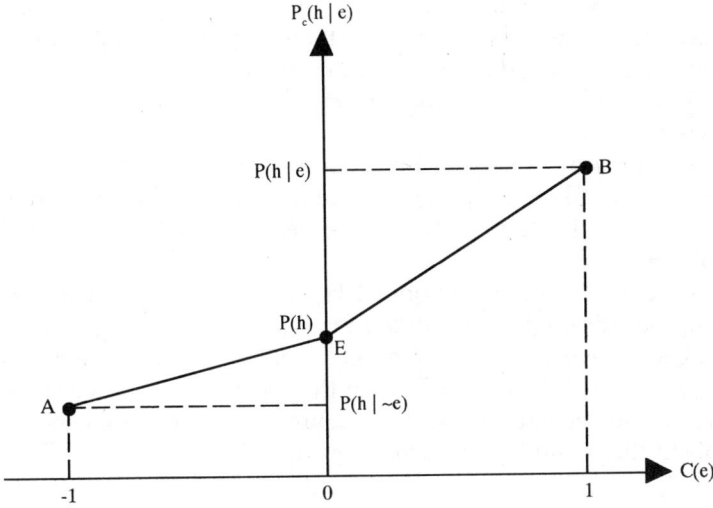

For piecewise linear interpolation, we derive the equations of straight lines AE and EB.

$$P_c(h \mid e) = \begin{cases} (P(h) - P(h \mid {\sim}e))\,C(e) + P(h) & \text{if } -1 \leqslant C(e) \leqslant 0 \\ (P(h \mid e) - P(h))\,C(e) + P(h) & \text{if } 0 < C(e) \leqslant 1 \end{cases}$$

Figure 10.9 Plot of $P_c(h \mid e)$ versus $C(e)$.

For other values of $C(e)$ we can evaluate $P_c(h \mid e)$ by piecewise linear interpolation as in Figure 10.9.

To illustrate, let $P(h) = 0.2$, $N = 0.2105$, $S = 16$ and $P(e) = 0.1$. We are to evaluate $P_c(h \mid e)$ for $C(e) = -0.2$ and for $C(e) = 0.5$. Then from the equations of Figure 10.4:

$$P(h \mid {\sim}e) = \frac{NP(h)}{1 + (N - 1)P(h)} = 0.05$$

$$P(h \mid e) = \frac{SP(h)}{1 + (S - 1)P(h)} = 0.8.$$

Now from the equations of Figure 10.9:

for $C(e) = -0.2$,
$P_c(h \mid e) = (P(h) - P(h \mid {\sim}e))C(e) + P(h) = 0.17$,
for $C(e) = 0.5$,
$P_c(h \mid e) = (P(h \mid e) - P(h))C(e) + P(h) = 0.5.$

In the above example: when $C(e) < 0$, then $P_c(h|e) < P(h)$, and so h is discouraged; when $C(e) > 0$, then $P_c(h|e) > P(h)$, and so h is encouraged. If needed, we can next obtain $C(h|e) = -0.15$ for $P_c(h|e) = 0.17$ and $C(h|e) = 0.375$ for $P_c(h|e) = 0.5$, as shown in the example of section 10.2.6.

You may have noticed that whereas the value of $P(e)$ was required for the calculations in section 10.2.7, it was not required for the calculations in this section. The results in the two sections are, however, the same.

Incidentally, the equations of Figure 10.9 can be derived in another way. Substitute $((1 + C(e))P(e))$ for $P_c(e)$ in the first equation of Figure 10.8 to derive the first equation of Figure 10.9. Similarly, substitute $(P(e) + (1 - P(e))C(e))$ for $P_c(e)$ in the second equation of Figure 10.8 to derive the second equation of Figure 10.9. The justification for these substitutions can be seen from Figure 10.5.

10.2.9   Evaluating $C(h|e)$ given $C(e)$

As an alternative to section 10.2.8, we shall next derive equations by which we can evaluate $C(h|e)$ directly from $C(e)$ without first evaluating $P_c(h|e)$. We establish the following relationship between $C(e)$ and $C(h|e)$.

1. When $C(e) = -1$, then one is fully certain that e is absent, so
$$C(h|e) = \frac{P(h|\sim e) - P(h)}{P(h)}.$$

2. When $C(e) = 0$, then one does not know whether e is absent or present, so $C(h|e) = 0$.

3. When $C(e) = 1$, then one is fully certain that e is present, so
$$C(h|e) = \frac{P(h|e) - P(h)}{1 - P(h)}.$$

For other values of $C(e)$ we can evaluate $C(h|e)$ by piecewise linear interpolation as in Figure 10.10.

To illustrate, let $P(h) = 0.2$, $N = 0.2105$, $S = 16$ and $P(e) = 0.1$. We are to evaluate $C(h|e)$ for $C(e) = -0.2$ and for $C(e) = 0.5$. Then from the equations of Figure 10.4:

$$P(h|\sim e) = \frac{NP(h)}{1 + (N - 1)P(h)} = 0.05$$

$$P(h|e) = \frac{SP(h)}{1 + (S - 1)P(h)} = 0.8$$

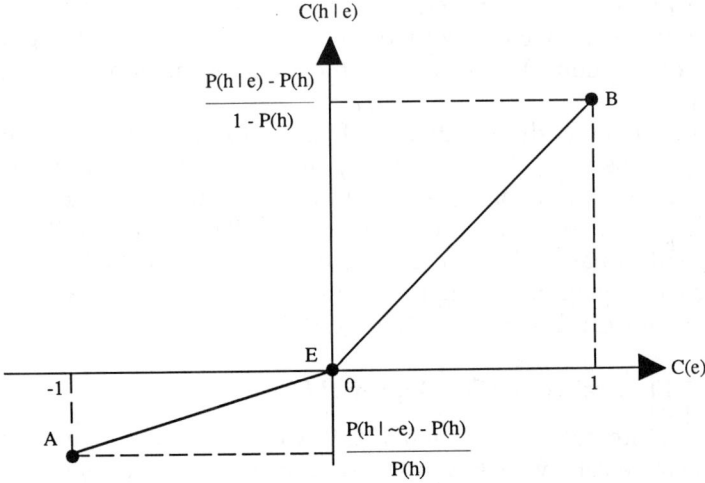

For piecewise linear interpolation, we derive the equations of straight lines AE and EB.

$$C(h \mid e) = \begin{cases} \dfrac{(P(h) - P(h \mid \sim e))\, C(e)}{P(h)} & \text{if } -1 \le C(e) \le 0 \\[2em] \dfrac{(P(h \mid e) - P(h))\, C(e)}{1 - P(h)} & \text{if } 0 < C(e) \le 1 \end{cases}$$

Figure 10.10   Plot of $C(h \mid e)$ versus $C(e)$.

Now from the equations of Figure 10.10:

for $C(e) = -0.2$,

$$C(h \mid e) = \frac{(P(h) - P(h \mid \sim e))C(e)}{P(h)} = -0.15,$$

for $C(e) = 0.5$,

$$C(h \mid e) = \frac{(P(h \mid e) - P(h))C(e)}{1 - P(h)} = 0.375.$$

In the above example: when $C(e) < 0$, then $C(h \mid e) < 0$, and so h is discouraged; when $C(e) > 0$, then $C(h \mid e) > 0$, and so h is encouraged. If needed, we can next obtain $P_c(h \mid e) = 0.17$ for $C(h \mid e) = -0.15$, and $P_c(h \mid e) = 0.5$ for $C(h \mid e) = 0.375$, as shown in the example in section 10.2.6.

You may have noticed that, just as in section 10.2.8 but unlike section 10.2.7, we did not require the value of $P(e)$ for the calculations in this section. The results in the three sections are, however, the same.

Incidentally, the equations in Figure 10.10 can be derived in another way. Substitute $(1 + C(h|e))P(h))$ for $P_c(h|e)$ in the first equation of Figure 10.9, and solve for $C(h|e)$ to derive the first equation of Figure 10.10. Similarly, substitute $P(h) + (1 - P(h))C(h|e)$ for $P_c(h|e)$ in the second equation in Figure 10.9, and solve for $C(h|e)$, to derive the second equation of Figure 10.10. The justification for these substitutions can be seen from Figure 10.7.

10.2.10 Evaluating $C(h|e)$ given $P_c(e)$

As an alternative to section 10.2.9, we shall next derive equations by which we can evaluate $C(h|e)$ having been given the value of $P_c(e)$. We establish the following relationship between $P_c(e)$ and $C(h|e)$.

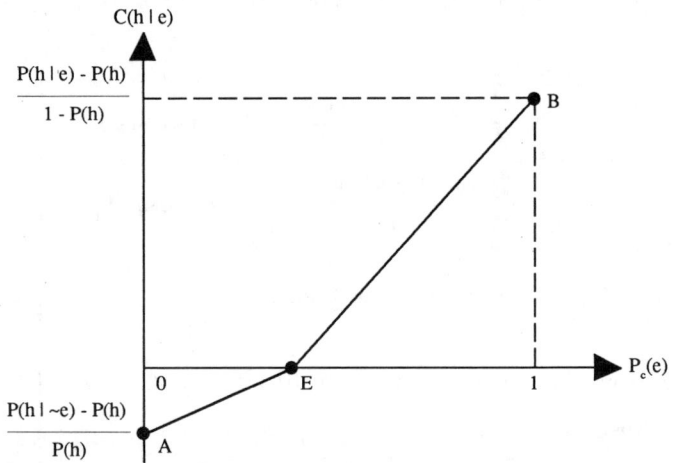

For piecewise linear interpolation, we derive the equations of straight lines AE and EB.

$$C(h\,|\,e) = \begin{cases} \dfrac{(P(h) - P(h\,|\,\sim e))(P_c(e) - P(e))}{P(h)\,P(e)} & \text{if } 0 \leq P_c(e) \leq P(e) \\[2ex] \dfrac{(P(h\,|\,e) - P(h))(P_c(e) - P(e))}{(1 - P(h))(1 - P(e))} & \text{if } P(e) < P_c(e) \leq 1 \end{cases}$$

Figure 10.11   Plot of $C(h\,|\,e)$ versus $P_c(e)$.

1. When $P_c(e) = 0$, then one is fully certain that e is absent, so

$$C(h|e) = \frac{P(h|\sim e) - P(h)}{P(h)}.$$

2. When $P_c(e) = P(e)$, then one does not know whether e is absent or present, so $C(h|e) = 0$.

3. When $P_c(e) = 1$, then one is fully certain that e is present, so

$$C(h|e) = \frac{P(h|e) - P(h)}{1 - P(h)}.$$

For other values of $P_c(e)$ we can evaluate $C(h|e)$ by piecewise linear interpolation as in Figure 10.11.

To illustrate, let $P(h) = 0.2$, $N = 0.2105$, $S = 16$ and $P(e) = 0.1$. We are to evaluate $C(h|e)$ for $P_c(e) = 0.08$ and for $P_c(e) = 0.55$. Then from the equations of Figure 10.4:

$$P(h|\sim e) = \frac{NP(h)}{1 + (N-1)P(h)} = 0.05$$

$$P(h|e) = \frac{SP(h)}{1 + (S-1)P(h)} = 0.8.$$

Now from the equations of Figure 10.11:

for $P_c(e) = 0.08$,

$$C(h|e) = \frac{(P(h) - P(h|\sim e))(P_c(e) - P(e))}{P(h)P(e)}$$

$$= -0.15,$$

for $P_c(e) = 0.55$,

$$C(h|e) = \frac{(P(h|e) - P(h))(P_c(e) - P(e))}{(1 - P(h))(1 - P(e))}$$

$$= 0.375.$$

In the above example: when $P_c(e) < P(e)$, then $C(h|e) < 0$, and so h is discouraged; when $P_c(e) > P(e)$, then $C(h|e) > 0$, and so h is encouraged. If needed, we can next obtain $P_c(h|e) = 0.17$ for $C(h|e) = -0.15$ and $P_c(h|e) = 0.5$ for $C(h|e) = 0.375$, as shown in the example in section 10.2.6.

You may have noticed that, just as for section 10.2.7 but unlike sections 10.2.8 and 10.2.9, we required the value of $P(e)$ for the calculations in this section. The results in the four sections are, however, the same.

Incidentally, the equations in Figure 10.11 can be derived in another way. Substitute

$$\frac{(P_c(e) - P(e))}{P(e)}$$

for $C(e)$ in the first equation of Figure 10.10 to derive the first equation of Figure 10.11. Similarly, substitute

$$\frac{(P_c(e) - P(e))}{(1 - P(e))}$$

for $C(e)$ in the second equation of Figure 10.10 to derive the second equation of Figure 10.11. The justification of these substitutions can be seen from Figure 10.5.

Of the four alternative sets of equations displayed in Figures 10.8–10.11, you may choose the set that you find most convenient for your calculations.

10.2.11   Influence of multiple evidence on a hypothesis

Until now we have been discussing the influence of a single evidence e on a hypothesis h. In this section, we delineate a procedure to see how multiple evidence e_1, e_2, e_3, ... can cumulatively influence h. The procedure adapts equation 28. of section 10.2.1 according to which:

$$O(h\,|\sim e_1 \wedge \sim e_2 \wedge \ldots \wedge \sim e_k \wedge e_{k+1} \wedge \ldots \wedge e_m)$$

$$= \left(\prod_{i=1}^{k} N_i\right)\left(\prod_{i=k+1}^{m} S_i\right) O(h)$$

where the necessity measure

$$N_i = \frac{P(\sim e_i | h)}{P(\sim e_i | \sim h)} \quad \text{for } i = 1, 2, \ldots, k,$$

and the sufficiency measure

$$S_i = \frac{P(e_i | h)}{P(e_i | \sim h)} \quad \text{for } i = k + 1, k + 2, \ldots, m.$$

Suppose we have the following prodrules:

If e_1 then h.

If e_2 then h.

If e_3 then h.

.
.
.

Let the necessity and sufficiency measures of the prodrule 'If e_i then h' be N_i and S_i for $i = 1, 2, 3, \ldots$. We want to find the cumulative influence of all the e's on h. Without loss of generality, let us assume that:

1. $e_1, e_2, \ldots, e_k$ are known to be absent; in other words, $-1 \leq C(e_i) < 0$, or we can say $P_c(e_i) < P(e_i)$, for $i = 1, 2, \ldots, k$;
2. $e_{k+1}, e_{k+2}, \ldots, e_m$ are known to be present; in other words, $0 < C(e_i) \leq 1$, or we can say that $P_c(e_i) > P(e_i)$, for $i = k + 1, k + 2, \ldots, m$;
3. $e_{m+1}, e_{m+2}, \ldots$ are not known to be absent or present; in other words, $C(e_i) = 0$, or we can say that $P_c(e_i) = P(e_i)$, for $i = m + 1, m + 2, \ldots$.

Given $P(h) = 0.2$, for the following prodrules:

If e_1 then h [$N_1 = 0.101$, $S_1 = 90$, $P(e_1) = 0.3$].
If e_2 then h [$N_2 = 0.2105$, $S_2 = 16$, $P(e_2) = 0.1$].
If e_3 then h [$N_3 = 0.01$, $S_3 = 500$, $P(e_3) = 0.18$].

Further given that:

e_1 is absent with $P_c(e_1) = 0.24$;
e_2 is present with $P_c(e_2) = 0.55$;
e_3 is not known to be absent or present: that is, $P_c(e_3) = 0.18$. We ignore e_3 since it will not influence h.

To evaluate $P_c(h \mid e_1 \wedge e_2)$.

As you read the solution below, keep referring step by step to the description of the procedure in Section 10.2.11.

[Step 1]	$P(h \mid \sim e_1)$	=	0.0246
	$P(h \mid e_2)$	=	0.8
[Step 2]	$P_c(h \mid e_1)$	=	0.165
	$P_c(h \mid e_2)$	=	0.5
[Step 3]	$O_c(h \mid e_1)$	=	0.198
	$O_c(h \mid e_2)$	=	1.0
[Step 4]	$O(h)$	=	0.25
[Step 5]	E_1	=	0.792
	E_2	=	1.00
[Step 6]	$O_c(h \mid e_1 \wedge e_2)$	=	0.792
[Step 7]	$P_c(h \mid e_1 \wedge e_2)$	=	0.442

Figure 10.12 An example to show the influence of multiple evidence on a hypothesis.

We can ignore all e's that are not known to be either absent or present since they will not influence h. Accordingly, the only e's that will influence h are those that are known to be either absent or present.

Below you will read the description of a seven-step procedure to evaluate $P_c(h \mid e_1 \wedge e_2 \wedge \ldots \wedge e_m)$, given $P_c(e_1)$, $P_c(e_2)$, ..., $P_c(e_m)$. As you read the procedure, keep referring step by step to the example in Figure 10.12. That should help you understand the procedure better.

Step 1
Evaluate

$$P(h \mid \sim e_i) = \frac{N_i P(h)}{1 + (N_i - 1)P(h)} \quad \text{for } i = 1, 2, \ldots k$$

$$P(h \mid e_i) = \frac{S_i P(h)}{1 + (S_i - 1)P(h)} \quad \text{for } i = k + 1, k + 2, \ldots, m.$$

The above equations are from Figure 10.4.

Step 2
Evaluate

$$P_c(h \mid e_i) = P(h \mid \sim e_i)P(e_i) + \frac{P_c(e_i)(P(h) - P(h \mid \sim e_i))}{P(e_i)}$$
$$\text{for } i = 1, 2, \ldots, k$$

$$P_c(h \mid e_i) = \frac{P(h) - P(h \mid e_i)P(e_i) + P_c(e_i)(P(h \mid e_i) - P(h))}{1 - P(e_i)}$$
$$\text{for } i = k + 1, k + 2, \ldots, m.$$

The above equations are from Figure 10.8. Had we been given $C(e_1)$, $C(e_2)$, ..., $C(e_m)$ instead of $P_c(e_1)$, $P_c(e_2)$, ..., $P_c(e_m)$, we would have employed the equations of Figure 10.9 to evaluate $P_c(h \mid e_1)$, ..., $P_c(h \mid e_m)$.

Step 3
Evaluate

$$O_c(h \mid e_i) = \frac{P_c(h \mid e_i)}{1 - P_c(h \mid e_i)} \quad \text{for } i = 1, 2, \ldots, m.$$

The above is from equation 20. of section 10.2.1.

Step 4
Evaluate

$$O(h) = \frac{P(h)}{1 - P(h)}.$$

The above is from equation 17. of section 10.2.1.

Step 5

Evaluate *effective* influence measures:

$$E_i = \frac{O_c(h|e_i)}{O(h)} \quad \text{for } i = 1, 2, \ldots, m.$$

For $1 \leq i \leq k$, we can alternatively say that E_i is an effective necessity measure N_i'. Similarly, for $k + 1 \leq i \leq m$, we can alternatively say that E_i is an effective sufficiency measure S_i'.

Step 6

Evaluate

$$O_c(h|e_1 \wedge \ldots \wedge e_m) = \left(\prod_{i=1}^{m} E_i \right) O(h).$$

The above is an adaptation of equation 28. of section 10.2.1, to which we referred at the beginning of this section.

Step 7

Evaluate

$$P_c(h|e_1 \wedge \ldots \wedge e_m) = \frac{O_c(h|e_1 \wedge \ldots \wedge e_m)}{1 + O_c(h|e_1 \wedge \ldots \wedge e_m)}.$$

The above is from equation 21. of section 10.2.1.

It can be seen from the above procedure that the order in which we consider the different evidence does not affect our evaluation of $P_c(h|e_1 \wedge \ldots \wedge e_m)$. But here we also need words of caution. According to the above procedure if, say, e_1 encourages h and if e_2 encourages h then $(e_1 \wedge e_2)$ also encourages h. This should hold most of the time. In the literature, you may however find an example from subparticle physics, where e_1 encourages h and e_2 encourages h but $e_1 \wedge e_2$ discourages h. We shall ignore such rare examples in finding out the cumulative influence of multiple evidence on a hypothesis. You may, if you wish, consider the subparticle physics example to be more precisely saying that $(e_1 \wedge \sim e_2)$ encourages h, $(\sim e_1 \wedge e_2)$ encourages h and $(e_1 \wedge e_2)$ discourages h.

10.2.12 Propagation of probabilities

Suppose there is a hypothesis h_1 that is influenced by evidence e_1, $e_2, \ldots, e_m$. From our discussion in the previous section, we can evaluate $P_c(h_1|e_1 \wedge \ldots \wedge e_m)$. Now suppose that h_1 is an intermediate hypothesis so that it influences another hypothesis h_2. To find this influence on h_2, we rename h_1 as e' and we declare $P_c(e')$ to be equal to

$P_c(h_1|e_1 \wedge \ldots \wedge e_m)$. Then we can evaluate $P_c(h_2|e')$ as discussed in section 10.2.7. To illustrate, let us consider the following prodrules:

If e_1 then h_1. ($P(h_1) = 0.2$, $N_1 = 0.101$, $S_1 = 90$, $P(e_1) = 0.3$)

If e_2 then h_1. ($P(h_1) = 0.2$, $N_2 = 0.2105$, $S_2 = 16$, $P(e_2) = 0.1$)

If e_3 then h_1. ($P(h_1) = 0.2$, $N_3 = 0.01$, $S_3 = 500$, $P(e_3) = 0.18$)

If h_1 then h_2. ($P(h_2) = 0.15$, $N_4 = 0.05$, $S_4 = 475$, $P(h_1) = 0.2$)

We are also given $P_c(e_1) = 0.24$, $P_c(e_2) = 0.55$ and $P_c(e_3) = 0.18$. We ignore e_3 since it will not influence h_1. Note that $P_c(e_3)$ is equal to $P(e_3)$. Then according to the calculations in Figure 10.12, we get $P_c(h_1|e_1 \wedge e_2)$ = 0.442. We rename h_1 as e' and declare that $P_c(e') = 0.442$, so the fourth prodrule above becomes *If e' then h_2*. We proceed as in section 10.2.7. From the equation in Figure 10.4:

$$P(h_2|e') = \frac{S_4 P(h_2)}{1 + (S_4 - 1)P(h_2)}$$

$$= \frac{475 \times 0.15}{1 + (475 - 1) \times 0.15}$$

$$= 0.986.$$

Then from the equation of Figure 10.8:

$$P_c(h_2|e') = \frac{P(h_2) - P(h_2|e')P(e') + P_c(e')(P(h_2|e') - P(h_2))}{1 - P(e')}$$

$$= \frac{0.15 - 0.986 \times 0.2 + 0.442 \times (0.986 - 0.15)}{1 - 0.2}$$

$$= 0.403.$$

We have thus propagated the probability from h_1 to h_2. If h_2 itself is an intermediate hypothesis, then we can similarly propagate the probabilities all the way to the final hypotheses.

10.2.13 The special case of harmonious provisions

The values of $P(h)$, N, S and $P(e)$, supplied by the domain expert for the prodrule

If e then h

are called the **provisions** of the prodrule. The provisions of a prodrule are said to be **harmonious** if, and only if, they satisfy the following equation, derived in Figure 10.13:

In Section 10.2.3, we saw:

$$P(e \mid h) = \frac{S(1 - N)}{S - N} \qquad \text{<i>}$$

$$P(e \mid \sim h) = \frac{1 - N}{S - N} \qquad \text{<ii>}$$

Moreover, from equation [31] of Section 10.2.1, we know:

$$P(e) = P(h) \, (P(e \mid h) - P(e \mid \sim h)) + P(e \mid \sim h)$$

Substituting the right-hand sides of <i> and <ii> for their corresponding left-hand sides in the above equation, we get:

$$P(e) = \frac{(1 - N)((S - 1) \, P(h) + 1)}{S - N}$$

Figure 10.13 Derivation of the equation to be satisfied by harmonious provisions.

$$P(e) = \frac{(1 - N)((S - 1)P(h) + 1)}{S - N}.$$

One would presume that the provisions of a prodrule are always harmonious. They should be so, but in practice they often are not.

Let us assume that the domain experts have supplied the following provisions for a prodrule: $P(h) = 0.3$, $S = 500$, $N = 1$ and $P(e) = 0.08$. If we substitute these values in the equation above we can see that the provisions are not harmonious. We can view these values in another way. We saw in Figure 10.3 the constraint that $S > 1$ if, and only if, $N < 1$. Clearly, the provisions are violating this constraint. You may point this out to the domain experts, but since they may work by intuition (that is how they usually give the values of S and N), they may insist that their S and N are appropriate. In effect, the domain experts are saying that, although the presence of e influences h by encouraging it, the absence of e does not influence h (see Figures 10.1 and 10.2). Accordingly, you may be obliged to associate disharmonious provisions with a prodrule.

It may be of interest to know that piecewise linearization was required in Figure 10.8 to accommodate disharmonious provisions. If, however, the provisions are harmonious, then, as a special case, the plot of Figure 10.8 becomes a single straight line as shown in Figure 10.14.

It should be remembered that whereas the equations of Figure 10.8 can be used for both harmonious and disharmonious provisions, the equation of Figure 10.14 can be used only for harmonious provisions.

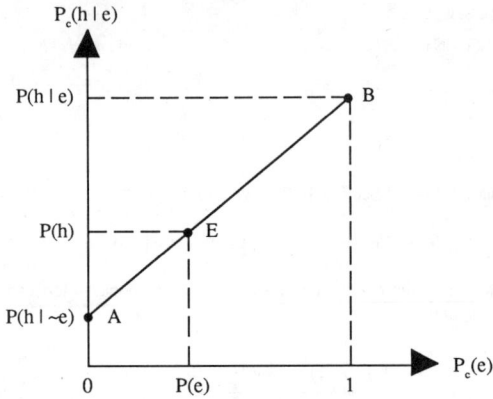

When the provisions are harmonious, it can be shown that the slope of AE is equal to the slope of EB, so that AB becomes a straight line. Note that

$$\text{Slope of AE} = \frac{P(h) - P(h \mid \sim e)}{P(e)}$$

$$\text{Slope of EB} = \frac{P(h \mid e) - P(h)}{1 - P(e)}$$

For linear interpolation, we derive the equation of AB:

$$P_c(h \mid e) = P_c(e)(P(h \mid e) - P(h \mid \sim e)) + P(h \mid \sim e)$$

Figure 10.14   Plot of $P_c(h \mid e)$ versus $P_c(e)$ when the provisions are harmonious.

When the provisions are harmonious the equations of Figure 10.8 and the equation of Figure 10.14 will produce identical results.

To illustrate, let $P(h) = 0.2$, $N = 0.2105$, $S = 16$ and $P(e) = 0.2$. We are to evaluate $P_c(h \mid e)$ for $P_c(e) = 0.15$ and for $P_c(e) = 0.4$. Then from the equations of Figure 10.4:

$$P(h \mid \sim e) = \frac{N \, P(h)}{1 + (N-1) \, P(h)} = 0.05$$

$$P(h \mid e) = \frac{S \, P(h)}{1 + (S-1) \, P(h)} = 0.8.$$

We notice that the provisions are harmonious since

$$P(e) = \frac{(1-N)((S-1)P(h) + 1)}{S - N}.$$

Let us first evaluate $P_c(h|e)$ by the equations of Figure 10.8:

for $P_c(e) = 0.15$,

$$P_c(h|e) = P(h|\sim e) + \frac{P_c(e)(P(h) - P(h|\sim e))}{P(e)}$$

$$= 0.1625,$$

for $P_c(e) = 0.4$,

$$P_c(h|e) = \frac{P(h) - P(h|e)P(e) + P_c(e)(P(h|e) - P(h))}{1 - P(e)}$$

$$= 0.35.$$

Now let us evaluate $P_c(h|e)$ by the equation of Figure 10.14:

for $P_c(e) = 0.15$,

$$P_c(h|e) = P_c(e)(P(h|e) - P(h|\sim e)) + P(h|\sim e)$$

$$= 0.1625,$$

for $P_c(e) = 0.4$, by using the same equation, we get

$$P_c(h|e) = 0.35.$$

Thus in the above example, since the provisions were harmonious, the equations of Figure 10.8 and the equation of Figure 10.14 have produced identical results.

In closing, you should take note that, even for harmonious provisions, the plots of Figures 10.9 to 10.11 may still remain only piecewise linear and not become a single straight line each.

10.2.14   Remarks on the Bayesian scheme

Since the provisions supplied by a domain expert are usually subjective estimates, and since the certainties of initial evidence supplied by the user are also subjective estimates, one can say that the scheme described above is only approximately Bayesian.

A strict application of Bayes theorem would require that, for any given evidence, the hypotheses be exhaustive and mutually exclusive. As discussed in section 9.3.2, the hypotheses in reality may not always be mutually exclusive, for example, with some symptoms, a patient may have more than one disease.

Moreover, in developing equations for finding the cumulative influence of multiple evidence on a hypothesis (as discussed in section 10.2.11), we assumed the conditional independence of e_1, e_2, e_3 ... as shown in equation 28. of section 10.2.1, which in reality may not hold. Because of the various adjustments made in applying Bayes theorem to plausible reasoning, the scheme described above is often known in the literature as modified Bayesian reasoning, or as subjective Bayesian reasoning.

10.3   AN *AD HOC* SCHEME

You may have found the Bayesian scheme somewhat intricate, yet the accuracy of the results banks on the accuracy of some subjective estimates (the provisions of the prodrules and the certainties of the evidence). Therefore a question that arises is this: Since we are working with subjective estimates, do we need a scheme as intricate as the Bayesean scheme? One can even debate the arguments offered to establish a relationship between certainties and probabilities, such as that in section 10.2.4.

Therefore, as an alternative to the Bayesian scheme, we describe below an *ad hoc* scheme. The *ad hoc* scheme, as its name suggests, is an improvization. It was developed empirically by researchers. Parts of the scheme are loosely grounded on probability theory, parts on the intuition of the researchers.

10.3.1   Reliability of a prodrule

The reliability of a prodrule *If e then h* is denoted by R, where $0 \le R \le 1$. If $R = 1$, then e validates h; if $R = 0$, then the influence of e on h is unknown. The value of R is supplied by the domain expert. It is supported by the intuition of the domain expert.

10.3.2   Certainty of an evidence

The certainty of an evidence e is denoted by $C(e)$, where $-1 \le C(e) \le 1$. The certainty of initial evidence is supplied by the user. As defined in section 10.2.4: if $C(e) = -1$, then one is fully certain that e is absent; if $C(e) = 0$, then one does not know whether e is absent or present; and if $C(e) = 1$, then one is fully certain that e is present. Note that $C(\sim e) = -C(e)$.

10.3.3   Certainty of a formula of evidence

What exemplifies a formula of evidence was explained in section 10.2.5. Suppose e is the formula:

$$e = e_1 \wedge e_2 \wedge \ldots \wedge e_n.$$

Then, based on fuzzy set theory, as by the first approach of section 10.2.5:

$$C(e) = \min(C(e_1), C(e_2), \ldots, C(e_n)).$$

Similarly, if

$$e = e_1 \lor e_2 \lor \ldots \lor e_n$$

then

$$C(e) = \max(C(e_1), C(e_2), \ldots, C(e_n)).$$

Then, for a typical formula like

$$e = e_1 \land e_2 \lor e_3,$$

we can evaluate

$$C(e) = \max(\min(C(e_1), C(e_2)), C(e_3)).$$

Given a prodrule

If e then h,

where e is any formula, we shall assume that $C(e)$, if needed, has been evaluated. From now on, whenever we refer to an evidence during the discussion on this *ad hoc* scheme, we shall be referring to the formula of evidence in the antecedent of a prodrule, unless otherwise stated.

10.3.4   The certainty of the hypothesis inferred

A prodrule *If e then h* gets heated (see sections 9.2.2 and 9.3.2), if, and only if, $C(e) > t$, where t is called a threshold value. Intuitively, if $C(e) > t$, then e is considered to be strong enough to heat the prodrule. The value of t is supplied by the domain expert. If e is evidence for, say, a heart attack, then t may have a low value like 0.05; if e is evidence for, say, a cold (considered to be less alarming than a heart attack), then e may have a higher value like 0.2. For our discussion we shall assume that t is always equal to zero. Unlike the Bayesian scheme, here only the presence of e is deemed to influence h, not its absence. If a heated prodrule with reliability R is fired (see section 9.4), then $C(h|e)$, the certainty of h conditioned on the certainty of e, is evaluated as follows:

$$C(h|e) = RC(e).$$

Suppose $R = 0.9$ and $C(e) = 0.6$. Then $C(h|e) = 0.9 \times 0.6 = 0.54$.

Figure 10.15 derives the condition under which the Bayesian and the *ad hoc* schemes will produce the same value for $C(h|e)$ for a given value of $C(e)$, provided $0 < C(e) \leq 1$.

In the Bayesian scheme, for $0 < C(e) \leq 1$,

$$C(h \mid e) = \frac{(P(h \mid e) - P(h))}{1 - P(h)} C(e) \qquad \text{[see Figure 10.10]}.$$

In the above equation, replace $P(h \mid e)$ by

$$\frac{S\, P(h)}{1 + (S - 1)\, P(h)} \qquad \text{[see Figure 10.4]},$$

to derive

$$C(h \mid e) = \frac{(S - 1)\, P(h)\, C(e)}{1 + (S - 1)\, P(h)} .$$

In the ad hoc scheme,

$$C(h \mid e) = R\, C(e).$$

Therefore, the Bayesian scheme and the ad hoc scheme will produce the same value of $C(h \mid e)$, for a given value of $C(e)$, provided $0 < C(e) \leq 1$, if the following condition is satisfied:

$$R = \frac{(S - 1)\, P(h)}{1 + (S - 1)\, P(h)} .$$

Note that as S tends to ∞, R tends to 1.

Figure 10.15   Derivation of the condition under which the Bayesian and the *ad hoc* schemes produce the same certainty of the hypothesis inferred.

To illustrate, if $S = 16$ and $P(h) = 0.2$ (as they were for the example in section 10.2.9), then to satisfy the condition of Figure 10.15,

$$R = \frac{(S - 1)P(h)}{1 + (S - 1)P(h)}$$

$$= 0.75.$$

10.3.5   The certainty of the hypothesis with multiple evidence

In this section, we present equations for evaluating the cumulative certainty of a hypothesis that is influenced by multiple evidence. There are two cases.

(1) Suppose we have the following prodrules:

    If e_1 then h.
    If e_2 then h.

If e_1 and e_2 are independent, then the cumulative certainty of h can be evaluated from the equation

$$C(h|e_1 \wedge e_2) = C(h|e_1) + C(h|2) - C(h|e_1)C(h|e_2).$$

You may have noticed that the above equation is grounded loosely on probability theory (equation 7. in section 10.2.1). To illustrate, given $C(h|e_1) = 0.9$ and $C(h|e_2) = 0.5$, then $C(h|e_1 \wedge e_2) = 0.9 + 0.5 - 0.9 \times 0.5 = 0.95$. We can say that $C(h|e_1)$ and $C(h|e_2)$ reinforce each other to produce $C(h|e_1 \wedge e_2)$.

If, however, e_1 and e_2 are not independent, then inspired by fuzzy set theory (section 10.2.2), we say:

$$C(h|e_1 \wedge e_2) = \max(C(h|e_1), C(h|e_2)).$$

So for $C(h|e_1) = 0.9$ and $C(h|e_2) = 0.5$, we would obtain $C(h|e_1 \wedge e_2) = 0.9$. Note that the above discussion will not hold for that rare example of subparticle physics mentioned in section 10.2.11.

(2) Now suppose that we have the following prodrules:

    If e_1 then h.
    If e_2 then $\sim h$.

If e_1 and e_2 are independent, then the cumulative certainty of h can be evaluated from the following empirically evolved equation:

$$C(h|e_1 \wedge e_2) = \frac{C(h|e_1) - C(\sim h|e_2)}{1 - \min(C(h|e_1), C(\sim h|e_2))}.$$

Suppose $C(h|e_1) = 0.9$ and $C(\sim h|e_2) = 0.5$. Then

$$C(h|e_1 \wedge e_2) = \frac{0.9 - 0.5}{1 - \min(0.9, 0.5)}$$

$$= 0.8.$$

The above equation is biased toward the higher certainty: as the example shows, the cumulative certainty of 0.8 is closer to the higher certainty of 0.9 than to the lower certainty of 0.5. If $C(h|e_1) = 1$ and $C(\sim h|e_2) < 1$, then $C(h|e_1 \wedge e_2) = 1$. Similarly, if $C(h|e_1) < 1$ and $C(\sim h|e_2) = 1$, then $C(h|e_1 \wedge e_2) = -1$; that is to say, $C(\sim h|e_1 \wedge e_2) = 1$. If, however, $C(h|e_1) = 1$ and $C(\sim h|e_2) = 1$, then we have a contradiction. We would need to confer with the domain experts to change the prodrules, or their reliability measures, or both.

If, however, e_1 and e_2 are not independent, then we need not bias the cumulative certainty, and we can evaluate it from the equation:

$$C(h|e_1 \wedge e_2) = C(h|e_1) - C(\sim h|e_2).$$

So for $C(h|e_1) = 0.9$ and $C(h|e_2) = 0.5$, we would obtain $C(h|e_1 \wedge e_2) = 0.4$.

In general, we could have many prodrules, some of which have h in the consequent, and some have $\sim h$ in the consequent. To find the cumulative certainty of h we first consider pairwise the prodrules that have h in the consequent, then we consider pairwise the prodrules that have $\sim h$ in the consequent, and finally we find the cumulative certainty from the certainties of h and $\sim h$. For example, let e_1, e_2, e_3, e_4 be mutually independent in the following prodrules:

If e_1 then h.
If e_2 then h.
If e_3 then $\sim h$.
If e_4 then $\sim h$.

After evaluating $C(h|e_1)$, $C(h|e_2)$, $C(\sim h|e_3)$ and $C(\sim h|e_4)$, we first consider the prodrules with h in the consequent to evaluate:

$$C(h|e_1 \wedge e_2) = C(h|e_1) + C(h|e_2) - C(h|e_1)C(h|e_2).$$

Then we similarly consider prodrules with $\sim h$ in the consequent to evaluate:

$$C(\sim h|e_3 \wedge e_4) = C(\sim h|e_3) + C(\sim h|e_4) - C(\sim h|e_3)C(\sim h|e_4).$$

Finally, we evaluate:

$$C(h|e_1 \wedge e_2 \wedge e_3 \wedge e_4) = \frac{C(h|e_1 \wedge e_2) - C(\sim h|e_3 \wedge e_4)}{1 - \min(C(h|e_1 \wedge e_2), C(\sim h|e_3 \wedge e_4))}.$$

10.3.6 Propagation of certainties

From our discussion in the previous section, we can evaluate $C(h_1|e_1 \wedge e_2 \wedge \ldots \wedge e_m)$ for a given hypothesis h_1. Now suppose that h_1 is an intermediate hypothesis so that it serves as evidence for another hypothesis h_2. To find the certainty of h_2, we rename h_1 as e', and we declare $C(e')$ to be equal to $C(h|e_1 \wedge \ldots \wedge e_m)$. Then we can evaluate $C(h_2|e')$ as discussed in section 10.3.4. To illustrate, let us consider the following prodrules:

If e_1 then h_1. ($R_1 = 0.5$)
If e_2 then h_1. ($R_2 = 0.9$)
If h_1 then h_2. ($R_3 = 0.85$)

We are told that e_1 and e_2 are independent, that $C(e_1) = 0.8$ and that $C(e_2) = 0.6$. We proceed as follows:

$C(h_1|e_1) = R_1 C(e_1) = 0.5 \times 0.8 = 0.4$
$C(h_1|e_2) = R_2 C(e_2) = 0.9 \times 0.6 = 0.54.$

Since e_1 and e_2 are independent, we evaluate

$$C(h_1|e_1 \wedge e_2) = C(h|e_1) + C(h|e_2) - C(h|e_1)C(h|e_2)$$
$$= 0.4 + 0.54 - 0.4 \times 0.54$$
$$= 0.724.$$

We rename h_1 as e' and declare that $C(e') = 0.724$. Then from the third prodrule above:

$$C(h_2|e') = R_3 C(e')$$
$$= 0.85 \times 0.724$$
$$= 0.615.$$

We have thus propagated the certainty from h_1 to h_2. If h_2 itself is an intermediate hypothesis, then we can similarly propagate the certainties all the way to the final hypotheses.

10.4   CLOSING REMARKS

Given some evidence, we can infer different final hypotheses h_1, h_2, h_3, ... together with their certainties. Since the evaluation of the certainties has a subjective basis, it may not be enough to inform the user of only the final hypothesis that has the highest certainty. It may be more befitting to inform the user of all the final hypotheses inferred together with their certainties, then let the user do the picking of the hypotheses. For example, in an expert system for medical diagnosis, one disease may be inferred with a certainty of 0.9, and another disease with a certainty of 0.3. The user, who most likely will be a doctor, may want to treat the patient for both diseases.

10.5   EXERCISES

1. As defined in section 10.2.3:

$$N = \frac{P(\sim e|h)}{P(\sim e|\sim h)}$$

$$S = \frac{(e|h)}{P(e|\sim h)}.$$

Prove the following:

$$P(e|h) = \frac{S(1 - N)}{S - N}$$

$$P(e|\sim h) = \frac{1 - N}{S - N}$$

$$N = \frac{1 - SP(e|\sim h)}{1 - P(e|\sim h)}.$$

2. Suppose you have the following prodrules and you know that e_1 and e_2 are present:

(I1) If e_1 then h.
(I2) If e_2 then h.

If you chill refractory prodrules as mentioned in section 9.4, then once prodrule I1 has fired, I2 will never fire. Thus h will not get influenced by e_2, although for plausible reasoning we want h to be influenced by e_2 also. Hence what changes should be made regarding the chilling of refractory prodrules so that after I1 has fired, it will not fire again, but I2 can be fired to further influence h?

3. Given the following prodrules:

If e_1 then h_1. ($P(h_1) = 0.01$, $S_1 = 70$, $N_1 = 0.01$, $P(e_1) = 0.1$)
If e_2 then h_1. ($P(h_1) = 0.01$, $S_2 = 300$, $N_2 = 0.0001$, $P(e_2) = 0.03$)
If h_1 then h_2. ($P(h_2) = 0.05$, $S_3 = 200$, $N_3 = 0.001$, $P(h_1) = 0.01$)
If e_3 then h_2. ($P(h_2) = 0.05$, $S_4 = 1000$, $N_4 = 0.00005$, $P(e_3) = 0.12$)

Let $C(e_1) = -0.25$, $C(e_2) = 0.8$ and $C(e_3) = 0.3$. Evaluate $C(h_2|h_1 \wedge e_3)$ and $P(h_2|h_1 \wedge e_3)$ by the Bayesian scheme.

4. For Figure 10.14, prove that when the provisions of a prodrule are harmonious, then the slope of line AE = slope of line EB, that is,

$$\frac{P(h) - P(h|\sim e)}{P(e)} = \frac{P(h|e) - P(h)}{1 - P(e)}.$$

5. Let $P(h) = 0.2$, $S = 16$ and $N = 0.2105$. Using the equation of Figure 10.14, evaluate $P_c(h|e)$ for the following two cases:
(a) $P_c(e) = 0.145$ when $P(e) = 0.1$,
(b) $P_c(e) = 0.24$ when $P(e) = 0.2$.
By looking at the values of $P_c(h|e)$, can you detect an anomaly in one of the values? What is the cause of this anomaly? Re-evaluate

$P_c(h|e)$ for the two cases by using the equations of Figure 10.8. Has the anomaly been removed?

6. Discuss the pros and cons for evaluating the certainty of a formula of evidence by the following equations:

$$C(e_1 \wedge e_2) = \max(0, C(e_1) + C(e_2) - 1)$$
$$C(e_1 \vee e_2) = \min(1, C(e_1) + C(e_2)).$$

Compare these equations with those given in section 10.3.3.

7. In Figures 10.8–10.11 and 10.14, to evaluate $P_c(h|e)$ or $C(h|e)$, we first have to evaluate $P(h|\sim e)$ or $P(h|e)$. Derive new equations so that we do not have to evaluate $P(h|\sim e)$ or $P(h|e)$ first. The new equations will contain either $P_c(h|e)$ or $C(h|e)$ on the left-hand side, and $P(h)$, N, S, $P(e)$, $P_c(e)$ and $C(e)$ on the right-hand side. As examples: (a) see the equation derived in Figure 10.15 from the second equation of Figure 10.10, and (b) it can be shown from Figure 10.8 that

$$P_c(h|e) = \frac{P(h)(NP(e) - P_c(e)(N - 1)(P(h) - 1))}{(1 + (N - 1)P(h))P(e)} \quad \text{if } 0 \le P_c(e) \le P(e).$$

8. In section 10.3.4, it was mentioned that for the *ad hoc* scheme, $C(h|e) = RC(e)$. Discuss the pros and cons of replacing this equation by any of the following:
(a) $C(h|e) = \max(0, C(e) + R - 1)$
(b) $C(h|e) = \min(R, C(e))$
(c) If $(R + C(e)) > 1$, then $C(h|e) = \min(R, C(e))$; otherwise $C(h|e) = 0$.

9. Given the following certainties:

$$C(h|e_1) = 0.8$$
$$C(\sim h|e_2) = 0.6$$
$$C(h|e_3) = 0.5$$
$$C(h|e_4) = 0.3$$
$$C(\sim h|e_5) = 0.4$$

by the *ad hoc* scheme, evaluate $C(h|e_1 \wedge e_2 \wedge e_3 \wedge e_4 \wedge e_5)$ for the two cases:
(a) e_1 to e_5 are mutually independent,
(b) e_1 to e_5 are not mutually independent.

10. Suppose you have the prodrules:

If e_1 then h.
If e_2 then h.

Based on the discussion of section 10.3.5, explain which will give you a higher cumulative certainty of h: when e_1 and e_2 are independent, or when e_1 and e_2 are not independent. Will your explanation remain unchanged if the second prodrule above is changed to 'If e_2 then $\sim h$'?

11. Suppose we have the following prodrules:

If e then h_1. $(R_1 = 0.8)$
If e then h_2. $(R_2 = 0.6)$
If h_1 then h_3. $(R_3 = 0.5)$
If h_2 then h_3. $(R_4 = 0.9)$

Evaluate $C(h_3 | h_1 \wedge h_2)$ for $C(e) = 0.7$ by the *ad hoc* scheme.

12. Extend the *ad hoc* scheme so that, like in the Bayesian scheme, not only the presence of e, but also the absence of e influences h.

13. In the expert system shell built for exercise 9 of chapter 9, incorporate both the Bayesian and the *ad hoc* schemes so that a user can choose the scheme he wants.

14. Suppose we amend the Bayesian scheme to establish the following relationship between $C(e)$ and $P_c(h | e)$: for $-1 \leq C(e) \leq 0$, let $P_c(h | e) = P(h)$; if $C(e) = 1$, then $P_c(h | e) = P(h | e)$. For other values of $C(e)$, evaluate $P_c(h | e)$ by linear interpolation. What influences h now: is it the presence or the absence of e?

10.6   SUGGESTIONS FOR FURTHER READING

Zadeh (1975) described how fuzzy set theory can be used for reasoning. Duda, Hart and Nilsson (1981) presented the Bayesian scheme. Salmon (1973) cited the example from subparticle physics mentioned in sections 10.2.11 and 10.3.5. Neapolitan (1990) and Pearl (1988) examined reasoning with probabilities. Cheng and Kashyap (1989) explored the associativity of multiple evidence. Shortliffe and Buchanan (1984) discussed the *ad hoc* scheme. Shafer (1976) explained another scheme, called the Dempster–Shafer scheme, for plausible reasoning.

1. Cheng, Y. and Kashyap, R. L. (1989) A study of associative evidential reasoning, *IEEE Transactions on Pattern Analysis and Machine Intelligence*, **PAMI-11**[6], 623–31.
2. Duda, R. O., Hart, P. E. and Nilsson, N. J. (1981) Subjective Bayesian methods for rule-based inference systems, in *Readings in Artificial Intelligence* (eds. B. L. Webber and N. J. Nilsson), Tioga Publishing Company, Palo Alto, California, pp. 192–99.

3. Neapolitan, R. E. (1990) *Probabilistic Reasoning in Expert Systems*, Wiley-Interscience, New York.
4. Pearl, J. (1988) *Probabilistic Reasoning in Intelligent Systems: Networks of Plausible Inference*, Morgan Kaufmann Publishers Inc., San Mateo, California.
5. Salmon, W. C. (1973) Confirmation, *Scientific American*, **228**, 75–83.
6. Shafer, G. (1976) *A Mathematical Theory of Evidence*, Princeton University Press, Princeton, New Jersey.
7. Shortliffe, E. H. and Buchanan, B. G. (1984) A Model of Inexact Reasoning in Medicine, in *Rule-Based Expert Systems: The MYCIN Experiments of the Stanford Heuristic Programming Project* (eds. B. G. Buchanan and E. H. Shortliffe), Addison-Wesley, Reading, Massachusetts, pp. 233–62.
8. Zadeh, L. A. (1975) Fuzzy logic and approximate reasoning, *Synthese*, **30**, 407–28.

11
Solving problems by searching state space

11.1 INTRODUCTION

The two common methodologies to solve many kinds of problems are by searching state space and by searching decompositions. In this chapter, we shall deal with searching state space; in the next chapter, with decompositions. As a preparatory example to understand the preliminary notions and terminology, we shall consider the following problem:

> λ (where $\lambda \geq 1$) missionaries and λ cannibals arrive on the left bank of a river. They have a rowing boat with them. The boat will be used for transporting them across the river to the right bank. Each of them knows how to row, but there are two constraints: (a) the boat, which requires one person to row, cannot carry more than two persons at a time; and (b) if the number of missionaries on a bank is one or more, then the number of cannibals on that bank cannot be more than the number of missionaries on the bank. How are the missionaris and the cannibals to be transported across the river? Note that when the boat is on a bank, then all persons in the boat are also considered to be on the same bank.

From the first constraint above, we realize that all the missionaries and the cannibals cannot be transported across the river in one sailing of the boat from the left to the right bank. The boat will need to sail back and forth between the banks a few times. Moreover, we shall have to ensure that, while the boat is sailing back and forth, we do not violate the second constraint above.

In attempting to solve the problem on a computer, we shall have to give the problem a formal representation. Accordingly, let m denote missionaries, c denote cannibals, L denote the left bank of the river, and R denote the right bank. Furthermore, let the situation before or after a sailing be denoted by a triple

$\langle \alpha_1, \alpha_2, \alpha_3 \rangle$

where α_1 tells us which persons are on the left bank at that time, α_2 tells us which persons are on the right bank, and α_3 is either L or R: if α_3 is L, the boat is on the left bank; if α_3 is R, the boat is on the right bank. We shall refer to $\langle \alpha_1, \alpha_2, \alpha_3 \rangle$ as a **state** of the problem at a particular time. We then say that the **source** state (the state at the beginning) is

$\langle \lambda m \lambda c, 0, L \rangle$

and the **destination** state (the state we ultimately want to reach) is

$\langle 0, \lambda m \lambda c, R \rangle$.

To reach the destination state from the source state, we shall traverse through a succession of intermediary states. To traverse from one state to another state we shall make a **move**, where a move is a sailing of the boat from either the left bank to the right bank, or vice versa. You may view a move as a function that maps states into states, or you may view it as an operator that transforms one state into another. When we are in a particular state, to traverse to some other state we shall need to select a move from amongst the following five alternative moves:

$1m$	(send one missionary in the boat to sail)
$2m$	(. . . two missionaries . . .)
$1m1c$	(. . . one missionary and one cannibal . . .)
$1c$	(. . . one cannibal . . .)
$2c$	(. . . two cannibals . . .)

To solve the problem, we are to find the sequence, if any, of moves by which we can traverse from the source state to the destination state.

So that our approach to solving the problem in general is easy to comprehend, we shall for now assume a small value of λ, namely 2. Hence the source state is $\langle 2m2c, 0, L \rangle$, and the destination state is $\langle 0, 2m2c, R \rangle$.

Let us now look at what happens when we are in the source state, and we select by turns each of the five alternative moves. We can illustrate this by the graph of Figure 11.1, where a state in the problem corresponds to a node in the graph, and a move in the problem corresponds to an arc in the graph. If we can traverse from a state x to a state y by a move μ, then in the graph:

1. an arc is directed from node x (more precisely, the node corresponding to state x) to node y;
2. the arc is labelled μ;

source node

| 2m2c, 0, L |

1m   2m   1m1c   1c   2c

| 1m2c, 1m, R | | 2c, 2m, R | | 1m1c, 1m1c, R | | 2m1c, 1c, R | | 2m, 2c, R |

renegade node: it
may be deleted

After the first move, we can be in one of these leaf nodes, for these are
the surviving children of the source node.

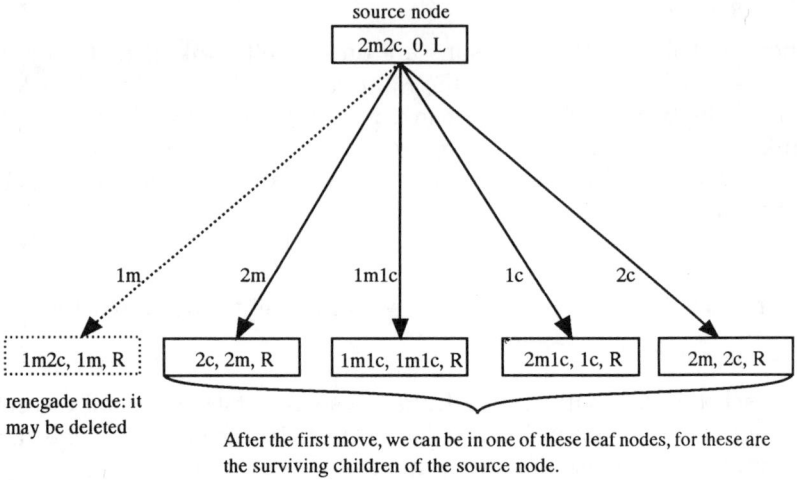

Figure 11.1   Expanding the source node to generate its children for the
problem of the two missionaries and two cannibals. A state in the problem
corresponds to a node above. We generate nodes that will result by making
each of the five moves from the source node. Each move is depicted by a
directed arc from the source node to the generated node, the arc being labelled
with the name of the move. The five nodes generated are the children of the
source node. The leftmost child [shown dotted] is renegade since it violates a
constraint of the problem: on the left bank, the number of cannibals becomes
more than the number of missionaries. A renegade node cannot be part of a
solution of the problem. If a node cannot be part of a solution, then any arc
directed toward it cannot be part of a solution either.

3. node *x* is known as a **parent** of node *y*; and
4. node *y* is known as a **child** of node *x*.

A source node has no parent. A child can be **generated** for each move
that can be made from a node. Thus the source node in Figure 11.1 has
five children. We say that the children of a node are generated by
expanding the node, and that the children are **sibling** of one another.
Hence, expanding the source node generated its five children, and
these five children are the siblings of one another.

One child of the source node in Figure 11.1 is a **renegade** node: it
violates a constraint of the problem. A renegade node and any arc
directed toward it cannot be part of a problem solution, and so they
may be deleted. Accordingly, the source node is said to have four
surviving children. These four children are leaf nodes (a leaf node has
no children) in the graph. Put another way, the leaf nodes constitute
the set of unexpanded nodes in the graph.

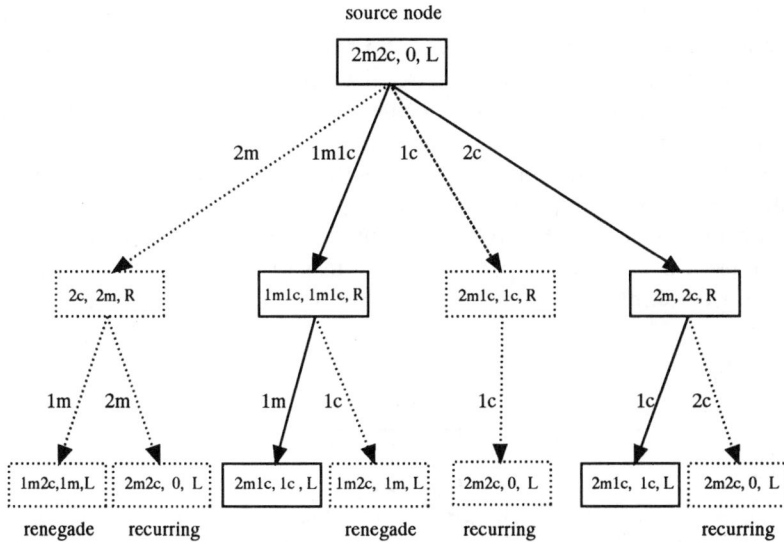

Figure 11.2 Continuing from Figure 11.1, we expand the children of the source node. These four siblings generate seven nodes to depict the states in which we may be after the second move. Of these nodes, only two nodes [both corresponding to the state ⟨2m1c, 1c, L⟩ since it is reachable from the source node by two paths: by the arc sequence 1m1c, 1m; or by 2c, 1c] may be part of a problem solution; the other nodes cannot be part of a problem solution because they are either renegade or recurring. All the recurring nodes above are identical to the source node, their ancestor. Since a recurring node brings us to a state in which we were earlier, considering a recurring node as part of a problem solution can lead to indefinite looping. If all the children of a node cannot be part of a problem solution, then the node itself cannot be part of a problem solution. Thus the nodes ⟨2c, 2m, R⟩ and ⟨2m1c, 1c, R⟩ above cannot be part of a problem solution either.

Now consider expanding the leaf nodes of Figure 11.1. Suppose we are in the node ⟨2c, 2m, R⟩. Then since the boat has to next sail from the right bank to the left bank and since there are two missionaries on the right bank, the moves we can make are either 1m or 2m; therefore, two children will be generated by expanding the node. We can similarly expand the other leaf nodes of Figure 11.1 to obtain the graph of Figure 11.2.

According to Figure 11.2, after the second move we shall be in the state ⟨2m1c, 1c, L⟩, which is depicted by two nodes. This is because we can traverse either of two paths to reach the state from the source node. As must have become apparent from the figure, a **path** is a sequence of one or more arcs, and we can traverse a path by traversing from node to node in the direction of the arcs. We can put it in a more formal manner: let $x_0, x_1, \ldots, x_n$ be nodes such that there is an arc directed from x_0 to x_1, another arc directed from x_1 to x_2, and so on; then the sequence of arcs constitutes a path from x_0 to x_n. We can traverse from x_0 to x_n by first traversing from x_0 to x_1, then from x_1 to x_2, and so forth. The **length** of the path is the number of arcs in the path; hence, the length of the path from x_0 to x_n is n.

A node y is said to be an **ancestor** of a node z if, and only if, either y is a parent of z, or y is a parent of an ancestor of z. A node z is said to be a **descendant** of a node y if, and only if, y is an ancestor of z. Thus,

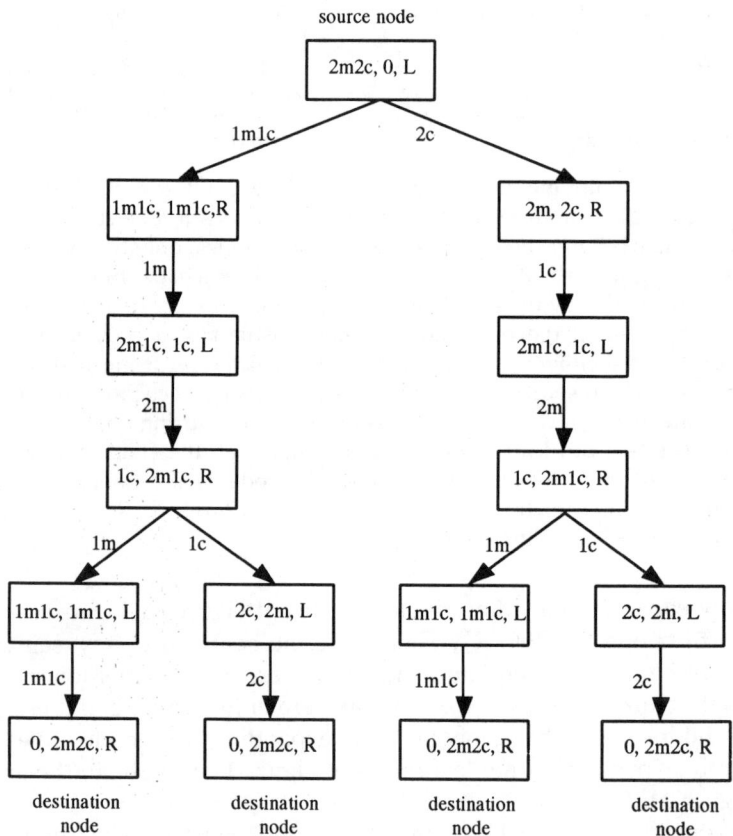

Figure 11.3 A tree-structured search graph for the problem of the two missionaries and two cannibals. The four solution paths are the following: (*a*) 1m1c, 1m, 2m, 1m, 1m1c, (*b*) 1m1c, 1m, 2m, 1c, 2c, (*c*) 2c, 1c, 2m, 1m, 1m1c, (*d*) 2c, 1c, 2m, 1c, 2c. Each solution path is of length 5.

for example, if there is a path from node x_0 to node x_n, then x_0 is an ancestor of x_n, and x_n is a descendant of x_0. A **recurring** node is defined to be a node that is identical to one of its ancestors; in other words, if node x_n is identical to any of the nodes $x_0, x_1, \ldots, x_{n-1}$ in the path from x_0 to x_n, then x_n is a recurring node. As explained in the legend of Figure 11.2, a recurring node cannot be part of a problem solution. Such a node may be deleted from the graph.

We continue to construct the graph of Figure 11.2 by successively expanding the leaf nodes at any particular time until we generate the destination nodes as shown in Figure 11.3. The graph, called a **search graph**, in effect searches the alternative arcs from every node to find paths from the source node to the destination nodes. Such paths are called **solution paths** and they denote the different solutions for the problem. The search graph of Figure 11.3 furnishes us with four solution paths, each of the same length. In general, however, should a problem have more than one solution path, then the different solution paths need not necessarily be of the same length. You will see one such specimen problem in section 11.2.

You may have noticed that the search graph of Figure 11.3 has identical nodes in different paths from the source node. To be precise, the graph of Figure 11.3 is a tree. The source node, which has no parent, is the root of the tree. Any other node in the tree has exactly one parent. In other words, every node in a tree has one parent at the most. To reduce the amount of memory required, you may prefer to store the nodes in a search graph that is not a tree. In such a graph, a node may have more than one parent. Such a search graph for the problem of two missionaries and two cannibals is shown in Figure 11.4. When a search graph is a tree, we may on occasion prefer to refer to it as a **search tree**.

The approach discussed above to solve the problem of two missionaries and two cannibals can be adopted in general to solve the problem of λ missionaries and λ cannibals, for any value of $\lambda \geq 1$. As an illustration, a search graph for $\lambda = 3$ is presented in Figure 11.5. Take note, however, that solution paths may not exist for all values of λ: there may be values of λ for which, as you construct the search graph, all of the nodes generated are either renegade or recurring.

We shall now bring in the notion of the cost of a path. Let us assume for the above problem that the missionaries are old men and the cannibals are young, so the cannibals are better equipped than the missionaries to handle the strain of repeatedly sailing across the river. To be more specific, let the cost of sending a missionary in the boat be 2 units, and the cost of sending a cannibal be 1 unit. Hence the cost of each of the five possible moves is the following:

source node

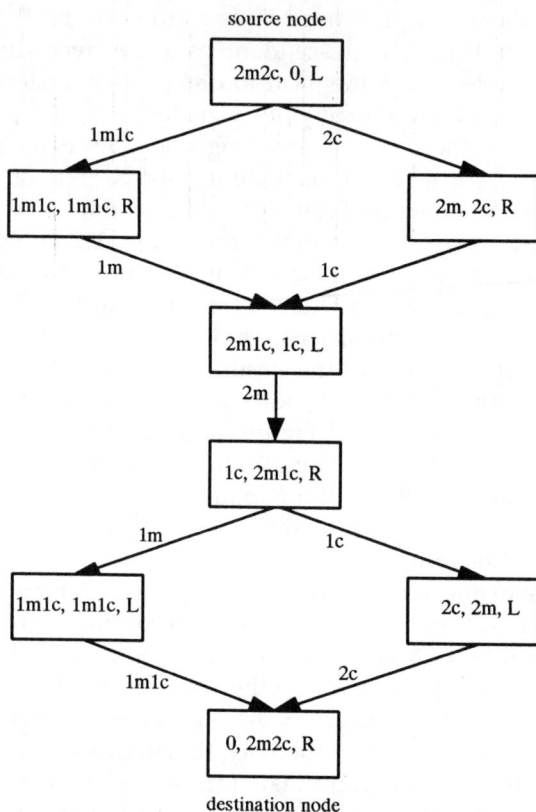

Figure 11.4 A non-tree-structured search graph for the problem of the two missionaries and two cannibals. Compare the above graph with the tree-structured graph [which we may refer to as a search tree] of Figure 11.3.

$1m$	2 units
$2m$	4 units
$1m1c$	3 units
$1c$	1 unit
$2c$	2 units

The cost of a move is the cost we associate with the corresponding arc in the search graph. We call it the **arc cost**. The arc cost is a positive value. The cost of a path is then defined to be the sum of the arc costs of the arcs in the path.

The four solution paths of Figure 11.5 have equal lengths, but their costs are different, as tabulated in Figure 11.6. Should we be interested

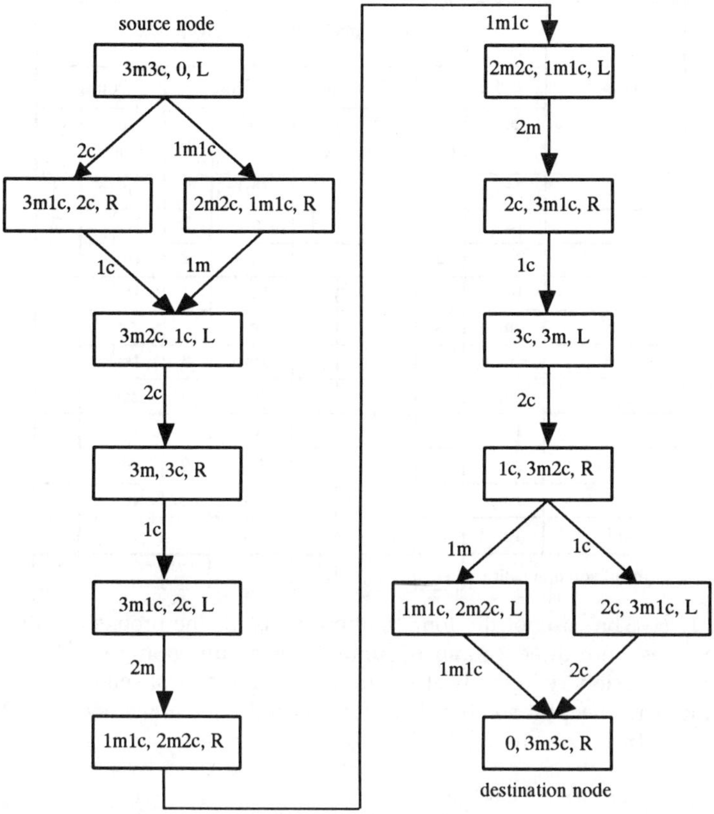

Figure 11.5   A search graph for the problem of the three missionaries and three cannibals.

in finding the *cheapest* solution path, that is, the solution path whose cost is the least among all the solution paths of the problem, then such a solution path for the problem of three missionaries and three cannibals can be found from Figure 11.6. Note that if, in a problem, the cost of each move is the same, then the cheapest solution path is identical to the *shortest* solution path, in other words, the solution path whose length is the least among all the solution paths of the problem. Thus we may view the shortest solution path as a special case of the cheapest solution path, when all moves cost the same.

Problem solving by searching alternatives in general entails constructing a search graph to find a solution path, if any, between some specified source and destination nodes. If there is more than one solution path, then the different solution paths may be of different

Number	The four solution paths from Figure 11.5							
	First		Second		Third		Fourth	
	arc label	arc cost	arc label	arc cost	arc label	arc cost	arc label	arc cost
1	2c	2	2c	2	1m1c	3	1m1c	3
2	1c	1	1c	1	1m	2	1m	2
3	2c	2	2c	2	2c	2	2c	2
4	1c	1	1c	1	1c	1	1c	1
5	2m	4	2m	4	2m	4	2m	4
6	1m1c	3	1m1c	3	1m1c	3	1m1c	3
7	2m	4	2m	4	2m	4	2m	4
8	1c	1	1c	1	1c	1	1c	1
9	2c	2	2c	2	2c	2	2c	2
10	1m	2	1c	1	1m	2	1c	1
11	1m1c	3	2c	2	1m1c	3	2c	2
Cost of solution path	25		23		27		25	

Figure 11.6 The costs of the four solution paths for the problem of the three missionaries and three cannibals, under the assumption that the cost of sending a missionary in the boat is 2 units, and the cost of sending a cannibal is 1 unit. The cheapest solution path [the second one shown above] is 2c, 1c, 2c, 1c, 2m, 1m1c, 2m, 1c, 2c, 1c, 2c. Its cost is 23 units.

lengths and costs, and we may typically be required to find any solution path, the shortest solution path, or the cheapest solution path.

It should be evident from Figures 11.1 and 11.2 that neither a renegade node nor a recurring node lies on a solution path. Another kind of node that does not lie along a solution path is known as an **inert** node. A node z that is not a destination node is said to be **inert** if, and only if, z can have no children at all. Such a node corresponds to a state in a problem from which, according to the given problem definition, we cannot make any moves. The missionaries and cannibals problem described above does not generate any inert nodes in its search graph. A problem that does generate inert nodes is defined in Figure 11.7. An unfinished search graph for the problem is displayed in Figure 11.8. The graph contains a few inert nodes. Such nodes, as mentioned in the legend of the figure, may be deleted.

We suggest that you attempt to finish manually the search graph of Figure 11.8. Maintain a record of the order in which you expanded the nodes; let your intuition guide you. If, at some time, there were many

A casing contains $(2\lambda + 1)$ cells, where $\lambda > 1$. A cell may either be empty, or it may be occupied by one coin. In the source state, the λ leftmost cells are each occupied by a one franc coin [F], the λ rightmost cells are each occupied by a one pound coin [P], and the middle cell is empty:

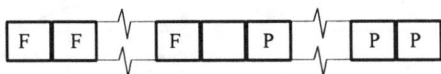

We are required to interchange the locations of the franc and the pound coins to reach the destination state:

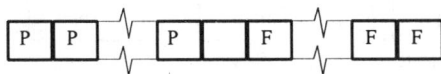

As a move in the puzzle, a coin can either [1] slide into an adjacent empty cell, or [2] hop over one other coin into an empty cell. The cell from which the coin slid or hopped becomes the new empty cell. The above moves must, however, be made under the following constraints:

[i]   a franc coin can slide or hop only toward the right, and
[ii]   a pound coin can slide or hop only toward the left.

Based on the above, we give the following names to the four possible moves:

F_H : a franc coin hops to the right,
F_S : a franc coin slides to the right,
P_H : a pound coin hops to the left, and
P_S : a pound coin slides to the left.

Figure 11.7   The problem definition of the λ franc and λ pound coins puzzle. An unfinished search graph for $\lambda = 2$ is displayed in Figure 11.8.

unexpanded nodes, make a note of the motivation that prompted you to select one node over another for expansion. You may find your record useful to your understanding when you refer to it, as you read below about methods for constructing search graphs to find solution paths. One obvious method is by searching exhaustively among all possible states, called the **state space** of the problem. Such an exhaustive search of a state space is described next.

11.2   EXHAUSTIVE SEARCH

The search graph for exhaustive search contains a node corresponding to every state of the problem's state space. For all pairs of nodes x_i and x_j in the search graph, there is an arc directed from x_i to x_j if, and only if, x_j is reachable from x_i in one move. To visualize exhaustive search, let us consider the problem of the three-tiles puzzle in Figure 11.9.

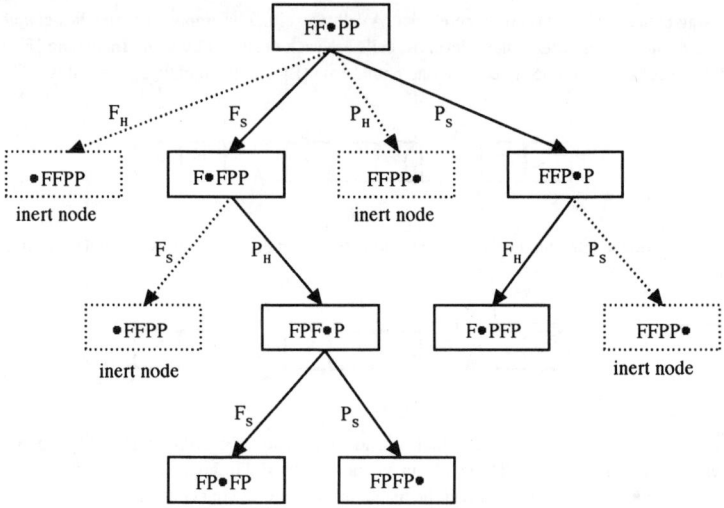

Figure 11.8   An unfinished search graph for the 2 franc and 2 pound coins puzzle, as defined in Figure 11.7. The symbol '•' denotes the empty cell. All the dotted nodes above are inert: none of them is the destination node and none of them can have any children. While traversing a path from a source node, if we reach an inert node, then we cannot traverse any further; intuitively, it is like being on a dead-end street. Thus an inert node cannot lie on a solution path, and such a node may be deleted.

The puzzle consists of a 2 × 2 tray of four cells. Three of the cells are each occupied by a mobile tile stamped with a number from 1 to 3. No two tiles are stamped with the same number and one cell is empty. Any configuration of the three tiles and the empty cell constitutes a state of the puzzle. A **move** in the puzzle is the sliding of a tile into the empty cell provided the empty cell is either vertically or horizontally adjacent to that tile. The cell from which the tile was slid becomes the

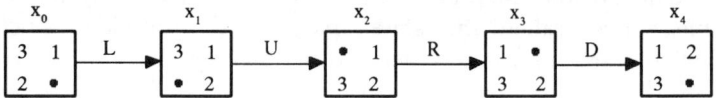

Figure 11.9   Examples of the four kinds of moves in the three-tiles puzzle. The symbol '•' denotes the empty cell. If, in node x_0 [more precisely, the state corresponding to node x_0], we slide the tile stamped 2 into the empty cell adjacent to it horizontally, then we traverse to node x_1. We say that we have made an L [leftward] move because, in effect, the empty cell has advanced to the left. As shown above, we can likewise make a U [upward], a R [rightward], or a D [downward] move.

new empty cell. As mentioned in the legend of Figure 11.9, the four kinds of moves are called L, U, R and D.

The state space of the three-tiles puzzle comprises 24 (factorial of 4) states. Thus the search graph for exhautive search contains 24 nodes, as shown in Figure 11.10. Toward the end of section 11.1, you were asked to finish the search graph of Figure 11.8. You may want to examine whether you conducted an exhaustive search.

We shall employ Figure 11.10 to bring in the notion of the **depth** of a node in a search graph. Associated with every node is a non-negative integer d, which is called the depth of the node; therefore $d \geq 0$. The smaller the value of d for a node, the **shallower** is the node. Similarly, the larger the value of d for a node, the **deeper** is the node. The source node in a search graph is defined to be at depth 0. The depth of any other node is defined to be 1 more than the depth of its shallowest

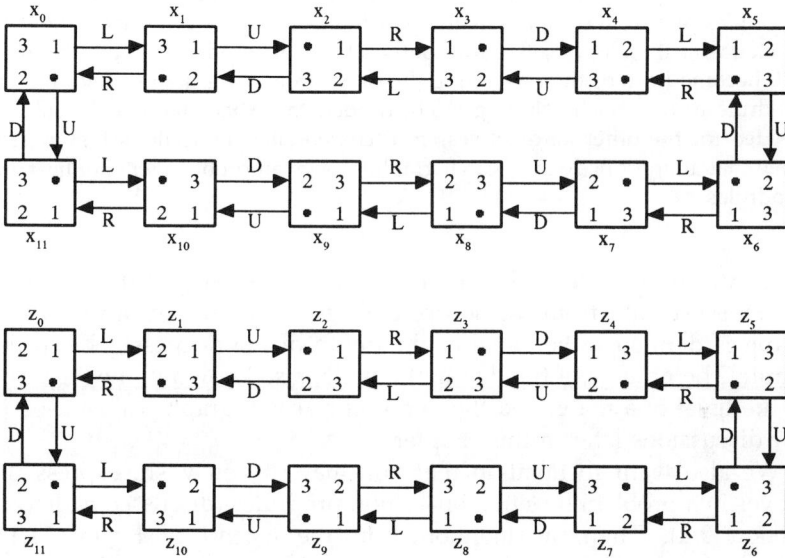

Figure 11.10 The 24 nodes corresponding to the state space of the three-tiles puzzle fall into two disjoint sets of 12 nodes each, x_0 to x_{11} and z_0 to z_{11}. No x node can ever reached from a z node, and vice versa. All x nodes are reachable from one another. Similarly, all z nodes are reachable from one another. Between reachable nodes more than one path exists: the different paths may not be of the same length. For example, if x_0 is the source node, and x_3 is the destination node, then the solution path along $x_0x_1x_2x_3$ is of length 3, and the solution path along $x_0x_{11}x_{10}x_9x_8x_7x_6x_5x_4x_3$ is of length 9. Hence, according to the definition given in section 11.2, the depth of x is 3, not 9. The depth of the search graph is 6 because that is the depth of the deepest node in the graph.

```
┌─────────┐
│ X   X   │
│ X   •   │
└─────────┘
```

[J1]   If   there is a tile to the left of the empty cell,
        then   make a L move.

[J2]   If   there is a tile above the empty cell,
        then   make a U move.

[J3]   If   there is a tile to the right of the empty cell,
        then   make a R move.

[J4]   If   there is a tile below the empty cell,
        then   make a D move.

Figure 11.11   Specimen situation–action prodrules to express the moves in the three-tiles puzzle. It does not matter which tile occupies a cell shown above by X. Hence, if the empty cell is the southeast corner, prodrules J1 and J2 above will become heated; then, selecting the move to make is akin to selecting the prodrule to fire. Such selecting is not needed for exhaustive search, but it is needed for the other kinds of search discussed later, in sections 11.3 to 11.5. Note that an inert node in a search graph for a given problem will not heat any prodrules.

parent. In other words, the depth of a node z is equal to the length of the shortest path from the source node to z. The depth of the search graph is defined to be equal to the depth of the deepest node in the graph. The notions of the depth of a node, also known in the literature as the **level** of a node, and the depth of a search graph will be used in our discussions later in this chapter.

We also want to mention that you may, if you wish, express the moves in a problem by situation–action prodrules (discussed earlier, in section 9.2). Then, as mentioned in the legend of Figure 11.11, selecting a move to make is akin to selecting a prodrule to fire. Expressing moves as prodrules will be useful when we discuss robotic planning in section 12.5.

Exhaustive search is jocularly known in the literature as the British Museum search procedure. According to an apocryphal canon, all the books in the British Museum can be begat over millennia by a monkey hammering away exhaustively at the keys of a typewriter, so if you want to read a particular book, you will just have to wait until the monkey hammers out the book.

We could solve the three-tiles puzzle by exhaustive search because the total number of states in the state space is 24, not a large number.

7	•	1
3	2	8
4	5	6

A sample source
state

3	7	1
2	8	6
4	5	•

A sample destination
state

Figure 11.12 The eight-tiles puzzle. It has 8 tiles and an empty cell in a 3 × 3 tray. The moves are L, U, R and D, as for the three-tiles puzzle. The state space of the eight-tiles puzzle comprises 362 880 [factorial of 9] states. These states fall into two equal sized disjoint sets, in a manner similar to the three-tiles puzzle. A typical problem would be to find a solution path between the source and the destination states such as those given above.

But if the number of states in the state space is larger, say thousands or millions, then exhaustive search is far too inefficient to be practical. Even if we had enough memory to store all the nodes for the states, we would take far too long to conduct the exhaustive search. Consider, for instance, extensions to the three-tiles puzzle: the eight-tiles puzzle (Figure 11.12) and the fifteen-tiles puzzle (Figure 11.13). It may not be practical to solve a typical problem in the eight-tiles or fifteen-tiles puzzles by exhaustive search.

So that searching a state space becomes more practical, we can adopt some strategy that will guide us to construct a search graph not in the entire state space, but only in a selected subspace of it. That is to say, we shall search only a selected part of the state space. Hence it would be unlike exhaustive search, in which we search the entire state space. There is, however, a caveat: if we happen to select that part of

1	13	5	3
9	7	•	10
2	12	4	8
14	6	15	11

A sample source
state

2	10	3	8
13	6	14	5
4	1	15	11
9	7	•	12

A sample destination
state

Figure 11.13 The 15-tiles puzzle. It has 15 tiles and an empty cell in a 4 × 4 tray. The moves are L, U, R, and D, as for the three-tiles and eight-tiles puzzles. The state space of the 15-tiles puzzle comprises 20 922 789 890 000 [factorial of 16] states. These states fall into two equal sized disjoint sets, in a manner similar to the three-tiles and eight-tiles puzzles. A typical problem would be to find a solution path between the source and the destination states such as those given above.

the state space in which no solution path exists, then we shall fail to find the solution path, even though the solution path exists in the entire state space.

A search strategy can be classified as being either **complete** or **incomplete**. A search strategy is said to be complete if, and only if, it is guaranteed to find a solution path provided such a path exists. Ideally, a strategy should be complete, but we can occasionally risk adopting an incomplete strategy, should we envision that, for a given problem, if the strategy does succeed in finding a solution path then it will do so with a sizeable increase in the efficiency of the search.

A search strategy that is complete may be further subclassified as any of the following:

1. an **admissible** strategy is guaranteed to find the cheapest solution path;
2. a **defensible** strategy is guaranteed to find the shortest solution path; and
3. a **concessible** strategy is not guaranteed to find the shortest or the cheapest solution path although it may occasionally do so; in other words, it is complete but neither admissible nor defensible.

Figure 11.14 summarizes the kinds of solution paths, if any, found for a given problem by a search strategy of a particular class or subclass.

Various search strategies, both complete and incomplete, are described in sections 11.3–11.5. For our description, we shall assume that in the search graphs constructed:

1. the number of children, if any, of a node is finite; and
2. a solution path, if it exists, is of finite length.

Therefore, any search graph we construct will be finite: it will contain a finite number of nodes and a finite number of arcs.

To get a preview of the search strategies to be described, let us look over the synopsis of a typical strategy. We begin by expanding the source node. Its children constitute a set of unexpanded nodes. From the set of unexpanded nodes, we select a node (different search strategies advocate different criteria for this selection), expand it, and add its children to the set of unexpanded nodes. We continue selecting one of the unexpanded nodes, expanding it, and adding its children to the set of unexpanded nodes, until one of the following conditions holds:

1. we cannot generate any new node since the set of unexpanded nodes has become empty; we then stop because we have failed in finding a solution path either because a solution path does not exist,

Number of solution paths in the problem	The cost of all moves is	The class or subclass of the search strategy, and the solution path found			
		Complete			Incomplete
		Admissible	Defensible	Concessible	
more than one	not the same	cheapest, which may not be the shortest	shortest, which may not be the cheapest	any solution path, which may be neither the cheapest nor the shortest	no solution path may be found even though it exists
	the same	cheapest, which will also be the shortest	shortest, which will also be the cheapest		
one	of no relevance	the single solution path			
zero		none, since no solution path exists			

Figure 11.14　The solution path, if any, found by a search strategy for a given problem depends on [1] the number of solution paths that exist in the problem, [2] the cost of the moves as compared to one another, and [3] the class or subclass of the search strategy. Since exhaustive search finds all solution paths that exist, it is both admissible and defensible. An admissible strategy can be adopted to find the shortest solution path in a problem where all moves are considered to cost the same.

or because our search strategy has been unable to find a solution path even though such a path exists, as may happen with an incomplete strategy;
2. we succeed in generating a destination node; we then trace back along our record of node expansions to find the solution path.

One of the above two conditions must ultimately hold since the search graph has been assumed to be finite. For implementing a strategy like that summarized above, we can maintain two lists named, say, OPEN and CLOSED. At any time during the execution of the strategy, unexpanded nodes are stored in OPEN provided such nodes are neither renegade nor recurring. From Figures 11.1 and 11.2, we know that renegade or recurring nodes need not be stored anywhere since such nodes cannot be part of a problem solution. The nodes in OPEN, being unexpanded, are considered to be open to, that is, available for, expansion. Nodes already expanded and hence considered to be closed to, that is, unavailable for, expansion are stored in CLOSED. So in expanding a node, not only do we generate its children, but we also transfer it from OPEN to CLOSED. If the node for expansion happens to be inert, we delete it from OPEN but we do not transfer it to CLOSED.

Furthermore, every node stored in either OPEN or CLOSED is stored with a pointer to its parent. These pointers, called **parentage pointers**, are put to use when we succeed in generating a destination node, and we are to trace back along our record of node expansions to find the solution path. The solution path will be found to lie along a subset of the nodes in CLOSED. Suppose we have generated a destination node y_0. We next look for its parent y_1 in CLOSED. Using the parentage pointer of y_1, we examine the contents of CLOSED to look for node y_2, the parent of node y_1. Then we continue to look for the parent of y_2, and so on, until we discover the source node y_n. Then the solution path lies along $y_n y_{n-1} \cdots y_0$.

Search strategies can also be classified depending on how they select a node for expansion from OPEN. Accordingly, the strategies described in sections 11.3–11.5 can be classified into the following:

1. **breadth-first** search strategies expand a shallower node before a deeper node;
2. **depth-first** search strategies expand a deeper node before a shallower node; and
3. **best-first** search strategies expand the node that is most likely to lie on the desired solution path.

We now commence our description of the search strategies with the breadth-first search strategies.

11.3 BREADTH-FIRST SEARCH

In breadth-first search, we begin by expanding the source node, which is at depth 0, to generate all its children, which now become nodes at depth 1. Then, one by one, we expand all nodes at depth 1 to generate all nodes at depth 2. Thus in general we generate nodes at depth $d + 1$ only after we have generated all nodes at level d, where $d \geq 0$. Generating nodes in the order discussed above, we may heuristically prune the search graph by deleting some of the nodes to reduce the memory and computation required for the search. Below, we first describe the strategy in which we do not prune the search graph, and then the strategy in which we prune the search graph.

11.3.1 Unpruned breadth-first

Figure 11.15 An unpruned breadth-first search tree for the eight-tiles puzzle. The children of a node may be generated in any order: above, we have generated

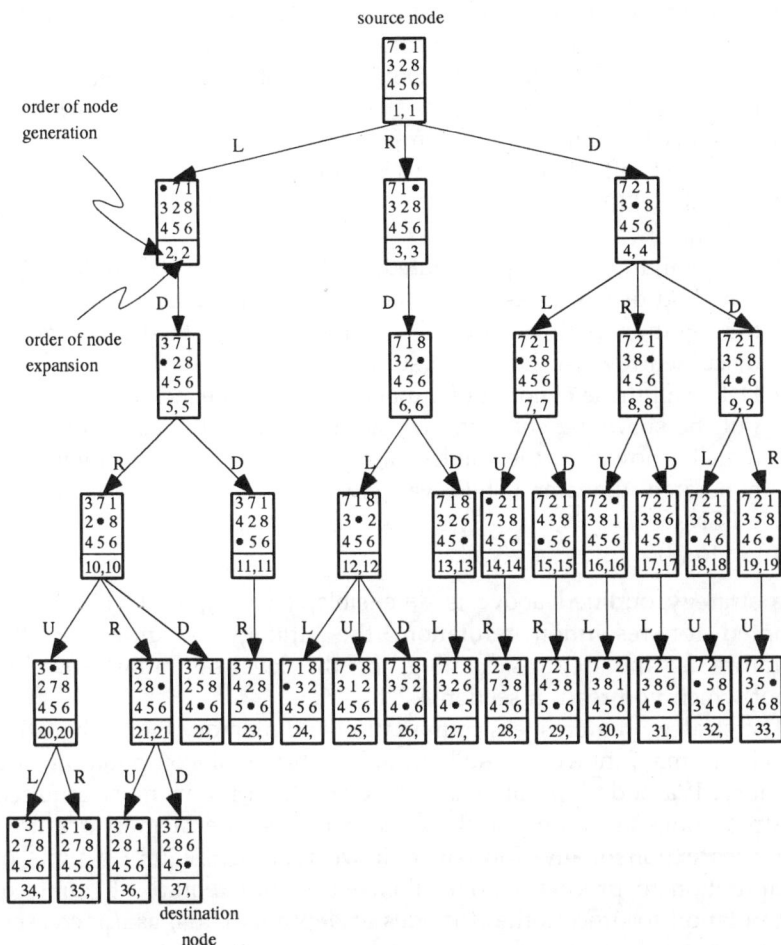

Figure 11.15 An unpruned breadth-first search tree for the eight-tiles puzzle. The children of a node may be generated in any order: above, we have generated them by making the moves possible in the order L, U, R, D [shown left to right]. The nodes are then expanded in the order in which they were generated. The source and destination nodes are as specified in Figure 11.12. Neither any renegade nodes nor any inert nodes were generated. Any recurring nodes generated were deleted; they are not shown above. The two-tuple below a node indicates the order in which the node was generated, and the order in which it was expanded.

(1) If the source node is identical to the destination node then return successfully with the empty solution path.
(2) Initialize lists OPEN and CLOSED to empty. Put the source node in OPEN.
(3) If OPEN is empty then return failure.
(4) Remove the frontmost node x from OPEN.
(5) Put x in CLOSED.
(6) Expand x.
(7) If no children of x are generated, that is, x is inert, then go to (3).
(8) If a child of x is a destination node, then return successfully with the solution path obtained by using the parentage pointers, as discussed toward the end of section 11.2.
(9) Delete all those children of x that are either renegade or recurring.
(10) Put the surviving children of x in any order at the back of OPEN; usually, however, the children are put in x in the order they were generated: the later a child was generated, the further back it is in OPEN.
(11) Go to (3).

The strategy outlined above is defensible, (see Figure 11.14). When adopted for resolution refutation, the strategy is known in the literature as the depth-saturating, or the level-saturating strategy, about which you read in section 4.2.1.

The strategy requires less computation and memory than exhaustive search; it may, however, still require substantial computation and memory. If a node typically has B children, then the memory required to store nodes at depth d is B^d. As d increases, the memory required increases exponentially. Moreover, if we typically require ρ units of computation to process a node, then we would require ρB^d units of computation to process the B^d nodes at depth d. Thus, as d increases, the computation required also increases exponentially.

To reduce the required computation and memory we can modify the above strategy by deleting some of the nodes generated. This modification is described next.

11.3.2 Pruned breadth-first

For pruned breadth-first search, we need a heuristic to measure how *promising* is a given node for being on the desired solution path. Then in essence we retain only a few of the most promising nodes, the rest being deleted.

The heuristic employs a function that maps a node into a numerical value, which serves as a measure of the promise of the node. There is

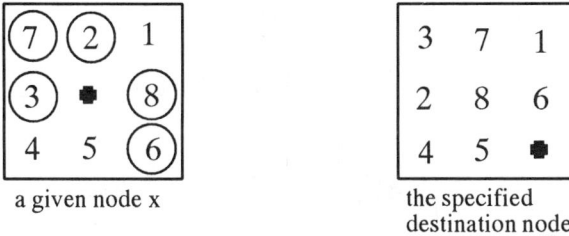

a given node x

the specified
destination node

Figure 11.16 How to count the number of dislocated tiles in a given node x.
Compare x with the destination node. If a tile in x is not in the same location
[that is, in the same row and the same column] as it is in the destination node,
then the tile is said to be *dislocated*. The tiles shown circled in x are dislocated.
Thus node x has 5 dislocated tiles.

no known heuristic that will measure the promise of nodes in general.
The heuristic will depend on the particular problem that one is trying
to solve. Later, in section 11.6, we shall give some suggestions for
developing such heuristics for problems in general.

A specimen heuristic for the eight-tiles puzzle is the **dislocated-tile**
heuristic. Figure 11.16 shows how we can count the number of
dislocated tiles in a given node. According to this heuristic, the fewer
the dislocated tiles in a node, the more promising is the node.

One way to conduct a pruned breath-first search is as follows. After
all the nodes at a particular depth have been generated, we retain β of
the most promising nodes, the rest being deleted. Typically, the value
of β, based on our intuition, is greater than zero but less than the total
number of nodes generated at a depth (not counting the renegade or
recurring nodes, if any, that were generated). Figure 11.17 shows an
example with β = 1.

For implementing the strategy, we would need a list, say, RESERVE
besides the usual lists OPEN and CLOSED. While nodes are being
generated they are stored in RESERVE. After all the nodes of a
particular depth have been generated, only the nodes to be retained,
that is, the β most promising nodes at that depth, are copied into
OPEN. Pruned breadth-first can then be outlined as follows.

(1) If the source node is identical to the destination node then return
successfully with the empty solution path.
(2) Initialize the lists OPEN, CLOSED and RESERVE to empty. Put
the source node in OPEN.
(3) If OPEN is empty, then do:
    (3.1) if RESERVE is empty then return failure.
    (3.2) if RESERVE is non-empty then select the β most promising

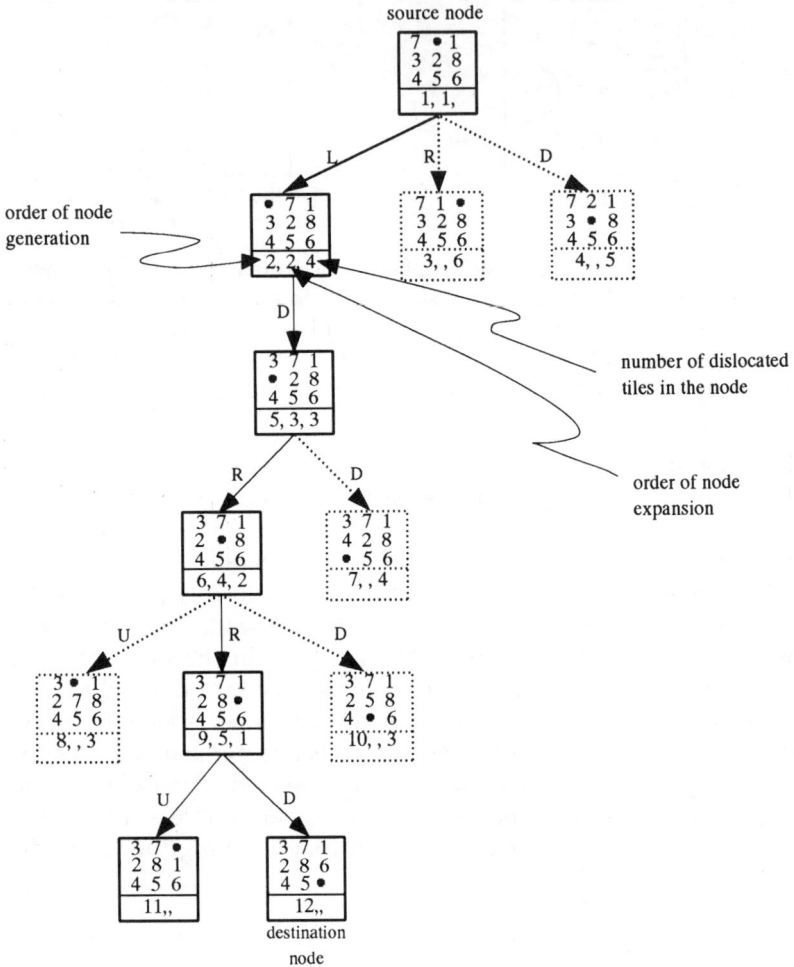

Figure 11.17   A pruned breadth-first search tree for the eight-tiles puzzle. Only the most promising node, as measured by the dislocated-tile heuristic, is retained at every depth. The deleted nodes are shown dotted above. Compare the above search tree with the search tree of Figure 11.15. The three-tuple below a node indicates the order in which the node was generated, the order in which it was expanded, and the number of dislocated tiles in it.

nodes from RESERVE and copy them into the back of OPEN in decreasing order of their promise, that is, the lower the promise of a node, the further back it is in OPEN (should RESERVE have fewer than β nodes, then all of them are copied into the back of OPEN, in descending order of their promise). Make RESERVE empty.

(4) Remove the frontmost node x from OPEN.

(5) Put x in CLOSED.

(6) Expand x.

(7) If no children of x are generated, that is, x is inert, then go to (3).

(8) If a child of x is a destination node then return successfully with the solution path obtained by using the parentage pointers, as discussed toward the end of section 11.2.

(9) Delete all those children of x that are either renegade or recurring.

(10) Put the surviving children of x in any order into RESERVE.

(11) Go to (3).

The strategy is incomplete (see Figure 11.14) because the heuristic, being fallible, may misjudge the promise of a node. Thus a node that lies on the solution path may be deleted.

The heuristic will require some computation to measure the promise of a node. Nevertheless, unless the heuristic itself is so complex that it needs excessive computation and memory, pruned breadth-first search is expected to require less computation and memory than unpruned breadth-first search.

You may, however, alter the pruned breadth-first search from that described above. For example:

1. rather than delete only those children of node x that are either renegade or recurring, in the ninth step of the above outline, delete also the inert children of x; then in the seventh step, you would not need to check every time whether the node to be expanded is inert;
2. rather than have a fixed value of β at all depths you may vary it: say, a smaller β for shallower nodes, and a larger β for deeper ones;
3. rather than generate all nodes at a particular depth d and then select some nodes, you may select a few children from every parent of depth $d-1$, and delete the rest.

Earlier in this section, it was said that typically the value of β is less than the total number of nodes generated at a depth. If, however, the value of β at a depth is equal to the number of nodes generated at that depth, then the strategy becomes unpruned breadth-first search, the nodes at a depth being expanded in decreasing order of their promise: the more promising a node, the earlier it is expanded.

In the literature, unpruned breadth-first search is often simply known as breadth-first search, and pruned breadth-first search is known as **beam search**. In calling it beam search, the source node is imagined to be a source of light; then by retaining only some nodes at each level, the beam of light supposedly emanating from the source node is visualized to have been narrowed.

By expanding a shallower node before a deeper node, the breadth-first search strategies in effect expand a node's siblings before expanding its descendants. But the depth-first strategies, described next, behave conversely: by expanding a deeper node before a shallower node, they in effect expand a node's descendants before expanding its siblings.

11.4   DEPTH-FIRST SEARCH

To adopt any of the depth-first search strategies described below, we ordinarily first estimate how long the solution path will be at the most. Heuristics similar to that presented in section 11.3.2 can be employed to make such an estimate. In the eight-tiles puzzle, for example, the more dislocated tiles there are in a source node, the more will be the estimate. This estimate is called the **length-bound**. We can also call it the **depth-bound** because it demarcates the maximum depth of the destination node according to our estimate. Alternatively, if we are interested in the cost of the solution path, but not in the length of the solution path, then we shall estimate the maximum cost of the solution path. This estimate shall be called the **cost-bound**. We can, of course, have both a depth-bound and a cost-bound. Then we are not interested in searching for a solution path whose length exceeds the depth-bound or whose cost exceeds the cost-bound.

A node z that is not a destination node is said to be **insipid** if, and only if,

1. the depth of z is greater than or equal to the depth-bound, if any, or
2. the cost of the path from the source node to z is greater than or equal to the cost-bound, if any.

Note that at least one of the values of depth-bound or cost-bound should be demarcated. While traversing a path from the source node, if we reach an insipid node z, then we are not interested in finding a solution path that passes through z because the length of the path will exceed the depth-bound, or the cost of the path will exceed the cost-bound, or both. We say that such a path itself is insipid, and we want to find a solution path other than an insipid path.

Moreover, as discussed in section 11.1, a solution path does not contain any renegade, recurring, or inert nodes. Now, suppose that while traversing a path from the source node, we reach a node that is inert, renegade, recurring or insipid. Then we say that the path has become **barricaded**. If a path becomes barricaded then we should look elsewhere in the search graph for a solution path.

In depth-first search we essentially traverse one path at time. Let us assume that the path we are traversing is along the nodes

1. $x_0 x_1 \ldots x_{j-1} x_j \ldots x_n$,
2. where x_0 is the source node, and that
3. the path becomes barricaded on reaching x_n.

Then we abandon the barricaded path and start traversing a new path $x_0 x_1 \ldots x_{j-1} x_j' \ldots$, for some j such that $1 \leq j \leq n$, and x_j' is a sibling of x_j. In sections 11.4.1 and 11.4.2 below, we describe the ways for selecting a new path to be traversed. If we are unable to find a new path for traversing, then we have failed in finding a solution path.

Be aware that all depth-first search strategies are incomplete (refresh your memory from Figure 11.14). What causes their incompleteness will become clear in section 11.4.3, only after you have read about the strategies themselves in the next two sections.

11.4.1 Depth-first with backtracking

To describe depth-first search with backtracking, we require the following definition. A node is said to be **partly expanded** during the time we have generated at least one of its children, but not all of its children. Being partly expanded is a status of the node: it becomes fully expanded when we cannot generate any more of its children.

In this strategy, we generate one child at a time of a given node. Beginning from the source node x_0, we generate x_1, which is one of the children of x_0. Next, we generate x_2, which is one of the children of x_1, and so on. The outcome of this is that $x_0 x_1 x_2 \ldots$ becomes our path of traversal. Suppose that, on generating some node x_n, our path becomes barricaded. Then we **backtrack**, that is, we go back over our path. There are two modes to backtracking: **chronological** and **hindsight**. We shall describe chronological backtracking before hindsight backtracking: the latter calls for an understanding of the former.

To backtrack chronologically after our path becomes barricaded at x_n, we scan the nodes x_{n-1}, x_{n-2}, $\ldots$ until we discover a partly expanded node x_{j-1}, where $0 < j \leq n$. Failure to discover such a node signifies that we have failed to find a solution path, and so we can stop. Node x_{j-1}, if discovered, is thus the partly expanded node that is chronologically the nearest to x_n. We next generate x_j', a new child of x_{j-1}; put another way, x_j' is a child that x_{j-1} has never generated earlier. Then $x_0, x_1 \ldots x_{j-1} x_j' \ldots$ becomes our new path of traversal.

In brief, we say that we have backtracked chronologically to x_{j-1} over the nodes $x_n, x_{n-1}, \ldots, x_j$. The nodes backtracked over should be deleted. Should our new path of traversal also become barricaded, then we again backtrack chronologically for yet another path. Thus we proceed. Figure 11.18 shows an example.

Remember that we had seen earlier the applications of depth-first

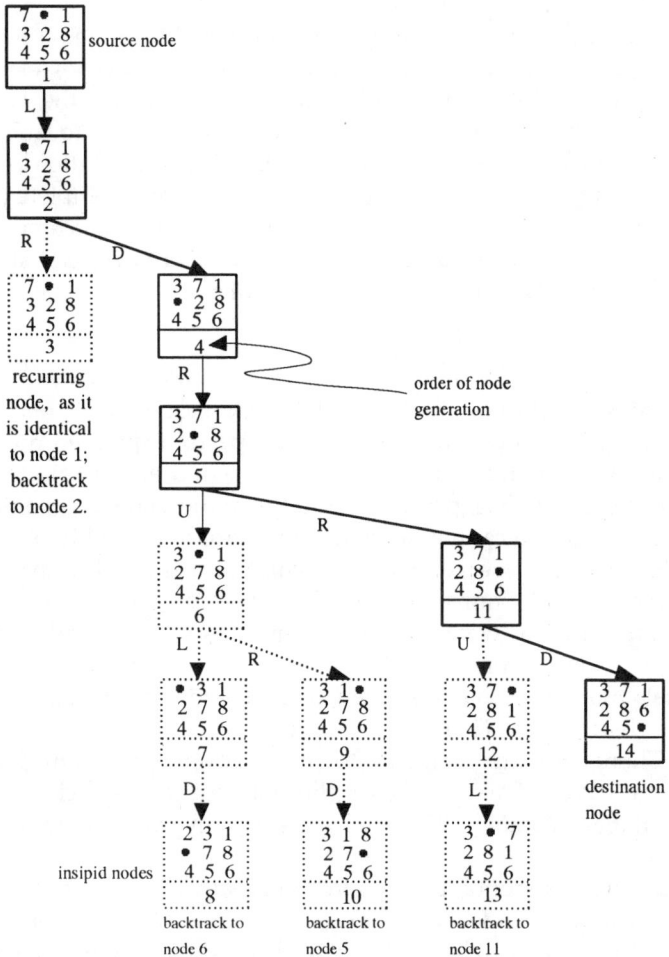

Figure 11.18 An example of depth-first search, with chronological backtracking and a depth-bound of six, for the eight-tiles puzzle. To prevent cluttering the figure, we have shown only one recurring node. Neither any renegade nodes nor any inert nodes were generated. The source and destination nodes are as specified in Figure 11.12.

strategy with chronological backtracking during the discussions on using logic to write programs (sections 5.2.3 and 5.3.3) and on using augmented transition networks to parse English sentences (section 7.2.1). Moreover, we saw in section 5.3.5 how, after finding the answer to a question, we can force chronological backtracking to find multiple answers to a question. Similarly, after finding a solution path here, we can force such backtracking to find multiple solution paths.

As an example of multiple solution paths, consider the four-queens puzzle: place four queens on the squares of a 4 × 4 chess-board, each queen on one square, so that no queen attacks another: in other words, no queen can capture another, or that no two queens share the same row, column or diagonal.

The four-queens puzzle exemplifies a problem in which the destination node is not explicitly specified: only the constraints that should be satisfied by the destination node are specified. Hence there can be more than one destination node that satisfies the constraints. Contrast this with the eight-tiles puzzle (Figure 11.12) or the missionaries and cannibals problem (section 11.1), in which the destination node is explicity specified.

Let us now discuss solving the four-queens puzzle by depth-first search with chronological backtracking. As you read the discussion below, keep referring to the problem solution illustrated in Figure 11.19. The columns of the chess-board are assumed to be numbered 1 to 4 from left to right. The squares in each column are then assumed to be numbered 1 to 4 from top to bottom. We begin by placing queen Q_1 in the first column, then we place queen Q_2 in the second column, and so on we proceed placing the queens in the columns from left to right. A queen can be placed on only one of the squares that are unattacked by any of the queens placed earlier. The depth-bound for solving the problem is obviously 4.

If a column has unattacked squares numbered, say, k and m, where $k < m$ (square k is above square m), then we place the queen in square k; if later we have to backtrack, we place the queen in square m. We backtrack when we cannot put a queen in a column since the column has no unattacked squares (every child of the corresponding node is renegade). On backtracking, we change the place of the queen for which we most recently selected one of the unattacked squares. Figure 11.19 also illustrates how, after finding a solution, we can force backtracking to find another solution, provided another solution exists.

Having described chronological backtracking, we shall now describe hindsight backtracking. To do that, we require the following definition. A node z is said to be **subversive** if, and only if, every path from the source node passing through z becomes barricaded at some descendant

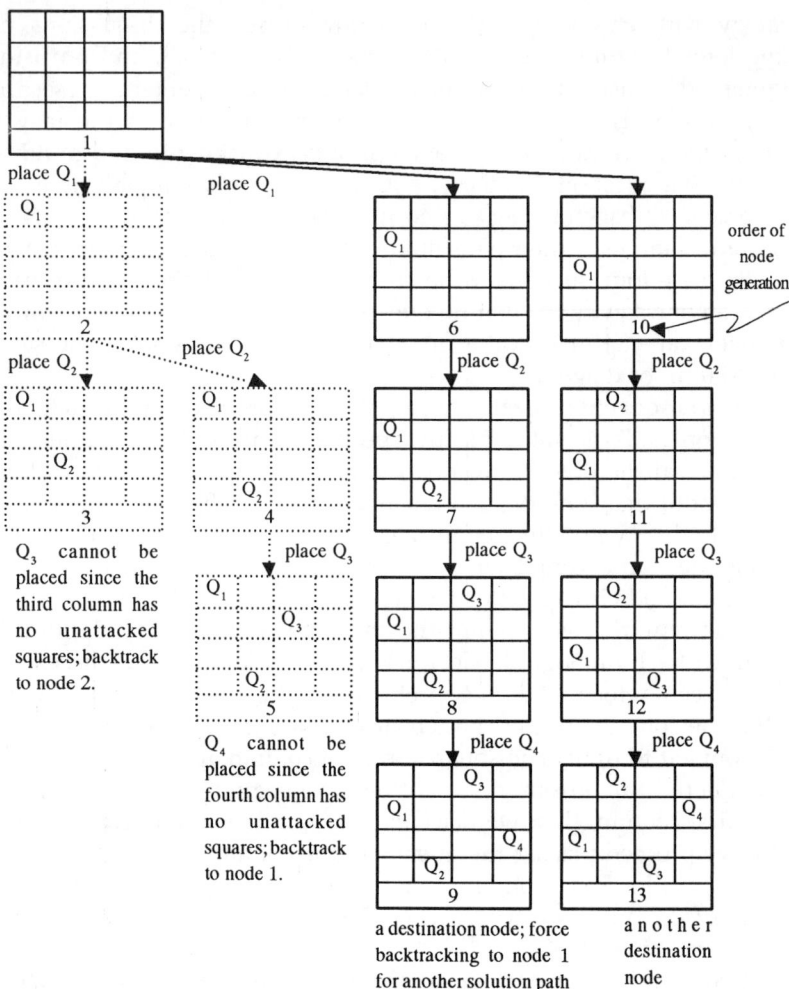

Figure 11.19   An example of depth-first search with chronological backtracking for the four-queens puzzle. On reaching a destination node, we forced backtracking to find another solution path. Note that the two destination nodes happen to be mirror images of each other.

of z. It should be apparent that a subversive node cannot lie on any solution path. Accordingly, if we realize that a particular node is a subversive, then we need not generate any more of its descendants.

Before we describe hindsight backtracking in detail, let us consider a preparatory example. Suppose our wallet contains 3 doubloons, which are to be spent for two meals: lunch and supper. We can spend 1, 2 or

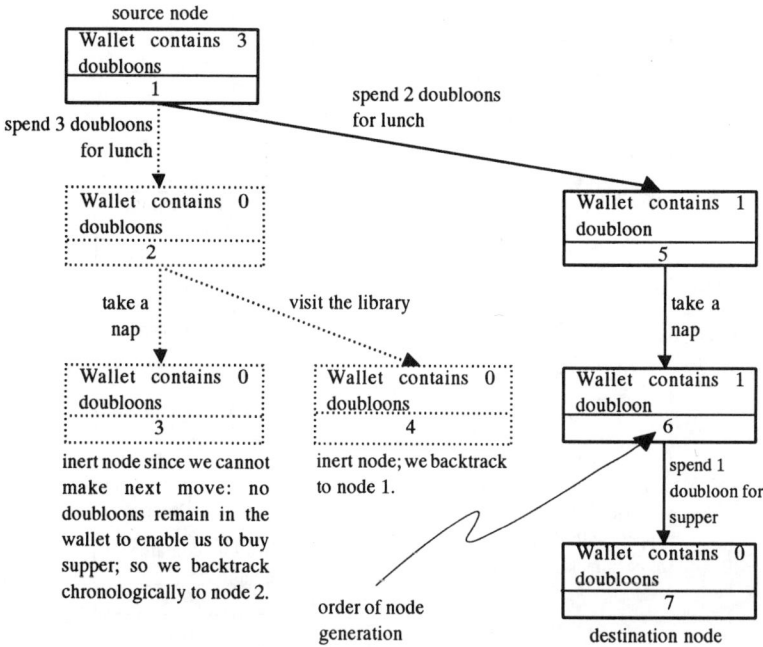

Figure 11.20 Depth-first search with chronological backtracking for planning our lunch, afternoon activity, and supper on a budget of 3 doubloons. We are to spend at least one doubloon for each meal. Compare the above figure with Figure 11.21.

3 doubloons on a meal. After lunch, we can either take a nap or visit the library. Neither activity requires our spending any doubloons. We are to plan our day. With a depth-bound of three, we plan by chronological backtracking in Figure 11.20, and by hindsight backtracking in Figure 11.21. We expect that constructing the search graph of Figure 11.21 will require less computation overall than the search graph of Figure 11.20. Hindsight backtracking is in general expected to be more efficient than chronological backtracking.

Ideally, we should replace hindsight by foresight. If we have foresight, then we have the ability to look ahead and thus avoid any kind of backtracking. The example above can be solved by the foresight that at the time of buying lunch, we should set aside at least one doubloon for supper. Nevertheless, in practice foresight is difficult to have for solving problems in general (see also the comments on foresight in section 2.3.4).

Let us now describe hindsight backtracking in a little more detail. As happens in our depth-first search, suppose that we are traversing a

source node

Wallet contains 3 doubloons
1

spend 3 doubloons
for lunch

spend 2 doubloons
for lunch

Wallet contains 0 doubloons
2

Wallet contains 1 doubloon
4

order of
node
generation

take a
nap

take a
nap

Wallet contains 0 doubloons
3

Wallet contains 1 doubloon
5

inert node since no
doubloons remain in our
wallet to enable us to buy
supper; with hindsight,
we backtrack to node 1.

spend 1
doubloon for
supper

Wallet contains 0 doubloons
6

destination node

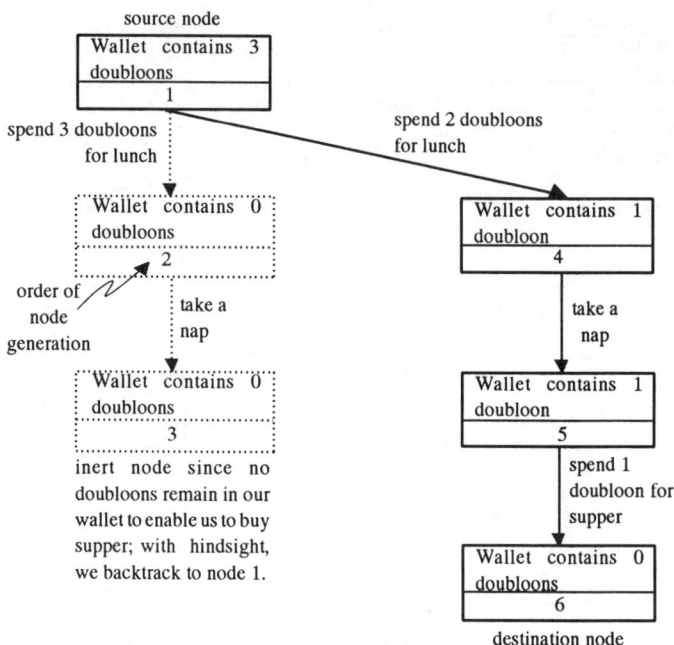

Figure 11.21 Depth-first search with hindsight backtracking for the same problem as in Figure 11.20. We ran out of doubloons at node 3 because we spent too many earlier: remember, we spend no doubloons regardless of what afternoon activity we undertake. With this hindsight wisdom, we assess node 2 to be subversive. We assume the path to be barricaded at node 2 itself: then we backtrack chronologically to node 1. Overall, we have backtracked with hindsight from node 3 to node 1. Hindsight backtracking thus contains a component of chronological backtracking.

path $x_0x_1x_2 \ldots$, where x_0 is the source node, and that the path becomes barricaded at some x_n. To attempt hindsight backtracking, we execute the following two acts.

1. Using the hindsight wisdom gained from whatever caused the path to be barricaded, we scan the nodes $x_0, x_1, x_2, \ldots$ looking for a node x_i (where $0 \leq i < n$) that we assess to be subversive. If we discover more than one subversive node, then the subversive node that is the nearest to x_0 comes to be x_i. If no subversive node is discovered, then we stipulate x_i to be the same as x_n. There are no known general techniques to assess that a node is subversive; such techniques will depend on the particular problem and the hindsight wisdom we have gained in attempting to solve it.

2. Backtrack chronologically from x_i. If x_i is a subversive node, then in executing this act we are implicitly assuming the path to be barricaded at x_i itself.

It should be apparent from above (also mentioned in the legend of Figure 11.21) that hindsight backtracking contains within it a component of chronological backtracking. Thus in backtracking with hindsight from node x_n, we shall backtrack over at least as many nodes (but often, more nodes) as we would in backtracking chronologically from x_n. All nodes backtracked over are deleted. Hindsight backtracking requires some computation to look for subversive nodes, but the overall computation in hindsight backtracking is expected to be less than that in chronological backtracking because hindsight backtracking prunes more of the search graph.

As another example in hindsight backtracking, consider an extension of the four-queens puzzle (Figure 11.19) you saw earlier in this section. It is the eight-queens puzzle: place eight queens on the squares of an 8 × 8 chess-board, each queen on one square, so that no queen attacks another. Figure 11.22 shows a board configuration from which hindsight backtracking would be preferable over chronological backtracking.

Depth-first search with any kind of backtracking requires less memory than breadth-first search (see section 11.3.1): at a given time, the former stores only one path in memory since the nodes backtracked over are deleted, whereas the latter stores many paths in memory.

For implementing depth-first search with backtracking, we need two lists: one will be the list OPEN to store unexpanded and partly expanded nodes; the other will be the list PROGENY to ensure that every time a child of a node x is generated, it is a new child. Note that we do not need the list CLOSED as we did for the breadth-first search described in sections 11.3.1 and 11.3.2. Depth-first search with backtracking can then be outlined as follows.

(1) If the source node is identical to the destination node, then return successfully with the empty solution path.
(2) Initialize lists OPEN and PROGENY to empty. Put the source node in OPEN.
(3) If OPEN is empty, then return failure.
(4) Generate a new child of the frontmost node x in OPEN, that is, the child generated should not be identical to some node y in PROGENY such that the parentage pointer of y designates x to be the parent of y.

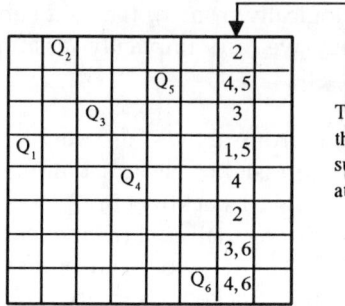

The numbers in a square in this column indicate the subscripts of the queens attacking the square.

Suppose that, by depth-first search with bactracking, we reach the above node. We have placed queens Q_1 to Q_6, and we have next to place Q_7. But Q_7 cannot be placed because the seventh column has no unattacked squares. The path thus becomes barricaded.

Under chronological backtracking, we would remove Q_6 and try to place Q_5 in another square in the fifth column. But that would not help because each square in the seventh column is attacked by one of the queens Q_1 to Q_4. A node with Q_1, Q_2, Q_3, and Q_4 as shown above is subversive. Under hindsight backtracking, we remove Q_5 and Q_6, and then we try to place Q_4 in another square in the fourth column.

Figure 11.22 A node from which hindsight backtracking would be preferable over chronological backtracking to solve the eight-queen puzzle by depth-first search. In solving the problem, we can alternatively include the foresight that place queen Q_i [for $1 \le i \le 7$] in an unattacked square such that every column to the right of the ith column has at least one unattacked square.

(5) If no new child of x can be generated, that is, x is inert, or it has been already fully expanded, then do:

   (5.1) remove x from OPEN;

   (5.2) if we have gained any hindsight wisdom, use it to look for a subversive node, starting from the back of OPEN; should such a node be discovered, then remove it from OPEN together with all the nodes in front of it in OPEN (this will remove the subversive node and all its descendants);

   (5.3) go to (3).

(6) If x has a new child, then put the child in PROGENY.

(7) If the child of x is a destination node, then return successfully with the solution path obtained from the nodes in OPEN, similar to that discussed toward the end of section 11.2.

(8) If the child of x is a renegade, a recurring, or an insipid node, then go to (4).

(9) Put the child of x at the front of OPEN.

(10) Go to (3).

According to the above outline if we can backtrack with hindsight we do so, otherwise we backtrack only chronologically. Expunging step (5.2) from the outline will prevent any attempt at hindsight backtracking: only chronological backtracking will remain. For saving memory, any time a node from OPEN is removed, all its children in PROGENY may also be removed. To find multiple solution paths, we can force backtracking after finding a solution path; more specifically, after finding a solution path in step (7) above, we shall delete the destination node generated, and then go to step (4).

Hindsight backtracking is known in the literature by various names: **dependency-based**, **dependency-directed** or **non-chronological** backtracking.

11.4.2 Depth-first with leap-frogging

In depth-first search with backtracking, described in the preceding section, we generate the children of a node, one child at a time. As an alternative, in the depth-first search described in this section, we generate the children of a node all at once.

To begin, we expand the source node x_0. From the children of x_0, we select one child x_1. Comments on the criteria to make this selection are given later in this section. For the time being, we shall assume that the child x_1 is selected arbitrarily. Node x_1 is next expanded. From the children of x_1, we select one child x_2 and expand it, and so we proceed. Thus $x_0 x_1 x_2 \ldots$ becomes our path of traversal. Suppose the path becomes barricaded at some x_n. Then we **leap-frog**, that is, we transfer to a sibling of one of the nodes $x_1, x_2, \ldots, x_n$. There are two modes to leap-frogging: **chronological** and **hindsight**. We shall describe chronological leap-frogging before hindsight leap-frogging. The notions of chronology and hindsight are the same as those discussed in section 11.4.1, and hence they will not be discussed again.

To leap-frog chronologically after our path becomes barricaded at x_n, we scan the nodes $x_n, x_{n-1}, \ldots$ until we discover a node x_j (where $0 < j \le n$) such that it has a sibling x_j' along which we have not traversed until now. Failure to discover such a node signifies that we have failed to find a solution path, and so we can stop. But if we discover such a node, then $x_0 x_1 \ldots x_{j-1} x_j' \ldots$ becomes our new path of traversal. We say that we have leap-frogged chronologically from x_n to x_j'. Should our new path of traversal also become barricaded, then we leap-frog chronologically again for yet another path, and so we proceed. Figure 11.23 shows an example.

Let us now describe hindsight leap-frogging. As before, suppose that, while traversing a path $x_0 x_1 x_2 \ldots$, our path becomes barricaded

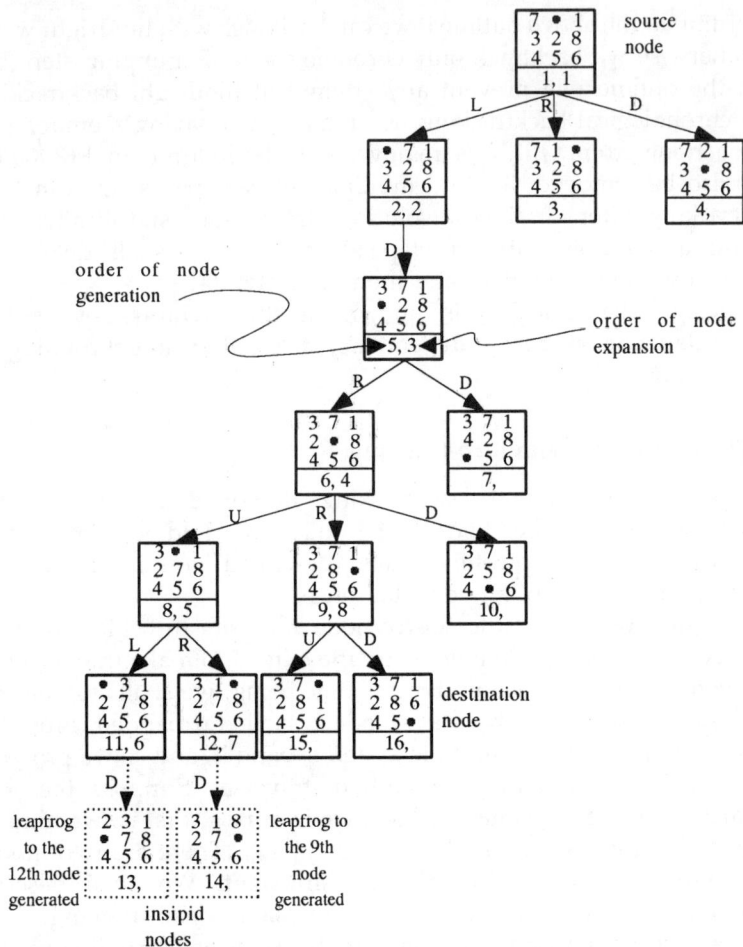

source node

```
7 • 1
3 2 8
4 5 6
1, 1
```

L   R   D

```
• 7 1      7 1 •      7 2 1
3 2 8      3 2 8      3 • 8
4 5 6      4 5 6      4 5 6
2, 2       3,         4,
```

order of node generation

```
3 7 1
• 2 8
4 5 6
5, 3
```

order of node expansion

R   D

```
3 7 1      3 7 1
2 • 8      4 2 8
4 5 6      • 5 6
6, 4       7,
```

U   R   D

```
3 • 1      3 7 1      3 7 1
2 7 8      2 8 •      2 5 8
4 5 6      4 5 6      4 • 6
8, 5       9, 8       10,
```

L   R   U   D

```
• 3 1      3 1 •      3 7 •      3 7 1
2 7 8      2 7 8      2 8 1      2 8 6
4 5 6      4 5 6      4 5 6      4 5 •
11, 6      12, 7      15,        16,
```

destination node

D   D

leapfrog to the 12th node generated

```
2 3 1      3 1 8
• 7 8      2 7 •
4 5 6      4 5 6
13,        14,
```

leapfrog to the 9th node generated

insipid nodes

Figure 11.23   An example of depth-first search, with leap-frogging and a depth-bound of six, for the eight-tiles puzzle. One child is arbitrarily selected [shown above in left to right order] for expansion from the children of a node. To prevent cluttering the figure, we have not shown any recurring nodes. Neither any renegade nor any inert nodes were generated. The source and destination nodes are as specified in Figure 11.12.

at x_n. To attempt hindsight leap-frogging, we execute the following two acts:

1. look for a subversive node x_i, exactly as explained in section 11.4.1 while describing hindsight backtracking;
2. leap-frog chronologically from x_i.

Accordingly, hindsight leap-frogging contains within it a component of chronological leap-frogging.

Early in our description of depth-first search with leap-frogging, we had assumed that whenever we select a node for expansion from among its siblings we shall select the node arbitrarily. Alternatively, we can employ a heuristic to measure the promise of a node. A given set of sibling nodes can then be sorted as $z_1, z_2, z_3, \ldots$ in decreasing order of their promise; thus, for example, node z_1 is more promising than node z_2, and node z_2 is more promising than node z_3. The first time we have to select one of the z's for expansion, we select z_1. If later we have to leap-frog to one of the z's, we leap-frog to z_2. If we have to leap-frog to one of the z's again, we leap-frog to z_3, and so on.

A depth-first search that selects siblings for expansion based on their promise, as described above, is known in the literature by the name **hill-climbing**. In giving the search this name, the destination node is imagined to be the peak of a hill. Then, the more promising a node, the closer it is viewed to the peak. A hill climber, having set out on a path on the face of the hill, then advances toward the point of highest slope, that is, the node with the most promise, in order to reach the peak. Figure 11.24 shows an example of the hill-climbing strategy.

It should be clear from our discussion above, and from Figures 11.23 and 11.24 as compared to Figure 11.18, that a depth-first strategy with leap-frogging would require more memory than a depth-first strategy with backtracking: for leap-frogging, all the children of a node are stored in memory; for backtracking, a child is generated when needed. But then, the strategy with leap-frogging may be faster than the strategy with backtracking: for leap-frogging, a node is expanded only once since its children are generated all together; for backtracking, more time may be consumed because a node may be expanded more than once, each time generating one child, and ensuring that the child generated is a new child.

For implementing depth-first search with leap-frogging, we need the lists OPEN and CLOSED to store unexpanded and expanded nodes, respectively, similar to those mentioned in sections 11.3.1 and 11.3.2. The search strategy can then be outlined as follow.

(1) If the source node is identical to the destination node, then return successfully with the empty solution path.
(2) Initialize lists OPEN and CLOSE to empty. Put the source node in OPEN.
(3) If OPEN is empty, then return failure.
(4) Remove the frontmost node x from OPEN.
(5) Put x in CLOSED.

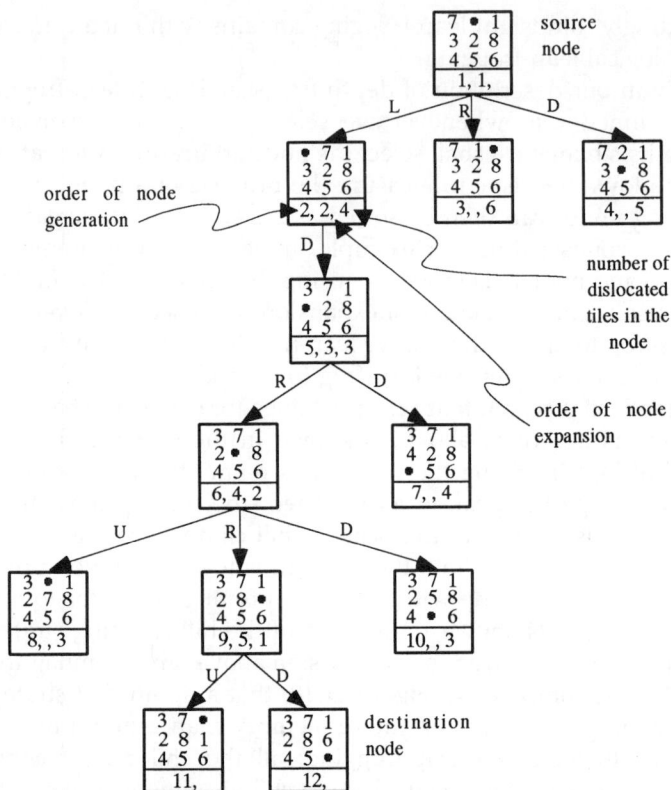

Figure 11.24　An example of the hill-climbing instance of depth-first search for the eight-tiles puzzle. The dislocated tile heuristic [see section 11.3.2] was employed to measure the promise of sibling nodes. Compare the above search tree with the search tree of Figure 11.23. Note that above we did not have to leap-frog at all. But in solving problems in general we may have to leap-frog, mainly because the heuristic employed may misjudge the promise of a node among its siblings.

(6) Expand x.

(7) If no children of x are generated, that is, x is inert, then do:

　　(7.1)　if we have gained any hindsight wisdom, use it to look for a subversive ancestor of x; should such an ancestor be discovered, then remove it from OPEN together with all its descendants in OPEN;

　　(7.2)　go to (3).

(8) If a child of x is a destination node, then return successfully with the solution path obtained by using the parentage pointers, as discussed toward the end of section 11.2.

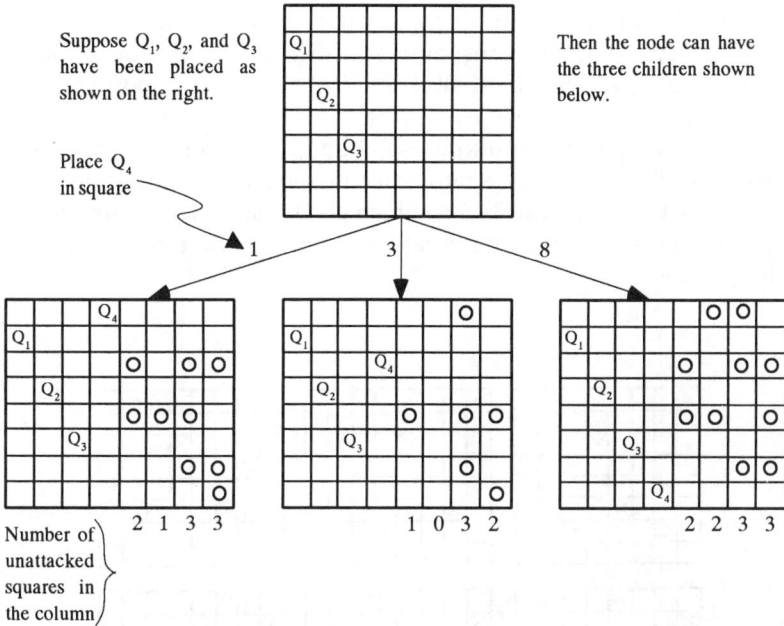

Suppose Q_1, Q_2, and Q_3 have been placed as shown on the right.

Then the node can have the three children shown below.

Place Q_4 in square

1   3   8

Number of unattacked squares in the column

2 1 3 3   1 0 3 2   2 2 3 3

Figure 11.25 A specimen heuristic to compare the promise of sibling nodes for the eight-queens puzzle. Let the promise of a node be equal to the minimum of the number of unattacked squares in each of the columns in which the queens are yet to be placed. Unattacked squares are denoted by the symbol 'O' in the three siblings above. Then the promise of the siblings from left to right are min(2,1,3,3), min(1,0,3,2), and min(2,2,3,3); that is, 1, 0, and 2. Thus the rightmost sibling is the most promising. The middle sibling is in fact a subversive node.

(9) Delete all those children of x that are either renegade, recurring or insipid.

(10) Put the surviving children of x in decreasing order of their promise at the front of OPEN, that is, the more promising the node, the further toward the front it is in OPEN. In case the promise of the children is not being considered, put them in arbitrary order at the front of OPEN.

(11) Go to (3).

According to the above outline if we can leap-frog with hindsight we do so, otherwise we leap-frog chronologically. Expunging step (7.1) from the outline will prevent any attempt at hindsight leap-frogging: only chronological leap-frogging will remain. In section 11.4.1, we saw how we can force backtracking to find multiple solution paths to a problem. Similarly, after finding a solution path here, we can continue to find multiple solution paths; more specifically, after finding a solution path in step (8) above, we shall delete the destination node generated and then go to step (9).

As an example for multiple solution paths, consider the eight-queens puzzle, which we saw earlier in section 11.4.1 and in Figure 11.22. Now look at Figure 11.25, which gives a specimen heuristic to be employed in a hill-climbing strategy for comparing the promise of sibling nodes.

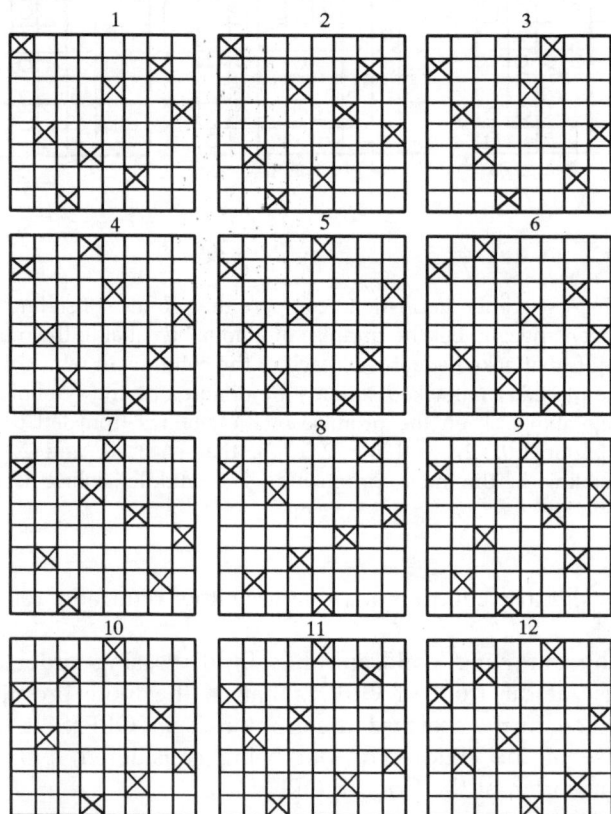

Figure 11.26   A solution from each of the twelve families of solutions for the eight-queens puzzle. Solutions within a family can be obtained from one another by rotation and by mirror images. See, for example, Figure 11.27 for the solutions that are members of the first family above. All families have eight members except the tenth family, which has only four members [see Figure 11.28]. The symbol 'X' denotes a queen.

We can repeatedly force leap-frogging to find the 92 solutions of the puzzle. These solutions can be thought to be members of 12 families. Figure 11.26 displays one member from each of the families. Eleven families have eight members each; one family has four members. This gives (11 × 8) + 4 = 92 solutions. Figure 11.26 cites Figures 11.27 and 11.28, which show how to obtain all the members of each family.

We are not giving the search graph for all the solutions because that will take up far too much space. Should you want to construct the search graph yourself, you may verify your solutions with those given in Figures 11.26 to 11.28.

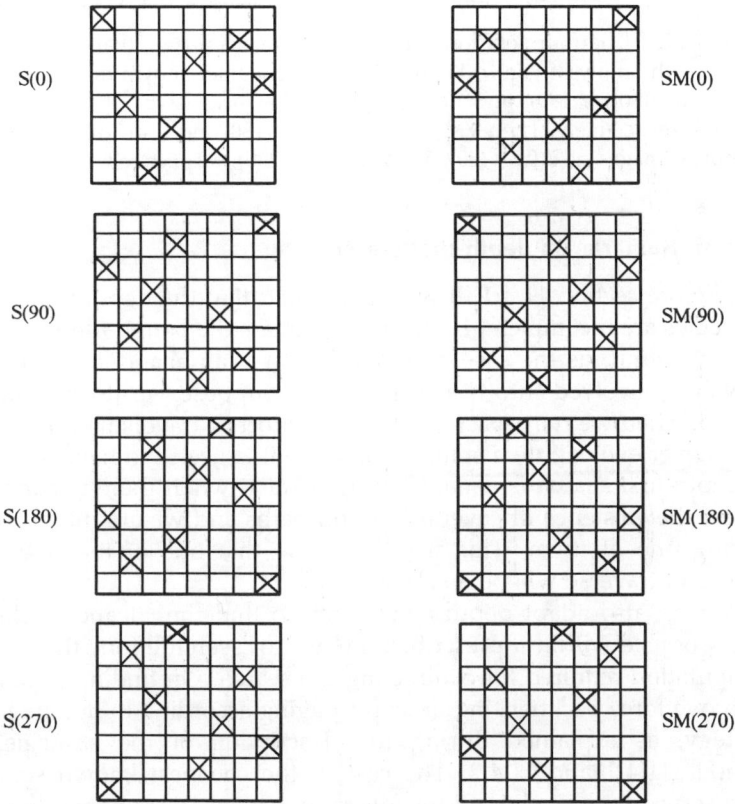

Figure 11.27   The eight solutions of the eight-queens puzzle that are members of the first family of Figure 11.26. S(0) is the member shown in Figure 11.26. To obtain S(90), S(180), and S(270), rotate S(0) clockwise by 90, 180, and 270 degrees, respectively. Then SM(0), SM(90), SM(180), and SM(270) are obtained as mirror images of S(0), S(90), S(180), and S(270), respectively.

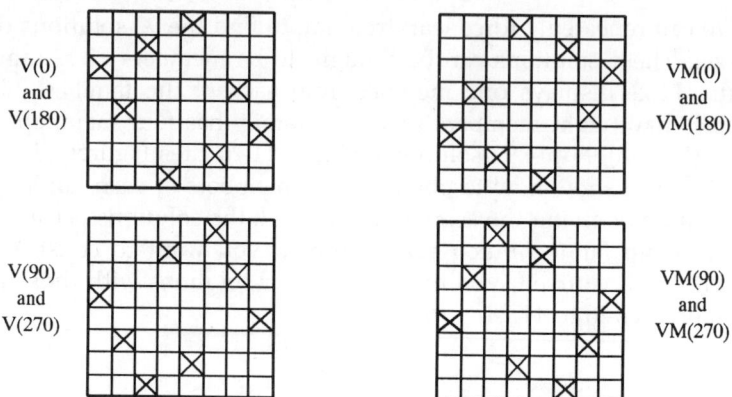

Figure 11.28 The four solutions of the eight-queens puzzle that are members of the tenth family of Figure 11.26. V(0) is the member shown in Figure 11.26. To obtain V(90), V(180), and V(270), rotate V(0) clockwise by 90, 180, and 270 degrees, respectively. Then VM(0), VM(90), VM(180) and VM(270) are obtained as mirror images of V(0), V(90), V(180), and V(270), respectively.

11.4.3   Remarks on depth-first search

Just before section 11.4.1, it was mentioned that the depth-first search strategies are incomplete. If we underestimate the bound (depth-bound or cost-bound, as the case may be) then we can abandon a path that may have evolved into a solution path. Suppose we do not have a bound. Then we may waste substantial effort in traversing a path that may never evolve into a solution path, so it is useful to have a bound.

Depth-first search is usually recommended when there is reason to expect the existence of several solution paths and we are interested in finding one of them. This way we hope that one of the paths we chance to traverse will be a solution path.

We can also adapt depth-first search to find the cheapest solution path possible within a prescribed amount of search effort, that is, the computation required for conducting the search. On finding a solution path, we force backtracking or leap-frogging according to our choice of strategy, as explained during the description of the strategies in sections 11.4.1 and 11.4.2. The cost of the cheapest known solution path serves as a cost-bound for future searching. We continue like this until the prescribed amount of search effort has been consumed. We can replace cheapest by shortest, cost by length and cost-bound by length-bound above, to similarly find the shortest solution path possible within a prescribed amount of search effort.

In the literature, you will also see an alternative version of the hill-climbing strategy discussed in section 11.4.2. In the alternative version, we begin as usual by expanding the source node x_0. From the children of x_0, we heuristically select the most promising child x_1. The other children of x_0 are deleted. Next we expand x_1, select one child x_2, delete the other children of x_1, and so on. From our path of traversal $x_0 x_1 x_2 \ldots$, we can neither leap-frog nor backtrack. Thus the strategy is said to be irrevocable. Because of the fallibility of the heuristic employed in selecting a node from its siblings, the irrevocable version of hill-climbing is more likely to fail in finding a solution path than the leap-frogging version. The irrevocable version will, however, require less memory than the leap-frogging one.

Incidentally, you can view irrevocable hill-climbing as a pruned breadth-first search (see section 11.3.2) in which only one node is retained at each depth. Accordingly, Figure 11.15 illustrates the irrevocable hill-climbing strategy.

11.5 BEST-FIRST SEARCH

Having described breadth-first and depth-first search, we now turn to describing best-first search. We shall assume for the time being that we have some means available to measure the promise of any given node, discussed in section 11.3.2.

We begin a best-first search by expanding the source node. From then on, at any given time, we select that node for expansion which is the best, that is, the most promising, among all the existing unexpanded nodes, thereby giving the search its name: best-first. The children of the node expanded are added to the set of unexpanded nodes. We proceed in this manner

We emphasize that the node for expansion is selected from all the unexpanded nodes then existing, regardless of where they are in the search graph. Contrast this with breadth-first search (section 11.3) in which the node for expansion is selected from only the unexpanded nodes that are at the same depth, and with depth-first search (section 11.4) in which the node for expansion is selected from only the unexpanded nodes that are siblings.

One way to measure the promise of a node x is to estimate the cost of the cheapest solution path constrained to pass through x; in other words, of all the solution paths that may pass through x, we are to estimate the cost of the cheapest of these paths. We discuss this in more detail below. Let:

$g^*(x)$ (pronounced g-star x) be the cost of the cheapest path from the source node to node x, where $g^*(x) \geq 0$;

$h^*(x)$ be the cost of the cheapest path from node x to the destination node, where $h^*(x) \geq 0$; and

$$f^*(x) = g^*(x) + h^*(x).$$

Therefore, $f^*(x)$ is the cost of the cheapest solution path that is constrained to pass through x. During the search, we shall not ordinarily know the value of $f^*(x)$, so we estimate it, and use the estimate to guide us during the search.

Accordingly, let $g(x)$ be the cost of the cheapest known path at any given time from the source node to node x. As the search progresses, we may find more than one path from the source node to x. We shall retain only the cheapest of these, discarding the rest. Hence the value of $g(x)$ may decrease as the search progresses, but the value of $g(x)$ can never be less than $g^*(x)$. Thus $g(x) \geq g^*(x) \geq 0$.

Moreover, let $h(x)$ be an estimate of $h^*(x)$ based on some heuristic, such that $h(x) \geq 0$. We next define

$$f(x) = g(x) + h(x),$$

so that $f(x)$ becomes an estimate of the cheapest solution path that is constrained to pass through x. We can say that $f(x)$ measures the promise of a node; the lower the value of $f(x)$, the better, that is, more promising, x appears to us. For our discussion, we shall be adopting such an $f(x)$ to measure the promise of a node x.

As mentioned above, in best-first search, at any given time we expand the best unexpanded node then existing. Thus in effect we expand the node with the lowest f value from all the unexpanded nodes. Before reading any further, look at Figure 11.29 for two special cases of our best-first search.

[1]   For this search, called the <u>incurred cost</u> search, we assume the h values of all nodes to be zero. Then, for all nodes x, we obtain f(x) = g(x). From all the unexpanded nodes, we thus expand the node that has the lowest g value; that is, the node to which we incurred the lowest cost in traversing from the source node. If all the moves cost the same, then the nodes are expanded depth by depth, as in the unpruned breadth–first search of Section 11.3.1. Incurred cost search is also known in the literature as the <u>uniform cost</u> search.

[2]   For this search, called the <u>predicted cost</u> search, we ignore the g values of all nodes. Then, for all nodes x, we obtain f(x) = h(x). From all the unexpanded nodes, we thus expand the node that has the lowest h value; that is, the node from which we expect the lowest cost in traversing to the destination node. The fewest literals preference strategy [Section 4.2.2] of resolution refutation exemplifies a predicted cost search for deducing the empty clause. Predicted cost search is also known in the literature as the <u>greedy</u> search.

Figure 11.29   Two special cases of our best-first search in which f(x) = g(x) + h(x).

It is an established mathematical result that for all nodes x, if $h(x) \leq h^*(x)$, then the above search strategy is admissible (see Figure 11.14 to refresh your memory). The search strategy is then known in the literature as the A* search strategy. Take note of the following: saying that $h(x) \leq h^*(x)$ for all nodes x is synonymous with saying that h is a lower bound on h^*, that $h(x)$ is never an overestimate of $h^*(x)$, that we are optimistic in h, or that h is an admissible heuristic. We shall next discuss a few details of the A* search strategy.

11.5.1 A* Search

As an example, let us first conduct an A* search to solve the eight-tiles puzzle of Figure 11.12. For simplicity, let every move have unit cost. We define $h(x)$ to be the number of dislocated tiles (defined in Figure 11.16) in node x. Since we shall need at least one move each for every dislocated tile of x to be put in its desired location in the destination node, we can say that h is an admissible heuristic. Figure 11.30 shows the search tree constructed by A*.

For implementing an A* search we need the lists OPEN and CLOSED to store unexpanded and expanded nodes, respectively, similar to those mentioned in sections 11.3.1, 11.3.2 and 11.4.2. Nodes in OPEN will be stored in increasing order of their f values from the front to the back of OPEN: thus the node with the lowest f value will be at the front of OPEN. If several nodes have equal f values, they may be stored in arbitrary order within themselves; nevertheless, it is preferable, but not essential, that if one of these nodes is a destination node, then such a node is stored nearest to the front of OPEN. Doing so requires comparing the node with a destination node before it is stored in OPEN, but it reduces the number of nodes generated to finish the search, since the node picked up from the front of OPEN is expanded if, and only if, it is not a destination node, as can be seen below. For brevity, we shall say that every node in OPEN should be in its **earmarked** position in OPEN. The A* search strategy can then be outlined as follows.

(1) Initialize lists OPEN and CLOSED to empty. Put the source node in OPEN.
(2) If OPEN is empty, then return failure.
(3) Remove the frontmost node x from OPEN.
(4) If x is a destination node, then return successfully with the solution path obtained by using the parentage pointers, as discussed toward the end of section 11.2. (For reasons given immediately below this outline, here we test for a node being a

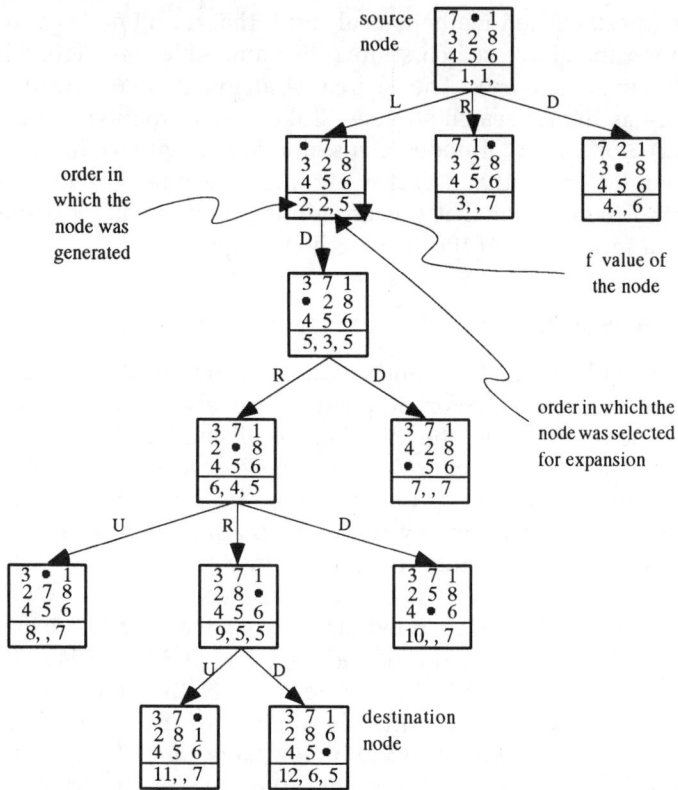

Figure 11.30　An example of A* search for the eight-tiles puzzle. The cost of the cheapest path from a node to the destination node was estimated to be equal to the number of dislocated tiles in the node. The source and destination nodes are as specified in Figure 11.12. Neither any renegade nodes nor any inert nodes were generated. Any recurring nodes generated were deleted; they are not shown above.

destination node before its expansion. This is unlike the breadth-first and depth-first strategies of sections 11.3 and 11.4, wherein we test for a node being a destination node right after its generation.)

(5) Put x in CLOSED.

(6) Expand x.

(7) If no children of x are generated, that is, x is inert, then go to (3).

(8) Delete all those children of x that are either renegade or recurring.

(9) For every surviving child y of x do the following.

(9.1) If a copy of y is neither in OPEN nor in CLOSED, then put y in its earmarked position in OPEN.

(9.2) If a copy y_c of y is either in OPEN or CLOSED then do the following.

    (9.2.1) If $f(y) \geq f(y_c)$, that is, a more costly path through the node has been estimated, then delete y.

    (9.2.2) If $f(y) < f(y_c)$, that is, a cheaper path through the node has been estimated, then delete y_c, and put y in its earmarked position in OPEN (thus, if y_c was in OPEN, then only one copy of the node is retained in OPEN; if y_c was in CLOSED, then it is in effect transferred to OPEN so that later it may be expanded again).

(10) Go to (2).

It can be shown mathematically that, since $h(x) \leq h^*(x)$, a node selected for expansion in step (3) above will appear to be at least as promising as it actually is, if not better; that is to say:

$$f(x) \leq f^*(x).$$

Thus, from the definition of $f(x)$ and $f^*(x)$:

$$(g(x) + h(x)) \leq (g^*(x) + h^*(x)).$$

If the node x selected for expansion in step (3) is a destination node, then $h(x) = h^*(x) = 0$. Hence, from the above equation:

$$g(x) \leq g^*(x).$$

But, in section 11.5, where $g(x)$ and $g^*(x)$ were defined, it was shown that $g(x) \geq g^*(x)$. Therefore

$$g(x) = g^*(x).$$

So when a destination node is selected for expansion in step (3) of the A* search, the cheapest solution path to the destination node has been found.

Step (9) in the A* outline above ensures that at any given time only the cheapest known path to a node is retained, discarding any other path to the node. The step may require substantial computation. Accordingly, in the literature, you may see the mention of the following two alternatives.

.. When a cheaper path to a node that is already in CLOSED is found, instead of transferring the node to OPEN, leave the node in CLOSED but change its parentage pointer and the f values of its descendants as shown in Figure 11.31.

[9]   For every surviving child y of x do:

[9.1]   If a copy of y is neither in OPEN nor in CLOSED, then put y in its earmarked position in OPEN.

[9.2]   If a copy y_C of y is either in OPEN or CLOSED then do:

[9.2.1]   If $f(y) \geq f(y_C)$ then delete y.

[9.2.2]   If $f(y) < f(y_C)$ and y_C is in OPEN, then delete y_C and put y in its earmarked position in OPEN.

[9.2.3]   If $f(y) < f(y_C)$ and y_C is in CLOSED, then delete y, change the parentage pointer of y_C to designate x to be the new parent of y_C, and update the f values of all descendants of y_C.

Figure 11.31   An alternative to step [9] in the A* outline of section 11.5.1. Substep [9.2.2] of section 11.5.1 has been replaced above by substeps [9.2.2] and [9.2.3]. The other substeps remain the same.

2. Allow the presence of multiple copies of a node in OPEN and CLOSED so that step (9) reads: Put every surviving child of *x* in its earmarked position in OPEN.

You may adopt any of the above alternatives depending on the particular problem you are trying to solve.

11.5.2   Informedness of A* search

Search strategies in general can be viewed as being either **informed** or **uninformed**. Strategies that are informed employ some heuristics specific to the problem being solved. Uninformed strategies do not employ any heuristics at all; the unpruned breadth-first search of section 11.3.1 exemplifies an uninformed strategy. In the literature, uninformed strategies are also known as **general-purpose, weak** or **blind** strategies.

Let us assume that to solve a particular problem we adopt two A* search strategies called A_1^* and A_2^*, such that for a node *x*

1. A_1^* uses the equation $f_1(x) = g_1(x) + h_1(x)$, and
2. A_2^* uses the equation $f_2(x) = g_2(x) + h_2(x)$.

Remember that both h_1 and h_2 are admissible heuristics, that is,

$h_1(x) \leq h^*(x)$, and
$h_2(x) \leq h^*(x)$.

Suppose that for all nodes *x* that are not destination nodes,

$h_2(x) > h_1(x)$.

Then it is an established mathematical result that A_2^* **dominates** A_1^*. This means that every node expanded by A_2^* will also be expanded by A_1^*, but the converse need not be so. Thus the search graph of A_2^* may not be equal to the search graph of A_1^*. In other words, the number of nodes in the search graph of A_2^* will be less than or equal to the number of nodes in the search graph of A_1^*. We say that the A_2^* search is **more informed** than the A_1^* search, or that h_2 is a **more informed** heuristic than h_1.

Consider, for example, the eight-tiles puzzle such that all moves cost the same, where for a node x

1. $h_1(x) = 0$, as in the incurred cost search of Figure 11.29, and
2. $h_2(x) = $ the number of dislocated tiles in x, as illustrated in Figure 11.16.

The search graph with $h_1(x)$ will be the same as that shown in Figure 11.15 for unpruned breadth-first search, and the search graph with $h_2(x)$ will be the same as that shown in Figure 11.30. Clearly, every node expanded in Figure 11.30 is also expanded in Figure 11.15, but it is not so conversely.

From the above, we can say that to enable an A^* to construct the smallest possible search graph, we should have h as the highest possible lower bound on h^*; in other words, we should be optimistic in h as pessimistically as possible.

In the rare instance that $h(x) = h^*(x)$ for all nodes x, the f values of the different nodes will be the same as we traverse the solution path: as we get nearer to the destination node, the h value of the node will decrease by the same amount that the g value increases. We shall be expanding only those nodes that lie on the cheapest solution path.

It may not, however, always be true that the smaller the search graph, the less is the computation required for the search, because A^* can expand the same node more than once, as is apparent from step (9) in the A^* outline of section 11.5.1. Each such expansion increases the computation required, but if we impose some constraints on the heuristic h, then we can ensure that A^* never expands the same node more than once. These constraints are discussed in the section below.

11.5.3 A monotonic heuristic for A^* search

A heuristic function h is said to be **monotonic** if, for all nodes x and y, where y is a child of x,

$h(x) \leq$ Cost of arc from x to $y + h(y)$,

and for a destination node z', $h(z') = 0$. A heuristic function h is said to be **consistent** if, for all nodes x and z, where z is a descendant of x,

$h(x) \leq$ Cost of cheapest path from x to $z + h(z)$.

Since every child of x is also a descendant of x, we can say that if h is consistent, then h is monotonic. Moreover, it can be shown by induction that if h is monotonic, then h is consistent. A heuristic function h is accordingly monotonic if, and only if, it is consistent.

Suppose we have a monotonic heuristic function h. Because h is also consistent from the above discussion, we can say that for any node x

$$h(x) \leq \text{Cost of cheapest path from } x \text{ to the destination node } z' + h(z')$$
$$= \text{Cost of cheapest path from } x \text{ to the destination node (since } h(z') = 0)$$
$$= h^*(x).$$

Hence $h(x) \leq h^*(x)$, that is, h is admissible. Therefore, if a heuristic function h is monotonic, then it is admissible, but if h is admissible, then it need not be monotonic. To conduct an A* search, it is thus sufficient for the heuristic function to be monotonic.

It is an established mathematical result that when employing a monotonic heuristic function h, if A* expands a node x, then A* has already found the cheapest path from the source node to x. Hence $g(x) = g^*(x)$, so A* never expands the same node more than once. Thus we never need to check whether a copy of a newly generated node is in the list CLOSED (see the A* outline of section 11.5.1) since such a copy cannot be in CLOSED. We can accordingly expunge all reference to CLOSED in step (9) of the A* outline.

It is also an established mathematical result that if h is monotonic, then any other admissible search strategy using the same h for a particular problem would require computation at least as much as A* does.

Let us summarize the above discussion. For A* to construct the smallest possible search graph such that no node in it is expanded more than once, you should ensure that

1. the heuristic function h is monotonic, and
2. h is the highest possible lower bound on h^*.

But it may not be useful to have an h so complicated that evaluating $h(x)$ requires so much computation as to neutralize any computation saved in constructing the above search graph. Figure 11.32 shows a typical plot of the computation required to conduct a search.

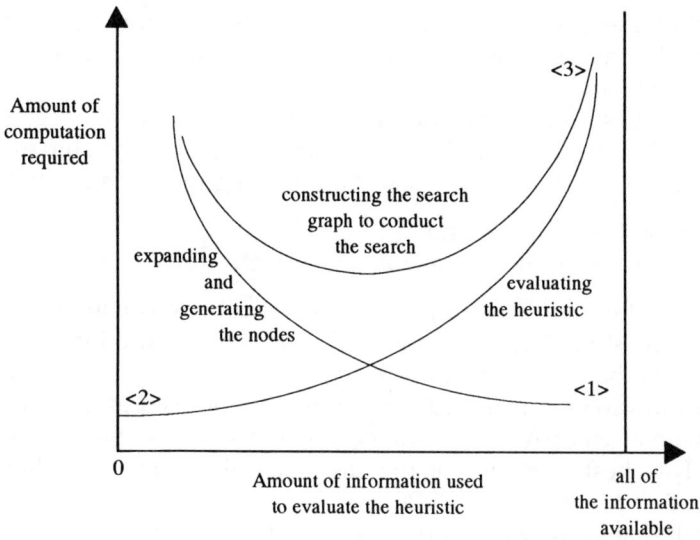

Figure 11.32 Plot ⟨3⟩ shows the usual trend of the computation required to conduct the search versus the amount of information used to evaluate the heuristic employed for the search. Plot ⟨3⟩ sums plots ⟨1⟩ and ⟨2⟩.

11.6 DEVELOPING HEURISTICS

From our discussion of the different search strategies, we can see the importance of heuristics in solving a problem. Heuristics help us solve a problem usually

1. when no algorithm to solve the problem is known (for example, UNPERS in section 9.3.1), or
2. when the algorithm known demands so much computation that the algorithm becomes impractical (for example, the exhaustive search in section 11.2).

Heuristics customarily take the form of either prodrules, as in UNPERS, or of a mathematical function that maps a state/node of the problem into a numeric value, as in the dislocated-tile heuristic of section 11.3.2.

There is no universal method to develop the heuristics that may help us solve a given problem. How to develop heuristics is itself a heuristic. Typically, you may consider solving a problem by using the experience you may have gained from solving similar problems.

A method often recommended to develop heuristics for solving a given problem is to think of a similar problem that is a simplified version of the problem given. The simplified version can often be obtained by relaxing, or loosening, some of the constraints of the original problem.

For an illustration, consider the eight-tiles problem as given in Figure 11.12. We can say that, in a move, a tile can be shifted from location p_1 to location p_2 provided the following two constraints hold:

1. the empty cell is at p_2, and
2. p_2 is either vertically or horizontally adjacent to p_1.

To simplify the problem suppose we relax both the constraints. A tile can thus be shifted from location p_1 to any other location p_2 in one move. Then the number of moves required to go from a given state to a specified destination state will be the number of dislocated tiles in the given state as compared with the destination state, as shown in Figure 11.16. This bestowed on us the dislocated-tile heuristic, which we employed as $h(x)$ in Figure 11.30.

An alternative way to simplify the eight-tile puzzle is to relax only the first constraint above. To shift a tile from location p_1 to location p_2 in one move, p_2 should thus be either verticaly or horizontally adjacent to p_1. Hence the number of moves required to shift a tile from its location of row r_1 and column c_1 in a given state to its location of row r_2 and column c_2 in a specified destination state will be

$$|r_2 - r_1| + |c_2 - c_1|,$$

which is known as the **city-block**, or **manhattan**, distance for the tile. Then the number of moves required to go from the given state to the destination state will be the sum of city-block distances for the dislocated tiles of the given state. An example is show in Figure 11.33. This bestows on us the city-block heuristic, which we could have employed as $h(x)$ in Figure 11.30.

Suppose the heuristic function h developed with the simplified problem is monotonic. Then, as mentioned in section 11.5.3, the heuristic function h will also be consistent. Accordingly, for all nodes x and z in the simplified problem, where z is a descendant of x,

$$h(x) \le \text{Cost of cheapest path from } x \text{ to } z + h(z).$$

Since the original problem is more constrained than the simplified problem, the cost of the cheapest path from x to z in the actual problem will either stay the same or increase. Thus if h is used as the heuristic function in the original problem, h will remain consistent. Hence, as shown in section 11.5.3, the heuristic function h will be admissible.

In closing this section, we can say that the above method of

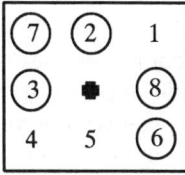

a given state x

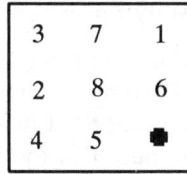

the specified
destination state

The dislocated tiles of x have been shown circled. We can then evaluate the sum of the city-block distances for the dislocated tiles of x, as follows:

the dislocated tile stamped with	location of tile in state x		location of tile in destination state		City-block distance of the tile $= \lvert r_1 - r_2 \rvert + \lvert c_1 - c_2 \rvert$
	row r_1	cloumn c_1	row r_2	column c_2	
7	1	1	1	2	1
2	1	2	2	1	2
3	2	1	1	1	1
8	2	3	2	2	1
6	3	3	2	3	1
Sum of the city-block distances for the dislocated tiles of state x =					6

Figure 11.33 An example to evaluate the sum of the city-block distances for the dislocated tiles of a given state in the eight-tiles puzzle.

developing heuristics from a simplified version of a given problem may be useful in developing admissible heuristics for the problem as originally given.

11.7 MODIFICATIONS TO BEST-FIRST SEARCH

It can happen that the amount of computation (for instance, in expanding the nodes and in evaluating the heuristic function) required to search for the cheapest solution path is so high that it may be more practical to search for a solution path of reasonable cost, provided the computation required for the search is reduced. There is no known precise definition of what constitutes reasonable cost: the definition of reasonable cost may vary from problem to problem. Such a solution path is often referred to in the literature as a **satisficing** solution path. In sections 11.7.1–11.7.5 below, we describe five modifications to best-first search to reduce the computation required for the search.

11.7.1   Bandwith search

In this modification, we let the heuristic function h be inadmissible if it requires less computation than if it were admissible, and if it is likely to reduce the number of node expansions. Suppose we overestimate $h(x)$ by some amount e at the most; that is to say, for any node x,

$$h(x) - h^*(x) \le e.$$

It is an established mathematical result that then the cost of the solution path found by the best-first search will not exceed the cost of the cheapest solution by more than e; in other words,

Cost of solution path found $-$ Cost of the cheapest solution path $\le$ e. This is known as the **admissibility of bandwidth** e. Moreover, the search and the heuristic function are both known as e-**admissible**.

11.7.2   Weighted search

Another modification to the best-first search is to allot weights to the functions g and h used in the search. Accordingly, in this **weighted search**, rather than evaluating

$$f(x) = g(x) + h(x),$$

we evaluate

$$f_W(x) = (1 - W)g(x) + Wh(x),$$

where W is a weighting coefficient, such that $0 \le W \le 1$. For $0 \le W < 0.5$, the search tends toward the incurred cost search, and for $0.05 < W \le 1$, toward the predicted cost search, shown in Figure 11.29. Having $W = 0.5$ is of no interest since it is akin to alloting no weights at all to the functions g and h. The value of W that will most reduce the computation for search is usually determined by experimentation with the class of problems that are expected to be solved by the weighted search.

11.7.3   Staged search

In this modification to the best-first search, we frequently examine the list OPEN, which contains the unexpanded nodes. We then retain only a subset (those with the lowest f values) of the nodes in OPEN. The remaining nodes are then deleted. The computation required for the search is reduced since the list of unexpanded nodes to be maintained in sorted order is pruned. Moreover, the pruning of unexpanded nodes may be useful when we notice while searching that the computer memory is about to be exhausted. Thus, in effect, the size of OPEN has been restricted. The search, however, becomes inadmissible. This search is known in the literature as **staged** search.

11.7.4   Limited children search

In another modification to the best-first search, we retain only a subset (those with the lowest f values) of the children generated from a node. The retained children are put in their respective earmarked positions in OPEN, the remaining children being deleted. The search is inadmissible. In the literature where children are called **successors**, this search is then known as the **limitation of successors** search.

11.7.5   Bidirectional search

In this modification to the best-first search, we conduct a bidirectional search by mingling two unidirectional searches: a forward search (or **foresearch**, for short, from the source node to the destination node) with a backward search (or **backsearch**, for short, from the destination node to the source node). When implementing a bidirectional search on the same processor,

1. we can alternate node expansions between foresearch and backsearch; or
2. at any particular time, we can proceed with the search that has fewer expanded nodes, thus attempting to prevent either search graph from becoming very much larger than the other.

We continue like this until there exists a node z that has been generated by both the searches. The solution path is obtained by concatenating the path from the source node to z, manifested by the foresearch, with the reverse of the path from the destination node to z, manifested by the backsearch.

Remember from section 11.3.1 that the number of nodes in a search tree grows exponentially with the depth of the tree. Therefore, the number of nodes in one search tree (constructed by a unidirectional search) of depth, say, D will be more than the number of nodes in two search trees (constructed by a bidirectional search) each of depth approximately $D/2$. Accordingly, the computation required by a bidirectional search is expected to be less than the computation required by a unidirectional search.

Be aware, however, that if no solution path is found, then bidirectional search will construct two search trees, each of depth approximately D. Compare this with a unidirectional search, which will construct a single search tree of depth D. In such a case, bidirectional search wil require about double the computation of a unidirectional search.

Moreover, note that bidirectional search can be attempted only when both the source and the destination nodes are explicitly specified. Consider, for example, the eight-queens puzzle mentioned in section 11.4.1. In the puzzle, the source node is explicitly specified: a chess-board with nothing placed on it. The destination node, however, is not explicitly specified: only the constraints are specified, according to which the queens are to be so placed such that no queen attacks another. We obviously cannot attempt a bidirectional search to solve the eight-queens puzzle. But, to solve the eight-tiles puzzle, wherein both the source and destination nodes are explicitly specified, as in Figure 11.12, we can attempt a bidirectional search.

As you have undoubtedly realized, a bidirectional search can also be implemented on two processors communicating with each other, one processor conducting the foresearch, and the other the backsearch. Suppose at any time during the search, $x_1, x_2, \ldots, x_k$ are the unexpanded nodes in the foresearch, and $y_1, y_2, \ldots, y_m$ are the unexpanded nodes in the backsearch. Then in the foresearch, we expand the x node that has the least f value among all the x nodes; similarly, in the backsearch, we expand the y node that has the least f value, among all the y nodes. Alternatively, we can expand that pair of nodes x_i and y_j for which $f'(x_i, y_j)$ is the minimum over $1 \leq i \leq k$ and $1 \leq j \leq m$, such that

$$f'(x_i, y_j) = g_1(x_i) + h'(x_i, y_j) + g_2(y_j),$$

where

$g_1(x_i)$ is the cost of the cheapest known path from source node to x_i;

$h'(x_i, y_j)$ is an estimate of the cheapest path from x_i to y_j, the estimate being based on some heuristic; and

$g_2(y_j)$ is the cost of the cheapest known path from y_j to the destination node.

The above equation for $f'(x_i, y_j)$ is an extension of the equation used by the unidirectional best-first search of section 11.5. With the above equation, we expect to reduce computation by expanding few nodes, but this reduction may be neutralized by the computation required to evaluate $f'(x_i, y_j)$ for different node pairs x_i and y_j.

Together with the bidirectional search, we can also adopt any of the other modifications described in sections 11.7.1–11.7.4. Thus, for instance, according to section 11.7.3, we can prune unexpanded nodes in the foresearch and backsearch components of bidirectional search.

11.8 APPRAISING THE PERFORMANCE OF A SEARCH STRATEGY

In this section, we discuss two measures that are often used to appraise the performance of a search strategy. Let T be the total number of nodes in the search graph, not counting the source node; note that the destination node is being counted. Let D be the length of the solution path. Alternatively, D is the number of nodes in the solution path, counting the destination node, but not the source node. If the solution path is the shortest solution path, then D will also be the depth of the destination node.

Then we define one measure of search performance as **penetrance** P by the equation

$$P = \frac{D}{T}.$$

If the search graph contains only those nodes that are on the solution path, then $T = D$, and hence $P = 1$; otherwise, $T > D$, and hence $0 < P < 1$.

The other measure of search performance is **branching factor** B, where B denotes the constant number of children each non-leaf node would have in a tree that contains T nodes (not counting the root, which corresponds to the source node), such that the deepest nodes in the tree are at depth D. The tree would have B nodes at the first depth, B^2 nodes at the second depth, and so on. Thus,

$$T = B + B^2 + \ldots + B^D$$
$$= \frac{B(B^D - 1)}{B - 1}.$$

When the search graph contains only those nodes that are on the solution path then, since $T = D$, we obtain $B = 1$. Otherwise, $T > D$, and hence $B > 1$.

From this discussion of the values of P and B, we can say that:

1. $B = 1$ if, and only if, $P = 1$; and
2. $B > 1$ if, and only if, $0 < P < 1$.

It can be informally said that B signifies a search tree's bushiness, and P its elongatedness.

Now let us consider an example. Suppose a search strategy solves a given problem and we observe that $T = 71$ and $D = 14$. We are to evaluate P and B. We evaluate P from the equation:

$$P = \frac{D}{T}$$
$$= \frac{14}{71}$$
$$= 0.197.$$

Next, we evaluate B from the equation:

$$T = \frac{B(B^D - 1)}{B - 1}$$

that is,

$$71 = \frac{B(B^{14} - 1)}{B - 1}$$

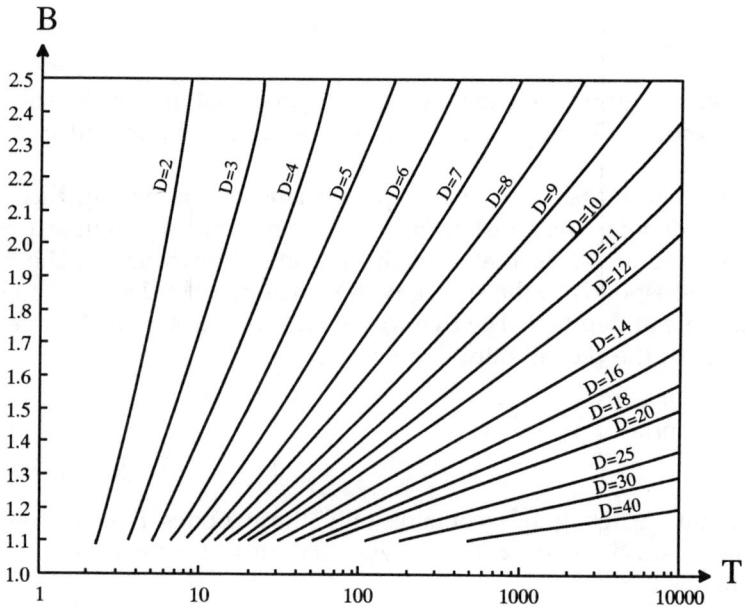

As mentioned in Section 11.8: $T = \dfrac{B(B^D - 1)}{B - 1}$

Figure 11.34 Plots of B versus T for the various values of D. The axis for T is on a log scale.

Calculating the value of B from the above equation is complicated. Instead, we read the value of B from Figure 11.34, because it is easier to do so. Accordingly, we obtain $B = 1.2$.

We can use the above value of B to estimate T', the number of nodes that would correspondingly be in the search graph if the search strategy were to solve an altered version of the problem, typically, different source and destination nodes. Let us assume that the branching factor remains unchanged, and that the length D' of the solution path is expected to be 20. Then

$$T' = \frac{B(B^{20} - 1)}{B}$$
$$= \frac{1.2(1.2^{20} - 1)}{0.2} \text{ since B = 1.2}$$
$$= 224,$$

and the corresponding penetrance

$$P' = \frac{D'}{T'}$$
$$= \frac{20}{224}$$
$$= 0.09.$$

Instead of doing the above calculations, we could have read the value of T' from Figure 11.34, and the value of P' from Figure 11.35. The figures may be helpful to you should you need them.

Having read of solving problems by searching the state space in this chapter, you will read of solving problems by decomposition in the next chapter.

11.9   EXERCISES

1. Write a program to solve the problem of λ missionaries and λ cannibals, as delineated in section 11.1, for $\lambda = 1, 2, 3, \ldots, 10$. Alter the program to solve the problem with the following new constraints: (a) the boat, which requires one person to row, cannot carry more than three persons at a time; (b) if the number of missionaries on a bank is one or more, then the number of cannibals on that bank cannot be more than the number of missionaries on the bank; and (c) if the number of missionaries in the boat is one or

P

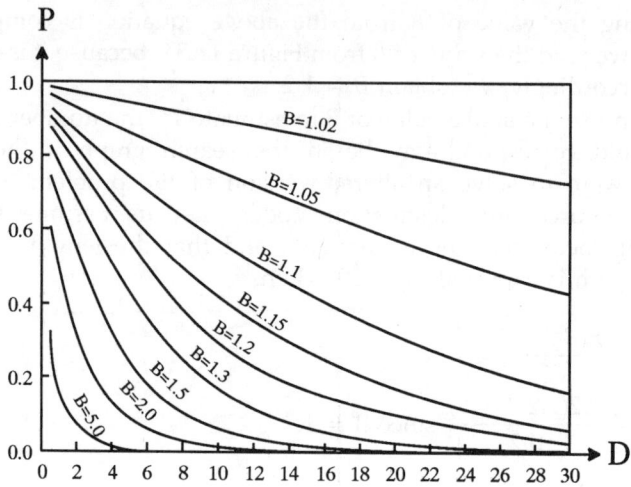

As mentioned in Section 11.8: $P = \dfrac{D}{T}$ and $T = \dfrac{B(B^D - 1)}{B - 1}$

Therefore, by algebraic manipulation: $P = \dfrac{D(B - 1)}{B(B^D - 1)}$

Figure 11.35   Plots of P versus D for various values of B.

more, then the number of cannibals in the boat cannot be more than the number of missionaries in the boat.

2. Consider the addition below with upper case letters:

```
    I  T  S
    S  E  T
       A  S
  _____

    T  E  S  T
```

Each letter denotes a numerical degit from 0 to 9. No two distinct letters denote the same digit, that is, distinct letters denote distinct digits. No number is written with its leftmost digit as zero. The addition is performed under the usual constraints of arithmetic. Which numerical digit is denoted by each letter? Which search strategy did you adopt? Why did you choose the strategy you adopted?

3. You are given two empty jugs whose capacities are X and Y litres,

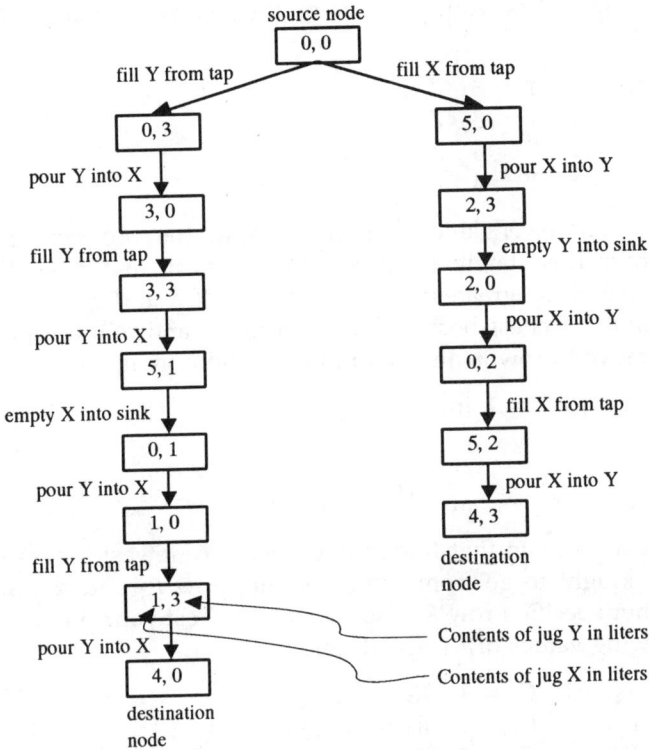

Figure 11.36 Two solution paths for the third exercise with specimen values of X = 5, Y = 3, and Z = 4. The two solution paths are not of the same length. For brevity, we are referring to the jug with capacity X litres as jug X, and the jug with capacity Y litres as jug Y. In a destination node, the contents of jug X should be 4 litres, since Z = 4. To prevent cluttering the figure, only the nodes on the solution paths are shown.

respectively, such that $X \neq Y$. A move is delineated to be any of the following:
(a) fill either jug with water from a tap;
(b) empty either jug into a sink;
(c) pour water from one jug into the other jug, until either the jug being poured from is empty, or the jug being poured into is full.

You are to measure off Z litres of water in either jug, where $Z \leq$ max(X,Y). Figure 11.36 shows an example. Note that the values of X, Y and Z are all positive integers. Write a program that finds the solution of the fewest moves possible, for some specified values of

X, Y and Z. Test your program on the following values of X, Y and Z:

$$X = 4 \quad Y = 3 \quad Z = 2$$
$$X = 7 \quad Y = 3 \quad Z = 2$$
$$X = 7 \quad Y = 4 \quad Z = 5$$
$$X = 8 \quad Y = 4 \quad Z = 5$$

After you have gained experience with the program, prove or disprove this statement: a solution exists if, and only if, Z is a multiple of the greatest common divisor of X and Y.

4. On an 8 × 8 chess-board a knight in row r_1 and column c_1 can go in one move to row r_2 and column c_2 if, and only if,

$$|r_1 - r_2| = 1 \text{ and } |c_1 - c_2| = 2,$$

or

$$|r_1 - r_2| = 2 \text{ and } |c_1 - c_2| = 1.$$

Write a program that finds the sequence of fewest moves possible for a knight to go from some specified row R_1 and column C_1 to another specified row R_2 and column C_2. Test your program on the following values of R_1, C_1, R_2 and C_2:

$$R_1 = 1 \quad C_1 = 1 \quad R_2 = 8 \quad C_2 = 8$$
$$R_1 = 1 \quad C_1 = 1 \quad R_2 = 7 \quad C_2 = 7$$
$$R_1 = 4 \quad C_1 = 5 \quad R_2 = 4 \quad C_2 = 4$$
$$R_1 = 2 \quad C_1 = 3 \quad R_2 = 1 \quad C_2 = 3$$
$$R_1 = 2 \quad C_1 = 3 \quad R_2 = 1 \quad C_2 = 4$$

Remember that all values of rows and columns are constrained to be integers from 1 to 8. Assume that the knight is the only piece on the chess-board.

5. Compare the fallibility of the following three heuristics for the eight-queens puzzle: the promise of a node is equal to the
   (a) reciprocal of the number of squares in the longest diagonal through the queen placed last;
   (b) total number of unattacked squares on the chess-board; or
   (c) minimum of the number of unattacked squares in each of the columns in which the queens are yet to be placed (note that this heuristic was employed in Figure 11.25).

6. An array X is of eight elements X(1) to X(8). You are to assign distinct positive integers 1 to 8 to the eight elements of the array such that

$$\text{if } |i - j| = m, \text{ then } |X(i) - X(j)| \neq m.$$

A specimen assignment is $\langle 1, 5, 8, 6, 3, 7, 2, 4 \rangle$, which signifies that $X(1) = 1$, $X(2) = 5$, ..., $X(8) = 4$. Write a program to find all possible assignments by conducting each of these: a breadth-first search, a depth-first search with backtracking, and a depth-first search with leap-frogging. Since no search terminates after finding one solution, but continues to find all solutions, you will have to modify the corresponding search outlines given in sections 11.3 and 11.4.

7. Give the step by step outline for the irrevocable version of the hill-climbing strategy discussed in section 11.4.3.

8. To solve a particular problem, suppose that you have developed monotonic heuristic functions h_1, h_2, ..., h_n that are mutually independent. Since they are monotonic they will be admissible too. Say you decided to calculate the h value of a node x from the equation

$$h(x) = \max(h_1(x), h_2(x), \ldots, h_n(x)).$$

This is your attempt to make h the highest possible lower bound on h^*. Clearly, $h(x)$ is admissible. Is it monotonic? Give reasons for your answer.

9. In section 11.6, two heuristics for the eight-tiles puzzle were developed: the dislocated-tile heuristic and the city-block heuristic. Is the city-block heuristic more informed than the dislocated-tile heuristic? Give reasons for your answer.

10. The transformation from the source state to the destination state as specified in Figure 11.12 for the eight-tiles puzzle can be depicted by the following four permutations:

(7 3 2 8 6 0)   (1)   (4)   (5)

The leftmost permutation can be read as follows: tile 7 in the source state is to go where tile 3 is in the destination state; tile 3 in the source state is to go where tile 2 is the destination state, ..., and the empty cell (written as 0 above) in the source state is to go where tile 7 is in the destination state. You can similarly read the other permutations. Since the leftmost permutation above contains 6 (an even number) elements, it is called an even-cardinality permutation. The other permutations are correspondingly of odd-cardinality. Argue for or against the following statement regarding the eight-tiles puzzle: A destination state can be reached from a source state if, and only if, the city-block distance between the empty cells in the two states and the number of even-cardinality permutations are both odd, or both even. The statement holds for Figure 11.12 because the city-block distance is 3 and the number of

Buildings	Cafeteria	Dispensary	Gym	Laboratory	Library
Cafeteria	0	120	130 ·	70	155
Dispensary	120	0	60	105	65
Gym	130	60	0	90	110
Laboratory	70	105	90	0	95
Library	155	65	110	95	0

Figure 11.37   Distances in metres between buildings for exercise 12; the distance between the cafeteria and the gym is, for instance, 130 metres. A route exists between every pair of buildings. The routes do not necessarily run in straight lines.

even-cardinality permutations is 1, both thus being odd. Does it hold in general? If not, can you develop some other statement? If so, do so.

11. Arbitrarily choosing a set of source and destination states for the eight-tiles puzzle, write programs to
   (a) determine the value of the weight W that most reduces the computation required for weighted search (discussed in section 11.7.2); and
   (b) compare the average computation required for unidirectional search with that for bidirectional search (discussed in section 11.7.5).

12. Every morning after breakfast in the cafeteria building you walk to visit once each of the following buildings: dispensary, gym, laboratory and library. You then walk back to the cafeteria for lunch. Figure 11.37 shows the distances between these buildings along routes on which you are constrained to walk. Write a program conducting a best-first search to find the sequence in which you should visit the buildings so that you have to walk the least possible. Would it be more efficient to solve the problem by a bidirectional search? Explain your answer.

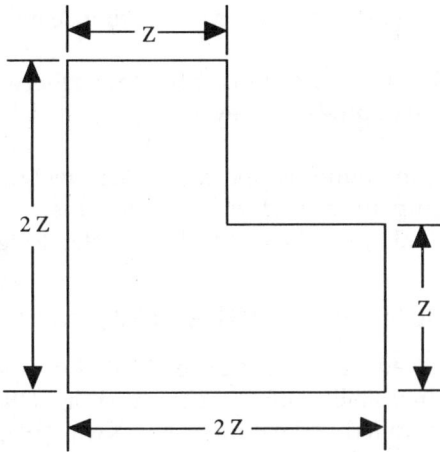

Figure 11.38 The L-shaped sheet required to solve the exercise 14. The dimensions of the sheet are shown above. Note that the area of the sheet is $3Z^2$, so the area of each segment will be $3Z^2/4$.

13. Draw manually the search graph to search exhaustively for the solution of the λ franc and λ pound coins puzzle, defined in Figure 11.7, where $\lambda = 2$. Then write a program to solve the puzzle for $\lambda = 2, 3, \ldots, 6$ by conducting a best-first search. For each value of λ find the cheapest solution path in which a coin hop costs three units and a coin slide costs one unit. Find also the shortest solution path for each value of λ.

14. You are given an L-shaped sheet as shown in Figure 11.38. Mark the sheet with dotted lines to divide the plate into four L-shaped segments of equal areas. Solve the problem manually. Can the problem be solved by any of the search strategies described in this chapter? If yes, how? If not, why not?

15. You are given 12 identical-looking coins. Eleven of the coins weigh the same. One coin, being a counterfeit, is either slightly lighter or slightly heavier. Using a two-pan scale, weigh the coins against one another so that in three weighings, you can detect the counterfeit coin, and whether it is lighter or heavier.

16. Comment on the effectiveness of appraising the performance of a search strategy by branching factor and penetrance. Can you suggest other measures? If so, do so, giving reasons as to why you consider them to be effective in appraising the performance of a search strategy.

17. Suppose you are given the following search strategy.
    (a) Set the depth-bound to be 1.

(b) Conduct a depth-first with backtracking search, as described in section 11.4.1.

(c) If a solution path is found, then stop; otherwise, increase the value of the depth-bound by 1.

(d) Go to (b).

Thus the depth-bound is increased iteratively. Is the strategy complete? Compare its performance with the unpruned breadth-first (section 11.3.1) for the eight-tiles puzzle of Figure 11.12.

11.10 SUGGESTIONS FOR FURTHER READING

Pearl (1984) reviewed search strategies. Nilsson (1980) presented a proof for the admissibility of A* search. Korf (1989) advanced a modified A* and called it real-time A*. Kwa (1989) described an admissible bidirectional search strategy. Polya (1957) discussed heuristics for solving mathematical problems.

1. Korf, R. E. (1989) Real-time heuristic search, *Artificial Intelligence*, **42**[2–3], 189–211.
2. Kwa, J. B. H. (1989) BS*: an admissible bidirectional staged search algorithm, *Artificial Intelligence*, **38**[1], 95–109.
3. Nilsson, N. J. (1980) *Principles of Artificial Intelligence*, Tioga Publishing Company, Palo Alto, California.
4. Pearl, J. (1984) *Heuristics: Intelligent Search Strategies for Computer Problem Solving*, Addison-Wesley, Reading, Massachusetts.
5. Polya, G. (1975) *How to Solve It* (2nd edition), Doubleday Anchor Books, Garden City, New York.

12

Solving problems by searching decompositions

12.1 INTRODUCTION

Chapter 11 presented the solving of problems by searching their state spaces. This chapter will present the solving of problems by searching their decompositions. Much of our terminology and notion will be the same as in Chapter 11. Therefore, we shall assume you have mastered that chapter.

Often a problem can be split into subproblems such that solving the subproblems leads us to solving the problem. In section 9.2.1, for example, the problem of packing a suitcase was split into two subproblems:

1. check the articles that are to be taken on the trip;
2. put the articles into the suitcase.

To solve a given problem by decomposition we split the problem into a set of subproblems. Each subproblem is expected to be simpler to solve than the given problem. We then solve the given problem by solving the subproblems. A subproblem can, of course, be further decomposed. We proceed this way until we obtain a set of **terminal** problems, that is, problems whose solutions we know; terminal problems are also referred to in the literature as **primitive** problems. In other words, the problem originally given is repeatedly decomposed into simpler and simpler problems, until we obtain terminal problems.

12.2 AND/OR GRAPHS

Problem decomposition is represented by kinds of graphs called AND/OR graphs, in which nodes denote problems to be solved. The inference nets you saw earlier in Figures 9.10–9.14 exemplified AND/OR graphs. You should look at those figures to refresh your memory and to get a preliminary idea about AND/OR graphs, which we shall

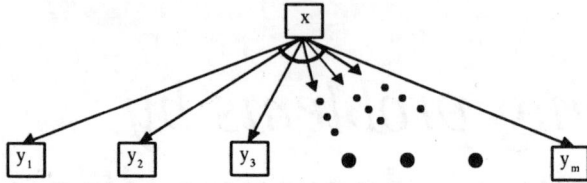

Figure 12.1 In an AND/OR graph representing problem decomposition, a node denotes a problem. A circular mark joining the arcs denotes conjunction [*and*]. The problem denoted by the node x above has been decomposed into a conjunction of m subproblems, denoted by the y nodes. To solve node x [which is a short form of saying, to solve the problem denoted by node x], we should solve each of the y nodes. The m arcs are collectively called a connector, whose cardinality is m, and which is directed from x to the y nodes. The y nodes are the children of their parent x and are said to be *sired* by the connector. A problem can be decomposed into alternative sets of subproblems. This is illustrated in Figure 12.2.

be discussing in this section. As the figures show, now and then a circular mark joins some of the arcs in an AND/OR graph. The purpose of the circular mark and some additional notation is explained in Figures 12.1–12.3.

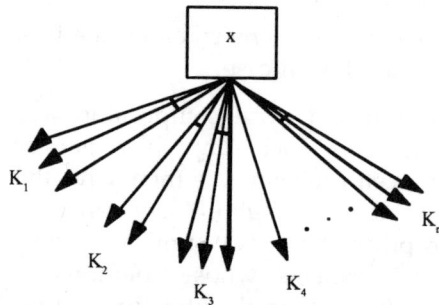

Figure 12.2 The problem denoted by the node x above has been decomposed into n alternative sets of subproblems. This is indicated by the connectors K_1, $K_2, \ldots, K_n$ directed from x. The cardinality of each connector may be different. When the cardinality of a connector is 1 [as K_4 above], then the circular mark joining the arcs of the connector is obviously not shown. On expanding x, we generate all its children sired by all the connectors directed from x. Then to solve node x, we need to solve all the children of x sired by any one of the connectors from it. Put another way, we need to solve all the children of x sired by K_1, or all the children of x sired by $K_2, \ldots$, or all the children of x sired by K_n. To remove any misconception, the above explanation is made more specific in Figure 12.3.

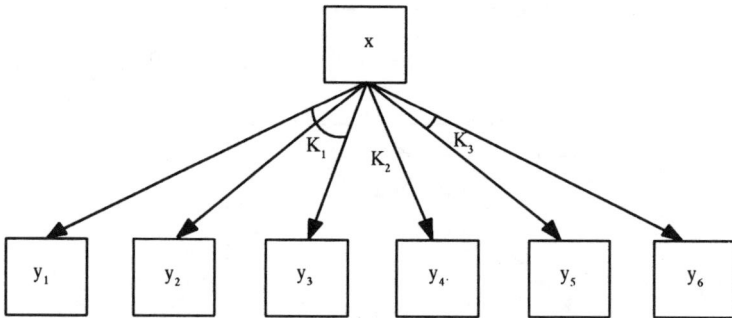

Figure 12.3 By expanding a given node x, say, we generated six children y_1 to y_6 sired by the connectors K_1 to K_3, as shown above. Then to solve x, we need to solve y_1 and y_2 and y_3; or we need to solve y_4; or we need to solve y_5 and y_6. Typically, we shall select one of the connectors and solve the children sired by that connector. The cost of the solution may depend on the connector we select. As discussed later in section 12.3, we may often be required to find the cheapest solution of x.

As a preparatory example, consider the following problem from integral calculus:

$$\int (2t + \sec^2 t \sin^2 t + 7)\, dt.$$

The problem can be decomposed into the following three subproblems:

$$\int 2t\, dt + \int \sec^2 t \sin^2 t\, dt + \int 7\, dt.$$

The solution of the problem by decomposition is illustrated in Figures 12.4 and 12.5.

The graph of Figure 12.5 exemplifies an AND/OR graph used to solve a problem by decomposition. Note, however, that the graphs you saw in Chapter 11 are not AND/OR graphs. To distinguish them from AND/OR graphs, the graphs of the kind in Chapter 11 are sometimes named in the literature as OR graphs. You may view OR graphs as those in which every connector has cardinality 1. We can alternatively say that an AND/OR graph contains at least one connector whose cardinality is more than 1. It should also be apparent from Figure 12.5 that every leaf node in an AND/OR graph is either a terminal node or a non-terminal node.

As another example, consider the problem of transforming a declarative active positive sentence in English into a declarative passive negative sentence. The gist of solving the problem by decomposition

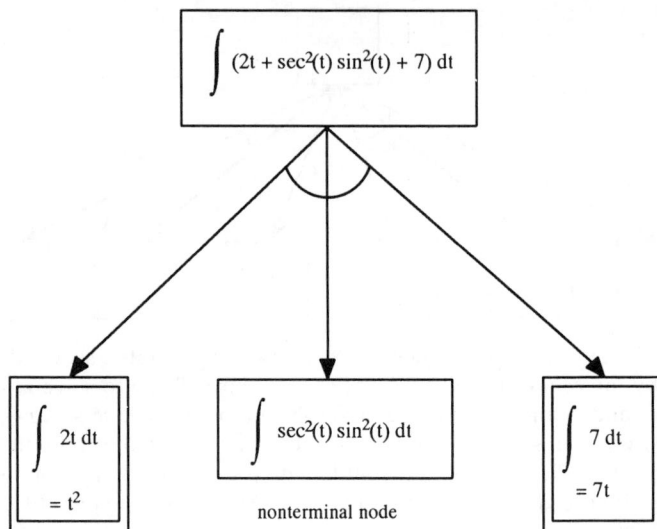

Figure 12.4   The problem of integrating the expression $(2t + \sec^2(t) \sin^2(t) + 7)$ can be decomposed into the subproblems of integrating the three subexpressions $2t$, $\sec^2(t) \sin^2(t)$, and 7 [shown above by the leaf nodes]. In an AND/OR graph, a node with no connector toward it is the root node of the graph. The root node above denotes the problem originally given. Note that in the above example, the subproblems of integrating the three subexpressions can be solved in any order, independently of one another. Problems that are considered to be terminal are depicted by doubly lined nodes, which are then referred to as terminal nodes. Of the three leaf nodes above, two are terminal, and one non-terminal. The non-terminal node is next expanded as shown in Figure 12.5.

is shown in Figure 12.6. If, perchance, you are not familiar with transformational grammar as discussed in Chapter 8, then you may skip the details of the example. You should, however, note that this is an example of a problem in which once a particular set of subproblems has been selected for solving, the subproblems must be solved in a prescribed order. This is unlike the problem in Figures 12.4 and 12.5, in which the subproblems may be solved in any order.

We shall assume for this chapter that none of our AND/OR graphs contain any recurring nodes: no node is identical to its ancestor. Reworded, no node is its own ancestor; that is, the AND/OR graph is acyclic. Thus we would not be considering a graph such as that in Figure 12.7.

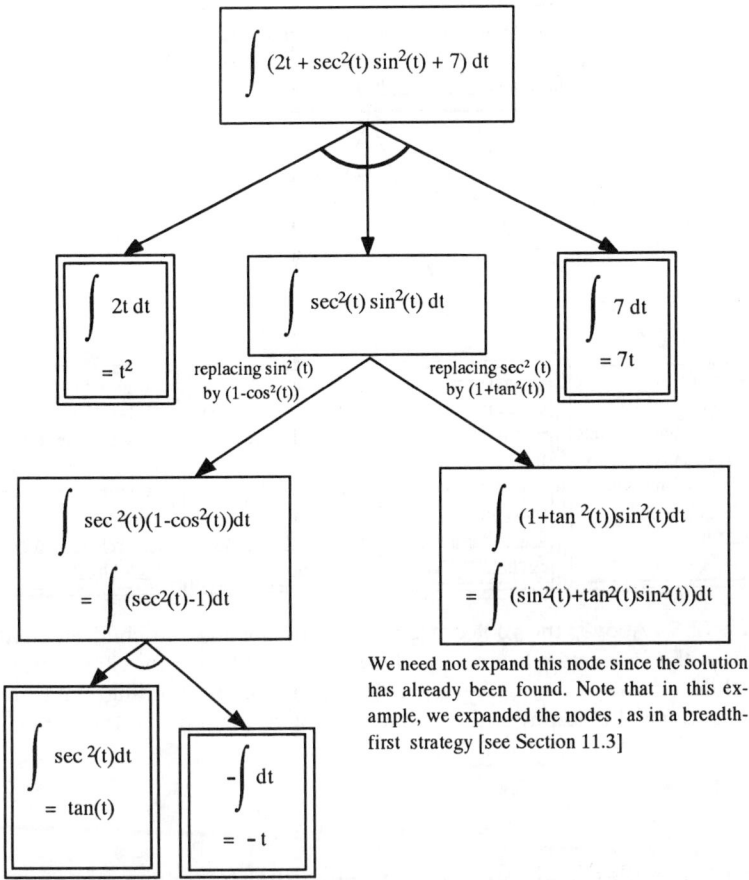

Figure 12.5 Expanding the non-terminal leaf node of Figure 12.4, we see that to integrate $\sec^2(t) \sin^2(t)$, we can integrate either $(\sec^2(t) - 1)$ or $(\sin^2(t) + \tan^2(t) \sin^2(t))$. We continue to expand non-terminal leaf nodes as shown above until we obtain the solution, which is $(t^2 + \tan(t) - t + 7t)$, which in turn can be simplified to $(t^2 - 6t + \tan(t))$.

12.3   SEARCHING AND/OR GRAPHS

A subgraph S_x of an AND/OR graph G is said to be a **solution graph** from a node x in G if

1. x is the root of S_x;
2. for every non-leaf node y in S_x, exactly one connector K going out from y, together with all the children of y sired by K, is in S_x;

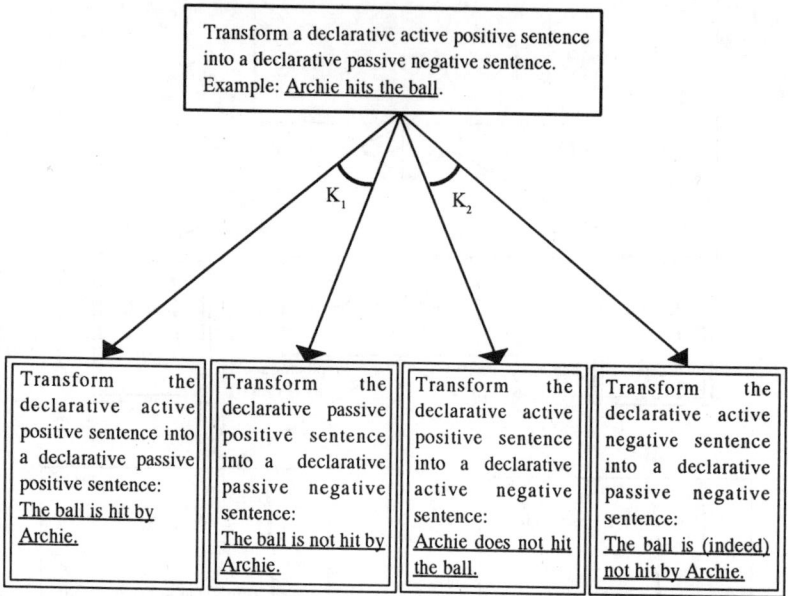

> Transform a declarative active positive sentence into a declarative passive negative sentence.
> Example: <u>Archie hits the ball.</u>

| Transform the declarative active positive sentence into a declarative passive positive sentence: <u>The ball is hit by Archie.</u> | Transform the declarative passive positive sentence into a declarative passive negative sentence: <u>The ball is not hit by Archie.</u> | Transform the declarative active positive sentence into a declarative active negative sentence: <u>Archie does not hit the ball.</u> | Transform the declarative active negative sentence into a declarative passive negative sentence: <u>The ball is (indeed) not hit by Archie.</u> |

Figure 12.6 Above, the root can be solved by solving the children sired by either of the connectors K_1 and K_2. Nevertheless, note that for either connector the child on the left must be solved before the corresponding child on the right, because the output of the left child becomes the input to the right child.

3. all leaf nodes in S_x are terminal, such that by solving the terminal nodes, we have solved x.

There can be more than one solution graph from x. Each such solution graph contains the alternative sets of terminal nodes that can be solved so as to solve x. The objective of searching an AND/OR graph from x is to find a solution graph S_x, provided such a solution graph exists. Figure 12.8 illustrates an AND/OR graph together with the different solution graphs from its root node.

To couple the notion of a solution graph with the solvability of a node, we say that a node x is **solvable** if, and only if,

1. x is a terminal mode, or
2. x is a non-terminal node such that all its children sired by at least one of the connectors from x are solvable.

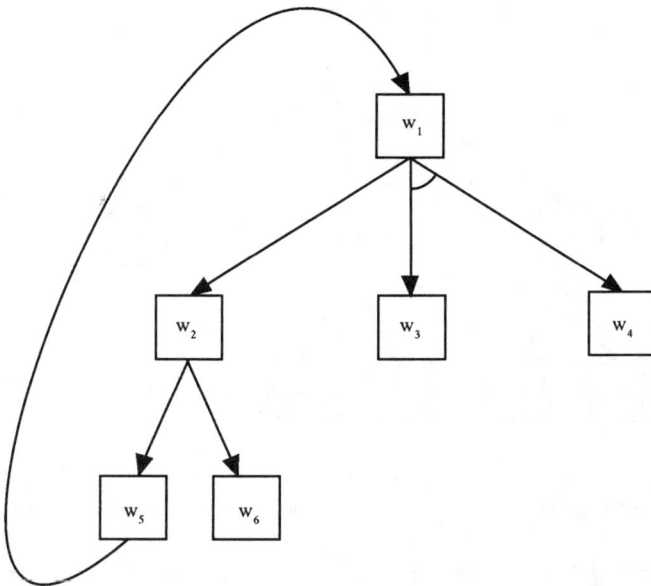

Figure 12.7 If we were to attempt solving w_1 by the above AND/OR graph, we could loop indefinitely. Node w_1 is recurring: by being its own ancestor, it is identical to its ancestor. Alternatively, we can say that the graph contains a cycle among the nodes w_1 w_2 w_5: according to the graph, node w_1 can be solved by solving w_2, node w_2 can be solved by solving w_5, and node w_5 can be solved by solving w_1. To prevent indefinite looping, we shall assume for this chapter that all our AND/OR graphs are acyclic.

Accordingly, a node x is **unsolvable** if x is a non-terminal node and there is no connector from x such that all the children of x sired by that connector are solvable. Based on our above discussion we can say that a node x is solvable if, and only if, there exists a solution graph S_x. Note that the solution graph from a terminal node contains only the node itself.

Thus to solve the node x, we should search the AND/OR graph for an S_x. Amplifying the comments in the legend of Figure 12.8, we describe below a depth-first strategy for searching AND/OR graphs.

12.3.1 Depth-first search

Suppose, in an AND/OR graph, a node x has n connectors directed from it as you saw in Figure 12.2. To find a solution graph S_x, that is,

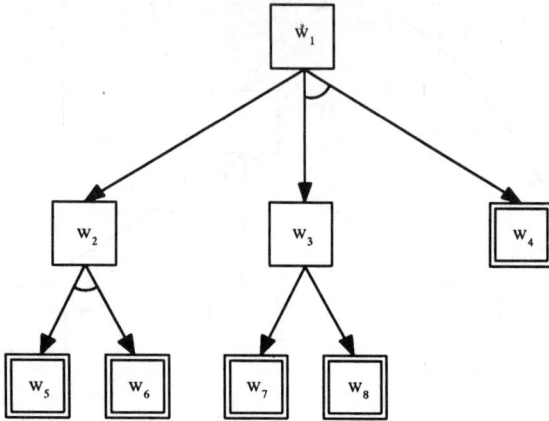

The three solution graphs that can be obtained from the root of the above AND/OR graph are shown below:

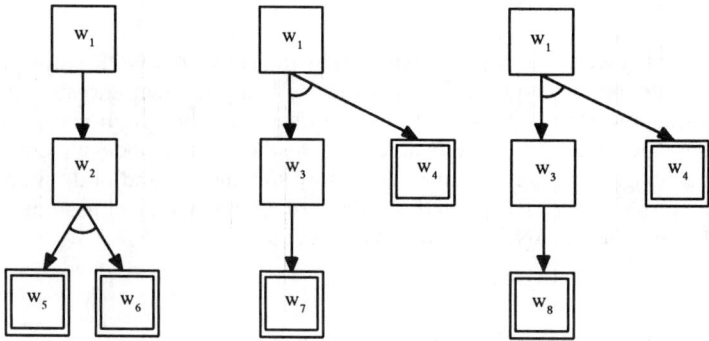

Figure 12.8 An AND/OR graph and the three solution graphs from its root. To search for such a solution graph, proceed as follows. Beginning from the root node, select an outgoing connector to its children. From each child, select in turn an outgoing connector to its children. Repeat executing the previous sentence until all the leaf nodes are terminal nodes. The cost of the solution of w_1 may vary with the solution graph we select to solve w_1. We can say that each solution graph above represents a particular decomposition of w_1. Typically, we shall be searching for a solution graph from the root of an AND/OR graph, because the root denotes the problem originally given to be solved.

to solve x, a recursive depth-first search strategy DFSAOG (Depth-First Search of AND/OR Graph) can be outlined as follows.

(1) Procedure DFSAOG(x);

(2) If x is a terminal node, then return *solved* with S_x containing only x.

(3) Select a connector K that is directed from x and that has not been selected before. If there is no such connector, then return *unsolved* since no S_x has been found; otherwise, do the following.

    (3.1) Select a child y of x that is sired by K and that has not been selected before. If there is no such child then return *solved*, with S_x containing the subgraph traversed; otherwise, do:

        (3.1.1) if DFSAOG(y) is *solved*, then go to (3.1); otherwise, go to (3).

(5) end.

In step (3) above, we can select a connector K arbitrarily. Similarly, in step (3.1) we can select a child y arbitrarily. If, however, the children sired by K should be solved in some prescribed order, as in the problem of Figure 12.6, then the children may be selected in that order.

We can also employ heuristics to make the above selections. We heuristically measure the promise of a node, where the more likely it is that the node will be solved, the more promising is the node. Alternatively, the more difficult it appears to be to solve a node, the less promising is the node.

Similarly we measure the promise of a connector, where the more likely it is that all the children sired by it are solvable, the more promising is the connector. Then in step (3) above, connectors are selected in decreasing order of their promise. Thus the more promising a connector, the earlier it is selected: the earlier we know that all the children sired by a connector are solved, the earlier we know that the parent of the children is solved.

However, once a connector has been selected in step (3), then in step (3.1) we select the children sired by it in increasing order of their promise. Thus the less promising a child, the earlier it is selected: the earlier we come to know that one of the children sired by the connector is unsolvable, the earlier we realize that the connector cannot be in the solution graph and hence the earlier we can backtrack to select another connector.

Nevertheless, take note that the above search strategy is inadmissible: it is not guaranteed to find the cheapest solution graph S_x, that is, the S_x with the least cost. The cost of an S_x is the cost of the solution of x according to the decomposition of x, as represented by S_x.

Often we may be required to find the cheapest S_x, so we need to

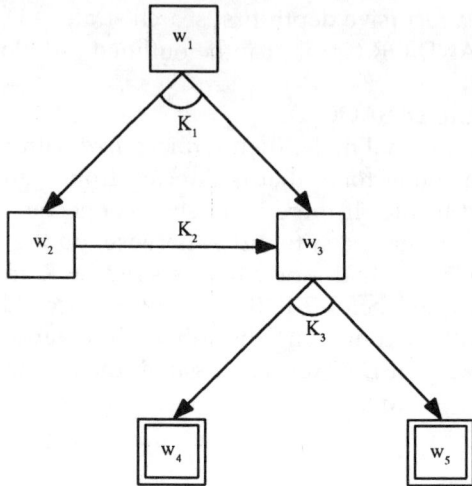

The cost of the solution graph from w_1 is equal to
  1 time the cost of connector K_1
  + 1 time   ... „ ... K_2
  + 2 times   ... „ ... K_3.

Note that the costs of the solution graphs from the terminal nodes w_4 and w_5 have been assumed to be zero.

We can say that, in general, if there are j paths from a node x to a node y, and if both x and y are in a solution graph, then in calculating the cost of the solution graph, the cost of the connector directed from y, such that the connector is in the solution graph, is counted j times.

Above there are two paths from w_1 to w_3: one along the arc $w_1 w_3$, and the other along the arcs $w_1 w_2$ and $w_2 w_3$. So the cost of K_3, the connector directed from node w_3, is counted twice.

Figure 12.9   Evaluating the cost of a solution graph.

learn of an admissible search strategy. To understand this, however, we should learn how to evaluate the cost of a solution graph.

Associated with every connector is a positive value called the cost of the connector. If a connector K is directed from a node x to nodes y_1, $y_2, \ldots, y_m$, then the cost of K is the cost of decomposing the problem at x into the subproblems at $y_1, y_2, \ldots, y_m$. The cost of a solution graph from x (where the solution graph contains K) is defined to be equal to the

$$\text{Cost of } K + \sum_{i=1}^{m} \text{Cost of a solution graph from } y_i.$$

It is assumed that the cost of a solution graph from a terminal node (that is, the cost of a solution of a terminal node) is known. Figure 12.9 shows that, in evaluating the cost of a solution graph, the costs of some of the connectors may be counted more than once.

12.3.2   A heuristic function for admissible search

Since there can be more than one solution graph from a node x, there can be more than one value for the solution graphs from x. Let

$h^*(x)$ be the cost of the cheapest solution graph from node x, where $h^*(x) \geq 0$; and

$h(x)$ be an estimate of $h^*(x)$ based on some heuristic (review section 11.6), such that $h(x) \geq 0$.

If $h(x)$ is infinite, then x has been judged to be unsolvable. For implementing on a computer, however, the h value of an unsolvable node is set to the largest positive number that the particular computer can process. Suppose that for all nodes x, and for all connectors directed from x,

$h(x) \leq$ Cost of the connector from x to the nodes $y_1, y_2, \ldots, y_m$

$$+ \sum_{i=1}^{m} h(y_i).$$

Then the heuristic function h is said to be **monotonic**. It can be shown, as in section 11.5.3, that if h is monotonic, and if the h value of all terminal nodes is zero, then h is a lower bound on h^*. In other words, $h(x) \leq h^*(x)$, for all nodes x.

The heuristic function h is employed by a search strategy called AO*, described in the next section. It is an established mathematical result that if h is monotonic, and if h is a lower bound on h^*, then AO* is admissible: in other words, AO* is guaranteed to find the cheapest solution graph, provided a solution graph exists.

But before we read about AO*, we should learn how to find the h value of a node, if we know the h values of the node's children. The **liability** of a connector directed from a node x to nodes $y_1, y_2, \ldots, y_m$ is defined to be equal to the

Cost of the connector $+ \sum_{i=1}^{m} h(y_i).$

If there are n connectors directed from x, the connector with the least liability is called the **prime** connector from x. Then $h(x)$ is evaluated to be equal to the liability of the prime connector from x. In doing this,

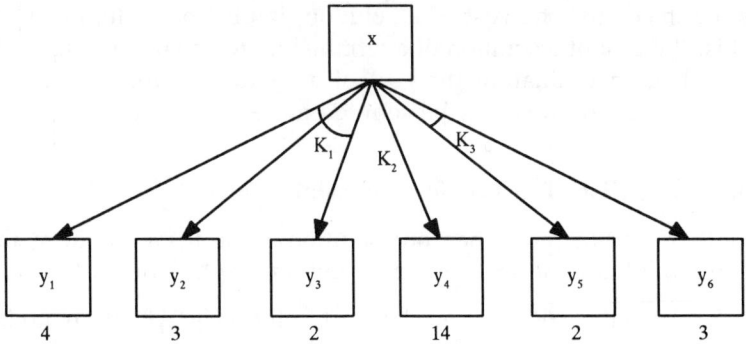

Suppose we are given that the h values of the y nodes are as written next to the nodes, and that the costs of the connectors K_1, K_2, K_3 are respectively 3,1, and 2. We are to find the value of h(x).

Liability of K_1 = Cost of K_1 + h(y_1) + h(y_2) + h(y_3) = 12.
Liability of K_2 = Cost of K_2 + h(y_4) = 15.
Liability of K_3 = Cost of K_3 + h(y_5) + h(y_6) = 7.

K_3 is the prime connector since it has the least liability.
Therefore, h(x) = Liability of K_3 = 7.

Figure 12.10   An example of propagating the h values of the children to their parent.

the *h* values of the children of a node are said to be propagated to their parent. An example is shown in Figure 12.10.

Knowing the *h* values of the leaf nodes, we can propagate the *h* values to their parents. Repeatedly propagating the *h* values from, say, depth *d* to depth *d*-1, then from depth *d*-1 to depth *d*-2, and so on, we can find the *h* value of the node at depth 0, that is, the root node. Thus the *h* value can be propagated from the leaf nodes of an AND/OR graph to the root node of the graph.

12.3.3   AO* search

The AO* searches an AND/OR graph G from a node x in G to find the cheapest solution graph S'_x. To find the cheapest solution for the problem at, say, the root of G, node x will be the root node. It is assumed that, during the search, all nodes have pointers to their parents as well as to their children. Hence from a node we can traverse in either direction: toward the parents, or toward the children, as needed. While reading the description of the AO* search below, keep continually referring to the example that stretches over Figures 12.11–12.16. By doing so, you will see that the solution graph is constructed

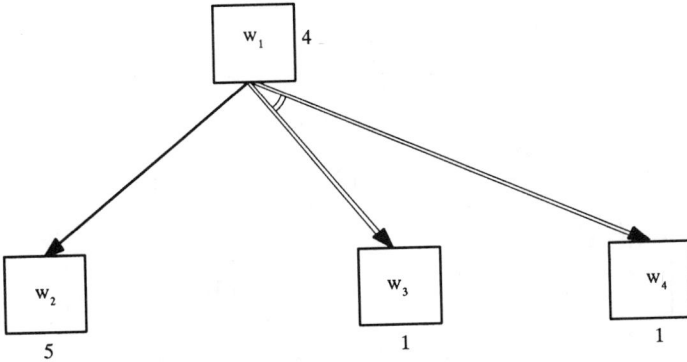

Figure 12.11 An example of AO* search for which we assume that the cost of a connector is equal to the cardinality of the connector. To begin, we expand w_1 to generate, say, w_2, w_3, and w_4. Suppose that the h values of w_2, w_3, and w_4 are calculated to be 5, 1, and 1, respectively. The prime connector is shown doubly lined. Propagating the h values of w_2, w_3, and w_4 to their parent, we obtain $h(w_1)$ to be equal to 4. Traversing along the prime connector from w_1, we should next expand either w_3 or w_4. Let us select w_3. Its expansion is shown in Figure 12.12.

stage by stage, and that will help you easily understand the AO* search strategy. For the example, we have assumed that the cost of a connector is equal to the cardinality of the connector.

As will become apparent below, AO* in essence runs in two phases. During the first phase it constructs a subgraph of G by traversing from node x along the prime connectors of G, expanding a selected non-terminal leaf and employing a heuristic function to calculate the h values of the newly generated children. Then, during the second phase, AO* propagates the newly calculated h values to node x. It alternates between two phases until, in traversing along the prime connectors of G, all the leaf nodes it reaches are terminal. Then the subgraph traversed is the cheapest solution graph S_x'. The search strategy AO* can then be outlined as follows.

(1) Put the node x into the graph G. Estimate $h(x)$. If x is a terminal node, then declare x as solved and let S_x' be equal to G.
(2) If x is solved, then return with S_x' and with $h(x)$ as the cost of S_x'.
(3) If $h(x)$ is infinite, then return with failure since no solution graph has been found.
(4) Let S_x' be the subgraph that is obtained by beginning from x and traversing along the prime connectors of G. (Some of the

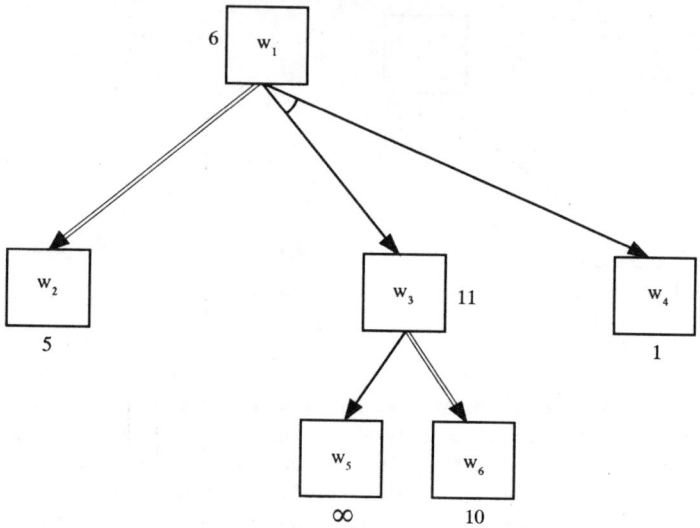

Figure 12.12   Continuing the AO* search from Figure 12.11, we expand w_3 to generate, say, w_5 and w_6. Suppose that the h values of w_5 and w_6 are calculated to be ∞ and 10, respectively. Propagating the h values, we obtain $h(w_3)$ to be 11, and $h(w_1)$ to be 6. Traversing along the prime connector from w_1, we should next expand w_2. This is shown in Figure 12.13.

connectors are flagged as being prime in step (10) below. When executing the current step the first time, G will contain only x, so S'_x also will contain only x.)

(5) Select a non-terminal leaf node x' from S'_x. (You may select this x' arbitrarily. Nevertheless, it is often recommended to select the x' with the largest h value. The reason will become apparent from our comments after you have read all the steps of the AO* search. When executing this step the first time, either way x' will be the same as x.)

(6) Expand x' to generate all its children. Delete all children that are recurring. If x' has no surviving children (that is, either x' has no children because x' is inert, or all the children of x' are recurring), then let $h(x')$ be infinite (node x' cannot belong to any solution graph). Otherwise, for every surviving child y of x', do the following.

(6.1) Add y to G as a child of x'.

(6.2) Calculate $h(y)$. If y is a terminal node, then declare y as solved.

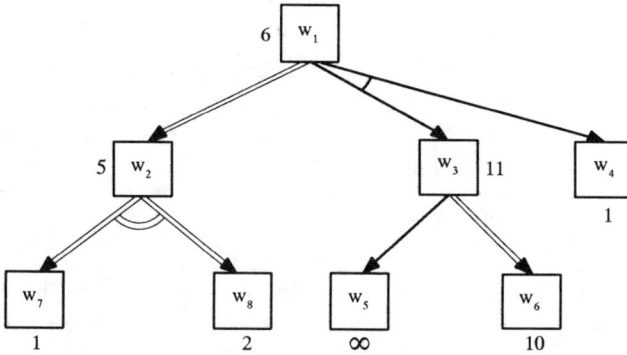

Figure 12.13 Continuing the AO* search from Figure 12.12, we expand w_2 to generate, say, w_7 and w_8. Suppose that the h values of w_7 and w_8 are calculated to be 1 and 2, respectively. Propagating the h values, we obtain $h(w_2)$ to be 5, which remains unchanged from Figure 12.12. Accordingly, $h(w_1)$ also remains unchanged at 6. Traversing along the prime connectors from w_1, we should next expand either w_7 or w_8. With $h(w_8)$ being larger than $h(w_7)$, let us, as recommended in step ⟨5⟩ of the AO* search, select w_8. Its expansion is shown in Figure 12.14.

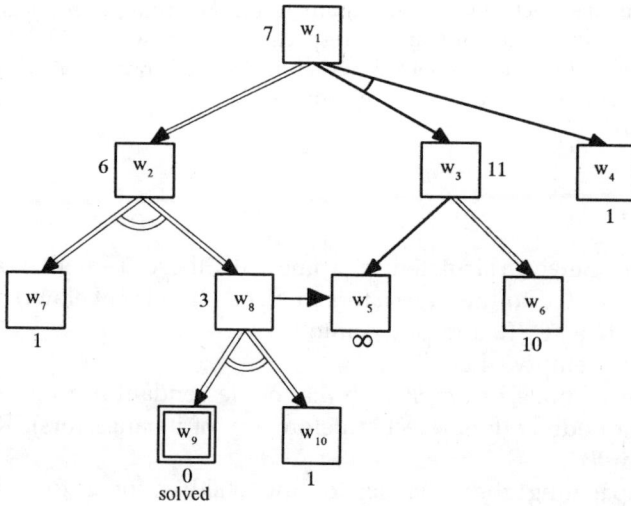

Figure 12.14 Continuing the AO* search from Figure 12.13, we expand w_8 to generate, say, w_5, w_9, and w_{10}. Of these, w_5 already exists. Suppose that the h values of w_9 and w_{10} are calculated to be 0 and 1, respectively. Since w_9 is noticed to be a terminal node, we declare it solved. Propagating the h values, we obtain $h(w_8)$, $h(w_2)$, and $h(w_1)$ to be 3, 6, and 7, respectively. Traversing along the prime connectors from w_1, we should next expand either w_7 or w_{10}. Let us select w_7. Its expansion is shown in Figure 12.15.

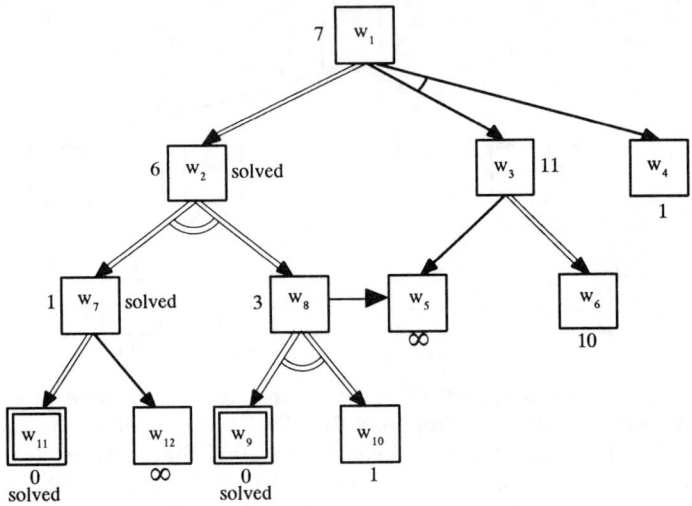

Figure 12.15 Continuing the AO* search from Figure 12.14, we expand w_7 to generate, say, w_{11} and w_{12}. Suppose that the h values of w_{11} and w_{12} are calculated to be 0 and ∞, respectively. Since w_{11} is noticed to be a terminal node, we declare it solved. Propagating the h values, we obtain w_7 to be 1, which remains unchanged from Figure 12.14. Accordingly, $h(w_2)$ and $h(w_1)$ also remain unchanged at 6 and 7, respectively. Since w_{11}, a child of w_7 sired by the prime connector, is solved, w_7 too is declared solved. Traversing along the prime connectors from w_1, we should next expand w_{10}. This is shown in Figure 12.16.

(The newly calculated *h* values of these *y* nodes are next propagated to their ancestors in steps (7) to (12) below.)

(7) Create a set Ψ, and put x' into it.

(8) If Ψ is empty, then go to (2).

(9) Select a node z from Ψ such that no descendant of z in G occurs in Ψ (a node is thus selected before any of its ancestors). Remove z from Ψ.

(10) Propagating the *h* values of the children of z to z itself, as explained in section 12.3.2, flag the prime connector from z. If all the children of z sired by this prime connector are solved, then declare z as solved. (Note that the *h* values of the children of z would have been calculated either in an earlier iteration in steps (8) to (12), or in step (6.2) above.)

(11) If z is solved, or if the value of $h(z)$ changed in step (10) above,

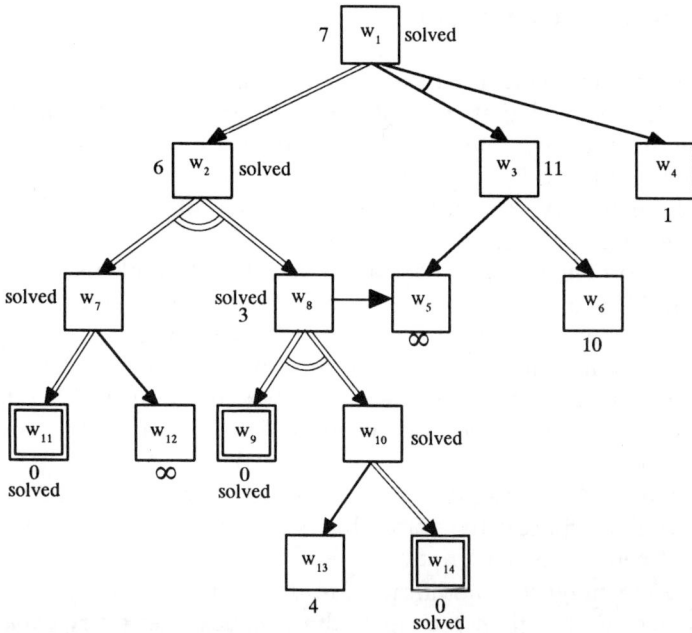

Figure 12.16 Continuing the AO* search from Figure 12.15, we expand w_{10} to generate, say, w_{13} and w_{14}. Suppose that the h values of w_{13} and w_{14} are calculated to be 4 and 0, respectively. Since w_{14} is noticed to be a terminal node, we declare it solved. Propagating the h values, we obtain $h(w_{10})$ to be 1, which remains unchanged from Figure 12.15. Accordingly, $h(w_8)$, $h(w_2)$, an $h(w_1)$ also remain unchanged at 3, 6, and 7 respectively. Moreover, w_{10}, w_8, w_2, and w_1 are declared solved. The solution graph, whose cost is 7, consists of all the nodes shown as solved.

then add to Ψ all parents z' of z, such that z had been sired by a prime connector from z'. (This is done so that the new h value of z can be propagated to its parents z'.)

(12) Go to (8).

Since we assume h to be monotonic, when we propagate the h values in steps (7)–(12) above, the h value of a node can either remain the same, or it can increase; that is, the h value of a node cannot decrease. So in step (5) it was recommended to select the x' with the largest h value, for such an x' is the most likely to change the h values of its ancestors.

12.3.4   Remarks on AO* search

Looking at Figures 12.11–12.16 for the example of AO* search, you may have observed that the full AND/OR graph may be larger than what was ultimately constructed in Figure 12.16. In general, we need not construct the full AND/OR to find the cheapest solution graph by the AO* search. We construct only the portion of the AND/OR graph that is required to find the solution graph.

When a problem x can be decomposed into subproblems y_1, y_2, ... , y_m, then AO* considers each subproblem independently of the others as if they can be solved in any order, although in reality the subproblems may need to be solved in some prescribed order.

If, for all nodes x, we assume $h(x)$ to be zero, then AO* conducts a breadth-first search (described in section 11.3) to find the cheapest solution graph.

Comparing A* search (described in section 11.5.1) with AO* search, we notice that whereas the graph that A* constructs is a tree, the graph that AO* constructs need not be a tree.

Below we suggest a modification to try to improve the efficiency of AO* search. Rather than propagate the h values after every expansion of a non-terminal leaf node, we expand several of these nodes, and then we propagate the h values. On the one hand we may reduce the computation required since we shall be propagating the h values fewer times, but, on the other hand, we may increase the computation required since we shall be expanding more nodes that may ultimately not be in the desired solution graph.

12.4   MEANS–END ANALYSIS

Until now, our discussion has focused on finding a solution once we know how to decompose a problem. Now our discussion will focus on how to decompose a given problem. The details of how to decompose a problem will, of course, depend on the particular problem. Here we present a technique that should in general help you in decomposing a given problem. The technique is referred to in the literature as **means–end analysis**: it analyses the means to be adopted for obtaining a specified end.

As mentioned in section 11.1, a move in a problem lets us traverse from one state to another. A typical problem has a set of possible moves. If we want to traverse from a state z, then we should select one of the moves whose requisite is matched by z. The **requisite** of a move specifies the situation that must prevail to enable us to make the move.

The move to make ↘ Distance to be traveled	16 kilometers or more	2 kilometers or more, but less than 16 kilometers	2 kilometers or less	Requisites of the move
Ride a bus	Yes	Yes	No	Be at the bus station, and have the bus fare
Ride our bicycle	No	Yes	Yes	Be where our bicycle is parked
Walk	No	No	Yes	None

Figure 12.17 A table to guide us in selecting a move for solving the problem of travelling from home to school. To travel, say, 2 kilometres or more but less than 16 kilometres, we can either ride a bus or ride our bicycle. Before making any move we must, however, satisfy the requisites of the move. Thus to ride a bus, we should be at the bus station, and we should have the bus fare. 'Being at the bus station,' and 'having the bus fare' can be viewed as subproblems we must solve before we can make the move of riding a bus. Suppose we do not have the bus fare, and we are unable to beg, borrow, or earn. Then we cannot ride a bus, and we should look at moves other than that of riding a bus.

Thus if a move is expressed as a prodrule, as in the specimen in Figure 11.11, then the requisite of the move is specified in the antecedent of the prodrule.

Before we read a description of means–end analysis, let us consider a preparatory example. So that our example is easy to understand, we shall avoid many of the details. Suppose that we are to travel from our living room at home in the town of Laval to the gym at school in the town of Westmount, a distance of 12 kilometres. As the set of possible moves, we can travel by bus, by bicycle or by walking. Our selection of moves is guided by Figure 12.17. In the literature where a move is known as an operator, a table such as Figure 12.17 is known as a difference-operator table. It is the table from which we select an operator to reduce the difference between a given problem's source and destination states. The problem decompositions for the above example are illustrated in Figure 12.18.

Let us now discuss means–end analysis more formally. As we saw

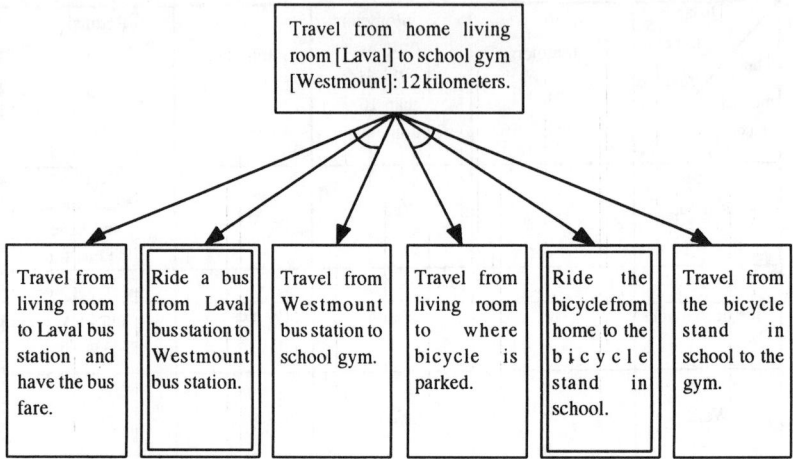

Figure 12.18   Alternative problem decompositions for travelling from home to school. Suppose that we can solve the problem according to either of the two decompositions above. Also suppose that the more time we take for travelling, the higher is the cost of the solution. Then by conducting an AO* search for the cheapest solution, we may prefer to ride a bus over riding our bicycle. This may be corroborated by our intuition.

in Chapter 11, solving a problem typically entails traversing from some state x to some other state y. In means–end analysis, we look for a move μ that will bring us to a state y' such that y' is closer than x to y. Now suppose that according to the requisite of the move μ we should be in state x' to enable us to make the move. Then the problem of traversing from state x to state y can be decomposed into the following three subproblems (also shown in Figure 12.19):

1. the subproblem of traversing from x to x', the subproblem being terminal if either $x = x'$ or there exists a single move to take us from x to x';
2. the terminal subproblem of traversing from x' to y' by the move μ; and
3. the subproblem of traversing from y' to y, the subproblem being terminal if either $y' = y$ or there exists a single move to take us from y' to y.

If the first and the third subproblem above are non-terminal, they can be further decomposed by means–end analysis. Thus means–end analysis can be used recursively to decompose a given problem, as shown in Figure 12.20.

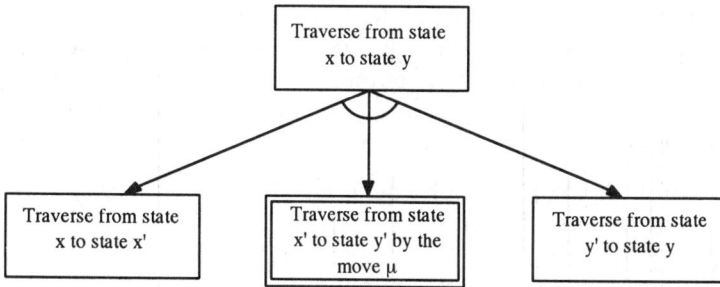

Figure 12.19 Problem decomposition by means–end analysis. The non-terminal subproblems above can be further decomposed by means–end analysis. If either of the non-terminal subproblems is found to be unsolvable, then, as described in section 12.3.1, we can backtrack and select another move μ'. Alternatively, we can consider the different ways that the problem can be decomposed with moves $\mu_1, \mu_2, \ldots$, and then we can conduct an AO* search, as described in section 12.3.3. Note that if $x = x'$ always, then our search becomes a foreward state space search from the node x to the node y. Likewise, if $y' = y$ always, then our search becomes a backward state space search from the node y to the node x. State space search was discussed in Chapter 11.

[1]   procedure MEA (x,y);

[2]   If x=y, then return successfully with the empty solution path ;

[3]   If there is no untried move μ to bring us to y' such that y' is closer than x to y, then return failure;

[4]   If there is an untried move μ to bring us to y' such that y' is closer than x to y, then do:

    [4.1]   x' := requisite of μ;
    [4.2] α := MEA (x,x');
    [4.3]   If α is equal to failure, then consider all moves whose requisite is x' as having been tried, and go to [2];
    [4.4] β := MEA (y',y);
    [4.5]   If β is equal to failure, then consider all moves which bring us to y' as having been tried, and go to [2];
    [4.6]   Return the concatenation of α, μ, and β;

[5]   end.

Figure 12.20 The recursive procedure for means–end analysis [MEA] to traverse from a state x to a state y.

You may have noted that the decomposition we obtain depends on the move μ that we select. Ideally, we should select a μ such that its requisite x' is closer than x to y, but it may not always be possible to do so. For our preparatory example, presented earlier in this section, suppose we take up the following instance:

x = our living room at home in Laval,
x' = Laval bus station,
μ = ride a bus,
y' = Westmount bus station, and
y = the school gym.

It may happen that x' (the Laval bus station) is a little further away than x (our living room) from y (the school gym), but we may still have to go from x to x' so that we can ride the bus.

Now suppose that we are at the Westmount bus station. The remaining problem to be solved is to reach the school gym, and we can either ride a bicycle or walk. But the bicycle is at home and it obviously makes no sense for us to go back home to the bicycle so that we can ride it. We would rather walk.

To sum up, in selecting a move consider giving preference to a move whose requisite brings us closer to our destination. If, however, the requisite does take us away from our destination, then it should not do so by more than some threshold.

12.4.1   The towers of Hanoi

In this section we shall apply means–end analysis to solve as an example the problem of the towers of Hanoi. In essence, the problem consists of transferring n (where $n \geq 1$) rings of varying radii from a tower T_1 to another tower T_3, one ring being transferred in each move so that a bigger ring never rests on a smaller ring, with another tower T_2 being used to stack rings temporarily. The details of the problem are given in Figure 12.21.

Let the n rings in ascending order of their radii be $r_1, r_2, \ldots, r_n$. Hence r_1 is the smallest and r_n the largest.

Let $H(n, i, j)$ be the sequence of moves to transfer the n rings from tower T_i to T_j, where $1 \leq i, j \leq 3$. If $i = j$ then $H(n, i, j)$ is the empty sequence, so we shall consider the case when $i \neq j$.

Let $\mu(i, j)$ be a move in which the topmost ring from T_i is transferred to T_j. The problem of finding $H(1, i, j)$ is terminal since $H(1, i, j) = \mu(i, j)$, so in our discussion below, we shall consider the case when $n \geq 2$ in $H(n, i, j)$.

To transfer the n rings from T_1 to T_3, at sometime we shall have to

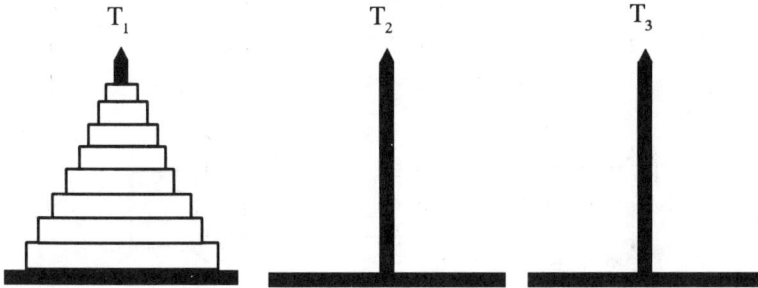

There are three towers T_1, T_2, and T_3. In the source state, n [where n ≥ 1] rings are stacked in T_1. Each ring is of a different radius, and the rings in T_1 form a pyramid: from top to bottom the rings are in ascending order of their radii, the smallest at the top, and the largest at the bottom. In the destination state, the n rings are to be stacked as a pyramid in T_3.

The only move permitted consists of sliding the topmost ring from a tower and sliding it into another tower, such that at no time may a bigger ring rest on a smaller ring . Tower T_2 may be used temporarily to stack the rings.

Figure 12.21 The towers of Hanoi problem.

transfer ring r_n from T_1 to T_3. Since r_n will be the topmost ring in T_1 at that time, and since a bigger ring can never rest on a smaller ring, the rings r_1 to r_{n-1} then cannot be in T_1 or T_3: they must be in T_2. Generalizing the above, we can say that when r_n is transferred from T_i to T_j, rings r_1 to r_{n-1} should be in $T_{(6-i-j)}$.

Thus the problem of transferring the n rings $r_1, r_2, \ldots, r_n$ from T_i to T_j can be decomposed by means–end analysis into the following three subproblems:

1. the subproblem $H(n - 1, i, 6 - i - j)$ of transferring $(n - 1)$ rings r_1, $r_2, \ldots, r_{n-1}$ from T_i to $T_{(6-i-j)}$;
2. the terminal subproblem of transferring the single ring r_n from T_i to T_j by the move $\mu(i, j)$; and
3. the subproblem $H(n - 1, 6 - i - j, j)$ of transferring $(n - 1)$ rings r_1, $r_2, \ldots, r_{n-1}$ from $T_{(6-i-j)}$ to T_j.

We can summarize the above discussion by saying the following. If $n = 1$, then

$$H(n, i, j) = \mu(i, j).$$

If $n \geq 2$, then

$$H(n, i, j) = H(n - 1, i, 6 - i - j), \mu(i, j), H(n - 1, 6 - i - j, j).$$

The solution for the specimen value of $n = 3$ is given in Figure 12.22.

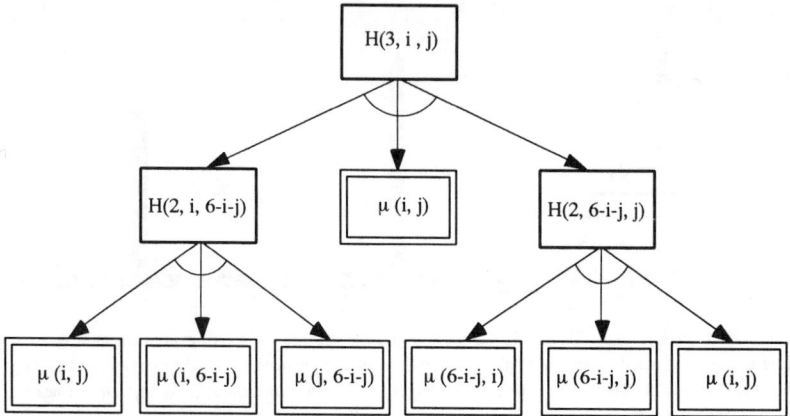

The sequence of moves to transfer 3 rings from T_i to T_j is $\mu(i,j)$, $\mu(i,6\text{-}i\text{-}j)$, $\mu(j,6\text{-}i\text{-}j)$, $\mu(i,j)$, $\mu(6\text{-}i\text{-}j, i)$, $\mu(6\text{-}i\text{-}j,j)$, $\mu(i,j)$.

For i=1, and j=3, the sequence of moves, therefore, is $\mu(1,3)$, $\mu(1,2)$, $\mu(3,2)$, $\mu(1,3)$, $\mu(2,1)$, $\mu(2,3)$, $\mu(1,3)$.

Figure 12.22 The solution for transferring three rings from T_1 to T_3 in the problem of the towers of Hanoi. The number of moves [that is, the length of the solution path] required is 7. It can be shown by induction that the length of the solution path for n rings is 2^n-1.

12.4.2 The towers of Brahma

As another example for applying means–end analysis, we shall consider the problem of the towers of Brahma. The three towers, the n rings, the source state, and the destination state in the towers of Brahma are the same as in the towers of Hanoi. However, there is now one extra constraint in the making of a move: the only move permitted consists of sliding the topmost ring from a tower and sliding it into the *adjacent* tower such that at no time may a bigger ring rest on a smaller ring. Thus in one move a ring can be transferred from T_1 to T_2, from T_2 to T_3, from T_3 to T_2, or from T_2 to T_1. Put another way, no ring can be transferred in one move from T_1 to T_3 or from T_3 to T_1.

Let $B(n, i, j)$ be the sequence of moves to transfer n rings from T_1 to T_j, where $1 \leq i, j \leq 3$, and where $|i - j| = 2$.

Let $\mu(i, j)$ be a move in which the topmost ring from T_i is transferred to T_j, provided $|i - j| = 1$. The problem of finding $B(1, i, j)$ is terminal since

$$B(1, i, j) = \mu(i, 6 - i - j), \ \mu(6 - i - j, j).$$

With reasoning similar to that for the towers of Hanoi, the problem of transferring the n rings $r_1, r_2, \ldots, r_n$ from T_i to T_j (where $|i - j| = 2$) in the towers of Brahma can be decomposed by means–end analysis into the following three subproblems:

1. the subproblem $B(n - 1, i, j)$;
2. the terminal problem $\mu(i, 6 - i - j)$; and
3. the subproblem of arranging the $(n - 1)$ rings in T_j and the single ring in $T_{(6-i-j)}$ into a pyramid in T_j.

The third subproblem above can be further decomposed by means–end analysis as follows:

(3.1) the subproblem $B(n - 1, j, i)$;
(3.2) the terminal problem $\mu(6 - i - j, j)$; and
(3.3) the subproblem $B(n - 1, i, j)$.

We can then summarize the above discussion by saying the following. If $n = 1$ and $|i - j| = 2$, then

$$B(n, i, j) = \mu(i, 6 - i - j), \mu(6 - i - j, j).$$

If $n \geq 2$ and $|i - j| = 2$, then

$$B(n, i, j) = B(n - 1, i, j), \mu(i, 6 - i - j), B(n - 1, j, i),$$
$$\mu(6 - i - j, j), B(n - 1, i, j).$$

The solution for the specimen value of $n = 2$ is given in Figure 12.23.

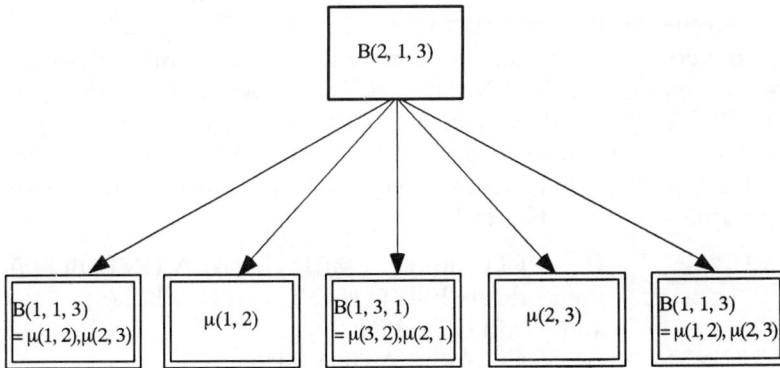

The sequence of moves to transfer 2 rings from T_1 to T_3 is $\mu(1,2)$, $\mu(2, 3)$, $\mu(1, 2)$, $\mu(3, 2)$, $\mu(2,1)$, $\mu(2, 3)$, $\mu(1, 2)$, $\mu(2, 3)$.

Figure 12.23 The solution for transferring two rings from T_1 to T_3 in the problem of the towers of Brahma. The length of the solution path is 8. It can be shown by induction that the length of the solution path for n rings is 3^n-1.

12.5 PLANNING A ROBOT'S MOVES

Problem decomposition can also be employed for planning a robot's moves. To discuss how this can be done we shall consider the following problem, which we shall call the *three-cubes* problem.

We are given a table and three equal-sized cubes a, b and c. A cube may rest on the table or on another cube. As moves, a robot hand can pick up a cube from the table or from another cube. It can also place it on the table or on another cube. We assume that the table is large enough to accommodate all the cubes so that while making any of the above moves the robot does not have to check whether there is enough space on the table for a cube.

Typically, we are given a source state and a destination state, where a state denotes an arrangement of the cubes. As a solution, we are to find a sequence of robotic moves that will enable us to reach the destination state from the source state. The sequence is known in the literature as the plan for the robot. It is in fact the same as what we have been calling a solution path. Conforming to the terminology of the literature, we too may refer to the move sequence as a plan.

To discuss how a robot can generate its plan for solving a problem, we shall have to formalize our discussion. The formalization will be in predicate logic. Make sure that you are conversant with predicate logic as discussed in Chapter 3.

Any state of the cubes can be delineated by a conjunction of predicate logic literals. The literals that we shall be using for the three-cubes problem are enumerated in Figure 12.24. Then the source state and the destination state for us are given in Figure 12.25.

To traverse from one state to another the robot can make these four kinds of moves: PICKUP(u) to pick-up a cube u from the table, PUTDOWN(u) to put down a cube u on the table, STACK(u, v) to put a cube u on top of a cube v, and UNSTACK(u, v) to remove a cube u from the top of a cube v. These moves can be expressed more precisely by prodrules (see also Figure 11.11).

PICKUP(u):   **If**   CLEAR(u) $\wedge$ EMPTYHAND $\wedge$ ONTABLE(u),
                then delete EMPTYHAND $\wedge$ ONTABLE(u),
                and   add GRASPING(u).
PUTDOWN(u): **If**   CLEAR(u) $\wedge$ GRASPING(u),
                then delete GRASPING(u),
                and   add EMPTYHAND $\wedge$ ONTABLE(u).
STACK(u, v):   **If**   CLEAR(u) $\wedge$ CLEAR(v) $\wedge$ GRASPING(u),
                then delete CLEAR(v) $\wedge$ GRASPING(u),
                and   add EMPTYHAND $\wedge$ ON(u, v).
UNSTACK(u, v): **If**   CLEAR(u) $\wedge$ EMPTYHAND $\wedge$ ON(u, v),

Literal	Explanation of the literal.	A specimen pictorial representation of the literal
CLEAR (v)	Cube v is clear; that is, there is nothing on top of v.	
EMPTYHAND	The robot is empty handed; that is, it not grasping anything.	
GRASPING (v)	The robot is grasping cube v.	
ON (u, v)	Cube u is resting on the top of cube v.	
ONTABLE (v)	Cube v is resting somewhere on the table.	

Figure 12.24   Literals that will be used to delineate the state of the cubes. In a typical state, more than one literal may be true; for example, the topmost pictorial representation can be delineated as CLEAR (v) ∨ ONTABLE (v). Variables u and v above can be replaced by constants a, b, c, which are the names of the cubes in our three-cubes problem.

source state

destination state

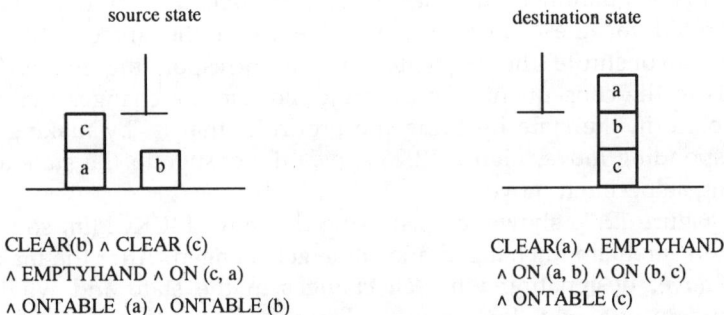

CLEAR(b) ∧ CLEAR (c)
∧ EMPTYHAND ∧ ON (c, a)
∧ ONTABLE (a) ∧ ONTABLE (b)

CLEAR(a) ∧ EMPTYHAND
∧ ON (a, b) ∧ ON (b, c)
∧ ONTABLE (c)

Figure 12.25   The source and the destination states for our three-cubes problem.

Line	A state	A pictorial representation of the state
1	CLEAR(b) ∧ CLEAR (c) ∧ EMPTYHAND ∧ ON (c, a) ∧ ONTABLE (a) ∧ ONTABLE (b)	
2	CLEAR(b) ∧ CLEAR (c) ∧ GRASPING (b) ∧ ON (c, a) ∧ ONTABLE (a)	

Figure 12.26   Change in state after making a specimen move in our three-cubes problem. Suppose the state is as in the first line above. The antecedent of the prodrule PICKUP (u) can be unified with a subset of the literals that delineate the state, by the most general unifier, mgu, δ = {b/u}. Hence the PICKUP (b) instance of the prodrule can be fired: that is, the robot can make the corresponding move. The resulting state is as in the second line above. As specified by the PICKUP (b) instance of the prodrule, we delete the literals EMPTYHAND and ONTABLE (b) from the first line, and we add the literal GRASPING (b), to obtain the second line.

> **then**   delete EMPTYHAND $\wedge$ ON(u, v),
> **and**   add CLEAR(v) $\wedge$ GRASPING(u).

Note that in the above prodrules variables u and v are assumed to be existentially quantified: the names of our cubes a, b and c can be substituted for these variables. The literals in the antecedent of a prodrule constitute the requisite for the corresponding move. The literals in the consequent of a prodrule indicate the changes that will take place in the state by firing the prodrule, that is, by making the corresponding move. Figure 12.26 shows the change in the state after making a specimen move.

As Figure 12.26 shows, after making the move PICKUP(b), some of the literals remain unchanged and some get changed. After the making of a move, designating what all changes in the state and what all remains unchanged is known in the literature as the 'frame problem.'

Take note, however, that there are certain constraints that must not be violated by any state of the three cubes. To illustrate, we cannot say that a cube is clear and at the same time say that there is another cube on it. For our three cubes we shall assume the following seventeen constraints.

1. If a cube is clear, then there is no other cube on it.
2. If the robot is empty-handed, then it is not grasping any cube.
3. If the robot is grasping a cube, then the cube is clear.
4. If the robot is grasping a cube, then it is not empty-handed.
5. If the robot is grasping a cube, then it is not grasping any other cube.
6. If the robot is grasping a cube v, then there is no other cube on v.
7. If the robot is grasping a cube v, then v is not on any other cube.
8. If the robot is grasping a cube, then the cube is not on the table.
9. If a cube u is on cube v, then v is not clear.
10. If a cube u is on cube v, then u is not the same as v, that is to say, no cube can be on itself.
11. If a cube u is on cube v, then the robot is not grasping u.
12. If a cube u is on cube v, then the robot is not grasping v.
13. If a cube u is on cube v, then v is not on u, in other words, no two cubes can be mutually on each other.
14. If a cube u is on cube v, then u is not on any other cube, that is, a cube cannot be on two other cubes.
15. If a cube u is on cube v, then on other cube w is on v; reworded, two cubes cannot be on one cube.
16. If a cube is on the table, then it is not being grasped by the robot.
17. If a cube is on the table, then it is not on any other cube.

It is hoped that none of the above constraints go against your intuition. Nevertheless, you may have noted that some of the constraints are redundant since they can be deduced from others. To illustrate, the sixth constraint above can be deduced from the third and the first constraints. Such redundancy will be useful for our discussion later: whenever a constraint is violated, we can indicate which specific constraint is violated. The constraints are displayed as predicate logic formulae in Figure 12.27.

Suppose a state is delineated by the formula

$$L_1 \wedge L_2 \wedge L_3 \ldots ,$$

where the L's are literals. A theorem prover (as in Chapters 2–5) in the robot can check whether the state is renegade: that is, whether it violates one of the constraints. If the state is renegade, then it cannot exist. To illustrate, let the formula

[1]	$\forall v$ (CLEAR (v)	$\rightarrow$	$\sim \exists u$ ON (u, v))
[2]	EMPTYHAND	$\rightarrow$	$\sim \exists u$ GRASPING (u)
[3]	$\forall v$ (GRASPING (v)	$\rightarrow$	CLEAR (v))
[4]	$\forall v$ (GRASPING (v)	$\rightarrow$	~EMPTYHAND)
[5]	$\forall v$ (GRASPING (v)	$\rightarrow$	$\sim \exists u$ (GRASPING (u) $\wedge \sim$ EQUAL (u, v))
[6]	$\forall v$ (GRASPING (v)	$\rightarrow$	$\sim \exists u$ ON (u, v))
[7]	$\forall v$ (GRASPING (v)	$\rightarrow$	$\sim \exists u$ ON (v, u))
[8]	$\forall v$ (GRASPING (v)	$\rightarrow$	~ONTABLE (v))
[9]	$\forall u \forall v$ (ON (u, v)	$\rightarrow$	~CLEAR (v))
[10]	$\forall u \forall v$ (ON (u, v)	$\rightarrow$	~EQUAL (u, v))
[11]	$\forall u \forall v$ (ON (u, v)	$\rightarrow$	~GRASPING (u))
[12]	$\forall u \forall v$ (ON (u, v)	$\rightarrow$	~GRASPING (v))
[13]	$\forall u \forall v$ (ON (u, v)	$\rightarrow$	~ON (v, u))
[14]	$\forall u \forall v$ (ON (u, v)	$\rightarrow$	$\sim \exists w$ (ON (u, w) $\wedge \sim$ EQUAL (v, w)))
[15]	$\forall u \forall v$ (ON (u, v)	$\rightarrow$	$\sim \exists w$ (ON (w, u) $\wedge \sim$ EQUAL (u, w)))
[16]	$\forall u$ (ONTABLE (u)	$\rightarrow$	~GRASPING (u))
[17]	$\forall u$(ONTABLE (u)	$\rightarrow$	$\sim \exists v$ ON (u, v))

Figure 12.27 Constraints for the three-cubes problem.

CLEAR(*b*) $\wedge$ ON(*c*, *b*)

delineate a state. A theorem prover can show that the formula is inconsistent: it violates the first constraint of Figure 12.27. Accordingly, the state is renegade and it cannot exist.

Before we solve the three-cubes problem by decomposition, we shall solve it by state space search. That way you can compare state space search with problem decomposition and improve your understanding of problem solving methodologies. The solution of the problem by a breadth-first state space search (discussed in section 11.3) is shown in Figures 12.28 and 12.29. As we can see from the two figures, the plan (solution path) is UNSTACK(*c*, *a*) PUTDOWN (*c*), PICKUP(*b*), STACK(*b*, *c*), PICKUP(*a*), STACK(*a*, *b*).

source node

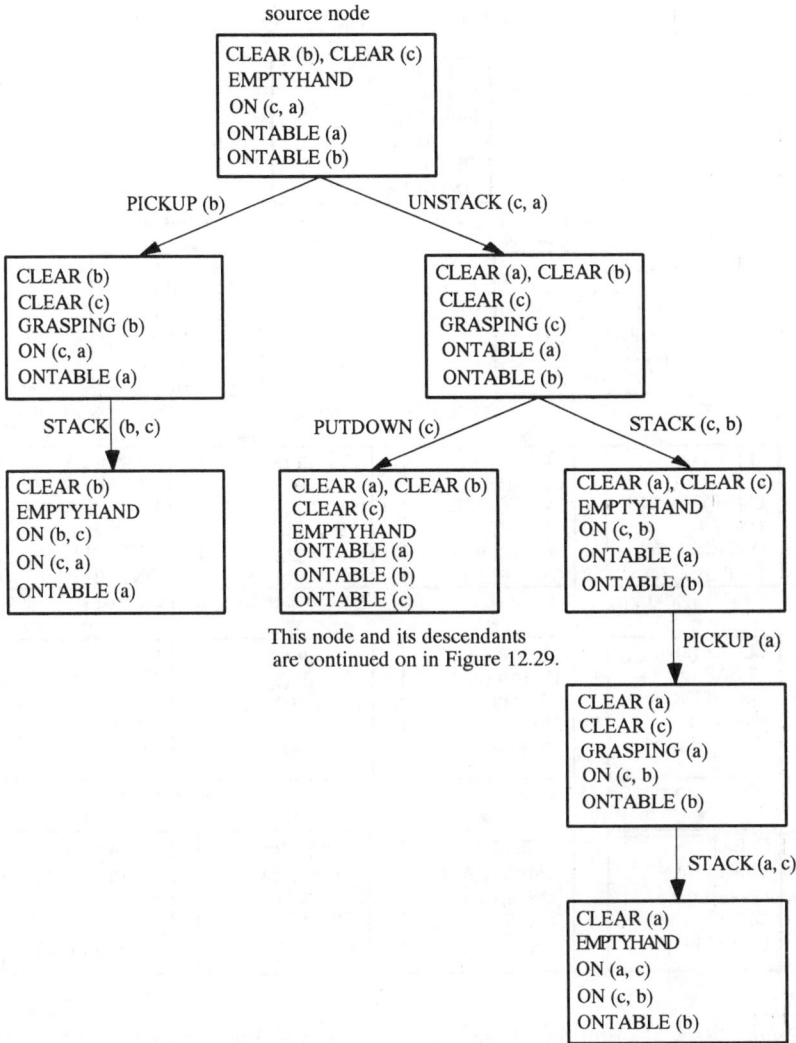

Figure 12.28 Breadth-first search of the state space for the three-cubes problem. To prevent cluttering, the logical operator '∧' between the literals is not shown. The figure is continued on in Figure 12.29.

12.5.1 Backchaining with regression

In Figures 12.28 and 12.29 we searched from the source node to the destination node, but, as mentioned in section 11.7.5, we can also search from the destination node to the source node. For such

This node is from Figure 12.28

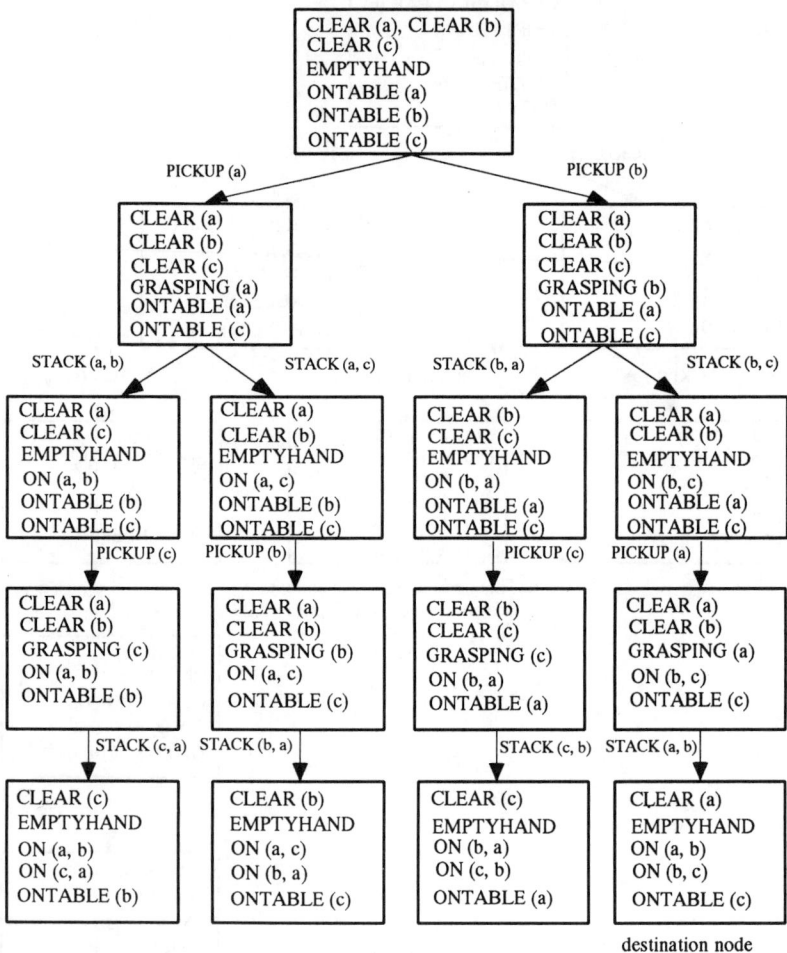

Figure 12.29 Continuing from Figure 12.28, the breadth-first search of the state space for the three-cubes problems.

searching, we have to backchain through the prodrules. Backchaining here is more complicated than the backchaining you saw earlier in sections 5.3.2 and 9.5 because backchaining here involves regression, too. We shall first discuss regression.

Suppose we want to find out how the firing of a prodrule affects a literal G. We then regress G through the prodrule. Figure 12.30 explains how to regress G and what the regression signifies. G can

G is identical to	G regresses to	Comments on what the regression signifies.
one of the literals to be deleted by the firing of the prodrule	FALSE	G will be false after the firing of the prodrule.
one of the literals to be added by the firing of the prodrule	TRUE	G will be true after the firing of the prodrule.
none of the literal to be added or deleted	G	G is not affected by the firing of the prodrule: if G is true [false] before the firing, it will be true [false] after the firing.

Figure 12.30   Regressing a literal G through a prodrule.

regress to FALSE, TRUE or G itself. If G regresses to FALSE (TRUE), then G is false (true) after the firing of the prodrule. If G regresses to itself, then the truth value of G after the firing is the same as it was before the firing.

Below we give two examples of regression. While reading the examples, refer continually to Figure 12.30 to make sure that you have understood regression.

Example 1
Suppose we have the following ground instance of a prodrule (note, b is a constant):

PUTDOWN(b): **If**   CLEAR(b) $\wedge$ GRASPING(b),
        then   delete GRASPING(b),
        and   add EMPTYHAND $\wedge$ ONTABLE(b).

Through the above prodrule GRASPING(b) will regress to FALSE, EMPTYHAND will regress to TRUE, and ONTABLE(a) will regress to ONTABLE(a).

Example 2
Suppose we have the following instance of a prodrule (where b and c are constants and v is a variable):

UNSTACK(b, v): **If**   CLEAR(b) $\wedge$ EMPTYHAND $\wedge$ ON(b, v),
         then   delete EMPTYHAND $\wedge$ ON(b, v),
         and   add CLEAR(v) $\wedge$ GRASPING(b).

Through the above prodrule EMPTYHAND will regress to FALSE, and GRASPING(b) will regress to TRUE.

Let us now regress CLEAR(c) through the prodrule. If $v = c$, then CLEAR(c) will regress to TRUE, but if $v \neq c$, then CLEAR(c) will regress to CLEAR(c).

Similarly, if $v = c$, then ON(b, c) will regress to FALSE, but if $v \neq c$, then ON(b, c) will regress to ON(b, c).

Having discussed regression, we shall now discuss how regression is incorporated into backchaining. Suppose we have a formula J and a prodrule I as follows.

(J) $G_1 \wedge G_2 \ldots \wedge Gj$

(I) **If** $F_1 \wedge F_2 \ldots \wedge F_k$,
   then   delete $L_1 \wedge L_2 \wedge \ldots \wedge L_m$,
   and   add $M_1 \wedge M_2 \wedge \ldots \wedge M_n$.

Formula J can be backchained through prodrule I if there exists a G_i (where $1 \leq i \leq j$) such that G_i is unifiable with one of the M's by an mgu δ. (section 3.3.5 explains mgu's, that is, the most general unifiers.) Then by backchaining formula J through the prodrule I, we obtain the following formula J′.

(J′) $F_1\delta \wedge F_2\delta \wedge \ldots \wedge F_k\delta$
   $\wedge$ Regression of $G_1\delta$ through Iδ
   $\wedge$ Regression of $G_2\delta$ through Iδ
   .
   .
   .
   $\wedge$ Regression of $G_{i-1}\delta$ through Iδ
   $\wedge$ Regression of $G_{i+1}\delta$ through Iδ
   .
   .
   .
   $\wedge$ Regression of $G_j\delta$ through Iδ

Formula J′ is called a **precursor** of formula J. More precisely, J′ is the precursor produced by using the **bellwether** literal G_i to backchain formula J through prodrule I.

Suppose J and J′ denote states in our three-cubes problem. Then the above backchaining signifies that if we want to reach state J (more precisely, the state delineated by formula J) by firing prodrule I, we should first reach state J′; that is, state J′ is a precursor of state J. It may be of interest to you to compare the notion of a precursor discussed here with the notion of a bourne discussed in section 5.3.2.

We give below four examples of the backchaining that we have discussed above. Since, in this section, we have given two examples of regression, the examples below are numbered from 3 onward.

Example 3
By using ONTABLE(b) as the bellwether literal, backchain

EMPTYHAND $\wedge$ ONTABLE(a) $\wedge$ ONTABLE(b)

through the prodrule

PUTDOWN(u): **If** CLEAR(u) $\wedge$ GRASPING(u),
then delete GRASPING(u),
and add EMPTYHAND $\wedge$ ONTABLE(u).

ONTABLE(b) unifies with ONTABLE(u) of the prodrule by mgu $\delta =$ $\{b/u\}$. Applying δ to the prodrule, we obtain the literals in the antecedent of the prodrule to be CLEAR(b) $\wedge$ GRASPING(b). Literal EMPTYHAND regresses to TRUE and ONTABLE(a) regresses to ONTABLE(a). Therefore, we obtain the precursor

CLEAR(b) $\wedge$ GRASPING(b) $\wedge$ TRUE $\wedge$ ONTABLE(a),

which can be simplified to the equivalent formula:

CLEAR(b) $\wedge$ GRASPING(b) $\wedge$ ONTABLE(a).

Example 4
By using CLEAR(b) as the bellwether literal, backchain

CLEAR(b) $\wedge$ EMPTYHAND $\wedge$ ONTABLE(c)

through the prodrule

UNSTACK(u, v): **If** CLEAR(u) $\wedge$ EMPTYHAND $\wedge$ ON(u, v),
then delete EMPTYHAND $\wedge$ ON(u, v),
and add CLEAR(v) $\wedge$ GRASPING(u).

CLEAR(b) unifies with CLEAR(v) of the prodrule by mgu $\delta = \{b/v\}$. Applying δ to the prodrule we obtain the literals in the antecedent of the prodrule to be CLEAR(u) $\wedge$ EMPTYHAND $\wedge$ ON(u, b). Literal EMPTYHAND regresses to FALSE and ONTABLE(c) regresses to ONTABLE(c). Therefore, we obtain the precursor

CLEAR(u) $\wedge$ EMPTYHAND $\wedge$ ON(u, b) $\wedge$ FALSE $\wedge$ ONTABLE(c).

The precursor is inconsistent. Hence, by firing the prodrule, we shall not obtain the formula that was given for backchaining.

Example 5
By using ON(b, c) as the bellwether literal, backchain

$$ON(a, b) \land ON(b, c) \land ONTABLE(c)$$

through the prodrule

STACK(u, v): **If**   CLEAR(u) $\land$ CLEAR(v) $\land$ GRASPING(u),
    then   delete CLEAR(v) $\land$ GRASPING(u),
    and   add EMPTYHAND $\land$ ON(u, v).

ON(b, c) unifies with ON(u, v) of the prodrule by mgu $\delta = \{b/u, c/v\}$. Applying δ to the prodrule, we obtain the literals in the antecedent of the prodrule to be CLEAR(b) $\land$ CLEAR(c) $\land$ GRASPING(b). Literal ON(a, b) regresses to ON(a, b) and ONTABLE(c) regresses to ONTABLE(c). Therefore, we obtain the precursor

CLEAR(b) $\land$ CLEAR(c) $\land$ GRASPING(b) $\land$ ON(a, b)
    $\land$ ONTABLE(c).

A state corresponding to the above precursor is renegade, since it violates the sixth constraint of Figure 12.27. Hence, by firing the prodrule we shall not obtain the formula that was given for backchaining.

Example 6
By using GRASPING(b) as the bellwether literal, backchain

CLEAR(c) $\land$ GRASPING(b) $\land$ ONTABLE(a)

through the prodrule

UNSTACK(b, v): **If**   CLEAR(b) $\land$ EMPTYHAND $\land$ ON(b, v),
    then   delete EMPTYHAND $\land$ ON(b, v),
    and   add CLEAR(v) $\land$ GRASPING(b).

We proceed as we did in the earlier examples in this section. If $v = c$, we obtain the precursor

CLEAR(b) $\land$ EMPTYHAND $\land$ ON(b, c) $\land$ TRUE $\land$ ONTABLE(a),

which can be simplified to the equivalent formula:

CLEAR(b) $\land$ EMPTYHAND $\land$ ON(b, c) $\land$ ONTABLE(a).

But if $v \neq c$, then the precursor we obtain can be rewritten as

CLEAR(b) $\land$ EMPTYHAND $\land$ ON(b, v) $\land$ ~EQUAL(v, c)
    $\land$ CLEAR(c) $\land$ ONTABLE(a).

It is hoped that with the above examples you have understood the backchaining that incorporates regression within it. Such backchaining can be illustrated by a graph wherein nodes correspond to formulae and arcs to prodrules. As a specimen, the graph in Figure 12.31

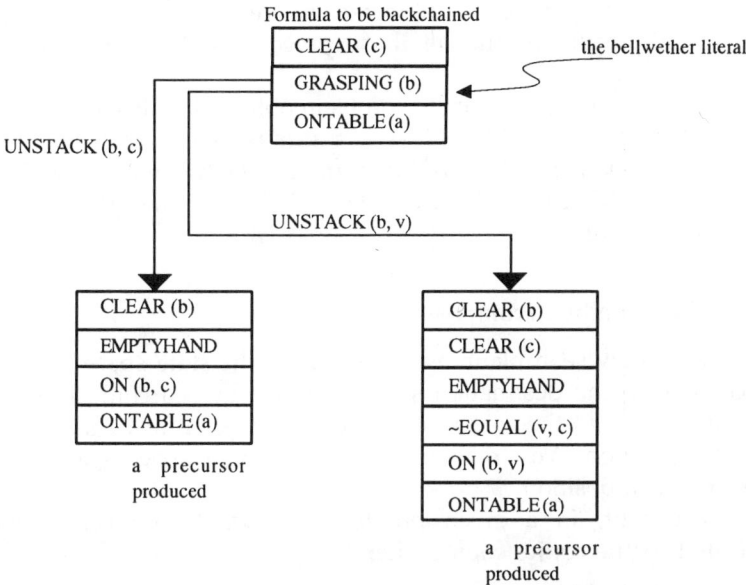

Figure 12.31 The graph to illustrate the backchaining of the sixth example of section 12.5.1. Each node corresponds to a formula delineating a state of our three-cubes problem. An arc is directed from the bellwether litheral in the formula to be backchained. The arc is labelled with the prodrule through which the formula is backchained. The arc is directed toward the precursor produced. To prevent cluttering, the logical operator '∧' between the literals of a formula is not shown.

illustrates the backchaining of the last example above. The legend in the figure explains the notation.

Suppose we have a formula

$$G_1 \wedge G_2 \wedge \ldots \wedge Gj$$

and a set of prodrules. Typically, with a given G_i as the bellwether literal, the formula can be backchained through more than one prodrule. Moreover, if each of the G_i's (where $1 \leq i \leq j$) is considered to be the bellwether literal by turn, then the formula can have several precursors.

A state space search from the destination state of a given problem to the source state can then be outlined as follows. Generate all precursors of the destination state. Remember that each precursor is itself a state. In some order (say, breadth-first or depth-first), select these states and produce their precursors. Continue to do this until the source state is produced. In between, remember to delete all inconsistent precursors and all those precursors that correspond to renegade states.

The solution of the three-cubes problem obtained by backchaining is illustrated in Figures 12.32–12.34. As can be seen from the three figures, the plan is UNSTACK(c, a), PUTDOWN(c), PICKUP(b), STACK(b, c), PICKUP(a), STACK(a, b). This is the same plan that we had obtained earlier from Figures 12.28 and 12.29.

12.5.2   Planning by decomposition

We have by now seen planning by searching the state space from the source state to the destination state, and also by searching from the destination state to the source state. Below, we shall discuss planning by decomposition. You may then compare state space search with problem decomposition.

Suppose that, in a given problem, we want to reach a state delineated by the conjunction of literals:

$$G_1 \wedge G_2 \wedge \ldots \wedge G_j.$$

In problem decomposition, we treat each of the literals as a subproblem. We then attempt to make each literal to be true one by one. We say that we attempt to **attain** each of the G's one by one. When we have attained each of the G's, then we have reached the desired state.

Nevertheless, in a given problem it can happen that we can reach the desired state if we attempt to attain the G's in one order, but we are unable to reach the desired state if we attempt to attain the G's in another order. In the literature, such G's are said to be **interactive** or **non-linear**. To wear shoes and socks it is conventional to attain the wearing of socks before the wearing of shoes, not the other way round. In other words, subproblems should be solved in a prescribed order, but we may not always know the prescribed order.

Accordingly, we can attempt to attain the G's in, say, some arbitrary order. If we do not succeed in attaining all the G's, we can backtrack and attempt the G's in another order. We can continue such backtracking and attempt different orderings of G's until either all the G's are attained or we realize that it is not possible to attain all of the G's.

As an alternative to ordering the G's arbitrarily, we can employ heuristics to measure the difficulty of attaining each of the G's. Then we attempt to attain the G's in decreasing order of their difficulty: the more difficult a G, the earlier it is attempted to be attained. This way,

destination node

UNSTACK (u, a)

CLEAR (a)

EMPTYHAND   PUTDOWN (u)   precursors not
                                                  shown to avoid
STACK (a, b)   ON (a, b)   STACK (u, v)   clutter

ON (b, c)

ONTABLE (c)

STACK (b, c)   PUTDOWN (c)

CLEAR (u)	CLEAR (a)	CLEAR (a)	CLEAR (a)
EMPTYHAND	CLEAR (b)	CLEAR (c)	CLEAR (c)
ON (a, b)	GRASPING (a)	GRASPING (b)	GRASPING (c)
ON (b, c)	ON (b, c)	ON (a, b)	ON (a, b)
ON (u, a)	ONTABLE (c)	ONTABLE (c)	ON (b, c)
ONTABLE (c)			

renegade node since for u=b it violates the thirteenth constraint, and for u=c it violates the seventeenth constraint, of Figure 12.27

This node and its precursors are continued on in Figure 12.33

renegade node since it violates the sixth constraint of Figure 12.27

renegade node since it violates the first constraint of Figure 12.27

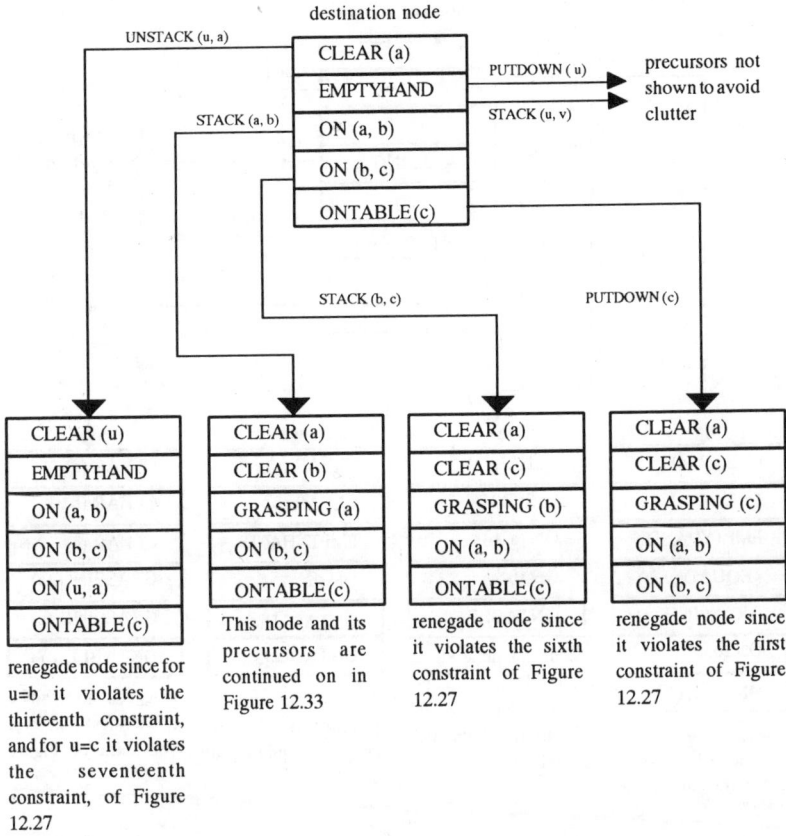

Figure 12.32 Backchaining the destination node of the three-cubes problem. To prevent clutter, not all of the precursors have been shown. The renegade nodes are deleted. The backchaining continues on in Figure 12.33.

the earlier we come to know that one of the *G*'s is unattainable under the present ordering, the earlier we can backtrack and attempt another ordering of the *G*'s. You may have noticed that this reasoning is similar to that mentioned in section 12.3.1 for the depth-first search of AND/ OR graphs.

For our three-cubes problem, we shall assume that the literals (whose different conjunctions delineate different states) are in the following order of decreasing difficulty:

ON(u, v)
CLEAR(v), GRASPING(v), ONTABLE(v)
EMPTYHAND

This node is from
Figure 12.32

UNSTACK (u, b)

UNSTACK (a,b)	CLEAR (a)	UNSTACK (u, a)
	CLEAR (b)	
PICKUP (a)	GRASPING (a)	UNSTACK (a, v)
	ON (b, c)	
	ONTABLE (c)	PUTDOWN (u)

} precursors not
shown to avoid
clutter

STACK (b, c)

CLEAR (a)	CLEAR (a)	CLEAR (a)	CLEAR (a)
CLEAR (u)	EMPTYHAND	CLEAR (b)	CLEAR (b)
EMPTYHAND	ON (a, b)	EMPTYHAND	CLEAR (c)
~EQUAL (u, a)	ON (b, c)	ON (b, c)	GRASPING (a)
GRASPING (a)	ONTABLE (c)	ONTABLE (a)	GRASPING (b)
ON (b, c)		ONTABLE (c)	ONTABLE (c)
ON (u, b)			

renegade node since
it violates the second
constraint of Figure
12.27

recurring node since
it is identical to the
destination node of
Figure 12.32, and so it
is deleted

This node and its
precursors are
continued on in Figure
12.34

renegade node since
it violates the fifth
constraint of Figure
12.27

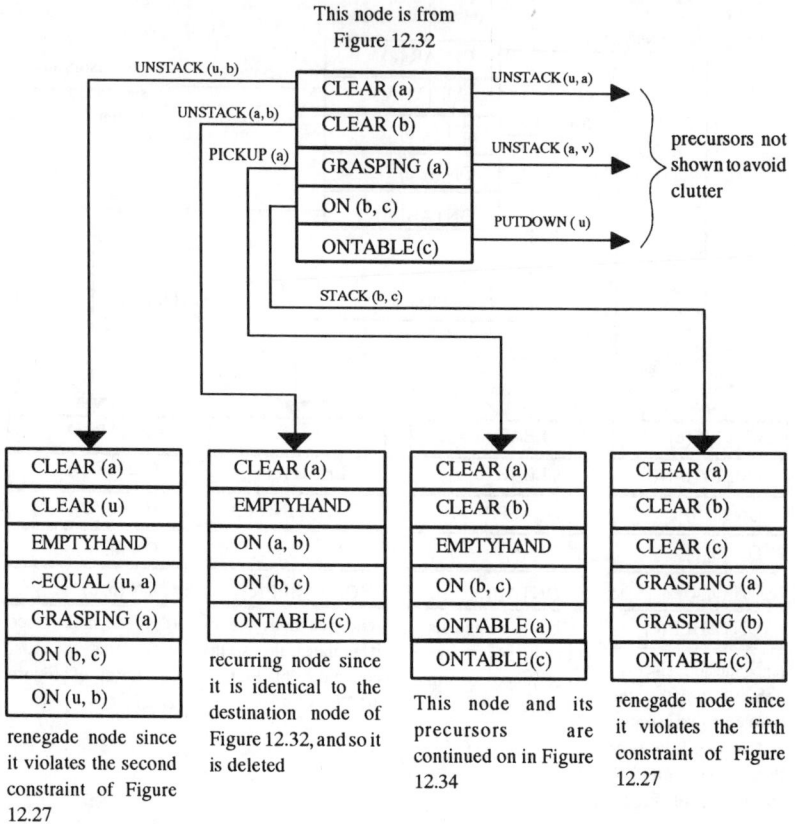

Figure 12.33   Continuing on from Figure 12.32, backchaining for the three-cubes problem. The renegade nodes are deleted. The backchaining continues on in Figure 12.34.

Thus ON(u, v) is assumed to be the most difficult to attain, and EMPTYHAND the least difficult. CLEAR(v), GRASPING(v) and ONTABLE(v) are assumed to be equally difficult among themselves, less difficult than ON(u, v), but more difficult than EMPTYHAND. We assumed EMPTYHAND to be the least difficult because it can be easily attained by putting down whatever the robot hand is grasping.

As we proceed with solving the three-cubes problem, we shall maintain at all times a record of the following:

1. the current state, which tells us the state of the cubes at a given time, and
2. the G-list, which contains the literals yet to be attained.

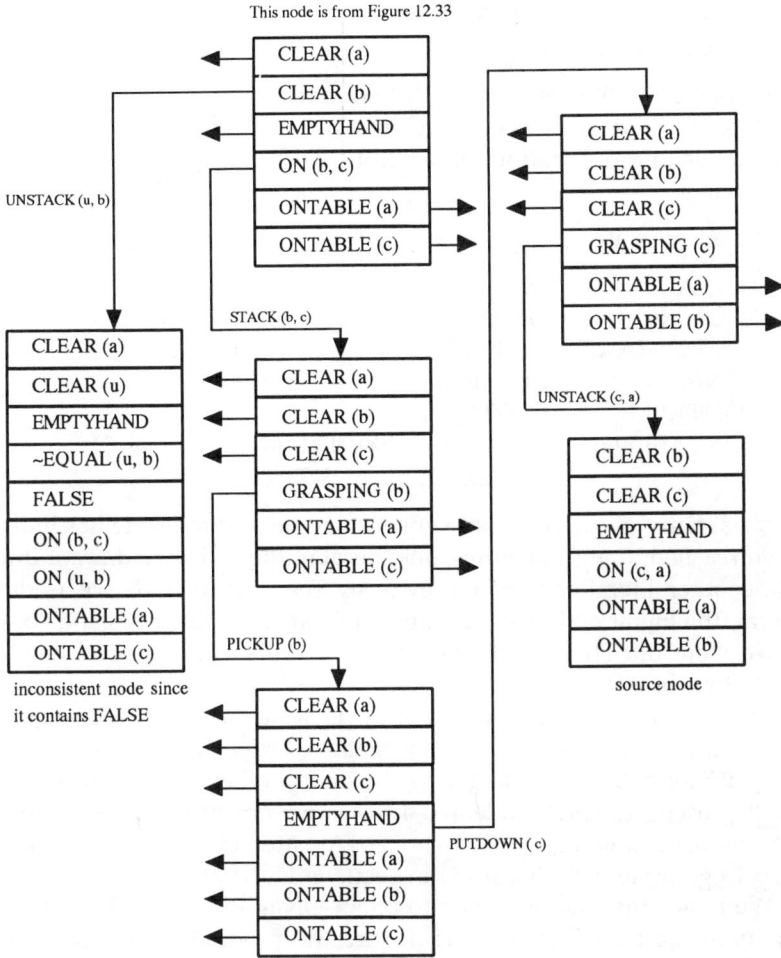

This node is from Figure 12.33

Figure 12.34   Continuing on from Figure 12.33, backchaining for the three-cubes problem. We stop on generating the source node. For the solution, read the labels of the arcs from the source node to the destination node. To prevent clutter, not all of the precursors have been shown.

In the beginning, the current state is the same as the source state,

CLEAR(*b*) ∧ CLEAR(*c*) ∧ EMPTYHAND ∧ ON(*c*, *a*)
  ∧ ONTABLE(*a*) ∧ ONTABLE(*b*),

and the list *G*-list contains the destination state,

CLEAR(*a*) ∧ EMPTYHAND ∧ ON(*a*, *b*) ∧ ON(*b*, *c*) ∧ ONTABLE(*c*).

We reorder the literals of the G-list so that the more difficult a literal, the closer it is to the top of the G-list. We shall then attempt to attain the literals in top to bottom order in the G-list. Accordingly, we obtain the node

(1A) Current state   G-list

CLEAR(*b*)	ON(*a*, *b*)
CLEAR(*c*)	ON(*b*, *c*)
EMPTYHAND	ONTABLE(*c*)
ON(*c*, *a*)	CLEAR(*a*)
ONTABLE(*a*)	EMPTYHAND
ONTABLE(*b*)	CLEAR(*a*) ∧ EMPTYHAND ∧ ON(*a*, *b*)
	∧ ON(*b*, *c*) ∧ ONTABLE(*c*)

The last entry in the G-list is to ensure that the desired state has indeed been reached; that in attaining one literal of the G-list we did not undo some other literal that had previously seen attained. If we undo a literal, the literal no longer remains attained. To wear shoes and socks, if we wore our shoes first, then to wear the socks, we shall have to undo the shoes.

Since the topmost two entries of the G-list are assumed to be equally difficult, we could have had ON(*b*, *c*) above ON(*a*, *b*), as shown in node 1A' of Figure 12.35. Node 1A' is thus an alternative to node 1A. We shall proceed to solve node 1A. In case we are unable to solve node 1A, we can attempt to solve node 1A' after either backtracking or leap-frogging to it as discussed in sections 11.4.1 and 11.4.2.

We notice that the only way to attain ON(a, *b*) in node 1A is to fire the prodrule STACK(a, *b*), but, to fire the prodrule, we should first satisfy the requisite of the prodrule. Note the similarity of this ap-

[1A']   Current State   G-LIST

CLEAR (b)	ON (b, c)
CLEAR (c)	ON (a, b)
EMPTYHAND	ONTABLE (c)
ON (c, a)	CLEAR (a)
ONTABLE (a)	EMPTYHAND
ONTABLE (b)	CLEAR (a) ∧ EMPTYHAND ∧ ON (a, b)
	∧ ON (b, c) ∧ ONTABLE (c)

Figure 12.35 Node 1A' is an alternative to node 1A of section 12.5.2.

proach with the means–end analysis discussed in section 12.4. We remove ON(a, b) from the G-list, and add STACK(a, b) and the literals in the antecedent of the prodrule to the G-list. Accordingly, we obtain the node

(1B) Current state   G-list

CLEAR(b)   CLEAR(a)
CLEAR(c)   CLEAR(b)
EMPTYHAND   GRASPING(a)
ON(c, a)   CLEAR(a) ∧ CLEAR(b) ∧ GRASPING(a)
ONTABLE(a)   STACK(a, b)
ONTABLE(b)   ON(b, c)
              ONTABLE(c)
              CLEAR(a)
              EMPTYHAND
              CLEAR(a) ∧ EMPTYHAND ∧ ON(a, b)
                ∧ ON(b, c) ∧ ONTABLE(c)

To attain CLEAR(a) in node 1B, we need to fire UNSTACK(u, a), so we remove CLEAR(a) from the G-list, and add UNSTACK(u, a) and its antecedent literals to the G-list. Accordingly, we obtain the node

(1C) Current state   G-list

CLEAR(b)   ON(u, a)
CLEAR(c)   CLEAR(u)
EMPTYHAND   EMPTYHAND
ON(c, a)   CLEAR(u) ∧ EMPTYHAND ∧ ON(u, a)
ONTABLE(a)   UNSTACK(u, a)
ONTABLE(b)   CLEAR(b)
              GRASPING(a)
              CLEAR(a) ∧ CLEAR(b) ∧ GRASPING(a)
              STACK(a, b)
              ON(b, c)
              ONTABLE(c)
              CLEAR(a)
              EMPTYHAND
              CLEAR(a) ∧ EMPTYHAND ∧ ON(a, b)
                ∧ ON(b, c) ∧ ONTABLE(c).

We notice that for $u = c$, the topmost four entries of the G-list in node 1C are matched by the current state, that is, these entries are among the literals that delineate the current state, so we fire the prodrule UNSTACK(u, a) for $u = c$, and remove the topmost five entries from the G-list. The firing of the prodrule changes the current state. Accordingly, we obtain the node

(2A) Current state   G-list

CLEAR(*a*)	CLEAR(*b*)
CLEAR(*b*)	GRASPING(*a*)
CLEAR(*c*)	CLEAR(*a*) ∧ CLEAR(*b*) ∧ GRASPING(*a*)
GRASPING(*c*)	STACK(*a*, *b*)
ONTABLE(*a*)	ON(*b*, *c*)
ONTABLE(*b*)	ONTABLE(*c*)
	CLEAR(*a*)
	EMPTYHAND
	CLEAR(*a*) ∧ EMPTYHAND ∧ ON(*a*, *b*)
	∧ ON(*b*, *c*) ∧ ONTABLE(*c*)

CLEAR(*b*) from the G-list is matched by the current state, so it is removed. To attain GRASPING(*a*), we can fire either UNSTACK(*a*, *v*) or PICKUP(*a*). We remove GRASPING(*a*) from the G-list. If we choose to fire UNSTACK(*a*, *v*), we add it and its antecedent literals to the G-list, as shown in Figure 12.36.

If, however, we choose to fire PICKUP(*a*), then we add it and its antecedent literals to the G-list. Accordingly, we obtain the node

(2B) Current state   G-list

CLEAR(*a*)	CLEAR(*a*)
CLEAR(*b*)	ONTABLE(*a*)
CLEAR(*c*)	EMPTYHAND
GRASPING(*c*)	CLEAR(*a*) ∧ EMPTYHAND ∧ ONTABLE(*a*)

[2B']	Current State	G-list
	CLEAR (a)	ON (a, v)
	CLEAR (b)	CLEAR (a)
	CLEAR (c)	EMPTYHAND
	GRASPING (c)	CLEAR (a) ∧ EMPTYHAND ∧ ON (a, v)
	ONTABLE (a)	UNSTACK (a, v)
	ONTABLE (b)	CLEAR (a) ∧ CLEAR (b) ∧ GRASPING (a)
		STACK (a, b)
		ON (b, c)
		ONTABLE (c)
		CLEAR (a)
		EMPTYHAND
		CLEAR (a) ∧ EMPTYHAND ∧ ON (a, b)
		∧ ON (b, c) ∧ ONTABLE (c)

Figure 12.36   Node 2B' is an alternative to node 2B of section 12.5.2.

[2C']   Current State   G-list

    CLEAR (a)   CLEAR (u)
    CLEAR (b)   CLEAR (v)
    CLEAR (c)   GRASPING (u)
    GRASPING (c)   CLEAR (u) ∧ CLEAR (v) ∧ GRASPING (u)
    ONTABLE (a)   STACK (u, v)
    ONTABLE (b)   CLEAR (a) ∧ EMPTYHAND ∧ ONTABLE (a)
                                    PICKUP (a)
                                    CLEAR (a) ∧ CLEAR (b) ∧ GRASPING (a)
                                    STACK (a, b)
                                    ON (b, c)
                                    ONTABLE (c)
                                    CLEAR (a)
                                    EMPTYHAND
                                    CLEAR (a) ∧ EMPTYHAND ∧ ON (a, b)
                                       ∧ ON (b, c) ∧ ONTABLE (c)

Figure 12.37   Node 2C' is an alternative to node 2C of section 12.5.2.

ONTABLE(*a*)   PICKUP(*a*)
ONTABLE(*b*)   CLEAR(*a*) ∧ CLEAR(*b*) ∧ GRASPING(*a*)
               STACK(*a*, *b*)
               ON(*b*, *c*)
               ONTABLE(*c*)
               CLEAR(*a*)
               EMPTYHAND
               CLEAR(*a*) ∧ EMPTYHAND ∧ ON(*a*, *b*)
                  ∧ ON(*b*, *c*) ∧ ONTABLE(*c*)

The topmost two entries of the G-list in node 2B are matched by the current state; so we remove these entries. To attain EMPTYHAND we can fire either STACK(*u*, *v*) or PUTDOWN(*u*). We remove EMPTY-HAND from the G-list. If we choose STACK(*u*, *v*), we add it and its antecedent literals to the G-list as shown in Figure 12.37.

If, however, we choose PUTDOWN(*u*) then we add it and its antecedent literals to the G-list. Accordingly, we obtain the node

(2C) Current state   G-list

    CLEAR(*a*)   CLEAR(*u*)
    CLEAR(*b*)   GRASPING(*u*)
    CLEAR(*c*)   CLEAR(*u*) ∧ GRASPING(*u*)
    GRASPING(*c*)   PUTDOWN(*u*)
    ONTABLE(*a*)   CLEAR(*a*) ∧ EMPTYHAND ∧ ONTABLE(*a*)
    ONTABLE(*b*)   PICKUP(*a*)

CLEAR(a) $\wedge$ CLEAR(b) $\wedge$ GRASPING(a)
STACK(a, b)
ON(b, c)
ONTABLE(c)
CLEAR(a)
EMPTYHAND
CLEAR(a) $\wedge$ EMPTYHAND $\wedge$ ON(a, b)
    $\wedge$ ON(b, c) $\wedge$ ONTABLE(c)

We notice that for $u = c$, the topmost three entries of the G-list in node 2C are matched by the current state, so we fire the prodrule PUTDOWN(u) for $u = c$, and remove the topmost four entries from the G-list. The firing of the prodrule changes the current state. Accordingly, we obtain the node

(3A) Current state   G-list

CLEAR(a)   CLEAR(a) $\wedge$ EMPTYHAND $\wedge$ ONTABLE(a)
CLEAR(b)   PICKUP(a)
CLEAR(c)   CLEAR(a) $\wedge$ CLEAR(b) $\wedge$ GRASPING(a)
EMPTYHAND   STACK(a, b)
ONTABLE(a)   ON(b, c)
ONTABLE(b)   ONTABLE(c)
ONTABLE(c)   CLEAR(a)
                        EMPTYHAND
                        CLEAR(a) $\wedge$ EMPTYHAND $\wedge$ ON(a, b)
                            $\wedge$ ON(b, c) $\wedge$ ONTABLE(c).

The topmost entry of the G-list in node 3A is matched by the current state, so we fire the prodrule PICKUP(a) and remove the topmost two entries from the G-list. The firing of the prodrule changes the current state. Accordingly, we obtain the node

(4A) Current state   G-list

CLEAR(a)   CLEAR(a) $\wedge$ CLEAR(b) $\wedge$ GRASPING(a)
CLEAR(b)   STACK(a, b)
CLEAR(c)   ON(b, c)
GRASPING(a)   ONTABLE(c)
ONTABLE(b)   CLEAR(a)
ONTABLE(c)   EMPTYHAND
                        CLEAR(a) $\wedge$ EMPTYHAND $\wedge$ ON(a, b)
                            $\wedge$ ON(b, c) $\wedge$ ONTABLE(c)

The topmost entry of the G-list of node 4A is matched by the current state, so we fire the prodrule STACK(a, b) and remove the topmost two entries from the G-list. The firing of the prodrule changes the current state. Accordingly, we obtain the node

(5A) Current state   G-list

CLEAR(a)	ON(b, c)
CLEAR(c)	ONTABLE(c)
EMPTYHAND	CLEAR(a)
ON(a, b)	EMPTYHAND
ONTABLE(b)	CLEAR(a) $\wedge$ EMPTYHAND $\wedge$ ON(a, b)
ONTABLE(c)	$\wedge$ ON(b, c) $\wedge$ ONTABLE(c)

By now you must have understood how to continue. The literal to attain in node 5A is ON(b, c). You may now proceed on your own. Nodes 1A', 2B' and 2C' shown in Figures 12.35–12.37 serve as alternatives in case you have to backtrack or leap-frog.

You may have noticed that above we generated nine nodes: 1A, 1B, 1C, 2A, 2B, 2C, 3A, 4A and 5A; but we made only four moves: from 1C to 2A, from 2C to 3A, from 3A to 4A, and from 4A to 5A. Between the other nodes we changed the contents of the G-list but not the current state. If you proceed in the manner shown above and stop when the G-list becomes empty you will obtain the following ten moves:

1. UNSTACK(c, a)
2. PUTDOWN(c)
3. PICKUP(a)
4. STACK(a, b)
5. UNSTACK(a, b)
6. PUTDOWN(a)
7. PICKUP(b)
8. STACK(b, c)
9. PICKUP(a)
10. STACK(a, b)

But then you will notice that the current state after the second move (PUTDOWN(c)) above is identical to the current state after the sixth move (PUTDOWN(a)). You can then condense the plan by deleting the third, fourth, fifth and sixth moves, for they are unnecessary. Accordingly, the condensed plan will be UNSTACK(c, a), PUTDOWN(c), PICKUP(b), STACK(b, c), PICKUP(a), STACK(a, b). This is the same plan as that obtained from Figures 12.28 and 12.29, and also as that obtained from Figures 12.32–12.34.

The unnecessary moves above were obtained because, in proceeding from node 1A, we chose to attain ON(a, b) before ON(b, c). Because of that you will attain ON(a, b), undo it, attain ON(b, c), and then attain

ON(a, b) again. It is likely that you may not generate the unnecessary moves if you proceed from node 1A' of Figure 12.35. In proceeding from node 1A', you will choose to attain ON(b, c) before ON(a, b). By looking at the pictorial representation of the destination state in Figure 12.25, it should be intuitively obvious that ON(b, c) should be attained before ON(a, b), but incorporating such intuitive foresight in a computer program in general is difficult. At times, the plans you generate may contain unnecessary moves. It is suggested that, after you generate a plan, you scan it to locate unnecessary moves and accordingly condense the plan. Appearance of the same state more than once during the execution of a plan is an indication that the plan contains unnecessary moves. For the rest of this chapter, any reference to a plan is that to a condensed plan, unless otherwise stated.

12.5.3   Triangular matrices for planning

You may have felt that a fair amount of computation could be required in developing a plan no matter whether we search the state space or the decompositions. Often a robot is needed to perform tasks that are either repeated or similar. It is not necessary that a robot develop a plan from scratch every time it is called to perform a task. Once a robot develops a plan, it can store the plan in its memory in the form of a triangular matrix as described below.

Suppose, to perform some task, the robot developed a plan that required the firing of N prodrules. For the three-cubes problem of Figure 12.25, the plan required the firing of six prodrules: UNSTACK(c, a), PUTDOWN(c), PICKUP(b), STACK(b, c), PICKUP(a), STACK(a, b). Thus $N = 6$. We shall number these prodrules from 1 to 6; hence UNSTACK(c, a) is the plan's first prodrule and STACK(a, b) the sixth. For a better understanding, continually refer to the triangular matrix in Figure 12.38, as you read the description below.

The triangular matrix M contains $N + 1$ rows and $N + 1$ columns, where

1. row i (where $1 \leq i \leq N$) contains the literals that constitute the requisite of the plan's ith prodrule;
2. row $N + 1$ contains the literals whose conjunction delineates the destination state;
3. column 1 contains the literals whose conjunction delineates the source state;
4. column j (where $2 \leq j \leq N + 1$) contains those literals that are added by the plan's $(j - 1)$th prodrule.

	1	2	3	4	5	6	7
1	CLEAR (c) EMPTYHAND ON (c, a)	UNSTACK (c, a)					
2		CLEAR (c) GRASPING(c)	PUTDOWN (c)				
3	CLEAR (b) ONTABLE (b)		EMPTYHAND	PICKUP (b)			
4			CLEAR (c)	CLEAR (b) GRASPING(b)	STACK (b, c)		
5	ONTABLE (a)	CLEAR (a)			EMPTYHAND	PICKUP (a)	
6					CLEAR (b)	CLEAR (a) GRASPING(a)	STACK (a, b)
7			ONTABLE (c)		ON (b, c)		CLEAR (a) ON (a, b) EMPTYHAND

Figure·12.38 The triangular matrix M depicting the plan developed for our three-cubes problem. To illustrate the notion of kernels, the second kernel comprises rows 2 to 7, and columns 1 to 2; the fifth kernel comprises rows 5 to 7, and columns 1 to 5.

The outcome of the above is that, in the triangular matrix M (for $2 \leq i$, $j \leq N$), the element

$M(i, j) =$ those literals added by firing the plan's $(j - 1)$th
prodrule that are contained in the requisite of the
plan's ith prodrule.

The kth **kernel** (where $1 \leq k \leq N + 1$) in M is defined to comprise all elements $M(i, j)$ such that $k \leq i \leq N + 1$ and $1 \leq j \leq k$. A state is said to be in the kth kernel if the conjunction of the literals in the kernel delineates that state, that is, all the literals in the kernel are **matched** by the state. Thus, the first kernel contains the source state; the mth kernel (where $2 \leq m \leq N$) contains the state after the firing of the plan's $(m - 1)$th prodrule but before the firing of the plan's mth prodrule; the $(N + 1)$th kernel contains the destination state. The procedure to find the kernel in which a given state x is contained can be outlined as follows.

(1) Let i and k be equal to $N + 1$.
(2) If $i < 0$, then state x is not contained in any kernel of the triangular matrix M.
(3) Scan the ith row of M left to right from columns 1 to k.
(4) If in column j (note, $j \leq k$) of the ith row we find a literal that is not matched by the state x (that is, state x can be contained in only kernel $j - 1$ or less), then let k be equal to $j - 1$, decrease i by 1, and go to (2).
(5) If there are no literals in columns 1 to k of the ith row that are not matched by the state x, then do:
    (5.1) if $i = k$, return since the state x is contained in the kth kernel;
    (5.2) otherwise, decrease i by 1, and go to (2).

Let us consider an example in which to apply the above procedure. Suppose that a given state x in our three-cubes problem is denoted by:

CLEAR(a) $\wedge$ CLEAR(b) $\wedge$ CLEAR(c) $\wedge$ EMPTYHAND
$\wedge$ ONTABLE(a) $\wedge$ ONTABLE(b) $\wedge$ ONTABLE(c)

In the triangular matrix of Figure 12.38, we are to find the kernel that contains state x. We proceed as follows.

1. Scan the seventh row from the left to the right. The literal in the fifth column, ON(b, c), is not matched by state x. Let $k = 5 - 1 = 4$.
2. Scan the sixth row from columns 1 to 4. There are no literals that are not matched by state x.
3. Scan the fifth row from columns 1 to 4. There are no literals that are not matched by state x.
4. Scan the fourth row from columns 1 to 4. The literal in the fourth column, GRASPING(b), is not matched by state x. Let $k = 4 - 1 = 3$.
5. Scan the third row from columns 1 to 3. There are no literals that are not matched by state x. Thus, state x is contained in the third kernel.

Now note that if it is required to traverse from the state in the mth kernel to the state in the nth kernel, where $m < n$, we need to fire prodrules $m, m + 1, \ldots, n - 1$. To illustrate, if we are to traverse from the state in the third kernel of Figure 12.38 to the state in the sixth kernel, we shall fire the third, fourth and fifth prodrules, that is, PICKUP(b), STACK(b, c) and PICKUP(a).

Triangular matrices are also useful in recovering from robotic accidents. Suppose that in Figure 12.38, after the firing of the fourth prodrule, STACK(b, c), the cube b falls off cube c and lands on the table. The sensors built into the robot can ascertain that the state now actually existing is contained in the third kernel, so the robot can continue on from firing the third prodrule, PICKUP(b).

12.6   CLOSING REMARKS

In the last two chapters you have read about solving problems by searching state space and searching decompositions. The two methodologies can be mixed. Say you are given a problem to solve. You may decompose it into subproblems. Some of the subproblems may be solved by further decomposition, while the other subproblems may be solved by state space search.

In the next chapter we discuss another kind of problem to solve: the problem of playing games.

12.7   EXERCISES

1. Your problem is to write an essay on artificial intelligence. How will you attempt to solve the problem: by searching the state space, by decomposition or by some other approach you have developed? Discuss.
2. Argue for or against: Any recursive procedure exemplifies problem solving by decomposition.
3. Can you solve the problem of λ missionaries and λ cannibals, introduced in section 11.1, by decomposition? If not, why not? If yes, then write a program to solve the problem for $\lambda = 1, 2, 3, \ldots,$ 10.
4. Write a program to solve the eight-tiles puzzle according to the decomposition given in Figure 12.39. Compare the efficiency of this approach with that of the A* search, which was discussed in section 11.5.1.
5. The problem of the λ franc and λ pound coins puzzle in Figure 11.7 contains $2\lambda + 1$ cells. We can solve the problem by decomposing it into the following two subproblems.
   (a) Obtain a state such that the rightmost cell contains a franc coin and the leftmost cell contains a pound coin.
   (b) Ignoring the leftmost and the rightmost cells, solve the subproblem of the $\lambda - 1$ franc and $\lambda - 1$ pound coins puzzle that now contains $2\lambda - 1$ cells.
   The second subproblem above can be further decomposed. Write a program to solve the problem by the decomposition discussed above for $\lambda = 2, 3, \ldots, 6$. Compare the efficiency of this approach with that of the A* search, which was discussed in section 11.5.1.

For the 8-tiles puzzle [see Figure 11.12], the problem of traversing from the source state

$$
\begin{array}{|ccc|}
\hline
7 & \bullet & 1 \\
3 & 2 & 8 \\
4 & 5 & 6 \\
\hline
\end{array}
\quad \text{to the destination state} \quad
\begin{array}{|ccc|}
\hline
3 & 7 & 1 \\
2 & 8 & 6 \\
4 & 5 & \bullet \\
\hline
\end{array}
$$

can be decomposed into the following two subproblems:

[1]   Traverse from the source state to

$$
\begin{array}{|ccc|}
\hline
3 & 7 & 1 \\
2 & X & X \\
4 & X & X \\
\hline
\end{array}
$$

The X's can be the empty cell, or any of the tiles stamped 5, 6, or 8. Hence, in this subproblem, the tiles in the gnomon not containing the empty cell are brought to where they would be in the destination state.

[2]   Traverse from the above state to the destination state by manipulating only the X's as if they constituted a 3-tiles puzzle [see Figure 11.10].

Figure 12.39 The problem decomposition of the eight-tiles puzzle for exercise 4.

6. Develop an outline for the breadth-first search of an AND/OR graph to find a solution graph.
7. In Chapter 2 you read about natural deduction to prove theorems. Discuss how means–end analysis can be employed to select inference rules for proving theorems by natural deduction in mathematical logic.
8. Write a program to find the plan of the three-cubes problem by solving node 1A′ of Figure 12.35.
9. Write a program to solve the four-cubes problem, illustrated in Figure 12.40, by (a) a state space search from the source state to the destination state, (b) backchaining with regression, and (c) problem decomposition. Compare the efficiency of the three approaches and construct the triangular matrix for the plan generated. Redo the exercise after interchanging the source and the destination states. While redoing the exercise, does the computation required to generate the plan by decomposition depend on the order in which you attempt to attain ON(d, c), ON(c, b) and ON(b, a)?
10. You are given the prodrule:
TRANSFER(X, Y, a, b):

> **If**   register X contains the value a,
> **and**   register Y contains the value b,
> **then** register X contains the value b.

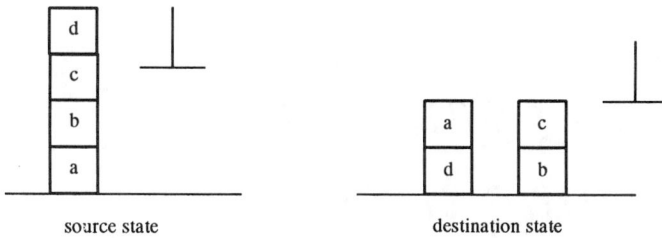

source state   destination state

Figure 12.40 The source and the destination states for the four-cubes problem of exercise 9.

In other words, the value of register Y is transferred to register X while the value in register Y remains unchanged. Let CONTAIN(X, a) be a literal to denote that register X contains the value a. Then the above prodrule can be written as follows:

If   CONTAIN(X, a) $\wedge$ CONTAIN(Y, b),

then   delete CONTAIN(X, a),

and   add CONTAIN(X, b).

You are given three registers X, Y and Z. Can you employ means–end analysis to exchange the contents of X and Y? If yes, show how it can be done. If not, discuss why it cannot be done.

12.8 SUGGESTIONS FOR FURTHER READING

Martelli and Montanari (1978) discussed AO* search and its admissibility. Ernst and Newell (1969) explored GPS, a General Problem Solver, based on means–end analysis. Chapman (1987), Korf (1987) and Nilsson (1980) presented refinements to planning.

1. Chapman, D. (1987) Planning for conjunctive goals, *Artificial Intelligence*, **32**[3], 333–77.
2. Ernst G. and Newell, A. (1969) *GPS: A Case Study in Generality and Problem Solving*, Academic Press, New York.
3. Korf, R. E. (1987) Planning as search: a quantitative approach, *Artificial Intelligence*, **33**[1], 65–88.
4. Martelli, A. and Montanari U. (1978) Optimizing decision trees through heuristically guided search, *Communications of the ACM*, **21**[2], 1025–39.
5. Nilsson, N. J. (1980) *Principles of Artificial Intelligence*, Tioga Publishing Company, Palo Alto, California.

13

Playing games by searching trees

13.1 INTRODUCTION

In the kinds of problems studied in the last two chapters you faced no opponent in solving the problem: no one was deliberately trying to prevent you from reaching your objective of solving the given problem. But if you are playing the game of, say, chess, and your objective understandably is to win the game, then you face another player, your opponent. Your opponent deliberately tries to prevent you from reaching your objective. In this chapter, you will read how you can get a computer to be a player in certain types of games and how it can attempt to defeat its opponent. Such games are usually played interactively with the computer.

For our discussion the terminology on graphs will be the same as that in the last two chapters. Hence you should be conversant with those chapters; that terminology will not be defined again. Any extension to that terminology or any new terminology will, of course, be defined.

We shall confine our discussion to games of two players. The objective of each player is to win. During the game, the players alternate in making a move. For our purposes, a **move** is the action performed by either player to transform the game from one state into another. This extends slightly the definition of a move from that given in section 11.1. Books aimed at teaching their readers how to play some of the two-player games occasionally define a move as a player's action followed by his opponent's action. Do not be confused. Our definition of a move will make our discussion easier to comprehend. Furthermore, it is the definition that is customary in the literature on computer game playing.

We shall assume for our discussion that the games are zero-sum games: one player's win is the other player's loss. If the game terminates with neither player winning, then the game is a draw.

We shall also assume for our discussion that the outcome of the game depends solely on the moves made by the two players, not on chance. Hence we shall disregard games like backgammon and rummy: in the former, the outcome depends partly on the chance result of the roll of dice; in the latter, on the chance result of the distribution of playing cards.

Lastly, we shall assume for our discussion that the games are perfect-information games: at any given time during the game, each player knows fully about all the moves that either player has made until then, the state of the game then existing, and the moves available to the player whose turn it is to play at that time. Rummy is not an instance of a perfect-information game: a player does not know the cards held by his opponent, and thus he does not fully know the current state of the game.

Our discussion will accordingly be confined to two-player, zero-sum, non-chance, perfect-information games. Such games are, for example, draughts (also known as checkers), chess, Go, Grundy's, Kalah, Nim, Othello, and noughts and crosses (also known as tic-tac-toe). You need not be skilled in any of the above games to understand our discussion. It will, however, be helpful if you are familiar with the above class of games in a general sense.

13.1.1 Comprehensive game trees

As a preparatory example to understand the preliminary notions for this chapter, let us consider the λ-coin (where $\lambda \geq 1$) Grundy's game, which is played as follow.

> Two players C_1 and C_2 have a pile of λ coins between them. Moving first, C_1 splits the pile into two unequal piles. To illustrate, a pile of 6 coins can be split into two piles of either 5 and 1 coins, or of 4 and 2 coins, but not of 3 and 3 coins. After C_1 has moved, C_2 similarly splits one of the piles. The game proceeds with the two players alternating so that each player likewise splits one of the piles at his turn to move. The game terminates when no pile can be further split into two unequal piles. The player whose turn it then is to move is declared the loser, and the other player the winner.

It should perhaps be obvious that, when the above game terminates, each pile between the players will have either one coin or two coins.

For our discussion, we shall consider the game when the number of coins in the pile at the beginning of the game is seven; in other words, $\lambda = 7$. To look at the possible move sequences we search the state

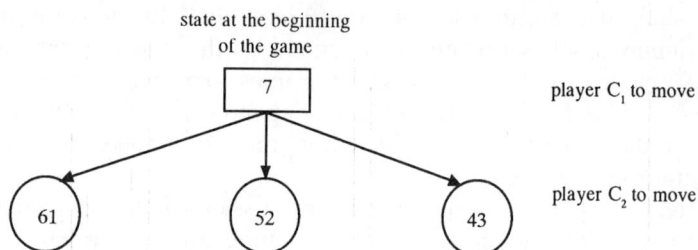

state at the beginning
of the game

7   player C_1 to move

61   52   43   player C_2 to move

Figure 13.1   The possible game states after the first move of player C_1 in the seven-coin Grundy's game. These states are <61>, <52>, and <43>, depending on the move made by C_1. As may be apparent from the above, the nodes correspond to game states, and the arcs to moves. Remembering the terminology of graphs from Chapter 11, we know that the leaf nodes <61>, <52>, and <43> are siblings. They are the children generated by expanding their parent node <7>. The root node <7> is at depth, or level, 0. Its three children are at depth 1. It is now the turn of player C_2 to move. We expand the nodes at depth 1 to obtain the possible game states after C_2 has moved. This is shown in Figure 13.2.

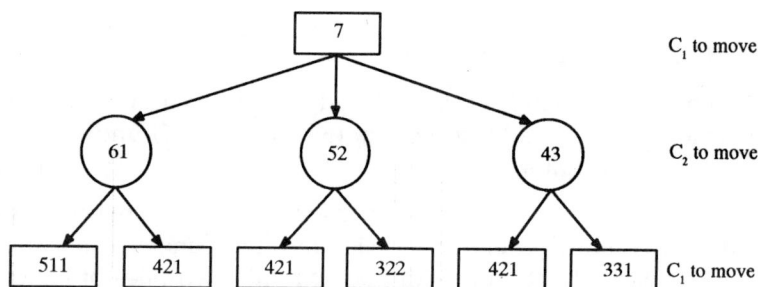

7   C_1 to move

61   52   43 C_2 to move

511   421   421   322   421   331 C_1 to move

Figure 13.2   Continuing from Figure 13.1, we obtain the possible game states after player C_2 has moved. These states correspond to the leaf nodes, which are at depth 2 above. The arcs between depth 0 and depth 1 nodes correspond to the moves of player C_1, and the arcs between depth 1 and depth 2 nodes correspond to the moves of player C_2. By convention, nodes at even depths are shown to be rectangular, and nodes at odd depths are shown to be circular. The player who moves from odd depth nodes is the opponent of the player who moves from even depth nodes, and vice versa. From the graph terminology of Chapter 11, remember that the root node is the ancestor of all the non-root nodes. Conversely, all the non-root nodes are descendants of the root node. We can continue to expand the leaf nodes depth by depth, until we generate *terminal* nodes; that is, until we generate nodes at which the game terminates. This is shown in Figure 13.3.

space by constructing a graph in the form of a tree, called a **comprehensive game tree**. In such a tree for the seven-coin Grundy's game, let the node

$$\langle j_1 \ j_2 \ j_3 \ \ldots \rangle$$

correspond to that state of the game in which each of the piles between the two players contains j_1, j_2, $j_3 \ldots$ coins. Thus the node $\langle 3211 \rangle$, for instance, corresponds to that game state in which there exists one pile of three coins, one pile of two coins and two piles of one coin each. The node corresponding to the game state at the beginning of the game is $\langle 7 \rangle$. The comprehensive game tree is then constructed in stages from Figures 13.1–13.3. We can see from Figure 13.3 that the game is *biased*

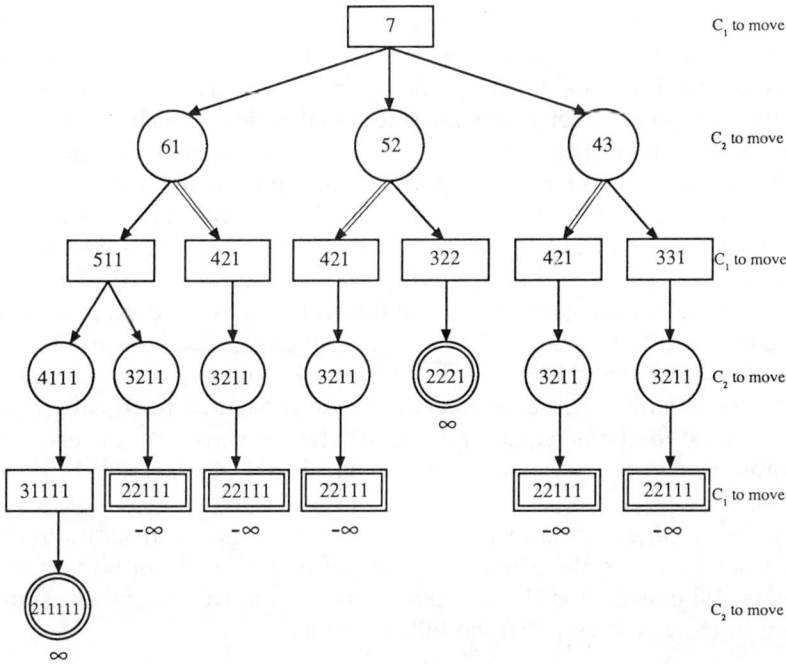

Figure 13.3   To construct the comprehensive game tree for the seven-coin Grundy's game, we continue from Figure 13.2 to expand the leaf nodes depth by depth. We stop when all the leaf nodes become terminal nodes. Such nodes are shown doubly lined above. A value of ∞ written alongside a terminal node indicates player C_1 wins at that node, and a value of $-\infty$ indicates C_1 loses. Depending on what first move C_1 makes, if C_2 makes the move corresponding to a doubly lined arc, then C_2 will win the game: we, therefore, say that the seven-coin Grundy's game is biased in favour of C_2.

in favour of player C_2: a game is said to be *biased* in favour of a player if, and only if, he can win regardless of what moves the other player makes. The bias in the λ-coin Grundy's game for $\lambda = 7$ does not, however, necessarily imply that the game has a similar bias for other values of λ. It should be apparent from Figure 13.3 that in the comprehensive game tree for a given game

1. the root node corresponds to the beginning game state, and
2. the leaf nodes are terminal, thus corresponding to the game states at which the game terminates.

At each terminal node, we would know the outcome of the game played if the game were to traverse along the sequence of arcs from the root to that terminal node; that is to say, we know which player would win, or whether the game would be a draw.

It may seem that to play a given game, all a computer needs to do is to construct a comprehensive game tree and then make suitable moves so that the game traverses toward a terminal node at which it wins. But for many a game, the comprehensive game tree is far too large to be stored in the computer memory. According to estimates mentioned in the literature, a node in the tree for chess has typically 35 children and the game lasts typically 80 moves: the comprehensive game tree would thus contain about 35^{80} nodes, which is approximated as 10^{120} nodes. The comprehensive game tree for draughts has likewise been estimated to contain 10^{40} nodes and the comprehensive game tree for Go to contain 10^{180} nodes. Even if we were to miraculously come upon the memory to store such large trees, the time consumed to construct the tree would perhaps equal the life of the universe, so instead the computer constructs smaller trees, which we shall call **abridged game trees**.

In an abridged game tree, the root node need not correspond to the beginning game state. Moreover, the leaf nodes need not be terminal nodes. Whenever it is the computer's turn to move in a given game, then in essence it executes the following steps:

1. constructs an abridged game tree rooted in the current game state, that is, the game state from which it is to move;
2. searches the tree by looking at the nodes that correspond to the game states possible over the next few moves; and
3. makes the move to enable the game to traverse toward the node that appears to be the most potent to it (by definition, the more potent a node is to a player, the more likely it is that the player can win from that node).

Before discussing in detail the constructing and the searching of an abridged game tree, we shall discuss the measuring of the potency of a node.

13.1.2   The potency of a node

A **potency function** (also known in the literature as a **static evaluation function**) is a heuristic function with respect to one of the players to measure how potent is the node to that player. The function maps the node into a numerical value, which is named the **potency value** (also known as the **static value** in the literature) of the node. If the potency function is with respect to a player C, then the potency value obtained is also said to be with respect to C. By convention, the higher the potency value of a node with respect to a player, the more potent is the node to that player.

As an example for developing a potency function, let us consider a game in which you may be a wizard, to wit noughts and crosses:

On a 3×3 grid of empty spaces two players C_1 and C_2 move alternately, C_1 putting an 'X' symbol and C_2 putting a 'O' symbol. Either player may move first at the beginning of the game. The winner is the player who is able to put three identical symbols in a line, that is, in a row, column or diagonal. If there are no empty spaces remaining in the grid, and if neither player has been able to put three identical symbols in a line, then the game terminates in a draw.

Figures 13.4 and 13.5 illustrate two different potency functions for noughts and crosses. The function of Figure 13.5 requires more computation than that of Figure 13.4. Comparing the computation required by the two functions and your intuitive assessment of which function is more accurate in its purpose, you may choose either function, or you may develop your own. Remember that potency functions are heuristic.

You will have noticed that the potency functions of Figures 13.4 and 13.5 are both polynomials. The potency function for many a game is expressed in practice as the polynomial

$$W_1 u_1 + W_2 u_2 + W_3 u_3 \ldots ,$$

where the u's are **features** to be extracted from a given node and the W's are weighting coefficients. The W's reflect the weighting that has been allocated to the different features: the more important a u_i is the greater is the allocated W_i.

For instance, in Figure 13.5, more weight has been allocated to

Let the potency function with respect to C_1, the player who puts the 'X' symbols, be $u_1 - u_2$, where for $1 \le i \le 2$,

u_i =   number of lines that are still unblocked for player C_i; a line is said to be <u>unblocked</u> for C_i if at some stage of the game C_i can have three of his symbols on that line.

Then for, say, the following given node

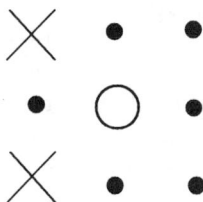

we observe that

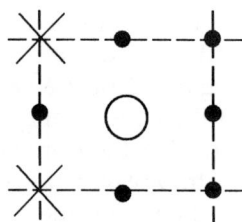   and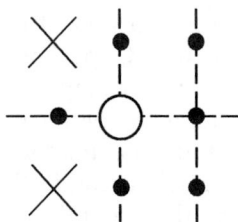

$u_1 = 4$ and $u_2 = 3$.

Therefore, the potency value of the given node is $u_1 - u_2 = 1$.

Figure 13.4   A specimen potency function for noughts and crosses.

having three symbols in a line than to having two symbols in a line. We can view this another way: since we can have three symbols in a line only after having two symbols in that line, we allocate more weight to the former. Reworded, a feature desired in the long run is allocated more weight than a feature desired in the short run, because ultimately (in the long run) we want to win.

As further examples, let us consider the games of draughts and chess, both played on an 8 × 8 board. At any particular time in draughts, a player has at the most two types of pieces: king and non-king. In chess, a player at any time has one king and at the most

We are to develop a potency function different from that in Figure 13.4. This function is also with respect to C_1, the player who puts the 'X' symbols. According to this function, let the potency value of a node be equal to

$$(u_{11} - u_{21}) + 5(u_{12} - u_{22}) + 30(u_{13} - u_{23})$$

where for $1 \le i \le 2$ and $1 \le j \le 3$,

u_{ij} = number of unblocked lines for player C_i in which C_i has already put j of his symbols.

Then for the following given node:

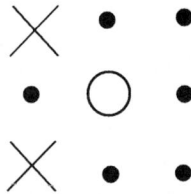

we observe that

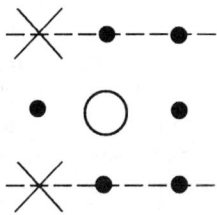 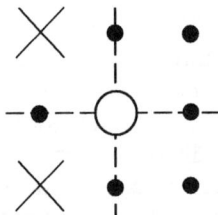 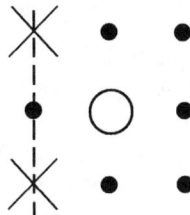

$$u_{11} = 2, \qquad\qquad u_{21} = 2, \qquad \text{and} \qquad u_{12} = 1.$$

Moreover, $u_{22} = u_{13} = u_{23} = 0$. Therefore, the potency value of the given node

$$= (u_{11} - u_{21}) + 5(u_{12} - u_{22}) + 30(u_{13} - u_{23})$$
$$= (2 - 2) + 5(1 - 0) + 30(0 - 0)$$
$$= 5.$$

Figure 13.5   A potency function for noughts and crosses different from that in Figure 13.4.

five types of pieces: queen, rook, bishop, knight and pawn. In either game, the number of pieces of each type on the board changes as the game progresses, since a player can capture the other's pieces and remove them from the board, and some pieces can be transformed from one type into another. With the two players being C_1 and C_2, let

u_v = number of pieces of type v that player C_1 has
   − number of pieces of type v that C_2 has.

Then a specimen potency function for draughts, with respect to C_1, is

$$5u_{\text{king}} + u_{\text{non-king}}.$$

Similarly, a specimen potency function for chess, with respect to C_1, is

$$9u_{\text{queen}} + 7u_{\text{rook}} + 5u_{\text{bishop}} + 3u_{\text{knight}} + u_{\text{pawn}}.$$

The above potency functions take into account the difference in the number of pieces of the two players but not the placements of the pieces in relation to one another. In a node, if a piece of C_1 can capture a piece of C_2, then the potency value of the node with respect to C_1 should typically be higher than that obtained from the above functions. Conversely, if a piece of C_1 can be captured, then the potency value should typically be lower. If you wish to do so you may augment the above potency functions to take into account features that consider the placements of the pieces in relation to one another. The question arises: what weightings should be allocated to these features?

Usually the relative values of the W's in a polynomial potency function

$$W_1u_1 + W_2u_2 + W_3u_3 + \ldots$$

are initially based on our intuition. As our experience with the game grows we can change the values of the W's to improve the potency function. It is not essential that the values of the W's remain the same for the entire game. We can divide the game into phases, say, early, middle and late. These phases may depend on the number of moves made: fewer moves in the early phase, and more in the late phase. In games like draughts and chess, the phases may depend on the number of pieces on the board: more pieces in the early phase, and fewer in the late phase. Then the values of the W's in the potency function may vary from phase to phase.

It is, of course, not imperative that the potency function be a polynomial. For a given game, you should develop a function that appeases your intuition. Taking into account the features present in a node, the function should map the node into a numerical value to measure as accurately as possible the potency of the node. As will become clear later in this chapter, if the computer employs a potency function that is lax in measuring the potency of a node, then the computer is apt to play the game poorly. You will find in section 13.2.3 some suggestions on improving the accuracy of a given potency function. The suggestions will make more sense there because by then you will have read about procedures for searching game trees.

We shall assume that the computer's opponent is employing the negative of the computer's potency function. We do not know whether it is actually so in reality because we have no control over the opponent's behaviour. But, in fairness, we should give the opponent the benefit of the doubt; in other words, the opponent is as meticulous as the computer in measuring the potency of a node. The upshot of this is that if the potency value of a node is m with respect to the computer, then the potency value of the node is $-m$ with respect to the computer's opponent, and conversely. Accordingly, the more potent is a node to the computer, the equally less potent it is to the computer's opponent, and vice versa.

It is a convention that, at a terminal node, if the game is a draw, then the potency value of the node is 0 with respect to either player; otherwise, it is ∞ with respect to the player who wins, and consequently it is $-\infty$ with respect to the player who loses. For implementation purposes, you could replace the infinity symbol ∞ by the largest number the computer can process. Having discussed potency functions and potency values, we shall now discuss the constructing and searching of abridged game trees.

13.2 ABRIDGED GAME TREES

Suppose that we are playing the game of chess. From a particular state in the game, it is our turn to move. We notice that if we move our queen, we can capture our opponent's bishop. Should we move, or should we pause to think of the opponent's countermove in response? Most likely the latter, for suppose that in response the opponent can capture our queen. In such a case, we may be reluctant to capture the opponent's bishop with our queen.

To decide on a move to make while playing a game in general, we should usually think of our move, our opponent's countermove in response, our move avenging the opponent's countermove, and so on. In brief, we should look ahead. We should ideally look ahead all the way to the termination of the game, but that may often take too long a time, or it may be too much for our mental capacity, or both, so, in practice, we look ahead only a few moves from the current state of the game.

The above notion is implemented in computer game playing as an abridged game tree. For the rest of our discussion in this chapter, any reference to game trees would mean abridged game trees, unless otherwise stated.

Whenever the computer is to make a move it constructs a game tree whose root corresponds to the current game state. The tree displays the alternative moves the computer can make from the root, the opponent's alternative countermoves in response to each move of the computer, the computer's alternative moves avenging each countermove of the opponent, and so on. The leaf nodes in the tree may all be at the same depth. Alternatively, they may be at varying depths, the computer thus looking ahead further along some moves than along others. For the time being, we shall assume that the depth of the game tree is solely constrained by the computing time and memory resources available. You will find more comments on the depths of game trees later, in sections 13.2.3, 13.7.4 and 13.7.5. By then, you will have become more familiar with game trees.

The computer will also need to search the game tree it constructs. By conducting the search, it can decide on the optimal move to make from the root of the tree. The **optimal move** from a node y is that which enables the game to traverse toward the leaf node that is expected to be the most potent for the player moving from y. To illustrate, in chess, the optimal move for the computer may not ordinarily be such that its pawn be captured, but if by having its pawn captured the computer is sure of capturing the opponent's rook when the game reaches a leaf node, then the optimal move for the computer could be to let its pawn be captured.

It should be obvious that the optimal move from a node y can be only to a child of y. Node y' is said to the **heir** of node y if, and only if, the optimal move from y is to y'. The sequence of arcs from node y_0 to node y_j is said to be the **principal path** from y_0 to y_j if, and only if, there exist nodes $y_0, y_1, y_2, \ldots, y_j$ such that y_i is the heir of y_{i-1}, for $1 \leq i \leq j$. The principal path thus contains the nodes through which the game would traverse if both players make optimal moves from $y_0, y_1, \ldots, y_{j-1}$. Later in this chapter, we shall be interested in the principal path from the root of the game tree to a leaf node. Such a path is said to be the principal path of the tree. In the literature, the principal path is also known as the **principal variation** or **principal continuation**.

The player who moves from the root of the game tree is usually referred to in the literature as the root player. Since in our discussion, it is the computer that moves from the root, you may think of the root player as synonymous with the computer.

Suppose that, for some game, the root player does a **two-ply** lookahead; that is, the player looks ahead by 2 moves. In other words, the depth of the game tree construced is 2. Figure 13.6 explains informally how the root player searches the game tree to discover the optimal move from the root.

The explanation of Figure 13.6 can be expressed more formally as a procedure called **minimax** for searching game trees in general. Before reading of minimax, however, you should make sure that you have understood the discussion in this section. If you have any doubts about

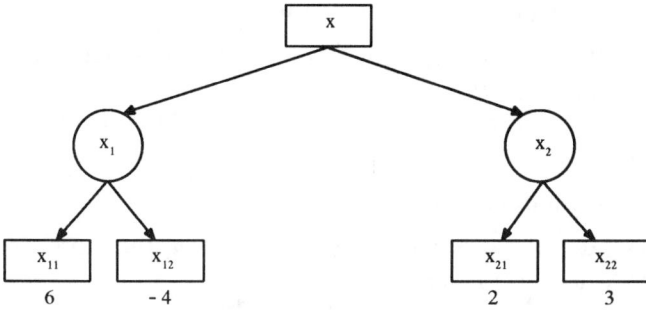

Figure 13.6 A specimen game tree of depth 2. Let the potency value of a leaf node be as written alongside the node. The potency values are with respect to the root player. Suppose that the root player were to move from node x to node x_1. Then the opponent is expected to move to node x_{12}: since x_{12} is less potent than x_{11} to the root player, x_{12} is more potent than x_{11} to the opponent. Alternatively speaking, the optimal move from x_1 is to x_{12}, or that x_{12} is the heir of x_1. Reasoning similar to that above, we say that if the root player were to move from x to x_2, then the opponent is expected to move from x_2 to x_{21}; that is, the optimal move from x_2 is to x_{21}, or that x_{21} is the heir of x_2. Node x_{21} being more potent than x_{12} to the root player, the optimal move for the root player is to move from x to x_2. Hence, x_2 is the heir of x. The principal path in the above tree is accordingly through the nodes x, x_2, and x_{21}. It will be our custom in illustrating game trees that sibling nodes such as $x_1, x_2, \ldots, x_n$ will be displayed from left to right. Then a node x_i [where $1 \le i < n$] is a *left sibling* of nodes $x_{i+1}, x_{i+2}, \ldots, x_n$. Similarly, a node x_j [where $1 < j \le n$] is a *right sibling* of nodes $x_1, x_2, \ldots, x_{j-1}$.

your having understood the discussion, you should read this section again, referring continually to Figure 13.6. You may then go on to the minimax procedure, which is described next.

13.2.1 Searching by the minimax procedure

Nodes at even depths are named as MAX nodes and nodes at odd depths as MIN nodes. The root player moves from MAX nodes and the opponent from MIN nodes.

Every node x has a value $M(x)$, called the **minimax value** of x, associated with it. If x is a leaf node, then $M(x)$ is defined to be equal to the potency value of x with respect to the root player. If, however, x is a non-leaf node with children $x_1, x_2, \ldots, x_n$, then the minimax value $M(x)$ depends on whether x is a MAX node or a MIN node.

Let us first consider the case when x is a MAX node. Then, by definition:

$$M(x) = \max(M(x_1), M(x_2), \ldots, M(x_n)).$$

The higher the value of $M(x_i)$ for $1 \leq i \leq n$, the more **worthy** we say is MIN node x_i to its parent x.

We now consider the case when x is a MIN node. Then, by definition:

$$M(x) = \min(M(x_1), M(x_2), \ldots, M(x_n)).$$

Now, the lower the value of $M(x_i)$ for $1 \leq i \leq n$, the more worthy we say is MAX node x_i to its parent x.

To summarize we can say the following: if x is a non-leaf node, then the minimax value of its worthiest child is propagated to x. This child is declared to be the heir of x. A node x, however, can have more than one worthiest child: since such children are siblings, their minimax values will be equal to one another's. If node x has more than one

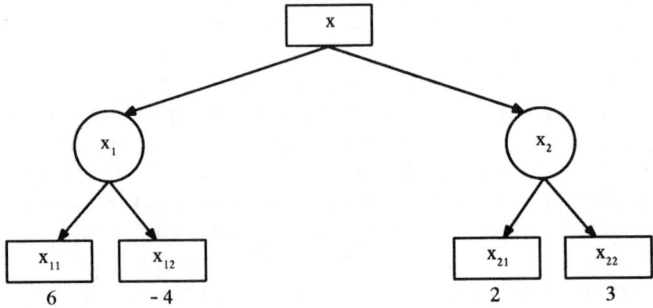

Figure 13.7 Searching a specimen game tree of depth 2 by the minimax procedure. The potency values written alongside the leaf nodes are with respect to the root player. Adhering to the convention mentioned in Figure 13.2 of showing even-depth nodes to be rectangular and odd-depth nodes to be circular, we observe that, for the minimax procedure, MAX nodes are rectangular, and MIN nodes are circular. The minimax values of the leaf nodes are equal to their corresponding potency values, as shown above. Propagating the minimax values from the leaf nodes to the root, we see that:

$$M(x_1) = \min(M(x_{11}), M(x_{12})) = \min(6, -4) = -4,$$
$$M(x_2) = \min(M(x_{21}), M(x_{22})) = \min(2, 3) = 2, \text{ and}$$
$$M(x) = \max(M(x_1), M(x_2)) = \max(-4, 2) = 2.$$

Since it was the maximum value of x_2 that was propagated to the root x, node x_2 is the heir of node x, and the optimal move from x is to x_2. Also note that x_{12} is the heir of x_1, and x_{21} is the heir of x_2. The principal path is through the nodes x, x_2, and x_{21}. You may have noticed that the above game tree is the same as that in Figure 13.6.

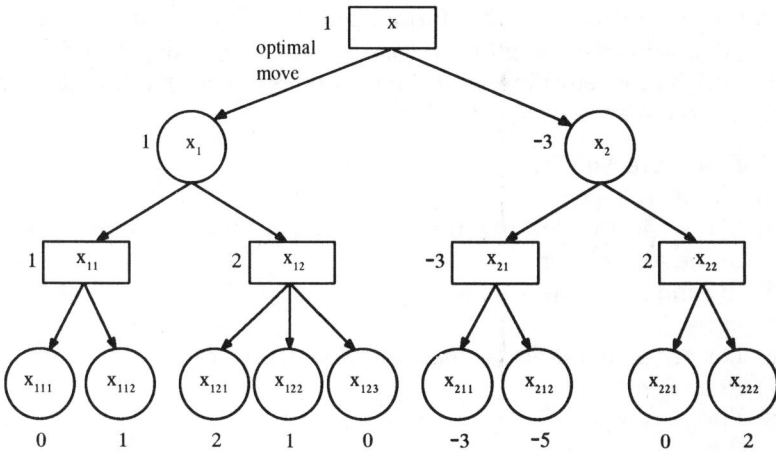

Figure 13.8 Searching a specimen game tree of depth 3 by the minimax procedure. The minimax value of any node is written alongside the node. The optimal move from root x is to x_1. The principal path is through the nodes x, x_1, x_{11}, and x_{112}.

worthiest child, then by convention the leftmost of such children is selected to be the heir of x. To put it another way, let us suppose that the worthiest children of node x are nodes x_i and x_j. If $i < j$, we select x_i to be the heir of x; otherwise, we select x_j. Once we know the heir of x, we also know that the optimal move from x is to the heir of x.

In the minimax procedure we first calculate the minimax values of the leaf nodes from some potency function, as described in section 13.1.2. We then repeatedly propagate these values from depth d, say, to depth d-1, next from depth d-1 to depth d-2, and so on, until we obtain the minimax value of the node at depth 0, that is, the root node. The optimal move from the root is accordingly to its heir.

The game tree that was given in Figure 13.6 is now searched by the minimax procedure in Figure 13.7. Compare the explanations presented in the two figures, and then see another example of searching by the minimax procedure in Figure 13.8.

It should be apparent from Figures 13.7 and 13.8 that in essence it is a leaf node whose minimax value is finally propagated across the depths to the root. Suppose that it is some leaf node z whose minimax value is finally propagated to the root. Then it can be seen that the principal path is the sequence of arcs from the root to z.

You must have undoubtedly guessed that the procedure is called minimax because we are required to find the *mini*mum and *max*imum of values at alternate depths.

Minimax search can be formulated by these two procedures: MINIMAXE for returning the *minimax* values of *e*ven-depth nodes, and MINIMAXO for returning the *minimax* values of *o*dd-depth nodes. The two procedures are outlined below.

(1) Procedure MINIMAXE(*x*: node): integer;
(2) *i*, *m*, *n*: integer;
(3) If *x* is a leaf node, then return the potency value of *x* with respect to the root player.
(4) Expand *x* to generate its children $x_1, x_2, \ldots, x_n$.
(5) $m := -\infty$.
(6) For $i := 1$ to *n* do $m := \max(m, \text{MINIMAXO}(x_i))$.
(7) Return *m*.
(8) End.

(9) Procedure MINIMAXO(*x*: node): integer;
(10) *i*, *m*, *n*: integer;
(11) If *x* is a leaf node, then return the potency value of *x* with respect to the root player.
(12) Expand *x* to generate its children $x_1, x_2, \ldots, x_n$.
(13) $m := \infty$.
(14) For $i := 1$ to *n* do $m := \min(m, \text{MINIMAXE}(x_i))$.
(15) Return *m*.
(16) End.

In the above procedures variable *x* symbolizes a node. Of the integer variables, *i* is used as a counter in looping, *m* stores the minimax value of node *x*, and *n* is the number of children of *x*.

On invoking MINIMAXE(root) we return with the minimax value of the root node. We have made the following assumptions in outlining the above procedures

1. The potency values of the leaf nodes are integers and hence all minimax values are integers, too. In practice, however, such values may be real, that is, non-integers.
2. When a procedure returns the minimax value of a node it also identifies the heir of the node. Accordingly, when we come to know of the minimax value of the root we also know its heir and hence the optimal move from the root. Such identifying of the heir is not shown above to keep the procedure outlines simple.
3. Built-in functions 'max' and 'min' return, respectively, the maximum and minimum values of their arguments.

Unless otherwise stated, the above notation and assumptions will be retained for all search procedures formulated in this chapter.

Minimax value of the root in a comprehensive game tree	The player in whose favor the corresponding game is biased
∞	The root player
-∞	The root player's opponent
0	Neither player

Figure 13.9 Comments on the bias in a game if in the rare instance we are able to search the comprehensive game tree of the game. Since the leaf nodes in a comprehensive game tree are terminal nodes with potency values ∞, −∞, or 0, the minimax value of the root will also be ∞, −∞ or 0. For example, the minimax value of the root in Figure 13.3 is −∞. Nonetheless, as mentioned in section 13.2, in many games, we are able to search only abridged game trees, not comprehensive game trees, so we might not be aware whether a given game is biased. It is an open question whether games like draughts and chess are biased.

In Figure 13.3, you saw the presence of bias in a game. Figure 13.9 tells us how, in some rare instances, we can find out about the bias in a game by conducting a minimax search.

13.2.2 Searching by the negamax procedure

A variant of the minimax procedure is the **negamax** procedure. Every node x has a value $N(x)$, called the **negamax value** of x, associated with it. If x is a leaf node, then $N(x)$ is defined to be equal to the potency value of x with respect to the player who is to move from x. If, however, x is a non-leaf node with children $x_1, x_2, \ldots, x_n$, then by definition:

$$N(x) = -\min(N(x_1), N(x_2), \ldots, N(x_n)).$$

The lower the value of $N(x_i)$ for $1 \le i \le n$, the more **worthy** we say is x_i to its parent x. Hence, the negamax value of the worthiest child of x is propagated to x. This child is declared to be the heir of x. If node x has more than one worthiest child, then by convention the leftmost of such children is selected to be the heir of x. The optimal move from x is to the heir of x.

In the negamax procedure, the values are propagated depth by depth from the leaf nodes to the root. The optimal move from the root is accordingly to its heir. The principal path is the sequence of arcs from the root to the leaf node whose negamax value is finally

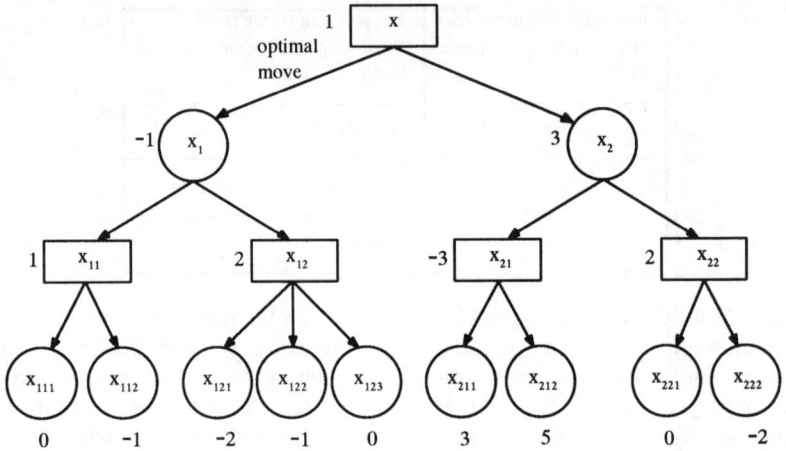

Figure 13.10 Searching a specimen game tree of depth 3 by the negamax procedure. The negamax value of any node is written alongside the node. The above tree is the same as that for minimax search in Figure 13.8. Comparing the values of the nodes in the two trees, we observe that at odd depth nodes, the values of the corresponding nodes have the same magnitude, but opposite signs; at even depth nodes, the values of the corresponding nodes are equal. For both the minimax and negamax procedures, not only is the value of the root same, but also the identity of the root's heir.

propagated to the root. An example of searching by the negamax procedure is shown in Figure 13.10.

It should be obvious that instead of defining

$$N(x) = -\min(N(x_1), N(x_2), \ldots, N(x_n)),$$

we had defined

$$N(x) = \max(-N(x_1), -N(x_2), \ldots, -N(x_n)),$$

we would propagate the same value from $x_1, x_2, \ldots, x_n$ to their parent x. The latter equation is more popular in the literature. Since, according to this equation, we are required to find the *max*imum of the *neg*ative of values, the procedure is called negamax.

Unlike the minimax procedure, the negamax procedure does not distinguish MAX nodes from MIN nodes. For a given game tree, if a node x is at an even depth, then the minimax value $M(x)$ of x is equal to the negamax value $N(x)$ of x, but if x is at an odd depth, then $M(x) = -N(x)$. Searching a game tree by either the minimax procedure or the negamax procedure is essentially the same. The negamax procedure, which on being invoked as NEGAMAX(root) returns the negamax value of the root of a game tree, is now outlined below.

(1) Procedure NEGAMAX(x: node): integer;
(2) i, m, n: integer;
(3) If x is a leaf node, then return the potency value of x with respect to the player who is to move from x.
(4) Expand x to generate its children $x_1, x_2, \ldots, x_n$.
(5) $m := -\infty$
(6) For $i := 1$ to n do $m := \max(m, -\text{NEGAMAX}(x_i))$.
(7) Return m.
(8) End.

13.2.3 Remarks on searching game trees

Now that you have read about both minimax and negamax procedures for searching game trees you may choose whichever you prefer. Remember, however, that minimax determines the potency value of a leaf node with respect to the root player, but then distinguishes MAX nodes from MIN nodes. In contrast, negamax determines the potency value of a leaf node with respect to the player who is to move from that node, but then does not distinguish MAX nodes from MIN nodes.

From now on, to evaluate a node is to find the node's valuation, where *valuation* designates either

1. the minimax value of the node, if we are searching by the minimax procedure, or
2. the negamax value of the node, if we are searching by the negamax procedure.

You should be adept at both the minimax and the negamax procedures, even though you may prefer one of them. Our subsequent examples in this chapter may be from whichever procedure is thought to be easier for discussing the topic under consideration. Moreover, for brevity, we shall at times refer to the valuation of the root of a game tree as the valuation of the game tree itself.

You may have noticed that both the minimax and the negamax procedures, as formulated in sections 13.2.1 and 13.2.2, are depth-first procedures (review section 11.4). The number of moves by which the root player looks ahead serves as the depth-bound for the search. Figure 13.11 displays the order in which the two tree search procedures generate and evaluate the nodes of a specimen game tree. Figure 13.12 then displays an alternative order in which the nodes can be generated if so desired.

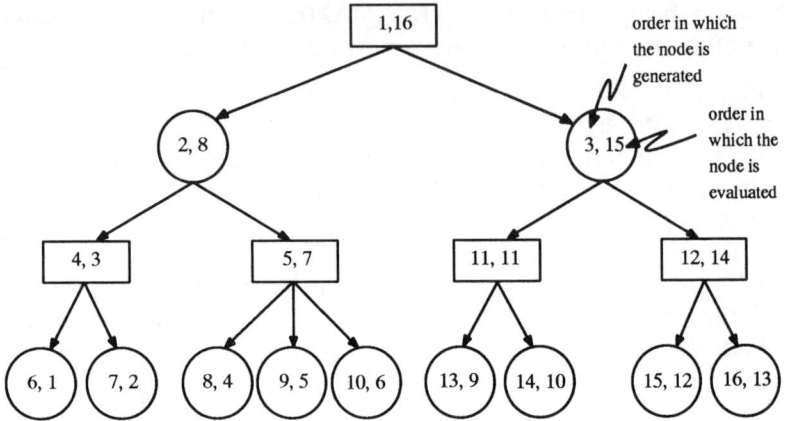

Figure 13.11   The order in which the nodes of the above specimen game tree will be generated and evaluated by either of the minimax and negamax procedures, as formulated in sections 13.2.1 and 13.2.2. The order in which the nodes are generated is different from the order in which they are evaluated. Both procedures generate nodes in the manner of depth-first with leapfrogging [described in section 11.4.2]. As an alternative, nodes may be generated in the order shown in Figure 13.12. We, however, prefer the order shown above, because we can then sort sibling nodes in an attempt to improve the efficiency of search, as discussed in section 13.3.3.

Suppose that the heuristic employed to measure the potency of a node is infallible; in other words, the potency function corresponding to the heuristic measures the potency of a node with unerring accuracy. We would then need to construct a game tree of depth only 1. The optimal move from the root would be to the most potent leaf node with respect to the root player. It is, however, difficult to develop such accurate potency functions for most games of interest, so the game trees we construct are usually of depth more than 1. In constructing such trees, we are implicitly assuming that our potency function evaluates the leaf nodes more accurately than it evaluates the non-leaf nodes. This is because the leaf nodes are expected to be closer than the non-leaf nodes to the termination of the game. As a general tenet, the more accurate the potency function, the more skillfully the computer can play, and the shallower is the game tree needed. Now, the shallower the game tree is, the less memory is required to store it, and the quicker it can be constructed and searched. It is therefore advisable to improve as much as practically possible the accuracy of a potency function.

We give below some suggestions that you may adopt to improve the

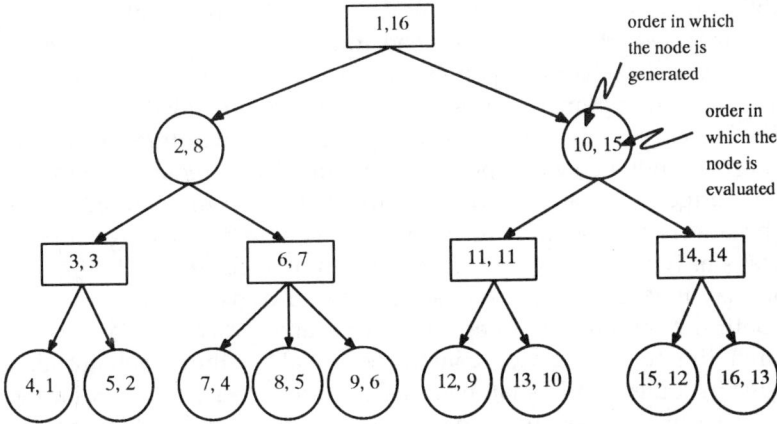

Figure 13.12   The order in which the nodes of the above specimen tree will be generated and evaluated by either of the minimax and negamax procedures of sections 13.2.1 and 13.2.2, if you were to modify them so that the children of a node are generated one at a time. The procedures would then generate nodes in the manner of depth-first with backtracking [described in section 11.4.1]. The nodes above are generated in an order different from that in Figure 13.11. Nevertheless, the nodes are evaluated in the same order as in that figure. If you prefer the above order for generating nodes, you can make the appropriate modifications to the minimax and negamax procedures. For instance, in NEGAMAX of section 13.2.2, rather than generate all the children of a node in line [4], you will generate them one by one within the loop of line [6].

accuracy of a potency function for a given game. The initial version of the potency function you develop will usually be based on your intuitive understanding of the game. Then consult publications that give recommended moves from typical states of the game. Construct game trees rooted at nodes corresponding to such game states and search the trees by either the minimax or the negamax procedure. Moreover, calculate the potency value of the root node with respect to the root player. For each tree, compare the potency value of the root node with the value propagated to it from the leaf nodes. The closer the two values in general, the more accurate is perhaps your potency function. Thus, over the trees searched if

|the potency value of the root node − the value propagated to it|

is on average greater than some threshold value, then you may need to amend your potency function.

In addition, compare the optimal moves from the roots as obtained by your tree searching with the moves recommended in the publications. If your optimal moves are often different from those recommended, then you may need to amend your potency function. You may also, of course, confer with human experts of the game and compare your optimal moves with those recommended by them. But there is a caveat: you will occasionally see in the literature stories about how such-and-such game-playing program discovered a move that was later judged to be superior to the move recommended by the publications or the human experts, so your optimal move does not always have to be the same as that recommended, for – who knows? – you may have discovered one such superior move.

Both the minimax and negamax tree search procedures as described search the full game tree constructed; that is, they evaluate all the nodes in the tree. We shall next discuss how to embody modifications in such full tree search so that at times we can prune the game tree thus searching only a portion of it. Then we do not evaluate all the nodes in the tree and yet we are able to evaluate the root node correctly. Evaluating fewer nodes is generally expected to improve the efficiency of the search.

Moreover, by pruning a game tree, some of the computer memory required to store the tree is released. Accordingly, in some given amount of memory we can store a deeper tree with pruning than without pruning. Searching a deeper tree is generally expected to improve the skill by which the computer plays.

The first method of pruning a game tree that we shall present is known as **alphabeta search**.

13.3　PRUNING BY ALPHABETA SEARCH

Suppose that, while searching a game tree, the root player discovers a move by which he will win over his opponent. The search by the root player can then be discontinued, because no other move will be better than the winning move already discovered. The winning move is the optimal move.

Now suppose that, while searching the game tree, the root player discovers that no matter what move he himself makes, his opponent can make a countermove by which the opponent will win. Then also the search by the root player can be discontinued because the optimal move for the opponent has been discovered. In being fair to the opponent, we assume that the opponent will make the optimal move available to him. Whether he actually does so is considered to be immaterial.

The above cases of discovering winning moves are extreme cases. In general, if the root player discovers, while searching the game tree,

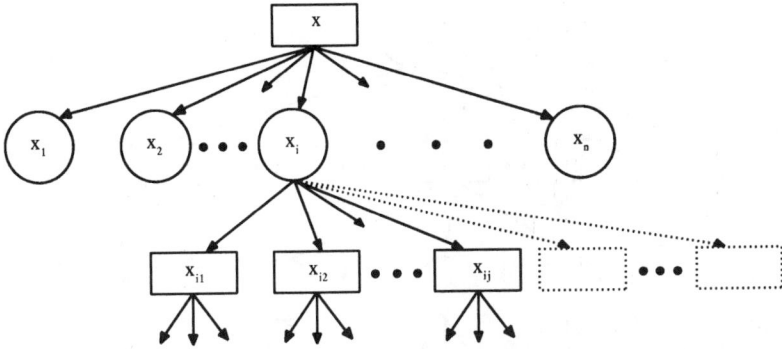

Figure 13.13   An instance of an alpha cut off in the above subtree rooted at x, while conducting an alphabeta search embodied in the minimax procedure. Let us consider the situation after the subtree rooted at x_{ij} has been searched. Since the search is depth-first [see Figure 13.11] nodes $x_1, x_2, \ldots, x_{i-1}$ would already have been evaluated. If the minimax value of the worthiest child among x_1, $x_2, \ldots, x_{i-1}$ has a value α, then α is said to be the provisional value of x. Being a MAX node, x will have a minimax value of α or more, since the value will be equal to the highest minimax value of all its children. If x_{ij} is the worthiest child among $x_{i1}, x_{i2}, \ldots, x_{ij}$, and if the minimax value of x_{ij} is m, then the provisional value of x_i is m. Being a MIN node, x_i will have a minimax value of m or less, since the value will be equal to the lowest minimax value of all its children. Now, if $m \leq \alpha$, then the minimax value of x_i will not be propagated to x. Hence x_i is not the heir of x. Accordingly, it is fruitless search any further the subtree rooted at x_i. In other words, all the right siblings [shown dotted above] of x_{ij} can be deleted. We say than an alpha cut off occurs below x_i. The provisional value of x_i is assumed to be its minimax value. Node x_{ij} is called the *arrogator* of x_i, and the move from x_i to x_{ij} is called a *refutation* move: it is said to refute the move from x to x_i.

that move μ_2 currently being investigated cannot be better than a move μ_1 investigated earlier, then he can cut off any further investigation of μ_2. There are two kinds of such cut-offs. If μ_1 and μ_2 are moves that the opponent would make, then it is called an **alpha** cut-off, but, if μ_1 and μ_2 are moves that the root player would make, then it is called a **beta** cut-off.

Having seen an intuitive foreglimpse of alphabeta search, we next discuss how it is embodied in the minimax procedure.

13.3.1   Alphabeta in minimax

Figure 13.13 explains an instance of nodes being deleted under an alpha cut-off and Figure 13.14 under a beta cut-off. The figures bring in the notion of the provisional value of a node. While evaluating one by

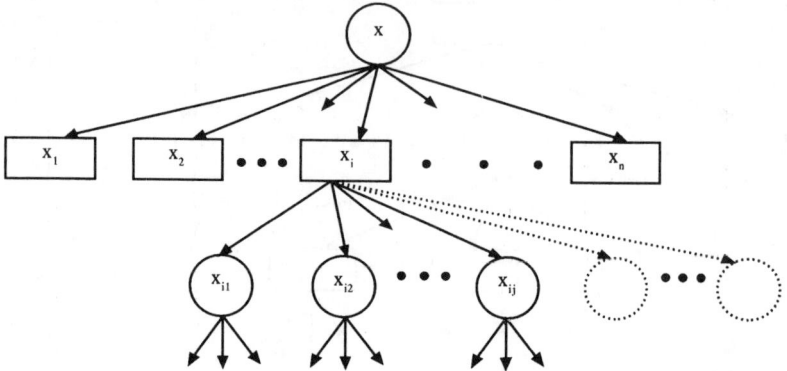

Figure 13.14   An instance of a beta cut-off in the above subtree rooted at x, while conducting an alphabeta search embodied in the minimax procedure. Let us consider the situation after the subtree rooted at x_{ij} has been searched. Since the search is depth-first [see Figure 13.11], nodes $x_1, x_2, \ldots, x_{i-1}$ would already have been evaluated. If the minimax value of the worthiest child among $x_1, x_2, \ldots, x_{i-1}$ has a value β, then β becomes the provisional value of x. Being a MIN node, x will have a minimax value of β or less, since the value will be equal to the lowest minimax value of all its children. If x_{ij} is the worthiest child among $x_{i1}, x_{i2}, \ldots, x_{ij}$, and if the minimax value of x_{ij} is m, then the provisional value of x_i is m. Being a MAX node, x_i will have a minimax value of m or more, since the value will be equal to the highest minimax value of its children. Now, if $m \geq \beta$, then the minimax value of x_i will not be propagated to x. Hence x_i is not the heir of x. Accordingly, it is fruitless to search any further the subtree rooted at x_i. In other words, all the right siblings [shown dotted above] of x_{ij} can be deleted. We say that a beta cut-off occurs below x_i. The provisional value of x_i is assumed to be its minimax value. Node x_{ij} is the arrogator of x_i, and the move from x_i to x_{ij} refutes the move from x to x_i.

one the children of a node y, the minimax value of the worthiest child found so far becomes the provisional value of y. It should be evident from the figures that if y is a MAX node, then its provisional value at any particular time is a lower bound on its minimax value; if, however, y is a MIN node, then its provisional value at any particular time is an upper bound on its minimax value.

Generalizing the explanation given in Figures 13.13 and 13.14, we say that in an alphabeta search the definitions for cut-offs are as follows.

1. An alpha cut-off occurs below a MIN node y if its provisional value is equal to α or less, where α is the highest provisional value of y's MAX node ancestors.
2. A beta cut-off occurs below a MAX node y if its provisional value is

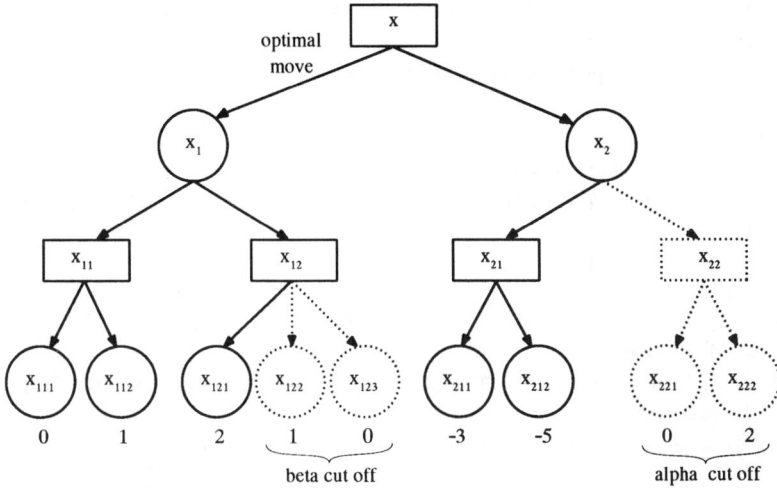

Figure 13.15 The pruning of the specimen game tree of Figure 13.8 by an alphabeta search embodied in the minimax procedure. The potency values written alongside the leaf nodes are with respect to the root player. Nodes x_{122} and x_{123} are deleted since MAX node x_{12}'s provisional value 2 is more than its MIN ancestor x_1's provisional value 1. Node x_{22} is deleted since MIN node x_2's provisional value -3 is less than its MAX ancestor x's provisional value 1. Nodes x_{221} and x_{222} are not even generated because x_{22} has been deleted. We thus say that five nodes [shown dotted] are cut-off by the alphabeta search of the above tree. The nodes cut off are not evaluated. The potency values of the leaf nodes cut off are written alongside them just to show what the values would have been, had the nodes been evaluated. Such will be our practice in this chapter.

equal to β or more, where β is the lowest provisional value of y's MIN node ancestors.

Both alpha and beta cut-offs cause the game tree being searched to be pruned. Figure 13.15 shows a specimen game tree being pruned by an alphabeta search embodied in the minimax procedure.

Alphabeta search, when embodied in the minimax procedure, can be formulated by these two procedures: ALPHABETAME for returning the minimax values of even-depth nodes, and ALPHABETAMO for returning the minimax values of odd-depth nodes. The two procedures are outlined below.

(1) Procedure ALPHABETAME(x: node; α, β: integer): integer;
(2) i, m, n: integer;

(3) If x is a leaf node, then return the potency value of x with respect to the root player.

(4) Expand x to generate its children $x_1, x_2, \ldots, x_n$.

(5) $m := \alpha$.

(6) For $i := 1$ to n do:

 (6.1) $m := \max(m, \text{ALPHABETAMO}(x_i, m, \beta))$.

 (6.2) If $m \geq \beta$ then return m (a beta cut-off occurs below node x).

(7) Return m.

(8) End.

(9) Procedure ALPHABETAMO(x: node; α, β: integer): integer;

(10) i, m, n: integer;

(11) If x is a leaf node, then return the potency value of x with respect to the root player.

(12) Expand x to generate its children $x_1, x_2, \ldots, x_n$.

(13) $m := \beta$.

(14) For $i := 1$ to n do:

 (14.1) $m := \min(m, \text{ALPHABETAME}(x_i, \alpha, m))$.

 (14.2) If $m \leq \alpha$ then return m (an alpha cut-off occurs below node x).

(15) Return m.

(16) End.

For obtaining the minimax value of the root, we should invoke ALPHABETAME(root, α, β), where α and β, the two values we supply to the procedure, are such that $\alpha < \beta$. The question arises: What values should we choose for α and β? The discussion below will help us in choosing these values. Suppose that to evaluate a node x in a game tree, we invoke ALPHABETAME(x, α, β) with some arbitrarily chosen values of α and β. Based on established mathematical results, we can then say the following.

1. If x's minimax value happens to be α or less, then the value returned by ALPHABETAME(x, α, β) will also be α or less. Hence, the value returned is not guaranteed to be the minimax value of x. We are said to have **failed low**.

2. If x's minimax value happens to be β or more, then the value returned by ALPHABETAME(x, α, β) will also be β or more. Hence, the value returned is not guaranteed to be the minimax value of x. We are said to have **failed high**.

3. If x's minimax value happens to be more than α, but less than β, then the value returned by ALPHABETAME(x, α, β) will be the minimax value of x. In other words, if x's minimax value lies within the **alpha-beta window**, that is, the open interval between α and β,

then we are guaranteed to return successfully with the minimax value of x.

Accordingly, an assured way of obtaining the minimax value of a game tree is by invoking ALPHABETAME(root, $-\infty$, ∞). So:

1. if the value returned is $-\infty$, then in spite of our having failed low, we know that the minimax value of the root is $-\infty$;
2. if the value returned is ∞, then in spite of our having failed high, we know that the minimax value of the root is ∞;
3. if the value returned is greater than $-\infty$, but less than ∞, then we know that we have returned successfully with the minimax value of the root.

Thus, no matter what the value returned, we are able to evaluate the root correctly.

13.3.2 Alphabeta in negamax

It should perhaps be obvious that the alphabeta search can also be embodied in the negamax procedure. Observing that the negamax procedure does not distinguish MAX nodes from MIN nodes, we can say that the provisional value of any node y is a lower bound on the negamax value of y. Moreover, the definition for any kind of cut-off can then be expressed as follows.

A cut-off occurs below a node y if its provisional value is

$$\geq$$

minus the highest provisional value among the ancestors of y that are above y by an odd number of depths.

If the node y is at an odd depth, then it is an alpha cut-off; otherwise, it is a beta cut-off. The criterion for both the cut-offs is, however, the same. To remove any misconception, Figure 13.16 describes an instance of a cut-off. Figure 13.17 then shows a specimen game tree being pruned by an alphabeta search embodied in the negamax procedure.

Alphabeta search, when embodied in the negamax procedure, can be outlined as follows.

(1) Procedure ALPHABETAN(x: node; α, β: integer): integer;
(2) i, m, n: integer;
(3) If x is a leaf node, then return the potency value of x with respect to the player who is to move from x.
(4) Expand x to generate its children $x_1, x_2, \ldots, x_n$.
(5) $m := \alpha$

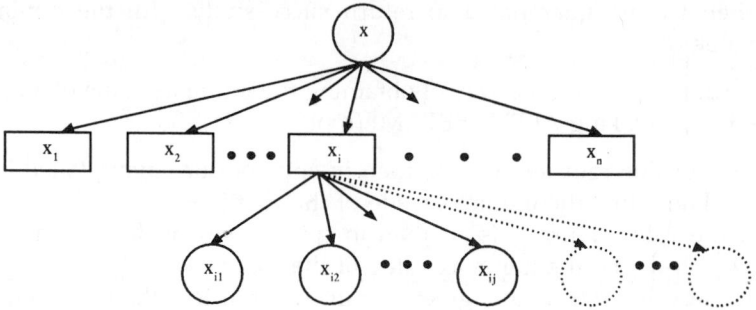

Figure 13.16   An instance of a cut-off in the above subtree rooted at x, while conducting an alphabeta search in the negamax procedure. Let us consider the situation after the subtree rooted at x_{ij} has been searched. Since the search is depth-first [see Figure 13.11], nodes $x_1, 2, \ldots, x_{i-1}$ would already have been evaluated. If the negamax value of the worthiest child among $x_1, 2, \ldots, x_{i-1}$ has a value β, then −β becomes the provisional value of x. Node x will have a negamax value of −β or more. If x_{ij} is the worthiest child among $x_{ij}, x_{12}, \ldots, x_{ij}$, and if the negamax value of x_{ij} is −m, then the provisional value of x_i is m. The negamax value of x_i will be *m* or more. Now, if $m \geq \beta$, then the negamax value of x_i will not be propagated to x. Hence x_i is not the heir of x. Since it is fruitless to search any further the subtree rooted at x_i, all the right siblings [shown dotted above] of x_{ij} are cut off. The provisional value of x_i is assumed to be its negamax value. Node x_{ij} is the arrogator of x_i, and the move from x_i to x_{ij} refutes the move from x to x_i. Note that the above cut off is a beta cut-off. A description similar to that above can be given to present an instance of an alpha cut-off.

(6) For $i := 1$ to n do:
   (6.1) $m := \max(m, -\text{ALPHABETAN}(x_i, -\beta, -m))$.
   (6.2) If $m \geq \beta$, then return *m* (a cut-off occurs below node *x*).
(7) Return *m*.
(8) End.

Suppose that, to evaluate a node *x* in a game tree, we invoke ALPHABETAN(*x*, α, β) by supplying the procedure with some arbitrarily chosen values of α and β, where $\alpha < \beta$. Based on established mathematical results, we can then say the following.

1. If *x*'s negamax value happens to be α or less, then we fail low since the value returned by ALPHABETAN(*x*, α, β) will also be α or less, there being no guarantee that the value returned is the negamax value of *x*.

2. If *x*'s negamax value happens to be β or more, then we fail high since the value returned by ALPHABETAN(*x*, α, β) will also be β or

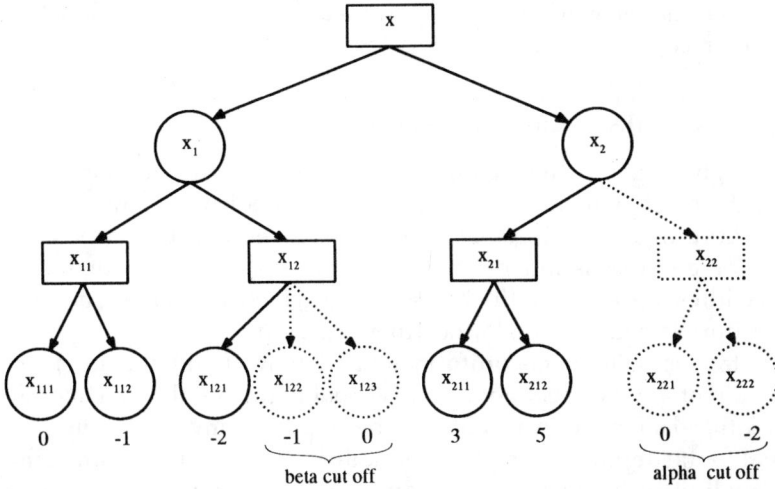

Figure 13.17 The pruning of the game tree of Figure 13.10 by an alphabeta search embodied in the negamax procedure. The potency values written alongside the leaf nodes are with respect to the player who is to move from these nodes. A cut-off occurs below x_{12} because x_{12}'s provisional value 2 becomes more than the negative of its ancestor x_1's provisional value -1, ancestor x_1 being above x_{12} by a depth of 1, an odd number. Similarly, a cut-off occurs below x_2 because x_2's provisional value 3 becomes more than the negative of its ancestor x's provisional value 1, ancestor x being above x_2 by a depth of 1, an odd number. If the above tree were searched by embodying alphabeta search in the minimax procedure, then the same nodes would be cut-off, as shown in Figure 13.15.

more, there being no guarantee that the value returned is the negamax value of x.

3. If x's negamax value happens to lie within the α-β window, (that is, more than α, but less than β) then we succeed since the value returned by ALPHABETAN(x, α, β) will be the minimax value of x.

Accordingly, an assured way of obtaining the negamax value of a game tree is by invoking ALPHABETAN(root, $-\infty$, ∞). So:

1. if the value returned is $-\infty$, then in spite of our having failed low, we know that the negamax value of the root is $-\infty$;
2. if the value returned is ∞, then in spite of our having failed high, we know that the negamax value of the root is ∞;
3. if the value returned is greater than $-\infty$, but less than ∞, then we know that we have returned successfully with the negamax value of the root.

Thus, no matter what the value returned, we are able to evaluate the root correctly.

13.3.3 Remarks on alphabeta search

On a given game tree, alphabeta search cuts off the same nodes regardless of whether the search is embodied in the minimax procedure or in the negamax procedure. Extending this, we can say that for our discussion below it is immaterial in which of the two procedures we embody the alphabeta search: whatever is true in one procedure is equally true in the other procedure.

A tree is said to be **uniform** if, and only if, (a) the number of children of any non-leaf node in it is equal to the number of children of any other leaf node in it, and (b) the depth of any leaf node in it is equal to the depth of any other leaf node in it. A tree is **non-uniform** if, and only if, it is not uniform. Figure 13.7 exemplifies a uniform tree; Figures 13.3 and 13.8 exemplify non-uniform trees. The **branching factor** of a uniform tree is the number of children of each non-leaf node in the tree. Uniform trees will be used in our discussion below.

But before that, let us suppose that the children $x_1, x_2, \ldots, x_n$ of a node x in a game tree are such that x_i is less worthy than x_{i+1} for $1 \leq i < n$. Then the sibling nodes x_1 to x_n are said to be **nugaciously ordered**.

To evaluate the siblings by alphabeta search, we shall first evaluate x_1, then x_2, and so on. Node x_n, the heir of node x, will be evaluated last. In other words, among the siblings, we shall always be evaluating a less worthy before a more worthy node. Alternatively, we can say that, in an intuitive sense, we shall be investigating worse moves from x before investigating better moves from x. As a general tenet, the more often siblings in a tree happen to be nugaciously ordered, the less likely it is for alphabeta search to cut off any nodes. A game tree in which all sibling nodes are nugaciously ordered is said to be **nugaciously deployed**. An alphabeta search will not cut off any nodes in a nugaciously deployed tree. An example is shown in Figure 13.18. If a nugaciously deployed tree happens to be a uniform tree of branching factor B and depth D, then an alphabeta search will evaluate B^d notes at depth d, for $0 \leq d \leq D$.

As a contrast to the above, we shall now look at game trees in which the children $x_1, x_2, \ldots, x_n$ of a node x are such that x_1 is the heir of x. The siblings x_1 to x_n are then said to be **flawlessly ordered** (also known as **perfectly ordered** in the literature). A game tree in which all sibling nodes are flawlessly ordered is said to be **flawlessly deployed**.

Figure 13.19 gives the number of nodes that will be evaluated at various depths in a flawlessly deployed uniform tree when we conduct

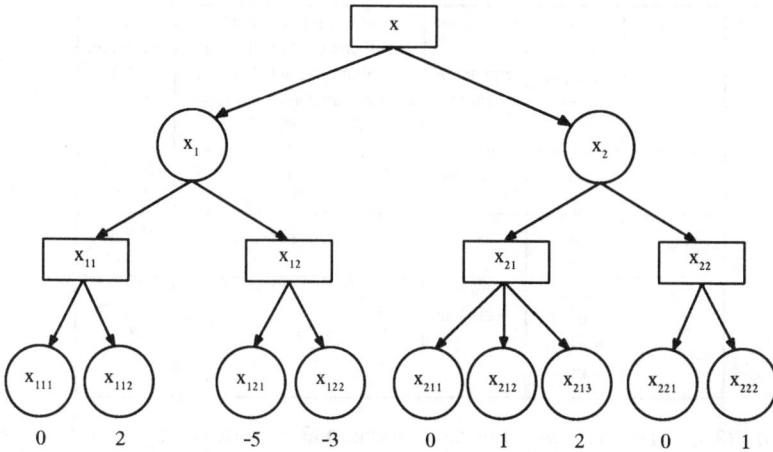

Figure 13.18   A specimen tree is which alphabeta search does not cut off any nodes. The potency values written alongside the leaf nodes are with respect to the root player. The above tree is essentially the same as the trees in Figures 13.15 and 13.17. The above tree, however, is nugaciously deployed.

an alphabeta search on the tree. Moreover, the Figure cites Figures 13.20–13.22 for examples, which we recommend that you study closely for a better understanding of tree pruning.

In a uniform tree, a successful alphabeta search always cuts off the most nodes when the tree is flawlessly deployed. In a non-uniform tree, however, a successful alphabeta search may on occasion cut off fewer nodes when the tree is flawlessly deployed than when the tree is not flawlessly deployed. One such example is given in Figure 13.23.

The above discussion about flawlessly deployed trees is mainly of theoretical interest. In practice, flawlessly deployed trees rarely, if ever, occur. In the remote instance that a tree is flawlessly deployed, and we know it to be so, then we need not search it at all. On expanding the root, the leftmost child of the root will be the root's heir.

Nonetheless, it should be apparent that to increase the likelihood of cut-offs, we should attempt as often as possible to evaluate more worthy siblings before less worthy siblings. You may wonder how we can make such an attempt since we do not know the worth of a node before the node is evaluated. One way to do so is described below.

Let us assume for the present that we have a heuristic available to estimate the worth of a node. This estimate is called the **promise** of the node: the more worthy we estimate a node to be, the more promising is the node. Then every time, we expand a node x, we sort its children

Case	Minimax value of the game tree	Comments on the alphabeta search	According to established mathematical results, the number of nodes that will be evaluated at every depth d, for $1 \leq d \leq D$.	For an example, see
1	$-\infty$	fails low	$B^{\lceil d/2 \rceil}$	Figure 13.20
2	∞	fails high	$B^{\lfloor d/2 \rfloor}$	Figure 13.21
3	more than $-\infty$, but less than ∞	returns successfully	$B^{\lceil d/2 \rceil} + B^{\lfloor d/2 \rfloor} - 1$	Figure 13.22

Figure 13.19 The number of nodes evaluated at various depths in a flawlessly deployed uniform tree of branching factor B and depth D, when it is searched by invoking ALPHABETAME (root, $-\infty$, ∞), as formulated in section 13.3.1.

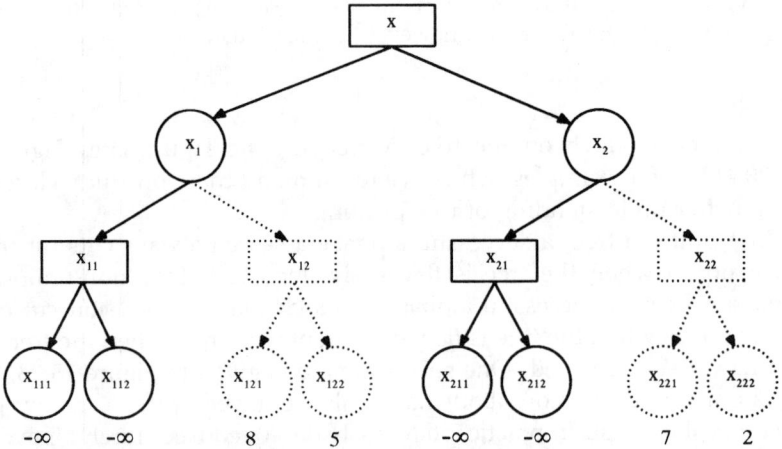

Figure 13.20 An example of invoking ALPHABETAME (root, $-\infty$, ∞) on a flawlessly deployed uniform tree whose minimax value is $-\infty$. The search, therefore, fails low. The potency values written alongside the leaf nodes are with respect to the root player. The nodes cut off are shown dotted. The number of nodes evaluated at depth d is

$B_{\lceil d/2 \rceil}$,

where B = 2, and $0 \leq d \leq 3$. Accordingly, the number of nodes evaluated is 1 at depth zero, 2 at depth one, 2 at depth two, and 4 at depth three. The cutoffs can be seen from this alternative viewpoint: if the provisional value of a MIN node becomes $-\infty$, then all its unevaluated descendants can be cut off, because none of them can change the value of the MIN node.

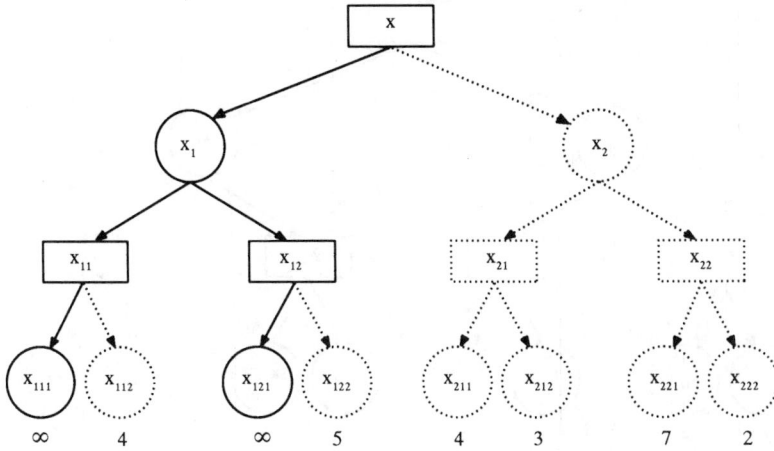

Figure 13.21   An example of invoking ALPHABETAME (root, $-\infty$, ∞) on a flawlessly deployed uniform tree whose minimax value is ∞. The search, therefore, fails high. The potency values written alongside the leaf nodes are with respect to the root player. The nodes cut off are shown dotted. The number of nodes evaluated at depth d is

$$B^{\lfloor d/2 \rfloor},$$

where B = 2, and $0 \le d \le 3$. Accordingly, the number of nodes evaluated is 1 at depth zero, 1 at depth one, 2 at depth two, and 2 at depth three. The cut-offs can be seen from this alternative viewpoint: if the provisional value of a MAX node becomes ∞, then all its unevaluated descendants can be cut off, because none of them can change the value of the node. Compare the above search with that in Figure 13.20.

as x_1, x_2, x_3, ..., such that they are in decreasing order of their promise; thus, for example, node x_1 is more promising than node x_2, and node x_2 is more promising than node x_3. You may have noticed that this ordering of siblings is akin to what we do for hill-climbing with leap-frogging, which was described in section 11.4.2.

Suppose that the siblings x_1, x_2, ..., x_n have been ordered on their promise as described above, and that after evaluating the siblings we discover x_i (where $1 \le i < n$) and x_j (where $j > i$) to be the worthiest nodes among the siblings. Then, according to our convention mentioned in sections 13.2.1 and 13.2.2, we shall be selecting x_i to be the heir, since $i < j$. But x_i also happens to be more promising than x_j. You may find this selection of the more promising node as the heir to be intuitively gratifying.

We can add this refinement to the ordering of siblings based on their

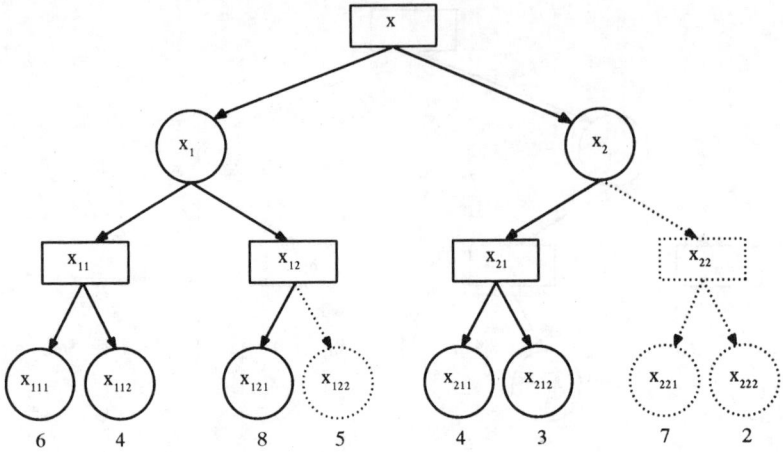

Figure 13.22   An example of invoking ALPHABETAME (root, $-\infty$, ∞) on a flawlessly deployed uniform tree whose minimax value is more than $-\infty$, but less than ∞. The search, therefore, returns successfully. The potency values written alongside the leaf nodes are with respect to the root player. The nodes cut off are shown dotted. The number of nodes evaluated at depth d is

$$(B^{\lceil d/2 \rceil} + B^{\lfloor d/2 \rfloor} - 1),$$

where $B = 2$, and $0 \le d \le 3$. Accordingly, the number of nodes evaluated is 1 at depth zero, 2 at depth one, 3 at depth two, and 5 at depth three. Compare the above search with that in Figures 13.20 and 13.21.

promise. If two siblings x_i and x_{i+1} are equally promising, than x_i will be the node that is expected to have fewer children than x_{i+1}. We shall then be searching the smaller subtree rooted at x_i before the larger subtree rooted at x_{i+1}. In case x_{i+1} is cut off we shall be cutting off a larger subtree and hence more nodes.

Let us now describe some recommended approaches to measure the promise of a node. Since the promise of a node is an estimate of its worth, and since the worth of a node depends on its valuation, discussed in sections 13.2.1 and 13.2.2, to measure the promise of a node we need to estimate the valuation of the node.

From section 13.2.3 it would have been evident that with a reasonably accurate potency function, a non-leaf node's potency value will be close to the value propagated to it. If we have such a potency function then we can calculate a node's potency value and consider this value to be an estimate of the value that will be propagated to it. To reduce the computation in calculating this estimate we may adopt a

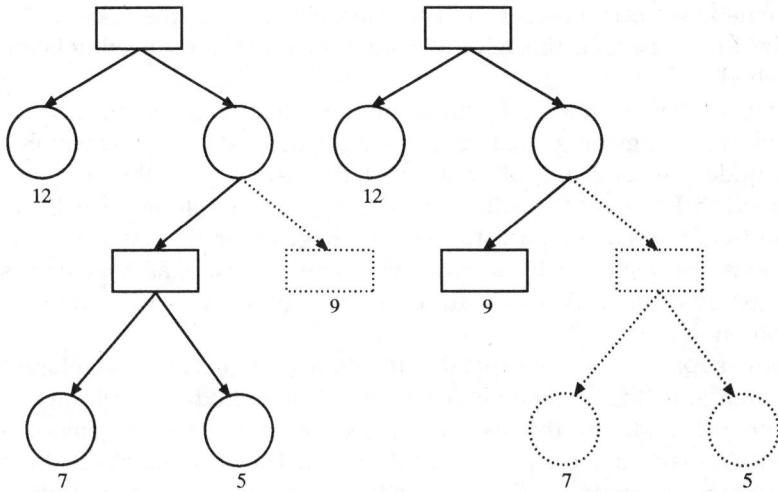

Figure 13.23   An example in which a successful alphabeta search cuts off fewer nodes in a flawlessly deployed non-uniform tree [the tree on the left] than in a non-flawlessly deployed non-uniform tree [the tree on the right]. The potency values written alongside the leaf nodes are with respect to the root player. The nodes cut off are shown dotted. Note that the two trees are essentially the same.

simplified version of the potency function. Suppose that the potency function is

$$W_1 u_1 + W_1 u_2 + \ldots + W_8 u_8,$$

then, as mentioned in section 13.1.2, the potency of function is using eight features u_1 to u_8. For the simplified version of the potency function, we can select a subset of these features. The features selected are thought to be more important then the features not selected for measuring the potency of a node. Suppose that from the above eight features, we select u_3, u_5 and u_8. Then a simplified version of the potency function could be

$$W_3 u_3 + W_5 u_5 + W_8 u_8.$$

The valuation of many a node can be estimated by another approach. Remember that, as the game progresses, a game tree is constructed after every two moves: one move by the root player and one move by the opponent. Thus there can be many a node in the game tree currently being searched that has appeared in the game tree constructed two moves earlier, and then such a node would have been evaluated. We can consider the valuation obtained for the node in the earlier tree to be an estimate of its valuation in the tree currently being searched.

Still another approach for estimating the valuation of many a node is as follows: in a given game tree, a node z is defined to be a **hegemonic** of a node y if, and only if, z is either the heir of y or the arrogator (defined in Figures 13.13, 13.14, and 13.16) of y. While we search the game tree, we maintain a list called the **hegemonic list**. As the name suggests, this list contains, at any given time, the list of all hegemonics already evaluated. Along with each hegemonic we also store its valuation.

Now suppose that we expand some node and generate its children. We then scan the hegemonic list to see if any child is identical to a hegemonic node in the list. If so, we consider the hegemonic's valuation to indicate the promise of the child. The belief here is that the hegemonic of a node y' is likely to be the hegemonic of another node y, so when we expand y, we try to find its hegemonic as quickly as possible. Doing so will give us either the heir of y or a cut-off below y.

Note that the move to a hegemonic node z will either be an optimal move (in case z is an heir) or a refutation move (in case z is an arrogator). Optimal moves and refutation moves are colloquially known as **killer** moves. Since the above heuristic is grounded on such moves it is known in the literature as the **killer heuristic**.

There are certain nodes in any game tree that are **indispensable**: they will never be cut off by a successful alphabeta search, no matter how infallible the heuristic employed to order the sibling nodes in the tree. We discuss below how to identify such nodes.

Let the nodes in a game tree be labelled in the **Dewey** style as follows: the children of a node labelled x_k, where the subscript k is empty for the root node, are labelled x_{k1}, x_{k2}, x_{k3}, ... You may have noticed that the nodes of the game trees in this chapter have indeed been labelled in the Dewey style. The subscript i of any non-root node x_i is accordingly a number string of the form $c_1c_2c_3\ldots$, where each of the c's is a positive integer; for example, if x_i is x_{4123}, then $i = 4123$ and $c = 4$, $c_2 = 1$, $c_3 = 2$, $c_4 = 3$.

It is an established mathematical result that in any game tree the root node x and all nodes x_1, x_2, x_3, ... at depth 1 are indispensable. At other depths, where i is the number string $c_1c_2c_3\ldots$, node x_i is indispensable if, and only if, c_j is equal to 1

1. for all odd values of j, or
2. for all even values of j, or
3. for all values of j.

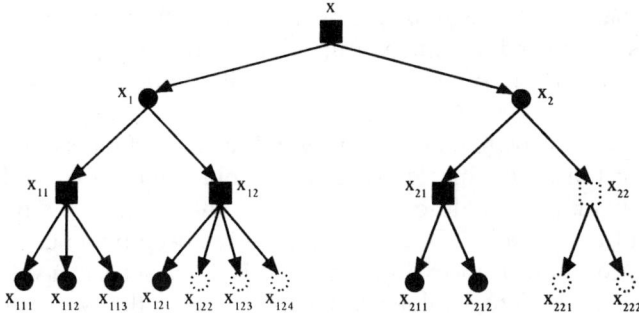

Figure 13.24 A specimen game tree to illustrate indispensable nodes. The indispensable nodes are shown darkened. The dotted nodes are not indispensable. While conducting an alphabeta search, if an indispensable node is cut off, then the search has failed. In Figure 13.20, for example, indispensable nodes are cut off since the search fails low; in Figure 13.21, indispensable nodes are cut off since the search fails high. In a uniform tree of branching factor B, the indispensable nodes at depth d are

$$(B^{\lceil d/2 \rceil} + B^{\lfloor d/2 \rfloor} - 1).$$

See Figure 13.19. Indispensable nodes are also known as *critical* nodes in the literature.

Thus, for instance, nodes x_{1312}, x_{41311}, x_{1111} and x_{113111} are indispensable, but nodes x_{1221} and x_{3124} are not indispensable.

We can alternatively say that a node z in a game tree is indispensable if, and only if, on the path from the root to z,

1. every odd-depth node, or
2. every even-depth node, or
3. every node

is the leftmost among its siblings. Figure 13.24 shows a pictorial illustration of indispensable nodes in a specimen game tree.

Until now our discussion in this section has been mainly about ordering sibling nodes. If we are able to sort the siblings $x_1, x_2, \ldots, x_n$ such that they become **deftly ordered** (in other words, x_i is usually worthier than x_{i+1} for $1 \leq i < n$), then we increase the likelihood of cut-offs. We shall now see another technique to increase the likelihood of cut-offs.

To conduct an alphabeta search, we have been declaring α to be $-\infty$ and β to be ∞. Then we have been invoking either ALPHABETAME (root, α, β) of section 13.3.1 or ALPHABETAN (root, α, β) of section 13.3.2. The α-β window around the root has thus been of infinite size.

But if we narrow this window, then more cut-offs become likely. A window is narrowed by increasing α or decreasing β, or both. A narrowed window is often known in the literature as an **aspirated window**.

One popular way to narrow the window is to first estimate the valuation of the root. This estimate can be obtained heuristically in a manner similar to that described earlier in this section for ordering siblings on their promise. Once an estimate has been obtained, we put a window around it. Hence, if the estimate is θ, we set α to a value less than θ, and we set β to a value greater than θ, such that we expect the valuation of the root to lie in the open interval between α and β.

By ordering sibling nodes on their promise and by narrowing the α-β window we can reduce the computation required to search a given game tree, since we expect to cut off more nodes. But note that the heuristics employed to order the siblings and to narrow the α-β window require some extra computation, too. Employing the heuristics becomes useless if this extra computation neutralizes the computation saved in cutting off more nodes. Accordingly, the heuristics employed should not be so complicated as to require too much computation.

13.4   PRUNING BY SCOUT SEARCH

In this section, we shall present another method for pruning game trees. The method is known as **scout search**. To understand the fundamental notion of this search, an analogy will be helpful. Suppose that you want to bake a cake. Before baking the cake, you will look around the kitchen to see whether it contains all the ingredients needed to bake the cake. If it does contain the ingredients, you bake the cake; otherwise, you do not. We shall refer to the kind of looking around mentioned above as **scouting**.

We already know from reading section 13.2 that, in searching a given game tree, we are typically required to evaluate sibling nodes x_1, $x_2, \ldots, x_n$. At such times in a scout search, we first evaluate x_1. Then, for i ranging from 2 to n, we scout node x_i (details of such scouting are given below) to see whether it can possibly be worthier than the worthiest node found so far among $x_1, x_2, \ldots, x_{i-1}$; if so, we evaluate x_i and it becomes the worthiest node found so far among $x_1, x_2, \ldots, x_i$; otherwise, we do not evaluate x_i.

You may have noted that in a scout search we may visit some nodes twice: the first time for scouting and the second time for evaluating. A node that is never visited is cut off.

As we shall find out below, in scouting a typical node, we expect to visit only a few descendants of the node. If the siblings $x_1, x_2, \ldots, x_n$

happen to be **deftly ordered**, we shall not be evaluating all the sibling of x_1. We can attempt to have the siblings deftly ordered by sorting them in decreasing order of their promise, as discussed in section 13.3.1. In **deftly deployed** trees, that is, trees in which sibling nodes are deftly ordered, we expect to cut off many nodes. In such trees, nodes that will be visited twice are expected to be few.

We can embody a scout search in either the minimax procedure or the negamax procedure. Section 13.4.1 describes the search being embodied in the minimax procedure and section 13.4.2 in the negamax procedure.

13.4.1   Scout in minimax

A scout search when embodied in the minimax procedure can be formulated by these three procedures: EVALSM for *eval*uating by a scout search the *m*inimax value of a given node, SCOUTMG for *scout*ing a given node to return TRUE if the node's *m*inimax value is seen to be *g*reater than another given value, and SCOUTML for *scout*ing a given node to return TRUE if the node's *m*inimax value is seen to be *l*ess than another given value. The three procedures are outlined below.

(1) Procedure EVALSM (x: node): integer;

(2) i, m, n: integer;

(3) If x is a leaf node, then return the potency value of x with respect to the root player.

(4) Expand x to generate its children and preferably sort them as x_1, x_2, . . . , x_n in decreasing order of their promise.

(5) $m := \text{EVALSM}(x_1)$

(6) If x is a MAX node, then for $i := 2$ to n do the following.

    (6.1) If SCOUTMG (x_i, m) is TRUE, then $m := \text{EVALSM}(x_i)$. (After scouting MIN node x_i, if its minimax value is seen to be greater than m, the minimax value of the worthiest node among x_1 to x_{i-1}, then evaluate x_i. Moreover, x_i now becomes the worthiest node among x_1 to x_i.)

(7) If x is a MIN node, then for $i := 2$ to n do the following.

    (7.1) If SCOUTML(x_i, m) is TRUE, then $m := \text{EVALSM}(x_i)$. (After scouting MAX node x_i, if its minimax value is seen to be less than m, the minimax value of the worthiest node among x_1 to x_{i-1}, then evaluate x_i. Moreover, x_i now becomes the worthiest node among x_1 to x_i)

(8) Return m.

(9) End.

(10) Procedure SCOUTMG (x: node; m: integer): boolean;

(11) i, n: integer;

(12) If x is a leaf node, then do:

    (12.1) if the potency value of x with respect to the root player is greater than m, then return TRUE;

    (12.1) return FALSE.

(13) Expand x to generate its children $x_1, x_2, \ldots, x_n$.

(14) If x is a MAX node, then do the following.

    (14.1) For i := 1 to n do the following.

        (14.1.1) If SCOUTMG (x_i, m) is TRUE, then return TRUE. (We return TRUE on finding a child x_i whose minimax value is greater than m, for then the minimax value of MAX parent x is greater than m.)

    (14.2) Return FALSE. (No child x_i found whose mimimax value is greater than m, and hence the minimax value of MAX parent x is not greater than m.)

(15) If x is a MIN node, then do the following.

    (15.1) For i := 1 to n do the following.

        (15.1.1) If SCOUTMG(x_i, m) is FALSE, then return FALSE. (We return FALSE on finding a child x_i whose minimax value is not greater than m, for then the minimax value of MIN parent x is not greater than m.)

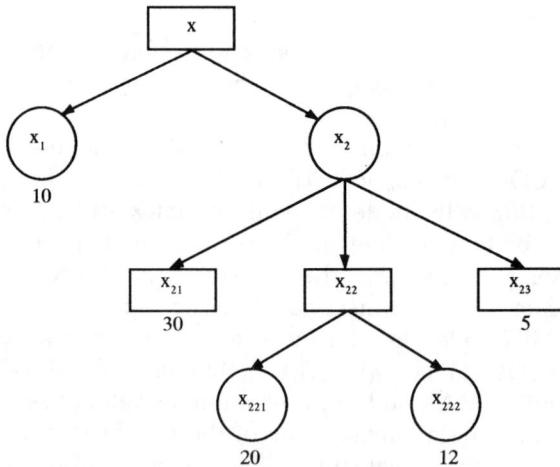

Figure 13.25 A specimen game tree in which a node, namely x_{222}, is cut off by EVALSM, but not by alphabeta search. The potency values written alongside the leaf nodes are with respect to the root player.

(15.2) Return TRUE. (The minimax value of every child of MIN node x is greater than m, and hence the minimax value of x is greater than m.)

(16) End.

(17) Procedure SCOUTML (x: node; m: integer): boolean;

(18) i, n: integer;

(19) If x is a leaf node, then do:

(19.1) if the potency value of x with respect to the root player is less than m, then return TRUE;

(19.2) return FALSE.

(20) Expand x to generate its children x_1, x_2, ... , x_n.

(21) If x is a MAX node, then do the following.

(21.1) For $i := 1$ to n do the following:

(21.1.1) If SCOUTML (x_i, m) is FALSE, then return FALSE. (We return FALSE on finding a child x_i whose minimax value is not less than m, for then the minimax value of MAX parent x is not less than m.)

(21.2) Return TRUE. (The minimax value of every child of MAX node x is less than m, and hence the minimax value of x is less than m.)

(22) If x is a MIN node, then do the following.

(22.1) For $i := 1$ to n do the following.

(22.1.1) If SCOUTML(x_i, m) is TRUE, then return TRUE. (We return TRUE on finding a child x_i whose minimax value is less than m, for then the minimax value of MIN parent x is less than m.)

(22.2) Return FALSE. (No child x_i found whose minimax value is less than m, and hence the minimax value of MIN parent x is not less than m.)

(23) End.

To obtain the minimax value of a game tree we invoke EVALSM (root), Figures 13.25 and 13.26 each illustrate an example to compare the tree pruning by EVALSM with the tree pruning by an alpahabeta search. We suggest that you trace EVALSM through the trees in the two figures. That will improve your understanding of EVALSM.

The next section describes the embodying of a scout search in the negamax procedure.

13.4.2 Scout in negamax

A scout search when embodied in the negamax procedure can be formulated by these two procedures: EVALSN for *eva*luating by a *scout*

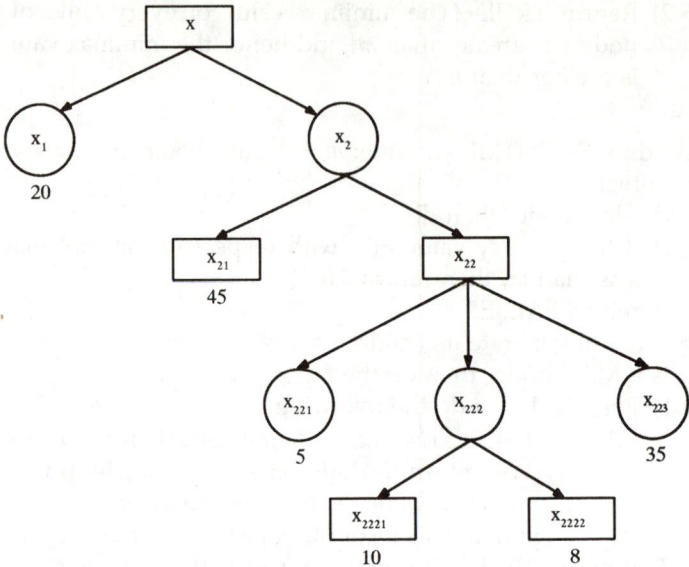

Figure 13.26   A specimen game tree in which a node, namely x_{2222}, is cut off by alphabeta search, but not by EVALSM. The potency values written alongside the leaf nodes are with respect to the root player.

search the *n*egamax value of a given node, and SCOUTNL for *scout*ing a given node to return TRUE if the node's *n*egamax value is seen to be less than another given value. The two procedures are outlined below.

(1) Procedure EVALSN(x: node): integer;

(2) i, m, n: integer;

(3) If x is a leaf node, then return the potency value of x with respect to the player who is to move from x.

(4) Expand x to generate its children and preferably sort them as x_1, x_2, ..., x_n in decreasing order of their promise.

(5) $m := -$EVALSN(x_1).

(6) For $i := 2$ to n do the following.

   (6.1) If SCOUTNL(x_i, $-m$) is TRUE, then $m := -$EVALSN(x_i). (After scouting node x_i, if its negamax value is seen to be less than $-m$, the negamax value of the worthiest node among x_1 to x_{i-1}, then evaluate x_i. Moreover, x_i becomes the worthiest node among x_1 to x_i.)

(7) Return m.

(8) End.

(9) Procedure SCOUTNL (x: node; m: integer): boolean;

(10) i, n: integer;

(11) If x is a leaf node, then do:

    (11.1) if the potency value of x with respect to the player moving from x is less than m, then return TRUE;

    (11.2) return FALSE.

(12) Expand x to generate its children x_1, x_2, ..., x_n.

(13) For $i := 1$ to n do the following.

    (13.1) If SCOUTNL(x_i, $-m$) is TRUE, then return FALSE. (We return FALSE on finding a child x_i whose negamax value is less than $-m$, for then the negamax value of parent x is not less than m.)

    (13.2) Return TRUE. (No child x_i found whose negamax value is less than $-m$, and hence the negamax value of parent x is less than m.)

(14) End.

To obtain the negamax value of a game tree we invoke EVALSN(root). On a given game tree EVALSM of section 13.4.1 will cut off the same nodes as EVALSN of this section. We suggest that you trace EVALSN through the game trees of Figures 13.25 and 13.26.

13.4.3 Adapting alphabeta for scouting

We can adapt alphabeta search to scout and evaluate a node in a manner somewhat similar to that described above in sections 13.4.1 and 13.4.2. For instance, let us formulate the procedure SALPHABETAN for scouting with an *alphabeta* search embodied in the *negamax* procedure. The procedure is outlined below:

(1) Procedure SALPHABETAN(x: node; α, β: integer): integer;

(2) i, k, m, n: integer;

(3) If x is a leaf node, then return the potency value of x with respect to the player who is to move from x.

(4) Expand x to generate its children and preferably sort them as x_1, x_2, ..., x_n in decreasing order of their promise.

(5) $m := -$SALPHABETAN(x_1, $-\beta$, $-\alpha$).

(6) For $i := 2$ to n do:

    (6.1) if $m \geq \beta$, then return m (a cut-off occurs below node x);

    (6.2) $\alpha := \max(\alpha, m)$ (this will narrow the α-β window);

    (6.3) $k := -$SALPHABETAN(x_i, $-\alpha-1$, $-\alpha$) (searching the subtree rooted at x_i with a unit-sized window is akin to scouting x_i);

    (6.4) if $k > m$, then do:

        (6.4.1) if ($k > \alpha$) and ($k < \beta$), then

$m := -\text{SALPHABETAN}(x_i, -\beta, -k)$; otherwise, $m := k$ (node x_i is evaluated with a wider window).

(7) Return m.

(8) End.

Suppose that, to evaluate to node x in a game tree, we invoke SALPHABETAN(x, α, β) by supplying the procedure with some arbitrarily chosen values of α and β, where $\alpha < \beta$. Based on established mathematical results, we can then say the following.

1. If the value returned by SALPHABETAN(x, α, β) is α or less, then the negamax value of x will be equal to the value returned, or less. We have failed low, there being no guarantee that the value returned is the negamax value of x.
2. If the value returned by SALPHABETAN(x, α, β) is β or more, then the negamax value of x will be equal to the value returned, or more. We have failed high, there being no guarantee that the value returned is the negamax value of x.
3. If the value returned by SALPHABETAN(x, α, β) is within the α-β window (that is, more than α, but less than β), then we succeed since the value returned is the negamax value of x.

Note that the above results are not the same as those given for ALAPHABETAN in section 13.3.2. Nonetheless, the assured way of obtaining the negamax value of a game tree is by invoking SALPHABETAN(root, $-\infty$, ∞).

Let us now discuss some highlights of SALPHABETAN formulated above. Given siblings $x_1, x_2, \ldots, x_n$, we evaluate x_1 in line (5). Later, in line (6.3), we search the subtree rooted at x_i (where $2 \le i \le n$) with a unit-sized window. The window being very small, we cut off so many nodes in the subtree that it is akin to scouting x_i. After such scouting of x_i, we return with a value of $-k$. You may have noticed that the negamax value of the worthiest sibling among x_1 to x_{i-1} is $-m$.

Now if $k > m$ (which is the same as saying that $-k < -m$), we have failed low. Then, from the results about SALPHABETAN given above, we know that the negamax value of x_i is $-k$ or less, and that accordingly x_i is the worthiest sibling among x_1 to x_i. So to evaluate x_i in line (6.4.1), we invoke SALPHABETAN with the upper bound of the window being $-k$.

We have not discussed every detail of SALPHABETAN to prevent confusing you. However, we suggest that you trace SALPHABETAN through several game trees of your choice. Doing so will improve your understanding of SALPHABETAN. You will observe, for instance, that in a given game tree SALPHABETAN may not always cut off the same nodes as EVALSN of section 13.4.2. This is because of minor differences in the manner in which SALPHABETAN and EVALSN carry out their respective scouting.

13.4.4 Remarks on scout search

A node that is indispensable (illustrated in Figure 13.24) will never be cut off by a scout search. In a deftly deployed tree, a scout search is expected to cut off more nodes than an alphabeta search. In a nugaciously deployed tree, neither a scout search nor an alphabeta search will cut off any nodes; the scout search will, however, be slower because it will be visiting nearly all nodes more than once.

Now that you have read about alphabeta search and scout search in sections 13.3 and 13.4, we shall present in the next section another method for pruning game trees. The method prunes game trees by conducting a best-first search (discussed in section 11.5) on the trees.

13.5 PRUNING BY BEST-FIRST SEARCH

Consider two nodes y and z in a game tree such that neither of them is an ancestor of the other. Then y is said to be a **left kinsman** of z if, and only if,

1. y is a left sibling of z, or
2. y is a left sibling of an ancestor of z, or
3. an ancestor of y is a left sibling of z, or
4. an ancestor of y is a left sibling of an ancestor of z.

Moreover, z is said to be a **right kinsman** of y if, and only if, y is a left kinsman of z. You will notice in our illustrations of game trees that the subtree rooted at node y is visually shown to the left of the subtree rooted at node z if, and only if, y is a left kinsman of z.

For the best-first search of game trees described below, we need to think of the tactics adopted by the players. The **tactics** for a player consist of specifying a response for every possible move of the opponent. Such tactics can be represented by subtrees of a given game tree. These subtrees are called **tactical trees**.

The search described in section 13.5.1 is based on *personal* tactical trees, that is, tactical trees representing the tactics of the root player. The search described in section 13.5.2 is, however, based on *adversary* tactical trees, that is, tactical trees representing the tactics of the root player's opponent. The description in both the sections will be in the minimax notation, but the description can be expressed in the negamax notation, too. Describing the search in the minimax notation is,

You can view a game tree as an AND/OR graph [see Section 12.2]. Consider each arc from a MAX node to be a connector of cardinality 1. Consider all the arcs from a MIN node to be one connector, its cardinality being equal to the number of arcs from the MIN node. Then constructing a personal tree is similar to constructing a solution graph [see Section 12.3]. Accordingly, to construct the personal tree:

[i]   Put the root of the game tree as the root of the personal tree.

[ii]   If a non-leaf node y is in the personal tree, then put all the children of y sired by one of the connectors from y into the personal tree.

Figure 13.27   Constructing a personal tree from a given game tree by viewing the game tree as an AND/OR graph.

however, believed to be easier to understand. If you wish, you may amend the description appropriately to suit the negamax notation. For brevity in our description, personal tactical trees will be referred to as **personal trees**, and adversary tactical trees as **adversary trees**.

13.5.1   SSS* in minimax

Since the search described in this section is based on personal trees, let us first study them. From a given game tree, you can construct a personal tree as follows:

1. put the root of the game tree as the root of the personal tree;
2. if a non-leaf MAX node y is in the personal tree, then put exactly one child of y into the personal tree;
3. if a non-leaf MIN node y is in the personal tree, then put all the children of y into the personal tree.

An alternative view of game trees and how to construct personal trees from them is given in Figure 13.27. Both the above technique and that of Figure 13.27 produce the same personal trees. Figure 13.28 shows a specimen personal tree.

As defined in Figure 13.28, the proficiency value of a personal tree is the value propagated to the root by the minimax procedure from the leaf nodes of the personal tree. Contemplate what happens when we propagate minimax values from the leaf nodes to the root of a personal tree. The value propagated to a MIN node is the minimum minimax value of its children. The value propagated to a MAX node is the minimax value of its solitary child. Remember that in a personal tree any MAX node has only one child. Accordingly, to propagate minimax values in a personal tree, we are required to find the minimum of values but not the maximum of values. As a result of this the

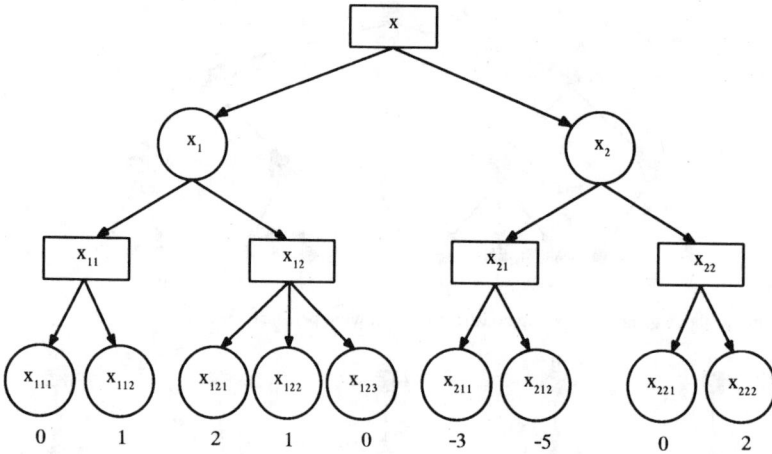

A specimen personal tree constructed from the above game tree is shown below:

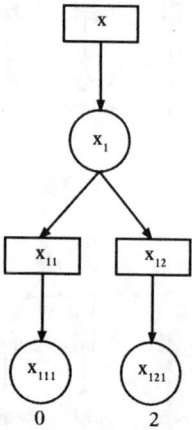

The proficiency value of a personal tree is defined to be the value propagated to the root by the minimax procedure from the leaf nodes of the personal tree. Hence, the proficiency value of the personal tree on the left is 0. As explained in Section 13.5.1, the proficiency value is always equal to the minimum potency value of the leaf nodes in the personal tree. The potency values written alongside the leaf node are with respect to the root player.

Figure 13.28   A specimen personal tree constructed from a given game tree. On adopting the tactics depicted by a personal tree, the root player moves from a non-leaf node according to the arc from that node. Thus on adopting the above personal tree, the root player will, for instance, move from x_{11} to x_{111}. Moreover, after three moves from the root, the game is expected to reach x_{111}, the node whose minimax value was propagated to the root of the personal tree.

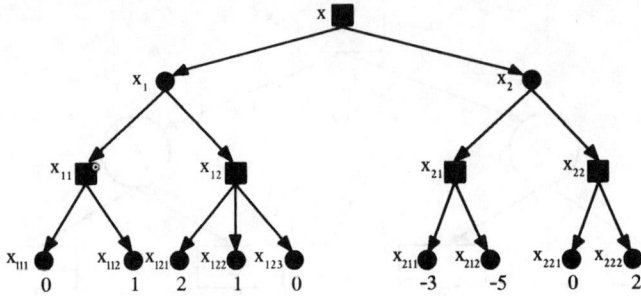

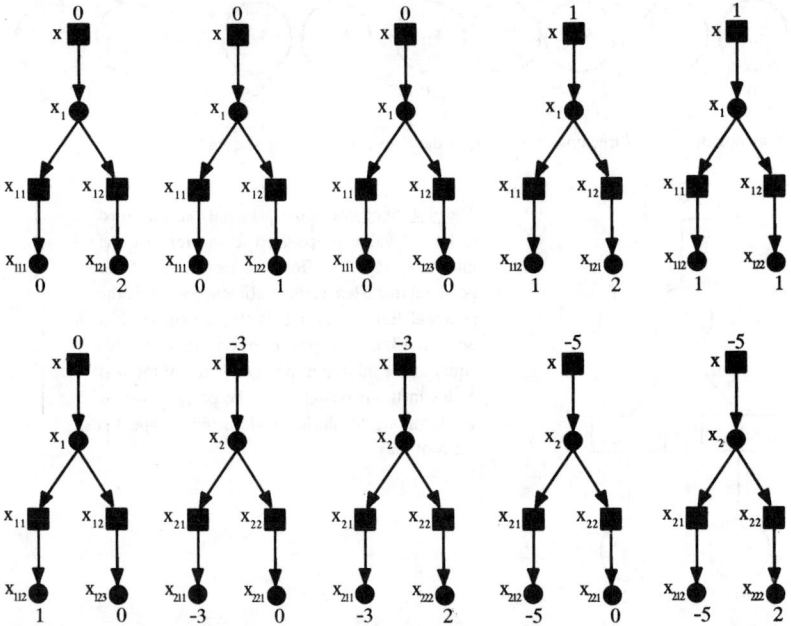

Figure 13.29 An example to show that the minimax value of a game tree is equal to the maximum proficiency value of the personal trees that can be constructed from the game tree. The potency values written alongside the leaf nodes are with respect to the root player. Each personal tree's proficiency value is written alongside its root. The minimax value of the game tree is 1.

proficiency value of a personal tree is always equal to the minimum potency value of the leaf nodes in the personal tree.

It is an established mathematical result that the minimax value of a game tree is equal to the maximum proficiency value of all the personal

Conditions in a comprehensive game tree	The player in whose favor the corresponding game is biased
There exists at least one personal tree whose proficiency value is ∞	The root player
The proficiency value of every personal tree is -∞	The root player's opponent
There does not exist any personal tree of proficiency value ∞, and there exists at least one personal tree of proficiency value 0	Neither player

Figure 13.30 Comments on the bias in a game if in the rare instance we are able to construct personal trees from the comprehensive game tree of the game. Compare the above with Figure 13.9. If all the leaf nodes in a personal tree are terminal nodes such that the root player wins, then the personal tree depicts a winning tactic for the root player.

trees that can be constructed from the game tree. An example is shown in Figure 13.29.

In Figure 13.3 you saw the presence of bias in a game. Figure 13.30 tell us how, in some rare instances, we can find out about the bias in a game by looking at personal trees.

Having studied personal trees, we shall now describe the search that is based on these trees. The search is known in the literature as SSS* (State Space Search Star).

In synopsis, SSS* evaluates the root of a given game tree by implicitly constructing personal trees, but it does not construct all the personal trees that can possibly be constructed. At any particular time it constructs the personal tree that appears to have the highest proficiency value from a set of partly constructed personal trees. When one personal tree has been fully constructed its proficiency value becomes the minimax value of the game tree. The personal trees that were not fully constructed contribute to cutting off some of the nodes in the game tree. SSS* can be implemented on parallel processors to construct the different personal trees simultaneously. Our description will, however, be for a single processor.

In searching for the personal tree with the highest proficiency value, SSS* is modelled on A*, the best-first search you read about in section 11.5.1. But there is a difference. A* minimizes over the values of the costs of solution paths. SSS* maximizes over the proficiency values of the personal trees.

Just as for A*, we need a list, called OPEN, to implement SSS*. The list for SSS* stores triples of the form

$$\langle x, s, m \rangle$$

where x is the label of a node in the game tree; s indicates the status of node x: the status is U if node x is unevaluated and it is E if node x has been evaluated; and m is the merit of node x. The **merit** of a node is defined to be the upper bound on the proficiency values of the personal trees that contain the node. Although the merit of a node may sometimes equal the minimax value of the node, it need not always be so.

In the list OPEN, the triples are stored in decreasing order of their merit from the front to the back of OPEN. Accordingly the triple containing the highest merit is stored at the front of OPEN, and the triple containing the lowest merit is stored at the back of OPEN. If triples $\langle y\ s_1, m_1 \rangle$ and $\langle z, s_2, m_2 \rangle$ are such that $m_1 = m_2$, then y will be stored closer than z to the front of OPEN if, and only if, y is a left kinsman of z. For brevity, we shall say that every triple should be in its **earmarked** position in OPEN.

To commence SSS*, we can assume the merit of the root to be ∞, so we shall put the triple

$$\langle \text{root, U,}\ \infty \rangle$$

in OPEN. Then, as described below, we search the game tree by iterating to delete and insert triples in OPEN, until OPEN contains the triple

$$\langle \text{ root, E, } m \rangle.$$

Since m is now the highest proficiency value of all the personal trees, it is also the minimax value of the game tree. SSS* can now be outlined as follows.

(1) Put the triple $\langle$ root, U, m $\rangle$ in OPEN, where m is usually assumed to be ∞. It can, however, be some other value as discussed toward the end of this section.
(2) Remove for examination the frontmost triple $\langle x, s, m \rangle$ from OPEN.
(3) If $x =$ root and $s =$ E (that is, the root has been evaluated), then return m as the minimax value of the game tree.
(4) Manipulate OPEN according to Figure 13.31
(5) Go to (2).

We suggest that you read the above steps again, while you look over the example given in Figure 13.32.

Note that for SSS* we always examine the frontmost triple in OPEN.

Case Number	In the triple <x, s, m> being examined,		The manipulation of OPEN
	status s is	node x is a	
1	E	MIN node	Put the triple <y, s, m> at the front of OPEN, and delete from OPEN all triples that contain descendants of y, where y is the parent of x.
2	E	MAX node such that x has a right sibling	Put the triple <z, U, m> at the front of OPEN, where z is the nearest right sibling of x.
3	E	MAX node such that x does not have any right siblings	Put the triple <y, s, m> at the front of OPEN, where y is the parent of x.
4	U	leaf node	Insert the triple <x, E, min(m, the potency value of x) > in its earmarked position in OPEN.
5	U	non-leaf MIN node	Expand x. Put the triple <x_1, s, m> at the front of OPEN, where x_1 is the leftmost child of x.
6	U	non-leaf MAX node	Expand x. For i : = n downto 1 do: put the triple <x_i, s, m> at the front of OPEN, where x_1, x_2,..., x_n are left to right the children of x.

Figure 13.31   Table to delineate how list OPEN is to be manipulated in step [4] of SSS*, as outlined in section 13.5.1. Among left to right siblings x_1, x_2, . . . , x_n, the *nearest* right sibling of x_i is x_{i+1}, for $1 \le i < n$.

Since the triples are stored in decreasing order of their merit from the front to the back of OPEN, we always examine the triple containing the highest merit. Remember that we are looking for the personal tree with the highest proficiency value. In OPEN if two nodes have equal highest merit, we examine the node that is the left kinsman of the other. In other words, if two personal trees have equal proficiency values we implicitly construct the personal tree on the left. If a triple $\langle w, s, m \rangle$ never appears at the front of OPEN, then node w is never examined, and thus w is cut off.

If a node is unevaluated, its children, if any, are yet to be evaluated.

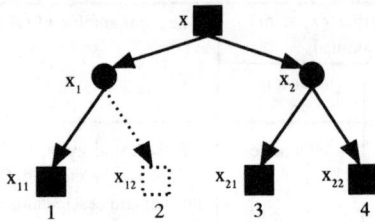

Iteration Number	Case Number	Contents of OPEN	
		front of OPEN...	...back of OPEN
0	-	$< x, U, \infty >$	
1	6	$< x_1, U, \infty > < x_2, U, \infty >$	
2	5	$< x_{11}, U, \infty > < x_2, U, \infty >$	
3	4	$< x_2, U, \infty > < x_{11}, E, 1 >$	
4	5	$< x_{21}, U, \infty > < x_{11}, E, 1 >$	
5	4	$< x_{21}, E, 3 > < x_{11}, E, 1 >$	
6	2	$< x_{22}, U, 3 > < x_{11}, E, 1 >$	
7	4	$< x_{22}, E, 3 > < x_{11}, E, 1 >$	
8	3	$< x_2, E, 3 > < x_{11}, E, 1 >$	
9	1	$< x, E, 3 >$	

Figure 13.32 An example to display the contents of OPEN during every iteration of SSS* while searching the above game tree. The potency values written alongside the leaf nodes are with respect to the root player. The case number for each iteration is identified from Figure 13.31. By convention, the front of OPEN is shown on the left, and the back of OPEN on the right. Node x_{12} [shown dotted] is cut off because it is never contained in any of the triples examined from the front of OPEN. The last triple to be examined before putting the evaluated root node x in OPEN contained node x_2. Hence x_2 is the heir of x. The minimax value of the game tree is 3. An alphabeta search on the above tree will not cut off any nodes. Thus, in the above game tree, SSS* cuts off a node that an alphabeta search does not.

A node becomes evaluated when on examination it is found to be either

1. a leaf node, or
2. a non-leaf node whose heir has already been evaluated.

The potency value of a leaf node with respect to the root player can at times also be the merit of the node, since the potency value is an upper bound on the proficiency value of any personal tree that contains the node.

After examining a triple $\langle x', E, m \rangle$, if $\langle \text{root}, E, m \rangle$ is put into OPEN, then x' is the heir of the root node, and the minimax value of the root is m.

It is an established mathematical result that SSS* dominates a successful alphabeta search, that is, an alphabeta search that neither fails low nor fails high. Reworded, in searching a tree, if a successful alphabeta search cuts off a node, then SSS* also cuts off that node, but SSS* might cut off nodes that a successful alphabeta might not cut off (an instance of this is shown in Figure 13.32).

SSS* does, however, not dominate an alphabeta search that fails. At such times, the alphabeta search might cut off nodes that SSS* might not cut off. An example is shown in Figure 13.33.

Let us consider game trees whose minimax value is greater than $-\infty$ but less than ∞. An alphabeta search will return successfully on these trees. A node that is indispensable (as discussed in Figure 13.24) will never be cut off by SSS*. When the principal path (defined in section 13.2) is toward the right in a game tree, then SSS* is expected to cut off substantially more nodes than either an alphabeta search or a scout search. A nugaciously deployed tree is an extreme example of such a game tree. Remember that both alphabeta and scout process the nodes left to right, thus discovering the principal path only toward the end of the search, but SSS* processes the most meritorious node available, be it on the left or the right. In a deftly deployed tree the principal path is toward the left in the tree. On such a tree, SSS* is expected to cut off the same number of nodes as alphabeta or scout, or at best only slightly more.

SSS*, however, requires more memory than alphabeta or scout, since SSS* has to store the list OPEN, a characteristic common to any best-first search. For many a game the list OPEN may become long.

Moreover, SSS* typically requires more computation than alphabeta or scout because SSS* has to maintain the list OPEN sorted. Overall, the processing of nodes by SSS* is more complicated than by alphabeta or scout. Hence, SSS* will usually be slower than the other two search methods. Nonetheless, if calculating the potency values of leaf nodes requires excessive computation, then SSS* may be faster than alphabeta or scout, for SSS* is expected to evaluate fewer such nodes.

One way to speed up SSS* is as follows. In commencing SSS* by putting $\langle \text{root}, s, m \rangle$ in OPEN, rather than assuming the merit m to be ∞, we let it be a finite upper bound on the minimax value of the root. Such as SSS* is known in the literature as an **aspirated SSS***. To obtain a value for m, we can first obtain a value for β, as mentioned during the discussion on narrowed α-β windows in section 13.3.3. We then set m to be equal to $\beta - 1$. The lower the value of m, the more nodes we

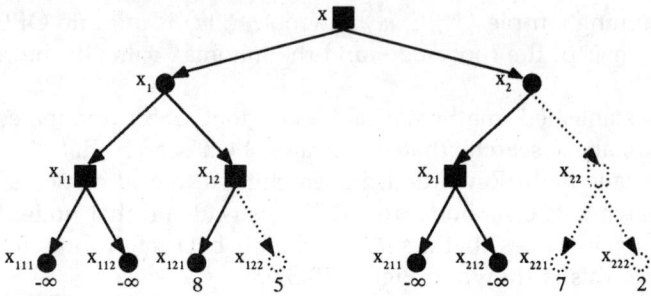

Iteration Number	Case Number	Contents of OPEN
0	-	$< x, U, \infty >$
1	6	$< x_1, U, \infty > < x_2, U, \infty >$
2	5	$< x_{11}, U, \infty > < x_2, U, \infty >$
3	6	$< x_{111}, U, \infty > < x_{112}, U, \infty > < x_2, U, \infty >$
4	4	$< x_{112}, U, \infty > < x_2, U, \infty > < x_{111}, E, -\infty >$
5	4	$< x_2, U, \infty > < x_{111}, E, -\infty > < x_{112}, E, -\infty >$
6	5	$< x_{21}, U, \infty > < x_{111}, E, -\infty > < x_{112}, E, -\infty >$
7	6	$< x_{211}, U, \infty > < x_{212}, U, \infty > < x_{111}, E, -\infty > < x_{112}, E, -\infty >$
8	4	$< x_{212}, U, \infty > < x_{111}, E, -\infty > < x_{112}, E, -\infty > < x_{211}, E, -\infty >$
9	4	$< x_{111}, E, -\infty > < x_{112}, E, -\infty > < x_{211}, E, -\infty > < x_{212}, E, -\infty >$
10	1	$< x_{11}, E, -\infty > < x_{211}, E, -\infty > < x_{212}, E, -\infty >$
11	2	$< x_{12}, U, -\infty > < x_{211}, E, -\infty > < x_{212}, E, -\infty >$
12	6	$< x_{121}, U, -\infty > < x_{122}, U, -\infty > < x_{211}, E, -\infty > < x_{212}, E, -\infty >$
13	4	$< x_{121}, E, -\infty > < x_{122}, U, -\infty > < x_{211}, E, -\infty > < x_{212}, E, -\infty >$
14	1	$< x_{12}, E, -\infty > < x_{211}, E, -\infty > < x_{212}, E, -\infty >$
15	3	$< x_1, E, -\infty > < x_{211}, E, -\infty > < x_{212}, E, -\infty >$
16	1	$< x, E, -\infty >$

Figure 13.33   SSS* on a game tree of minimax value $-\infty$. The potency values written alongside the leaf nodes are with respect to the root player. The nodes cut off are shown dotted. SSS* did not cut off nodes x_{12} and x_{121}, which were cut off by an alphabeta search that failed low in Figure 13.20.

expect to cut off, but remember that if the upper bound on the minimax value of the root is incorrect, then SSS* will return with a value that is not the minimax value of the root. Figures 13.34 and 13.35 show an example to compare SSS* with an aspirated SSS*.

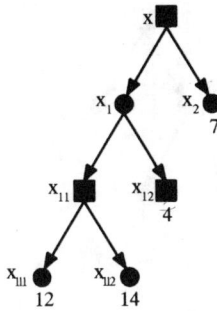

Iteration Number	Case Number	Contents of OPEN
0	-	$< x, U, \infty >$
1	6	$< x_1, U, \infty > < x_2, U, \infty >$
2	5	$< x_{11}, U, \infty > < x_2, U, \infty >$
3	6	$< x_{111}, U, \infty > < x_{112}, U, \infty > < x_2, U, \infty >$
4	4	$< x_{112}, U, \infty > < x_2, U, \infty > < x_{111}, E, 12 >$
5	4	$< x_2, U, \infty > < x_{112}, E, 14 > < x_{111}, E, 12 >$
6	4	$< x_{112}, E, 14 > < x_{111}, E, 12 > < x_2, E, 7 >$
7	1	$< x_{11}, E, 14 > < x_2, E, 7 >$
8	2	$< x_{12}, U, 14 > < x_2, E, 7 >$
9	4	$< x_2, E, 7> < x_{12}, E, 4 >$
10	1	$< x, E, 7 >$

Figure 13.34   An example of SSS* on a game tree in which no nodes were cut off. Compare the above search with Figure 13.35, in which an aspirated SSS* cut off one node in the same tree. The potency values written alongside the leaf nodes are with respect to the root player.

13.5.2   DSSS* in minimax

The search described in the previous section was based on personal trees. The search described in this section is based on adversary trees. From a given game tree, you can construct an adversary tree as follows:

1. put the root of the game tree as the root of the adversary tree;
2. if a non-leaf MAX node y is in the adversary tree, then put all the children of y into the adversary tree;
3. if a non-leaf MIN node y is in the adversary tree, then put exactly one child of y into the adversary tree.

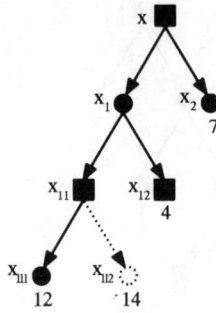

Iteration Number	Case Number	Contents of OPEN
0	-	$< x, U, 9 >$
1	6	$< x_1, U, 9 > < x_2, U, 9 >$
2	5	$< x_{11}, U, 9 > < x_2, U, 9 >$
3	6	$< x_{111}, U, 9 > < x_{112}, U, 9 > < x_2, U, 9 >$
4	4	$< x_{111}, E, 9 > < x_{112}, U, 9 > < x_2, U, 9 >$
5	1	$< x_{11}, E, 9 > < x_2, U, 9 >$
6	2	$< x_{12}, U, 9 > < x_2, U, 9 >$
7	4	$< x_2, U, 9 > < x_{12}, E, 4 >$
8	4	$< x_2, E, 7 > < x_{12}, E, 4 >$
9	1	$< x, E, 7>$

Figure 13.35 An example of an aspirated SSS* on a game tree in which one node [shown dotted] was cut off. Compare the above search with Figure 13.34, in which SSS* did not cut off any nodes in the same tree. The potency values written alongside the leaf nodes are with respect to the root player. We commenced the above aspirated SSS* by estimating the root to have a merit of 9. Had we commenced the aspirated SSS* with the root having a merit of, say, 3, then we would have returned with a value that is not the minimax value of the root, since 3 is not an upper bound on the minimax value of the root.

The proficiency value of an adversary tree is defined to be the value propagated to the root by the minimax procedure from the leaf nodes of the adversary tree. While propagating minimax values in an adversary tree we are required to find the maximum of values but never the minimum of values, since a MAX node can have many children but a MIN node can have only one child. Therefore, the proficiency value of an adversary tree is always equal to the maximum potency value of the leaf nodes in the adversary tree. It is an

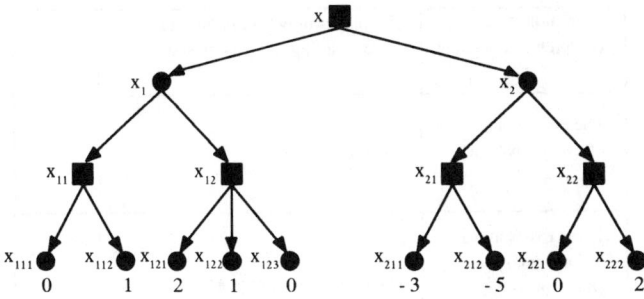

From the above game tree, we can construct the following adversary trees:

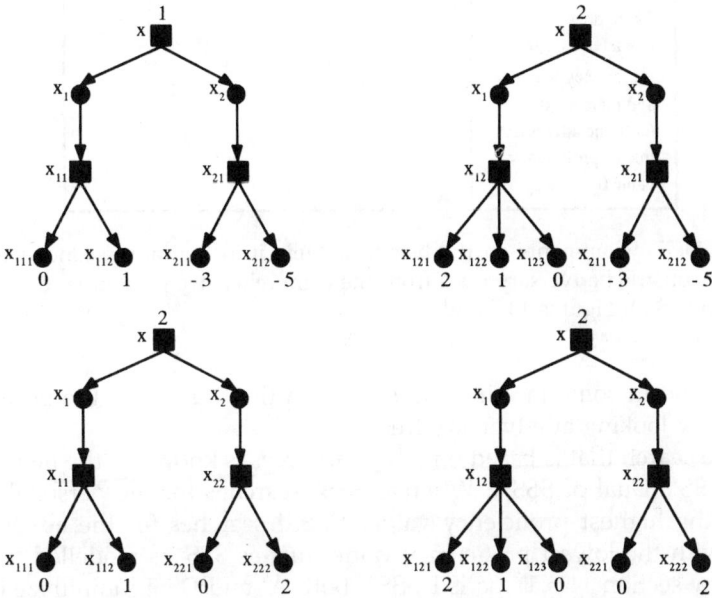

Figure 13.36 An example to show that the minimax value of a game tree is equal to the minimum proficiency value of the adversary trees that can be constructed from the game tree. The potency values written alongside the leaf nodes are with respect to the root player. Each adversary tree's proficiency value is written alongside its root. The minimax value of the game tree is 1.

established mathematical result that the minimax value of a game tree is equal to the minimum proficiency value of all the adversary trees that can be constructed from the game tree. An example is shown in Figure 13.36.

In Figure 13.3, you saw the presence of bias in a game. Figure 13.37

Conditions in a comprehensive game tree	The player in whose favor the corresponding game is biased
The proficiency value of every adversary tree is ∞	The root player
These exists at least one adversary tree whose proficiency value is -∞	The root player's opponent
There does not exist any adversary tree of proficiency value -∞, and there exists at least one adversary tree of proficiency value 0	Neither player

Figure 13.37 Comments on the bias in a game if in the rare instance we are able to construct adversary trees from the comprehensive game tree. Compare the above with Figures 13.9 and 13.30.

tells how, in some rare instances, we can find out about the bias in a game by looking at adversary trees.

The search that is based on adversary trees is known in the literature as DSSS* (Dual of SSS*). Whereas SSS* searches for the personal tree with the highest proficiency value, DSSS* searches for the adversary tree with the lowest proficiency value. Just as SSS* is modelled on A* (review section 11.5.1), so is DSSS*. Both A* and DSSS* minimize over values: A* over the values of the costs of solution paths, and DSSS* over the proficiency values of adversary trees.

The list OPEN needed to implement DSSS* stores triples of the form

$$\langle x, s, k \rangle$$

where x is the label of a node in the game tree; s, the status of node x, is U for an unevaluated x and E for an evaluated x; and k is the demerit of x. The **demerit** of a node is defined to be the lower bound on the proficiency values of the adversary trees that contain the node. Although the demerit of a node may sometimes equal the minimax value of the node, it need not always be so.

The triples in OPEN are stored in increasing order of their demerits from the front to the back of OPEN. The triple containing the lowest demerit is accordingly stored at the front of OPEN and the triple containing the highest demerit is stored at the back of OPEN. If triples $\langle y, s_1, k_1 \rangle$ and $\langle z, s_2, k_2 \rangle$ are such that $k_1 = k_2$, then y will be stored closer than z to the front of OPEN if, and only if, y is a left kinsman of z. As is our wont, we shall say for brevity that every triple should be in its earmarked position in OPEN.

To commence DSSS*, we can assume the demerit of the root to be $-\infty$. So we shall put the triple

$$\langle \text{root, U}, -\infty \rangle$$

in OPEN. Then, as described below, we search the game tree by iterating to delete and insert triples in OPEN until OPEN contains the literal

$$\langle \text{root, E, } k \rangle.$$

Since k is now the lowest proficiency value of all the adversary trees, it is also the minimax value of the game tree. DSSS* can now be outlined as follows.

(1) Put the triple $\langle \text{root, U, } k \rangle$ in OPEN, where k is usually assumed to be $-\infty$. It can, however, be some other value as discussed toward the end of this section.
(2) Remove for examination the frontmost triple $\langle x, s, k \rangle$ from OPEN.
(3) If $x = $ root and $s = $ E (that is, the root has been evaluated), then return k as the minimax value of the game tree.
(4) Manipulate OPEN according to Figure 13.38.
(5) Go to (2).

We suggest that you read the above steps again, while you look over the examples given in Figures 13.39 and 13.40.

Note that in DSSS* we always examine the triple containing the lowest demerit because we are looking for the adversary tree with the lowest proficiency value. In OPEN, if two nodes have equal lowest demerit, we examine the node that is the left kinsman of the other. The potency value of a leaf node with respect to the root player can at times also be the demerit of the node, since the potency value is a lower bound on the proficiency value of any adversary tree that contains the node.

SSS* and DSSS* might not cut off the same nodes in a given game tree. For instance, DSSS* does not cut off any nodes in the game tree of Figure 13.39, whereas SSS* does cut off a node in the same game tree (Figure 13.32). But then DSSS* cuts off a node in the game tree of Figure 13.40, whereas SSS* does not cut off any nodes in the same game tree (Figure 13.34). Coincidentally, the node cut off by DSSS* in

Case Number	In the triple <x, s, m> being examined,		The manipulation of OPEN
	status s is	node x is a	
1	E	MAX node	Put the triple <y, s, k> at the front of OPEN, and delete from OPEN all triples that contain descendants of y, where y is the parent of x.
2	E	MIN node such that x has a right sibling	Put the triple <z, U, k> at the front of OPEN, where z is the nearest right sibling of x.
3	E	MIN node such that x does not have any right siblings	Put the triple <y, s, k> at the front of OPEN, where y is the parent of x.
4	U	leaf node	Insert the triple <x, E, max(k, the potency value of x) > in its earmarked position in OPEN.
5	U	non-leaf MAX node	Expand x. Put the triple <x_1, s, k> at the front of OPEN, where x_1 is the leftmost child of x.
6	U	non-leaf MIN node	Expand x. For i : = n downto 1 do: put the triple <x_i, s, k> at the front of OPEN, where x_1, x_2, ..., x_n are left to right the children of x.

Figure 13.38   Table to delineate how list OPEN is to be manipulated in step [4] of DSSS*, as outlined in section 13.5.2. Comparing this figure with Figure 13.31, we notice that above k, MAX, MIN, and max have replaced m, MIN, MAX, and min, respectively.

Figure 13.40 is the same as the node cut off by aspirated SSS* in Figure 13.35.

Just as SSS* dominates a successful alphabeta search, so does DSSS*. Accordingly, in searching a tree, if a successful alphabeta search cuts off a node, then DSSS* also cuts off that node. But DSSS* might cut off nodes that a successful alphabeta search might not cut off (an instance of this is shown in Figure 13.40). Nevertheless, a node that is indispensable (described in Figure 13.24) will never be cut off by DSSS*.

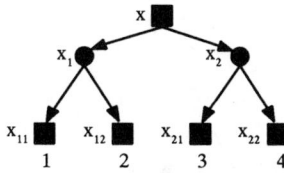

Iteration Number	Case Number	Contents of OPEN
0	-	$< x, U, -\infty >$
1	5	$< x_1, U, -\infty >$
2	6	$< x_{11}, U, -\infty >< x_{12}, U, -\infty >$
3	4	$< x_{12}, U, -\infty >< x_{11}, E, 1 >$
4	4	$< x_{11}, E, 1 >< x_{12}, E, 2 >$
5	1	$< x_1, E, 1 >$
6	2	$< x_2, U, 1 >$
7	6	$< x_{21}, U, 1 >< x_{22}, U, 1 >$
8	4	$< x_{22}, U, 3 >< x_{21}, E, 3 >$
9	4	$< x_{21}, E, 3 >< x_{22}, E, 4 >$
10	1	$< x_2, E, 3 >$
11	3	$< x, E, 3 >$

Figure 13.39 An example to display the contents of OPEN during every iteration of DSSS* while searching the above game tree. The potency values written alongside the leaf nodes are with respect to the root player. The case number for each iteration is identified from Figure 13.38. The last triple to be examined before putting the evaluated root node x in OPEN contained x_2. Hence x_2 is the heir of x. The minimax value of the game tree is 3. No nodes were cut off in the above tree by DSSS*. On the same tree, however, SSS* cut off one node, namely x_{12}, as illustrated in Figure 13.32.

DSSS* does not dominate an alphabeta search that fails. At such times, the alphabeta search might cut off nodes that DSSS* might not cut off. An example is shown in Figure 13.41.

DSSS* requires memory to store the list OPEN, just as SSS* does. The complicacy in processing of nodes by DSSS* is similar to that by SSS*. Hence, although DSSS* may cut off more nodes than alphabeta or scout search, it will usually be slower than those two search methods.

To speed up DSSS*, we can have an **aspirated DSSS***, by an approach similar to that for an aspirated SSS*. In an aspirated DSSS*, when we commence by putting $\langle$ root, s, k $\rangle$ in OPEN, we let k be a

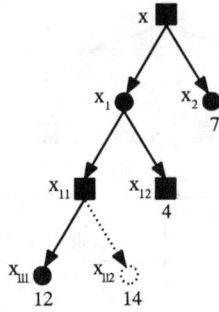

Iteration Number	Case Number	Contents of OPEN
0	-	$< x, U, -\infty >$
1	5	$< x_1, U, -\infty >$
2	6	$< x_{11}, U, -\infty >< x_{12}, U, -\infty >$
3	5	$< x_{111}, U, -\infty >< x_{12}, U, -\infty >$
4	4	$< x_{12}, U, -\infty >< x_{111}, E, 12 >$
5	4	$< x_{12}, E, 4 >< x_{111}, E, 12 >$
6	1	$< x_1, E, 4 >$
7	2	$< x_2, U, 4 >$
8	4	$< x_2, E, 7 >$
9	3	$< x, E, 7 >$

Figure 13.40   An example of DSSS* on a game tree. The potency values written alongside the leaf nodes are with respect to the root player. DSSS* cut off one node, namely x_{112} [shown dotted], in the above tree. An alphabeta search on the above tree will not cut off any nodes. Neither does SSS* cut off any nodes in the above tree, as illustrated in Figure 13.34.

finite lower bound on the minimax value of the root, rather than assuming k to be $-\infty$. To obtain a value for k, we can first obtain a value for α, as mentioned during the discussion on narrowed α-β windows in section 13.3.3. We then set k to be equal to $\alpha + 1$. The higher the value of k, the more nodes we expect to cut off. But, if the lower bound on the minimax value of the root is incorrect, then DSSS* will return with a value that is not the minimax value of the root. Figure 13.42 shows an example of aspirated DSSS*.

13.5.3   Remarks on personal and adversary trees

As we saw in the previous two sections, a best-first search is based either on personal trees or on adversary trees. We have also seen in

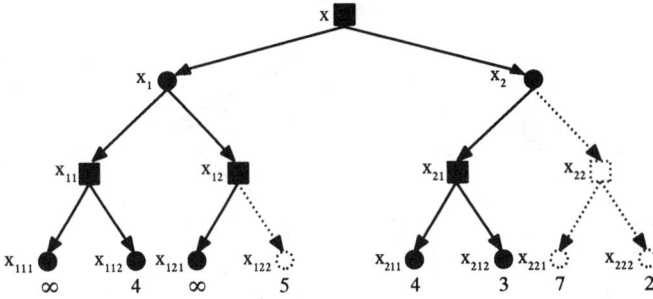

Iteration Number	Case Number	Contents of OPEN
0	-	$< x, U, -\infty >$
1	5	$< x_1, U, -\infty >$
2	6	$< x_{11}, U, -\infty >< x_{12}, U, -\infty >$
3	5	$< x_{111}, U, -\infty >< x_{12}, U, -\infty >$
4	4	$< x_{12}, U, -\infty >< x_{111}, E, \infty >$
5	5	$< x_{121}, U, -\infty >< x_{111}, E, \infty >$
6	4	$< x_{111}, E, \infty >< x_{121}, E, \infty >$
7	2	$< x_{112}, U, \infty >< x_{121}, E, \infty >$
8	4	$< x_{112}, E, \infty >< x_{121}, E, \infty >$
9	3	$< x_{11}, E, \infty >< x_{121}, E, \infty >$
10	1	$< x_1, E, \infty >$
11	2	$< x_2, U, \infty >$
12	6	$< x_{21}, U, \infty >< x_{22}, U, \infty >$
13	5	$< x_{211}, U, \infty >< x_{22}, U, \infty >$
14	4	$< x_{211}, E, \infty >< x_{22}, U, \infty >$
15	2	$< x_{212}, U, \infty >< x_{22}, U, \infty >$
16	4	$< x_{212}, E, \infty >< x_{22}, U, \infty >$
17	3	$< x_{21}, E, \infty >< x_{22}, U, \infty >$
18	1	$< x_1, E, \infty >$
19	3	$< x, E, \infty >$

Figure 13.41 DSSS* on a game tree of minimax value ∞. The potency values written alongside the leaf nodes are with respect to the root player. The nodes cut off are shown dotted. DSSS* did not cut off nodes x_{112}, x_2, x_{21}, x_{211}, and x_{212}, which were cut off by an alphabeta search that failed high in Figure 13.21.

our discussion in this chapter until now that the indispensable nodes of a game tree are not cut off, regardless of whether we conduct an alphabeta search, a scout search or a best-first search.

It may be of interest to know that we can detect indispensable nodes by constructing personal and adversary trees. Let us construct a

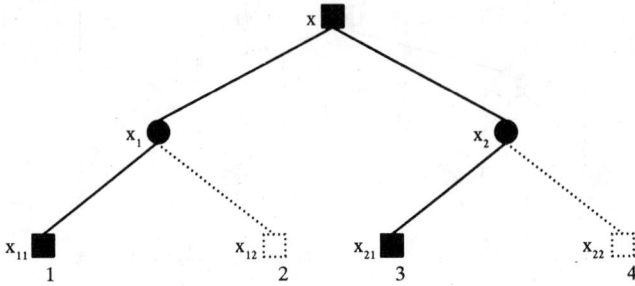

Iteration Number	Case Number	Contents of OPEN
0	-	$< x, U, 3 >$
1	5	$< x_1, U, 3 >$
2	6	$< x_{11}, U, 3 > < x_{12}, U, 3 >$
3	4	$< x_{11}, E, 3 > < x_{12}, U, 3 >$
4	1	$< x_1, E, 3 >$
5	2	$< x_2, U, 3 >$
6	6	$< x_{21}, U, 3 > < x_{22}, U, 3 >$
7	4	$< x_{21}, E, 3 > < x_{22}, U, 3 >$
8	1	$< x_2, E, 3 >$
9	3	$< x, E, 3 >$

Figure 13.42 An example of an aspirated DSSS* on a game tree in which two nodes [shown dotted] were cut off. Compare the above search with Figure 13.39, in which DSSS* did not cut off any nodes in the same tree. The potency values written alongside the leaf nodes are with respect to the root player. We commenced the above aspirated DSSS* by estimating the root to have a demerit of 3. Had we commenced the aspirated DSSS* with the root having a demerit of, say, 4, then we would have returned with a value that is not the minimax value of the root, since 4 is not a lower bound on the minimax value of the root.

personal tree such that we always select the leftmost child of a MAX node to be in the personal tree. Similarly, let us construct an adversary tree such that we always select the leftmost child of a MIN node to be in the adversary tree. We can then see that any node contained in either of the two trees constructed is indispensable.

It may also be of interest to know that a relationship exists between the sequence of moves made by the two players and the tactics adopted by them. If the tactics adopted by the root player is depicted by personal tree Z_1, and if the tactics adopted by the root player's opponent is depicted by adversary tree Z_2, then the sequence of moves made by the two players lies on the intersection of Z_1 and Z_2. In other words, the game traverses through the nodes that are common to Z_1 and Z_2. You may find it instructive to check the veracity of the above discussion by intersecting the different personal trees of Figure 13.29 with the different adversary trees of Figure 13.36.

13.6 APPRAISING SEARCH PERFORMANCE

Having read about alphabeta search, scout search and best-first search, we shall now read about the approaches for appraising the performance of a given search. Most of the computation required by a search is in the following three activities:

1. constructing the game tree by expanding nodes to generate their children,
2. calculating the potency values of the leaf nodes, and
3. propagating the values from the leaf node to the root of the tree.

Ideally, we like to reduce the overall computation required without any deterioration in the quality of the game played by the computer; for instance, the computer should always discover the optimal move from any given game state.

Game trees are mostly non-uniform. Even if the game trees for a given game were uniform, the trees will usually become non-uniform after some of the nodes have been cut off during the search. Let us posit that, for a given game, the typical non-uniform tree G' constructed by some particular searching method is experimentally observed to have, on average, depth D', number of leaf nodes L', and number of non-leaf nodes N'. We then conceive of a uniform tree G that supposedly requires the same amount of computation and memory to search as G'. We admit that the above supposition is debatable but such a supposition has become fairly acceptable in practice. The trees G and G' are said to be mutually **equipollent**. For a given G', its equipollent G may not be unique. The G we develop depends on what initial assumptions we make.

In sections 13.6.1–13.6.4, we discuss four approaches to develop a uniform tree G that is equipollent to a given non-uniform tree G'. In the discussion, we cite the equations derived in Figure 13.43, and we treat the non-uniform tree in Figure 13.44 as our example of G'. We obtain for each approach the values of the branching factor B, depth D, number of leaf nodes L, and number of non-leaf nodes N for a uniform

[1]   From our fundamental understanding of the number of nodes at each depth of a uniform tree:

$$N = B^0 + B^1 + \cdots + B^{D-1}$$

$$= \frac{B^D - 1}{B - 1}$$

[2]   Again, from our fundamental understanding of uniform trees:

$$L = B^D$$

[3]   We define T to be the number of nodes in the tree, not counting the root. Hence:

$$T = N + L - 1$$

[4]   By algebraic manipulation of [1], [2], and [3], it can be shown that:

$$T = \frac{B(B^D - 1)}{B - 1}$$

[5]   By algebraic manipulation of [1] and [4], it can be shown that:

$$B = \frac{T}{N}$$

[6]   From [3] and [5]:

$$B = \frac{N + L - 1}{N}$$

Figure 13.43   Equations for a uniform tree G of branching factor B, depth D, number of leaf nodes L, and number of non-leaf nodes N. Above, T can be alternatively viewed as the number of descendants of the root, or, as the number of arcs in the tree.

tree G that is equipollent to the G' of Figure 13.44. B is also known as the **effective branching factor** of G'.

13.6.1   Assuming $D = D'$ and $L = L'$

In this approach, we postulate that the amount of computation required depends mainly on the number of leaf nodes evaluated and on the number of depths across which the node valuations are propagated from the leaf nodes to the root. We accordingly assume that $D = D'$ and $L = L'$. To illustrate, the non-uniform tree G' of Figure 13.44 has $D' = 3$, $L' = 4$ and $N' = 4$. Its equipollent uniform tree G therefore has $D = 3$ and $L = 4$. Then, from equation 2. of Figure 13.43:

$$B = L^{1/D}$$
$$= 4^{1/3}$$
$$= 1.59.$$

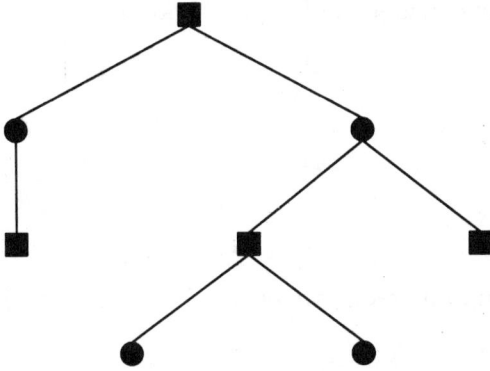

Figure 13.44 An example of a non-uniform tree G', in which depth D' is 3, the number of leaf nodes L' is 4, and the number of non-leaf nodes N' is 4. Moreover, T', the number of nodes not-counting the root node, is 7.

Moreover, from equation 1. of Figure 13.43:

$$N = \frac{B^D - 1}{B - 1}$$

$$= \frac{1.59^3 - 1}{1.59 - 1}$$

$$= 5.1.$$

Thus for the uniform tree G, we obtain B = 1.59, D = 3, L = 4 and N = 5.1.

13.6.2 Assuming L = L' and N = N'

In this approach, we postulate that the amount of computation required depends mainly on the number of nodes evaluated, but that the amount of computation required for evaluating a leaf node is different from the amount of computation required for evaluating a non-leaf node. We accordingly assume that L = L' and N = N'. To illustrate, the non-uniform tree G' of Figure 13.44 has D' = 3, L' = 4 and N' = 4. Its equipollent uniform tree G therefore has L = 4 and N = 4. Then, from equation 6. of Figure 13.43:

$$B = \frac{N + L - 1}{N}$$

$$= \frac{4 + 4 - 1}{4}$$

$$= 1.75.$$

Moreover, from equation 2. of Figure 13.43:

$$L = B^D;$$

that is

$$4 = 1.75^D;$$

and hence

$$D = 2.48.$$

Thus for the uniform tree G, we obtain $B = 1.75$, $D = 1.48$, $L = 4$ and $N = 4$.

13.6.3   Assuming $D = D'$ and $T = T'$

In this approach, we postulate that the amount of computation required depends mainly on the number of depths across which the node valuations are propagated from the leaf nodes to the root, and on the number of nodes evaluated, the amount of computation required for evaluating a leaf node being equal to the amount of computation required for evaluating a non-leaf node. We accordingly assume that $D = D'$ and $L + N = L' + N'$. Now,

$$
\begin{aligned}
T &= L + N - 1 && \text{from equation 3. of Figure 13.43,} \\
&= L' + N' - 1 && \text{by our above assumption,} \\
&= T' && \text{by defintion of } T'.
\end{aligned}
$$

To illustrate, the non-uniform tree G' of Figure 13.44 has $D' = 3$, $L' = 4$, $N' = 4$ and $T' = 7$. Based on our assumptions, the equipollent uniform G therefore has $D = 3$ and $T = 7$. Then, from equation 4. of Figure 13.43:

$$T = \frac{B\,(B^D - 1)}{B - 1;}$$

that is

$$7 = \frac{B\,(B^3 - 1)}{B - 1}$$

Calculating the value of B from an equation such as this can in general be complicated. Incidentally, we have seen the above equation in section 11.8 for appraising state space search strategies, and we had drawn plots for the equation in Figure 11.34. Reading the value of B from Figure 11.34 we obtain $B = 1.5$. Now from equation 2. of Figure 13.43:

$$L = B^D$$
$$= 1.5^3$$
$$= 3.375.$$

Moreover, from our assumption, $N + L = N' + L'$. Hence,

$$N = N' + L' - L$$
$$= 4 + 4 - 3.375$$
$$= 4.625.$$

Thus for the uniform tree G, we obtain $B = 1.5$, $D = 3$, $L = 3.375$ and $N = 4.625$.

13.6.4   Assuming $D = D'$ and $N = N'$

In this approach, we postulate that the amount of computation required depends mainly on the number of non-leaf nodes evaluated, and on the number of depths across which the node valuations are propagated from the leaf nodes to the root. This can happen when the computation required for evaluating the leaf nodes is negligible. We accordingly assume that $D = D'$ and $N = N'$. To illustrate, the non-uniform tree G' of Figure 13.44 has $D' = 3$, $L' = 4$ and $N' = 4$. Its equipollent uniform tree G therefore has $D = 3$ and $N = 4$. Then, from equation 1. of Figure 13.43:

$$N = \frac{B^D - 1}{B - 1} \; ;$$

that is

$$4 = \frac{B^3 - 1}{B - 1}$$

Calculating the value of B from an equation such as this can in general be complicated. We can, however, read the value of B from Figure 13.45. We obtain $B = 1.3$. Moreover, from equation 2. of Figure 13.43:

$$L = B^D$$
$$= 1.3^3$$
$$= 2.2.$$

Thus for the uniform tree G, we obtain $B = 1.3$, $D = 3$, $L = 2.2$ and $N = 4$.

13.6.5   Remarks on appraising search performance

You must have noticed that for the same non-uniform tree (that of Figure 13.44), the branching factor of the equipollent uniform tree varied from 1.3 to 1.75 by the above four approaches.

B

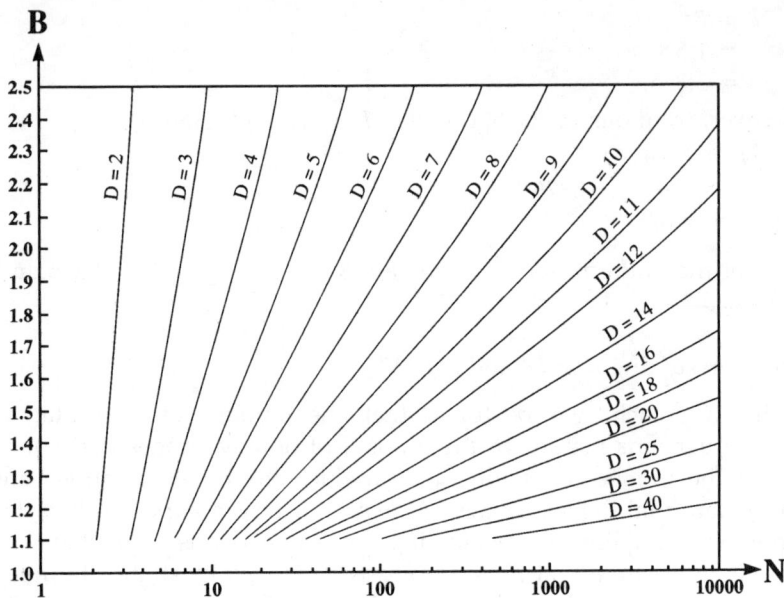

From Equation [1] of Figure 13.43: $N = \dfrac{B^D - 1}{B - 1}$

Figure 13.45   Plots of B versus N for various values of D. The axis for N is on log scale.

You may be wondering which approach to adopt. The approach of section 13.6.1 is popular in the literature. Nonetheless, you may adopt the approach that you think best reflects reality for the game playing program you have designed. For instance, if your potency function is so complicated that it requires substantial computation, then adopt an approach for which the computation required is postulated to be mainly in evaluating leaf nodes. You could then adopt the approach of either section 13.6.1 or section 13.6.2.

Once you have adopted an approach, carry out extensive experiments with the different search methods of sections 13.3–13.5. Suppose that you typically obtain non-uniform trees G_1' and G_2' by two search methods. With the approach you adopted, develop the corresponding equipollent uniform trees G_1 and G_2. You may then regard the search method that gives you the smaller equipollent tree as the preferred search method. Alternatively, you may prefer the search method that gives you a smaller effective branching factor, that is, a smaller branching factor for its equipollent uniform tree.

You may, of course, ignore all the four approaches described in sections 13.6.1–13.6.4. You could then use a clock to observe the typical speed of the different search methods. The fastest search method could then be your preferred method.

13.7 ENHANCEMENTS TO SEARCH PROCEDURES

In sections 13.7.1–13.7.5, we describe enhancements to improve the efficiency of the tree search or to improve the quality of the game played. You may choose the enhancements that you find appealing and incorporate them into any game playing program that you design.

13.7.1 Bandwidth pruning

Alphabeta, scout and best-first search are sometimes known in the literature under the generic appellation of **branch-and-bound** search, because there is this commonality in them: if a value associated with a node violates some bound, then a cut-off occurs; otherwise, we branch out to look at another node.

To increase cut-offs and thus hasten the search we can relax the bound by some heuristic bandwidth e. Then, in alphabeta search, for instance, we can redefine an alpha cut-off as follows: the cut-off occurs below a MIN node y if its provisional value is equal to $\alpha + e$ or less, where α is the highest provisional value of y's MAX node ancestors. Compare this revised definition with the original definition of alpha cut-off given in section 13.3.1.

Note, however, that such relaxation of the bound can result in our not discovering the optimal move, but some **near-optimal** move, that is, a move nearly as good as the optimal move. Hence the quality of the game played may deteriorate.

13.7.2 Forward pruning

The kind of pruning done by a branch-and-bound search is sometimes known in the literature as **backward pruning**. This is because, in essence, the search first proceeds forward from the root to the leaf nodes; second, it evaluates the leaf nodes; and then it cuts off nodes while proceeding backward to the root.

In contrast, a search that cuts off nodes while proceeding from the root to the leaf nodes does **forward pruning**. Such pruning is, however, heuristic. When we expand a node we retain only a few of its most promising children (see section 13.3.3), the rest being deleted. The number of children retained may vary in different parts of the game tree. Let us assume that we have sibling nodes x_1, x_2, x_3, ... sorted in decreasing order of their promise. On expanding these siblings we could retain more children of x_i (where $i \geq 1$) than of x_{i+1} because x_i is more promising than x_{i+1}. Usually the deeper a node is in the tree, the fewer of its children we retain. We thus prevent the tree from spreading out to become very bushy.

Accordingly, we can do forward pruning while proceeding from the root to the leaf nodes, and backward pruning while proceeding in reverse. Note, however, that forward pruning can cause the quality of the game played to deteriorate; for example, forward pruning may prevent a player from making a sacrifice for later gain. Suppose that in chess the optimal move for the root player is to let his pawn be captured so he can later capture the opponent's rook. Sacrificing the pawn may cause a temporary decrease in the promise of the corresponding node, and thus the node could be deleted. This would result in the root player not discovering his optimal move.

13.7.3　Transposition tables

In this enhancement to tree search, whenever we evaluate a node y we store in a data structure, called a **transposition table**, the following information:

1. the node y,
2. the valuation of y,
3. the heir z of y, and
4. the depth d of the subtree rooted at y, which was searched to evaluate y.

The above information about y is known as the **accoutrements** of y and is illustrated in Figure 13.46.

On coming across any other node y' later in the search, we scan the transposition table to see whether an identical node y exists in the table. If no such y is found we evaluate y' by the usual search and we store the accoutrements of y' in the transposition table. If, however, such a y is found in the transposition table, we execute the following steps.

1. If $d' \leq d$, where d' is the depth of the subtree rooted at y', then read off the valuation and the heir of y from the transposition table. The valuation and the heir of y are assigned as the valuation and heir, respectively, of y'.

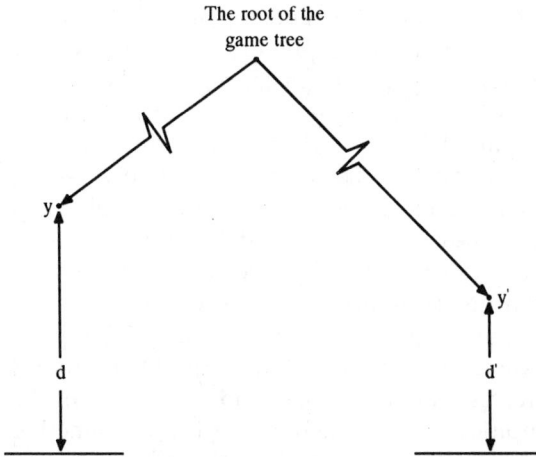

Figure 13.46 Using transposition tables to hasten the tree search. Let us assume that we have evaluated node y, and that we have stored its accoutrements in the transposition table. Later in the search, suppose that we come across a node y' that is identical to y. Rather than spend time evaluating y' by the usual tree search, we assign the valuation and the heir of y to be the valuation and heir, respectively, of y'. We do this provided d' ≤ d, where d' is the depth of the subtree rooted at y', and d is the depth of the subtree rooted at y.

2. If $d' > d$, then we need to evaluate y'. Hence expand y' and order its children so that the heir of y as read off from the transposition table becomes the leftmost child of y'. Evaluate y' by the usual tree search and store its accoutrements as the revised accoutrements of y in the transposition table.

Using a transposition talbe is expected to make our tree search faster. We shall, however, need some technique by which we can quickly scan the transposition table to see whether a given node exists in the table. The technique often recommended in the literature is hashing the table. Hashing is a vast topic in itself. We assume you are familiar with hashing from your understanding of computer science in general.

13.7.4 Curtailing the horizon effect

This enhancement to tree search is for improving the quality of the game played. Let us consider an example. Suppose that our game tree is of depth 5, in other words, we are looking five moves ahead. The optimal move from the root aims the game at the leaf node that is expected to be the most potent for us. There is, however, the possibility that what is most potent after 5 moves may no longer remain so potent later. For instance, in chess we capture the opponent's pawn 5 moves from now, but then 2 moves further he captures our queen. Such an aftermath arising from our inability to look beyond a certain number of moves is known is the literature as the **horizon effect**. The leaf nodes form our metaphorical horizon.

We cannot eradicate the horizon effect but we can attempt to curtail it by complying with this heuristic: do not have a non-quiescent node as a leaf. A **non-quiescent** node is one at which there is a sharp change of the situation in the game: say, a node at which a piece is captured. The potency value of a non-quiescent node differs from its parent's by an amount greater than some threshold. The value of the threshold is developed empirically: its value depends on the game being played (is it chess, or draughts, or . . .?), and on the potency function employed to evaluate leaf nodes. Accordingly, while searching the game tree, whenever we come across a non-quiescent node y that would have been a leaf node, we are advised to look deeper until we reach a quiescent descendant of y. This technique is known in the literature as **heuristic continuation** or as **feedover**.

We can augment heuristic continuation. After searching a game tree suppose we found that the principal path ends on the leaf node z (remember that our optimal move lies on the principal path). We now ignore the rest of the game tree but we look a few moves deeper from z to ensure that the move sequence we found does not later lead us to some adverse game states. It is akin to thinking ahead a few moves more after we have nearly decided our move, just to be doubly sure.

Of course, an adverse game state can lurk somewhere beyond no matter how deep we look unless we are able to look ahead all the way to the end of the game, which , as discussed in section 13.2, we can do only rarely. That is why we can attempt to curtail the horizon effect, but we cannot eradicate it.

13.7.5   Iterative deepening

In tournaments it is often the practice to prescribe the amount of time within which a player should make a move. By the enhancement to tree search described below, we attempt to play the game of the best possible quality within the prescribed time limit. In essence, we search the game tree by deepening it iteratively (also known as **progressive deepening** in the literature).

To find the optimal move from a given game state we commence by searching a game tree of depth 1. Next, we search a game tree of depth

2, then of depth 3, and so on. In general, considering the valuation of a node obtained from searching the tree of depth $d - 1$ as the promise of the node, we sort sibling nodes in decreasing order of their promise, to search a tree of depth d.

Suppose that we are searching the tree of depth d, when we notice that the prescribed time limit is about to be exceeded. We discontinue the search. The optimal move discovered by searching the tree of depth $d - 1$ is declared to be the optimal move for which we have been looking.

You may argue that this repeated propagation of values through the non-leaf nodes for trees of different depths is wasteful. The literature, however, presents a counter-argument: from equations 1. and 2. of Figure 13.43 in a typical tree of effective branching factor B, depth D, number of leaf nodes L and number of non-leaf nodes N, it can be said that

$$\frac{N}{L} = \frac{B^D - 1}{(B - 1)B^D}$$

$$= \frac{1}{B - 1} \text{ approximately.}$$

Thus for a game like chess, where B would usually be 35:

$$\frac{N}{L} = \frac{1}{34}.$$

Hence, evaluating non-leaf nodes repeatedly will increase the computation required only marginally, since most of the computation required will be for evaluating leaf nodes.

You may find the above counter-argument intuitively disagreeable. We suggest that for some particular game you empirically compare the quality of the game played when you carry out iterative deepening, with the quality when you do not carry out iterative deepening. You may then make up your mind based on your empirical results.

You may, of course, modify the iterative deepening described above. For instance, you may commence by searching a tree of depth 2. Next, search a tree of depth 4, then of depth 6, and so on. This way the leaf nodes always correspond to the game states immediately after the opponent has moved. This contrasts with the way, described earlier, in which the leaf nodes alternated between the game states after the root player's move and the game states after the opponent's move. It is believed that a player's position improves after his own move as compared to his position after the opponent's move. Thus the root player may make a wiser choice of optimal move if the leaf nodes always correspond to the game states immediately after the opponent has moved.

13.8   ALTERNATIVE SEARCH PROCEDURES

As mentioned in section 13.2.3, in general the more accurate the potency function, the more skillfully the computer can play. If the potency function is inaccurate, then no matter how the tree is searched the game played will not be of high quality. In sections 13.8.1 and 13.8.2 we present two alternative ways of instituting potency functions. Both these alternatives will be explained in the minimax notation. You may, if you wish, amend the alternatives appropriately to suit the negamax notation.

13.8.1   Optimistic and pessimistic potency values

In this alternative, known in the literature as the B* **algorithm**, we measure the potency of a node by two heuristic functions: one function measures the potency optimistically, the other function pessimistically. Accordingly, a leaf node has two potency values: one optimistic and one pessimistic. Since our discussion is in the minimax notation, both the values are with respect to the root player. Moreover, a node's optimistic value is either equal to the node's pessimistic value, or it is greater.

Whenever these values are propagated from the leaf nodes to the root by the minimax procedure, the optimistic and pessimistic values are propagated independently of each other, so each non-leaf node also has an optimistic value and a pessimistic value.

We can now combine the above with the idea of iterative deepening discussed in section 13.7.5. We iteratively construct deeper and deeper trees. For each tree, the values are propagated up from the leaf nodes. We continue to do so until we meet this stopping criterion: for some trees, the pessimistic value of a node y at depth 1 becomes greater than or equal to the optimistic values of all its siblings. The optimal move from the root is then to node y. An example is shown in Figure 13.47.

If we do not meet the above stopping criterion within some prescribed time limit, we then consider the values of the nodes as obtained from the deepest tree searched so far. The optimal move from the root is to that depth 1 node whose weighted value is the highest among the weighted values of all depth 1 nodes, where the weighted value of a node z is defined to be equal to

W times the optimistic value of $z + (1 - W)$ times the pessimistic value of z,

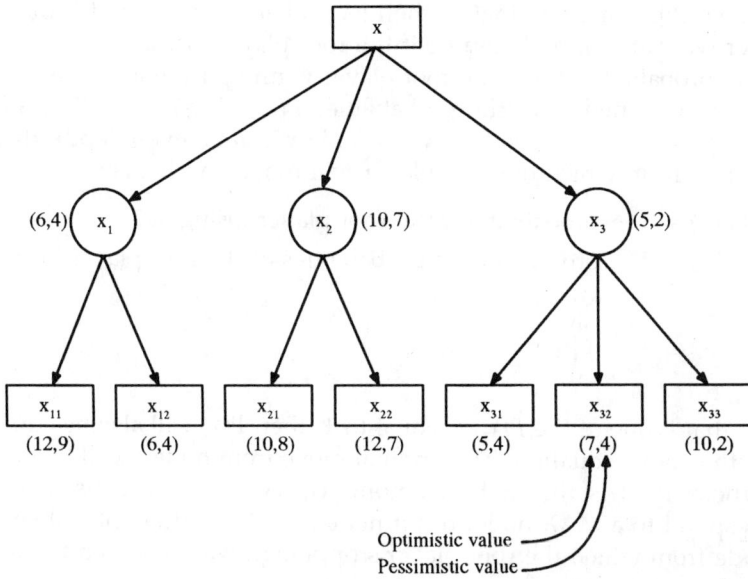

Figure 13.47 An example of propagating optimistic and pessimistic minimax values in the B* algorithm. Each node's optimistic and pessimistic values are written alongside the node. Propagating the optimistic and pessimistic values independently of each other from the leaf nodes, we notice that, at depth 1, the pessimistic value of node x_2 has become greater than or equal to either of the optimistic values of x_1 and x_3. Hence the optimal move from root node x is to node x_2.

in which W is an empirically developed weighting coefficient such that $0 \leq W \leq 1$. Nonetheless, if we are to use both the optimistic value and the pessimistic value of a node, we should have $0 < W < 1$.

13.8.2 The propagation of probabilities

In all our discussions and examples until now, the potency values of leaf nodes have been integers, but, as mentioned in section 13.2.1, these values can also be non-integers. Moreover, we can have a potency function such that the potency value of a leaf node lies in the closed interval between 0 and 1. The potency value of a leaf node can then be considered to be the probability of the root player winning from that node (section 10.2.1 contained a review of probability theory). The probabilities of sibling nodes are assumed to be independent of one another. If a leaf is a terminal node, that is, a node at which the game terminates, then its probability value is 1 if the root player wins at that node, and 0 if the root player loses.

The probability $P(x)$ of the root player winning from a non-leaf node x can be obtained from the probabilities $P(x_1)$, $P(x_2)$, ..., $P(x_n)$ of its children $x_1, x_2, \ldots, x_n$ as follows. If node x is at an even depth, then it is a node from which the root player will move and hence

$P(x) = 1 -$ probability of the root player losing at x

$\qquad = 1 -$ product of the probabilities of the root player losing at $x_1, x_2, \ldots, x_n$

$$= 1 - \prod_{i=1}^{n} (1 - P(x_i)).$$

Note that if one of the $P(x_i)$ is equal to 1, then $P(x)$ will also be equal to 1 by the above equation. The optimal move from node x will be to that x_i whose $P(x_i)$ is the highest among $x_1, x_2, \ldots, x_n$. Thus x would correspond to a MAX node. But if node x is at an odd depth, then it is a node from which the root player's opponent will move, and hence

$P(x) =$ product of the probabilities of the root player winning at $x_1, x_2, \ldots, x_n$

$$= \prod_{i=1}^{n} P(x_i).$$

Note that if one of the $P(x_i)$ is equal to 0, then $P(x)$ will also be equal to 0 by the above equation. The optimal move from x will be to that x_i whose $P(x_i)$ is the lowest among $x_1, x_2, \ldots, x_n$. Thus x would correspond to a MIN node.

By repeatedly applying the above formulae across the depths in a game tree, we can propagate the probability values from the leaf nodes to the nodes at depth 1. The optimal move from the root is then to the node with the highest probability value among the node's siblings. An example is given in Figure 13.48.

It can sometimes happen that the optimal move from the root node obtained by probability propagation is not the same as the optimal move obtained by the minimax procedure. This, in fact, happens in the example of Figure 13.49.

13.9   CLOSING REMARKS

You can surely think up extensions to the techniques for game playing described in this chapter. By borrowing ideas from problem decomposition (Chapter 12), you can, for instance, set up intermediate

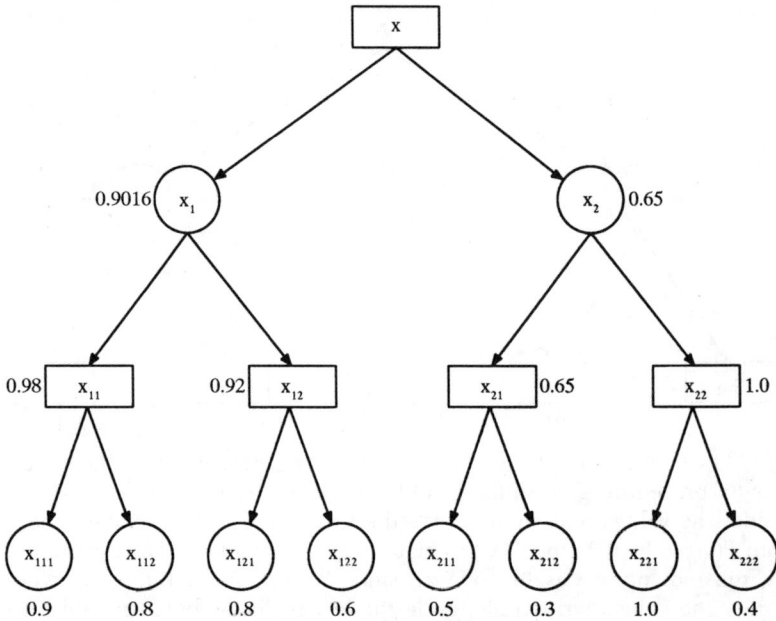

Figure 13.48 An example of propagating probability values from the leaf nodes in a game tree. The probability values of the leaf nodes and those propagated to the non-leaf nodes are written alongside the nodes. An instance of propagating the probability value to a non-leaf node at an even depth is the following:

$$P(x_{11}) = (1 - (1 - P(x_{111}))(1 - P(x_{112})))$$
$$= (1 - (1 - 0.9)(1 - 0.8)) = 0.98.$$

Likewise, an instance of propagating the probability value to a non-leaf node at an odd depth is the following:

$$P(x_1) = P(x_{11})P(x_{12}) = 0.98 \times 0.92 = 0.9016.$$

The optimal move from root node x is to node x_1, since $P(x_1) > P(x_2)$. Note that in the above example, had we considered the values to be propagated by the minimax procedure, then also we would obtain the same optimal move from the root node. Contrast this example with the example of Figure 13.49.

objectives that you want the computer to achieve. Such objectives, once achieved, should help the computer win the game. As an illustration, let us consider chess. To win, a player must checkmate his opponent's king. An intermediate objective that a player can have is to, say, capture the opponent's queen. Once an objective has been decided upon, the computer plays to achieve that objective first.

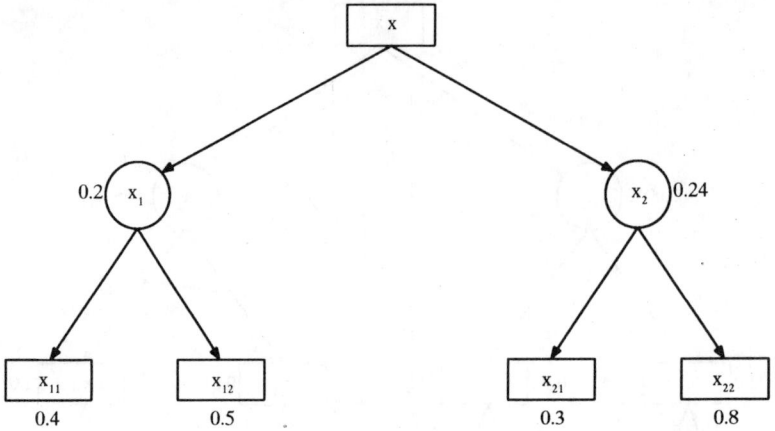

Figure 13.49   An example in which propagating probability values and the minimax procedure give different optimal moves from the root node. If we consider the values written alongside the leaf nodes as probabilities, then we obtain $P(x_1)$ to be 0.2, and $P(x_2)$ to be 0.24 as shown above. The optimal move from the root node x is to node x_2, since $P(x_2) > P(x_1)$. But if we were to consider the values written alongside the leaf nodes as potency values to be propagated by the minimax procedure, then we would obtain the move from node x to node x_1 as the optimal move from the root.

Another extension could possibly be the following. Every time, while the opponent is thinking of what move to make, the computer can go ahead constructing and pruning its tree based on the guess that the opponent is likely to make his optimal move. Whenever the computer's guess turns out to be correct, as may happen quite often, the computer will be able to search deeper trees in the time available.

Alternatively, rather than construct only one tree as above, the computer may construct a small number of trees based on the set of the most likely moves that the opponent might make. Then, once the opponent has moved, the computer commences to search the appropriate tree to greater depth.

Two games γ_1 and γ_2 may seem to be different, but they may essentially be the same. The two games are then said to be **isomorphic** to each other. One of the games, say, γ_2 may be easier to play than γ_1. Suppose that you are to write a program for playing γ_1. You can then write your program so that the computer appears to play γ_1, but it is actually playing γ_2.

As an illustration, suppose that you are to write a program for playing the game of **number scrabble**.

Figure 13.50 By viewing the counters of number scrabble placed as above, we can see that the game is isomorphic to noughts and crosses [see Figures 13.4 and 13.5]. The sum of the numbers in any line [that is, a row, column, or diagonal] is 15. To win, a player should pick up three counters from a line. Correspondingly, to win in noughts and crosses, a player should put three of his symbols in a line.

> Two players have a pile of 9 counters between them. Each counter is stamped with a number from 1 to 9. No two counters are stamped with the same number. Moving alternately, each player picks up a counter from the pile. The counter picked up is removed from the pile. The player·who is the first to pick up three counters such that the numbers on the counters add to 15 wins the game.

Figure 13.50 shows that the number scrabble game is isomorphic to noughts and crosses discussed in section 13.1.2. If you find noughts and crosses easier, your program may appear to play number scrabble while actually playing noughts and crosses.

To increase the speed of a game playing program, it can be implemented on processors operating in parallel. The different parts of a game tree can then be searched simultaneously by the different processors. On returning with their results, the processors communicate with one another to prune the tree, and to find the optimal move from the root node.

13.10 EXERCISES

1. As shown in section 13.1.1, the λ-coin Grundy's game for $\lambda = 7$ is biased in favour of player C_2. Find the smallest values of $\lambda > 7$ for which the game is

(a) biased in favour of player C_1;

(b) not biased in favour of either player.

2. In the game of Nim, two players C_1 and C_2 have a pile of 26 coins between them. Moving first, C_1 picks up and removes from the pile 1, 2, 3 or 4 coins. Next, C_2 moves likewise. The game proceeds with the two players moving alternately. The player who picks up the last coin loses. Analyse the game. Is the game biased in favour of C_1, or C_2, or neither player? If the game is biased, express concisely the winning tactics of the player in favour of whom the game is biased.

3. The procedures MINIMAXE(x) and MINIMAXO(x) of section 13.2.1 return with the minimax value of node x. In the discussion on the procedures it was assumed that the procedures also identify the heir of x. Modify the procedures so that they explicitly identify the heir of node x. Similarly, modify procedure NEGAMAX(x) of section 13.2.2.

4. We had conformed to the practice in the literature and used the equation

$$N(x) = \max(-N(x_1), -N(x_2), \ldots, -N(x_n))$$

in the procedure NEGAMAX(x) of section 13.2.2. Modify NEGAMAX so that, instead of the above equation, it uses the following equation:

$$N(x) = -\min(N(x_1), N(x_2), \ldots, N(x_n)).$$

5. The minimax and negamax procedures as formulated in sections 13.2.1 and 13.2.2 generate and evaluate nodes in the sequence shown in Figure 13.11. Modify the procedures so that they generate and evaluate the nodes in the sequence shown in Figure 13.12 instead.

6. For the procedures ALPHABETAMO of section 13.3.1, and ALPHABETAN of section 13.3.2, does the following relationship hold:

$$\text{ALPHABETAMO}(x, \alpha, \beta) = -\text{ALPHABETAN}(x, -\beta, -\alpha)?$$

Give reasons for your answer. If the relationship holds, does it hold when

(a) the search is successful, or

(b) the search fails either high or low?

7. Suppose that you embody the following procedure in the negamax procedure.

(1) Procedure QN(x: node; β: integer): integer;

(2) i, m, n: integer;

(3) If x is a leaf node, then return the potency value of x with respect to the player who is to move from x.

(4) Expand x to generate its children $x_1, x_2, \ldots, x_n$.

(5) $m := -\infty$.

(6) For $i := 1$ to n do:

    (6.1) $m := \max(m, -QN(x_i, -m))$.

    (6.2) if $m \geq \beta$, then return m.

(7) Return m.

(8) End.

Compare the above procedure QN with the procedure ALPHABETAN of section 13.3.2. Which of the two procedures is expected to cut off more nodes in a game tree? Give reasons for your answer.

8. Suppose that, on expanding a node x, we sort the children as x_1, x_2, x_3 in decreasing order of their promise, where the estimates of the negamax values of x_1, x_2, x_3 are respectively 1, 2, 4. Remember that the lower the negamax estimate of a node, the more promising is the node. According to the scheme (known as the **static scheme**) described in section 13.3.3, we shall expand and evaluate first x_1, next x_2, and lastly x_3. Let us modify the above scheme to be the **dynamic scheme**, as described below. We first expand x_1. Say, while searching the subtree rooted at x_1, the provisional value of x_1 becomes 3. Now x_2 looks more promising than x_1. We suspend searching the subtree rooted at x_1. Instead, we expand x_2 and start searching the subtree rooted at x_2. Overall, in the dynamic scheme, at any given time, we are searching the subtree rooted at the sibling node that is the most promising at that time. Modify procedure ALPHABETAN of section 13.3.2 to incorporate the dynamic scheme. Does the extra complicacy of the dynamic scheme justify the extra nodes that it may cut off as compared to the static scheme? To answer this question, you may need to compare empirically the two schemes on some specimen game trees.

9. The procedure in section 13.4.3 adapts alphabeta to a scout search embodied in the negamax procedure. Formulate the corresponding procedure to adapt alphabeta to a scout search embodied in the minimax procedure.

10. Suppose that line (6.4.1) in the procedure SALPHABETAN of section 13.4.3 is modified to read as follows:

    If $(k > \alpha)$,

    and $(k < \beta)$,

and   the subtree rooted at x_i has a depth of more than 2,
then $m := -\text{SALPHABETAN}(x_i, -\beta, -k)$; otherwise, $m := k$.

Will the modification hasten the search? Give reasons for your answer. What are the drawbacks, if any, of the modification?

11. Which nodes will be cut off in the game trees of Figures 13.8 and 13.18 by (a) SSS*, and (b) DSSS*?

12. Which nodes will be cut off in the game tree of Figure 13.42 by an aspirated DSSS* if we commence the search by estimating the root node to have a demerit of 2?

13. In your own words, explain the difference and the relationship among the potency, worth, promise, merit and demerit of a node in a game tree.

14. Express the following in the negamax notation:
    (a) SSS* of section 13.5.1,
    (b) DSSS* of section 13.5.2, and
    (c) B* of section 13.8.1.

15. Let us define $P(x)$ to be the probability of winning from node x for the player who moves from x. Will the formulae for propagating the probability values upward from the leaf nodes be the same as those given in section 13.8.2? If not, develop the formulae that will be needed to propagate the probability values.

16. Write a program to play interactively any one of the two games described below. In both games, the players alternate, the computer putting an 'X' symbol, and the opponent putting an 'O' symbol in an empty space. At the beginning of the game, the computer asks the opponent whether he wants to move first or second. The game proceeds according to the opponent's response. Whenever the computer moves, it displays its move and the state of the game after the move. Whenever the opponent enters his move, the computer checks whether it is a permitted move; if the move is not permitted, the computer asks the opponent to enter his move again. At the termination of the game, the computer declares the winner, if the game is not a draw. The two games from which you are to choose are the following.
    (a) The game is five in a line played on an 11 × 11 grid of empty spaces, which is an enlargement of the grid you saw in Figures 13.4 and 13.5. The opponent indicates his move by entering, say, (3 1) to signify that his symbol is being put in row 3 and column 1. A player wins if he is able to put five of his symbols in a line, that is, in a row, column or diagonal.
    (b) The game is cubic played on 4 × 4 grids of empty spaces on the six faces of a cube. The opponent makes his move by entering,

The computer shows the state of the game, whenever needed, by displaying the following planes:

Plane 1	Plane 2	Plane 3	Plane 4
(ABCD)	(EFGH)	(IJKL)	(MNPQ)

Figure 13.51 Pictorial representation for cubic, required for exercise 16 of Chapter 13. Note that there are altogether 16 planes: the 6 faces [ABCD, DCPQ, . . .] of the cube, the 4 diagonal planes [ABPQ, DCNM, . . .], and the 6 mid-planes [EFGH, IJKL, . . .].

say, (2 3 1) to signify that he is putting his symbol in plane 2, row 3 and column 1 as shown in Figure 13.51. A player wins if he is able to put four of his symbols in a line in any of the 16 planes.

In both of the above games, if there are no empty spaces remaining, and if neither player has won, then the game is a draw. After your program has been implemented discuss, with reasons, the following:

(a) the potency function you developed;
(b) the searching method you selected (you should experiment with the different searching methods in this chapter, and then select one of them);

(c) the scheme, static or dynamic, according to which sibling nodes were ordered (see exercise 8 above); and
(d) the enhancements to search that you adopted from section 13.7.

13.11 SUGGESTIONS FOR FURTHER READING

Bell (1972) detailed several games for computer playing. Samuel (1967) described signature tables in which subsets of features are combined to serve as a potency function for draughts. McAllester (1988) advocated a procedure for constructing a game tree based on a measure of the accuracy of its minimax value. Rivest (1988) suggested a technique to select those nodes for expansion that are most likely to affect the minimax value of the root. Althöfer (1990) advanced an incremental negamax procedure in which the negamax value of the root node depends on the potency values of both the non-leaf and leaf nodes, rather than only on the potency values of the leaf nodes. Nau (1983) argued why searching deeper in game trees of certain rare games can cause deterioration in the quality of play. Knuth and Moore (1975) analysed alphabeta search. Kumar and Kanal (1984) proposed DSSS*. Marsland, Reinfeld and Schaeffer (1987) empirically compared SSS* and DSSS* with some procedures based on the alphabeta search. Ibarki (1986) presented a generalized formulation for alphabeta search and SSS*. Palay (1982) elaborated on the B* algorithm. Horowitz and Sahni (1984) explained hashing, which you may extend to incorporate transposition tables in searching game trees. Shaeffer (1989) discussed different combinations of enhancements to alphabeta search. Pearl (1984) gave a mathematical analysis of game tree search. Frey and Atkin (1979) provided advice on writing a program to play chess. Newborn (1988) explored a variation of alphabeta search suitable for parallel implementation. Berliner and Ebeling (1989) described a system architecture for searching game trees.

1. Althöfer, I. (1990) An incremental negamax algorithm, *Artificial Intelligence*, **43**[1], 57–65. (This was a special issue of the journal on computer chess.)
2. Bell, A. G. (1972) *Game Playing with Computers*, George Allen and Unwin Ltd., London.
3. Berliner, H. and Ebeling, C. (1989) Pattern knowledge and search: The SUPREM architecture, *Artificial Intelligence*, **38**[2], 161–98.
4. Frey, P. W. and Atkin, L. R. (1979) Creating a chess player, in *The BYTE Book of Pascal* (ed. B. L. Liffick), BYTE/McGraw-Hill, Peterborough, New Hampshire, pp. 107–55.

5. Horowitz, E. and Sahni, S. (1984) *Fundamentals of Computer Algorithms*, Computer Science Press, Rockville, Maryland.
6. Ibarki, T. (1986) Generalization of alpha–beta and SSS* search procedures, *Artificial Intelligence*, **29**[1], 73–117.
7. Knuth, D. E. and Moore, R. W. (1975) An analysis of alpha–beta pruning, *Artificial Intelligence*, **6**[9], 293–326.
8. Kumar, V. and Kanal, L. N. (1984) Parallel branch-and-bound formulations for AND/OR tree search, *IEEE Transactions on Pattern Analysis and Machine Intelligence*, **PAMI-6**[6], 768–78.
9. Marsland, T. A., Reinfeld, A. and Schaeffer, J. (1987) Low overhead alternatives to SSS*, *Artificial Intelligence*, **31**[2], 185–9.
10. McAllester, D. A. (1988) Conspiracy search for MIN–MAX search, *Artificial Intelligence*, **35**[3], 287–310.
11. Nau, D. S. (1983) Pathology on game trees revisited and an alternative to minimaxing, *Artificial Intelligence*, **21**[1,2], 221–44.
12. Newborn, M. (1988) Unsynchronized iteratively deepening alpha–beta search, *IEEE Transactions on Pattern Analysis and Machine Intelligence*, **PAMI-10**[5], 687–94.
13. Palay, A. J. (1982) The B* tree search algorithm: new results, *Artificial Intelligence*, **19**[2], 145–63.
14. Pearl, J. (1984) *Heuristics: Intelligent Search Strategies for Computer Problem Solving*, Addison-Wesley, Reading, Massachusetts.
15. Rivest, R. L. (1988) Game tree searching by min/max approximation, *Artificial Intelligence*, **34**[1], 77–96.
16. Samuel, A. L. (1967) Some studies in machine learning using the game of checkers II, *IBM Journal of Research and Development*, **11**[6], 601–17.
17. Schaeffer, J. (1989) The history heuristic and alpha–beta search enhancements in practice, *IEEE Transactions on Pattern Analysis and Machine Intelligence*, **PAMI-11**[11], 1203–11.

Appendix
Fingers to symbulators

A1 INTRODUCTION

A speed-calculating contest, sponsored by the journal *Stars and Stripes*, was held in Tokyo on 12 November 1946, shortly after the Second World War. The contestants were both 22-year-old clerks: Kiyoshi Matsuzaki, with the Japanese government, and Private Thomas Ian Wood, with the US army. Matsuzaki used a Japanese abacus, then costing about 25 US cents; Wood, an electric desk calculator, about $700. Experts in wielding their respective devices, the two men were tested on addition, subtraction, multiplication, division and composite problems. Matsuzaki was declared the winner. Not only did he calculate more rapidly, but also more accurately. The age-old abacus had trounced the twentieth-century calculator.

It is not certain when humankind first started using devices for calculations. Many of the earlier developments were not recorded. If recorded, they were lost when libraries were destroyed. In 213 BC, Emperor Ch'in Shih Huang Ti burned ancient Chinese books to eradicate the works of the philosophers Lao-tzu, Confucius and Mencius. The Alexandrian library in Egypt was destroyed during the civil war in the third century. A subsidiary library, Serapeum, was burned in 391 AD by Bishop Theophilus. In Rome, the Octavian library was burned in 80 AD, and the Palatine library in 192 AD. In the twelfth century, Bhaktiar Khilji, a Turkish general, sacked the Nalanda library in India. The Maya records were burned in Mexico after the Spanish invasion in the sixteenth century. What we know today is mainly from the few records that survived the whim of an emperor, a conqueror or a fundamentalist.

Before we learn to calculate, we must learn to count. To add 17 to 5, we can count seventeen pebbles, then another five pebbles, and then count the entire lot. The pebbles thus serve as counters. To subtract 5 from 17, we match five pebbles against seventeen pebbles, remove all matched pebbles, and count the remaining. Having learned addition and subtraction, we can do multiplication and division. Multiplying 17 by 5 is tantamount to repeated addition of seventeen. Dividing 17 by 5 is tantamount to repeated subtraction of five.

To record the number of sheep he had traded, an unlettered peasant could keep a count by pebbles, scratches on a stone or pottery, knots on a string, or notches on a stick. He soon began to group numbers; for example, a V-shaped notch could be equal to five |-shaped notches. The Incas in Peru used different kinds of knots to denote grouping of numbers. Today we group numbers in tens. This is called the **base-10** or **decimal** or **denary** number system. Any number we write has digits ranked as units, tens, hundreds, and so on. The word **digit**, referring to any of the symbols from 0 to 9, also means **finger**. Our forebears used their fingers for counting and so learned to group by tens. Not everyone did that. A base-20 (vigesimal) number system was developed by the Maya in Central America, and by the Basques in Europe. These people used their fingers and their toes for counting. The Babylonians in the second millennium BC used a base-60 (sexagesimal) number system. The Greek astronomer Ptolemy (circa 200 AD), used such a system in his calculations. We still use it: sixty seconds to the minute, sixty minutes to the hour.

The notion of zero was not used in these systems in the manner in which we use it today. The zero appeared in decimal numbers around the sixth century in the writings of astronomers in India. It was introduced by the Arabs to Europe, where it gained acceptance after prolonged opposition. The Europeans, who had until then been using pebbles on wooden boards to calculate with Roman numerals, took to paper-and-pen arithmetic. Europe used unevenly graded weights and measures (sixteen ounces to the pound, fourteen pounds to the stone, twelve inches to the foot, three feet to the yard). These are gradually being replaced by metric weights and measures (milligrams to kilograms, millimetres to kilometres), which are graded uniformly in tens. The metric system, developed in France at the time of the Revolution, is used world-wide today.

Most of us may take calculating for granted, but it was not always so. This will become apparent from the review of historical calculating devices given below. Many of these devices originated as counting devices. From these beginnings emerged the mechanical calculator, which in time became the twentieth-century electronic computer. If these devices do not interest you, then go on to section A9, for the discussion on the challenge of artificial intelligence. Our review of historical calculating devices starts with the oldest device with which nature has provided humans, namely fingers.

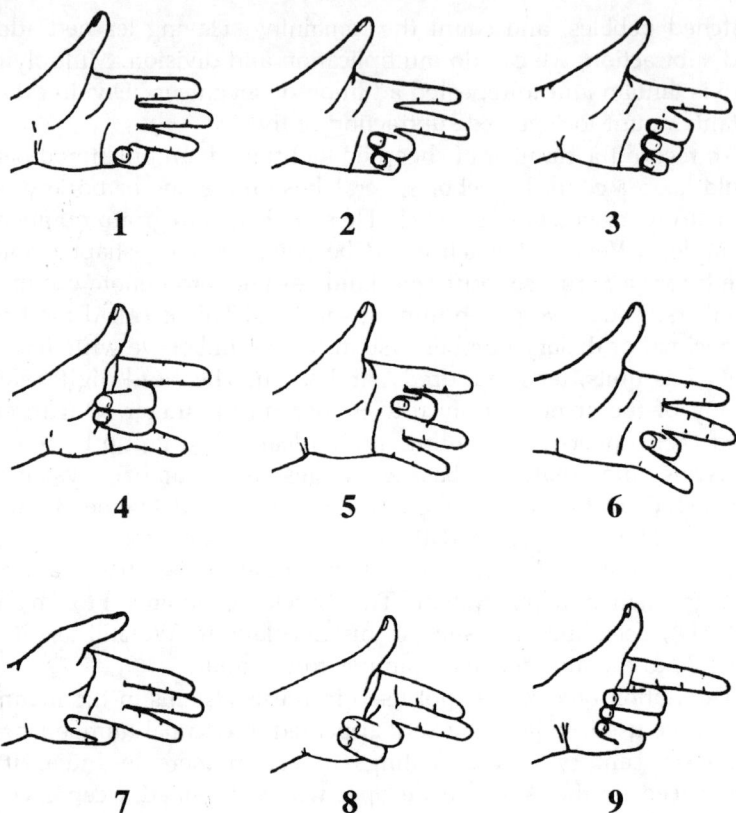

Figure A1   Gestures of the left hand [according to Bede] for the numbers 1 to 9.

A1.1   Finger counting

Using fingers to count developed independently all over the world: Babylon, China, Egypt, Greece, India, Persia, Rome. It is practiced to this day. As children, most of us used our fingers to do our sums. As adults, many of us count with our fingers, provided no one is looking.

By manipulating the fingers of both hands, the Romans were able to represent numbers from one to ten thousand. A British Benedictine monk, the Venerable Bede (673?–735), wrote a Latin manuscript, *De computo vel loquela digitorum* (On Calculating and Speaking with Fingers). He delineated rules on how to represent numbers on the fingers, and how to calculate. The rules are far too many to list here, but we can give you the general idea by naming the fingers used to show units, tens, hundreds, thousands, and by presenting examples.

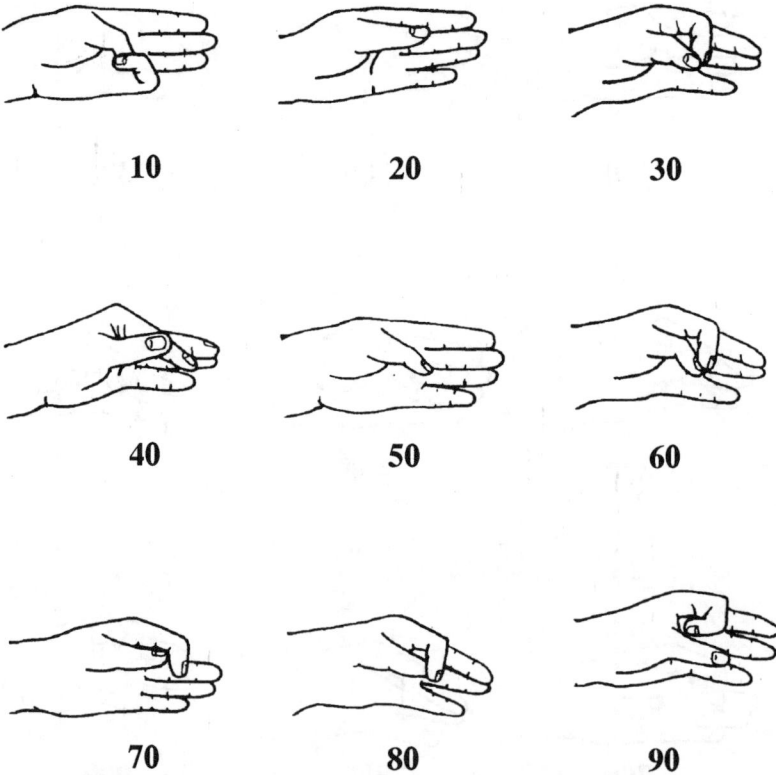

Figure A2   Gestures of the left hand [according to Bede] for the numbers 10, 20, . . . , 90.

Representing the units required the manipulation of the little, ring and middle fingers of the left hand (Figure A1). Thus number '1' was shown by bending the little finger to place its tip on the palm; '4' by similarly bending the ring and the middle fingers, but keeping the little finger straight. The tens needed the index finger and the thumb of the left hand (Figure A2). For '20', the tip of the thumb was placed between the index and the middle fingers. The hundreds required the index finger and the thumb of the right hand (Figure A3): '100' on the right hand was formed in the same way as '10' on the left, '200' as '20', and so on up to '900'. The thousands needed the little, ring and middle fingers of the right hand (Figure A4): '1000' on the right hand was formed in the same manner as '1' on the left, '2000' as '2', and so on up to '9000'.

Thus any number up to 9999 could be represented by these finger

| 100 | 200 | 300 |

| 400 | 500 | 600 |

| 700 | 800 | 900 |

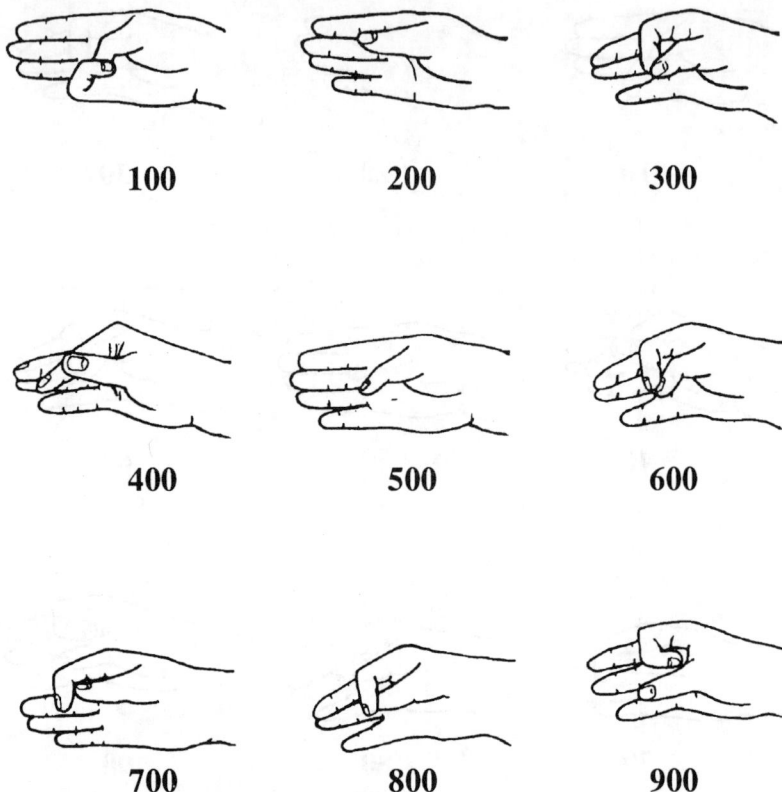

Figure A3   Gestures of the right hand [according to Bede] for the numbers 100, 200, . . . , 900.

gestures. For example, to represent 738, the fingers used for thousands were relaxed; all the other fingers would gesture to show 700 and 30 and 8. Bede went on to describe even finer gestures for numbers from ten thousand to one million. Bede's rules for representing numbers and calculating with them required nimble fingers, as does sign language for the deaf and dumb. His finger arithmetic was used mainly by the monks who had to calculate the changing dates of Easter, decreed in 325 AD by the Council of Nicaea to be the Sunday after the first full moon of spring (which was deemed to begin on March 21st). The dates of the other Christian festivals were then calculated relative to Easter: Pentecost was the seventh Sunday after Easter.

Five hundred years after Bede, the Italian mathematician Leonardo Pisano (also known as Fibonacci, 1170?–1250) wrote: '. . . multiplication with the fingers must be practiced constantly so that the mind like the hands becomes more adept at adding and multiplying various numbers.'

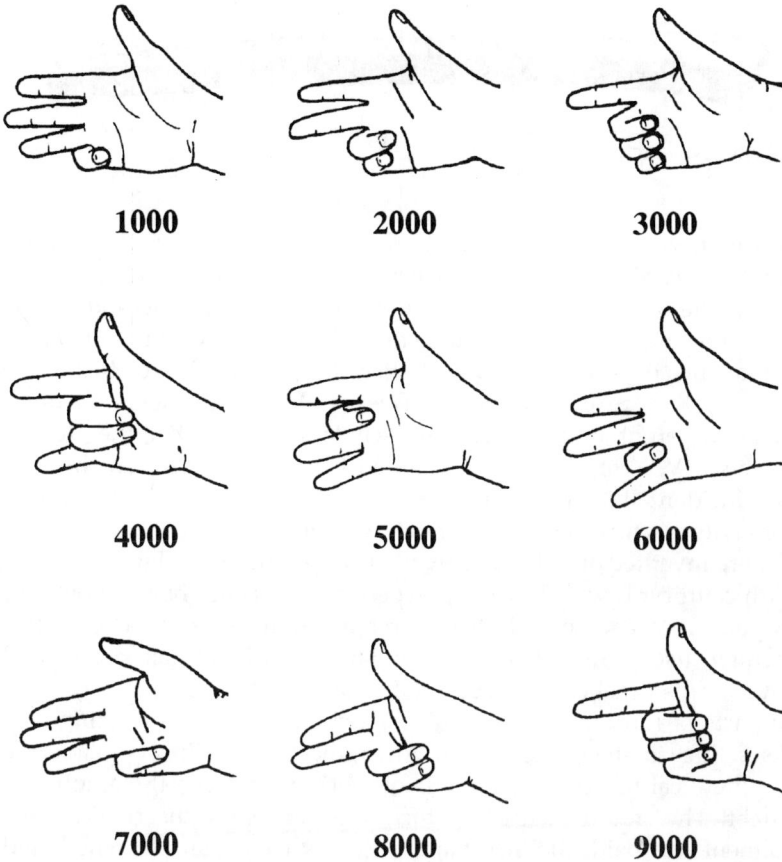

1000   **2000**   **3000**

4000   **5000**   **6000**

7000   **8000**   **9000**

Figure A4   Gestures of the right hand [according to Bede] for the numbers 1000, 2000, . . . , 9000.

In 1494, another Italian mathematician, Luca Pacioli, published in Venice his *Summa de Arithmetica*, which described finger arithmetic in detail, complete with sketches showing finger gestures for the various numbers. Pacioli, however, interchanged Bede's rules for the hundreds and the thousands.

As late as 1727, Jacob Leupold published *Theatrum Arithmetico–Geometricum*, in which he gave Bede's rules, together with sketches for numbers all the way up to one million.

A1.2   Tally sticks

One could use fingers for doing arithmetic, but one could not maintain a record with them. Once the fingers relaxed after the calculations were

Figure A5   A sketch of a tally stick.

over, one needed some other medium to maintain a record. A peasant needed to record the number of sheep he bought and sold, the amount of money he owed, and the amount owed to him. One method was to keep a pebble for, say, every sheep he owned. Another method was to make notches on sticks, called tally sticks (Figure A1.5). Notches of the form |, V, X were easy to carve. These different notches sometimes took on different meanings. Some scholars believe that the Roman numerals I, V, X for 1, 5, 10 descended from the notches on the tally sticks. Incidentally, the English word *write* is derived from the Anglo-Saxon *writan*, which meant to scratch or to notch.

Paper, invented in China, began to be produced in Europe in the twelfth century. It was, however, expensive and could be used only for important records, so tally sticks remained in service. The British exchequer used tally sticks to maintain records of taxes due and received. This practice survived until as late as 1826.

In parts of Europe, a creditor and a debtor used two matching tally sticks acting as stock and insert. After injecting the insert inside the stock, identical notches were made on both, to indicate the amount of the debt. The creditor kept the stock, the debtor the insert. When an instalment was paid, the insert and the stock were again matched, and notches were removed by chiselling or cutting both the sticks at the same time. This double bookkeeping discouraged cheating. Even Napoleon's *Code civile* of 1804 gave legal recognition to such tally sticks.

A2   THE ABACUS

The Roman numerals are not suited to arithmetic. Try adding LXVII to CIV. If we were to convert these numbers to Indo-Arabic numerals, we would get 67 and 104. Adding them is easy because there is the well-known procedure of starting from the right, summing digit by digit, and taking the carry, if any, across to the digits on the left. There are no such easy methods to do arithmetic in Roman numerals. During Roman times, arithmetic could be done by only a few scholars.

The Romans used pebbles as counters for arithmetic. In Latin, pebbles are called *calculi*, from which we get the word calculate. Later, counters made of glass, bone, ivory or brass were also used. The counters were put on a board or table, which the Romans called the *abacus*. The word abacus was derived from the Greek word *ábax*, which means round platter or stemless cup. The Greeks had used counting boards as far back as 500 BC. They called their board *abákion* and their counters were called *pséphoi* (pebbles). The Greek historian Herodotus (485–425 BC) mentioned the use of pebbles by his countrymen for their calculations.

In time, the word abacus took on a generic meaning for different kinds of physical calculating devices. Such abaci (plural of abacus) can be divided into three categories.

1. **Sand tablet** In India, a tablet covered with fine sand was used. The numbers employed in the calculation and the result were written on the sand by a stylus. After the calculation was over, the numbers were erased and the tablet could be used again. In Sanskrit, this process was called *dhuli* (sand) *karma* (work).
2. **Counting boards** Counters were placed and moved on a board. Different forms of counting boards were used in China, Greece, Europe and Peru.
3. **Sliding-bead abacus** Counters, in the form of beads, slide in grooves (Roman model) or on rods (Chinese, Japanese and Russian models).

Very little is known about the sand tablet, and so it cannot be discussed in any detail. The other devices, however, are described below. The use of the sliding-bead abacus survived into the twentieth century.

A2.1 The Chinese counting board

The genesis of the Chinese counting board is uncertain, as Emperor Ch'in Shih Huang Ti burnt the ancient Chinese books in 213 BC. Some indications of early calculating techniques come from the book *Collected Accounts of Mathematics* written by Hsü Y'ao early in the third century. Bamboo rods, three to six inches long, were used for counting even before the time of Confucius (551–478 BC). In time, these rods evolved into *chu suan phan* (Figure A6) meaning *ball arithmetic plate*. It was a board with nine horizontal rows and as many vertical columns as desired. The rows were numbered 1 to 9 from the bottom to the top. Starting from the right, the columns were ranked in units, tens, hundreds, and so on. A ball placed at the intersection of the seventh row and the hundreds column would then depict 700. A zero was indicated by an empty column.

Later, the counting board was reduced to only five rows (Figure

10⁷s	10⁶s	10⁵s	10⁴s	10³s	10²s	10 s	1 s	
							●	9
			●					8
					●			7
								6
								5
								4
								3
						●		2
								1

Figure A6   A Chinese counting board showing 80 729. Starting from the right, the columns were ranked in units, tens, hundreds, and so on, for as many columns as desired. The nine rows were numbered sequentially from the bottom to the top. Thus a ball in the seventh row and the hundreds [10^2s] column depicted 700. Zero was indicated by a blank column.

A7). This, however, necessitated the use of balls of two colours; say, yellow and blue. A yellow ball was used for values 1 to 5, and blue for 6 to 9. Thus a yellow ball placed in the second row indicated the value 2. A blue ball placed in the same row indicated five more than that; that is, the value 7.

A2.2   The Salamis (Greek) counting board

In the middle of the nineteenth century, a tablet (Figure A8) of white marble was found on the island of Salamis, near Athens. It is believed

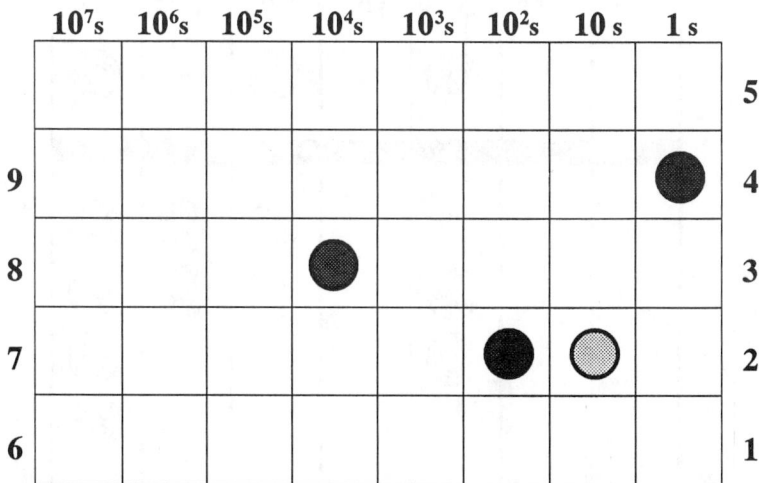

Figure A7 A half-size Chinese counting board showing 80729. ◉ and ●
denote balls of different colours. ◉ was used for indicating digits 1 to 5; ● for 6
to 9.

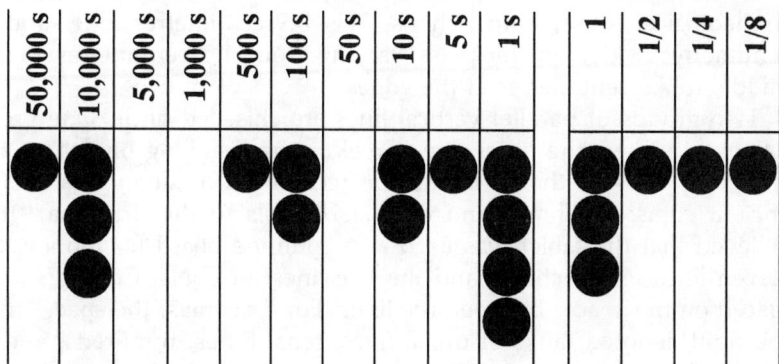

Figure A8 The Salamis counting board showing 80729 drachmas and 3⅞
obols. There were six obols to the drachma.

$$80729 = (1 \times 50000) + (3 \times 10000) + (1 \times 500) + (2 \times 100) + (2 \times 10)$$
$$+ (1 \times 5) + (4 \times 1)$$
$$3\tfrac{7}{8} = (3 \times 1) + \tfrac{1}{2} + \tfrac{1}{4} + \tfrac{1}{8}$$

10⁶s	10⁵s	10⁴s	10³s	10²s	10 s	1 s

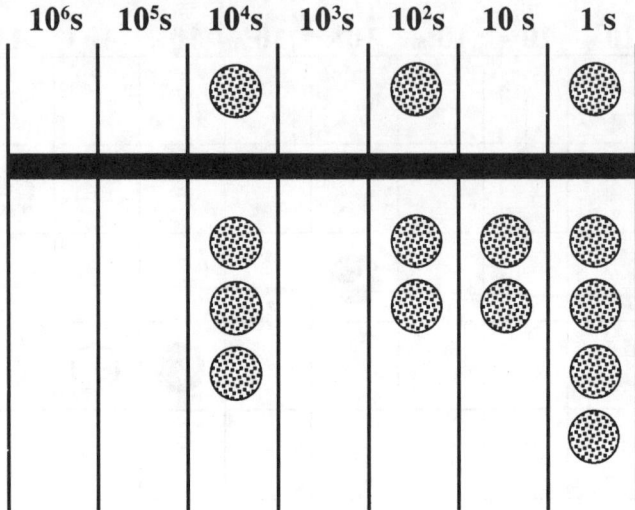

Figure A9   A Roman counting board showing 80 729. Starting from the right, the columns were ranked in units, tens, hundreds, and so on. A counter placed above the band was considered to be equal to five counters of the same rank [that is, in the same column] below the band.

to be from the fourth century BC and is now in the National Archeological Museum in Athens. It is 149 centimetres long, and 75 centimetres wide, its thickness varying from 4.5 centimetres in the middle to 7.5 centimetres at the edges.

Two groups of parallel vertical lines are chiselled on it. One group has eleven lines, the other five. Greek numerals along one short and two long sides of the tablet can be recognized as denominations of ancient coins: drachmas and obols (six obols to the drachma). It is believed that the tablet was used as a counting board for money, the eleven lines for drachmas and the five lines for obols. Counters were placed on the spaces between the lines. For drachmas, the spaces from the right denoted ranks of units, fives, tens, fifties, hundreds, and so on up to fifty thousands. Thus two counters in, say, the tens space depicted twenty drachmas. For obols, the spaces from the left signified coins with denominations of one, a half, a quarter and one eighth.

A2.3   The Roman counting board

In the Roman counting board, parallel vertical lines were drawn on a board (Figure A9). A horizontal band bearing Roman numerals cut

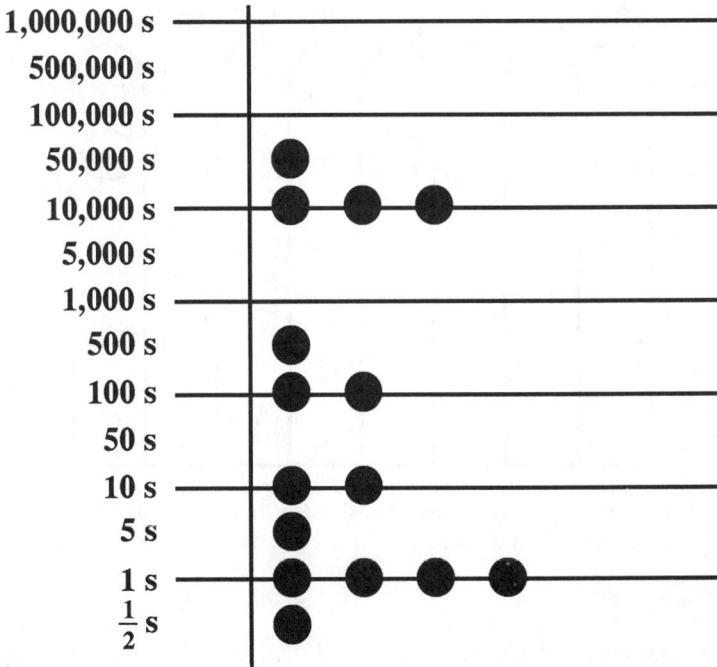

Figure A10   A European counting board showing 80 729 ½.

$$80\,729\ \tfrac{1}{2} = (1 \times 50\,000) + (3 \times 10\,000) + (1 \times 500) + (2 \times 100) + (2 \times 10)$$
$$+ (1 \times 5) + (4 \times 1) + \tfrac{1}{2}$$

across the lines. Counters, quinarily grouped, were placed in a space between the lines to indicate the value of a digit: a counter placed in a space above the band was considered to be equal to five counters in that space below the band. The spaces from the right were ranked as units, tens hundreds, and so on. Thus if in the hundreds space there was one counter above the band and two below, it would depict seven hundred. An empty space indicated an omitted rank (zero).

A2.4   The European counting board

The European counting board (Figure A10) was similar to the Salamis counting board, except for two differences.

1. The board was rotated clockwise by 90 degrees. It is believed the users preferred to move the counters horizontally rather than vertically. Thus the digit ranks (units, fives, tens, fifties, etc.) increased from bottom to top, rather than from right to left.

10⁷s 10⁶s 10⁵s 10⁴s 10³s 10²s 10 s 1 s

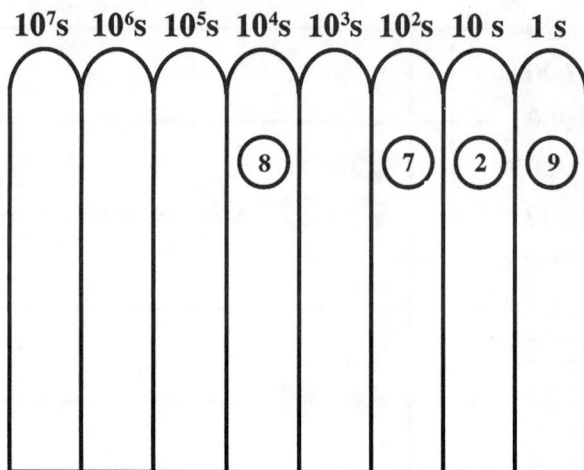

Figure A11   A Gerbert counting board with the labelled apices showing 80 729. The columns were ranked from the right as units, tens, hundreds, and so on.

2. The counters for units, tens, hundreds, etc. were placed on the lines; counters for fives, fifties, five hundreds, etc. were placed in the spaces between the lines. A counter placed below the lowest line indicated a half. Popular among the merchants of Europe in the Middle Ages, the counting board remained in use until the sixteenth century, when it was ousted by paper-and-pen arithmetic.

A2.5   The Gerbert counting board

Gerbert (950?–1003), born in the Auvergne, France, became Pope Sylvester II in 999 AD. In his youth he studied with the Arabs in Spain (who had been there since 713 AD) and learned of the Indo-Arabic numerals. He developed a counting board (Figure A11) having parallel columns with arches at the top. From the right, the columns were for units, tens, hundreds, and so on. He called his counters *apices* (plural of *apex*). Each apex was labelled with a numerical value from 1 to 9. Thus for a column to indicate the number 7, an apex labelled 7 was placed in the column. This differed from the European counting board in which seven unlabelled counters would have been used. Gerbert indicated a zero by an empty column.

He gave difficult, baffling rules to manipulate the apices for different arithmetic operations. For example, Gerbert described a method of division that became notorious as the **iron division**, because it was

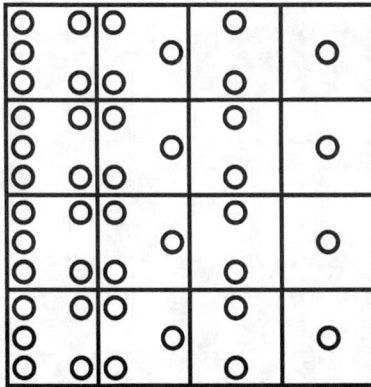

Figure A12 A Peruvian counting board. Each of the sixteen boxes had one to five holes. It is not known how the board was used.

rated to be harder than iron. The Gerbert board had another irksome trait: it required the apices to be kept sorted according to their labels. Contrast this with the European counting board, which required no such sorting.

Never well received save in some monasteries, the Gerbert board became known as the **monastic counting board**. Gerbert misinterpreted the principles of calculations with the Indo-Arabic numerals. This delayed the spreading of these numerals in Europe. For common usage Gerbert's knotty rules were just too much.

A2.6 The Peruvian counting board

Around 1600, Felipe Huaman Poma de Ayala, a Peruvian Indian, wrote a manuscript containing a sketch of a counting board (Figure A12) used in pre-Columbian Peru. The sketch shows a square divided into sixteen boxes. Each box has one to five holes. Unfortunately, it is not known how the board was used. There have been some speculations as to its use, none of them satisfactory.

A2.7 The Chinese sliding-bead abacus

Over time, the Chinese counting board (introduced in section A2.1) was transformed into a sliding-bead abacus called *suan pan*. It consisted of vertical rods inside a rectangular frame (Figure A13). A horizontal partition cutting across the vertical rods divided the frame. The Chinese abacus is said to be a (2, 5) abacus: on each vertical rod there

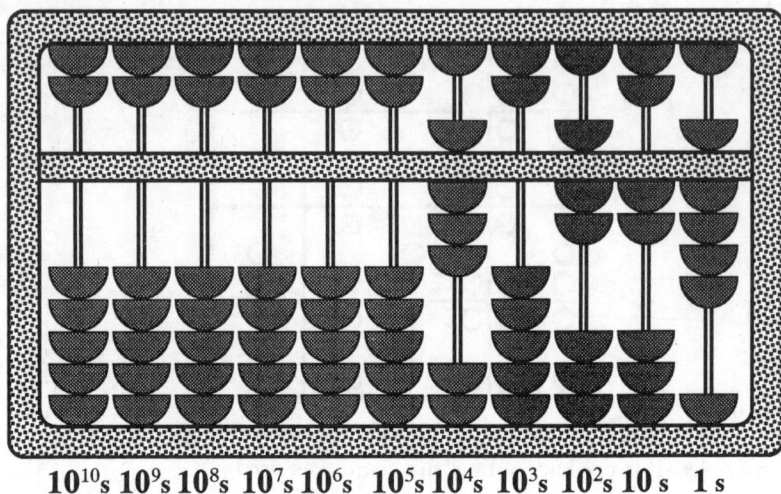

$$10^{10}\text{s } 10^9\text{s } 10^8\text{s } 10^7\text{s } 10^6\text{s } 10^5\text{s } 10^4\text{s } 10^3\text{s } 10^2\text{s } 10 \text{ s } 1 \text{ s}$$

Figure A13   A Chinese abacus showing 80 729. The rods were ranked from the right as units, tens, hundreds, and so on. The value of a digit was indicated by the number of beads touching the partition, except that one bead above the partition was considered to be equal to five beads below the partition.

were two beads above the partition and five below it. Starting from the right, the rods denoted the rank (units, tens, hundreds, etc.) of the digits of a number, with the position of the beads indicating the value of the digit. The value of a digit equalled the number of beads touching the partition, except that one bead above it was equal to the value five. Thus the abacus used a quinary grouping of beads, although its operation was decimal.

Chinese mathematicians had composed verses which described step by step procedures to perform various calculations; for example, addition, subtraction, multiplication, division, interest, annuity, square roots, etc. Knowing the problem and the corresponding verse, one could carry out the calculation by flicking the appropriate beads. These verses are akin to modern computer programs, which contain step by step instructions for solving a problem.

A2.8   The Japanese sliding-bead abacus

The sliding-bead abacus was brought to Japan from China. The Japanese modified it, and two models of the abacus (*soroban*) developed: one was a (1, 5) form, and the other was (1, 4). Like the

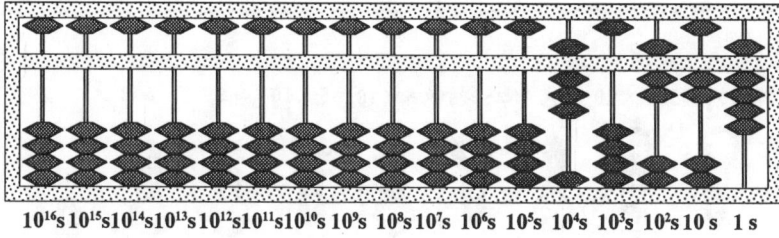

10^{16}s10^{15}s10^{14}s10^{13}s10^{12}s10^{11}s10^{10}s 10^9s 10^8s10^7s 10^6s 10^5s 10^4s 10^3s 10^2s10 s 1 s

Figure A14   A (1,4) Japanese abacus showing 80 729. The value of a digit was indicated as in the Chinese abacus of Figure A13.

Chinese abacus, it grouped beads quinarily, in spite of its operation being decimal.

The Japanese also made some physical changes (Figure A14). The frame was narrowed so that the beads moved a shorter distance, resulting in speedier calculations. The beads were bevelled to make pushing by the fingers easier. The frame had as many as seventeen rods (*keta*). Developed in the sixteenth century, this form of the Japanese abacus remained unchanged over the years. It was one such abacus that Kiyoshi Matsuzaki used when he beat Thomas Wood in the speed-calculating contest described at the beginning of section A1. Books, published mostly in Japan, described in detail how to do the various arithmetical operations on the abacus, including how to position the fingers. The use of the abacus, however, declined with the introduction of hand-held electronic calculators in the 1970s.

A2.9   The Roman sliding-bead abacus

The Roman abacus (Figure A15) consisted of a metal plate with long and short grooves, in which beads could slide. Its operation was similar to the Chinese sliding-bead abacus. Possibly the two abaci had a common pedigree. As early as the Han Dynasty (200 BC–200 AD), the Chinese and the Romans traded in silk, iron and hides, so give and take between them went on for a long time. The Roman abacus had grooves for integers and duodecimal fractions. For integers, there was a row of short grooves with matching long grooves below them; each short groove had one bead, whereas the long groove had four. The strip of metal dividing the long and the short grooves served the same function as the partition in the Chinese sliding-bead abacus. Roman numerals were impressed on this strip to indicate the rank of the digits represented by the corresponding grooves. Small enough to be held in the hand, different models of the abacus were used, depending on the number of grooves for the fractions.

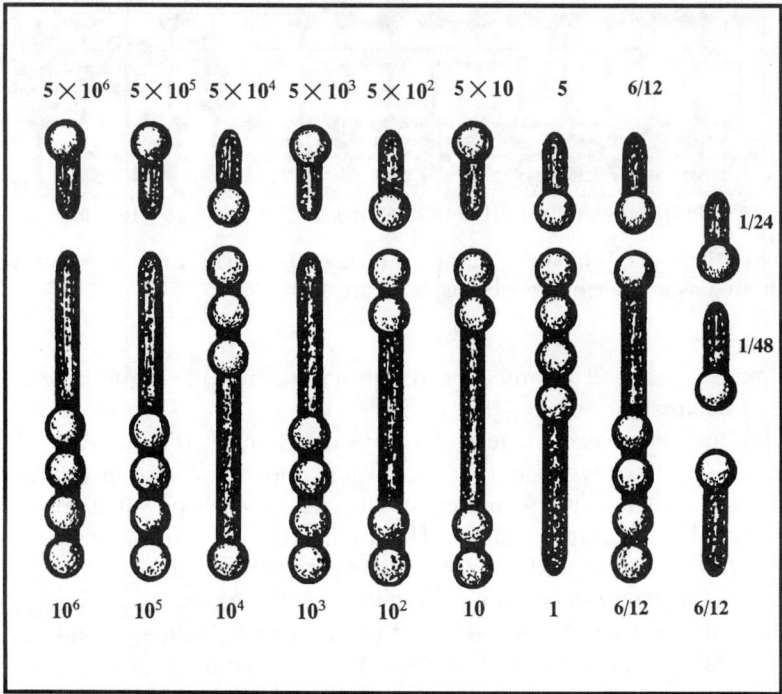

Figure A15   A Roman abacus.

A2.10   The Russian sliding-bead abacus

The Russian abacus (*s'choty*) had horizontal rods in a rectangular frame (Figure A16). From the bottom, the first and the fourth rods had four beads each. All the other rods had ten beads each. To make counting easier the middle two beads on each rod were coloured differently from the rest.

This abacus was used mainly for calculating financial transactions (roubles and kopeks, with 100 kopeks to the rouble). The first three rods from the bottom ranked the kopeks in quarters, units and tens; the fourth rod set the roubles apart from the kopeks (alternatively, it was used to designate quarter roubles); the fifth rod onward ranked the roubles in units, tens, hundreds, and so on. The number of beads touching the left edge of the frame indicated the value of the digit for that rod. In Turkey, the same abacus was called *coulba*; in Armenia, *choreb*.

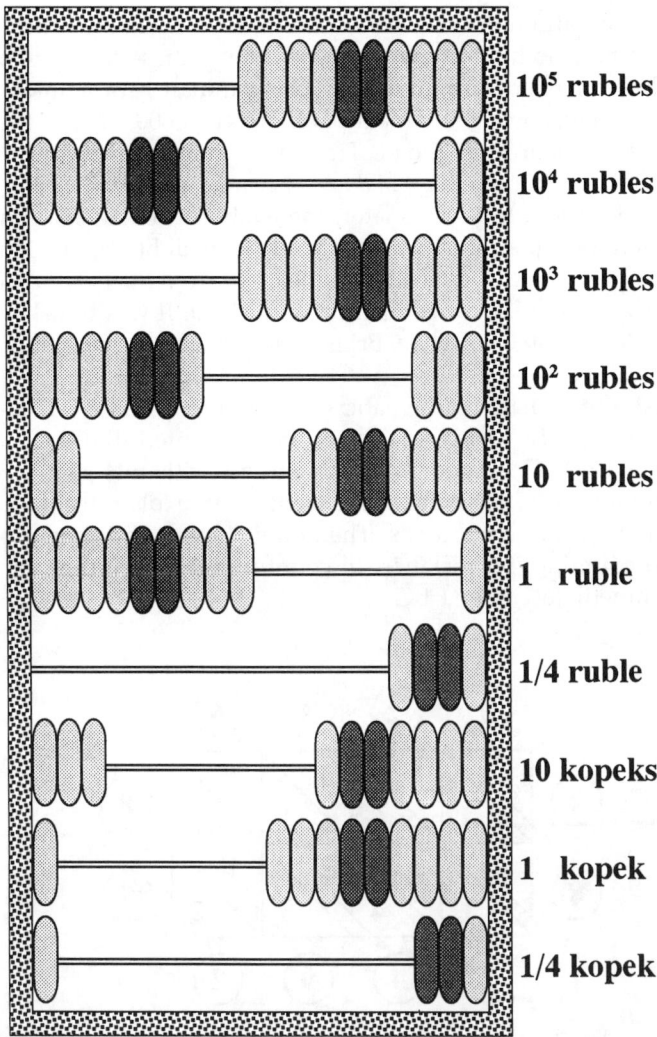

Figure A16   A Russian abacus showing 80729 roubles and 31¼ kopeks [a hundred kopeks to the rouble]. The middle two beads on each rod were coloured differently to make the counting easier. The number of beads touching the left edge of the frame indicated the value of the digit for that rod.

A3   INDO-ARABIC NUMERALS IN EUROPE

A new system of numerals appeared around the sixth century in India. It had nine symbols for 1 to 9, and a symbol for zero. The zero was called *shunya* (Sanskrit for empty). The adoption of zero in a decimal place-value notation of units, tens, hundreds, etc. enabled the writing of any number, no matter how large, with only these ten symbols.

In 773, a traveller brought a copy of an Indian astronomical book, *Sidhanta* (Principles) by Brahamagupta (born circa 600 AD), to the court of Caliph al-Mansur in Baghdad. Translated from Sanskrit into Arabic, the book, now known as *Sindhind*, became popular among Arab astronomers. About fifty years later, the Arab mathematician Abu Jafar Muhammad ibn Musa al-Khwarizmi wrote a small book explaining the use of Indian numerals, which he had learned from *Sindhind*. A copy of Al-Khwarizmi's book reached Spain around 1120. It was translated into Latin by Robert of Chester, a British mathematician who studied in Spain.

In 1202 the Italian mathematician Leonardo Pisano (1170?–1250) wrote a book *Liber Abaci* in which he presented the Indo-Arabic numerals 1 to 9. He stated: 'With them and with this sign 0 . . . any desired number can be written.' He went on to explain techniques for calculating with these numerals. The notion of zero had been absent in European counting; for instance, in counting the years, the year 1 AD follows immediately after 1 BC.

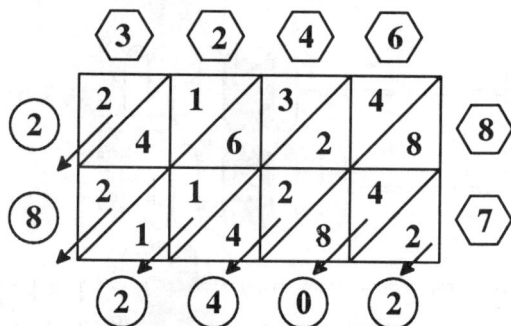

Figure A17   The Gelosia method of multiplication for the example 3246 × 87 = 282 402. In this method, write the multiplier and the multiplicand along the top and right edges, respectively, of a rectangle. Partition the rectangle into boxes, with a diagonal across each box. In each box, write the product of the digits of the multiplier and the multiplicand that appear above and to the right of the box. Write this product so that the tens digit appears above the diagonal and the units digit below it. Starting from the bottom right of the rectangle, add the digits that appear between the diagonals. Write the sum and take the carry, if any, across to the numbers between the next pair of diagonals to the left. Read the answer counter-clockwise along the left and bottom edges of the rectangle. The Italians called this the Gelosia method, because of the rectangle's supposed resemblance to a jalousie.

During the thirteenth century, calculations with the Indo-Arabic numerals spread among the merchants of Europe. The use of these numerals, however, faced obstacles. Paper and pen were required for doing the calculations. Since paper was scarce and expensive, most people still preferred counting boards. Moreover, many viewed these numerals with suspicion. For example, in Italy the city of Florence issued an edict in 1299 forbidding bankers to use these numerals; in 1348 the University of Padua decreed that a list of books for sale show the prices in Roman numerals, not Indo-Arabic. Even as late as Shakespeare's time (1564–1616), counting boards and Roman numerals were being used in Britain.

With the invention of printing in the fifteenth century, books began to circulate, some of which described how to calculate with Indo-Arabic numerals. Paper became available. Slowly the new numerals took root

	0	1	2	3	4	5	6	7	8	9
1	0/0	0/1	0/2	0/3	0/4	0/5	0/6	0/7	0/8	0/9
2	0/0	0/2	0/4	0/6	0/8	1/0	1/2	1/4	1/6	1/8
3	0/0	0/3	0/6	0/9	1/2	1/5	1/8	2/1	2/4	2/7
4	0/0	0/4	0/8	1/2	1/6	2/0	2/4	2/8	3/2	3/6
5	0/0	0/5	1/0	1/5	2/0	2/5	3/0	3/5	4/0	4/5
6	0/0	0/6	1/2	1/8	2/4	3/0	3/6	4/2	4/8	5/4
7	0/0	0/7	1/4	2/1	2/8	3/5	4/2	4/9	5/6	6/3
8	0/0	0/8	1/6	2/4	3/2	4/0	4/8	5/6	6/4	7/2
9	0/0	0/9	1/8	2/7	3/6	4/5	5/4	6/3	7/2	8/1

Figure A18 Napier's rods [or bones]. The multiplication table was written on narrow strips. Each strip carried the multiplication table for a number, written as in the Gelosia method. Shown in Figure A17.

in Europe. The numerals, however, had changed their shapes in their travel from India to Europe.

Paper-and-pen arithmetic with these numerals was, however, found to have its own problems. People doing the arithmetic often committed mistakes, so attempts were made to further simplify the calculations and to build mechanical calculators. One such early attempt led to the discovery of logarithms and the invention of the slide rule.

A4   THE SLIDE RULE AND NAPIER'S RODS

Logarithms were conceived of in 1614 by John Napier (1550–1617), a British mathematician. He showed that for every positive number x there exists another number y, such that y is called the logarithm of x, and x the antilogarithm of y. Then he proved that the product of two numbers p and q is equal to the antilogarithm of the sum of the logarithms of p and q. Thus if tables are available giving the logarithm and the antilogarithm of any number, a multiplication requires looking up these tables and doing an addition. Just as a multiplication is reduced to essentially an addition, a division is reduced to a subtraction. It is believed that people are less prone to committing mistakes in addition and subtraction than in multiplication and division.

A4.1   The slide rule

Logarithms became popular with British mathematicians. Henry Briggs (1561–1631), a professor of geometry at Gresham College in London, spent many years calculating and publishing logarithmic tables. Others began to develop methods to mechanize multiplication and division using logarithms. In 1620 Edmund Gunter (1581–1626) plotted logarithms on a two-foot straight line. Multiplication then consisted of using a pair of dividers to add logarithmically proportional distances on the line. For division, distances could similarly be subtracted. William Oughtred (1575–1660) improved Gunter's approach in 1621 by using two logarithmically graduated scales (one movable, the other fixed) which slide against each other. The movable scale slid against the fixed one to measure proportional distances. This device was called the **slide rule**. In 1654, Robert Bissaker refined it to make the movable scale slide in a fixed stock. In the mid-nineteenth century, a transparent cursor was added, which had a hairline to set one scale accurately against another. The hairline helped in reading the result.

The accuracy of a slide rule increases as the length of the scale increases. A long straight scale, however, makes the slide rule unwieldy. To reconcile these conflicting requirements, scales were

| 3 | 2 | 4 | 6 |

$\frac{0}{\ }3$	$\frac{0}{\ }2$	$\frac{0}{\ }4$	$\frac{0}{\ }6$	1
$\frac{0}{\ }6$	$\frac{0}{\ }4$	$\frac{0}{\ }8$	$\frac{1}{\ }2$	2
$\frac{0}{\ }9$	$\frac{0}{\ }6$	$\frac{1}{\ }2$	$\frac{1}{\ }8$	3
$\frac{1}{\ }2$	$\frac{0}{\ }8$	$\frac{1}{\ }6$	$\frac{2}{\ }4$	4
$\frac{1}{\ }5$	$\frac{1}{\ }0$	$\frac{2}{\ }0$	$\frac{3}{\ }0$	5
$\frac{1}{\ }8$	$\frac{1}{\ }2$	$\frac{2}{\ }4$	$\frac{3}{\ }6$	6

$\frac{2}{\ }1$ $\frac{1}{\ }4$ $\frac{2}{\ }8$ $\frac{4}{\ }2$ $\times$ **7** = 22722

$\frac{2}{\ }4$ $\frac{1}{\ }6$ $\frac{3}{\ }2$ $\frac{4}{\ }8$ $\times$ **8** = 25968 +

$\frac{2}{\ }7$ $\frac{1}{\ }8$ $\frac{3}{\ }6$ $\frac{5}{\ }4$ **9** **282402** **Result**

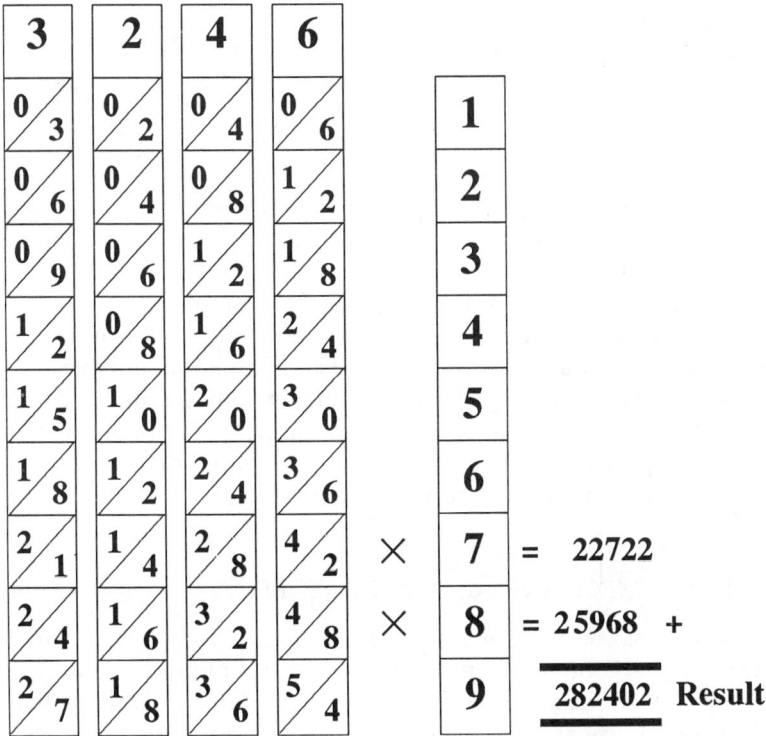

Figure A19 Multiplication using Napier's rods. Suppose we are to multiply, 3246 by 87. Put strips of 3, 2, 4, and 6 next to one another. Get the product of 7 and 3246 by the Gelosia method: it is 22722. Similarly, get the product of 8 and 3246; it is 25968. To determine the result, add these partial products, in the manner we all have learnt in primary school.

often engraved helically. The Otis–King slide rule of the twentieth century was about 15 centimetres long, but it contained a helical logarithmic scale of nearly 168 centimetres. Slide rules remained in use well into the twentieth century. It was only in the 1970s that the pocket electronic calculator edged out the slide rule.

A slide rule is an **analogue** calculator: numbers are represented as distances along a scale. Most of the other calculating devices discussed are **digital**: numbers are represented as discrete quantities.

A4.2 Napier's rods

John Napier, who had earlier discovered logarithms, published in 1617 a book called *Rabdolgia*. He described a new procedure of using the multiplication tables to transform a multiplication into a set of additions. Napier's procedure became known as **Napier's rods** (or **bones**). It was modelled on the *Gelosia* method of multiplication illustrated in Figure A17.

For his procedure Napier wrote multiplication tables on narrow strips, one strip for each number (Figure A18). A strip for, say, the number 3 carried the multiplication table for 3, written as in the Gelosia method. Numbers could then be multiplied by the method given in Figure A19.

Thus one did not need to memorize the multiplication tables. One needed to know addition. If, however, one could not even add, then one could use a counting board or read from an addition table.

Later, Napier built a small mechanism in which multiplication tables were inscribed on the sides of rods mounted in a wooden box. The rods could be rotated to expose whatever multiplication tables were required. Then the calculation proceeded as usual.

A5   EARLY MECHANICAL CALCULATORS

At the age of 29, Samuel Pepys (1663–1703) was appointed to take charge of the contracts branch of the British admiralty. Pepys, well-educated by the standards of his time, recorded in his diary that he would wake up at four o'clock in the morning to memorize the multiplication tables. His ignorance of the multiplication tables is not a reflection on himself but on the education he had received: most schools did not teach arithmetic in seventeenth-century Europe. It was in such a milieu that the early mechanical calculators were developed, the first one being in Germany.

A5.1   Schickard's calculator

Wilhelm Schickard (1592–1635), a professor of mathematics and astronomy at Tübingen, Germany, wrote to his compatriot, astronomer Johann Kepler (1571–1630), that he had designed a digital mechanical calculator capable of doing the four operations of arithmetic: addition, subtraction, multiplication and division. He had intended it for Kepler's use. He described the machine and enclosed drawings of it, but he notified Kepler that the prototype had been destroyed before completion in a fire. The State Library in Stuttgart has a sketch of the machine which was drawn by the mechanic who was fabricating the machine for Schickard in the early 1620s. However, Schickard did not build another model of his machine. Until 1957, when his letter was

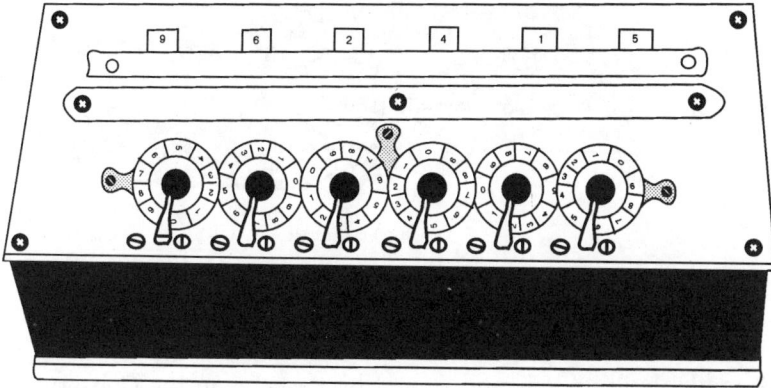

Figure A20   A sketch of Pascal's calculator.

found in Kepler's papers, it was not even known that Schickard had designed a mechanical calculator.

A5.2   Pascal's calculator

Unaware of Schickard's invention, the French mathematician Blaise Pascal (1623–62), built a calculating machine in 1642 to help his father, a tax officer. Father and son named the machine the *Pascaline*. It was principally a mechanical adder, consisting of a set of intermeshed ten-cog gears (Figure A20). The position of a gear in its rotation indicated the value of a digit in the number being added. This value was displayed in a window. One dialled in the numbers to be added; the dialling caused the gears to rotate appropriately.

When a gear completed one rotation, it turned the adjacent gear by one tenth of a rotation. This is equivalent to transporting a carry in written arithmetic. This mechanism functioned like an odometer in present-day motor cars.

Although its design was suited primarily for addition, the Pascaline could be used for subtraction by complement arithmetic. This entailed making an internal adjustment to make the machine count in reverse. Multiplication was done by repeated addition, division by repeated subtraction.

Patented in 1647, the machine failed commercially. It was expensive, and accountants resisted it, fearing it would replace them. Moreover, there was trouble in its manufacturing. The gears could be turned part way, to rest between digit positions which could then give wrong results.

Figure A21   A sketch of Leibniz's calculator.

A model built in 1652 and signed by Pascal is in the Conservatoire des Arts et Métiers in Paris. A copy of it is in the Science Museum in South Kensington, London.

A calculating machine with an arrangement of gears similar to the Pascaline was built in 1775 by Charles Stanhope (1753–1816), a British politician and scientist. Better constructed, the Stanhope machine operated more smoothly than the Pascaline.

A5.3   Leibniz's calculator

Gottfried Wilhelm Leibniz (1646–1716), a German scientist, improved on the Pascaline. In 1671 he built a machine in which, besides the Pascaline-like gears for addition and subtraction, he introduced a stepped wheel with nine teeth of different lengths (Figure A21). This wheel enabled multiplication and division to be distinct from addition and subtraction, unlike the Pascaline which required repeated addition for multiplication, and repeated subtraction for division. Thus multiplication and division were faster on the Leibniz machine than on the Pascaline.

The design of the Leibniz calculator was sound but, in the seventeenth century, industrial technology had not developed sufficiently to make such a complex set of gears with the desired precision. The machine was considered unreliable and was not an industrial success. Leibniz is reported to have built only two models of his calculator. The only one known to exist today is in the State Museum in Hannover.

Leibniz also studied binary (base–2) numbers, which are used in modern computers. Unfortunately he never incorporated binary numbers in his machine. Had he done so, it would have replaced the mesh of gears by two-position (binary) levers. The manufacturing skills of his day could have produced such a machine reliably.

About a hundred years later, a dependable calculator using the

Leibniz stepped wheel was built by mathematician Philipp Mathäus Hahn. The Leibniz stepped wheel survived even into the twentieth century: it was employed in many electromechnical calculators.

A5.4 The arithmometer

In Alsace, France, in 1822, Charles Xavier Thomas de Colmar built a calculator using the Leibniz stepped wheel, but he refined many of its moving parts. Numbers were entered into the machine by setting slides. To rotate the actuators, a belt was pulled; later models used a hand crank instead. Thomas started industrial production of his machine, called the *arithmometer*. This is the first known industrial production of a calculating machine. Later, other manufacturers based their calculators on the arithmometer. Such calculators were called Thomas-type machines.

The arithmometer sold initially in France and Germany. At the International Exhibition in London in 1862, it won a medal. It was reputed to multiply two eight-digit numbers in 18 seconds, divide a 16-digit by an eight-digit number in 24 seconds, and extract the square-root of a 16-digit number in 60 seconds.

The arithmometer continued to be manufactured until the 1930s. Just before the First World War, it was modified so that numbers could be entered from a keyboard. It was called the TIM arithmometer.

A6 BABBAGE AND BOOLE

John Napier had shown in 1614 that by using a table of logarithms a multiplication could be reduced to an addition, but soon a snag appeared. The tables of logarithms available were calculated manually, and they were thus spattered with mistakes.

To produce new tables of logarithms and the trigonometric functions, the French government in 1784 hired about a hundred people. Every calculation was double checked. It took two years to produce the manuscripts called *Tables de Cadastres*, but the manuscripts were never printed, for fear that errors may be introduced in them during the printing.

Since 1766, the Royal Observatory at Greenwich, England, had been publishing every year the *Nautical Almanac*. The calculations for the almanac were done manually, using the available logarithmic tables. The errors in the logarithms augmented the errors made in the manual calculations, giving rise to many mistakes in the almanac. For example, the 1818 and 1830 editions of the almanac each contained 58 errors. Such mistakes could cause shipwrecks.

Given that the values of the second degree polynomial $p = x^2 + x + 41$, for $x = 0, 1, 2$ are 41, 43, 47, respectively. By differencing, tabulate the polynomial for $x = 3, 4, 5 \ldots$

We build a difference table as follows:

x	$p = x^2 + x + 41$	first order difference D_1	second order difference D_2
0	41		
1	43	2	
2	47	4	2

The contents of the columns are as follows:

First column [x]: values of the independent variable x.
Second column [p]: values of the polynomial.
Third column [D_1]: difference between successive values of the second column.
Fourth column [D_2]: difference between successive values of the third column.

It is mathematically provable that all values in D_2 will be equal. In general, for an n-th degree polynomial, all values in the n-th order difference D_n will be equal. For each row of the difference table, fill the columns in the sequence D_2, D_1, p.

x = 3	$D_2 = 2$	$D_1 = 2 + 4 = 6$	$p = 6 + 47 = 53$
x = 4	$D_2 = 2$	$D_1 = 2 + 6 = 8$	$p = 8 + 53 = 61$
x = 3	$D_2 = 2$	$D_1 = 2 + 8 = 10$	$p = 10 + 61 = 71$

Thus we can extend the above table as shown below:

x	$p = x^2 + x + 41$	first order difference D_1	second order difference D_2
0	41		
1	43	2	
2	47	4	2
3	53	6	2
4	61	8	2
5	71	10	2
:	:	:	:

Figure A22   Example to show how to tabulate a polynomial by differencing. In his 1822 demonstration, Charles Babbage used the Difference Engine to tabulate $x^2 + x + 41$.

Irked by the errors in the manually calculated tables, the British mathematician Charles Babbage (1792–1871) set out to build a mechanical calculator to generate these tables. Exploiting the mathematical method of differencing, his calculator was to be called the **Difference Engine**.

A6.1   The Difference Engine

Tabulating a function $f(x)$ is finding the value of $f(x)$ for all values of the independent variable x that lie within a specified interval. In other words, tabulating a function is the same as producing a table of values for the function. The method of differencing can be applied to tabulate only polynomials. If $f(x)$ is not already a polynomial, we must find a polynomial whose values are as close to $f(x)$ as desired, for the values of x for which we are tabulating. Put another way, the polynomial is an approximation of the function $f(x)$. Mathematics has techniques for finding such a polynomial. The problem of tabulating the function $f(x)$ is now transformed to tabulating the polynomial. The polynomial we shall find will have a degree (the highest exponent of x) equal to some positive integer n. An example of differencing is given in Figure A22.

To start the procedure we must be given the values of the polynomial for $n + 1$ equally spaced values of x. In the method of differencing we use the given values to find the values of the polynomial for the remaining values of x. Differencing is attractive because the only arithmetical operation required is a series of additions for the tabulation, so a calculating device designed specially for differencing need only have the capability to add. Babbage's Difference Engine was to be such a device.

The principles of a Difference Engine were conceived in 1786 by J. H. Müller, a German military engineer. That year, an article entitled 'Description of a Newly Invented Calculating Machine,' written by E. Klipstein appeared in Frankfurt am Main. The article described Müller's ideas.

Nevertheless, Charles Babbage was the first to build a model of the Difference Engine. In 1822 he displayed it to the Royal Astronomical Society. The model could tabulate polynomials up to the second degree with an accuracy of six digits. It had gears and wheels, and it bore similarities to the Stanhope calculator of 1775. The Difference Engine was, however, larger and more complex.

Babbage proposed constructing a larger machine to tabulate polynomials up to the sixth degree with an accuracy of twenty digits. Not only would the machine do the calculations, but it would also set the results in type, thereby eliminating any errors in printing. He sought government funding to develop such a machine and, in 1823, the British government gave him an initial grant of £1500 to begin his project. He started with a workshop built on his estate. His venture was ambitious; his plans to set the results in type predated the invention of the typewriter or the typesetting machine. To tabulate sixth-degree polynomials, his machine required seven registers. For a

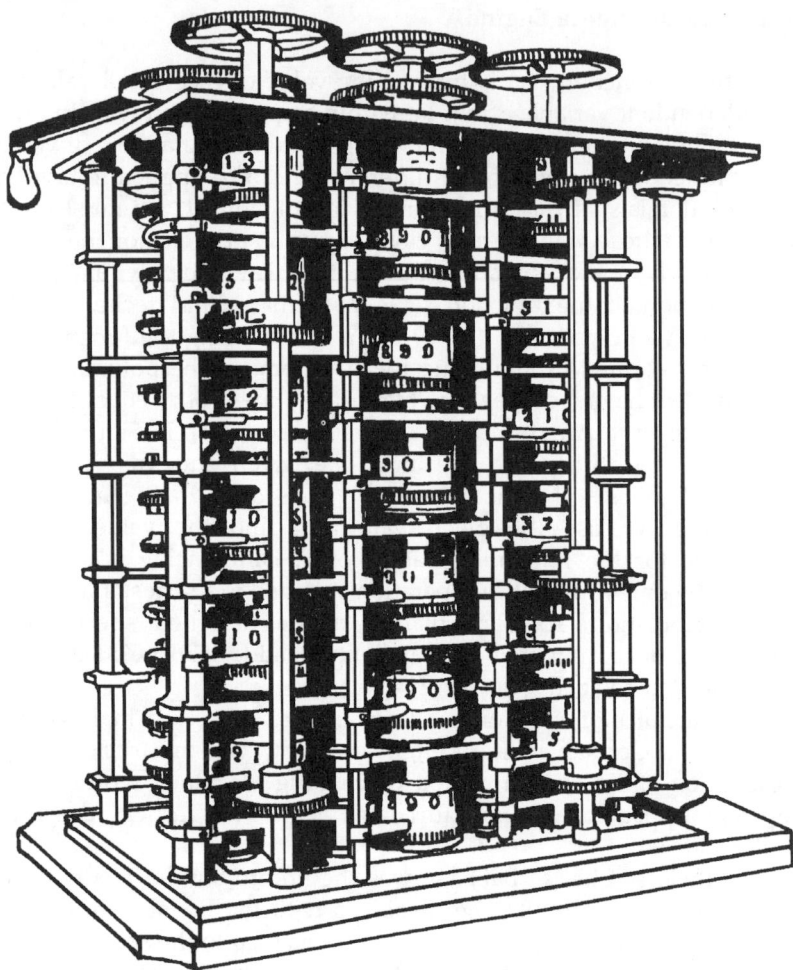

Figure A23   A sketch of a part of Charles Babbage's Difference Engine.

twenty-digit accuracy, each register was to have a capacity of that many digits. Each register added its contents to the one above it hierarchically. A carry propagating across twenty digits could slow the machine, so he devised a mechanical scheme to operate on all the carries simultaneously, a scheme which is implemented electronically in modern computers. The scheme is known as the **anticipatory carry**.

Metal casting techniques had not developed enough to mould to the required precision the numerous gears, ratchets, sprockets and rods. Minor defects here and there in the model he was building would

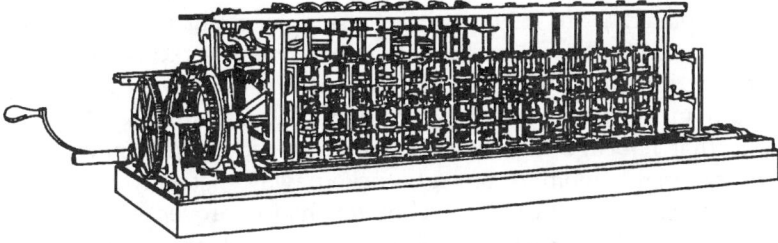

Figure A24 A sketch of the Scheutz Difference Engine.

compound to cause the machine to shake. In comparison, Thomas de Colmar's 1822 arithmometer was a simpler machine; nonetheless, Colmar was having trouble manufacturing it. However, Babbage's vexations were worse. Supported by government funds, he toiled on his Difference Engine year after year, but little was forthcoming and only parts of it were built (Figure A23). In 1842, after having spent £17 000 in all, a restive government cut off his funding. Babbage himself never built a complete Difference Engine, but others did (Figure A24).

Georg Scheutz (1785–1873), a printer and editor of a technical journal in Stockholm, read a description of Babbage's Difference Engine in the *Edinburgh Review* of July 1834. He perceived that the design was sound, so, working with his son, Edvard (1821–81), who was then a student at the Royal Technological Institute in Stockholm, Scheutz built a Difference Engine in 1843. It could tabulate polynomials up to the third degree with an accuracy of five digits, and print its results, but there were no buyers for the machine.

Scheutz then began building a bigger Difference Engine. Completed in 1853, it could tabulate polynomials up to the fourth degree with a 15-digit accuracy. After rounding the result it stereomoulded in lead the first eight digits. Plates for printing could then be fashioned from the lead stereomould. This Difference Engine could tabulate a polynomial at 120 lines per hour. It used base-10 arithmetic for its calculations but it could be adjusted to mix base-10 and base-6 arithmetic needed for astronomical, navigational and trigonometric tables, which contain measurements in degrees, minutes, seconds and decimals of seconds.

Scheutz succeeded over Babbage by setting himself a realistic goal. In 1855, his machine won a gold medal at the Paris International Exhibition. The British government, which at one time had cut off Babbage's funding, now placed an order for a Scheutz Difference

Engine. It was manufactured in Bermondsey by Messrs Bryan Donkin, who completed it in 1859, and was used to calculate actuarial life-expectancy tables based on the Registrar General's records of deaths and births for the years 1838–54. The machine is now in the Science Museum in South Kensington, London. The part of the Difference Engine that Babbage himself had built was shown in London at the 1862 Industrial Exhibition, but was tucked away obscurely.

By the 1870s, metal casting techniques had improved sufficiently to enable George Barnard Grant (1849–1917), an American mechanical engineer, to build an electrically driven Difference Engine. Displayed at the 1876 Centennial Exposition in Philadelphia, it was found to consume lots of electricity and demanded frequent human intervention during its calculations. Its huge size (that of a piano) prevented it from becoming popular.

A6.2   The Analytical Engine

Charles Babbage had given up building the Difference Engine but he was far from idle. By 1842, when the British government cut off his funds, he had already become engrossed in designing a new machine: the Analytical Engine. Whereas the Difference Engine could do only differencing, the Analytical Engine could be programmed to perform any sequence of arithmetic operations its user wanted. In modern shoptalk, the Difference Engine would be called a special-purpose machine; the Analytical Engine, general-purpose. Babbage spent the rest of his life working on the Analytical Engine. For it, he spent his own money (he had inherited over £100 000 from his banker father). In designing the machine, he drew numerous detailed sketches.

Babbage's design of the Analytical Engine is outlined in his essay dated 26 December 1837, and entitled, 'On the Mathematical Powers of the Calculating Engine.' Charles Babbage visited Italy in 1840–1. Based on Babbage's lectures there, Lugi F. Menabrea (1809–96), an engineer in the Italian army, wrote a paper titled, 'Sketch of the Analytical Engine Invented by Charles Babbage, Esq. It was published in the *Bibliothèque Universelle de Genève* in 1842. Ada Augusta Lovelace (1815–52), a British mathematician and an associate of Babbage, translated the paper into English, but annotated it by her own extensive commentary. It is from Babbage's own essay and from Lovelace's annotated translation that one can learn about the Analytical Engine. Babbage himself remarked that she 'seems to understand it better than I do, and is far, far better at explaining it.' The Analytical Engine had five components (Figure A25):

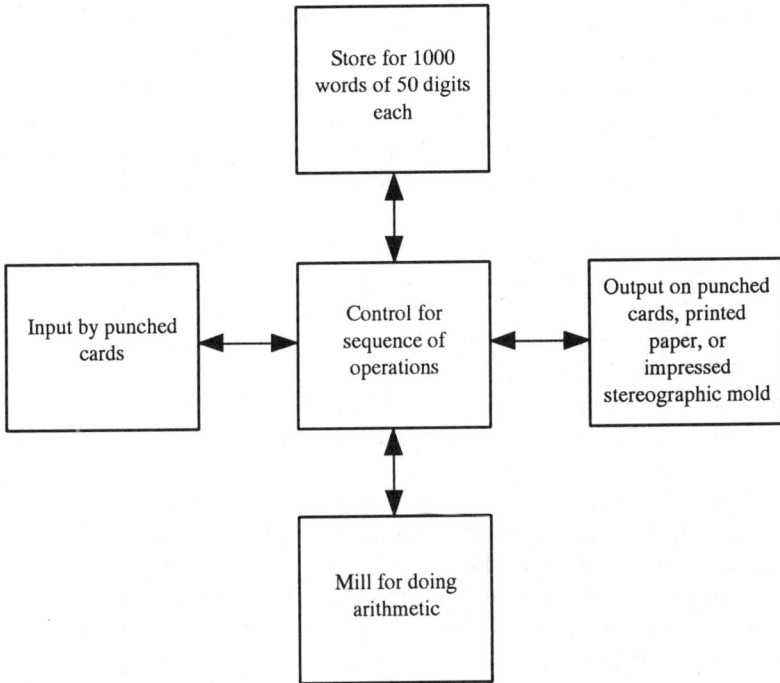

Figure A25 Outline of Babbage's Analytical Engine. In modern terminology, the store would be called the memory, and the mill would be the arithmetic unit.

1. *input*: to enter data (numbers) and program (instructions) into the machine;
2. *output*: to print results;
3. *store*: the memory to save the numbers;
4. *mill*: the arithmetic unit to do the calculations; and
5. *control*: to regulate the functioning of the machine.

Babbage planned to use punched cards for input. In this he was influenced by the achievement of Joseph Jacquard (1752–1834), a Frenchman who in 1801 had employed punched cards to control automatically the weaving of patterns on cloth. Ada Lovelace in her commentary on Menabrea's paper observed that 'the Analytical Engine weaves algebraical patterns just as the Jacquard loom weaves flowers and leaves.' The cards in the Analytical Engine were to be read by plungers passing through the holes.

The output could be punched cards, printed paper or impressed stereographic moulds for later printing, similar to modern computer-controlled typesetting.

The size of the store was one thousand registers, each capable of holding a 50-digit decimal number. In present-day terminology, this is about 20 000 bytes of memory. One can see how ambitious was the design when one notes that computers did not reach this memory size until the 1950s.

The mill could do all four arithmetical operations (addition, subtraction, multiplication and division). For any such operation on two numbers, the following procedure was performed: the two numbers were transferred from the store to the mill; the operation was executed in the mill to get the result; and the result was transferred to a register in the store. To speed up addition, Babbage used the scheme of anticipatory carry so that the mill added the corresponding digits of the two numbers simultaneously. Babbage gave the following estimates of time: one second for adding two 50-digit numbers, 60 seconds for multiplying them, and 60 seconds for dividing a 100-digit number by a 50-digit number.

For control, Babbage devised two kinds of punched cards: **operation cards** and **variable cards**. Calculating the value of a formula required a string of operation cards describing the arithmetic operations to be performed step by step. Each operation card needed three variable cards. Say the operation card called for addition. Of the associated variable cards, two cards indicated the operands (the registers in the store from which the numbers to be added are to be transferred to the mill), and the third card indicated the register in the store to which the result is to be transferred from the mill. Thus, if the variable cards contained R1, R2, R3, and the operation card called for addition, then in a twentieth-century programming language, FORTRAN, it would be synonymous to writing R3 = R1 + R2. Add R1 and R2; save the result in R3.

To feed initial numbers into the registers of the store, Babbage had conceived of using another set of punched cards called **number cards**. Since the registers were mechanical, he had planned to have them set manually, too.

The punched cards were to be read in sequence by the Analytical Engine. Nevertheless, Babbage intended to have mechanical means to allow the string of cards to be moved forwards or backwards by more than one card at a time. This would allow the control to jump across several cards. Such a jump could be done when, after subtraction, the result in the mill was negative. Should the result be non-negative, control proceeded sequentially. Thus the Analytical Engine had what is known as a **conditional jump** in modern computers.

In her commentary, Ada Lovelace explains how the Analytical Engine could be programmed. She recognized what in present-day programming terminology is called a **loop**, but which she called a **cycle**. If a set of operations was to be done more than once, those operations needed to be specified on only one set of punched cards. Using a conditional jump, these operations could be executed more than once. This eliminated the preparation of many sets of cards that specified identical operations.

Lovelace gave an example of a program to compute Bernoulli numbers. Babbage acknowledged that she had corrected one of his own mistakes in the analysis of these numbers. She is believed by some to be the world's first programmer. For those who may wonder whether the machine could be creative, Lovelace made a telling comment: 'The Analytical Engine has no pretensions whatever to originate anything. It can do whatever we know how to order it to perform. It can follow analysis; but it has no power of anticipating any analytical relations or truths.' In other words, the machine could do only what it was programmed to do.

In an era when many believed that women could not think because of the way nature has designed their anatomy, Lovelace had been advised by her tutor, Augustus De Morgan (1806–71), to discontinue studying mathematics, lest she become unable to bear children. Lovelace deserves our gratitude for having ignored the advice.

One can see that in his design of the Analytical Engine, Babbage had thought of all the basic components found in computers today. The Analytical Engine, had it ever been built (it never was), would have been a complex mechanism weighing several tons, and Babbage had planned to use steam to drive it. Its myriad moving parts would have had to fit accurately, but technology just did not exist then to build such complicated machinery with such precision. Charles Babbage was ahead of his time. He succeeded in constructing only a part of the Analytical Engine. Later, his son Henry built a portion of the mill (arithmetic unit) together with a mechanism to print results. It is now in the Science Museum in South Kensington. London, and is illustrated in Figure A26.

Besides his calculating devices, Babbage also had other interests: helping to develop the penny post, inventing the speedometer, designing the cowcatcher on locomotives, criticizing the Royal Society and the Royal Observatory, and campaigning against street singers because their noise bothered him.

Babbage died in 1871, disappointed, ridiculed and isolated; he told a friend that he had not had a single completely happy day in his life. Toward the end of his life, he had become incoherent in his public

Figure A26 A sketch of a part of the mill of Charles Babbage's Analytical Engine built by his son Henry.

speaking. By the time of his death, Babbage was reported to hate 'mankind in general, Englishmen in particular, and the English Government and Organ Grinders most of all.'

Charles Babbage was without honour in his own land. The Indian philosopher Vinoba Bhave was wont to say: when a king speaks, his army moves; when a prophet speaks, his beard moves. For clean-shaven Charles Babbage, not even his beard moved.

Long after his death, he was honoured, but strangely. In 1907, his brain was extracted and surgically examined to see why he was so brilliant. Nothing unusual was found. In the Hunterian Museum of the Royal College of Surgeons, his brain rests pickled in two jars, each hemisphere of the brain in a separate jar.

A6.3   Boolean algebra

While Babbage was wrestling with his Analytical Engine, George Boole (1815–64), a self-taught British mathematician with formal education limited to elementary school and a brief stint in a commercial school, was progressing on another front. Although without a university degree, Boole had been appointed in 1849 as a professor of mathematics at Queen's College in Cork, Ireland. In 1854, he published *An Investigation of the Laws of Thought on Which are Founded the Mathematical Theories of Logic and Probabilities*, often referred to briefly as Boole's *Laws of Thought*. In the preface, Boole called his work 'the mathematics of the human intellect.' He had developed an algebra, nowadays known as **Boolean** algebra, in which logical propositions were expressed by mathematical symbols. Furthermore, he showed that logic was a part of mathematics: until then, logic was considered to be a part of philosophy. The foundation of mathematical logic was thus laid by Boole. Mathematical logic was to become a pillar of support for the twentieth-century development of artificial intelligence.

A7   IMPROVED CALCULATORS

A century before their time, the basic components of a modern computer had been visualized by Charles Babbage. Other inventors did not dream such impossible dreams. They contented themselves mainly by building ordinary calculators, their effort directed usually toward hastening the calculations and facilitating the entry of data. The attainments of the trail-blazers we read of in this section laid the groundwork of today's computing industry. The popular calculators in the 1870s were the Thomas-type machines based on the arithmometer described in section A5.4. One of the early attempts made was in improving these machines.

A7.1   Baldwin-type machines

In 1872, Frank Stephen Baldwin of the USA replaced the Leibniz stepped wheel in the Thomas-type machines by a wheel with nine spring-loaded pins. He eliminated the reversing gears that were

Figure A27   A sketch of Frank Baldwin's calculator of the 1870s.

necessary for switching from addition and multiplication to subtraction and division. He received the patent for his machine in 1875, although he had already commenced commercial production two years earlier from Philadelphia, thus starting the mechanical calculator industry in the US. His calculator is shown in Figure A27.

In 1878, Willgodt Theophil Odhner, a Swedish engineer developed a calculator similar to Baldwin's. In Germany this was incorporated in a hand calculator, the *Brunsviga*, which became popular in Europe for both business and scientific use. A skilled user could operate this machine faster than its competitor, the arithmometer. Moreover, the Brunsviga was cheaper. First manufactured in 1892, it remained in use until the middle of the twentieth century.

Because of their common design characteristics, the Baldwin, Ohdner and Brunsviga calculators are usually considered to be of one kind. These machines could execute all the four operations of arithmetic.

Baldwin continued making improvements to his machine. In 1908, he received a patent for an improved version called the recording calculator. The digital actuators were redesigned so that numerical values could be entered from a keyboard. The results could also be printed. In 1912, Baldwin and Jay Randolph Monroe, once an auditor with the Western Electric Company in the US, built a compact recording calculator, but without the printing mechanism. This was called the **Monroe calculator**. It succeeded commercially.

A7.2   The Thomason tide predictor

William Thomson, also known as Lord Kelvin (1824–1907), a British mathematician and physicist, employed a wheel and disc integrator in 1878 to build an analogue device for predicting the times and heights of the flood and ebb tides on British shores for any number of years to come. The integrator had been invented by his brother James (1822–92) who was then a professor of engineering at Glasgow University. The tide predictor (an intricate contrivance of cables, dials, drums, gears and rods) and its modified forms were soon in use throughout the world.

A7.3   The Millionaire machine

Otto Steiger (1858–1923), a Swiss engineer in Zurich, built in 1887 a calculator called the *Millionaire*, which multiplied directly. The direct multiplier was implemented by mechanically incorporating Napier's rods (described in section A4.2). This approach had been proposed earlier by Léon Bollée of France. The machine proved popular when it started selling in 1894. Compared to the arithmometer (described in section A5.4), the Millionaire was faster. Operated manually, the Millionaire could multiply two eight-digit numbers in 6 to 7 seconds; divide a six-digit number by a three-digit number in the same time of 6 to 7 seconds; and find to five places the square-root of a nine-digit number in 18 seconds. Models driven by small electric motors were available from 1910. The Millionaire machine continued to sell until 1935.

A7.4   The comptometer

Dorr E. Felt (1862–1930) of the USA built a calculator, called the **comptometer**, in which keys rather than slides or levers were used to enter numbers. The demand for such keyboard machines arose after the invention of the typewriter in the early 1870s. By 1887, within two years of the first model being built, the comptometer was being commercially produced (Figure A28), and a mechanism was attached in 1889 to enable the printing of results on a role of paper. The comptometer was principally a rapid adding and subtracting machine; multiplication was done by repeated addition, division by repeated subtraction.

For each digit rank (units, tens, hundreds, . . .), the comptometer had nine keys labelled 1 to 9. Depressing the appropriate keys caused a mechanical linkage to enter the number in a register. No key was to be

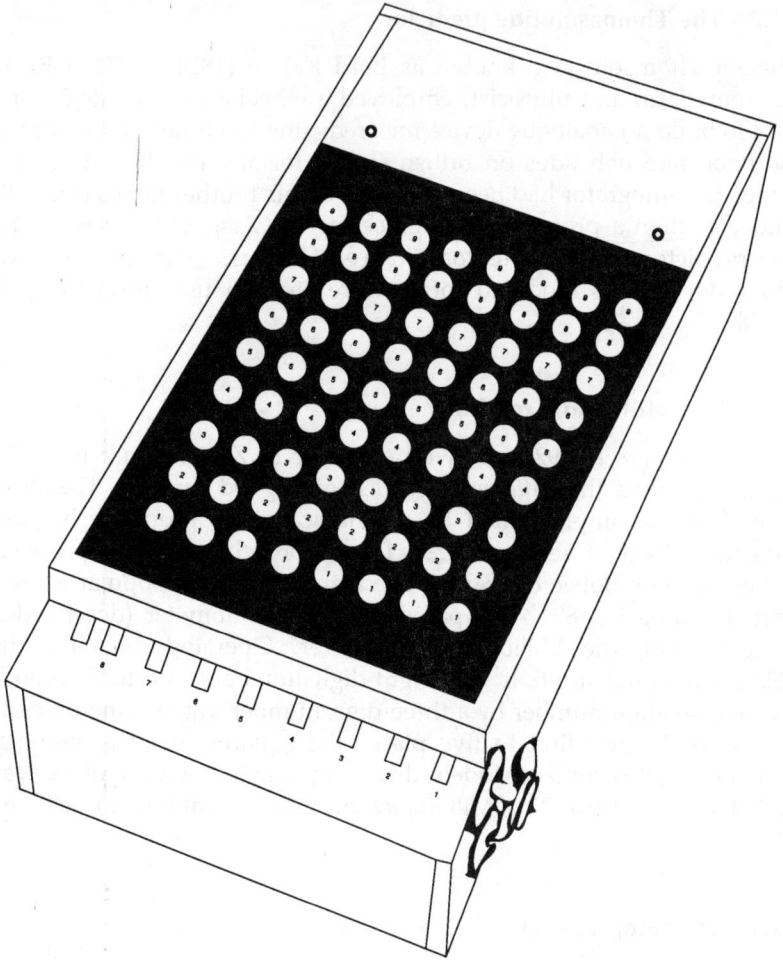

Figure A28   A sketch of Dorr E. Felt's comptometer of the 1890s.

depressed for entering a zero. In the earlier models, only one key could be depressed at one time. In 1903, Felt introduced a model in which all the keys required for entering a number could be depressed simultaneously. The comptometer sold well.

A7.5   The Burroughs accounting machine

William Seward Burroughs (1857–98), an American inventor, developed a keyboard adding machine somewhat different from the

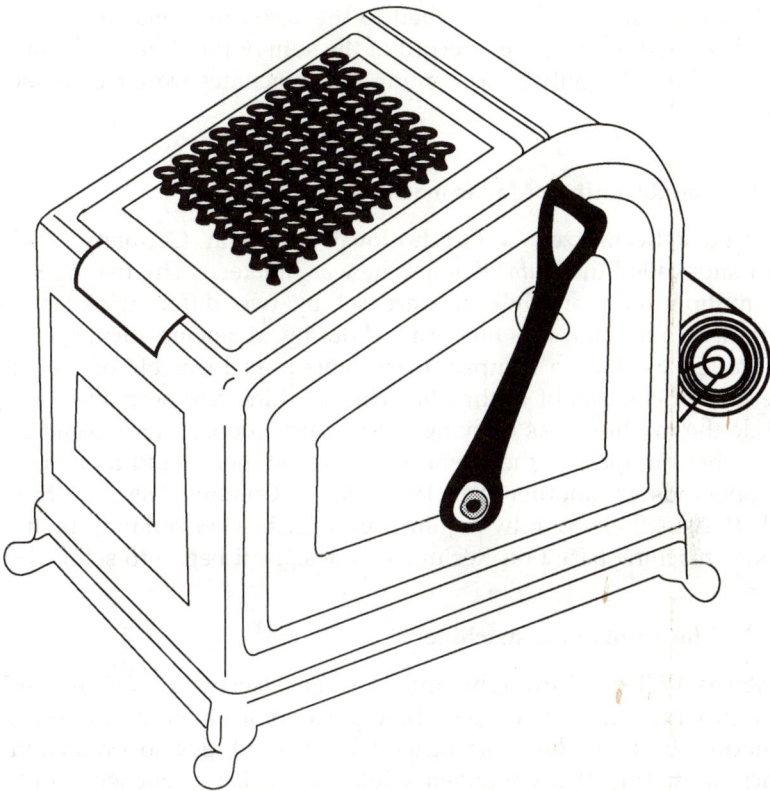

Figure A29   A sketch of Willam S. Burroughs' adding machine of the 1890s.

comptometer. In his machine, the number to be entered was first set by depressing the appropriate keys (there were nine keys for each digit rank); after checking the correctness of the number set, the user pulled a handle to enter the number in a register. The machine then printed the number entered. Figure A29 illustrates Burroughs' machine.

The first machine was manufactured 1890, but it took nearly two years for the machines to become reliable. In 1892 Burroughs received a patent. With their growing popularity, fifteen thousand units a year were being produced by 1909. By 1906, the machines had been modified to be driven by electric motors. After the First World War, a typewriter carriage and tabulators were attached to the machines. Named *Burroughs accounting machines*, these became popular in banks and businesses. Such machines were able to print numbers across a page, rather than only in a narrow column. If required, a number of adding registers could be attached to the accounting machines. These could be used for keeping a record of the sum of the different columns, a much desired facility in accounting. The machines were a commercial success.

A7.6   The Rechnitzer Madas machine

Alexander Rechnitzer, a Czechoslovak living in Germany, built a calculator called the *Autorith* when he was nineteen. The two operands in multiplication or division were set by two different slides. The arithmetic operation was then carried out by advancing a lever. In 1912 he started work on a compact marketable model capable of executing the four operations of arithmetic. This machine had a small memory. While the machine was carrying out its calculations, a user could enter two other numbers in the memory. These numbers could then be used as operands in another calculation later. Commercially, Rechnitzer failed. Nonetheless, Edwin Jahnz in Zürich, Switzerland, built the Madas machine based on Rechnitzer's design. It began to sell in 1914.

A7.7   The Sundstrand machine

Whereas William Burroughs and Dorr Felt (sections A7.4 and A7.5) had provided nine keys per digit position in their machines, two American brothers, Oscar and David Sundstrand, developed an adding machine in 1914 that contained a total of ten keys, labelled 0 to 9. A user depressed the appropriate keys to enter a number digit by digit, starting from the most significant digit. A register on a carriage moved as each digit was entered. The machine proved commercially popular.

A7.8   The Quevedo machine

Leonardo Torres y Quevedo (1852–1936) of Madrid, Spain, developed a division-by-comparison mechanism in an electromechanical calculator, which he displayed at the Paris Centennial in 1920. During division, the dividend was modified by subtracting the divisor from it. This was iteratively done until the dividend became less than the divisor. The quotient was then the number of iterations.

A7.9   Hollerith equipment

Manually counting, checking and recording the data from the 1880 US census took seven years to tabulate. It was feared that with each succeeding census and a larger population to count, the time taken in

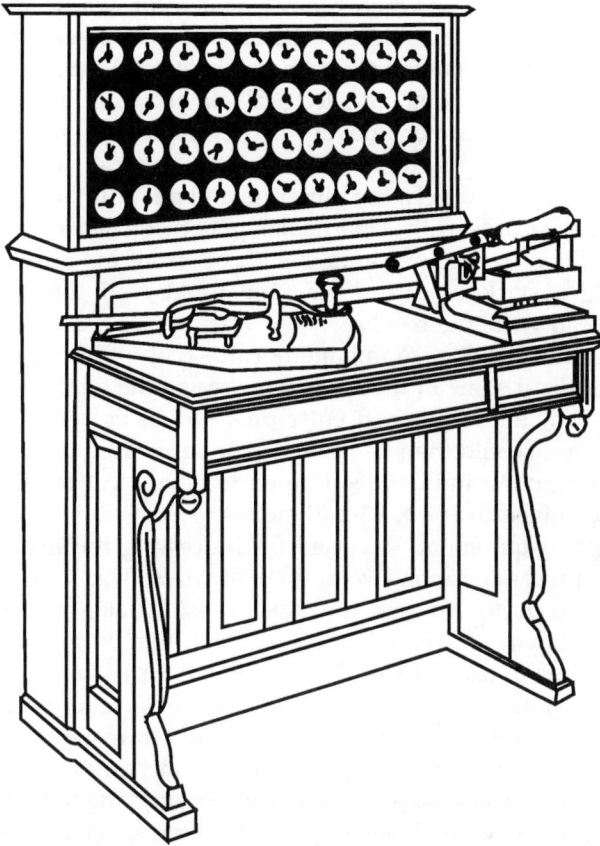

Figure A30   A sketch of the Hollerith tabulator used in the US Census of 1890.

tabulating the data would increase. By the time the results of a census were analysed, the analyses would be out of date. Herman Hollerith (1860–1929), a statistician with the US Census Bureau, turned to mechanizing the analyses of the data. Initially, he experimented with putting the data on perforated rolls of paper. Then he developed an electromechanical system of using punched cards. An individual's data (male or female, city or village dweller, age, profession, etc.) were coded as holes on these cards.

Hollerith's equipment consisted of a card punch, a non-printing tabulator (Figure A30) and a sorting box. Appropriate holes in a card were made by the card punch. To have it read, it was placed on a reading tray consisting of a pin press. The press contained a mercury cup below each position where a hole could occur. On closing a hinged cover, spring-loaded pins descended on the card. Some were blocked by the card. Others passed through the holes and made contact with the mercury, completing an electrical circuit. This incremented an electromechanical counter, moved the pertinent dial on the tabulator, and unlatched the appropriate bin cover on the sorter. The user would then remove the card from the pin press and put it in the unlatched bin of the sorter. Cards with a particular pattern of holes could thus be counted. Fifty to eighty cards could be read in a minute. After processing a stack of cards, the user could read the dials on the tabulator and write the results.

Hollerith used 127 × 76 millimetre cards, cut off in one corner. In a stack of cards, if some of the cards were facing the wrong way or were upside down, the misaligned cut corner would be seen by the user, and such cards could then be righted. The cards used in the twentieth-century computing industry continued to have a cut corner, but their size was changed to 187 × 83 millimetres.

Hollerith's equipment was used for processing the 1890 US census data. The processing took two-and-a-half years. This was one third of the time taken to process the 1880 census data, in spite of the population having increased to 63 millions from 50 millions over the ten years. Russia used Hollerith's equipment for its 1897 census.

In 1896, Hollerith quit the US Census Bureau and established the Tabulating Machine Company. He continued to make improvements: for reading a card, he replaced the pins and mercury by metal brushes which made contact with a metallic plate through the holes in the card; the tabulators were modified to print the results, thus eliminating the likelihood of a user making a mistake while copying the result; and a card punch was developed which could be operated conveniently from a numerical keyboard. The Hollerith system was used in the 1911 British census. In the same year, Hollerith's company merged with the International Time Recording Company and the Dayton Scale Company to become the Computing-Tabulating-Recording Company. In 1924, the company changed its name to International Business Machines (IBM) Corporation.

Hollerith's machines began to find users in the scientific world, too. In 1928 Leslie John Comrie of Britain used Hollerith machines to calculate the positions of the moon from 1935 to the year 2000.

A7.10   Powers equipment

To develop machines faster than the Hollerith machines, the US Census Bureau appointed another statistician, James Powers, as the

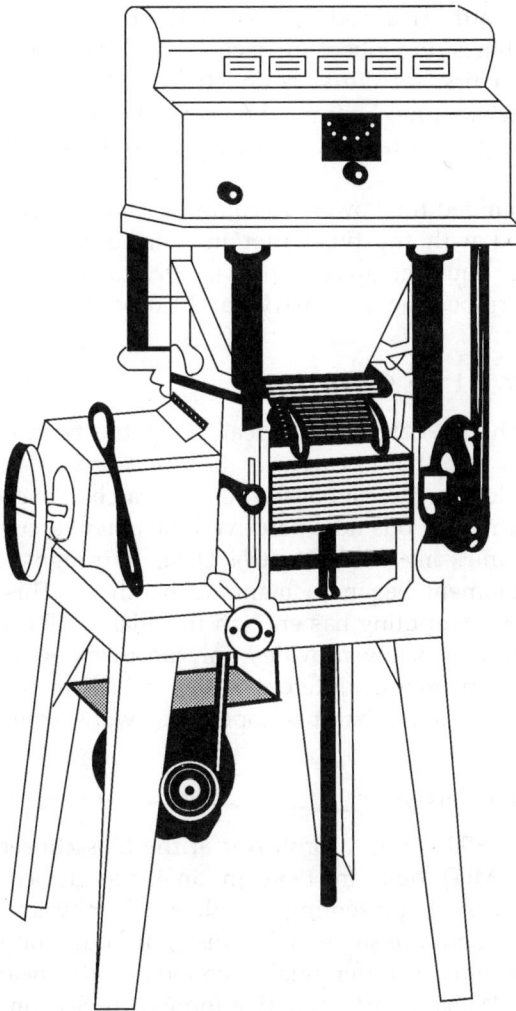

Figure A31 A sketch of James Powers' tabulator of 1910.

director of a new laboratory. Hollerith had built electromechanical equipment; Powers differed and developed purely mechanical equipment.

In 1908 he developed a keyboard card-punching machine in which all the holes to be punched in the card were first set by depressing the appropriate keys. The user could check to see whether he had depressed the right keys. If all the keys were correct, he would depress a punch key. All the required holes were then punched simultaneously on a 20-column card. This notion was similar to the one used in the Burroughs machines described in section A7.5 where, to enter a number, the user first set the keys and then pulled a handle. James Powers also developed mechanical tabulators (Figure A31) and sorters. All his machines proved reliable, and they were used in the 1910 US census.

In 1911, he founded the Powers Accounting Machine Company. His company merged with the typewriter manufacturer Remington and some other office equipment companies in 1927 to become Remington Rand. This in turn became the Sperry Rand Corporation in 1955.

A8   THE GROWTH OF COMPUTERS

The dream of Charles Babbage was realized in the twentieth century when computers were born. This was the result of years of research. The Second World War gave a boost to this research, as needs arose to fulfil wartime demands. Business perceived the potential of computers, and soon companies like IBM, Control Data, Burroughs, Honeywell and Digital Equipment began to manufacture them. This history of twentieth-century computing has enough material to fill a voluminous book. The discussion below provides only an overview of the work done by different people in different places, which made computers what they are today, and what it is hoped they will become.

A8.1   Differential Analysers

Vannevar Bush (1890–1974), a professor at the Masschusetts Institute of Technology (MIT) built in 1930 an analogue device called the *Differential Analyser*. Representing numbers as physical quantities (positions on a continuously rotating disc), it could find particular solutions for systems of differential equations, both linear and non-linear. Britain's William Thomson (mentioned in Section A7.2) had described the fundamentals of a mechanical Differential Analyser in a paper of the 1876 *Proceedings of the Royal Society*. Bush, however, maintained that while building his analyser, he was unaware of Thomson's paper.

Bush's analyser was partly mechanical and partly electronic. The electronic tubes consumed excessive electricity and emitted excessive heat, so they were placed far apart and were provided with coolers. This was the first time ever electronic tubes had been employed in a computing device.

Two British scientists, Douglas Hartree (1897–1958) and his student Arthur Porter, saw the Differential Analyser at MIT in 1933. On

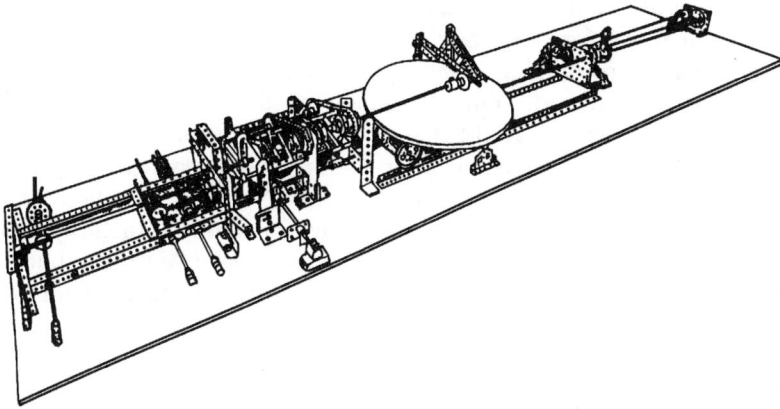

Figure A32 A sketch of Douglas Hartree and Arthur Porter's Differential Analyzer built in 1935 from Meccano parts.

returning to Britain they built in 1935 at Manchester University a small motor-driven analyser from the parts of a £20 Meccano set. (Figure A32). Its accuracy was within 2% of Bush's device. Later, Hartree built a full-size analyser, also at Manchester University. Both of the Hartree analysers are now in the Science Museum, in South Kensington, London.

In 1937 a student, Claude Elwood Shannon (born 1916), showed in his master's thesis at MIT that Boolean algebra (introduced in section A6.3) could be applied to design relay and switching circuits. Shannon had also been working as an operator of Bush's Differential Analyser, and Bush had urged him to take on this investigation for his thesis. Shannon also showed that circuits could be designed to carry out the arithmetic of adding, subtracting, multiplying and dividing. Moreover, Shannon noted that these circuits were simplified if arithmetic was carried out in binary, that is, by employing only the symbols 0 and 1. Remember that binary numbers had also been studied more than 200 years earlier by Gottfried Leibniz (section A5.3).

A8.2 The Turing machine

In 1936, the year before Shannon was to present his momentous thesis, a paper entitled 'On Computable Numbers with an Application to the Entscheidungs Problem' appeared in the *Proceedings of the London Mathematical Society*, volume **42**, pp. 230–65. The paper was by Alan Turing, the same person who was to later bring forth the Turing test of intelligence, which we had mentioned in section 1.2. In the paper,

Turing proposed a theoretical machine with an infinitely long tape. The tape could move forwards and backwards under an element called a head. The head could read binary symbols from the tape, it could erase them, and it could write binary symbols on the tape. Turing showed that if any problem could be programmed at all, it could be programmed on his machine after coding the program into binary symbols.

The machine has come to be known as the Turing machine. Since the machine is theoretical, it has, of course, never been built, but the notion of the Turing machine has served as a bedrock of theoretical computer science.

A8.3   Remote computing

George Stibitz, a mathematician at Bell Telephone Laboratories in New York, began in the late 1930s to build a machine for doing arithmetic on complex numbers. The input and output were in teleprinter code. Delivering a paper in 1940 at the Mathematical Society in Dartmouth College, New Hampshire, he gave a demonstration: users at Dartmouth could feed their arithmetical problems into a teleprinter linked to the machine in New York; the machine sent the results back to the teleprinter. Stibitz intended to show that users in any location, however remote, could communicate with his machine over teleprinter circuits. Remote computing was later to become commonplace.

A8.4   The Harvard Mark I

After having read the works of Charles Babbage (see section A6.1), Howard Hathaway Aiken (1900–73), a professor at Harvard University in the US, set out in 1937 to build a general-purpose digital calculator with an architecture similar to Babbage's Analytical Engine. IBM gave Aiken a million-dollar grant and a team of engineers to assist him. Begun in 1939, the machine was completed in 1943 at the IBM Development Laboratories in Endicott, New York. In August 1944, IBM presented the machine to Harvard. The machine was taken apart, partly redesigned and then reassembled in the physics laboratory at Harvard, where it worked for fifteen years. It was named the *Automatic Sequence Controlled Calculator* (ASCC), but it is now better known as the *Harvard Mark I.*

Smaller than Babbage's Analytical Engine, it had a store of 72 registers, each with the capacity of a sign and 23 decimal digits. It also had 60 more registers of the same capacity on which manual switches were used for setting values of constants. These 60 registers were not part of the store. Addition and subtraction were done directly on the 72 registers of the store by electromagnetic clutches. Aiken implemented the anticipatory carry proposed by Babbage. Multiplication and division were done in the mill (arithmetic unit) by looking up a multiplication table similar to Napier's rods (described in section A4.2). The machine had electromechanical tables for finding sines, exponents of ten, and base-10 logarithms of a value. The various operations and their execution time given in seconds within parentheses were the following: addition (0.3), subtraction (0.3), multiplication (3.0), division (11.4), sine (60.0), exponent of ten (61.2), logarithm (72.6).

Instructions for execution were punched on a continuous roll of paper. Numbers were entered in the 72 registers of the store by punched cards. Results could be printed by two electric typewriters or could be punched on cards. Unlike Babbage's Analytical Engine, the Harvard Mark I could not make a conditional jump across instructions.

It was over 15 metres long, nearly 2.5 metres high, contained nearly a million components and 800 kilometres of wiring, and weighed 5 tonnes. While it worked, the clicking of its electromagnetic relays was reputed to sound like a roomful of people 'knitting away with steel needles.'

After Harvard Mark I was complete, Aiken and his team built Mark II. It was delivered to the US Naval Proving Ground at Dahlgren, Virginia, in 1947. The capacity of its store registers was 10 digits, compared to 23 for Mark I. Adding took 0.2 seconds and multiplication 0.7. Thus it was a smaller machine than Mark I, but faster. Instructions were punched on three teletype paper tapes. At any one time the machine was executing the instruction sequence from one tape, say, Tape 1. If a condition set in the instructions was satisfied, the machine transferred control and started executing the instruction sequence from one of the other tapes, say, Tape 2, which would then have an instruction to transfer control back to Tape 1. This transfer of control from one instruction sequence to another and back is equivalent to conditional call of a subroutine followed by return in current jargon.

A8.5   The SSEC

IBM's *Selective Sequence Electronic Calculator* (SSEC) was built at the company headquarters in New York in 1948. It contained 23 000 relays and 13 000 electronic tubes. It was more than a hundred times faster than Harvard Mark I, as all its arithmetic was electronic. Punched tape was used for input. It had a conditional transfer instruction, similar to Babbage's Analytical Engine. The machine had three types of memory: (a) a small high-speed, electronic-tube memory, (b) a slightly larger memory of relays, and (c) an even larger memory on 80-column paper tape. It was used for research in astronomy, in the geology of oil wells, and for the US Atomic Energy. The machine was in use until 1952.

A8.6   The British war effort

During the Second World War, the British developed a series of machines to mechanize the breaking of German codes. The first such eletromechanical machine, called the *Heath Robinson*, was designed by Wynn-Williams. The machine could read and compare two paper tapes at 2000 characters per second. The subsequent improved machines were called *Peter Robinson, Robinson and Cleaver* and *Super Robinson*, but the machines were plagued by mechanical problems. Then a team led by M. H. A. Newman designed *Colossus*, an electronic computer. Colossus began functioning in December 1943. It could read punched paper tape at 5000 characters per second. Patterns for comparison required for code breaking were generated electronically by the machine. Electric typewriters were used for output at about 15 characters per second.

In June 1944, a Mark II Colossus was completed, which was five times faster than the first Colossus. By the end of the war, ten Colossus machines were in use. These were faster than Howard Aiken's Harvard Mark I (section A8.4) built in the US. The Colossus machines were, however, special-purpose (dedicated to code cracking), whereas Aiken's machine was general-purpose.

A8.7   Zuse machines

Konrad Zuse (born 1910), a German design engineer, built in 1936 a machine called Z1 in his parent's living room in Berlin. It used binary arithmetic and had a memory. Numbers were fed in from a keyboard and results were displayed by electric bulbs. It used cheap, commonly available mechanical components as switches.

Zuse then modified Z1. The mechanical switches were replaced by electromagnetic relays, as used in telephone switching, and the slow keyboard input by punched cinema film. The film, gathered from discarded stock, was a substitute for paper tape, which was not then available in Germany. Completed in 1939, the machine was called Z2. Zuse's friend Helmut Schreyer, then a doctoral candidate in electrical engineering, had suggested using electronic tubes instead of electromechanical relays. The tubes would give speed, but tubes were unreliable, used a lot of electricity, and generated a lot of heat. Moreover, they were costly and scarce. So Zuse had to make do with magnetic relays. In 1938, Schreyer received his doctorate for a thesis on how to use tubes in digital computers. The German government failed to see the value of using Schreyer's ideas to build high-speed, electronic Zuse machines in their war effort. This was unlike the British, who had independently developed their own machines and used them successfully.

On his own, Zuse built Z3 in 1941. It could add, subtract, multiply, divide, find square roots, and carry out binary-to-decimal conversion. Numbers were entered from a keyboard. A relay memory had the capacity of 64 words. A light panel displayed a four-decimal-digit output, together with a decimal-point indicator. Program control was by eight-bit, one-address instructions punched on cinema film. The arithmetic used 22-bit binary floating-point numbers. Of the 22 bits, one bit was for sign, seven bits for exponent and fourteen bits for mantissa. Its speed was nearly equal to that of Harvard Mark I, then being built by Howard Aiken in the US. Completed before Harvard Mark I, Z3 is now reputed to be the world's first general-purpose, programmable digital computer. Harvard Mark I was the second.

In 1942 Zuse began to work on an improved model, Z4. Models Z1, Z2 and Z3 were destroyed during the air raids in the closing days of the war in 1944. Z4 was installed in 1949 at the Eidgenössische Technische Hochschule in Zürich, Switzerland.

A8.8 ENIAC

The *Electronic Numerical Integrator and Computer* (ENIAC) was designed and built by John William Mauchly (1907–80) and John Presper Eckert (born 1919) at the Moore School of Engineering, University of Pennsylvania, USA. When Mauchly and Eckert started the design of ENIAC in 1943, they did not know (because of wartime secrecy) about the Robinson and Colossus machines that had been built in Britain. Neither had they any intimation about the Z series machines built by Konrad Zuse in Germany. Completed in 1946, ENIAC was built under a contract from the US government for the Ballistic Research Laboratory at Aberdeen Proving Grounds, Maryland. It was intended for calculating ballistic tables.

Its memory consisted of 20 registers, each with the capacity of a sign and 10 decimal digits. Of these registers, four were reserved for multiplication, which used multiplication tables similar in principle to Léon Bollée's mechanical tables used in the Millionaire machine (section A7.3). Thus only sixteen registers were available to store values. Nevertheless, hand switches were provided to feed in an additional 104 values manually. Input and output was by punched cards. Using decimal arithmetic, it could multiply two 10-digit numbers in 0.003 seconds, add in 0.0002 seconds, and divide or find a square-root in 0.01 seconds. It could read a card in 0.3 seconds and punch one in 0.6 seconds. Since it was designed specifically for calculating ballistic tables, it required manual rewiring if any change was to be made in the program to be run. Its programming was thus awkward. Nonetheless, ENIAC could be reprogrammed, whereas the British Colossus, designed only for cracking codes, could not be reprogrammed. Moreover, the ENIAC was slightly faster than the Colossus.

ENIAC was even larger than the Harvard Mark I: over 30 metres long, its 18 000 electronic tubes consumed over 100 kilowatts of electricity, discharging a great deal of heat. Used for nearly ten years, it was later placed in the Smithsonian Institution in Washington, DC.

A8.9   Development of stored-program computers

Even before the ENIAC was completed at the Moore School, work had started on an improved machine called the *Electronic Discrete Variable Computer* (EDVAC). This work began in January 1945 under the direction of S. Reid Warren. In 1946 Johann von Neumann (1903–57), a Hungarian-born mathematician and chemical engineer, joined the ENIAC team as a consultant. Von Neumann is usually credited for the idea that program instructions could be numerically coded and then stored in the computer memory, just like data. This view is disputed by other members of the ENIAC team (mainly John W. Mauchly and John Presper Eckert), who say that the stored program idea was developed jointly by the team. Once the program was stored in the memory, the control mechanism of the computer could then execute the instructions one by one sequentially, unless there was an instruction to branch to another instruction. Moreover, by storing the program in the memory the computer could be switched from one program to another without having to rewire the machine. Completed in 1952, the EDVAC was a stored-program computer. It contained 3600 electronic tubes, employed binary arithmetic, had a memory of 1000 words (compared to 20 for ENIAC), and was ten times faster than ENIAC. The EDVAC was, however, not the first stored-program computer in the world. As far back as 1948, the ENIAC had been modified so that a 312-word read-only memory could hold program instructions. Moreover, by the time the EDVAC was completed, the following two stored-program computers had already been built in Britain.

1. *Mark I* (not to be confused with Aiken's Harvard Mark I) by Frederick Calland Williams (born 1911) and Tom Kilburn (born 1921) at the University of Manchester in 1948.
2. *Electronic Delay Storage Automatic Computer* (EDSAC) by Maurice Vincent Wilkes (born 1913) at Cambridge University in 1949. Wilkes had once worked with the ENIAC team. During his stay at the Moore School, he had attended lectures on automatic computers in the summer of 1946.

As for Mauchly and Eckert of the EDVAC team, they were later to start the computer company UNIVAC.

A8.10 Advancements in computer memories

The earlier computers used mercury delay lines for memory. In 1948 Frederick Calland Williams at the University of Manchester developed a technique for storing information as spots of charge on the inside faces of cathode ray tubes. This form of memory, called the *Williams tube*, became popular in computers built in the US and Europe. It became obsolete in 1956 when it was displaced by *magnetic core* memory, developed by Jay Wright Forrester of the Massachusetts Institute of Technology. Magnetic core memory was conceived from the knowledge that magnetization in ferrites (crystalline compounds containing ferric oxide) could be instantaneously reversed. Thus ferrites could be used to store information coded in binary. Magnetic core memory was quickly adopted by computers, till it was replaced by semiconductor memory (electronic circuits integrated on a chip) in the 1970s.

Another advancement resulted in easier access to different parts of a computer's memory. In 1949, Tom Kilburn at the University of Manchester had developed the notion of an index register. An index register can store a number which can be added to that part of an instruction which indicates the memory location to be accessed. Thus, by varying the contents of an index register, the same instruction can be used to access different locations in the memory. The resulting programming convenience caused index registers to be widely incorporated in computers.

A8.11 Progress in programming languages

In the early days of computers, all programming was numerically coded. Needless to say, programming was tedious. Around the 1950s, computers began to be commercially manufactered and their use expanded. It became essential that programming be made more convenient. In 1957 John Backus and his collegues at IBM developed FORTRAN, a high-level language. In it, the programmer wrote algebra-like statements, which were then compiled by the machine into the required numerical representation called machine code. This made programming much easier. Other high-level languages were also developed: ALGOL in 1960, COBOL in 1961, BASIC in 1964, PASCAL in 1971, and ADA in the 1980s. The last language, named in honour of Ada Lovelace (Section A6.2), was sponsored by the United States Department of Defense.

A8.12   Generations of computers

Computer hardware (electronic components) has been improving since the days of ENIAC. Each dramatic improvement in hardware has led to a so-called new generation.

In the **first generation** of computers (1946–59), the logical circuits were of electronic vacuum tubes, the memories being of mercury delay lines and Williams tubes. The tubes could be unreliable, so the more tubes a machine had, the greater was its unreliability. The UNIVAC 1103, built in 1953, had nearly 2000 tubes; the IBM 701 of the same year had 4000. The tubes often failed. Moreover, such machines consumed large amounts of electricity and they generated lots of heat, necessitating forced-air cooling. Some of the first-generation computers were ENIAC, EDVAC, Burroughs 220, IAS, SEAC, SWAC, UNIVAC 1103, Whirlwind, and IBM's 650, 701, 704 and 705.

In the **second generation** of computers (1959–64), the logical circuits were of transistors. The transistor was invented in 1948 at Bell Telephone Laboratories by American scientists John Bardeen (born 1908), Walter Houser Brattain (born 1902) and William Bradford Shockley (born 1910). The transistors were more reliable than vacuum tubes and consumed less electricity. The memories in this generation were of magnetic cores, and index registers had been incorporated into the machines. Some of the machines of this generation were the CDC 3600, Honeywell 800, Ferranti Atlas, UNIVAC 1107, RCA 501, Philco 2000, and IBM's 7000 and 1400 series.

The **third generation** of computers (1964–75) used integrated circuits. For a specific operation the various components (resistors, capacitors and transistors) were incorporated on a silicon chip. These chips could be manufactured under strict control of quality which improved the reliability of the machine hardware. Moreover, the cost of hardware began to decrease. Some of the third-generation machines were the CDC 6000, UNIVAC 9400, DEC PDP-11, Honeywell 6000, and IBM's 360 and 370 series. A by-product of the development of integrated circuits was the introduction of the calculator-on-a-chip in 1971. It became the basis of hand-held calculators, which quickly became popular. Over the years, the number of electronic parts in the calculator has decreased, the size has become smaller, and several calculators have memory and are programmable.

The **fourth-generation** computers (1975 onward) used large scale integration (LSI) in which more and more electronic components were incorporated on a single chip. Examples of such computers are the Cray-1 and Cyber 205.

A8.13   Different sizes of computers

Computers are classified into three main sizes: mainframes, mini-computers and microcomputers. With advancing technology, the distinction between them is becoming blurred.

The **mainframe** computers are huge, expensive and consume lots of electricity. They can serve many users at the same time. In the late 1950s and early 1960s, the notion of time-sharing was developed. In this, if many users are interacting with the machine, it serves each user for a fraction of a second, and then serves the next user. This way it seems to each user as if the machine is working for him all the time, whereas in reality the machine is working for him for only a part of the time. Examples of mainframe computers are the Cyber 170 and the IBM 370.

The computing power of **minicomputers** is less than that of main-frames. The earlier minicomputers could serve only one user at a time, but the later minicomputers could serve many users (though fewer than mainframes) at the same time. Examples of minicomputers are the IBM System/38 and the DEC PDP-11.

The central processing unit of a **microcomputer** is built on a single silicon chip, usually less than 5 millimetres square and 0.5 millimetres thick. Thus both the arithmetic unit and the control circuit are on a single chip. Microcomputers became popular because they are cheap, portable, and consume little electricity. Since 1975, they have increasingly been used as personal computers. In them, one may save one's recipe for strawberry shortcake, or the record of transactions of one's bank account. The computing power of a microcomputer is less than that of a minicomputer. Examples of microcomputers are the IBM PC, TRS 80 and Apple Macintosh.

A9   THE CHALLENGE OF ARTIFICIAL INTELLIGENCE

With the growth of computers, the challenge soon arose whether computers could be built or programmed to display intelligence. This gave birth to the field of artificial intelligence.

A six-week conference was held in the summer of 1956 at Dartmouth College, New Hampshire. As far as is known, this was the first time that the term *artificial intelligence* (AI) was used. The conference was named 'The Dartmouth Summer Research Project on Artificial Intelligence.' The first usage of the term is ascribed to John McCarthy, then teaching at Dartmouth, and an organizer of the conference.

A highlight of the conference was the presenting of the program *Logic Theorist* developed at the Carnegie–Mellon University (at that time known as the Carnegie Institute of Technology) in Pittsburgh, Pennsylvania. The Logic Theorist was devised by Allen Newell, Herbert Alexander Simon and John Cliff Shaw. Employing heuristics instead of exhaustive search, the program could prove theorems in propositional logic. The creators of Logic Theorist took the term *heuristics* from George Polya's book *How to Solve It* (see section 11.6).

British mathematicians Alfred North Whitehead (1862–1947) and Bertrand Russell (1872–1970) had extended George Boole's work on logic by publishing the three-volume *Principia Mathematica* (Cambridge University Press, 1913). Newell, Simon and Shaw took some theorems from the first volume of the *Principia* and tried to have them proved by the Logic Theorist. The program succeeded in proving several of them. Actually, for one theorem, numbered as Theorem 2.85 in the *Principia*, the program found a proof shorter than that given in the book. The theorem, in effect, called for proving the formula

$$((A \lor B) \to (A \lor C)) \to (A \lor (B \to C))$$

to be a tautology. A paper, in which the Logic Theorist was named as the co-author, was submitted for publication to the *Journal of Symbolic Logic*. The paper presented the shorter proof found by the program. Surprisingly, the paper was rejected.

Newell, Simon and Shaw were later to develop the technique of means–end analysis, described in section 12.4, to solve problems. Based on this technique, they implemented a program called the *General Problem Solver*.

In the latter half of the 1950s, John McCarthy invented Lisp (*list* processing), a programming language that became popular with AI researchers. The other programming language popular with AI researchers is Prolog (*pro*gramming in *log*ic). It was invented in the early 1970s by Alain Colmerauer and his associates at the University of Marseilles, France.

Meanwhile, in 1961, James Slagle at MIT wrote a program called SAINT for solving problems of indefinite integrals. Constructing AND/ OR graphs (explained in section 12.2), the program manipulated non-numerical symbols to carry out the integration. In 1968, the program was augmented by Joel Moses. The augmented program, now called MACSYMA, could solve problems in algebra and calculus. Later still, in the 1980s, MACSYMA became commercially available from Symbolics, Inc., Burlington, Massachusetts. The program could solve many kinds of problems: differential and integral equations, Laplace and Fourier transforms, even vector and tensor calculus.

An interest shared by many AI researchers has been in the building of intelligent robots. The word robot descended from the Czech word *robota*, which means 'forced labour.' The word came into English usage in 1923, after Karel Čapek's play *Rossum's Universal Robots*. An essential component of a robot is a mechanical arm that can pick up, hold, carry and put down objects. In some robots, the arm is designed to execute repeatedly a specified sequence of actions; for example, pick up an object from spot A, turn it upside down and put it down in spot B. Such robots are not considered to be intelligent. They are on occasion called industrial robots. Having been employed since the 1960s, these robots have proved useful mainly in industrial jobs that humans find tedious because of the repetitive nature of the job, for instance, assembly line production, and removing parts from die casting apparatus.

Intelligent robots are computer controlled and they also have sensors; say, a television camera to photograph the objects around the robot. The images of the objects photographed by the camera are processed by the computer to recognize the objects. The computer then plans the sequence of actions required to finish an assigned task and to correct any errors made.

Projects to build intelligent robots were carried out from the mid-1960s to the early 1970s at MIT, Stanford University and Stanford Research Institute in the USA, and at the University of Edinburgh in Britain. All the robots built in these projects had television cameras as sensors. The robots operated in restricted domains, for example, a domain of toy blocks. The robot built at the Stanford Research Institute was the only mobile one of the four robots built at the different places. It would roll from room to room at the institute, avoiding obstacles. The robot was named SHAKEY because it would shake vigorously while rolling around. On being given a problem, SHAKEY conducted an A* search (described in section 11.5.1) to discover the solution path.

It is hoped that one day intelligent robots will be used liberally to work in environments that are hazardous to humans; for instance, repairing equipment in a territory contaminated by nuclear radiation, mining from an ocean bed, and exploring distant planets. In such places, the robot should be able to handle any sudden occurrences; say, extricate itself if it gets stuck in the mud. Nonetheless, before one begins to use robots in the above manner, one would be wiser to establish laws that all robots must obey. This is to prevent the harm that robots can do. American writer Isaac Asimov proposed three such laws in his book *I, Robot* (Gnome Press, New York, 1950). After making some modifications to the three laws, we have paraphrased them as follows:

1. a robot must protect itself except when ordered not to do so by its human commander or when, by protecting itself, it will hurt someone;
2. in fact, a robot must always obey its human commander except when such obedience will hurt someone;
3. in fact, a robot must never hurt anyone by any act of commission or omission.

Generalizing the above laws, we hope that no development in AI is such that it causes any harm. An area whose developments are not expected to cause any harm is game playing.

A9.1   Game playing

In 1950, the same year that Isaac Asimov proposed his laws for robots, Claude Shannon, whom we earlier saw in Section A8.1, published a paper entitled 'Programming a Computer for Playing Chess' in the *Philosophy Magazine*, volume **41**, pp. 256–75. Shannon described how a program to play chess could be designed. He also developed the notion of game trees, which we discussed in sections 13.1 and 13.2. Shannon estimated that a comprehensive game tree for chess would contain 10^{120} nodes. Some time after Shannon's paper, a paper entitled 'Digital Computers Applied to Games' was printed in the book *Faster than Thought*, edited by B. V. Bowden (Pitman Publishing Corporation, New York, 1953, pp. 286–310). Authored by Alan Turing, whom we earlier saw in sections 1.2 and A8.2, the paper described how computers could play games. The papers of Shannon and Turing became the basis of computer game playing. Since then many programs have been written to play games like draughts, chess, Go, Go-Moku and Kalah.

A famous program to play draughts was written by Arthur L. Samuel at IBM. Samuel began working on the program in the 1950s. By

1961, the program was playing at the master's level. Ultimately, the program became a better player than Samuel himself.

Nonetheless, the game playing programs that have received a lot of attention in the literature are those for chess. The first program to play chess was written in 1958 at IBM. It was written by Alex Bernstein, Tom Arbuckle, Michael Belsky and Michael De V. Roberts.

The first program to play chess successfully against humans was, however, written at MIT by Richard D. Greenblatt, Steven D. Crocker and Donald E. Eastlake. The program was named MAC HACK. In 1967 the US Chess Federation estimated MAC HACK to have a rating in the 1400s. This is the rating received by most people who have been playing chess regularly for three years.

The first world championship for computer chess was held in Stockholm in 1974. It was won by the program KAISSA, written by Mikhail Donskoy and Valadimir Arlazarov from the USSR's Institute of Control Sciences. The program was estimated to have a rating of about 1850, which is higher than that of MAC HACK.

A prominent chess playing program, continually refined from year to year in the 1970s, was named CHESS. It was written by David Slate and Larry Atkins of Northwestern University, Illinois. The later versions of the program searched game trees by iterative deepening (described in section 13.7.5). In 1979, when the program had been named as CHESS 4.9, it was estimated to have a rating of about 2050.

In 1980 a program named BELLE, written by Ken Thompson and Joe Condon of the Bell Telephone Laboratories, was estimated to have a rating of about 2100, which is higher than that of CHESS 4.9. BELLE won the world computer chess championship of 1983.

A still better program was written by Hans Berliner of Carnegie–Mellon University. The program, named HITECH, received a rating of 2407. In a match in New York in September 1988, HITECH defeated Arnold S. Denker, an international grand master and a former US chess champion with a rating of 2410. Writing in the Spring 1989 issue of the *AI Magazine* (p. 83), Berliner said: 'This was the first time a machine had defeated a grand master; at the time of the match, however, Denker was not playing as actively as he had at the peak of his career when he earned the grand master title. DEEP THOUGHT, a later program of F. Hsu, T. Anantharaman, M. Campbell and A. Nowatzyk, also from Carnegie–Mellon, received a rating of 2551.

As you may see from the above, chess playing programs have progressively improved over the years. They are expected to improve even further in the future.

Programs to play games are usually fun for those who write such programs, for those who play against the program, and for those who watch the game being played. But there may be those who consider computer game playing frivolous. For them, a serious area of AI would perhaps be natural language processing.

A9.2   Natural language processing

As mentioned in sections 1.1 and 6.1, by natural language processing we attempt to communicate with a computer in an everyday language like English. A few programs for natural language processing are noted below. In all these programs a user could communicate with a computer in English.

One of the earliest such programs came about in 1961. Named BASEBALL, it was written by Bert F. Green, Jr., Alice K. Wolf, Carol Chomsky and Kenneth Laughery at Lincoln Laboratories, Lexington, Massachusetts. BASEBALL could answer questions about the American League baseball games for one season.

In the early 1960s, Daniel G. Bobrow, a student at MIT wrote a program named STUDENT. The program could read typical problems of high-school algebra expressed in a restricted form of English. The program would then set up the required equations and solve them.

By 1966, Joseph Weizenbaum, a professor at MIT had written a conversational program named ELIZA. According to Weizenbaum, the program was named after George Bernard Shaw's heroine Eliza in the play *Pygmalion* because, like the heroine, the program could be 'taught to speak increasingly well.' The program would pick up some key words from what its conversational partner, that is, the user, said. It would then transform these words into some canned response. If no key words were found, ELIZA would refer to something the user had said earlier, and respond, 'Earlier you said . . .'. In effect, the program mimicked a Rogerian psychoanalyst who is not expected to contribute anything to a conversation, apart from letting his patient talk. Alternatively, it can be said that the program mimicked the typical chatter heard at parties. Conversing through a teletype with ELIZA, many people are reported to have been fooled into thinking that they were talking to another human. In a sense, the program passed the Turing test (of section 1.2), Yet it cannot be said that the program possessed any intelligence.

In October 1970, William A. Woods published a paper entitled 'Transition Network Grammars for Natural Language Analysis' in the *Communications of the ACM*, volume **13**, pp 591–606. To parse English sentences, Woods proposed the augmented transition networks (described in section 7.2). In 1972, Woods developed an English interface named LUNAR, which incorporated augmented transition networks.

A conversational program named SHRDLU (an arbitrary name, not based on any meaning) was written by Terry Winograd at MIT in 1972. The program simulated a robot arm and some blocks (boxes, cubes and pyramids) resting on a table. The robot arm and the blocks were displayed as line drawings on a television screen. On receiving an English instruction, the arm would move the blocks as instructed; for instance, 'Put the red pyramid in the box.' At any given time, the program knew the configuration of the blocks existing at that time. SHRDLU could answer questions about the configuration; for example, 'Where is the red pyramid?' The program could assimilate new definitions. Suppose that the user defined a steeple as a pyramid resting on a cube. Then the user could use the word steeple later in the conversation. If the user ever said anything ambiguous, SHRDLU would seek clarification as to what the user meant.

An English interface named LIFER was developed in 1977. It was written by Gary G. Hendrix, Earl D. Sacerdoti, Daniel Segalowicz and Jonathan Slocum. LIFER incorporated template fitting, or semantic grammar, which was discussed in section 6.1.1. LIFER was used to query a distributed database called LADDER at the Stanford Research Institute.

Also in 1977, Larry R. Harris developed ROBOT, an English interface to query databases. Later renamed as INTELLECT, the interface came to be sold by Artificial Intelligence Corporation, Waltham, Massachusetts.

It would be apparent from the above that by the late 1970s the area of natural language processing had begun to appear fruitful. Another such area of AI was expert systems.

A9.3   Expert systems

The first successful expert system is reputed to be DENDRAL. It was written in 1965 by Joshua Lederberg, Bruce Buchanan and Edward Feigenbaum at the Stanford Heuristic Programming Project. Given the mass spectrogram and the chemical formula of a compound, DENDRAL could derive the molecular structure of the compound.

Another expert system, also developed at the Stanford Heuristic Programming Project, was MYCIN. It was written in 1976 by Edward Shortliffe. MYCIN could diagnose blood infections and prescribe appropriate antibiotic therapy. MYCIN incorporated an *ad hoc* scheme of plausible reasoning (explained in section 10.3).

In 1979, Richard O. Duda, Peter E. Hart and associates developed the expert system PROSPECTOR at the Stanford Research Institute. Examining data about the soil at a site, PROSPECTOR could predict the minerals to be found at that site. It helped discover the mineral molybdenum near Mount Tolman in the state of Washington. PROSPECTOR incorporated a Bayesian scheme of plausible reasoning described in section 10.2.

All of the above expert systems solved problems of analyses (see section 9.3). An expert system developed to solve a problem of synthesis (section 9.2) was named R1. The system was developed in 1980 by John McDermott of Carnegie–Mellon University for Digital Equipment Corporation. The system configured VAX computer systems to satisfy the requirements put forward by Digital's customers. The system was later renamed XCON and used extensively by Digital Equipment.

With the success of expert systems such as those mentioned above, the use of expert systems began to spread in business and industry in the 1980s.

A10   CLOSING REMARKS

As we said in Chapter 1, the objective of AI is to build intelligent machines. Some may say that intelligent machines are unrealistic. In the nineteenth century, many considered Babbage's Analytical Engine to be unrealistic. The twentieth century, however, showed that the Analytical Engine is not unrealistic. It is hoped that one day intelligent machines, too, will not be considered unrealistic.

It may be apparent from reading this book that for a machine to display intelligence in some domain, we need to first store the knowledge about the domain in the machine. This knowledge is essentially in the form of both numerical and non-numerical symbols. Having stored the knowledge, the machine will have to manipulate these symbols of knowledge.

Techniques for manipulating numerical symbols, that is, calculations, were a challenge at one time; for instance, in Bede's time (Section A1.1), calculation required nimble fingers. Today's challenge, however, is for techniques that manipulate non-numerical symbols. A machine that can manipulate both numerical and non-numerical symbols with equal ease and efficiency is a desideratum for displaying intelligent behaviour. Let us call such a machine a **symbulator** (*symb*ol *manip*ulator) to distinguish it from a computer.

The hardware of a computer is designed for rapid computation. Likewise, the hardware of a symbulator should be designed for rapid symbulation. Ideally, a symbulator should be as able in making, say, a logical inference as it is in carrying out arithmetic.

The above history demonstrated that it took a long time to develop computers. Similarly, it may take some time to develop symbulators, but that should not discourage us, for any long journey is completed only step by step. Today effort is going on worldwide in Europe, Japan and the USA to build a generation of symbulators. As you saw in the above history, international effort brought us computers. We hope that international effort will bring us symbulators.

A11 SUGGESTIONS FOR FURTHER READING

Huskey and Huskey (1976) listed many of the computing devices developed since circa 500 BC. Li (1959) examined some fundamental notions of the abacus. Moon (1971) discussed techniques for calculating with different kinds of abaci. Menninger (1969) presented the history of numerical symbols and explained Gerbert's iron division, which was mentioned in section A2.5. Menabrea (1842) and Babbage (1982) delineated the Analytical Engine. Hyman (1982) penned a biography of Charles Babbage. Goldstine (1972) and Evans (1981) narrated the history of computing devices. Metropolis, Howlett and Rota (1980) edited a collection of papers on the twentieth-century history of computing. Cortada (1983) provided an annotated bibliography on the history of computing. Gardner (1968) explored the history of devices for mechanizing logic. Cohen (1967) portrayed humankind's view of robots from ancient times. Ralston and Reilly (1983) gathered essays on computing, some of which give the history of computing. Weizenbaum (1966) described his conversational program ELIZA, which was mentioned in Section A9.2. McCorduck (1979) wrote a history of artificial intelligence up until the 1970s. Berliner and Beal (1990) briefly reviewed the history of computer chess.

1. Berliner, H. J. and Beal, D. F. (1990). Introduction, *Artificial Intelligence*, **43**[1], 1–5. (This was as special issue of the journal on computer chess.)
2. Babbage, C. (1982) On the mathematical powers of the calculating engine, in *The Origins of Digital Computers* (3rd edition), (ed. B. Randell), Springer-Verlag, New York, pp. 19–54.
3. Cohen, J. (1967) *Human Robots in Myth and Science*, A. S. Barnes and Co. Inc., Cranbury, New Jersey.
4. Cortada, J. W. (1983) *An Annotated Bibliography on the History of Data Processing*, Greenwood Press, Westport, Connecticut.

5. Evans, C. (1981) *The Making of the MICRO: A History of the Computer*, Van Nostrand Reinhold Company, New York.
6. Gardner, M. (1968) *Logic Machines, Diagrams and Boolean Algebra*, Dover Publications Inc., New York.
7. Goldstine, H. H. (1972) *The Computer from Pascal to von Neumann*, Princeton University Press, Princeton, New Jersey.
8. Huskey, H. D. and Huskey, V. R. (1976) Chronology of computing devices, *IEEE Transactions on Computers*, **C-25**[2], 1190–9.
9. Hyman, A (1982) *Charles Babbage: Pioneer of the Computer*, Oxford University Press, New York.
10. Li, S. (1959) Origin and development of the Chinese abacus, *Journal of the ACM*, **6**[1], 102–10.
11. McCorduck, P. (1979) *Machines Who Think: A Personal Journey into the History and Prospects of Artificial Intelligence*, W. H. Freeman and Company, San Francisco, California.
12. Menabrea, L. F. (1842) Sketch of the Analytical Engine invented by Charles Babbage, Esq. *Bibliothèque Universelle de Genève*, 82. Translated into English with annotations by Ada Augusta Lovelace, and printed in *Taylor's Scientific Memoirs*, Volume III, pp. 666–731. Annotated English translation reprinted (1953): *Faster than Thought* (ed. B. V. Bowden), Pitman Publishing Corporation, New York, pp. 341–408.
13. Menninger, K. (1969) *Number Words and Number Symbols*, MIT Press, Cambridge, Massachusetts. (Translated from the revised German edition (1958) entitled *Zahlwort und Ziffer* by Paul Broneer, Vandenhoeck and Ruprecht Publishing Company, Götingen, West Germany.)
14. Metropolis, N., Howlett, J. and Rota, G. (eds.) (1980) *A History of Computing in the Twentieth Century*, Academic Press, New York.
15. Moon, P. (1971) *The Abacus*, Gordon and Breach Science Publishers, New York.
16. Ralston, A. and Reilly Jr., E. D. (eds.) (1983) *Encyclopedia of Computer Science*, Van Nostrand Reinhold Company, New York.
17. Weizenbaum, J. (1966) ELIZA – a computer program for the study of natural language communication between man and machine, *Communications of the ACM*, **9**[1], 36–45.

Index